STRATEGIC ORGANIZATIONAL
COMMUNICATION

STRATEGIC ORGANIZATIONAL COMMUNICATION

Into the Twenty-First Century

Charles Conrad

Texas A&M University

Marshall Scott Poole

Texas A&M University

Harcourt Brace College Publishers

Fort Worth   Philadelphia   San Diego   New York   Orlando   Austin   San Antonio
Toronto   Montreal   London   Sydney   Tokyo

Publisher	Earl McPeek
Acquisitions Editor	Carol Wada
Product Manager	Julie McBurney
Developmental Editor	Eric Carlson
Project Editor	John Haakenson
Production Manager	Diane Gray
Art Director	Garry Harman
Cover Image	Ron Lusk

ISBN: 0-15-503570-3

Library of Congress Catalog Card Number: 97-72835

Address for Editorial Correspondence: Harcourt Brace College Publishers, 301 Commerce Street, Suite 3700, Fort Worth, TX 76102.

Address for Orders: Harcourt Brace & Company, 6277 Sea Harbor Drive, Orlando, FL 32887-6777, 1-800-782-4479 (in Florida).

Website Address:
http://www.hbcollege.com

Harcourt Brace College Publishers may provide complimentary instructional aids and supplements of supplement packages to those adopters qualified under our adoption policy. Please contact your sales representative for more information. If as an adopter or potential user you receive supplements you do not need, please return them to your sales representative or send them to:

Attn: Returns Department
Troy Warehouse
465 South Lincoln Drive
Troy, MO 63379

Printed in the United States of America

890123456 039 98765432

To:
Helen and Cecil
who gave me a love of knowledge,
BJ
who has given me knowledge of love,
and
Travis and Hannah,
our gifts of love.

To:
Ed, Helen and Kim,
who are the foundation,
Lisa,
who built the home,
and
Sam,
who keeps it warm,
with all my love.

PREFACE

From its beginnings in 1983, the goal of *Strategic Organizational Communication* has been to provide a unified description of the incredibly diverse array of ideas that comprise our rapidly-expanding field. Responses to the first three editions have been especially gratifying. Readers are particularly complimentary about the *level of sophistication* of the book and its ability to *integrate research* from a number of academic disciplines. High praise is also given to the emphasis on organizations and organizational communication within a broader social, economic, and cultural context and for maintaining a relaxed, first-person writing style. Of course, we have retained or expanded each of these characteristics.

RESPONDING TO READER SUGGESTIONS

Readers also have been very open about changes that they would like to see made. As a result, each new edition really has been a *new* edition. The illustrations on the cover reflect these changes.

The New and Improved

Strategic Organizational Communication now has two authors. Marshall Scott Poole, who was one of the first people to adopt this book almost fifteen years ago, has contributed extended sections on **communication systems and networks, the communication processes of organizational groups,** and **organizational design,** as well as an entire chapter on **Communication Technology** (Chapter 5). But readers who know Scott's work well will see his influence throughout the book. The lightning bolt on the cover reflects the transformation that technology has brought to organizations.

A second change involves the theoretical frame underlying the book. Previous editions focused on the concept of **strategic choice** and employed sociologist Anthony Giddens' concept of the **duality of structure** as a basis for understanding choice-making behavior. People make choices about the kinds of societies and organizations in which they will live. Those choices create the **situations** that people encounter—the **challenges** they face, the **resources** they have available to manage those challenges, and the **guidelines** and **constraints** that limit the options that are available to them. People **adapt strategically** to the situations that they have created. Ironically, in adapting people tend to reproduce those situations, creating a complicated cycle of acting, creating situations, and adapting to them. Understanding this action-situation-adaptation cycle requires people to realize three key ideas:

*Organizations are embedded in societies and cannot be understood outside of a society's beliefs, values, structures, practices, tensions, and ways of managing those tensions. For example, U.S. society is defined in part by a tension between **community** and **individuality.** This tension is inherent to many of the challenges faced by contemporary U.S. organizations, challenges as diverse as the attitudes of "Generation X" (Chapter 1), organizational ethics (Chapter 12), and the dynamics of a diverse workforce (Chapters 10 and 11). The person on the cover symbolizes the society in which organizations exist.

*Organizations emerge through choices among various strategies of organizing. Each strategy includes a characteristic organizational **design,** a system of **motivation and control,** and a particular form of **leadership.** But, each strategy of organizing is a choice—for example, bureaucracies are bureaucracies because people in them **choose** to act like bureaucrats. And each strategy includes opportunities to **resist** the organization's strategy of organizing.

*Employees can manage organizational situations strategically. They can resist strategies of organizational control. They can manage organizational situations in ways that achieve their personal goals and the goals of other members of their organizations.

The third enhancement to this edition involves an expanded treatment of many of the concepts treated in earlier editions. For example, **critical theories** of organizational communication, including extended discussions of strategies of **resistance, feminist organizational theory** (Chapter 7), and **feminist forms of organizing** (Chapter 12) are treated in more detail. We also have expanded efforts to integrate social and critical theory with more traditional concepts such as systems and networks. Although these perspectives often are viewed in opposition to one another, we believe that a critical approach can reinvigorate older concepts and that traditional concepts can in turn be used to clarify and give a solid foundation to social/critical analyses. The organizational chart on the cover signifies the structure that people in organizations work within.

Other changes are less obvious. We have streamlined the discussion of strategies of organizing; in the third edition each of these topics took two chapters. They now take one chapter each and we have reorganized these discussions so that they follow a common format as much as possible. We have replaced many of the case studies included in the third edition with new ones, but have retained the old ones in the *Instructor's Manual.* As in the third edition, the cases are placed at the point in the text where they are most relevant rather than being gathered together in an appendix or workbook. Finally, the extended discussion of the Hawthorne studies that appeared in the three previous editions has been moved to the *Instructor's Manual.* Instructors who find that their favorite section of the third edition has disappeared are welcome to photocopy it for their classes and to do so without suffering through the usual copyright clearance process.

Oldies but Goodies

There are two aspects of *Strategic Organizational Communication* that we never want to change. One is the extensive research base for the book. The bibliography for this edition is as extensive as it was in the earlier editions, and like them it identifies readings that are especially appropriate for graduate students. The endnotes for each chapter provide a number of additional readings on virtually every aspect of contemporary organizational communication research and theory.

The second aspect that we always plan to retain is the conceptual coherence of the analysis. Two beliefs underlie all that we say in this book. One is that organizations (and societies) are **sites** in which various tensions and contradictions are negotiated through communication (this idea is explained at length in Chapter 1). The second belief is that **understanding organizations and organizational communication requires an analysis of both symbolic and structural processes.** We consistently balance various perspectives and indicate how each can be enriched by the key concepts of the others. Life is simply too complex for either/or thinking to capture its nuances; organizations are far too fluid and complicated for bimodal or trimodal paradigms to reveal much of importance.

ORGANIZATION OF THE BOOK

Like the first edition, this book is divided into two units. Unit I introduces the theoretical framework that unifies the book and develops the concept of **strategies of organizing** in detail. It concludes with an extended discussion of **communication technologies** which treats them not as a separate topic, but as processes that modify and expand the strategies of organizing available to members of organizations.

Unit II examines a number of situations that employees encounter in contemporary organizations and discusses the communicative strategies that they might use to **strategically manage** those situations. Chapter 7 examines strategies for **managing membership** in organizations, including the complex process of **entering an organization.** Subsequent chapters examine organizational **power and politics; individual, group, and organizational decision making; organizational conflict;** issues related to workforce **diversity;** and **organizational ethics.** It is inevitable that readers will encounter challenges related to these topics at some point in their careers.

THANKS

If they are to be effective, all communicative acts must be interactive. This dictum includes the writing of books. Consequently, our greatest vote of thanks goes to the many readers of the earlier editions who made thoughtful and valuable suggestions for improvement.

We also thank colleagues who provided advice on the different drafts of this edition: Marshall Prisbell, University of Nebraska at Omaha; Nick Trujillo, California State University - Sacramento; Roger L. Garrett, Central Washington University; Joseph Chilberg, State University of New York at Fredonia; Brenda J. Allen, University of Colorado - Boulder; David E. Switzer, Indiana University - Purdue University at Fort Wayne; Michael W. Kramer, University of Missouri at Columbia; and Lori A. Collins-Jarvis, Rutgers University. Linda Putnam is a constant source of support, providing insight, expertise, and resources that only she can provide, and providing constant evidence that truly transformational leadership is possible in even highly bureaucratic organizations. Karen Taylor contributed in important ways to the discussions of feminist theory, feminist organizations and discussions of race, gender, and ethnicity. She also is the author of the *Instructor's Manual.* Eric Carlson, Carol Wada, Terri House, John Haakenson, Diane Gray, Garry Harman, and Julie McBurney have made working with Harcourt Brace College Publishers a joy—we have never encountered more supportive and capable people in any organization. Private encouragement was provided by Betty Webber Conrad and Lisa O'Dell, and in even the most hectic of times Travis, Hannah, and Sam help us keep our priorities straight. A special thanks goes to each person who provided examples and case studies. In many cases they were donated by people who took some very real career risks in order to help us explain what organizational life is "really like."

Charles Conrad

Marshall Scott Poole

College Station, Texas
March, 1997

CONTENTS

Chapter 4
CULTURAL STRATEGIES OF ORGANIZING   112

Chapter 5
COMMUNICATION TECHNOLOGY AND NEW STRATEGIES OF ORGANIZING   149

UNIT II
Strategies of Organizational Communication   197

Chapter 6
MANAGING MEMBERSHIP IN ORGANIZATIONS   198

Chapter 7
COMMUNICATION, POWER AND POLITICS
IN ORGANIZATIONS   238

Chapter 8
COMMUNICATION AND DECISION-MAKING: INDIVIDUAL, GROUP,
AND ORGANIZATIONAL CONSIDERATIONS   270

Chapter 9
COMMUNICATION AND THE MANAGEMENT OF ORGANIZATIONAL
CONFLICT   312

UNIT 1

Strategies
of
Organizing

Chapter 1

STRATEGIC ORGANIZATIONAL COMMUNICATION

Don't ask me. I just work here.
—ANONYMOUS

CENTRAL THEMES

- Developing communication skills and understanding the communicative processes of organizations is related positively to individuals' career success and their ability to contribute positively to their organizations. As important, it helps people empower themselves.
- Organizational communication is *strategic* in two senses. Organizations emerge from strategic choices about how they will be designed and how their members will treat one another. These choices create the situations that employees face. Employees then make strategic choices about how to best pursue their own goals in these situations and in the process create, maintain, and sometimes transform the situations they face.
- Societies and organizations face a key dilemma. In order to function they must control and coordinate the activities of their members. But doing so frustrates the members' needs for autonomy, creativity, and sociability.
- Organizations exist within societal *contexts.* The beliefs, values, and expectations that employees bring with them into their organizations influence organizational communication in important ways.
- In societies and organizations, communication is used to manage tensions within and among the beliefs, values, and expectations of their members. If these tensions are managed effectively, the beliefs, values, and expectations are a powerful form of social and organizational control.
- Organizations are open systems, and viewing them as systems helps us understand the complex communication processes that take place in them.

KEY TERMS

Taking a critical perspective	Hegemony
Organizational communication	Organizations
Communication	Emergence
Autonomy	System hierarchy
Creativity	Networks
Sociability	Liaisons
Bureaucracy	Isolates
Chain of command	Gatekeepers
Guidelines	Boundary spanners
Constraints	Strong ties
Resources	Weak ties
Duality of structure	Uniplex ties
Externalization	Multiplex ties
Naturalization	System process
Normalization	Equifinality
Objectification	Homeostasis
Internalization	Unanticipated consequence
Proximity effect	Self-renewal
Myths	Environment

At one time or another almost everyone has responded to the question, "How did this (disaster) happen?" with a statement like, "Don't ask me. I just work here." In some cases the excuse is legitimate. The person giving the answer is not allowed by his or her organization to make even simple decisions required by his or her job. "I just work here" means that the person knows the answer or is aware of a solution to the problem but has too little power to make the necessary changes. In other cases someone else failed to inform the person of the policy, problem, or procedure that is in question. "I just work here" means that the speaker simply does not have the information needed to answer the question. But sometimes the person did act in ways that caused the problem and the response is merely an excuse. Although viable excuses often are available in organizations, in the final analysis it is an employee's own choices that create the situations she or he faces.

This book is about the choices and choice-making behaviors of members of formal organizations. It concentrates on *communication* because it is through communication that employees obtain information, make sense of the situations they encounter, and decide how to act. And, it is by communicating that employees translate their choices into action. Organizations must maintain at least an adequate level of communication effectiveness in order to survive and prosper. People who understand how communication functions in an organization, who have developed a wide repertory of written and oral communication skills, and who have learned when and how to use those skills seem to have more successful careers and contribute more fully to their organizations than people who have not done so.[1]

As a result, the number of college courses and professional training programs concerned with organizational communication has mushroomed. Of course, employees cannot function effectively unless they possess the technical skills that their positions require. But more and more it appears that being able to recognize, diagnose, and solve communication-related problems is vital to the success of people in even the most technical occupations. Accountants must be able to gain complete, accurate, and sometimes sensitive information from their clients. Supervisors of production lines must be able to obtain adequate and timely information on which to base their decisions. Managers of all divisions must be able to give their subordinates clear instructions, make sure those instructions are understood, create conditions in which their commands will be carried out, and obtain reliable feedback about the completion of the tasks that they have assigned. In a recent survey of 700 middle managers, almost 85 percent of the responses reported that it was their subordinates' communication skills (or lack of them) that determined their success or failure in critical situations. Although these managers also noted that factors such as loyalty and job-related skills also are important, it was their subordinates' abilities to communicate effectively that was most crucial.[2]

As important as the career-oriented benefits of studying organizational communication is the level of understanding that it brings. At many times during their organizational careers people feel powerless because they simply do not understand the events that are taking place around them. In some cases they are victimized by those events. And often, they are unable to determine what factors led to their becoming victims. As the title of a popular book says, bad things do happen to good people (and vice versa), both in our lives as a whole and in our organizations. Being able to **take a critical perspective** on those events, that is, to be able to examine the situations we find ourselves in and understand the many pressures and constraints that make up those situations, is necessary if we are to learn from our experiences and prevent their happening again. In short, understanding the communicative processes of organizations is itself empowering—it allows us to determine what events are our responsibility and what events were outside of our control, to realize that some strategies that we overlooked were available to us and will be available to us in the future.

The primary goal of the book is to give readers a sense of how organizational communication is used strategically, that is, how employees can analyze the situations they face at work and choose appropriate communication strategies. It assumes that all employees are goal-oriented and that if they understand how communication functions in their organizations they will be better able to achieve their objectives and those of their organizations. It explains when it is appropriate to use a variety of communication strategies, including the denial of responsibility and the claim of ignorance ("Don't ask me. I just work here"), and as important, when not to use them.

In this chapter I will introduce the three concepts that underlie the ideas presented in the rest of the book. First, I will explain organizational communication is *strategic* and explain the two dimensions of that concept. Then I will suggest that organizations and organizational are *contextualized* within particular social and economic conditions. These contexts include the beliefs and values that employees hold, but they also involve a characteristic set of tensions that must be managed successfully. Finally, I will argue that organizations and organizational communication are *systemic,* that is, they are made of complex networks of interpersonal relationships, information exchange, and interpretive processes.

These are difficult concepts and this is a challenging chapter. Although I will provide a number of concrete examples of each central concept, some of them may still seem to be abstract when the chapter ends. As the book progresses they will become more and more clear—additional examples and expanded explanations will help you understand even the most complex ideas. Good things do come to those who wait, and read.

ORGANIZATIONAL COMMUNICATION AS *STRATEGIC* DISCOURSE

One way of understanding a complicated phenomenon is to begin with definitions of key terms. The simplest definition of **organizational communication** is that it is communication that occurs within organizations, but that definition is not very informative. **Communication** generally is defined as a process through which people, acting together, create, sustain, and manage meanings through the use of verbal and nonverbal signs and symbols within a particular context. Of course, the key terms in this definition are *people, acting together, meaning,* and *context.* In even a simple communicative interchange between two people both parties bring a number of things with them to the episode—histories of past communication with the other person or with people who they perceive are similar to the other person, expectations about future interactions with one another, goals for the interchange and for the relationship, assumptions about how people are supposed to communicate with one another, certain levels of communicative skills, and so on. During the interchange people create and exchange a complex set of messages with one another and by doing so create meanings for each message and for the interaction itself. Some of the meanings that emerge are consistent with what the communicators intended their messages to mean; others are not. The systems of meanings that they create together influence their interpretations of one another, their relationship, and their communication. In turn, their communication influences their meaning systems, interpretations, and relationships. Their goals may change as they discover that the other person was more (or less) sympathetic to their position than they expected the person to be; their assumptions about how civil they should be toward the other person may change when they notice that she or he is more civil today than ever before, and so on.

For example, one of my graduate students and I recently studied a group that was charged with designing guidelines for the sex education program of a city school district. Both sides came to the first meeting with little direct knowledge of one another. But they came armed with solid expectations about what the others would be like based on their interpretations of the public debate in this nation over teenage sexuality and abortion. Conservatives feared that the liberals would want a program that encouraged sexual promiscuity among teenagers and would advocate abortion as a primary method of birth control; liberals were convinced that the conservatives would want a program that gave students little information and a great deal of fear and guilt.

During an early meeting the conservative group gave a number of long speeches arguing that the district's sex education program should persuade students to abstain from sexual activity. To their surprise, everyone in the room—even the liberals—agreed. Although it took a while for the two groups to recover from the shock of finding that they agreed on something important, the rest of the group's deliberations were very different than they otherwise would have been. Although they continued to be suspicious of one another throughout the next six months, they at least listened to one another and in doing so discovered many other areas of disagreement and some additional areas of agreement. In the process of communicating with one another they acted together to create, sustain, and modify a system of meaning that was uniquely their own. Their discussions always were influenced by the context in which they took place—both the local situation faced by the school board and the national debate over sexual issues—but the messages they exchanged and the meanings that they attributed to those messages could only be understood within the communicative process that they created.[3] In short, people with varying degrees of communicative skills acted together through the use of verbal and nonverbal cues to create, sustain, and modify systems of meaning. That is, they communicated.

Organizational communication differs from this definition of communication primarily in terms of the complexity of the context and people dimensions. Organizational relationships are both like and unlike "normal" interpersonal relationships. We communicate with people at work because we like them and because our tasks require us to do so. Thus, our relationships at work have both an interpersonal and an organizational dimension. As later chapters will explain, we constantly have to negotiate an appropriate "mix" of these two dimensions. We may have a strong personal relationship with our supervisor, but have to maintain the kind of relational distance, detachment, and subservience that is appropriate to our organizational relationship. We may like one of our subordinates very much, but his or her inability to do the job well creates constant stresses in our interpersonal relationship. Consequently, the process of creating shared meanings is more complicated in organizational relationships than in those that occur naturally.

Defining *Strategic* Organizational Communication

The concept of *strategy* enters into my perspective on organizational communication at two levels. One level is that of the organization. Most of us have learned to think of organizations as places where large numbers of people efficiently cooperate with one another to achieve some shared objectives. But organizations also are sites in which multiple different tensions exist, tensions that must be managed successfully if the organization is to succeed in meeting the goals of its members. Some tensions are specific to individual organizations; others are characteristic of the relationship between organizations and the surrounding society. But, there is at least one fundamental tension that faces all organizations, a tension between individual members' needs and the needs of their organizations. People have needs for **autonomy** (the feeling that we are in control of our actions and our destinies), **creativity** (feelings of pride that comes from making something that did not previously exist or in doing something better than or in a different way than anyone else), and **sociability** (feeling that we have meaningful interpersonal relationships with other people). We also need an adequate degree of *structure, stability,* and *predictability* in our lives—we need to know who we are, where we fit in our organizations and society, and how we and our peers are likely to act in various social and organizational situations.

Organizations also have needs that must be met. The most fundamental of these are *control* and *coordination*. Organizations exist because the tasks that people must perform are sufficiently complex that they must cooperate with one another to achieve their goals. In essence, organizations require us to sacrifice some of our *independence*—our ability to be self-sufficient—and replace it with *interdependence*. In modern societies very few persons have the skills, experience, or opportunities to personally do everything that is necessary to live a productive life. The vast majority of us actually can do very little—we are constantly at the mercy of electricians, plumbers, appliance repair technicians, auto mechanics, and on the organizations in which they work. What we can do we do very well. We have traded independence for *specialization* and become far more efficient as a result. But our efficiency depends almost wholly on coordinating our activities with the activities of others. Different cultures vary in the degree of interdependence that exists within them. So do organizations and the various departments within them. Research-and-development divisions usually have low interdependence, relying only on computer operators, purchasing and receiving departments (which order and deliver raw materials), and the physical plant operators (who keep equipment secure and functioning).

For them, coordination within the division is crucial; coordinating their activities with outsiders is less important. For other divisions, coordination is a more complex and critical problem. But to some degree all organizations need some coordination.

This *coordination* is achieved *through mechanisms of control*. All societies and all organizations need to influence the behaviors of their members. But this need creates a fundamental dilemma. If a society or organization successfully controls its members and relationships, *their individual* needs for *autonomy, creativity,* and *sociability* will be frustrated to some degree. Our societies and organizations provide us with needed structure and stability by telling us who we are and how we should act toward other people. But these messages inevitably limit our autonomy; direct our creative activities toward meeting the needs of the society/organization but not toward meeting our own needs; and guide and limit our interpersonal relationships.

But, conversely, if individual employees had unlimited autonomy, creativity, and control over their interpersonal relationships, the needs of their organization would be frustrated. This *dilemma* is the fundamental problem faced by societies and their organizations. To manage the dilemma successfully, they must create contexts in which their members will choose to act in ways that adequately meet their individual needs while also meeting the organization's needs for *control* and *coordination*.[4] Those contexts are created through various *strategies of organizing*.

Organizations as Strategic Creations.   Organizations are designed and operated as they are because of the choices their members make. Employees are constantly making choices about the goals they should pursue, the activities they should engage in, the kinds of relationships they should form, the kinds of rewards they should receive for their contribution to their organization, and how those rewards should be distributed. For example, in Western capitalist democracies, a common strategy of organizing is commonly called a **bureaucracy**. With its clear lines of authority, reliance on written policies and procedures, and focus on rational decision-making, bureaucracies can be a highly efficient strategy of organizing. (Of course, bureaucracies often are not highly efficient, for reasons that I will explain in detail in Chapter 2.)

But, it is important to keep three things in mind about the bureaucratic—or any other—strategy of organizing. First, it is a *strategy*—a choice—among a large number of possible options. There are a number of attributes of Western capitalist democracies that encourage members of organizations to choose bureaucratic strategies, but it is neither inevitable nor always preferable to organize according to this particular strategy. Bureaucratic organizations are so common in Western societies that we often do not realize that there *are* alternative organizational strategies and that our organizations are bureaucracies because we *choose* to organize our activities in that way.[5] Western organizations do not *have* to be bureaucratic; they are because we choose, consciously or not, to make them that way.

Second, modern organizations rarely are designed and operated according to a single strategy of organizing. Even the omnipresent bureaucratic strategy almost never appears in a pure form in real organizations. Instead, every individual organization is a distinctive, maybe even unique, mixture of the different strategies of organizing that I will discuss in Unit I of this book.

Finally, the particular organizational strategy chosen and enacted in an organization has an important effect on communication processes. Each organizational strategy asks the employees to accept a certain set of beliefs and values, creates a particular system of exchanging information, encourages the development of some kinds of leadership and leader–follower relationships while discouraging others, and legitimizes only certain means of motivating, controlling, and coordinating employees' actions. In addition, each strategy places particular requirements and burdens on the organization's communication systems and practices. For example, the bureaucratic strategy largely restricts communication to the formal **chain of command** (each employee communicates information to his or her supervisor and *only* to her or his supervisor, who then communicates it to his or her supervisor, and so on) and in doing so places a great deal of pressure on that communication system. But, ironically, the formal communication system is one of the weakest parts of bureaucratic strategies, especially when an organization exists in highly competitive, rapidly changing environment. As a result, certain kinds of communication breakdowns are inevitable and predictable, which in part explains why most people do not think of bureaucracies as highly efficient entities. Other strategies of organizing place other kinds of pressures on the organization's communication system, and thus make other kinds of communication breakdowns more (or less) likely.

In summary, organizations are strategic creations. They emerge through strategic choices, are sustained through strategic choices, and are changed when their members begin to make different choices.

Organizational Life as Strategic Communication.   The second sense in which organizational communication is *strategic* involves individual employees. For more than 2000 years communication scholars have believed that people communicate most effectively if they adapt their communication strategies to the situations they face. For example, Plato's intellectual rival Gorgias argued that knowing how to adapt to different life situations is the only kind of knowledge that is available to human beings. Some equivalent of Gorgias' concept of adaptation (which he labeled *kairos*), has been important to the study of communication since his time.[6] In order to communicate effectively, employees must be able to analyze the situations they encounter in their organizations, determine which communication strategies are available to them in those situations, select the most appropriate strategies, and enact those strategies successfully.

However, selecting appropriate communicative strategies is much more complex than the previous paragraph suggests. Strategies of organizing create particular kinds of organizational situations. All organizational situations contain **guidelines** that tell employees how they are supposed to act and communicate and **constraints** that tell them how they are *not* to act and communicate.[7] But, fortunately, organizational situations also *enable* us to communicate. They provide us with **resources** for acting—potential lines of argument, acceptable forms of persuasive appeal, and so on—that allow us to strategically pursue our goals.[8] The *relative* importance of guidelines/constraints and resources differs in different situations. Usually the particular combination of

FIGURE 1-1

PEANUTS reprinted with permission of UFS, Inc.

guidelines, constraints, and resources that exist in a given situation gives employees clear and workable options for acting. In most organizational situations employees have available resources that will allow them to simultaneously meet at least some of their goals while fulfilling at least some of their organization's objectives. In these cases choosing productive communication strategies is not particularly difficult.

In other situations, however, choosing appropriate communication strategies is more difficult, perhaps impossible. Organizational situations sometimes *paralyze* employees, at least momentarily. One kind of paralysis occurs when the guidelines and constraints in a situation are clear but the resources available to meet them are unclear, unknown, or insufficient.

Organizational situations may include commands for psychotherapists to "do good work," hospital administrators to "cut costs," or elementary schoolteachers to "stimulate all the students' interests." These "guidelines" may tell employees what they are supposed to do but they tell them very little about how they are supposed to do those things. As a result they may become paralyzed while they make sense out of their situations and discover the resources that are available to them. For example, a newly graduated student who had become a stockbroker once called me asking "What do I do next?"

after being given a desk and a "training session" that included only the comment "I hope you'll like it here. Just don't screw up like George (your predecessor) did."[9] This kind of paralyzing situation seems to be very common for new employees and has been shown to be a major source of organizational stress.

A more extreme form of paralysis occurs when action is called for but constraints leave the employee with no available resources. Like Lucy in the cartoon in Figure 1-1, organizational situations sometimes leave some employees with few realistic options. Presumably, Linus' purpose is to gain the childlike fun that comes from a friendly snowball fight. But Lucy's comments leave him with both a command to act (since dropping the snowball is an act) and no productive way to achieve his purpose. Throwing the snowball will fail; so will not throwing it. Lucy has taken the fun out of snowball fights and has robbed Linus of any opportunity for meaningful choice.

Organizational situations often parallel the Peanuts situation. Supervisors may find that they have only one position to allocate and two departments that desperately need help, have equally strong claims on the position, and will be justifiably angry if they do not receive it. Subordinates may be told to do one thing by one superior and the opposite by another. Even if they know that one supervisor has a higher rank than the other and that their organizational situation includes the guideline/constraint that they should follow the orders given by the higher-ranking person, they also may know that the other supervisor may retaliate in ways that will never be detected by anyone else. In this kind of situation the subordinate has no realistic options, because she or he has no adequate resources available. Between the two extremes of simple situations and paralyzing ones are the situations that employees normally face at work—situations that provide a range of options that can serve both the employees' purposes and those of their organizations, situations where employees can act and communicate strategically.

Finally, and perhaps ironically, employees' strategic choices create, reproduce, and in some cases, change the guidelines/constraints and resources that they face. For example, bureaucratic strategies of organizing continue to exist only because employees act like bureaucrats. The organizational strategy of making decisions only by applying established, written policies and regulations (a key element of the bureaucratic strategy) exists only because members of those organizations actually *make* decisions based on established policies and regulations *and* have come to believe that decisions *should* be made in this way. In doing so they choose to follow a "rule" that limits their actions to those prescribed by the organizational situation. And, in doing so, they use that rule as a "resource" for managing demanding people. But, in the process they reproduce and legitimize the guidelines and constraints that they face. Theorist Anthony Giddens has called this process of reproducing the guidelines and constraints that we face the **duality of structure**.[10]

CASE STUDY:
RESPECT THE DIVINE AND LOVE PEOPLE*

EngineerCorp is a multibillion dollar Japanese firm with a high-tech manufacturing plant in Southern California. It has a highly multicultural workforce—production workers are Hispanic or Filipino-Americans, upper management is Japanese, and the technical and engineering employees are Anglo-Americans. Each of its divisions (which are called "amoebas") operates pretty much independently from the others, although upper management makes policy decisions and sets goals for the amoebas and for the plant.

Two members of the human relations amoebae asked for a meeting with upper management to discuss what they saw as a serious problem for the firm—high turnover among top-flight engineers. The following is a paraphrase of part of their conversation:

HR MANAGERS: We're losing all of this talent because they think that the company doesn't care about them. They have no established career paths and they're falling behind their classmates in pay and advancement.

PLANT AND ENGINEERING MANAGERS: No, the problem is that Americans work for money. We feel that our lives are supported by the company; I can live because the company supports me. What is a career path?

HR MANAGERS: That's where the engineer knows what job he will move into next as he advances, what his salary and responsibilities will be, how long he will wait until being promoted. . . .

PLANT AND ENGINEERING MANAGERS: We are not concerned about our *next* job; we just want to do our current job the best way we can. We will be grateful when and if the president asks us to serve in a new job; we will be grateful. We are successful when the company is successful; we advance when we get better at our current jobs and learn new things; our careers *are* the company. Americans need dedication and loyalty; they do not understand commitment.

This brief interchange reveals a number of the rules and resources present in this organizational situation. Some of them were accepted by all parties: (1) Everyone knew and accepted a rule that all public discussions would be conducted in an atmosphere of politeness and nonconfrontation, at least when Japanese employees were present, even when they found other people's comments to be offensive; and (2) upper management would make all major policy decisions, although it was appropriate for amoeba managers to request that a

---

*This case study is based on Stephen Banks and Patricia Riley, "Structuration Theory as an Ontology for Communication Research," in Stanley Deetz, ed. *Communication Yearbook 16* (pp. 167–196). Newbury Park, CA: Sage.

(continued)

(continued from the previous page)

decision be made on a particular issue. Both sides also *seemed* to share the view that Americans were motivated by money and individual advancement, not by commitment, although they used this *resource* in different ways. Management drew on it as a basis for dismissing the HR managers' concerns; the HR managers drew on it as the basis for arguing that the organization needed to change in order to accommodate their talented engineers. The two groups challenged other resources. Management, especially during other parts of the conversation, expressed pride in the much-heralded success that Japanese firms have had in world markets and in ways that the company did things. They drew on that pride as a reason for deferring to present systems. HR refused to accept the notion that they should defer to the status quo, and tried to use another resource, the commonly held assumption among Americans that it is bad business for an organization to unnecessarily lose its best talent. Not only did management refuse to accept this assumption, they re-defined "best talent" in terms of loyalty—people who leave organizations are disloyal and selfish, and thus aren't the "best" people regardless of their technical expertise.

Eventually the contest ends, not because the parties are able to overcome differences in their understandings of the rules and resources that were available to them, but because of differences in power. Both groups refused to accept the legitimacy of key resources used by the other group. But, both groups did accept the legitimacy of upper management's right to make policy, and management's use of that rule as a resource determined the outcome of the conversation.

In the process the two groups enacted, and thus reproduced the rules and resources that guided and constrained their communication. The HR managers acted like Americans (at least as the Japanese managers defined Americans) and argued that their engineers did the same. Doing so meant that the Japanese managers' views of American workers would be available as a resource in future interactions. And, the Japanese managers acted in ways that "proved" they were irrational (being willing to lose talented engineers). This allows the HR managers to continue to say "I told you so" when talented engineers leave the firm, thus reproducing their reliance on the "bad business" resource. It also absolves them of responsibility for the turnover problem or for the race discrimination lawsuits that continue to be filed against the firm by exiting engineers.

Discussion Questions

1. Are there other resources available to either group in this case that could have been used to reach a different outcome?
2. What impact, if any, would a successful lawsuit have on the rules and resources operating in this organization? Would a successful suit make upper management's positions more flexible? Why or why not?

ORGANIZATIONAL COMMUNICATION AS *CONTEXTUALIZED* DISCOURSE

Organizational communication is *strategic;* it also is contextual. Organizations do not exist in a vacuum and societies do not exist without organizations. Even the ancient civilizations of the Middle East relied on church and state organizations, and they relied on effective communication. But societies and the organizations that exist within them are linked together in two other ways. One link is through core values and beliefs.

Communication and Societal/Organizational Beliefs and Values

Probably the most influential modern discussion of the relationship between a society and the organizations that develop within it was provided by the German sociologist Max Weber.[11] Weber observed that when people enter formal organizations they bring with them a long history of living within their society, of learning how members of their societies typically make sense out of events and respond to the situations they encounter. More recently, sociologist Peter Berger has described a three-phase process through which people learn and accept these core values and beliefs.

In the first phase, **externalization**, people notice the ways in which others interpret and respond to their surroundings. In order to "fit in," we begin to act in similar ways. Eventually we may begin to think of those actions as **natural** (that is, inevitable) and **normal** (which means *morally acceptable,* among other things).

Eventually, we may enter the second phase, **objectification**. We may begin to forget that we (and our peers) *choose* to act in the ways we do, and that any number of different choices are available to us. We begin to believe that the way *we* act and the way *we make sense out of* our actions is the only "correct" (that is, normal and natural) way of interpreting/acting. We begin to *objectify* the patterns of our society, to take them for granted, to not even be consciously aware of them in our everyday lives.[12] The concept of objectification implies that societies (and organizations) are maintained nonconsciously, as much through habit as through conscious deliberation. Routine decisions can be made nonconsciously, automatically, and with little expenditure of time or energy.

Societies (and organizations) benefit from objectification because it means that the vast majority of their members will act in acceptable ways. Only when individual members of the culture deviate from these assumptions does it become necessary to exert overt control. Only when circumstances change in ways that render "tried-and-true" patterns of action (habits) inappropriate do members of the society even become aware that their taken-for-granted assumptions are choices and thus can be changed. Individuals also benefit from objectification because it allows them to live in a stable world in which they know how to act and how others will act. Part of the "objective" reality of a society or organization is a matrix of explicit and implicit social contracts that bind members together in cooperative activities. In Western societies the notion of reciprocity is one such contract. We have learned that we have an obligation to reciprocate when we receive gifts or services from others. In "business" relationships we fulfill our contract to reciprocate by exchanging money or "items" whose value can be translated into a monetary code. In personal relationships the exchange usually is "in kind." Dinner invitations lead to reciprocal dinner invitations. In fact, the Internal Revenue Service officially defines entertainment costs in these terms. If two persons who are business associates rotate dinner invitations (that is, they reciprocate), then the relationship is "personal" and the entertainment costs are not deductible as business expenses. Only if they violate the cultural contract to reciprocate and do not rotate invitations is it nonpersonal (that is, business) entertaining.

In the final, **internalization** phase of learning a culture we begin to evaluate ourselves and our actions in terms of these taken-for-granted assumptions. We begin to see ourselves as "good" or "productive" or "righteous" only if we enact those values. Our self-concept depends on our thinking and acting in ways that are normal. Our self-esteem develops as we observe ourselves doing what is valued by our culture (and thus by ourselves). If we act in ways that violate core beliefs and values we may view ourselves negatively and be motivated to change our behavior.

Societies function smoothly largely because their members must act in accord with their values if they are to maintain their self-esteem and sense of self-worth. Organizations function most smoothly if they are designed and operated in ways that are consistent with the core beliefs and values of the societies from which they draw their members.

Of course, Weber, Berger, and their successors realized that even within the same society, people have different core beliefs and values. Every member of a given society has had unique experiences, has been involved in relationships with different people who have influenced their development in different directions, and has processed these experiences through her or his own unique personality. However, within all this diversity and individuality lies a common core that employees bring when they enter an organization. In short, each employee has been exposed to many conversations about what they should expect from life and from their organizations. Those expectations guide the ways in which people communicate at work and the ways in which they make sense out of the information they obtain. For example, someone who has repeatedly heard business described as being like the military—a clear chain of command, strict regulation of thought and behavior, premium placed on following orders without question—will have different expectations about organizational life than someone who has learned to think of businesses as being like families—high concern for one another, commitment to the group rather than to individual achievement, and so on.[13]

Other conversations involve the act of working. Persons who have learned that work is boring, unending toil with few rewards other than a paycheck will expect different treatment at work than people who have learned that work is and should be one's primary route to self-fulfillment. The society from which an organization draws its members provides a context—a complex web of taken-for-granted assumptions, meanings, expectations, and sense-making processes—through which people make sense out of their experiences at work. This context guides and constrains their actions at work and in turn guides and constrains the kinds of organizational strategies they will enact.

Communication and Societal/Organizational Tensions

Core beliefs and values make up only one dimension of the context surrounding organizations. Just as societies are made of dominant values and beliefs, they also are composed of *tensions, contradictions,* and *means of managing them.* For example, a number of social scientists long have observed that in U.S. society there is a fundamental tension between *individuality* and *community.*[14] Soon after the United States became a nation Alexis de Tocqueville toured the United States and repeatedly noted that we were *so* committed to the idea of *individual* achievement and *individual* responsibility for one's success or failure that we had very little basis for recognizing our *common* needs and interests, for developing a sense of *community.* Almost 200 years later sociologist Robert Bellah and his associates interviewed hundreds of people from all walks of life. They found that our obsession with individualism and our isolation from one another had expanded and deepened during the era since the end of World War II. As U.S. society and U.S. organizations have become more diverse, these tensions have increased further.[15] So prevalent is this tension that the strategies of organizing used in the United States have oscillated between an individualistic strategy that focuses on unemotional, rational decision-making and individual rewards for performance and a "communitarian" strategy that focuses on shared beliefs and values and group solidarity.[16]

Of course, societal tensions can be managed. Sometimes they are managed organizationally. For example, de Tocqueville concluded that the United States remained cohesive because so many of us were involved in informal nonwork organizations that provided a sense of community—churches, lodges, and so on. These experiences compensated for the extreme individuality that we face in our work organizations. But today, some observers suggest, we have become so marginally involved in community or religious organizations that we now must depend on our work organizations for much of our sense of community and "connectedness" (see Chapter 4). And, those informal organizations that we do join increasing focus on meeting individual needs and less and less on creating a sense of community and connectedness.[17]

Societal/organizational tensions also are managed communicatively. All societies have characteristic **myths**, expressions of the core beliefs and values of the society that rarely are even questioned, much less tested, by their members. Myths may or may not be "true" in an empirical sense, but they are treated as if they are true by members of a society. Articulated in stories and rituals, societal myths both express the core values and beliefs of the society and manage its core tensions.[18] For example, two of the most important myths in U.S. society are the "Horatio Alger" myth and the myth of the United States as a "melting pot." The former myth is named after the writer of a series of short books published during the late nineteenth century. In them the key character, always someone from a highly disadvantaged background, faced a series of challenges, but, thanks to his personal grit, talent, and determination and the unbounded opportunity provided by the U.S. economy, eventually overcame them to become an economic and social success. Unlike Europe, the stories go, the United States is a classless society in which the only limit to one's success is one's *individual* competence. Modern versions of the story, with a high-tech twist, are Apple Computer's Steve Jobs and Microsoft CEO Bill Gates.

The "melting pot" myth suggests that all people—regardless of their race, gender, or ethnicity—can become Horatio Alger figures if they only embrace distinctively U.S. values of hard work, determination, and loyalty. When combined the two myths manage the individuality–community tension by telling us that the United States is an economic and social *community* unified by *individual* opportunity.[19]

Societal myths are important because they function as a powerful form of control. Social theorists have labeled this kind of control **hegemony**, a concept that is quite complex.[20] It begins with the observation that societies are hierarchical in many ways, the most important of which are *race, ethnicity, gender,* and *class*. When we internalize the taken-for-granted assumptions of our society, we also internalize its hierarchical relationships, that is, we come to see them as *normal* and *natural*. In some cases, the taken-for-granted assumptions of a society express hierarchical relationships directly— blacks are assumed to be superior to whites, women to men, men to women, and so on. Some cultures assume that male homosexual relationships are superior to heterosexual or lesbian relationships (although it probably is safe to say that this is not an assumption held by most people in the United States today).

Societal assumptions often lead to some very concrete differences in the ways in which people are treated by a society and its organizations. For example, in the United States women long have been and still are paid substantially less than men for the same or for comparable work (see Chapter 10 for a more detailed analysis of differences in wage rates). This is partly because women tend to be concentrated in sectors of the economy that have relatively low salary rates (for example, teaching, nursing, and so on). Over time, the proportion of women in different occupations change. As the proportion of women in an occupation increases, the level of prestige afforded the occupation, and the wage rates paid to the people in it fall steadily until the occupation is approximately 50 percent women. When the proportion exceeds 50 percent, wages plummet.[21] There are two possible explanations for this: (1) an explanation based on societal myths, in this case the myth that "women's work" is worth less than "men's work," and (2) an economic explanation that says that when the number of applicants for a particular type of job increase, the heightened competition will force wages down. The cultural explanation has been shown to be more valid. Women are paid less than men in comparable jobs because their work is perceived to be less valuable; and we "know" women's work is less valuable because they are paid less. Again, the taken-for-granted assumptions of our society/organizations lead us to believe that hierarchical relationships are *normal* and *natural.* In turn we act and think in ways that support those assumptions.

In other cases, the effect is more complicated because it emerges from a combination of assumptions, not from one assumption alone. For example, the dominant ideology of the United States still assumes that men are more "rational" than women (and that women and African Americans and Latinos/Latinas[22] are more "emotional" than white men). These assumptions alone have little relevance to organizations. But our culture also assumes that organizations are (and should be) rational enterprises, especially at managerial levels (in spite of substantial evidence to the contrary that is summarized in Chapter 8). This assumption, in itself, has little relevance for race, gender, or ethnicity. But, when the two assumptions are combined, they generate a further assumption that white men are inherently better managers than white women, African Americans, or Latinos/Latinas. Whether they are direct or indirect, the dominant assumptions of a culture establish hierarchical relationships, and as long as the members of a culture *believe* that the hierarchies are *normal* and *natural,* they will tend to act in ways that perpetuate those hierarchies.

Supervisors tend to not offer married women managers promotions that require relocation because they *assume* that wives are not willing to ask their husbands and families to endure the stresses that involve moving, even when accepting transfers is necessary for promotion. Eventually these supervisors, their supervisors, and their employees notice that women managers do not move very often, and in turn *assume* that this is because women managers value their families more than their careers. It *seems* natural and normal to them to promote and reward those employees who put their careers first (and it *seems* that men are more likely than women to do so), especially if we also *assume* that sacrificing one's family life to one's firm is evidence that one is sufficiently loyal to warrant being promoted. After all, the supervisors making the decisions are supervisors in part because they were willing to make these sacrifices, and not requiring their subordinates to make the same sacrifices would make it difficult for them to rationalize their own career choices. As many sections of this book will indicate, there is little objective evidence to support any of these societal myths. Today women managers *do not* turn down promotions that involve relocating any more often than men do.[23] But the empirical verifiability of those assumptions is of secondary importance—they are dominant values/assumptions within contemporary U.S. society, and those societal taken-for-granteds serve as powerful guidelines and constraints on our beliefs and actions.

Of course, no set of assumptions is taken for granted by all of a society's members all of the time. Some people will constantly question some of the assumptions, and during times of social change large numbers of people may question many of the taken-for-granted assumptions of a society. But taken-for-granted assumptions are amazingly stable, in part because we constantly are exposed to messages that support them. As Chapter 10 explains in more detail, we seek out and attend to information—in both everyday experience and in the media—that confirms the hierarchical assumptions of our societies. We interpret ambiguous information so that it confirms them, and we tend to ignore or rationalize information that disconfirms them.[24] By doing so, by learning and accepting the taken-for-granted assumptions of our society and organizations, we become *qualified* to participate in them. We learn how we *should* think and act. But at the same time we *subject* ourselves to them—we accept limitations on how we think and act.[25]

In summary, organizations exist within societal contexts.[26] The strategies that their members choose are related strongly to the economic situations and taken-for-granted assumptions of the societies from which the organizations draw their members. And, the strategies in turn lead us to act in ways that make our economic situations seem to be "normal" and "natural." In turn they provide "evidence" for the legitimacy of those taken-for-granted assumptions. Societal myths provide people with stable and predictable lives, both inside and outside of their organizations. This concept is difficult to understand because doing so forces us to quit taking for granted the taken-for-granted assumptions of our society. It asks us to treat our most basic beliefs about what is natural and normal as cultural *choices,* not as absolute *truths.* Doing so is difficult both because it requires us to think critically about beliefs that we normally do not think about at all and because it asks us to question assumptions that make our worlds seem to be stable and predictable. Normally we do not think about such things, and as a result they provide powerful guidelines and constraints on our actions and the actions of our organizations. They are a powerful form of social control that can readily be adapted as powerful forms of organizational control.

CASE STUDY:
CAN YOU TRUST ANYONE UNDER THIRTY?

For decades white-collar workers in U.S. organizations have believed and acted as if they had an unspoken "contract" with their organizations. If they worked hard, were loyal and productive employees, and followed the rules of their organizations, they could expect to stay with their organizations as long as they chose to do so, to be rewarded for their contributions, and, eventually, to be supported during their "Golden Years" by an adequate pension. But, after a decade and a half of mergers, "downsizing," and "restructuring" that contract is almost extinct. A Towers-Perrin consulting firm survey in late 1995 found typical results: two-thirds of white-collar employees reported that their companies had downsized or undergone major restructuring during the past two years; only 46 percent believe that they will retire from their current firm (30 percent among employees aged 34 or less).* More than 43 million jobs were lost in the United States between 1979 and 1995, and, although even more jobs were created during that era, about 35 percent of full-time workers who lose their jobs are unable to locate new jobs with comparable salaries and benefits. Workers who earn at least $50,000 a year now fill twice as big a part of the unemployment line as they did during the 1980s. The fastest growing sector of the labor market between 1990 and 1995 was the category of "temp/employment agencies" (the next fastest growing categories were restaurants and bars, local government, recreation, and hospitals). Because these jobs do not include benefits like health insurance or pension plans, they seem to be relatively well paid (about $3–$4 per hour more than comparable permanent jobs), but the extra income still is not enough to buy health insurance.**

Adding to the fear and insecurities that workers feel is a growing resentment that stems from the disparity between skyrocketing firm profits and upper-management incomes and the experiences of both white-collar and blue-collar workers. Productivity in U.S. organizations has significantly and steadily increased during the 1980s and early 1990s, 19.5 percent in all. Until the late 1970s productivity increases were shared with workers at all levels. But since the early 1980s those increases have gone to fuel profits (up 57 percent between 1992 and 1994 alone; up even more in 1995) and upper management's compensation. In 1995 average wage and benefits for U.S. workers rose 2.9 percent, the smallest increase since 1981, while the incomes of CEOs soared. The CEOs of the 20 companies with the largest announced layoffs rose an average of 25

---

*Jim Barlow, "Will Managers Follow Own Lead?," *Houston Chronicle,* May 16, 1996, C1.

**Frank Emspak, "Where Have All the Jobs Gone?" *Chronicle of Higher Education,* April 4, 1996, B1–B2.

(continued)

(continued from the previous page)

percent. In fact, the number of jobs cut by a CEO now is a better predictor of his or her compensation than is the overall performance of the firm. When adjusted for inflation and taxes, real spendable incomes have fallen steadily since 1972 for all workers and since 1989 for male workers with college degrees. Consequently, the ratio of the base salaries of CEOs of U.S. firms to their average employee's salary in 1992 was 140:1 compared to 15:1 in Germany, 13:1 in Japan, and 40:1 in the United States twenty years earlier. In 1995 the ratio in the United States rose to 187:1 overall and 212:1 at the 30 largest U.S. companies.***

As a result of these trends, the attitudes and behaviors of white collar workers have changed markedly. Although the Tower-Perrin survey found that a huge majority of workers wanted to help their firms succeed, the figure was much lower for workers who did not anticipate retiring from their current firms than among those who did. In a 1990 study, Donald Kanter and Philip Mirvis found that 72 percent of workers believed that management takes advantage of their workers, 68 percent believe management makes an unfair salary compared with average employees, 66 percent say that management does not tell the truth, 42 percent say that it does not pay to work hard. The authors conclude that loyalty, which is a two-way street, is decreasing and there is an enormous mistrust of management that keeps workers from feeling involved in and committed to their companies.**** As a result, seminars with titles like "13 Dirty Tricks Companies Use to Get Rid of You (and how to protect yourself from them)" (offered by Houston's Social Systems Institute) have become very popular. And, in firms with large pay gaps between upper management and workers turnover is higher, and product quality, service quality, job satisfaction, and innovation are lower.

Into this situation steps a new generation, people now in their 20s and early 30s. Everywhere they turn, "Generation Xers" are advised to "consider themselves to be free agents," keeping their resumes polished and their network connections alert to opportunities in other firms. They must plan their own careers, seek out opportunities to develop new, marketable skills and opportunities to grow. And they seem to be listening. Traditional values like long-term commitment and loyalty to the firm aren't very popular with them. They refuse to make the kinds of sacrifices that their parents made—being subservient to their bosses, accepting multiple cross-country moves, putting in long hours, or accepting overnight travel. Some supervisors call them slackers. But they aren't—

***David Gordon, *Fat and Mean*. (New York: The Free Press, 1995); Charles Boisseau, "Workers Foot the Bill for Boosts in Bosses' Pay," *Houston Chronicle*, June 9, 1996, A1.

****Donald Kanter & Philip Mirvis, *The Cynical American: Living and Working in an Age of Discontent and Disillusionment* (San Francisco: Jossey-Bass, 1990 and Chip Walker and Elissa Moses, "The Age of Self-Navigation," *American Demographics* (September, 1996): 36–42.

(continued)

(continued from the previous page)

they are aggressive, hard-working entrepreneurs, even if they are working in corporate structures. They concentrate on developing computer, leadership, and communication skills, in part to make them valuable to their current firms, but also as a means of going out on their own as soon as possible. They are willing to take the risks of self-employment or job changes, in order to get the greater rewards and freedom that accompanies being their own bosses. But they also tend to form relatively superficial and inauthentic relationships in the workplace. Knowing that they may not be around very long, they make little investment in getting to know their supervisors and coworkers as people, and their supervisors and coworkers spend little energy getting to know them. This makes it easier to exit the organization—they can do so without leaving close friends or commitments behind—and makes it more likely that they will do so.*****

Discussion Questions

1. Are the strategies chosen by Generation Xers appropriate to the situations they face?
2. What effects are their strategies likely to have on their relationships with their supervisors in traditional firms? their relationships with their coworkers? with their subordinates?
3. What effects are their strategies likely to have on the situations that they face? Why?

*****See, for example, Daniel Feldman, *Managing Careers in Organizations* (Glenview, IL: Scott, Foresman, 1988); James Challenger, *Job Hunt* (Chicago, IL: Challenger, Gray & Christmas, Inc., 1995; L.M. Sixel, "Workers Should Consider Themselves Free Agents," *Houston Chronicle,* November 20, 1995, C1 and "Xers Want to Be Their Own Bosses," *Houston Chronicle,* November 2, 1995, C1.

ORGANIZATIONAL COMMUNICATION AS *SYSTEMIC* DISCOURSE

For at least 25 years scholars have thought of organizations as complex, open systems. Formally defined, a system is a network of interdependent components that is separated from its environment by a boundary. The components linked together in an organizational system may be individual members, organizational units such as departments, or a mixture of the two. A defining characteristic of a system is the pattern and types of relationships components have with each other. A number of different types of relationships can exist in systems: information exchange, power, work interdependence, political alliances, friendship, to name a few. Communication between components is an integral part of all of these relationships. In a very real sense, communication is the glue that holds organizational systems together. The interacting components give the system a wholeness that creates a boundary around the system. This boundary is sometimes formal or tangible, as when organizations give members security passes and only those with passes can get in, but it is more often intangible and a bit unclear.

Organizations are open systems, systems that exchange information and matter with their environments. An open system obtains the energy, materials, ideas, and information it needs to survive, maintain its complex structure, and grow through this exchange. To be effective organizational systems must adapt to their environments. They must be structured in a way that enables them to get what they need from their environment, to relate to their environment in a way that legitimates them to other organizations, and to respond to threats or problems in the environment.

The systems perspective is attractive because it allows scholars and practitioners to simultaneously consider all of the complicated processes that make up human action in organizations. In fact, the "systems theory" perspective dominated organizational communication research during the 1960s and 1970s. It lost popularity somewhat after 1980 because the perspective was so complex that it was very difficult to conduct truly systemic research and because the versions of systems theory that had been developed did not seem to recognize adequately that human *action* and the processes through which employees create meanings and construct and interpret messages are central to organizational communication systems.[27] But, the systems perspective recently has been revived as scholars have recognized that it is possible to incorporate notions of meaning-creation and action into a systems framework. In fact, one of the major themes of Unit I of this book will be that an organization's *communication systems* strongly influence the processes through which its employees make sense out of the experiences they have, the messages they receive, and how they respond strategically to those events and messages.

Organizations are systems of individuals pursuing multiple goals by creating and interpreting menages within complex networks of interpersonal and task relationships. Organizational strategies and situations emerge and are reproduced and transformed through systems of influence and information exchange, and the taken-for-granted assumptions of different societies and different relational groups tell people how to interpret the communication system that exists in their organizations. Conversely, characteristics of the organization's communication system influence employees' interpretations of events and messages. For example, if employees take it for granted that dishonesty is the normal way of conducting interpersonal relationships in their organization, breakdowns in systems of information exchange (like those discussed in Chapter 2) are likely to be interpreted as dishonest manipulation. It matters little that communication breakdowns might be an inevitable part of organizational communication systems. Within the interpretive frameworks of employees of this organization, inevitable structural breakdowns are interpreted as intentional manipulation. Conversely, in an organization whose employees value openness and honesty, the same breakdowns might be interpreted quite differently. In short, the systems perspective provides a framework for understanding why processes of creating, exchanging, and making sense out of messages function as they do. The description of organizational communication systems presented in this chapter is not intended to be comprehensive. Like the brief summary of *strategy* and *context* presented earlier, it is intended to provide readers with a *perspective* for understanding the interrelated processes that make up organizations and organizational communication.[28] It is based on the four key concepts of *wholeness, hierarchy, networks,* and *process.*

System Wholeness

It is often said in systems theory that the whole is greater than the sum of its parts. Systems are made up of components, but once those components are put into relation with one another, the entire assembly functions as a whole that is qualitatively different from any of its parts. An automobile engine functions on an entirely different level than do any of its individual parts. A cake is created from separate ingredients, but once baked (i.e., once the ingredients are joined to each other) the cake is an entity totally different from any of its ingredients. In the same way, an organizational system is more than the sum of its individual members and units or their particular relationships to one another.

For example, most charitable fundraising agencies are composed of office staff, telephone and personal fundraisers, advertising and promotion staff, accountants and bookkeepers, managers, and a board of directors. Each individual member has particular skills and values, strengths and weaknesses. Joined into units, such as the accounting department, individuals' skills and strengths can compensate for each other's weaknesses, and together they can achieve things they could not on their own. The units become wholes in their own right; they evolve their own goals and operating procedures, and they develop a set of values and culture of their own. Joined into an organization, the units, too, can achieve different outcomes and have different values than they could on their own. Accounting units keep the fundraisers honest. Advertising and promotion keeps the whole charity visible in the community, increasing revenues. But advertising and promotion would have no budget for their operations without the fundraisers (nor would the accountants get paid without those they monitor). In a very real sense, the charity functions as it does only because of its *entire* configuration of people and units. But the people and units would not be what they were without the whole. It is through their place in the charity that they realize their potential. This process, through which a dynamic interdependence of parts and whole creates a unique overall system has been called **emergence** by systems researchers.

System Hierarchy

The concept of **system hierarchy** is the notion that every system is embedded in a group of larger systems (suprasystems) and that every system is made of a number of smaller, interdependent subsystems—in short, a system is more than the sum of its parts. For example, the loading crew of a freight company is a system made up of a number of subsystems (workers, their interpersonal relationships, and so on), which are made up of smaller subsystems (each worker's perceptual processes, tasks, information-processing activities, memories, expectations, family, church, and social ties, and so on). But the loading crew is only one part of the production suprasystem of the organization, which is only one part of the freight company (supra-suprasystem), which is part of the even larger trucking industry, and so on. At any given time, the actions of any of the many employees or subsystems of employees in the organization (the loading crew, for example) may be influenced by the actions of any of the other interrelated subsystems or suprasystems of people. Information is *input* into a system through one or more of its subsystems. It is "processed" as it moves through the system and eventually becomes *output* that is processed by other systems and subsystems.

However, this depiction of organizations as systems of information exchange can lead people to forget that subsystems, systems, and suprasystems are not made of things, they are made of people. Each person carries with her or him a complex set of beliefs and values—about the organization, the nature of work, the other people in his or her immediate work group and the other work groups with which she or he has contact. Each person also has a different history and different expectations regarding their future with their organizational system, other subsystems and suprasystems, and all of the people with which they have relationships. These beliefs, values, histories, and expectations have an important influence on the information that people pay attention to, the ways in which they interpret ("process") that information, and what they decide to do with that information. And, as I will explain at length in the following section, people also are involved in a complex set of interpersonal relationships both within their immediate work group and with other people both inside and outside of their organization. Their attention, interpretations, and actions in part depend on how a given item of information is located in their relational networks.

Consequently, employees define the situation(s) they face in their own individual ways, and those definitions change as they perform new and different tasks, participate in interpersonal relationships that develop and grow, receive and interpret new information, and have interpretations are confirmed or disconfirmed. Their strategic choices are influenced by the entire matrix of pressures, goals, and concerns that they experience, all of which also are emerging and changing. As a result, individual employees may make decisions that are difficult for other employees to understand. Their choices probably make sense to them, and they usually *do* follow a characteristic pattern, although an outsider who does not know every nuance of the individual's situation often will find it difficult to see the "rationality" of her or his choices (I will examine rational and "nonrational" aspects of organizational decision-making at length in Chapter 7).

System Networks

The third key concept of the systems perspective—after *wholeness* and *hierarchy*—is **networks**.[29] Traditional systems perspectives tended to conceptualize communication networks in narrow terms—as *channels* or *conduits* through which chunks of information "flowed." The key concepts in this perspective were *boundaries,* and *roles.*

A boundary defines the limits of a system. Although this concept often is thought of in concrete terms (the physical walls of a freight company's building, for example), it really is an intangible barrier—more information flowed inside of this barrier than across it. Organizations (systems and subsystems) are *containers* whose boundaries isolated their members from outside information to one degree or another.[30] Tightly sealed boundaries were *impermeable* and organizations with them were *closed;* other boundaries were more or less permeable and their organizations were more or less open.

People played more or less stable roles in these networks of information exchange. Different systems (or subsystems) were linked together by **liaisons**, people who connect two systems or subsystems but are not members of either one. For example, in universities librarians often play this role. They may have worked with researchers in the medical school who are conducting research on a communicable disease and with people in social psychology who are studying the social and economic backgrounds of victims of the same disease. When one group makes an important discovery the librarian may pass that information to members of the other subsystem. Other people are **isolates** who rarely exchange information with other people; others are **gatekeepers** who control the flow of information throughout the network; others are **boundary spanners** (sometimes called *cosmopolites*), people who transmit information across system or subsystem boundaries.[31]

This version of systems theory had two very positive effects on our understanding of organizations and organizational communication. It focused attention on the environment surrounding organizational systems and subsystems; in short it forced researchers to recognize that organizational communication was *contextual,* embedded in a complex social and economic context. And, by outlining the multiple roles and functions played by people in communication networks, it indicated just how complicated information flow actually is.

But, traditional systems theories tended to underestimate the complexity of communication networks. Fortunately, recent versions of systems/network analysis have started to confront both weaknesses. They recognize that each member of an organization is simultaneously involved in multiple networks. We are part of networks based on friendships (affective networks), of other networks based on our desire to accomplish our goals (power and influence networks), of other networks that we create in order to deal with an immediate crisis, challenge, or task. Some of these networks overlap because some of the people we form relationships with are attractive to us (and we are attractive to them) for many reasons—they are friends who also have power in our organizations, for example. Communicating with people in some of our networks has an important effect on our beliefs, values, and ways of perceiving reality; communicating with people in other networks does not.[32]

Some of our networks involve people who are tightly connected with one another. In them, everyone knows how members of the network are supposed to think and act, people talk about the appropriateness of the behaviors of other members, and people reward one another based on the extent to which they communicate and act in approved ways. People who are members of only tightly connected networks tend to resist change and fall prey to "groupthink" processes. Expertise tends to be limited and shared, that is, everyone knows everything that everyone else knows, but not much of anything else. Others of our networks are more diverse, more loosely connected, more contentious.

The ties that we have within each network also vary. We have **strong ties** to some of the people in the network; we have weaker ties to other members. We talk more frequently with people with whom we have strong ties and they provide us with emotional support and the resources needed to accomplish everyday tasks. However, they provide us with little new information or encouragement to try new things.

Those with whom we have **weak ties** are more likely to provide us with new ideas and expertise, and encourage us to take risks and break out of old patterns of behavior. They also tend to have more extensive connections with people who are outside of our own networks. For example, Mark Granovetter found that white-collar employees are more likely to hear about job opportunities through weak ties than through strong ones.[33]

We also talk about different things to different "ties." Some relationships are **uniplex**, in which the parties always talk about the same topic (for example, work or sports). Others are **multiplex** relationships in which the parties communicate about a wide variety of topics and play a number of different roles with one another (for example, boss, collaborator on a key project, tennis partner, and so on). Multiplex relationships tend to be long-term, emotionally intense, influential, trusting, and more predictable than uniplex relationships. Communication tends to be deep, involving a good deal of self-disclosure, and rich, providing much emotional and cognitive detail. They provide us with social support and opportunities to vent our frustrations, thus helping us manage stress and make positive changes. And they also may increase our stress because it takes time and emotional energy to maintain intense relationships.

Finally, contemporary systems/network perspectives view networks and the roles that people play in them as emergent and changing. Cynthia Stohl says flatly that "*network boundaries are always permeable and never stable* . . . we are all *boundary spanners* . . . we move into [networks] and influence one another through an endless series of textured lengths."[34] The networks in which we participate, and the interpersonal relationships that make up those relationships, are constantly changing as our communication needs evolve and change. We play different roles in different networks at any given point in time, and each of those roles and networks is constantly changing. This does not mean that networks are chaotic, however.

Like any other aspect of organizational communication, networks are *strategic.* The strategy of organizing that is operating in an organization guides and constrains our relationships and the networks we form because it influence the activities that we are involved in. Activities are focused around persons (birthday parties, for example), places (the mythical "Cheers" bar), organizational positions (managers meeting with other managers), tasks that need to be performed, and so on. Our activities lead us to communicate with some people and not with others. These contacts are repeated, leading us to form more permanent links with some people and not with others, and these links become our communication networks. In effect, existing networks, psychological factors, situational barriers, and activities form guidelines and constraints for network emergence, and our networks and activities reproduce those guidelines and constraints.

Steve Corman and Robert McPhee have illustrated these concepts in a study of a local church. People who study religious organizations long have recognized that participating in church activities is interrelated with commitment to the organization—members who actively participate in the church's activities are highly committed to the church, and people who are highly committed to the church are actively involved in activities. But, Corman and McPhee found that the networks that emerged in the church also influence members' commitment and activity levels. Some church activities involve only an "elite" group of members. Sometimes this elite was formally defined—deacons (elders) meet together without other people being present. But sometimes the elite resulted from the amount of effort required by the activity itself. Only certain people become Sunday School teachers because it requires so much time and effort; a very different group joins the church basketball team because it requires a different level (and kind) of effort. Eventually networks form around these activities among the "elite" participants. Although these networks help create commitment to the church and its activities by those who participate in them, they also make it difficult for people who are not part of the elites to participate in them. Unless someone is involved in the activity, she or he is excluded from the network and unless he or she is part of the network, it is difficult to be involved in the activity. Sometimes new people are able to enter into the networks. Someone who already is a member invites them to join in the activity, where they meet highly committed members who encourage them to take the effort to be involved in demanding activities, and they become part of the network. But, people who do not receive these invitations find it difficult to enter into the core activities, do not become part of influential networks, and are unlikely to develop the level of commitment needed to participate in even more demanding activities. Eventually they give up and the churches lose many potentially valuable members.

Networks also are *contextual.* Part of that context involves preferences that employees bring with them to their organizations. We tend to invite people who are like us to join in our activities, people of the same race, gender, ethnic and socioeconomic background, citizenship, residence (even in terms of the same suburban subdivision), and education (degree, major, and school) and not to issue invitations to "different" people from those networks. It simply is easier to communicate with people who are like us. They will provide information that we think is important in a form that we can easily understand

and base their recommendations of beliefs, values, and interpretive processes we share. When we are surrounded by similar people our lives are more stable and predictable, and misunderstandings are less likely. When we encounter complex problems or crisis situations these advantages are multiplied.

For organizations, this preference for forming network ties with similar people may cause problems. Networks of similar persons tend to be tightly connected, and thus have all of the related problems. In addition, similarity-based networks tend to create artificial advantages for some employees and artificial disadvantages for others. Since the members of elite networks in organizations tend to be Anglo males, the network emergence process tends to close out women and members of minority groups (this idea is developed at length in Chapter 10). Because they are filled with people who think alike and have similar expertise, they often make lower quality decisions than more diverse groups would.[35]

Other parts of the context within which networks emerge involve concrete aspects of the work situation. For example, 3M's upper management has said publicly that they moved their research and development activities from Minneapolis, Minnesota, to Austin, Texas, because the weather in Minneapolis-St. Paul made it difficult for people to get together with one another. People just did not go from one building to another in the cold of a Minneapolis winter. So, valuable networks and network links never were formed. (As far as I know 3M's management never has publicly explained why their employees are willing to go outside in the middle of a Texas summer, but the example makes my point anyway—concrete things like weather, noise, distance, and schedules all influence network development).

Systems in Process

The first three ways in which organizational communication is systemic involved the concepts of wholeness, of hierarchy, and of networks. The final key concept is that of system process, the ways in which communication systems adapt, change, or remain the same. Three types of processes can be distinguished: self-regulation, adaptation, and self-renewal.

Self-regulation refers to the process by which systems achieve certain goals or attain certain desirable states of stability. All open systems have two types of goals: survival and purposive goals. Survival is the basic, lowest-order goal of all systems: ensure that the system maintains itself in a viable state. Survival involves maintaining the system's integrity and, in some cases, reproducing the system. To survive, a fast food restaurant chain must keep customers coming in so that it can generate the revenues needed to sustain it. But in today's competitive environment, it is also important for chain restaurants to be represented in as many cities and towns as possible, because this wins customers who will patronize other outlets for the chain when they travel or move. So fast food restaurants not only want to ensure patronage, but they also want to "reproduce" themselves by setting up franchises far and wide. Systems also have purposive goals, that is goals or standards they set up to achieve that go beyond survival. For example, the fast food chain might set two goals: 10 percent profit per annum and 15 percent growth in number of franchises per year. These help the chain act purposively and, if attained, ensure its growth and continued fitness in the future.

Traditional systems theorists developed the principle of **equifinality**, the idea that in complex situations there are a number of avenues to the same objectives. The application to organizational communication is a bit more complicated. It assumes that employees naturally develop communication processes that meet what they perceive are their needs and the needs of their organizations. When these patterns of communication are repeated over and over, they become stable parts of the organization. When situations change, the patterns also change temporarily as people adapt to new pressures. But eventually the patterns return to much the same circumstance as before—people act in ways that reproduce their communication systems.

Consequently, in terms of self-regulation, communication systems tend to be **homeostatic**, that is, they are constantly adapting, but in doing so they are staying much the same. They strive to maintain a stable state around a certain balance of inputs and outputs and a certain level of goal attainment. These stable but continually emerging patterns also help organizations by (1) constraining (controlling) the actions of employees, and (2) allowing the organization and its component subsystems to meet their needs for information and coordination. Of course, the patterns of communication that emerge in one organization may be both similar to and different from those that emerge in another organization—this is the essence of the principle of *equifinality.* Even when two organizations are alike in most respects, their patterns of communicating may be different. Organizations and units of organizations tend to develop their own "personalities." Of course, organizations do change. Organizational change is related to the second major systems process, *adaptation.* To thrive, it is necessary for organizations to adapt to their environments. If their environment changes, or if they move into a new environment, the organization must change as well. Our fast food chain will have to change if society begins to decide, as ours has recently, that much fast food is too fatty and not healthy. The chain may decide to change the types of food it offers, for example, put in salad bars and offer baked dishes. Or the chain may move into another type of business, for example, concentrate on serving meals in high schools, where the younger students are not as concerned with health issues and regularly go through "french fry withdrawal." Or the chain may shut down its outlets in health-conscious areas and reopen new ones where health is not such a hot issue. When the fast food chain decides to open franchises in China—definitely a different environment for organizations than the United States—it may have to change the structure and operation of these franchises in many respects, from the types of food served to how personnel are treated.

In adapting, the organization must balance change with the stability provided by the older structures. Because organizational systems are made up of people and not parts, they cannot always change "on a dime." People who have worked in the organization may resist some types of changes, and they may be slow in adopting even those they accept. The organization's culture may preclude some types of change, or at least make them very difficult to implement. Organizations that successfully adapt are able to acknowledge that stability as well as change is needed.

The degree to which an organization can control how it adapts and changes varies widely. Sometimes the changes are intentional and "planned." More often they are **unanticipated consequences** of strategic choices. But, even then the changes are predictable if one only knows the characteristics of the communicative systems that have emerged in the organization.

A vigorous, adaptive organizational system remains so because of the third process, **self-renewal**. Organizations, made up as they are of people and machines, need to replace these parts as they grow old, unable to perform, or unwilling to adapt. One way in which organizations renew themselves is by making sure to bring in fresh, new people and new technology. The danger in this case is that the new people and machines will challenge too radically a structure and culture that has worked well, simply for the sake of newness. In many cases self-renewal is most effective if it replenishes and refreshes rather than changes the organization. How new members can be integrated into organizational relationships and how cultures can be produced and sustained are important topics discussed in later chapters.

However, an organization must learn too, and this is also an important part of self-renewal. It is not only important to maintain, but to expand perspectives, to try out new things, to experiment. Much evidence suggests that organizational learning cannot be planned, but occurs in part through trial and error and in part through taking advantage of unexpected opportunities that arise. To innovate and learn, organizations have to build in a certain amount of slack resources and allow members to use these resources for experiments. The organization should be open to these trials and should not penalize members for mistakes, because mistakes lead to learning and improvement. For years 3M Corporation has maintained a reputation for being one of the most innovative firms in the United States. A standard policy at 3M is to give members license to steal time to work on new ideas and to reward people even for failures, as long as they keep trying to generate new ideas and products.

The other way to learn is to take advantage of unexpected opportunities and events. Open systems expose themselves to their environments and thus are open to many unanticipated happenings. They can use these to make themselves stronger and more adaptive. Sometimes these unexpected opportunities come by accident. The story is told that one of 3M's biggest successes, the ubiquitous Post-It Note, came about because of an accident that produced an adhesive that held only temporarily and could be easily peeled off. Rather than throwing out this batch of adhesive, creative 3M staff tried to figure out what it could be used for. The result has replaced many a thumbtack, paper clip, or piece of tape. In other cases unexpected opportunities for learning comes from failure. In his book *Groupthink*[36], Irving Janis recounts the story of the disastrous failure John F. Kennedy's administration created when it planned the Bay of Pigs invasion. This humiliating defeat stung Kennedy deeply, and he and his advisors used it to learn how to do things differently. This learning paid off when the same set of people performed excellently during the Cuban Missile Crisis, widely regarded as a major victory for Kennedy.

Opening up organizational systems to learning is critical to their growth and survival. Remaining open to new ideas and opportunities to learn is not always easy or even pleasant. But the organizations that are able to do so reap great benefits.

SUMMARY: THE COMPLEXITIES OF ORGANIZATIONAL COMMUNICATION

Organizations emerge through communication, are maintained through communication, and change through communication. Simultaneously, communication is a societal creation. Persons' interpretations of the messages that they encounter and produce at work are influenced by the taken-for-granted assumptions of their societies and those interpretations in turn form the situations that guide and constrain their communication. Consequently, the *context* surrounding an organization both influences and is influenced by the *strategic choices* made within the organization. Similarly, the context surrounding the organization influences the formation, maintenance, and modification of its communication *systems*. Our networks depend in part on our notions of whom we should communicate with and how we should communicate with them— *networks* are influenced by societal myths, just as the interpretive frameworks that we use to make sense out of the information flowing through those networks are socially constructed. Communication systems also are influenced by strategies of organizing and by individual employees' strategic choices. Together, these three core concepts provide a coherent view of organizational communication. But, understanding organizational communication fully involves recognizing that it is *strategic, contextual,* and *systemic,* and that each of these components is related to one another in complex ways.

An example of these complex relationships comes from the U.S. Senate.[37] Originally the Senate was designed to be a body characterized by deliberate, careful decision-making by people who were relatively impervious to the whims and pressures of public opinion (at least in comparison to the U.S. House of Representatives). In systems theory terms, the Senate was intended to be a relatively *closed* system. This *strategy of organizing* was implemented in a number of ways—long terms in office and rules making it difficult to stop debate (and thus encouraging and allowing filibusters to occur), for example. As times changed, so did the Senate. The growth of political parties, and later the two-party system led to a number of changes—the growth of the committee system and the role that seniority played in committee appointments—but even these changes *reproduced* the overall organizational strategy. In fact, perhaps the most important *rule* of the Senate was that junior senators, and especially first-term senators, were to be seen and not heard. Hubert Humphrey, who eventually authored more successful legislation than almost any senator in history, did not introduce a single bill during his first six-year term—he obeyed the rule perfectly. Senators also had opportunities to develop complex, *multiplex* relationships with one another. They had offices across from one another and thus saw one another frequently at work, dined in one another's homes, spent weekends together in a variety of activities, and did so across party lines and political ideologies, creating a number of *weak ties.* So, when a young Senator Richard Nixon heard that the young senator whose office was across the hall (John Fitzgerald Kennedy) was planning a trip to Paris, he provided him with a list of "folks to see in gay Paree" (network researchers call the effects of having adjoining offices a **proximity effect**). When Bob Dole resigned from the Senate, he could talk honestly about the close personal friendships that he had made with senators with *very* different political views—people like George McGovern and Hubert Humphrey.

But, today the Senate is a very different place. The same strategy of organizing still is in place, but the *context* has changed. Party control has weakened substantially, as party endorsements and funds from party coffers have become less important determinants of being re-elected. The omnipresence of the electronic media in Washington has forced the Senate to become a more open system. Even first-term senators can affect events directly, as California Senator Barbara Boxer did when she rejected the Senate Judiciary Committee's decision not to hold public hearings on improper actions of Oregon Senator Robert Packwood. She could do so only because the media provided a *resource* that she could use to overwhelm the Senate's traditional rules regarding seniority and party control. In addition, they spend relatively little time interacting informally with one another. Skyrocketing campaign costs combined with some provisions of campaign finance reform mean that senators must spend almost every weekend, and many evenings, in their home states raising funds. For a number of reasons the two parties have become more and more homogeneous and less and less tolerant of dissent (and of people who spend time with members of the other party). They have been forced to depend on their staffs rather than on one another for information on bills that are coming up for a vote. As a result they are more and more dependent on the *tight, uniplex* relationships that they have with their staffs and party colleagues for the information that they receive and the beliefs, values, and frames of reference that influence their interpretations of that information. Ironically, many of these changes were the *unintended consequences* of actions taken by the Senate, actions like reforming campaign finances, televising Senate debates, and relying on provocative "press conferences" as a means of getting free television news coverage. And, as the Senate has changed, senior members, especially those who are politically moderate or who relished the interpersonal ties possible in the "old" Senate have resigned—people like Nancy Kassebaum and Sam Nunn. In short, the strategic choices of the senators have transformed the Senate, creating new *rules* and *resources* that promise to continue the growing polarization of the organization, and increasing the likelihood that "gridlock" will continue. Of course, these changes are even more complex than the description that I have provided. But, they do suggest that understanding the Senate as an organization (or even understanding one of its key processes, "gridlock") requires a careful analysis of the *strategic, contextual,* and *systemic* nature of communications and organizational communication.[38]

At this point, all of these ideas may seem to be a little overwhelming. At least, at this point I hope that most readers feel a little overwhelmed. Communication is an exceptionally complex process; organizational communication is an especially complex type of communication. There are a depressingly large number of books, training programs, and consultants' gimmicks that depict effective organizational communication as the simple application of "five foolproof techniques" or some equivalent. Unfortunately, these depictions are as glib as they are misleading. There are a number of principles that employees can use in most organizational situations. But they are neither simple, foolproof, nor applicable in every case. My goal in this book is to explain those principles and to indicate how people can analyze the complexities they face at work and choose appropriate strategic responses, recognizing all the while that the choices they make usually will serve to reproduce the complexities they face.

THE DESIGN OF THIS BOOK

The following chapters are divided into two units. In Unit One I will expand the conceptualization of strategic organizational communication that was introduced in this chapter. Chapters 2 through 4 will examine the three dominant strategies of organizing that are used in contemporary organizations, what I will call the "Traditional," "Relational," and "Cultural" strategies. In Chapter 5, Marshall Scott Poole will expand the perspective to describe the impact that new communication technologies have had on strategies of organizing and the impact that strategies of organizing have had on the use of communication technologies.

The chapters that make up Unit Two discuss a number of challenges that members of modern organizations face. Chapter 6 examines the communication strategies that employees can use to manage membership in organizations, using the experience of entering and adapting to a new organization as an organizing framework. Chapter 7 expands the discussion of organizational power and control that permeates Unit I, while focusing on ways to deal with organizational politics. Chapters 8 and 9 examine decision-making and conflict from the perspective of strategic communication. The final three chapters deal with some of the most important developments facing organizations as we move into the twenty-first century—the increasing diversity of our population and workforce and increasing concerns about ethical issues surrounding organizations.

NOTES

[1] These conclusions are supported by the results of surveys of college graduates who majored in speech communication that recently were conducted by the Speech Communication Association and the International Communication Association. More systematic studies that reach the same conclusion are summarized in Patricia Hayes Andrews and Richard T. Herschel, *Organizational Communication* (Geneva, IL: Houghton-Mifflin, 1996, pp. 16–18); Theodore Zorn, "Communication-related Abilities and Upward Mobility," *Human Communication Research, 12* (1986):420–431; and Virginia P. Richmond and K. David Roach, "Willingness to Communicate and Employee Success in U.S. Organizations," *Journal of Applied Communication Research, 20* (1992): 95–115.

[2] Cal Downs and Charles Conrad, "A Critical Incident Study of Effective Subordinancy," *Journal of Business Communication, 19* (1982):27

[3] See Nina Anderson Legg, Other People's Kids: Decision-making About Sexual Education, Master's Thesis, Texas A&M University, 1992.

[4] Organizations need to control more than employees' overt actions. They also strive to control their interpersonal relationships. Some version of the military command that "officers cannot fraternize with enlisted personnel" exists within almost all organizations. Often the command is never spoken, because it need not be. Associates (recent graduates) in law firms learn by observation that they should not initiate conversations with senior partners, but should respond immediately when partners initiate communication with them. Assembly workers at Dana Corporation learn that they are expected to have lunch with upper management, and upper management learns that they are expected to have friendly but relatively superficial interpersonal relationships with rank-and-file workers. In both cases the organization subtly controls the kind of interpersonal relationships that employees form and maintain. Organizations do vary in how tightly they control their members' actions and relationships, but all organizations place people in interdependent roles, and consequently all organizations rely on control for coordination, and thus for survival.

[5] Stewart Clegg provides an excellent explanation of how bureaucratic organizations became the dominant organizational strategy in Western democracies (see *Modern Organizations,* London: Sage Publications, 1990), especially Chapters 2 and 3.

[6] See George Kennedy, *Classical Rhetoric in Its Christian and Secular Traditions from Ancient to Modern Times* (Chapel Hill: University of North Carolina Press, 1980).

[7] A similar concept has been developed by rhetorical theorist Lloyd Bitzer in "The Rhetorical Situation," *Philosophy and Rhetoric, 1* (1968): 1–14. Since its publication, a heated debate has taken place about his ideas. This interchange led him to modify his original position to focus on the dynamic nature of situations. Coincidentally, many of the examples that he used in his later articles involve organizations and organizational communication. See, for example, "Functional Communication," in *Rhetoric in Transition,* Eugene White, ed. (University Park, PA: Pennsylvania State University Press, 1980), especially pp. 27, 36–37.

[8] Anthony Giddens uses the term "rules" to encompass what I call "guidelines" and "constraints." I do not use his term because readers might confuse it with the much simpler (and very different) use of the term "rule" in the bureaucratic models of organizational control that are discussed in Chapter 2. My conception of "resources" and their relationship to guidelines/constraints is based on his work. See, for example, *Central Problems in Social Theory* (Berkeley: University of California Press, 1979) and *The Constitution of Society* (Berkeley: University of California Press, 1984).

[9] Fortunately, we were able to develop an appropriate strategy for him. He was an excellent basketball player. We decided that he should "play sandlot ball," which meant to assume the organization was completely unstructured, and that he should

watch for opportunities as they developed, pursue the opportunities that developed (for example, take what the opposition gives you), be flexible, and watch out for blind-side screens (that is, protect yourself). I assumed that over time his job would be less of an anarchy, that he would eventually find stable patterns that made life simpler, but my impression now is that chaos is a normal state of affairs for stockbrokers and that "playing sandlot ball" may be good advice for their entire careers. Eventually he decided that the chaotic and stressful life of a major college basketball coach was preferable to the chaos of his new job, and he now is in a career where he gets paid to "play sandlot ball."

[10] For a case study of how face-to-face communication reproduces strategies of organizing, see Teresa Harrison, "Communication and Interdependence in Democratic Organizations," *Communication Yearbook 17,* Stanley Deetz (ed.) (Newbury Park, CA: Sage, 1995, pp. 247–274).

[11] Clegg, *Organizations.* The most important of Weber's works on the relationship between the characteristics of Western societies and its organizations is *The Protestant Ethic and the Spirit of Capitalism* (New York: Charles Scribner's and Sons, 1958).

[12] Clifford Geertz, "Common Sense as a Cultural System," in *Local Knowledge* (New York: Basic Books, 1983).

[13] For an extended discussion of organizational metaphors, see Chapters 4 and 6 of this book and Cynthia Stohl, *Organizational Communication: Connectedness in Action* (Thousand Oaks, CA: Sage, 1995), pp. 10–13.

[14] Recently Warren Bennis, Jagdish Parikh, and Ronnie Lessem have argued that this tension is characteristic of many societies (*Beyond Leadership: Balancing Economics, Ethics, and Ecology* [Cambridge, MA: Basil Blackwell, 1994], especially Chapter 10).

[15] See the introduction to the second edition of Robert Bellah, et al., *Habits of the Heart,* 2nd ed. (Berkeley: University of California Press, 1995). A number of excellent case studies of how the tension between individuality and community are enacted in organizations are available. See, for example, Connie Kubo Della-Piana, "Performing Community," paper presented at the International Communication Association Convention, Chicago, 1996, and C.W. Reynolds and R.V. Norman (Eds.), *Community in America: The Challenge of Habits of the Heart* (Berkeley: University of California Press, 1988). Tensions related to workforce diversity will be examined at length in Chapter 11. For a summary of de Tocqueville's observations and their applicability today, see John Cawelti, *Apostles of the Self-Made Man* (Cambridge, MA: Harvard University Press, 1974) and Stanley Deetz, *Democracy in the Age of Corporate Colonization* (Albany, NY: SUNY Press, 1992).

[16] Stephen Barley and Gideon Kunda, "Design and Devotion: Surges of Rational and Normative Ideologies of Control in Managerial Discourse," *Administrative Science Quarterly, 37* (1992): 363–399. Although I do not agree with all of Barley and Kunda's conclusions—particularly their analysis of historical "waves" of theorizing—their arguments about the tension between individuality and community are compelling.

[17] See, for example, William Ouchi and A. Jaeger, "Type Z Organization," *Academy of Management Review, 3* (1978): 301–312 and William G. Scott and D.K. Hart, *Organizational America* (Boston: Houghton Mifflin, 1979). Unfortunately, the available evidence suggests that today these organizations play a much weaker role in our lives than they did in de Tocqueville's time.

[18] Organizational myths, stories and rituals will be discussed at length in Chapter 4.

[19] Sonia Ospina has persuasively argued that the central tension in U.S. culture is this conflict between the myth of individual opportunity and merit and the realities of different opportunities based on one's race, gender, class, and ethnicity (*Illusions of Opportunity* [Ithaca, NY: ILR/Cornell University Press, 1996]).

[20] For an extended explanation, see Stewart Clegg, *Frameworks of Power* (Newbury Park, CA: Sage, 1989); Charles Conrad, "Was Pogo Right?" in Julia Wood and Richard Gregg (Eds.), *Communication Research in the 21st Century* (Creskill, NJ: Hampton Press, 1995, pp. 183–208); and Charles Conrad, "Work Songs, Hegemony, and Illusions of Self," *Critical Studies in Mass Communication, 5* (1988): 179–201; and T.J. Lears, "The Concept of Cultural Hegemony," *American Historical Review, 90* (1985): 567–593. An excellent treatment of the complicated relationship between class and gender is available in Karen Hansen and Ilene Philipson, (Eds.), *Women, Class, and the Feminist Imagination* (Philadelphia: Temple University Press, 1990).

[21] Jeffrey Pfeffer and Alison Davis-Blake, "The Effect of the Proportion of Women on Salaries," *Administrative Science Quarterly, 32* (1987): 1–24; Robin Clair and Kelly Thompson, "Pay Discrimination as a Discursive and Material Practice," *Journal of Applied Communication Research, 24* (1996): 1–20.

[22] In general, I have chosen to use the terms that I do to refer to different groups of non-white employees because they seem to be preferred by members of each group. The reasons for my choice of terminology for persons of Spanish descent is a bit more complex. I use the terms "Latino" and "Latina" as *generic* terms to refer to men and women of Spanish descent respectively. I use the term "Mexican American" to refer to residents of the United States who were born in Mexico or whose families immigrated from Mexico. I do not use the term "Hispanic" at all because it is used in so many different ways, even in the scholarly literature, that its use is inevitably confusing. These terminological distinctions are important because the experiences of Latino and Latina persons in American organizations are very different depending on their heritage. In particular, people who immigrated from or whose families immigrated from Central and South America or the Caribbean face different attitudes and have had different experiences than those with roots in Mexico. I also use the pronoun "persons" instead of "people," because it better reflects the wide diversity and individuality of people who typically are identified by their race or ethnicity.

[23] Lynn Martin, *Pipelines of Progress* (Washington, D.C.: U.S. Department of Labor, August 1992, p. 12); also see "Corporate Women," *Business Week* (June 8, 1992) and Korn/Ferry International, "The Decade of the Executive Woman" (New York: 1993).

[24] See, for example, Stuart Hall, "Encoding/decoding," in *Culture, Media, Language,* S. Hall, D. Hobson, A. Lowe, and P. Willis, eds. (London: Hutchinson, 1982).

[25] Goran Therborn, *The Ideology of Power and the Power of Ideology* (London: Verso, 1980). For an extended treatment of how this notion compares to and contrasts with different concepts of hegemony, see Dennis Mumby, *Communication and Power in Organizations* (Norwood, NJ: Ablex, 1988), especially Chapter 4.

[26] In short, organizations are stratified social systems embedded in stratified societies (B. Schneider, S. Gunnarson, and J. Wheeler, "The Role of Opportunity in the Conceptualization and Measurement of Job Satisfaction," in C.J. Cranny, et al. (eds.), *Job Satisfaction* (New York: Lexington Books, 1992).

[27] Extended summaries of the history of the systems theory perspective are available in Eric Eisenberg and H.L. Goodall, Jr., *Organizational Communication* (New York: St. Martin's Press, 1993) and Terrance Albrecht and Betsy Bach, *Communication in Complex Organizations: A Relational Perspective* (Fort Worth, TX: Harcourt, 1996).

[28] The basic outline of systems theory was proposed by German philosopher and biologist Ludwig von Bertalanfy and applied to organizations by American scholars Talcott Parsons, Daniel Katz, and Robert Kahn. Like Max Weber and Thorstein Veblen, von Bertalanfy rarely is read by U.S. students. This unfortunate state of affairs

results, I think, from the kindness of professors who seem to realize that the original works of philosophers and many social scientists are almost unreadable for most students. As a result these works are assigned to graduate students, because professors also seem to believe that mastering pain is an important part of graduate school. For readers who want this experience, the bibliography at the end of this book contains a number of appropriate citations.

[29] This section is based largely on Cynthia Stohl, *Organizational Communication: Connectedness in Action* (Thousand Oaks, CA: Sage, 1995) and on conversations with Scott Poole.

[30] A now-classic summary/critique of this version of systems theory was provided by Steve Axley, "Managerial and Organizational Communication in Terms of the Conduit Metaphor," *Academy of Management Review, 9* (1984): 428–437.

[31] The latter group plays four important functions for a system. First, they provide the system and its subsystems with information about the organization's **environment** (all those people, events, organizations, and natural forces that impose pressures on the organization or its members) Second, they control the distribution of this information through the organization (thus playing a gatekeeping function), thus preventing the *information overload* that would occur if employees were deluged with all of the information that is available in the system's environment. In a sense, boundary-spanners *absorb some of the uncertainty* that is created when people confront new information. Third, they *protect people inside the organization from outsiders* who would like to influence their behavior, as anyone knows who has ever tried to communicate directly with the head of a large, bureaucratic organization. The final function played by boundary spanners is *representing the organization to outsiders*. Boundary spanners *legitimize* their organization by providing outsiders with evidence that the organization is striving to meet the outsiders' needs. They also *influence* the activities and attitudes of outsiders through carefully planned and executed persuasive communication. Of course, the functions played by boundary spanners are not independent of one another. They obtain information about how outsiders view their organizations, diffuse that information throughout the relevant parts of the organization, and persuade the outsiders that the organization has adapted to or is in the process of adapting to their concerns. Information gathering, information buffering, diffusion, and image management all are interrelated elements of the boundary spanner's organizational role. See J. Stacy Adams, "The Structure and Dynamics of Behavior in Organizational Boundary Roles," in *Handbook of Industrial and Organizational Psychology,* Marvin Dunnette, ed. (Chicago: Rand-McNally, 1976); Michael Tushman, "Impacts of Perceived Environmental Variability on Work-Related Communication," *Academy of Management Journal, 22* (1979): 482–500; and Howard Aldrich and D. Herker, "Boundary Spanning Roles and Organizational Structures," *Academy of Management Review, 2* (1977): 217.

[32] James Danowski, "Group Attitude Uniformity and Connectivity of Organizational Communication Networks for Production, Innovation and Maintenance Content," *Human Communication Research, 6* (1980): 299–308.

[33] Mark Granovetter, *Getting a Job* (Cambridge, MA: Harvard University Press, 1974). For an interesting application of this idea to the lives of recently widowed women, see Bryan Hirsch, "Psychological Dimensions of Social Networks," *American Journal of Community Psychology, 7* (1979): 263–277.

[34] Stohl, pp. 26, 39. Networks also seem to be "in our heads," not "out in our organizations" as traditional systems theories suggested, see Steve Corman, "A Model of Perceived Communication in Collective Networks," *Human Communication Research, 16* (1990): 582–602.

[35] Rosabeth Moss Kanter, *Men and Women of the Corporation* (New York: Harper & Row, 1977) and *A Tale of "O:" On Being Different in an Organization* (New York:

Harper & Row, 1980). For analyses of how network inclusion/exclusion is related to organizational power, see Robert Jackall, "Life Above the Middle," *Harvard Business Review* (September-October, 1982): 47–54, and Jeffrey Pfeffer, *Power in Organizations* (Marshfield, MA: Pitman, 1981).

[36] Irving Janis, *Groupthink,* 2nd edition (Boston: Houghton-Mifflin, 1982).

[37] A number of distinguished Washington reporters have recently written about the changes that have taken place in the U.S. Senate. For example, see David Broder, "Congress *Sans* Personal Relationships is Gridlock," *Houston Chronicle,* June 23, 1996: 3C; Haynes Johnson, *Divided We Fall: Gambling with History in the 1990s* (New York: W.W. Norton, 1994). The Nixon-Kennedy example that follows is taken from Christopher Matthews, *Kennedy & Nixon* (New York: Simon & Schuster, 1996).

[38] Similar changes have taken place in the U.S. House of Representatives, so much so that by mid-1996 Representatives David Skaggs (D-CO) and Ray LaHood (R-IL) proposed that all members of the House and their spouses participate in a retreat to "restore a bit of fellowship in a Congress whose poisonous partisanship has sickened, not just the votes, but many of the members" (David Broder, "Retreat May Be a Tonic for Acrimonious Congress," *Houston Chronicle,* July 21, 1996, 3F). Ironically, during the 1970s and 1980s after each election first-term representatives of both parties joined together for a week's discussion with one another at Harvard's Kennedy School of Government. But, as relationships got more acrimonious during the 1990s the Republicans pulled out of the Harvard retreats, and members of each party began meeting only with one another. Fortunately, the tradition has been renewed in 1997.

The leaders of each party regularly played cards with one another during the week and played golf together on weekends. Rep. Larry Combest (R-Texas) noted that in the old days, representatives "had intense debates, but they would walk off the floor arm in arm, because they were friends. That's the way it ought to be, but it's not the way it is here" (quoted in Broder).

Chapter 2

TRADITIONAL STRATEGIES
OF ORGANIZING

*The foreman should never be authorized to enforce his discipline
with the whips if he can accomplish it with words.*

—VARRO OF ROME, C. 100

*If the words of command are not clear and distinct, if orders are
not thoroughly understood, the general is to blame.*

—SUN TZU OF CHINA, 500 B.C.

CENTRAL THEMES

- Since the beginning of recorded history, people who work in organizations have recognized the crucial role that communication plays in their success.
- By the early 1900s a number of scholars and practicing managers realized that Western organizations faced serious problems. Their search for an alternative led to the development of "traditional" strategies of organizing.
- Traditional strategies of organizing attempt to control employees through rules, norms, and systems of rewards and punishments, all of which rely heavily on communication. But all control systems lead to resistance.
- If information is filtered as it passes through the formal chain of command, decision-makers may have too little relevant information to make good decisions; if it is not filtered, they may be too overloaded with information to make good decisions.
- Both structural and personal/interpersonal factors lead to omission and distortion of information as it passes through formal channels.
- When the environment surrounding an organization is stable or not competitive, traditional strategies of organizing may function well; when the environment is turbulent or competitive, weaknesses in formal communication systems make it difficult for traditional strategies to succeed.

- In traditional strategies of organizing, "leadership" primarily involves "managing," that is, designing and implementing formal systems of communication, motivation, and control.

KEY TERMS

Formal communication	Absorbing uncertainty
Special expertise	Trained incapacity
Hierarchy	Lateral communication
Centralized decision-making	Redundancy
Scientific job design	Counterbiasing
Legal authority	Malicious obedience
Structural barriers	Regressing
Trained incapacity	Management by objectives
Condensing	Equity theory
Simplifying	Organizing
Assimilating	Commanding
Whitewashing	Coordinating
Reductively coding	Controlling

As the ancient comments at the beginning of this chapter suggest, neither the study of organizations nor of communication in organizations is terribly new. Whenever people have depended on one another to complete tasks or meet their needs, they have formed *organizations*. By the time human beings joined together into families and clans, they had become involved in the economic activities of hunting and gathering. They had started to organize, which required them to communicate with other workers. Still later, after humans had become farmers, they developed more complex organizations with more complicated communication needs. With farming came villages and the need to govern groups of people; with villages came the concepts of citizenship and community welfare, which created the dual needs of defense and the management of the village's economy. As organizations became more complex, the nature and functions of organizational communication changed.

THE CONTEXT SURROUNDING THE DEVELOPMENT OF TRADITIONAL STRATEGIES

As villages became city-states it became necessary for their managers to plan the operation of the society and to keep permanent records of the rules and procedures that they developed. The oldest written documents in existence deal with religion, management, and government, a combination that makes great sense when one realizes that the earliest managers also were governors and priests. As ancient religious and political civilizations expanded, their needs for effective economic organizations and effective organizational communication multiplied. As early as 2000 B.C. leaders recognized the importance of communication. Pharaoh Ptah-hotep instructed his sons and managers in the importance of listening skills, the need to seek advice and information from their subordinates, the importance of staying informed about what was taking place around them, and the necessity of clearly explaining each worker's tasks and documenting these instructions in writing. The Chinese emperors Yao and Shun (c. 2300 B.C.) also searched for ways of opening communication channels between themselves and the peasants and advocated consulting their subordinates about the problems faced by the government. By the time of Christ, Greek and Roman scholars had suggested many of the key concepts of modern organizational communication theory. But it was the growth of the nation-state and the mercantile system that created separate roles for governors, managers, and priests. The large and complex firms of the Industrial Revolution made it clear that control and coordination could be achieved only through effective communication.[1]

Communication in Preindustrial and Early Industrial Organizations

Before the Industrial Revolution, the Western world was dominated by a domestic system of production. Small groups of workers, almost always families, obtained equipment and produced something (usually textiles) for a small local market. Because every member of these family organizations performed simple, repetitive tasks within sight of every other member, the communication needs of these "organizations" were minimal. Coordinating the activities of family members was simple; technological advancement and sophisticated managerial techniques were neither needed nor possible. Eventually these family businesses started to "put out" their products, contracting with local merchants to purchase their goods at an agreed-on price.

At some point these merchants started to provide the families with both the raw materials they needed and with a market for their finished goods. Family entrepreneurs had become employees. They no longer were involved in a cooperative family enterprise in which each member shared profits and losses. Instead, they were "hired help" whose interests coincided with their employees, but only to a limited degree. They soon learned they could increase their profits by weaving their cloth less tightly. This minor change in quality allowed them to produce more cloth *and* to sell the raw materials they saved on the black market. In spite of strict laws against it, this kind of fraud became so widespread that it ended the system.

The history of the putting-out system is important because it reveals three concepts central to organizations: (1) Employees have their own goals, desires, and incentives and, all other things being equal, they will act in ways that are consistent with what they perceive is in their self-interest; (2) in order to have adequate levels of control, organizations must be able to make workers be *accountable* for both the quantity and quality of their output; and (3) supervisors must be able to obtain accurate information about the activities of their subordinates.

With the invention of power-driven machinery, home production was replaced rapidly by large factories.[2] The cost of the new machinery was far beyond all but a few families, and improvements in transportation enabled factories to have access to a large enough market to sell all their production. Although the owners of these early factories paid little attention to effective management, even the managers of the late 1700s discussed the key concepts of division of labor, planning, job design, controlling employees, creating acceptable working conditions, and rewarding employees in ways that would increase their productivity.

The first systematic design of an organization took place during an expansion of the Soho Engineering Foundry in Great Britain in 1800. Equipment purchases, factory layout, job design, and incentive systems all were based on carefully obtained information. One of the primary concerns of the designers of the Soho plant was effective **formal communication**, that is, the exchange of particular kinds of information, through formally established channels for purposes defined and accepted by the organization. A detailed accounting system was devised so that supervisors could have accurate and up-to-date *information* about the performance of their units. In addition, a combination of weekly wages and bonuses based on the number of items produced by each worker was implemented. Because this wage system was complicated, the designers realized that it would succeed only if it was *easily and clearly communicated to workers.* Thus, as early as 1800, managers realized that *control*—guiding and constraining employees' actions—and *coordination* depended on effective communication.

Unfortunately, the people who operated these organizations had few reliable guidelines. Each of them had some experience in business and could rely on hunch and intuition. But people's memories often omit or redefine their failures and overemphasize successes, so experience often is not a reliable guide. Managers also could try to apply the principles used to run military organizations, not so much because their factories were like armies, but because armies were the only large, complex organizations that existed before the Industrial Revolution. And in both cases—businesses and military organizations—people often were appointed and promoted more on the basis of their political ties to owners or government officials (including royalty) than on the basis of their competence. Owners' decision-making suffered from a lack of concern for efficiency, a virtual absence of reliable information, and an ever-present ability to blame the effects of their foolish decisions on the workers.

In addition, owner-managers often treated their employees in arbitrary, capricious, and even inhumane ways. Proslavery politicians of the 1800s defended that institution by arguing that the lives of slaves were better than the lives of workers in Northern textile mills. There was enough of a parallel to make the argument credible. As a result workers began to organize politically and by forming unions. Labor–management relations became increasingly hostile and confrontations between labor and management often were violent. The broad, rapid economic growth of the 1800s came to a screeching halt in a series of economic depressions during the 1890s. By the early 1900s both managers and scholars recognized that Western organizations faced serious problems in design and operation. In response to these observations, a group of organizational theorists proposed an alternate form strategy of organizing, one that sought to manage the paradox between organizational and individual needs through efficient operation, the elimination of arbitrary supervisory behavior, and motivation of workers through economic rewards and a sense of personal achievement.

TRADITIONAL STRATEGIES OF ORGANIZATIONAL DESIGN

A large number of people were involved in the development of the "traditional" strategy of organizing. One group (which I will call the "scientific managers") tried to improve organizations from the bottom up, by reforming workers' tasks, efficiency, and rewards. A second group, the "bureaucratic theorists," attempted to improve organizations from the top down, by improving the effectiveness of administrative employees. Both groups had the same primary concern—replacing the arbitrary, capricious, and inefficient practices of contemporary organizations with systematically designed, objective, and fair systems of management and supervision.

Centralization, Specialization, and Hierarchicalization

Although they approached organizations differently, both the scientific managers and the bureaucratic theorists believed that organizational efficiency would come through segmenting an organization into specific tasks that were performed by people with the **special expertise** required by those positions, arranging those positions in a **hierarchy**, and **centralizing decision-making** at the top of that hierarchy. The former group was led by Frederick Taylor; the key figure in the latter group was Max Weber.

Frederick Taylor and Scientific Management.   Taylor believed in a new strategy of organizing that was based on a new set of attitudes and a group of scientific managerial techniques. Managers' primary goal, he argued, should be to create a cooperative relationship with their workers. This kind of relationship could exist if managers accepted responsibility for *both* their successes and their failures, instead of blaming and punishing workers for their errors, and if they fairly shared the economic rewards that would come from increasing organizational efficiency. Although these attitudes may not seem to be all that radical today, they were to Taylor's contemporaries. They were attractive only because they were coupled with a set of efficiency-enhancing techniques. Through these techniques firms would be able to increase their profits, the income of *all* their employees (including managers) and to reduce their prices, thus benefiting all consumers.[3]

Implementing Taylor's "principles" of scientific management began with a survey of all the tasks that needed to be performed for a particular organization to function. Each of those tasks was then assigned to a particular employee or group of employees who would be taught the most efficient means of accomplishing them. But, before workers could be trained, managers had to discover the most efficient techniques, a process that Taylor labeled **scientific job design**. Managers started by consulting with workers about the best ways of doing their jobs. It then involved redesigning tasks through "time-motion" studies, in which the supervisor or a consultant observed workers completing each task, broke the process down into its elements or motions, and then redesigned it so that the number of movements necessary to complete the task was minimized. Part of time-motion study was determining the attributes— mental and physical—that workers needed to possess in order to most efficiently complete each task. I once was transferred to a different division of a foundry because a time-motion study discovered that workers taller than six feet could not efficiently run the drill presses that I was operating. Today a number of consulting firms, armed with video technology, still conduct time-motion studies and make recommendations that improve efficiency and reduce worker strain and fatigue.[4]

Once tasks were scientifically designed, workers could be selected based solely on the extent to which they possessed the necessary attributes. Workers who were too tall—my foundry immediately quit hiring drill press operators who were more than six feet tall—or too short, too weak or too strong, would not be placed in jobs that were difficult to perform.[5] Once selected, workers would be trained in the most efficient techniques of completing their assigned tasks and rewarded for their individual productivity. Not only would everyone involved reap financial rewards from the increased efficiency that came from these techniques, workers also would begin to feel a sense of *achievement* from succeeding in their tasks.[6] Through a *combination* of careful selection, effective communication of the best means of completing a task (training), adequate incentives, and supervisory communication that both gave workers feedback on their performance and supported their efforts, organizational productivity and labor-management cooperation could be enhanced.

Of course, the cooperation was to be based on the mutual self-interest and economic rewards that came from increased organizational efficiency. Techniques like time-motion studies, scientific selection of workers, and rational decision-making by supervisors were important elements of scientific management. But the techniques were meant to be used within an organizational context that was humane, consultative, efficient, and rewarding. The strength of scientific management was its careful integration of a number of organizational subsystems. He recognized that selection, training, job design, consultation between supervisors and subordinates, and the administration of reward systems all influenced one another in important ways. If communication broke down within any of these subsystems, the efficiency of the others would be reduced. Although Taylor was not familiar with systems theory itself, he devised a form of organizing consistent with the complex, interactive nature of human systems.

The Bureaucratic Theorists.   Taylor and the scientific management group primarily were concerned with making the people at the bottom of the organizations more efficient, productive, and satisfied. Other theorists of Taylor's generation were concerned with increasing efficiency at the top of the organization, in the administrative staff. They were more concerned with communicating because most of a manager's time is spent doing it. The most important of these theorists was Max Weber.

Today Max Weber is known mostly for his lengthy discussion of *bureaucracies,* the kind of organization that seemed to him to best "fit" the cultures of Western democracies.[7] As people in Western democracies mature, they learn that formal rules are necessary for the efficient operation of their societies and its organizations, and serve to protect them from arbitrary or harmful treatment by more powerful people. We are taught to view societies of "law, not men [sic]" as normal and natural. We also learn that the individual is most important, that *individuals* have rights and that *individuals* should be rewarded or punished for their actions. We learn to accept what Weber called **legal authority**, the notion that societies and organizations should be organized around a formal, impersonal (and thus objective) written set of rules, policies, and procedures.

Weber believed that administration could be made most efficient through processes of specialization, hierarchicalization, and centralization; in fact, he was very much concerned that organizations designed and operated in this way would inevitably eliminate other types of organizations and the social goods that those non-bureaucratic organizations provided to society. In this highly efficient strategy of organizing, people would be selected solely on the basis of their *technical expertise* for positions with clearly defined responsibilities that required that expertise, that is they would be *specialists.* They would base their decisions *solely* on the written policies, procedures, and rules of the organization, and all of their actions should be documented in writing. Only those employees at the top of the organization would be empowered to actually establish policies and procedures or make major decisions. But, in order to prevent favoritism, even they would have only detached, impersonal relationships with clients and coworkers and keep emotional considerations from influencing their actions. Employees should be *evaluated* solely on the basis of their performance.

The positions should be arranged in a *hierarchy,* usually shaped like a pyramid, in which the supervisors are directly responsible to their own immediate supervisor for their own actions and for those of their immediate subordinates. Each supervisor would be responsible for ensuring a free flow of job-related information between their subordinates and their own supervisor. Communication should be limited to this chain of command, because only then can responsibility for communication breakdowns be assessed and remedies taken.

Today firms like the ones Taylor envisioned often are viewed as sweatshops where workers are treated like inhuman cogs in a giant industrial machine and the term "bureaucracy" has a number of negative connotations—images of inefficient bureaucrats producing little save exhaustive expense accounts; of customers and employees alike being buried in red tape and treated as nonhuman cogs in a vast administrative morass; and of stubbornness when action is required, blind obsession with unchangeable policies when flexibility is necessary, and interminable delays when speed is crucial. These images of the traditional strategy of organizing really are quite ironic. The original purpose of this strategy was to create efficient and productive organizations in which people were treated fairly and equitably. The arbitrariness and capriciousness that Taylor and Weber observed in the organizations of their time were to be replaced by policies and procedures that treated everyone—workers and customers/clients—in the same way. The inefficient decision-making of early firms was to be replaced by careful, data-based considerations. Although the strategy focused on meeting the organizations' needs for coordination and control, it also was intended to meet individual employees' needs for stability and autonomy.

People need stable and predictable lives. Organizational structure provides stability and predictability.[8] Bureaucratic structure is clear and predictable. It also allows managers to supervise their employees more loosely. In the family organizations that existed before the Industrial Revolution, a supervisor (father) was always present "looking over the shoulders" of his employees (wife and children) and maintaining control. Supervision was almost as tight in the firms of the early Industrial Revolution. However, effective formal communication, coupled with clear and enforced rules, procedures, and policies and an effective reward system, allows supervisors to monitor their employees without having to watch over them as constantly. Consequently, as long as employees act within the broad policies and procedures that their organizations established, they can experiment with different ways of completing their assigned tasks. They are given some room—both figuratively and literally—to be creative, although this latitude is quite small by modern standards.

But the traditional strategy also is problematic in two ways. Perhaps most important, its key elements—specialization, hierarchicalization, and centralization—place a great deal of pressure on an organization's formal communication system. Consequently, communication breakdowns are highly likely. Second, the strategy sacrifices flexibility and responsiveness for consistency and predictability. Although this is an appropriate trade-off in some organizational contexts, it creates serious problems in others.

Communication Breakdowns in Formal Communication Systems

For the traditional strategy of organizing to succeed, a number of communicative requirements must be met. First, a number of different kinds of information must flow from subordinates to the decision-makers at the top of the organization, information about the extent to which orders have been carried out and tasks have been completed and information about problems that have developed or are likely to develop in the future. In addition, each employee along the chain of command has his or her own unique areas of expertise (that is the purpose of specialization), and thus can provide unique insights into the challenges faced by the organization. If that expertise is not made available to upper management, their decision-making will suffer. Similarly, information must flow from supervisors to subordinates, information about policies, procedures, reward/rule systems, and the optimal means of performing each subordinate's assigned tasks. And, this information must be *accurate, timely,* and *both complete and concise.* If any of these communication processes breaks down, the organization will function at less than optimal efficiency.[9] If the margin of error available to the organization is small, these communication breakdowns may threaten its survival.

The Filtering Paradox.   Unfortunately, processes of information exchange create a fundamental paradox. On the one hand, upper-level decision-makers depend on a free flow of information from employees located lower in the hierarchy. However, if information did flow freely through the chain of command, the upper-level managers soon would be overloaded and overwhelmed by the information generated in their organization. For example, in a moderate-sized hierarchical organization (for example, one in which each supervisor had only four subordinates and the organization chart had seven levels) in which each employee sent only one message a day to be sent up the chain of command, 4,096 messages would reach upper management each day. Therefore at each level some messages must be screened out and others must be abbreviated.[10] But, if every employee screens out only half of the information received, 98.4 percent of the information generated in the organization would never reach its decision-makers. Consequently, the traditional strategy of organizing requires employees to simultaneously (1) rely on formal channels for the information they need and (2) restrict the flow of information through these channels. Of course, the paradox exists for all organizations.[11] But, the key elements of the traditional strategy makes it more of a problem than it is with other strategies of organizing. Fortunately, employees of even organizations using strict traditional strategies are able to cope with this paradox in a number of ways that I explain later.

Structural Barriers to Information Flow.   A number of factors complicate the filtering paradox. Some of these barriers to information flow involve the people who make up the organization—their background and training, personal characteristics, and interpersonal relationships. But others involve the formal structure of the organization and the nature of human communication. These **structural barriers** would exist regardless of who worked in the organization.

When one person communicates a message to another, each of them interprets it. The words that make up the message are meaningless until some human being makes sense out of them.[12] When we communicate we exchange our interpretations of information, not information in a "pure" form. When we interpret messages we alter their meaning. We **condense** messages, making them shorter and simpler; we **simplify** messages into good or bad, all or none, or other extreme terms; we **assimilate** new messages so that their meaning is similar to the meaning we attributed to information received in the past or expect to receive in the future; we **whitewash** messages, making them conform to the frames of reference of the people to whom we will send the messages; and we **reductively code** messages by combining them with other information to form a sensible overall picture, especially when the message is complex or ambiguous. In the process of interpreting we simplify and clarify the message, that is, we **absorb some of the uncertainty** and ambiguity in the message. But, we also change it.

Interpreting information is inevitable because all messages carry some degree of ambiguity, some degree of uncertainty about how they should be interpreted. In fact, this ambiguity can be valuable (see Chapter 6). But, each time a message is exchanged, the meaning is altered. If an organization is *centralized,* messages will be exchanged (and interpreted and altered) many times before they reach the decision-makers at the top of the organization. Many messages only slightly resemble their original form when they reach their destination. Interpretation/uncertainty absorption are natural and inevitable processes, but they also limit the flow of information through the organizational hierarchy.

Finally, the value of information to decision-makers is reduced when it is provided at the wrong time, particularly when it is too late to be used. Communicating through the chain of command is very time-consuming, as any student who has needed to change a registration for a course or searched for a "lost" student aid check is painfully aware. None of the barriers to information flow described in this section involve intentional actions by employees. They stem from the nature of communication processes and are exacerbated by key elements of traditional strategies of organizing. But, as I will explain later in this chapter, intentional withholding or distorting of communication does occur, and it also is made more likely by key attributes of traditional strategies.

Trained Communication Incapacity.   Another element of the traditional strategy of organizing is *specialization.* Specialization is intended to increase organizational efficiency by making sure that tasks are performed by people with the most relevant expertise. But, specialization also complicates information flow.[13] As people are trained in an increasingly specialized set of skills, they become less and less capable of performing other tasks, both because they lack the information and training necessary to perform them and because they eventually become incapable of learning the alien skills or adopting the alien patterns of thinking. They develop **trained incapacity**. Employees playing specialized roles tend to interpret the messages they receive in a manner appropriate to those roles. For example, personnel officers interpret messages in terms of what they imply about future needs for hiring, firing, or training employees; and financial officers attribute meaning to messages based on the economic impact that they imply. As their training and experience progress, employees become less capable of taking the perspectives of other members of the organization when interpreting or sending messages. They also create their own languages.

As employees become literate in the artificial language of their position or unit, they become less capable of translating their ideas into a language that other people can understand.[14] Of course, computer operators do not develop a "foreign" language because they want to be misunderstood. They do it because it allows them to communicate among themselves rapidly and efficiently. A frequent complaint heard by communication consultants is that people in specialized areas—computer operations and the legal department seem to be mentioned regularly—cannot be understood by people outside their units and do little to try to be understood. Although these complaints probably are exaggerated, they do reflect the difficulties that nonspecialists or people with different specialties encounter when attempting to communicate with these specialists. In fact, some recent research indicates that effective specialty units often assign someone (usually the manager of the unit) the specific job of communicating, or translating, to people outside the unit.

This phenomenon exists across different units of an organization and across different levels of the hierarchy. Supervisors perceive messages differently than do their subordinates, even when they once held their subordinates' positions. As a result, misunderstanding often is more common than understanding. Robert Miner found that in 63 percent of the superior–subordinate conversations that he studied, there was less than a 50 percent chance that the two parties shared the same information. Norman Maier found that supervisors and subordinates often did not even agree on whether they had met with each other during the past week.[15] In general, supervisors perceive that their subordinates are much better informed than they really are and as a result pass less information on to them than they need. When the organization has a large number of levels, subordinates receive even less information from other sources, making communication with their supervisors even more important and problems of distortion of downward communication more damaging.[16] The size of an organization in itself does not seem to increase problems of trained incapacity, but when an organization has a large number of units or tasks that are highly specialized trained incapacity can create severe problems.[17]

Specialization and trained incapacity also complicate **lateral communication** (between employees of one unit and employees of another), making it more difficult for employees to develop sources of information outside of the formal chain of command. Specialization creates efficiency *within* each specialty, but reduces the effectiveness of communication *across* specialties. It may reduce flexibility and the ability to cooperate with people who have other kinds of expertise that could be used to solve pressing organizational and societal problems.

Interpersonal Barriers to Information Flow.   A number of personal and interpersonal factors also complicate information flow (see Table 2-1). The *amount of communication* flowing through the chain of command is restricted by status differences among members of an organization. Since the traditional strategy highlights status differences, especially between managers and non-managers, less communication takes place and when communication does take place, it is more formal. Messages are communicated in writing instead of face to face, and they focus on tasks, with little informal or social content. Written messages are more ambiguous than those exchanges in open, face-to-face encounters, making differences in interpretation more likely. In general, interpretations of task-related information is greatest when the parties use *both* written and face-to-face communication.[18]

Differences in interpretations tend to reduce trust, which leads employees to rely more heavily on written communication in order to protect themselves, and so on in a downward spiral. Focusing solely on task information creates *uniplex* relationships, which also impede communication.[19] Supervisors can offset these effects by de-emphasizing status differences, training their subordinates in communication skills, rewarding their subordinates for keeping them informed, and encouraging them to seek clarification of ambiguous messages. However, supervisors often do the opposite by verbally or nonverbally communicating "I don't want to hear about it now" (talking while "on the run," using an annoyed tone of voice, physically moving away from the subordinate, and allowing other people to interrupt the conversation) or by failing to acknowledge or act on the information their subordinates provide.[20] Subordinates who lack trust in their supervisors send less information up the chain of command, especially if they desire promotions or recognition for their past accomplishments. This apparently is because they fear reprisals and assume that if their supervisors do not know what is going on, they are less likely to react negatively.[21] In highly political organizations, withholding information is even more likely, especially when it is negative. As Chapter 7 explains, information is a potent source of power, but only if it is not widely available. Political battles—between individual employees and between units of the organization—often are information battles, and the side that has obtained and exploited secret information wins.

Although this section has focused on barriers to the upward flow of information through the chain of command, downward communication also is limited by the same factors and processes. One of the most consistent findings in research on organizations is that subordinates want their supervisors to "keep them informed" and feel that they receive too little relevant and useful information from their supervisors, especially about events, policies, and changes directly involving them or their jobs. Many supervisors simply do not provide their subordinates with sufficient amounts of job-related information, especially feedback about the subordinates' performance.[22] Although some supervisors may convey as much as 80 percent of the available relevant information to their subordinates, others provide as little as 4 percent. Downward communication is selected, filtered, and interpreted in much the same way as upward communication. In addition, when supervisors believe that they should give their subordinates only the absolute minimum necessary amount of information, they filter an even higher proportion of downward communication, frequently withholding even crucial information.[23]

However, it also rarely is accurate to blame individual employees for withholding information. Doing so violates the process concept underlying a systems-theory view of organizations. No systems or subsystems are wholly independent of one another. Actions taken by one human system are interpreted by other systems, and their choices of how to respond are interpreted by still other systems, and so on in complicated, interactive cycles.[24] Subordinates "mirror" their supervisors' communication. Consequently, supervisors whose communication is considerate, frequent, and reliable tend to have subordinates whose communication is similar. Because they better understand their supervisors' information needs, they can better summarize the information they receive without leaving out important details. These subordinates keep their supervisors informed, which makes them seem trustworthy, and perceptions of trustworthiness reduce the distorting effects of status differences. In some supervisor–subordinate relationships positive cycles of open information exchange occur, but it is because of the nature of the communication *relationship* rather than because of the characteristics of any one individual. Conversely, supervisors who withhold information from their subordinates have subordinates who withhold information from them. The subordinates may interpret their own actions as an appropriate way to defend themselves against an untrustworthy supervisor; the supervisor may see the subordinates' actions as compelling evidence that they are hostile or unmotivated, which justifies the supervisor's withholding information, and so on in a destructive cycle. No individual is to blame (or should receive credit) for these patterns of action, although supervisors' higher formal power means that they have a greater effect on the direction the cycle will take. These patterns result from complex, interacting systems of meaning-creation and should be understood as complex systems of communication.

The *accuracy* of information flowing through the chain of command also is limited by interpersonal factors. As a general rule, little information that is negative or deals with controversial or sensitive issues is exchanged. Both supervisors and subordinates tend to be defensive during discussions of these topics, so interpersonal pressures against extended discussions in which both parties strive to fully understand one another are unlikely (Chapter 9 will examine this limitation in the context of organizational conflict). The likelihood of withholding information about negative or controversial topics is greater when (1) there are sizable differences in power or status between two people, and (2) they do not trust one another. If low levels of trust exist between a supervisor and a particular subordinate, other factors come into play. Subordinates who wish to be promoted, recognized for past advancement, and believe that the supervisor will have an influential voice on promotions also tend to withhold negative information from supervisors they do not trust.[25] The negative effects of these factors seem to be present even when the subordinate and the supervisor generally communicate in a free and open fashion. Those effects

TABLE 2–1
Factors That Distort Vertical Communication

STRUCTURAL	PERSONAL AND RELATIONAL

1. Processes of interpreting messages
  Condensation
  Accenting
  Assimilation to past
  Assimilation to future
  Assimilation to attitudes and
    values
  Reduction
	1. Power, status differences between
	parties

2. Number of links in communication chain	2. Mistrust between parties

3. Trained communication
  Incapacity
  Perceptual sets
  Language barriers
	3. Subordinates' mobility aspirations

4. Large size of the organization	4. Inaccurate perceptions of information needs of others
5. Problems in timing of messages	5. Norms or actions that discourage requests for clarification
6. Problems inherent in written communication	6. Sensitivity of topics

are increased when subordinates believe that their supervisors do not pass negative information on to them.[26]

Summary: How Traditional Strategies Complicate Information Flow.
When organizational roles are formalized, specialized, and distinct, differences in power and status between supervisors and their subordinates are increased. When relationships between supervisors and subordinates are impersonal and governed by established policies and procedures, trust and shared interpretations of information tend to be reduced. When supervisors are responsible for enforcing policies, procedures, rules, and reward systems, and written communication dominates, it is difficult to develop high levels of trust. It is precisely in this kind of situation that the flow of adequate amounts of accurate information through the chain of command is least likely. But it also is precisely the kind of situation that is fostered by traditional strategies of organizing. In short, traditional strategies rely heavily on formal, chain of command communication, and *paradoxically* create a number of barriers to successful information flow. If organizational communication really was restricted to formal channels, most people, in most organizations, most of the time could honestly say that they do not know what is going on.

CASE STUDY:
THE *CHALLENGER* CASE

Almost everyone knows the story of the January 28, 1986, launch of the space shuttle *Challenger.* Although the story tells us some important things about how difficult it is to design complicated equipment, it tells us a great deal more about how breakdowns occur in the formal communication systems of complex organizations. In fact, the *Challenger* case is not especially notable in itself—virtually all traditional organizations have the same kind of problems every day. What is notable is that the effects of NASA's communication problems were made public on national television. The immediate cause of the disaster was the failure of two O-rings, which were used to seal one of three joints in each of the two solid-fuel booster rockets that were produced by the Morton Thiokol company in Utah. From the instant of liftoff the damaged seals allowed a stream of super-heated gas to escape, burn a hole in the main fuel tank, and ignite its contents, turning the most technically advanced vehicle ever produced into a flaming coffin. Less well known are the events leading up to the launch, especially the communication breakdowns that led up to the decision to launch. The Presidential Commission on the Space Shuttle *Challenger* Accident concluded tersely that "the testimony reveals failures in communication that resulted in a decision to launch [mission] 51–L based on incomplete and sometimes misleading information" (Commission, p. 82).* This case explores those communication processes.

Safety always had been a major concern at NASA, so much so that separate safety oversight divisions were created in the shuttle project so that safety personnel could not be pressured into certifying unsafe equipment or missions. But independence carries a price. It means that the safety officers had to depend on the other divisions for information, and those divisions had incentives to withhold or reinterpret negative information. It also means that safety information had to pass through a lengthy chain of command before reaching the decision-makers in upper management. Safety officers were so independent that they were perceived as being unimportant. When NASA faced budget constraints after 1970, it fired safety officers—the total number declined 71 percent between 1970 and 1986. No safety officer was invited to participate in the prelaunch decision-making process for *Challenger.*

---

*This case is based on the report of the Presidential Commission, especially Chapter V, "The Contributing Cause of the Accident," Diane Vaughn, "NASA and the *Challenger,*" *Administrative Science Quarterly, 35*(1990): 225–257 and Diane Vaughn, *The "Challenger" Launch Decision* (Chicago: University of Chicago Press, 1996). For an interesting analysis of this case, see Judith Hoover, "NASA as a Myth System," paper presented at the Speech Communication Association Convention, Boston, 1987 and for an extended analysis of changes in NASA during its existence, see Phillip Tompkins, *Organizational Communication Imperatives: Lessons from the Space Program* (Los Angeles: Roxbury House, 1993).

(continued)

(continued from the previous page)

Finally, independence meant that the safety oversight groups had no power to reward or punish employees for their actions; in fact, NASA's overall reward/punishment system encouraged people to sacrifice safety for speed and low costs. Even after the *Challenger* disaster, no managers at NASA "were terminated or even publicly castigated by NASA" (Vaughn, p. 247). Similarly, there had been more than 25 occurrences of O-ring erosion and related SRB anomalies [booster rocket equipment problems] at the time of the accident.

> Thiokol had never been penalized, nor was there any evidence that punishment had been threatened. . . . Even after these [and other] violations became public, Thiokol was not penalized. . . . When rewards were great for cost savings and meeting deadlines and punishment was not forthcoming for safety infractions, contractors [like Thiokol] would tend to alter their priorities accordingly. Thiokol did comply, but with NASA production interests, not with safety standards (Vaughn, p. 248).

In December 1982, the O-rings were added to NASA's list of "criticality 1" features, a term meaning that a failure in this part could "cause a loss of life or vehicle" because it had no or insufficient backup systems. Unfortunately, this change was not communicated to all of NASA's division managers, so many of them believed that there were adequate backup systems. On at least three previous shuttle flights (in January, April, and October 1985) the seals had failed significantly. Lawrence Mulloy (manager of the Solid Rocket Booster division at the Marshall Space Flight Center) testified that "everyone" in NASA knew of these partial failures and the concern that they raised about the safety of the shuttles, especially when launched in cool weather (around 50 degrees). But "everyone" did not know. NASA had no centralized procedures or rules for reporting in-flight problems or any system for detecting trends across different launches. Consequently, each division and manager knew about problems in her or his area, but not about the overall picture of problems. Similarly, no one seems to have recognized that there had been O-ring problems on more than half of the flights. Presumably the safety group would be responsible for gathering, consolidating, and communicating the overall picture, but it had no way of extracting the information from the various divisions of NASA. After 1983, middle managers no longer were required to report safety problems to upper management, and when they did report problems Mulloy routinely waived the requirement that the problems be solved before the next flight (Vaughn, p. 236). Consequently, each of the subsystems designed to facilitate effective communication in the traditional strategy of organizing—the chain of command, centralized decision-making, and reward/punishment processes—was in some way missing at NASA.

(continued)

(continued from the previous page)

Other communication breakdowns occurred during the hours immediately before the launch. At 6 p.m. on January 27, a teleconference was held between NASA and Morton Thiokol. Weather forecasts were for a low temperature of 22 degrees during the night, rising to 26 degrees by launch time. Lawrence Ebeling, manager of Thiokol's booster engineering division, testified that "the meeting lasted one hour, but the conclusion of that meeting was that Engineering . . . were very adamant about their concerns on this lower temperature, because we were way below our data base [lowest temperature for a successful firing was 53 degrees]" (Commission, p. 86). The engineers' recommendation: "O-ring temp must be > 53 degrees F at launch" (Commission, p. 90). However, key figures remembered different interpretations. Committee member Keel asked Dr. Judson Lovingood of the Marshall Center, "So as early as that first afternoon conference at 5:45, it appeared that Thiokol was basically saying delay. Is that right?"

LOVINGOOD: That is the way it came across to me. . . .

DR. KEEL: Mr. Reinartz [manager of the shuttle project, Marshall Center], how did you perceive it?

MR. REINARTZ: I did not perceive it that way. I perceived that they were raising some questions and issues which required looking into by all of the parties, but I did not perceive it as a recommendation delay" (Commission, p. 87).

Three hours later a second teleconference began. It started with Thiokol's engineers presenting a set of charts on the "history of O-ring erosion" on previous flights and in tests that had been forwarded to the Kennedy Space Center. The engineers were worried that if the rings were too cold they would not be flexible enough to instantly seal the joint if they were needed. Engineer Boisjoly explained, "It would be like trying to shove a brick into a crack versus a sponge" (Commission, p. 89). He summarized the conversation:

> there was never one positive, pro-launch statement ever made by anybody [the engineers]. There have been some feelings since then that folks have expressed that would support the decision, but there was not one positive statement for launch ever made in that room.
>
> At about this time Hardy [NASA] was asked what he thought about the MTI [Thiokol engineers'] recommendation, and he said he was appalled. Hardy, also asked about launching, said that if the contractor recommended not launching, he would not go against the contractor (Commission, p. 90).

Soon after, Thiokol managers asked for a brief recess so they could caucus with their engineers in private. A 30–minute conversation followed. Boisjoly continued:

(continued)

(continued from the previous page)

Those of us who opposed the launch continued to speak out, and I am specifically speaking of Mr. [Arnie] Thompson and myself. . . . Arnie actually got up from his position which was down the table, and walked up the table . . . in front of the management folks, and tried to sketch out once again what his concern was with the joint, and when he realized he wasn't getting through, he just stopped. [Later] Mr. Mason [Thiokol management] said we have to make a management decision. He turned to Bob Lund [Thiokol vice-president of engineering] and asked him to take off his engineering hat and put on his management hat. From this point on management formulated the points to base their decision on. . . . I was not even asked to participate in giving any input to the final decision. . . . This was a meeting where the determination was to launch, and it was up to us to prove beyond a shadow of a doubt that it was not safe to do so. This is in total reverse to what the position usually is in a preflight conversation or a flight readiness review. It is usually exactly the opposite of that (Commission, p. 93).

Lund explained why Thiokol management had interpreted NASA's comments as pressure to launch:

We have dealt with Marshall for a long time and have always been in the position of defending our position to make sure that we were ready to fly. . . . But that evening I guess I had never had those kinds of things come from the people at Marshall. We had to prove to them that we weren't ready, and so we got ourselves in the thought process that we were trying to find some way to prove to them that it wouldn't work, and we were unable to do that (p. 94).

At approximately 11:00 p.m. Thiokol rejoined the conference and recommended that the shuttle be launched. Hardy [NASA] requested that the recommendation be put in writing and sent by fax immediately to Marshall and Kennedy.

However, the Thiokol engineers did have converts. Between 11:15 and 11:30 Allan McDonald [Thiokol's manager at Kennedy] argued against launching until being told that the launch decision was not his concern (Commission, p. 109). At later conferences within NASA lower-level managers either did not mention the O-ring discussion to upper management or discussed the concerns briefly, instead forwarding copies of the Thiokol fax recommending launch (Commission, pp. 109–110). The commission's findings included:

The Commission is troubled by what appears to be a propensity of management at Marshall to contain potentially serious problems and attempt to resolve them internally rather than communicate them forward. This tendency is altogether at odds with the need for Marshall to function as part of a system working toward successful flight missions . . . communicating with the other parts of the system. The Commission concluded that the Thiokol management reversed its position . . . at the urging of Marshall and contrary to the views of its engineers in order to accommodate a major customer (Commission, p. 104).

(continued)

(continued from the previous page)

The low temperatures also created concerns that falling icicles at launch would damage the shuttle, its main engine, or its fuel tank. The discussions between NASA and the shuttle contractor, Rockwell, were similar to the communication with Thiokol. The commission found that instead of reversing positions, Rockwell gave NASA only a highly ambiguous recommendation, which "was not clearly communicated to NASA officials in the launch decision chain" (Commission, p. 116).

Discussion Questions
1. Which of the sources of withholding/distorting information discussed in this chapter were present in the *Challenger* case? How were they related to the reward/punishment structure of the organization? How did they influence the decision to launch?
2. Did any of the participants show characteristics of "trained communication incapacity"? If so, how?
3. How did formal roles and reliance on the chain of command influence the events?
4. Are the communication problems that led up to the launch decisions inevitable in complex, hierarchical organizations? What changes could be made to prevent recurrence? Are these changes feasible in this kind of organization?

Inflexibility in Competitive and Turbulent Environments

So far in this chapter I have argued that traditional strategies of organizing rely heavily on formal systems of communication and that it is normal for these systems to break down. That analysis may lead readers to wonder just how these organizations manage to survive. The answer is that many organizations have minimal needs for rapid and accurate task-related communication. Some organizations exist in very stable environments, which place limited demands on organizational communication. Problems can be anticipated and situations can be understood rather easily, because they almost always are like those faced in the past, and tried-and-true solutions generally are available. Expertise, decision-making, and authority can be centralized; communication can be restricted to the chain of command; and so on. Information usually can be obtained through formal channels, and the kinds of communication breakdowns that are discussed in this chapter can be anticipated and offset. In stable environments, traditional strategies of organizing cope quite well with the limited amount of uncertainty that they face.

In contrast, organizations in highly competitive, rapidly changing, turbulent environments are effective when their work and communication structures allow a free, open, and rapid flow of information, not the restricted, formal, and slow chain of command. Organizations in turbulent environments often face complicated problems unlike any they have faced in the past. Open communication structures (such as those of the "relational" and "cultural" strategies of organizing described in Chapters 3 and 4) allow information about sudden environmental changes to be rapidly diffused throughout the organization. In addition, their employees can be involved in communication networks that include a large number of ties to people outside of the organization, and decision-making should involve any employees who have relevant information or expertise, not just upper management.[27]

For example, firms that manufacture plastics products face rapidly changing environments. Sources of raw materials (such as petroleum) are not particularly stable or predictable, as American plastics firms learned repeatedly during the 1970s. Production technology and research advance almost daily, and customer preferences and market demands change even more rapidly. For instance, what would you have done with a warehouse full of unsellable Hula-Hoops in 1985? If you had sold or destroyed them in 1986, how would you have felt in 1989 when they again became popular? How would you feel today if you had purchased more of them in 1987?

Of course, environmental pressures do not impinge on every member of an organization in the same way or to the same degree. Some employees perform tasks that place them closer than others to the source of the environmental uncertainties—"boundary spanners" who link the organization with outsiders. Employees who perform complex tasks are more vulnerable because they can be disrupted by many kinds of environmental changes. Sometimes environmental pressures quickly transform simple tasks into complex ones. Consider automobile mechanics, who often complain that today's complex, computerized vehicles are unrepairable. Their task once required a great degree of skill, but the analytical approaches involved were relatively straightforward. Fuel-efficient and pollution-reducing technologies have created engines in which the many subsystems are so highly interrelated that there no longer is any direct way to diagnose problems. As a result mechanics now have to rely on computerized equipment to analyze the malfunctions of other computerized equipment. The mechanics' task has become highly ambiguous, complex, and time-consuming, almost wholly because environmental factors have forced changes on them.

In the long run employees who deal with environmental pressures may find that they become more important to their organizations, and that this increased importance leads to rewards that offset the increased stress that accompanies dealing with environmental pressures. What is important is how employees interpret and respond to environmental turbulence, not the pressures themselves.[28] When employees choose communicative strategies that are appropriate to the information needs of the organization's environment, they can be most effective. When organizations adapt to the information and uncertainty-management needs of their employees, they are more effective than when they do not adjust.

Compensating for Communication Problems of Traditional Strategies of Organizing

Fortunately, there are a number of steps that members of organizations can take to compensate for the communication problems that are inherent in the traditional strategy of organizing. Since competition and turbulent environments magnify these communication problems, managers can take steps to reduce those pressures. Large firms can purchase, and then dissolve, competitors. Or, they can become even larger—monopolies and oligopolies are able to influence (perhaps even control) the prices and availability of inputs and sales in ways that reduce the environmental turbulence they face. Managers also often can persuade government to insulate them against environmental pressures, by placing patent or copyright restrictions on their competitors, or by using tariffs or other restrictions to make foreign competitors' products excessively expensive. Or they can focus some of the organization's activities on sectors of the economy that have relatively stable environments. For example, the largest U.S. tobacco firms diversified their activities during the 1980s, often being linked with stable industries like food production. Not only does diversification reduce the impact of a volatile environment, it allows firms to apply political and financial pressure on potentially problematic elements of their environment. For example, television news organizations might be tempted to air highly popular "exposes" of the tobacco industry if it was not for the massive advertising revenues that they receive from the tobacco companies' food subsidiaries. Of course, in a society that presumably values "free and open competition," many of these activities raise important ethical and legal questions (see Chapter 12). But, they help reduce the environmental pressures that organizations face.

Managers also can adjust requirements that employees follow the chain of command to create more flexible and adaptive communication systems. One of the early bureaucratic theorists, Henri Fayol, realized that there are times when following the chain of command is unwise. For example, customers of many health insurance firms currently are required to get the company's permission before having inpatient surgery. In emergencies this requirement is waived, although in order to receive payment, the patient and the surgeon must demonstrate that the case actually was an emergency. Fayol recognized that employees also sometimes face crisis decisions that make it impractical to enter into the time-consuming process of following the chain of command. In times of legitimate crisis, management should allow employees to bypass the formal chain and communicate directly with people in other divisions. They should be encouraged to form a temporary communication "bridge" across the formal hierarchy of the organization, provided that they can demonstrate to the people they bypassed that a legitimate crisis had occurred. Supervisors would still be able to limit and control their subordinates' communication, but the bridge would allow employees to communicate rapidly during crises. This does not mean that the chain of command can be abandoned. Fayol realized that the traditional strategy requires an appropriate balance between the stability that comes with following formal channels and the flexibility of bridging communication. Today, many organizations that seem to be organized around traditional strategies also use many of the nontraditional strategies that I will discuss in the remainder of this unit. What emerges are a number of hybrid organizational forms, each with its own strengths and weaknesses (see especially Chapter 5).

In addition, non-managerial employees also can choose *communication strategies* that compensate for problems in their organization's overall strategy of organizing. Most employees find that the same kind of information is withheld or distorted over and over again. Once employees find recurring patterns of communication breakdowns, they can compensate. They can offset problems of filtering and structural distortion by building **redundancy** into their own communication networks, that is, they establish links that allow them to obtain information about an issue from a number of different people before taking action. They offset personal and interpersonal barriers through **counterbiasing**, in which they determine the probable biases of each person who communicates with them, adjust their interpretation of the message to compensate this bias, and then talk about the topic with people who have different biases. In short, they can establish complex, overlapping communication networks so that they do not have to rely on the formal chain of command. (Informal communication networks were introduced in Chapter 1 and will be discussed in detail in Chapter 3.) Networks of communication are constantly emerging as people act in what they perceive are their self-interests.[29] Unless managers actively suppress these informal ties, they emerge naturally as people try to compensate for problems in formal communication. In meeting our own information needs, we often compensate for the communication problems of their organizations. Raymond Miles has summarized this process effectively:

> People violate their positional constraints for many reasons. They do so because of their own needs and desires—for security from threat and pressure, to develop or modify social ties, to satisfy needs for recognition and esteem, and so forth. They also do so simply because their position appears [to be] unclear or unworkable. . . . Thus, organizations not only may work less well than they were designed to work because of the interaction of people and their positions, but they also work much better than they have a right to perform . . . precisely because people do not accept their roles, relationships, and responsibilities as immutable.[30]

The paradox underlying the traditional strategy of organizing is managed through the strategic actions of individual employees.

TRADITIONAL STRATEGIES OF MOTIVATION AND CONTROL

One of the goals of the traditional strategy of organizing was to replace the arbitrary and capricious treatment of workers that often took place in turn-of-the century organizations with a scientifically designed and rationally implemented system of incentives and disincentives. All employees work in order to achieve goals, primarily economic ones, and a system that rewarded them following established rules and procedures and for maximizing their individual performance would be in everyone's self-interest. If appropriate rule and reward systems could be created, workers would *choose* to act in ways that met their needs and the needs of their organizations. Labor–management hostility would be replaced with cooperative, mutually rewarding relationships. But rule and reward systems succeed if and only if they are supported by effective communication.[31]

Motivation and Control through Rules Systems

Many people find rules systems to be an acceptable means of influencing their actions. This may be because of the way they were socialized—recall Weber's notion that in Western democracies children learn to accept rule-based systems—and it may be because they make our worlds stable, predictable, and in some ways simpler. Organizational theorist Karl Weick has noted that rules make it much simpler to negotiate organizational relationships. If rules are in place they place parameters around our choices of how to act, thus reducing the amount of time and energy we need to spend negotiating our actions. If few rules are available, it takes much more time and energy to negotiate our actions and relationships. For example, Rebecca Adams and Roxanne Parrot found that providing parents of pediatric patients with a written list of rules about how they would be expected to share caretaking with nurses while their children were hospitalized increased both the parents' satisfaction with the care provided their children and the nurses' job satisfaction. The rules made the ambiguous situation less confusing, and allowed the nurses to spend their time providing the parents with more information about the details of their children's care.[32]

But, even with these advantages, it still is difficult to fulfill the communicative requirements of rule systems. Employees will obey formal rules *only* if they *understand* the rules, are persuaded that the rules are *legitimate,* and believe that the rules are *supported by appropriate sanctions.* To succeed, rules must be expressed in clear and precise terms and be both general enough not to be seen as nit-picking and specific enough to define some actions as vital and others as forbidden. When rules are excessively constraining, employees rebel, covertly or overtly. Often supervisors respond to resistance by tightening the rules, which increases the probability of further resistance. The organization then finds itself immersed in destructive cycles of disobedience and dictatorial management.[33] Rules will be *seen as legitimate* only if they are believed to *apply equally* to everyone in the organization, are *fairly enforced,* and are *produced by the organization,* rather than by an individual. In addition rules will be perceived as illegitimate if they are applied outside an accepted range of activities. For example, rules about employees' private lives will not be accepted if employees perceive that their employer does not have a legitimate right to enforce them. At one time employees, especially managerial and supervisory personnel, gave their organizations the right to control much of their private lives. Today employees often refuse to accept company rules about where they should live, how they should spend their income, or what they should do with their leisure time. Municipal employees refuse to live within their city's boundaries, employees sometimes reject dress codes, and priests and nuns are beginning to reject canon law concerning celibacy and marriage, just as their parishioners long have rejected canon law about divorce and birth control. These changes do not mean that employees no longer obey those rules that they perceive as legitimate. Rather, the changes indicate that the range of actions over which employees grant their employers the legitimate right to enforce rules has changed. Finally, rules must be linked directly to sanctions—*punishments* or *rewards*.[34]

Resistance is an inevitable aspect of social or organizational control, because efforts to control employees' actions inevitably reduce their autonomy and creativity (recall the dilemma discussed in Chapter 1). Organizational communication transmits, produces, and reproduces organizational control, but it also reveals points at which control can be resisted. People can and do resist control systems, often doing so covertly because resistance often can be penalized or suppressed. But it is inherent in the nature of control and will occur whenever organizations guide and constrain employees' actions.[35]

The simplest forms of resistance are withdrawal and open rebellion. The former leads people to be progressively less involved in and committed to their jobs; the latter can culminate in sabotage. The disastrous chemical leak at Bhopal, India, in 1985 resulted in part from an employee's rebelling against being punished (fired) for breaking what he perceived as illegitimate rules. A cleaning woman once admitted that she retaliated against an especially controlling employer by cleaning her commodes with her toothbrush—for years.

Other forms of resistance are more complex. Employees sometimes rebel against their organizations by following rules exactly. Employees usually have a high degree of common sense and often ignore or revise inappropriate or counterproductive rules. As a result they give the organization a degree of flexibility that improves its effectiveness.[36] Rules must not be so specific nor obeyed so blindly that they eliminate this flexibility. During 1991, American Airlines pilots resisted management by following FAA regulations to the letter—filing *very* complete flight plans, requesting detailed weather reports, and engaging in other activities that are completely legal but rarely are absolutely necessary for flight safety (while denying in public that they were doing so). Turnaround time and flight delays skyrocketed, especially at American's Dallas–Fort Worth hub. Management retaliated by giving pilots they suspected of "working to rule" route assignments that reduced their income (while denying in public that they were doing so). Pilots countered by following the rules even more exactly, eventually paralyzing the airline through their strategy of **malicious obedience**. Employees also may respond to rules by **regressing**, that is, reducing their performance to the minimum acceptable standard the rules allow.

Whether the consequences are massive or minor, all forms of resistance serve the same purpose: They allow employees to rebel against rule systems with little chance of being detected. Some degree of resistance is inherent in all rule systems; the likelihood and degree of resistance depends on the extent to which rules are perceived to be legitimate and fairly enforced. Interestingly, while resistance may complicate an organization's operations in major ways, it rarely leads to major changes in organizations or organizational rule systems. The nature of the traditional strategy makes it difficult to locate and resist real sources of organizational control.[37] And, if resistance does threaten high-powered people, they usually are able to change the rules. For example, strikes long have been a potent way for unionized workers to resist management. But, first in the 1981 air traffic controllers' strike and increasingly since then, management has been able to hire (or threaten to hire) permanent replacements for striking workers, thus virtually eliminating strikes as a viable means of resisting management.[38] In addition, resistance is exhausting, much more so than is enforcing control systems. Eventually workers lose the strength necessary for further resistance. And finally, resisting focuses attention on control systems and in effect legitimizes them. While simple resistance may create questions about the legitimacy and appropriateness of a particular rule or control system it accepts the legitimacy of *some* system of organizational control.[39] Thus the relationship between control and resistance is paradoxical: Control inevitably creates resistance, which often supports the existence of systems of control.

Motivation and Control through Reward Systems

When coupled with efficient job design and effective selection and training, reward systems can increase employee effort and productivity. But they will do so only if supplemented by effective communication. This concept is explained effectively in *expectancy theory* proposed by Lyman Porter and Edwin Lawler. Employees' efforts depend on their perceptions of the value of the rewards they may receive, the degree of effort necessary to obtain the rewards, and the fairness of the reward system. Creating these perceptions depends on (1) persuading employees that their past efforts have been rewarded adequately and they can *expect* their efforts to be rewarded appropriately in the future, (2) convincing them that the reward system is, and will continue to be, fair and equitable; and (3) explaining the reward that they will receive in a way that maintains their self-esteem.[40] Employees must perceive that the rewards they receive are both substantial and important. Pay seems to have these characteristics, especially for employees whose incomes are low, whose tenure in the organization has been brief, whose commitment to the firm is low, and who feel that their pay is inappropriate when compared to the pay of other workers. The promotions and status that usually accompany pay increases also seem to be important to most people, especially those with a high need for achievement. Praise also is salient to most people and is positively related to both improved performance and job satisfaction. Although the idea that praise is rewarding is not new, its visibility has increased during recent years because of the increased use of behavior modification systems of management.[41]

Employees will perceive that a reward system is fair only if they believe that rewards are based on performance, rather than on friendships or biases, and that the employee is primarily responsible for her or his level of performance. It is difficult to persuade employees that this is true because people tend to attribute their successes to themselves or to factors within their control and their failures to others or to factors they cannot control.[42] Complex goal-setting and feedback systems called **management by objectives** (MBO)[43] are one means of addressing this problem. MBO systems assume that employees and their supervisors will negotiate mutually acceptable goals and will maintain a cooperative relationship while evaluating their performance. Goals are most successful if they are difficult but achievable, if employees are allowed to participate actively in setting their goals, and if supervisors and subordinates communicate well during the goal-setting process. Unless goals, strategies, and roles are clarified and unless the subordinate accepts the goals and means of achieving them, participatory goal-setting will have little if any effect on performance.

MBO reward systems also depend on the quality of performance feedback. Some employees—good performers, people with high self-esteem and who are self-directed—want feedback. Especially for them, positive feedback (praise) alone does seem to enhance performance, although the effects are increased if praise is combined with effective goal-setting. The positive effects of feedback also depend on successful superior–subordinate communication during appraisal sessions.[44]

Appraisals often are difficult exercises because (1) supervisors and subordinates generally evaluate the subordinate's performance differently, (2) they attribute the performance to different factors, and (3) supervisors artificially inflate their evaluations of poorly performing subordinates in anticipation of appraisal meetings. Because the success of reward systems relies on agreement on both evaluations *and* the causes of good or bad performance, the problems just mentioned are serious. They can be offset somewhat by using evaluative criteria that are quantifiable or in some way independently verifiable. Negative feedback is emotionally charged and will be perceived as credible to the extent that the supervisor focuses on describing specific behaviors instead of offering vague or general evaluations.[45]

Typically people who give feedback to others are advised to begin by creating a positive atmosphere by exchanging pleasantries, being direct and honest, and creating a coequal atmosphere by using first names and stating the purpose of the conversation. Feedback messages should be clear, specific, and considerate.[46] However, feedback should *both* clearly confront a problem (or clearly encourage continuation of excellent performance) and allow all parties to maintain face (see Chapter 6). Face management is complicated by an employee's status, race, gender, and ethnicity. For example, providing clear, detailed feedback to a person with higher status (for example, one's supervisor) may in itself threaten his or her face. Similarly, face-saving seems to be more important to women, Latinos, and Asian Americans than to white men and less important to African American than to white employees. Consequently, what may be an appropriate degree of clarity or detail and an adequate amount of care in saving face seems to vary widely across different situations and with different employees.[47]

Finally, employees must be persuaded that the reward system is fair and equitable.[48] People seem to evaluate the gains they receive from being part of a relationship or organization by comparing the reward they receive to the costs they incur. While making these comparisons, people also compare their net gains to those received by other people. When applied to organizational reward systems, this **equity theory** suggests that people will compare their efforts to the rewards they receive *and* to the efforts expended and rewards received by other employees. If they feel they are being treated inequitably, that is, if they feel that their net gains are lower than those of other employees, they will feel frustration and will try to resolve it by reducing their effort, attempting to increase their rewards, leaving the organization, or rationalizing the inequity by changing their perceptions of what net gains other people are receiving. Supervisors may use overt strategies to persuade their subordinates that the reward system is just (by giving workers information that proves that they are being treated equitably), or covert strategies like withholding the information that employees need to compare their rewards to others'. It is difficult to employ the first strategy successfully, as professors remember each time they try to respond to a student's complaint that "I worked much harder than so-and-so and received a lower exam grade."

It is equally difficult to implement the second strategy, although organizations often try to do so through rules that forbid employees from discussing their raises (or salaries) with others. The primary effect of these rules seems to be to encourage employees to obtain the forbidden information, since the very existence of the rules creates the impression that the reward system is inequitable. Thus the confidentiality rules give employees incentive to share salary information covertly. The fact that these rules often fail may be the best evidence in support of the equity theory's assumption that people are very much concerned with the equity of reward systems.[49]

There is no doubt that organizational control systems influence employees' actions and attitudes. However, there also is a great deal of evidence that control systems may have many consequences that are very different from those that were intended by the people who design and implement the systems. Implementing control systems requires that a number of requirements—communicative and otherwise—be met, and even if these requirements are met, employees still will make their own decisions about how to respond.

NEIMAN MARCUS IS THE COMPANY STORE*

Industry International is a manufacturing firm with about 2,500 employees in a number of plants. It often is touted as a monument to the power of financial reward systems. In an industry that has been battered by foreign competition for three decades it has remained highly profitable, in large part because its workers are 2 1/2 to 3 times as productive as those of its competitors. Their compensation also is three times the average salary for U.S. manufacturing employees. They are not unionized, have no paid vacations, and work 45–50 hours per week. Much of their income comes from a year-end cash bonus. Each year, after company taxes and dividends have been paid, the board of directors determines the size of the bonus pool, which is divided among the employees based on their base salary and individual merit ratings. From 1943 to 1994 the bonus percentage ranged from 55 percent to 104 percent; in 1994 it was 61 percent, meaning that an employee earning a $30,000 base salary and receiving a 100 percent merit rating would receive a bonus of $18,300. The bonus is kept secret from October until a meeting/celebration in December. When the meeting ends the employees rush to their cars, bonus checks in hand, and tie up traffic for hours going to their favorite places of celebration.

Most employees use the money to pay accumulated bills, in fact many spend far in excess of their base salaries and then put off paying bills and loans until the bonus checks come in. Other employees use the money for less mundane activities—one got his bonus in $100 bills, spread them on the living room floor and, along with his wife, rolled around on them (among other activities) in celebration; some make major purchases like houses, cars, and luxury items in cash; a few (mostly younger employees) use the money to gamble, hire prostitutes, or buy illegal drugs. When asked why they *spend* the money as they do, three answers are given—to live the "good life" so valued in the United States, to assert their autonomy (one said "spending bonus money is the one thing they [management] ain't telling me what and how to do"), and for the status money provides: "As soon as they [friends and neighbors] find out you work there, they think you have money coming out of your ears"; [another said] "They think I'm the richest s...o...b [ellipsis mine] in the world"; [another recalled that] years ago we made more money than professional football players."

What they don't tell their envious neighbors is what they went through to get the bonus. Merit points are based on output, quality, dependability, and personal characteristics. The first two can be quantified, leading employees to

---

*This case is based on Melissa Hancock and Michael Papa, "Employee Struggles with Autonomy and Dependence: Examining the Dialectic of Control through a Structurational Account of Power," Paper presented at the International Communication Association Convention, Chicago, 1996.

(continued)

(continued from previous page)

"work like dogs" until dangerously exhausted by long hours and difficult working conditions; the latter two cannot, creating a highly political atmosphere in the plant: [most echoed one worker's conclusion that] "if you don't go along with the system [managers], you could be the hardest worker in the world . . . and you would still be way short because you have not gone with the flow and you would be blackballed, and they give you what they want to give you."

But, things have changed for Industry International. The recession of the mid-1980s led to low bonuses (55 percent). Many workers lost their homes and cars because they were relying on large bonuses to pay mortgages and loans. Workers attributed the decline to many things, but primarily to management greed and incompetence—a "fat managerial level and more men at the top," embezzlement, and mismanagement of overseas accounts. Whatever the reason, the recession made it clear to workers just how dependent they were on Industry International, and how much things had changed: "The whole philosophy [established by the founder and maintained until 1983] was that you worked hard and got compensated for it. You busted your ass, but you got compensated. Now you bust your ass and you don't get compensated for it." But, they have very few options. Most are too old to start over somewhere else, and are limited by their education and training to manufacturing jobs, and high-paying manufacturing jobs are becoming very rare in the United States (see Chapter 12).

So, they talk about resisting management. They fear that management will eliminate the bonus system, replacing it with a form of profit-sharing that is not as lucrative for the workers. Many predict a massive walkout or work stoppage if that happens. Others talk about unionizing the firm. Management has persuaded them that the bonus system relies on a non-union shop, but if the bonus system is eliminated they have no reason not to unionize. Others predict that employees would quit the company; still others predict plummeting productivity and quality, others threaten physical violence against management and sabotage of the plant. "If they go rid of bonus, they wouldn't have the control over anyone. Bonus is what they have to keep the hold on you."

Discussion Questions

1. There is a substantial amount of research evidence indicating that pay is the most powerful motivator for U.S. workers.** Why? What functional and psychological factors make monetary reward systems work so well?

**See John Campbell and Robert Pritchard, "Motivation Theory," in *Handbook of Industrial and Organizational Psychology*, Marvin Dunnette, ed. (Chicago: Rand-McNally, 1976) and Charles Greene and Philip Podsakoff, "Effects of Withdrawal of a Performance-contingent Reward on Supervisory Influence and Power," *Academy of Management Journal, 24*(1981): 527–542.

(continued)

(continued from previous page)

2. How might these employees resist this particular motivation/control system? How could they keep from being dependent on the system? How likely are the forms of resistance that they describe in the final paragraph? What effects would those actions have on the system? Why?

3. Would this kind of motivation/control system work differently in different societal contexts, for example, in a society that was not as consumption-oriented as the United States or in a country with extensive social support systems for unemployed workers and their families?

4. If you were the CEO of Industry International, what kinds of public economic policies would you want the government to follow (Would you want the Federal Reserve Board to focus on keeping inflation low or keeping unemployment low? Would you want corporate income taxes to be a primary source of government funding or personal income taxes?)? Why?

TRADITIONAL STRATEGIES OF LEADERSHIP

Many contemporary organizational theorists view "leadership" and traditional strategies of organizing as contradictory ideas. The traditional strategy dictates that supervisors will be "managers," not "leaders." Bennis and Naus conclude that "managers do things right, but leaders do the right thing" and Tom Peters and Nancy Austin note that management is about "arranging" and "telling"; while leadership is about growing and enhancing.[50] However, traditional notions of supervision *do* include leadership, although it defines the term in a much different sense than Bennis, Naus, Peters, or Austin do. Traditional leadership is about designing, implementing, and adapting formal structures—policies, procedures, rules, rewards (including evaluation and feedback systems), and the chain of command. Decision-making tends to be reactive problem-solving rather than proactive and visionary. It does not ignore communication, since communication is crucial to the maintenance of all of these formal structures, but it tends to de-emphasize communication, especially direct, face-to-face interpersonal communication. Supervisor–subordinate relationships are intended to be relatively impersonal, based more on task responsibilities than on personal attraction and thus are relatively superficial and static.

Even some of the early proponents of the traditional strategy of organizing dealt with these issues. One was Henri Fayol, who argued that managing consists of five key activities, four of which directly involve communication:

> **Organizing** includes explaining employees' duties clearly, controlling the use of written communication, and providing clear and effective statements of managerial decisions.

Commanding involves conducting both periodic assessments of the organization's success through systems of performance feedback and conferences with employees to *direct* and *focus* their efforts.

Coordinating depends on making certain that all employees understand the nature and limits of their responsibilities.

Controlling involves administering rewards and punishments and persuading employees that their rewards are based on the quality of their performance.[51]

Clearly this is a much more restricted view of leadership communication than the "transactional" perspective of the relational model of organizing (Chapter 3) or the "transformational" perspective of the cultural strategy (Chapter 4), which involve higher personal relationships and charismatic, inspirational leadership. Managers do lead, but they do it through systems and structures that are consistent with the other attributes of the traditional strategy.

SUMMARY: COMMUNICATION AND TRADITIONAL STRATEGIES OF ORGANIZING

I have spent a substantial amount of space discussing traditional strategies of organizing because it is so relevant to modern employees. The traditional strategy, with its tight hierarchy, controlled and formal communication, and written policies and procedures, still is the dominant strategy used in the United States for governmental agencies, educational institutions, and many private firms. Although very few organizations conform completely to the strategy, many employees entering U.S. organizations today will find themselves in situations much like the traditional bureaucracy. Procedures and policies will be documented in writing; job-related communication will flow through the chain of command; positions will require specialized skills and will be filled at least in part because applicants fulfill established, written criteria; and decision-making will be centralized near the top of the organization. Of course, real organizations—even those in which the traditional strategy is in evidence—deviate in a number of important but predictable ways from what the traditional theorists envisioned. But, understanding the traditional strategy is important because many people will spend most of their lives working in organizations that are "traditional" in many ways.

NOTES

[1] Claude George, *The History of Management Thought* (Englewood Cliffs, NJ: Prentice-Hall, 1972), p. 52. The quotations from ancient managers that appear in this chapter and some of the historical summary are from this work.

[2] For an excellent summary and analysis of these processes, see Alfred Chandler, *The Visible Hand* (Cambridge: Harvard University Press, 1977) and Alfred Chandler and H. Daems, eds., *Managerial Hierarchies* (Cambridge: Harvard University Press, 1980).

[3] Frederick Taylor, "The Principles of Scientific Management," in *Classics of Organizational Theory,* Jay Shafritz and Philip Whitbeck, eds. (Oak Park, IL: Moore, 1978).

[4] However, the technique often was (and still is) used without consulting workers, often by outside consultants who the workers perceive are a threat to their jobs. Both in the 1930s and today time-motion studies are resisted by workers, especially when there is a lack of trust in management. However, if these techniques are used in the way that Taylor suggested, in a context of openness and consultation with workers, very little employee resistance is encountered (Edwin Locke, "The Ideas of Frederick Taylor," *The Academy of Management Review,* 7 [1982]: 14–24.)

[5] Modern uses of these techniques, often stimulated more by legal pressures in affirmative action suits than by a concern for scientific selection, have opened many jobs to women and members of minority groups who once were discriminated against because they were incorrectly *assumed* to lack sufficient strength, verbal skills, and so on.

[6] Taylor, "Principles."

[7] Weber was primarily interested in the relationships between a culture and the institutions—religious, political, and economic—that its members create. Societies and their organizations are alike in many respects, the most important of which are (1) the ways in which they are structured, (2) the processes through which employees make decisions, and (3) the means through which the organization influences and controls its members' actions.

[8] James March and Herbert Simon, Organizations (New York: John Wiley, 1958); Robert McPhee, "Vertical Communication Chains," *Management Communication Quarterly, 4* (1988): 455–493 and "Organizational Forms and Configurations," in L. Putnam & F. Jablin, eds., *The New Handbook of Organizational Communication* (Thousand Oaks, CA: Sage, 1997).

[9] Robert Snyder and James Morris, "Organizational Communication and Performance," *Journal of Applied Psychology, 69* (1984): 461–465.

[10] This is why computerized management information systems, recently installed in virtually every major organization, have had perplexing effects. Computer information systems do not filter information; in fact, that is why they were developed. In theory they allow every employee, no matter where in the organization, to instantly access any part of its information base. However, no one can process all the information. Unfiltered formal communication will literally bury upper-level managers in information, at least until they learn to use the equipment to screen out messages. High-speed computer systems may only allow them to be buried more quickly. The "solution" to communication overload is for upper management not to use the systems, which defeats the purpose of installing them in the first place. See Ron Rice and Urs Gattiker, "Communication Technologies and Structures," in L. Putnam and F. Jablin, eds. *The New Handbook of Organizational Communication* (Thousand Oaks, CA: Sage, 1997).

[11] Anthony Downs, *Inside Bureaucracy* (Boston: Little, Brown, 1967). The paradox is felt most acutely by middle managers, who suffer from filtering from two directions, feel uninformed more often, probably because they have greater communication needs (See Fred Jablin, "Formal Organizational Structure," in *Handbook of Organizational Communication,* Fred Jablin, et al., eds. [Newbury Park, CA: Sage, 1987]).

[12] Eric Eisenberg, "Ambiguity as Strategy in Organizational Communication," *Communication Monographs, 51* (1984): 227–242.

[13] Jablin, "Structure." Interestingly, the size of an organization itself does not seem to be important; it is the degree of specialization that creates these problems.

[14] Fredric Jablin, "Communication Competence and Effectiveness," in L. Putnam and F. Jablin, eds., *The New Handbook of Organizational Communication* (Thousand Oaks, CA: Sage, 1997); Michael Tushman and Thomas Scanlan, "Boundary Spanning Individuals," *The Academy of Management Review, 5* (1980): 123–138.

[15] Cited in John Campbell, "Systematic Error on the Part of Human Links in Communication Systems," *Information and Control, 1* (1958): 334–369. Also see Herbert Simon, *The New Science of Management Decision* (New York: Harper & Row, 1960) and Cynthia Stohl and Charles Redding, "Messages and Message Exchange Processes," in *Handbook of Organizational Communication,* Fred Jablin, et al., eds. (Newbury Park, CA: Sage, 1987).

[16] Jablin, "Structure".

[17] Jablin, "Structure," p. 397.

[18] Redding; Daniel Katz and Robert Kahn, *The Social Psychology of Organizations,* 2nd ed. (New York: John Wiley, 1978). Also see Albrecht and Bach's discussion of "co-orientation."

[19] Terrance Albrecht and Bradford Hall, "Facilitating Talk about New Ideas," *Communication Monographs, 58* (1991): 273–289 and "Relationship and Content Differences Between Elites and Outsiders in Innovation Networks," *Human Communication Research, 17* (1991): 535–562.

[20] Cal Downs and Charles Conrad, "A Critical Incident Study of Effective Subordinancy," *Journal of Business Communication, 19* (1982): 27–38; Gail Fairhurst, "Dialectical Tensions in Leadership Research," in L. Putnam and F. Jablin, eds. *The New Handbook of Organizational Communication* (Thousand Oaks, CA: Sage, 1997). For an extended analysis of how one's nonverbal cues influence interpersonal communication, including communication by the other members of the relationship, see Judee Burgoon, David Buller, and W. Gill Woodall, *Nonverbal Communication: The Unspoken Dialogue* (New York: Harper & Row, 1989), especially Chapters 9, 11, and 12, and Valerie Manusov and Julie M. Billingsley, "Nonverbal Communication in Organizations," in Peggy Yuhas Byers (ed.), *Organizational Communication: Theory and Behavior* (Boston: Allyn and Bacon, 1997).

[21] The studies on which I base this discussion are summarized in detail in W. Charles Redding, *Communication Within the Organization* (New York: Industrial Communication Council, 1972). For an interesting analysis of the political dimensions of trust, see Samuel Culbert and John McDonough, *Radical Management: Power Politics and the Pursuit of Trust* (New York: The Free Press, 1985).

[22] Gerald Goldhaber, *Organizational Communication,* 4th ed. (Dubuque, IA: William C. Brown, 1986); Jablin.

[23] However, employees often help create the feelings that they are "kept in the dark." In general, the more information people receive, the more they believe they need to have. Consequently, until they reach a point of extreme information overload, employees may always feel that they are not kept informed, regardless of what their supervisors do.

[24] This idea is developed best in Fulk and in Dennis Gioia and Henry Sims, "Cognition-Behavior Connections: Attribution and Verbal Behavior in Leader-Subordinate Interactions," *Organizational Behavior and Human Performance, 37* (1986): 197–229.

[25] Peter Monge, Jane Edwards, and Kenneth Kirstie, "The Determinants of Communication and Communication Structure in Large Organizations," in *Communication Yearbook 2,* Brent Ruben, ed. (New Brunswick, NJ: Transaction Books, 1978); Samuel Bacharach and Michael Aiken, "Communication in Administrative Bureaucracies," *Academy of Management Journal 3* (1977): 365–377; and Karlene Roberts and Charles O'Reilly, "Failures in Upward Communication: Three Possible Culprits," *Academy of Management Journal, 17* (1974): 205–215.

[26] Janet Fulk and Sirish Mani, "Distortion of Communication in Hierarchical Relationships," *Communication Yearbook 9,* Margaret McLaughlin, ed. (Newbury Park, CA: Sage, 1986).

[27] Paul Lawrence and Jay Lorsch, *Organizations and Environment* (Boston: Harvard Business School, 1967); Henry Mintzberg, *The Structuring of Organizations* (Englewood Cliffs, NJ: Prentice-Hall, 1978); Kathy Sutcliffe, "Information Processing and Organizational Environments," in L. Putnam and F. Jablin, eds., *The New Handbook of Organizational Communication* (Thousand Oaks, CA: Sage, 1997).

[28] Alan Meyer, "How Ideologies Supplant Formal Structures and Shape Responses to Environments," *Journal of Management Studies, 19* (1982): 45–61. Also see Janice Beyer, Roger Dunbar, and Alan Meyer, "Comment: The Concept of Ideology in Organizational Analysis," *The Academy of Management Review, 13* (1988): 483–489; and Robert Dewar and James Werbel, "Universalistic and Contingency Predictions of Employee Satisfaction and Conflict," *Administrative Science Quarterly, 4* (1979): 426–447. Chapter 7 explains how the degree to which an employee helps an organization cope with environmental pressures influences his or her organizational power.

[29] See Peter Monge and Noshir Contractor, "Emergent Communication Networks," in L. Putnam and F. Jablin, eds., *The New Handbook of Organizational Communication* (Thousand Oaks, CA: Sage, 1997).

[30] Miles.

[31] Katz and Kahn, p. 297. This section is based on pp. 307–331 of their book. Also see Amatai Etzioni, "Organizational Control Structures," in *Handbook of Organizations,* James March, ed. (Chicago: Rand-McNally, 1965).

[32] Karl Weick, *The Social Psychology of Organizing*, 2nd. ed. Rebecca Adams and Roxanne Parrot, "Pediatric Nurses' Communication of Role Expectations of Parents to Hospitalized Children," *Journal of Applied Communication Research, 22* (1994): 36–47.

[33] McPhee.

[34] For a provocative discussion of punishment in organizations, see Richard Arvey, Gregory Davis, and Sherry Nelson, "Use of Discipline in an Organization," *Journal of Applied Psychology, 69* (1984): 448–460; Richard Arvey and John Ivanevich, "Punishment in Organizations," 123–134, and Henry Sims, "Further Thoughts on Punishment in Organizations," *The Academy of Management Review, 5* (1980): 123–138.

[35] See Michel Foucault, *Discipline and Punish* (Harmondsworth, U.K.: Penguin, 1977), *Power/Knowledge*, ed. C. Gordon (Brighton, U.K.: Harvester Press, 1980), and *The Practice of Everyday Life* (Berkeley: University of California Press, 1984); Hannah Arendt, *The Human Condition* (Chicago: University of Chicago Press, 1958); Stewart Clegg, *Frameworks of Power* (Berkeley, CA: University of California Press, 1989); Jean Lipman-Blumen, *Gender Roles and Power* (Englewood Cliffs, NJ: Prentice-Hall, 1984); and Michael Mann, *The Sources of Social Power,* vol. 1. (Cambridge: Cambridge University Press, 1986). An excellent summary of Foucault's ideas is available in James Barker and George Cheney, "The Concept and Practices of Discipline in Contemporary Organizational Life," *Communication Monographs, 61* (1994): 20–43.

[36] D. Zimmerman, "The Practicalities of Rule Use," in *Understanding Everyday Life,* J. Douglas, ed (Chicago: Aldine, 1970).

[37] Charles Conrad, "Was Pogo Right? Communication, Power and Resistance," in *Communication Research in the 21st Century,* Julia Wood and Richard Gregg, eds. (Creskill, NJ: Hampton Press, 1995); Michel de Certeau; Michael Burawoy, *Manufacturing Consent* (Chicago: University of Chicago Press, 1979); and Stewart Clegg, "Power, Theorizing and Nihilism," *Theory and Society, 3* (1976): 65–87.

[38] This practice has been made possible in part by processes of deskilling, of making jobs progressively more simple, thus making it easier to replace workers with only a short-term loss of efficiency. Deskilling is discussed in more detail later in this book.

[39] Mann.

[40] Edwin Lawler, *Pay and Organizational Effectiveness* (New York: McGraw-Hill, 1971). Porter and Lawler admit that a number of factors other than motivation influence employee performance (for example, their skills, training, equipment, and access to information) and recognize that it is very difficult to design reward systems that actually reward the behviors that the system intends to reward. These problems are illustrated very effectively in what has become a classic essay on reward systems, Steven Kerr's "The Folly of Rewarding A While Hoping for B" (*Academy of Management Journal, 19* [1975]: 769–783). William Ouchi demonstrated just how difficult it is to design reward systems in a study of retailing firms. He found that those salespersons who were rewarded on a commission basis sold a lot of merchandise, but "have no incentive to arrange stock, take inventory, or train new salespeople, who become their competitors." People paid by the hour keep a tidy store but sell much less merchandise ("The Relationship Between Organizational Structure and Control," *Administrative Science Quarterly, 22* [1977]: 95–113).

[41] See Edwin Locke, Karyl Shaw, Lise Saari, and Gary Latham, "Goal Setting and Task Performance: 1969–1980," *Psychological Bulletin, 90* (1981): 125–152. For example, in a now-famous series of studies at Emery Air Freight, Edward Feeney applied a system of behavior modification in an attempt to improve performance. His system involved three steps: supervisors specify a "standard" level of performance, preferably in quantifiable terms; workers get immediate feedback about how their performance relates to this standard; and workers get positive feedback when their performance exceeds the standard and encouragement when their performance falls short. Average productivity at Emery improved significantly, more because workers were provided with performance feedback than because they were given positive feedback.

[42] Explanations of these processes are part of "attribution theory," a model summarized effectively and applied to organizational reward systems in J. Bettman and B. Weitz, "Attributions in the Board Room," *Administrative Science Quarterly, 28* (1983): 165–183; and B. Staw, P. McKechnie, and S. Puffer, "The Justification of Organizational Performance," *Administrative Science Quarterly, 28* (1983): 582–600.

[43] The communicative requirements of feedback systems are discussed at length in Cal Downs, Kenneth Johnson, and Kevin Barge, "Communication Feedback and Task Performance in Organizations," in *Organizational Communication,* Howard Greenbaum, Raymond Falcione,

and Susan Hellweg, eds. (Beverly Hills, CA: Sage, 1982). An excellent summary of MBO systems in available in Locke, et al., "Goal Setting."

[44] Lawrence Hanser and Paul Muchinsky, "Performance Feedback Information and Organization Communication," *Human Communication Research, 7* (1980): 68–73; and Timothy Downs, "Predictors of Communication Satisfaction with Appraisal Interviews," *Management Communication Quarterly, 3* (1990): 334–354.

[45] Louis Cussella, "The Effects of Feedback Source, Message and Receiver Characteristics on Intrinsic Motivation," *Communication Quarterly 32,* (1985): 211–221.

[46] See, for example, W.C. Donaghy, *The Interview* (Glenview, IL: Scott, Foresman and Company, 1984) and H.L. Goodall, Jr. *Small Group Communication in Organizations* (Dubuque, IA: W.C. Brown, Publishers, 1985).

[47] Karen Tracy and Eric Eisenberg, "Giving Criticism," *Research on Language and Social Interaction, 24* (1990/1991): 37–70. In addition to these factors, subordinates evaluate appraisal processes more highly if they have opportunities to discuss their career progress with their supervisors (Barry Nathan, Allan Mohrman, and John Milliman, "Interpersonal Relations as a Context of the Effects of Appraisal Interviews," *Academy of Management Journal, 34* (1991): 352–369). Also see Linda Smircich and R. Chesser, "Superiors and Subordinates' Perceptions of Performance," *Academy of Management Journal, 24* (1981): 198–205; and Arthur Brief, "Differences in Evaluations of Employee Performance," *Journal of Occupational Psychology, 50* (1977): 129–134.

These requirements indicate that some common reward systems used in traditional organizations may be doomed to failure. Systemwide rewards, in which equal rewards either are distributed to all employees regardless of their level of performance or are based on criteria not related to performance (for example, the length of time an employee has been in the organization), do not generate increased performance. At most, systemwide rewards increase job satisfaction and loyalty to the organization, neither of which consistently or significantly increases individual performance. In most cases they encourage people to work at the minimum level required to stay in the organization. In some cases they may be counterproductive. Marginal or poorly motivated workers who are rewarded beyond the level warranted by their performance will be encouraged to stay in the organization, whereas highly motivated employees will be encouraged to leave.

In time, low-producing employees begin to expect rewards in spite of their performance. If system rewards are reduced or discontinued, these workers will be alienated and their performance further reduced. This possibility makes it difficult for firms to shift away from system rewards to performance-producing rewards. In time the organization may have only poorly motivated, unproductive employees who also are dissatisfied.

In addition, system rewards may be inappropriate to the motivations of different groups of employees. For instance, research with college professors has found that although monetary rewards are motivating with younger, untenured professors, they are less motivating for older, perhaps more loyal employees. If employees receive across-the-board percentage-based salary increases, most of the reward budget will go to those employees who will be least motivated by them. During the 1980s many major firms shifted away from systems rewards in order to increase productivity and reduce costs. For many professionals and managers, a large proportion of their total income now comes in the form of year-end performance bonuses rather than salary increases. In the face of increased competition, performance-based reward systems seem to have returned to American companies. But even these reward systems will succeed only if they are supported by communication that persuades employees that their rewards will be *contingent* on their actions, that they will be substantial and salient, and that they will continue to be provided over the long run (Katz and Kahn, pp. 412–414).

[48] Exchange theories have been summarized effectively by Michael Roloff, *Interpersonal Communication* (Beverly Hills, CA: Sage, 1981). For an excellent critique from a traditional perspective, see Joseph Folger, M. Scott Poole, and Randall Stuttman, *Working Through Conflict,* 3rd ed. (New York: HarperCollins, 1996); for a critique from a critical theory perspective, see Nancy Hartsock, *Money, Sex and Power* (New York: Longman, 1983).

[49] Evidently, supervisors also are concerned about equity issues when making decisions about rewards. If they have reliable performance information on their employees, and if they can realistically determine which employee was responsible for which outcomes (positive and negative), they try to allocate rewards based on performance, although doing so can create com-

petition and hostility within a work group. Doing so is, of course, consistent with the highly individualistic orientation of American culture. But when the situation is less clear-cut, or when the supervisors are very concerned about "team building," they tend to give approximately equal rewards to each of their subordinates (James Meindl, "Managing to Be Fair," *Administrative Science Quarterly, 34* (1989): 252–276. For a discussion of the role of individualism in American culture, see Edward E. Sampson, "Justice, Ideology, and Social Legitimation," in *Justice in Social Relations,* H.W. Bierhoff, R.L. Cohen, and J. Greenberg, eds. New York: Plenum, 1986). However, more personal considerations also influence managers' decisions. Equity considerations are especially important in large departments in which people work alone and do not have close personal ties with one another. In departments in which people work closely together and are similar to one another in backgrounds, experience, and interests, rewards are more alike and as a result there is less difference among the salaries of the various employees (Jeffrey Pfeffer and Nancy Langton, "Wage Inequality and the Organization of Work." *Administrative Science Quarterly, 33* [1988]: 588–606).

To complicate matters even further, employees' responses to issues of equity seem to be culture-bound and seem to vary according to both the reward process and its outcomes. In a study of employees in two individualistic and masculine cultures (the United States and Japan) and a culture that is less individualistic and less masculine (South Korea), Kim and his associates found that all preferred equity-based reward systems, although three groups of employees preferred equity-based systems over across-the-board systems, more so in the United States and Japan (Ken Kim, Hun-Joon Park, and Nori Suzuki, "Reward Allocations in the United States, Japan, and Korea," *Academy of Management Journal, 33* [1990]: 188–198). In addition, McFarlin and Sweeney found that it is the *outcomes* of reward processes that influence employees' satisfaction with their pay and with their job while it was the perceived fairness of the *procedures* for allocating rewards that influence their commitment to the organization and their evaluations of supervisors (Dean McFarlin and Paul Sweeney, "Distributive and Procedural Justice as Predictors of Satisfaction with Personal and Organizational Outcomes," *Academy of Management Journal, 35* (1992): 626–637).

[50] William Bennis and B. Naus, *Leaders: The Strategies for Taking Charge* (New York: Harper & Row, 1985); Fairhurst, "Tensions;" Tom Peters and Nancy Austin, *A Passion for Excellence* (New York: Random House, 1987). Peters and Austin go on to suggest that "management" involves the roles of cop, referee, dispassionate analyst ("devil's advocate"), naysayer, and pronouncer (as in pronouncing judgment) while "leadership" involves the roles of cheerleader, enthusiast, nurturer, coach, and facilitator. I will examine this and related conceptions of leadership in Chapter 4 under the title of "transformational leadership."

[51] Henri Fayol, *General and Industrial Management* (London: Pitman, 1949). The other functions were regulating technical processes, purchasing and marketing, obtaining and using capital, protecting employees and property, and accounting.

Chapter 3

RELATIONAL STRATEGIES OF ORGANIZING

If thou art one to whom petition is made, be calm as thou listeneth. . . . Do not rebuff him before he has . . . said that for which he came. . . . It is not [necessary] that everything about which he has petitioned should come to pass, [but] a good hearing is soothing to the heart.

—PHARAOH PTAH-HOTEP TO HIS MANAGERS, C. 2700 B.C.

If a leader maintains close relationship with his soldiers they will "be more eager to be seen performing some honorable action, and more anxious to abstain from doing anything that was disgraceful."

—A LESSON LEARNED BY ALEXANDER THE GREAT
FROM THE PERSIAN KING CYRUS, C. 325 B.C.

CENTRAL THEMES

- Relational strategies of organizing substitute decentralization and participatory decision-making for the centralized, hierarchical, specialized organizational design of the traditional strategy. Employees sometimes resist these strategies, and their effects depend on a number of factors.
- Informal communication networks are an inevitable aspect of organizations and they can benefit organizations and their members in many ways.
- Relational strategies of motivation strive to fulfill employees' "upper level" needs through job enrichment and enlargement. They reject the "deskilling" tactics often used as part of the traditional strategy of organizing.
- Relational strategies rely on creating open and supportive supervisor-subordinate relationships, achieved through "transactional" or "contingency" leadership tactics.

KEY TERMS

Decentralization	Routinized tasks
Empowered	Job enlargement
Span of control	Job enrichment
Traditional authority	Ratebusters
Quality of Working Life	Transactional leadership
Gossip	Consideration
Cliques	Legitimation
Rumors	Disconfirming communication
Physiological needs	Co-orientation
Safety needs	Accommodation
Belongingness needs	Maturity
Esteem/ego needs	Willingness
Self-actualization	Telling style
Hygiene factors	Selling style
Motivators	Delegating style

Like Chapter 2, this chapter begins with a brief description of the context surrounding the development of a strategy of organizing—in this case "relational" strategies—and then discusses relational strategies of organizational design, of motivation and control, and of leadership. A brief look at the Table of Contents will indicate that the amount of space that I devote to each of these topics is quite different than in Chapter 2. It examined organizational design and motivation/control at length, but de-emphasized leadership. This chapter de-emphasizes organizational design, spends about the same space on strategies of motivation and control, and deals much more extensively with leadership. This difference in focus results from the perspectives themselves. Traditional strategies focus on design and motivation/control and assume that if those things are taken care of leadership is pretty simple. Relational strategies are much less concerned with design and instead focus on interpersonal relationships, particularly between supervisors and their subordinates. As a result, leadership communication is an important part of the strategy.

THE CONTEXT SURROUNDING THE DEVELOPMENT OF RELATIONAL STRATEGIES OF ORGANIZING

Traditional strategies of organizing rapidly came to dominate U.S. firms during the first third of the twentieth century. Indeed, as the conclusion to Chapter 2 indicated, the overall bureaucratic structure—specialization and, to a somewhat lesser degree, hierarchicalization—continue to be present in the majority of U.S. organizations. Rationality and efficiency had long been distinctive American values, and a reward system based on individual self-interest was especially appropriate to a society based on "rugged individualism." And, early uses of the traditional strategy left additional legacies for U.S. firms. They helped create a special class of workers, *managers,* who supposedly make "rational" decisions that are intended to increase organizational efficiency (short-term profit maximization). Bureaucratic organizations operate on the basis of scientific principles, and problems are to be solved through technical procedures and technological innovations. Unfortunately, this perspective de-emphasizes or ignores the differing individual needs of workers and treats considerations like "long-term social impact" as largely irrelevant to managerial decision-making (see the discussion of organizational ethics in Chapter 12).[1]

The system of motivation and control proposed by Taylor and his successors was less successful over the long term, in part because of the ways in which traditional strategies were used and in part because of changes in the U.S. workforce. In many firms that used scientific management, a brief time of labor-management cooperation was achieved. But as "scientifically managed" firms became more successful, workers demanded a larger proportion of the income pie and managers found ways to cheat them out of the rewards that they deserved. Issues over the proper distribution of increased profits eventually reduced labor-management harmony and led to intense opposition to Taylor's ideas by organized labor. Taylor showed great concern for the well-being of his employees. His followers often did not. They often used the techniques of scientific management to unfairly manipulate workers. Increases in efficiency through techniques like time-motion studies often were used to justify *reducing* workers' incomes, benefiting management alone, rather than increasing them as the traditional strategy envisioned. Labor hostility supported the growth of national unions, which added to the alienation between labor and management.[2] By the time of the Great Depression, the promises of increased well-being through improved efficiency and enhanced labor–management co-operation that formed the basis of the traditional strategy seemed hollow indeed. So, by the early 1930s, the climate was ripe for the introduction of another new strategy of organizing.

After the Depression and World War II were over, the U.S. workforce changed in ways that undermined the traditional strategies of motivation and control. The most important changes were the increased education and the altered expectations of our workforce. In Taylor's day, only a small proportion of the workers had completed even eight years of formal education. Today only a tiny proportion has not done so. Most have finished high school, and a large percentage have college degrees. In August 1983, one quarter of employed Americans held bachelor's degrees, the first time in history that such a high proportion of the workforce had college educations; in 1993 the figure was almost one-third. Highly educated workers generally expect to have jobs that use their creative talents and training in decision-making, something that is denied all but top management in the traditional strategy. By 1970 many supervisors understood the implications of these changes. One foreman from General Motors exclaimed, "The old-type tactics of being a supervisor don't work with these guys. In the past a man didn't need much motivation to do a job like this—the paycheck took care of that. But these guys, they're different."[3] The origins and development of the relational strategy of organizing can only be understood within this changed context.

RELATIONAL STRATEGIES OF ORGANIZATIONAL DESIGN

The primary focus of the relational strategy is on devising broader strategies of employee motivation and control and on improving supervisor–subordinate communication. Issues regarding organizational design are much less central to the strategy. However, there is one important design-related difference between relational and traditional strategies—**decentralization**. Two of the key features of the traditional strategy were *centralization* and *hierarchicalization,* the notion that organizations should be shaped like a multilevel pyramid in which only those employees at the top of the pyramid would make decisions about policies, procedures, and so on. Lower-level employees would be allowed to make decisions, but only in the restricted sense of applying the rules, policies, and procedures established by upper management to everyday situations. The relational strategy relaxes both assumptions, asserting instead that organizational hierarchies should be "flattened" and decision-making should be decentralized. This means that lower-level employees would be **empowered** to make decisions about a wide range of issues that directly affect them and their jobs, and that there would be far fewer links in the formal chain of command.[4]

Decentralization and Participation

Decentralization and participatory decision-making (PDM) are like two sides of the same coin. If an organization adopts a decentralized organizational structure the number of managers drops significantly, as does the number of levels of management.[5] As a result, lower-level employees *must* be allowed to make everyday decisions because there is no one else available to do so. (If top managers tried to make all of the everyday decisions they would soon experience serious overload problems.) In addition, the managers that are left in the organization are required to supervise much more "loosely" than are managers in the traditional strategy.

In the traditional strategy, supervisors are responsible for a relatively small number of subordinates (usually four to six). With this small "**span of control**" they could supervise tightly, making certain that their subordinates carried out their instructions precisely as they were intended. But, "tight" supervision increases the likelihood that workers will resist traditional systems of control because it robs them of a sense of autonomy and creativity. In short, tight supervision makes the tension between individual and organizational needs that was discussed in Chapter 1 more visible and more alienating. Granting workers more autonomy, allowing them to determine how to accomplish their assigned tasks, expecting them to make the decisions that influence them most, and supervising them loosely would allow each supervisor to manage a much larger

FIGURE 3–1
FIGURE 3–1
Likert's Multiple Overlapping Groups

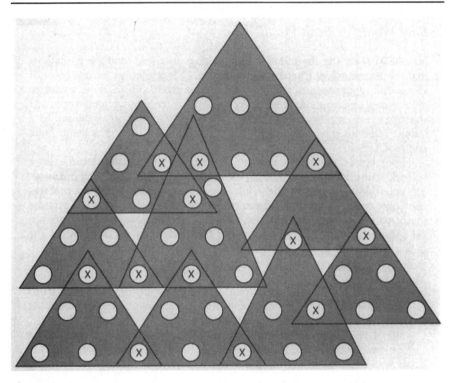

$\bigotimes$ *Linking pins.*

span of control. The number of managers needed is reduced and organizational efficiency is increased. Furthermore, decisions would be made by the workers who are most concerned with them and most expert in the day-to-day activities of the organization. Formal communication would cross fewer levels, thus reducing the potential for distortion (recall Chapter 2).

One of the primary advocates of the relational strategy, Rensis Likert, developed a model of relational organizational design that may help clarify these concepts. He proposed that organizations should be structured around overlapping groups of employees instead of with the independent divisions of the bureaucratic model. Each group would make any decisions that affect it or its members. Each group would be linked to every other group with which it was interdependent by a "linking pin," an employee who was a member of both groups (see Figure 3-1). In this structure each group could better understand the needs and problems of the other groups. The groups would minimize the problems of "trained communication incapacity" and specialized languages (discussed in Chapter 2) because they would always have a "translator" available. Intergroup conflict could be reduced because communication breakdowns between the two groups would be less frequent. Group decision-making would be enhanced because each linking pin would have access to different kinds of information as a result of his or her contact with other groups. In effect, this system (which Likert called System Four) created an organizational structure designed around the concept of PDM. Unfortunately, linking pins are placed in difficult and stressful positions. When things go wrong, they are handy scapegoats, and they rarely are rewarded for their efforts.[6]

Participatory decision-making comes in a variety of different forms and a number of different labels ("workplace democracy," "employee involvement," and "Total Quality Management" are some common examples). But, for PDM to increase organizational performance a number of requirements must be met:

1. Subordinates must want to be involved in decision-making, must be involved in complex tasks, and must be given substantial control over how they complete their tasks.

2. Supervisors must be willing to allow their subordinates legitimately to participate, to listen and respond to their ideas, and to encourage them to contribute.

3. The issues being discussed must be important to the participants. Workers usually believe that any decisions that directly affect them or their jobs are important and that decisions about more general company policies are less important. They especially would like to have influence over decisions about how to do their own work, scheduling of work, awarding raises and promotions, and hiring and firing of coworkers.

4. All the participants must have expertise and information relevant to the problems being discussed.

5. Managers must foster and support the beliefs, values, and attitudes necessary to legitimize participatory systems.[7] Publicly recognizing employees' contributions and creating positive feelings of success make employees feel that they really *do* have the authority to act on their own, and thus are important determinants of feeling empowered.[8]

In sum, participation is most successful when people are given the power to make decisions that are meaningful to them, provided with the expertise and skills to make decisions effectively, given all of the information that is relevant to the decision, and provided with significant and salient rewards, including public recognition, for their effort.[9] Unless these factors all are present, and often even when they are, participatory systems will be resisted.

Resistance to Participatory Decision-Making.   Participatory decision-making usually is implemented through problem-solving groups made up of subordinates and their supervisors. Making decisions in groups (see Chapter 9) is time-consuming and costly for organizations, but advocates of participation argue that these costs will be more than offset by the increased morale, improved quality of the decisions, and improved information flow that results from the systems made when subordinates' expertise is made available. But, even with these advantages, resistance occurs.

Sometimes resistance stems from the societal context surrounding an organization. Weber recognized that some societies are based on **traditional authority**, the notion that hierarchical relationships are legitimate because they "always" have existed. "Children, obey your parents" and "Because I [parent] said so" are commands that, as they typically are interpreted by members of Judeo-Christian societies, succeed because of the child's belief that parents should be obeyed simply because they are parents, or supervisors should make and enforce decisions simply because they are supervisors. Asian Americans also may find it difficult to challenge higher-status members of decision-making groups. For them, participatory decision-making is alien and frustrating.[10] In other social contexts—like the United States described by de Tocqueville (Chapter 1)—workers have more than enough opportunities to influence decisions in their families, churches, lodges, or civic organizations.[11] In others, a preference for individuality may make *group* decision-making and *group* responsibility seem to be alien. In these situations PDM can be offensive because it upsets traditional authority relationships or undermines individuality or it may provide psychological rewards that simply are not salient to workers who are actively involved in informal organizations.

Sometimes resistance is based on a lack of trust or skill. Many workers, especially blue-collar workers, do not wish to participate in decision-making because they would rather not share the responsibilities that accompany the systems. This is especially true early on, before workers are persuaded that management will not use the systems to penalize them when they make inevitable mistakes.[12]

People with high levels of expertise but weak speaking skills often are frustrated by group decision-making. Their expertise leads them to expect to have much more impact on decisions than their communication skills allow them to exert. People with high levels of communication anxiety also may find participation threatening and may respond by withdrawing. The group loses their expertise, and their satisfaction with their jobs drops. In less participatory arrangements, these people would have opportunities to communicate privately with a single supervisor. Since privacy provides "back stages" where they can plan and rehearse their messages for this single, known listener, their anxiety may be reduced. For them nonparticipatory decision-making may be more satisfying and may allow the organization to better benefit from their expertise.[13]

Participation also may increase employee stress by creating communication overload. When participatory strategies are used, everyone who is involved is required to increase his or her communication. Some PDM systems ask employees to meet after work or on weekends. Especially when their jobs place extreme demands on them, they may not be able to handle the increased communication and the time it takes away from other activities. The problem is even greater when employees, for whatever reasons, wish to participate less than they are asked to do. When the amount of participation is either more or less than employees desire, they have higher stress, lower job satisfaction, and poorer performance than when participation matches their preferences.[14]

Supervisors are even more likely to resist PDM. People become supervisors at least in part because they have a desire for power and an ability to ob-

tain and use it to their advantage. They gain substantial rewards from their superior positions—salary, status, and most important, the legitimate right to exercise authority over others. People maintain positive self-images by comparing
themselves, their positions, their power, and their achievements to others.
Power-sharing strategies, including PDM, are designed to reduce the power
"gap" between supervisors and their subordinates. If the strategies succeed,
they threaten the superiority, and thus the self-esteem and self-images, of powerful people. Thus, PDM threatens precisely those people who hold power
most dear and who have the greatest personal and practical reasons to want to
hold on to the power they have gained over the years.[15]

Power holders resist sharing their power in a number of ways. Some
methods may be overt: refusing to use participatory strategies, using them
only for trivial issues, acting in ways that split the group or otherwise impede
its ability to make effective decisions, refusing to carry out the group's decisions, or sabotaging the decision when it is implemented.[16] Other methods
are more subtle, for example, withholding valuable information from the
group. Because of their positions, supervisors have greater amounts of information and a better ability to take a broad perspective on problems. As a result
of their possessing this information supervisors usually can better anticipate
the effects a decision will have on the organization as a whole. By withholding
information, power holders can lead their group to make bad decisions. Because they possess private information they also can predict that the group's
decisions will fail. When their self-fulfilling predictions come true, their expertise and competence as perceived by other members of the group will be increased. Thus their ability to control the group's decisions in the future is increased. In this way power holders may actually be able to use participation to
increase their influence and enlarge the power gap between them and their
subordinates.

In a series of studies of power-sharing strategies in European firms, Mauk
Mulder found that in addition to having greater access to information, supervisors typically also have greater communication skills than their subordinates.
They are more persuasive, argue positions more effectively, and are more adept
at interpreting other employees' communication and responding appropriately.
In participatory systems these advantages allow them to influence the views of
other employees. In time a "power elite" develops whose membership *seems*
to be determined by their greater communication skills, but also is related to
their formal positions. Eventually less powerful members communicate less
and less and more powerful members begin to dominate the decision-making
process. Thus, the *opportunity* for more open communication, which is the
strength of participation, may lead to increased power gaps rather than to
power sharing.[17] In a study of communication in a lumberyard, Michael Huspek found that workers often were left powerless by their inability to express
their concerns in the technical language of management—they often literally
were not able to say a word during grievance sessions. As important, their inability to express themselves led them to believe that they did not *know*
enough to have the right to challenge their supervisors.[18]

CASE STUDY:
NO PILLSBURY DOUGH BOYS HERE

Resistance is both an individual and a group phenomenon. Different groups of people interpret and respond to the same organizational strategies in different ways. This concept will be discussed at length in Chapter 4, but its relevance to the concept of resistance can be discussed now. For example, let's look at a **quality of working life** (QWL) program in a large food processing company.*

QWL programs are focused participatory decision-making systems. They are designed to improve productivity and the quality of working life by encouraging labor and management to cooperatively find solutions to everyday concerns that are not addressed in formal labor contracts. But, like every other aspect of organizational life, the way a QWL program is perceived, interpreted, and enacted depends on the frames of reference of the different groups of employees who are involved. At Foodcom (a pseudonym, of course) various groups interpreted the program in terms of their own short-term interests, and in doing so probably doomed the program to failure from the beginning.

Top management saw the program as a threat to their control of the organization and to short-term profitability. It took months for the consulting group that was hired to help create the program to negotiate seemingly minor issues. Upper management, which operated on the basis of a strict accounting procedure, had institutionalized an obsession with minimizing costs. Because, like all participatory systems, QWL programs incur initial costs greater than their short-term returns, department heads were placed in an impossible situation: They were expected to make the system work while being punished for allowing their employees to spend the time necessary to make it work.

Plant managers described their organization as a "family," but defined that word in paternalistic terms: managers were parents, workers were children. Managers were supposed to control all aspects of "children's" lives. Dress codes and arrival times were strictly enforced, regardless of their actual effect on productivity, and no one was allowed to communicate with anyone else in the plant without the manager's explicit approval. The QWL committees were expected to serve as "rubber stamps" for the plant managers' projects rather than propose or implement their own solutions to the problems they

*This case study is based on Michael K. Moch and Jean Bartunek, *Creating Alternative Realities at Work* (New York: Harper Business, 1990). A summary of this book is available in Jean M. Bartunek and Michael Moch, "Multiple Constituencies and the Duality of Working Life," in *Reframing Organizational Culture*, Peter Frost, et al., eds. (Newbury Park, CA: Sage, 1991).

(continued)

(continued from the previous page)

encountered. Just as the plant managers enacted the role of dictatorial parents, the workers accepted their place as dependent children. They saw the QWL committees as a mechanism for getting perks—new uniforms, better cafeteria food, athletic facilities, and so on—instead of a way to resolve problems encountered at work. Even the workers' union representative accepted this version of the family metaphor: "I'm not saying they're children; I'm saying, you know, that sometimes you gotta police it like they were children." Just as plant managers refused to give their employees any power or responsibility, workers were unwilling to accept any responsibility, instead expecting that someone else would solve their problems for them. For both groups, the QWL program was simply a mechanism for continuing their paternalistic family.

But one group of workers, the machinists (who constructed, repaired, and maintained the plant and its equipment) saw the program differently. There were two unions in the plants, one representing the bakers and packers (FWIU) and one representing the machinists. The FWIU, long dominated by women, had successfully pressed for wage equality. The machinists were all men, and resented the women and their salaries. They regularly engaged in sexually harassing communication and made it as difficult as possible for the FWIU employees to do their jobs. Their primary objective seemed to be to assert their power whenever possible. When equipment broke down they refused to repair it until the request went through the entire chain of command; when the FWIU asked that a holiday be changed from Thursday to Friday in order to create a three-day weekend, the machinists refused. They also refused to participate in the QWL project out of fear that they would be outvoted by nonmachinist members. When the committee developed proposals that required the use or adaptation of machinery, the machinists refused to go along unless the proposal benefited them alone. As a result, most of the QWL group's proposals were never implemented or were implemented in a way that doomed them to failure. Through each of these processes the competitive relationships among upper management, plant managers, FWIU workers, and machinists were maintained through the implementation of a program that was supposed to foster labor-management cooperation.

Discussion Questions
1. Given all that you know about traditional organizations and the taken-for-granted assumptions that support them, is it realistic to expect power-sharing systems to *ever* be accepted without intense resistance?
2. Given all that you know about control and resistance, what are the likely effects of attempting to implement a power-sharing system and failing to do so? Why are those effects likely?

Summary: The Effects of PDM and Decentralization. Research since Tannenbaum's studies has indicated that PDM does have a number of positive effects. In U.S. firms, formal, company-wide programs of participation still are rare, although their popularity has increased during the last decade (see Chapter 5). Informal programs of participation, where supervisors ask their most productive employees for advice or information, are more widespread. Subordinates respond with useful advice, which increases their supervisors' trust in their judgment and encourages them to seek further advice, and their job satisfaction increases, which reduces absenteeism and voluntary turnover. Somewhat surprisingly, these positive effects do not result from subordinates' feeling that participation gives them greater power. Instead, it results from their being better *informed* about what is going on in the organization. During participatory interactions supervisors provide information and a more open and satisfying communicative relationship is created.[19]

Systems of participation have more limited effects on performance and productivity. In general, the quality of decisions made by participatory groups is better than that of decisions made by the "average" member of the group but is worse than the decision that would be made by the group's most expert individual. This does not suggest that better decisions would be made by a supervisor acting alone, for the simple reason that the supervisor may or may not be the most expert member of a work group. It just suggests that the positive effects of PDM depend on a number of factors, including the distribution of expertise in the group. Research on the effects of participation on productivity is less favorable. Some studies have found that participation does motivate workers to perform more effectively and more efficiently. In other cases participation gives supervisors an opportunity to persuade their subordinates to accept high performance goals. But, overall, research on participation indicates that "with respect to productivity . . . there is no trend in favor of participative leadership as compared to more directive styles."[20]

CASE STUDY:
BING WOULD'VE BEEN PROUD*

In spite of all of the complications and limitations that I have discussed, there are a large number of examples of successful applications of the relational strategy of organizing. Often these successes involve new organizations, since it

---

*This case is based on Theodore Zorn, "Implementing Self-Management at Holiday Inn," in *Case Studies in Organizational Communication,* Beverly Sypher, ed. (Guilford Press, 1991).

(continued)

(continued from the previous page)

seems to be easier to build relational strategies into organizations than to change traditional organizations to operate on a relational strategy. One such new organization is part of a major hotel and motel chain.

Long before any of us was born, Bing Crosby (if the name doesn't ring a bell, ask your professor who he was) starred in a movie titled *Holiday Inn* about a wonderful little hotel and nightclub hideaway in upstate New York that was open only on major holidays. (If you would like to see it for yourself, I promise that it will be broadcast during the Christmas holidays, sandwiched between yet another showing of *It's a Wonderful Life* and *Frosty the Snowman*.) The movie is known today for one of its songs, which went on to become the biggest-selling tune in history (again, if you can't guess the title, ask your professor). Years later a young entrepreneur, Kemmon Wilson, decided to name his chain of hotels after the movie, hoping that all the warm feelings generated by its love story would attract customers. Evidently the strategy worked. Today, Holiday Inn is one of the largest hotel chains in the world.

All of Holiday Inn's telephone reservations are handled in reservations centers near Chicago, Memphis, and Raleigh, North Carolina. When Dave Milidonis was hired to start and manage the Raleigh center he visited the other branches to see what problems they encountered. He found that most of their problems resulted from a Theory X management style, which focused on giving employees negative feedback whenever they violated one of a long list of rules. Since upper management had given him a mandate to create a unique reservations center that competitors could not copy, he went about creating an organization that was based on Theory Y assumptions and operated through team management.

The Raleigh center was designed to have each characteristic discussed in this chapter. It has a decentralized structure—Milidonis, eight call-service managers, and 200 to 600 reservations agents, depending on the season—giving it 50 to 70 percent *lower* administrative costs than other centers. Of course, eight supervisors cannot closely supervise 600 agents, even using computerized records systems. The agents are self-managed and seek assistance from their supervisor when they encounter problems. For example, one new agent asked his supervisor to monitor some of his telephone calls: "I wanted to know how I was coming across on the phone, because at this job . . . your pay is based on how quickly and efficiently you get the reservation done and you tend to rush. But you don't want the guest to know that you are rushing."

Agents are given points based on their performance (transactions per hour), timeliness and attendance (points are deducted for unexcused tardiness or absences), quality (error-free work), confirmation rate (number of sales per call), and safety. Their points are translated into salary bonuses and extra days off or

(continued)

(continued from the previous page)

preferential scheduling. They also receive extensive recognition, both for their own performance and for the center's overall performance. But most important is the atmosphere of trust and supportiveness in the plant: Workers take breaks when they want, can knit or perform hobbies while they work, visit a comfortable lounge, or spend time talking informally about work or personal topics with managers or other workers. Agents are *expected* to form informal communication ties—to go to the appropriate people when they need information. This openness even includes helping employees prepare their resumes and apply for jobs at other firms. Managers do not spend their time issuing warnings and punishments; employees know that their income and status within the group will be determined by their performance, so they make sure they spend their time wisely. Finally, employees have wide access to performance information about the center and participate in decision-making about major policies and procedures. As a result, applicants for jobs at the center are plentiful, even in an area that has 2 to 3 percent unemployment.

Of course, the system has its own complications. Managers are under a great deal of pressure to treat *every* employee equally. They not only need to be consistent in their own actions, but they also must be consistent with the actions of the other managers. This requires the managers to develop and maintain close ties with one another, as well as with their agents. Like children who go from one parent to another trying to get the answer they want, agents sometimes try to play one supervisor off the others. If a manager shows preferential treatment, "I'd have a riot right there. . . . And that's the key to making the grapevine work for us. For us to be consistent . . . the second we're not consistent, it's brought to that manager's attention, usually by that agent or group of agents who say, 'Now wait a minute' " (p. 215). Newcomers find the experience a little bewildering, because they are not used to the degree of freedom and responsibility that exists in the center. No one tells them what to do, and they are expected to confront and solve their own problems. For most newcomers, that is motivating in itself, but for employees whose lives have involved lengthy preparation for participation in traditional bureaucracies, it takes a bit of getting used to. But the system does seem to work. Performance equals or exceeds other centers', while operating costs have been lowest at Raleigh *every week* for the last four years. The biggest problem Milidonis faces is finding new ways to meet the changing needs of the organization and its employees.

Discussion Questions
1. Would you be satisfied in an organization like the Raleigh center? Would you be productive? Why?
2. Which of the "requirements" for human relations models to succeed that have been discussed in this chapter are present at Raleigh? Which ones are absent?

(continued)

(continued from the previous page)

3. What kinds of problems do you think will develop at Raleigh during the next few years? Over the long run?

4. A year or so ago the Raleigh center was purchased by the Bass corporation (makers of Bass Ale, among other things). Bass immediately transformed the center into a traditional, bureaucratic organization. Dave Milidonis, and many of the other people who made the Raleigh center what it was, now are gone. Why would such a decision be made? What effects is the change likely to have? Why?

Developing Informal Communication Networks

Chapter 1 explained the processes through which communication networks emerge. Traditional strategies of organizing largely ignored communication networks other than the formal chain of command; indeed, because communication through informal ties is outside of management's control supervisors operating on the basis of traditional strategies often tried to suppress their development. But, researchers as early as Chester Barnard (whose most influential book was published in 1938) realized that informal networks are inevitable and invaluable. They were present even in the prisons and concentration camps of World War II. Through them employees form meaningful interpersonal relationships, gain a sense of self-respect, meet their sociability needs, and exercise some degree of control over their working lives. People who are actively involved in informal networks have higher morale, job satisfaction, commitment to their organizations, know more about how their organizations operate, and are better able to meet other people's communication needs than employees who are not actively involved.[21]

However, it takes effort to develop and sustain informal networks. It takes time for people to find one another and much successful communication for them to come to understand and trust one another. Sometimes they will be members of units that have their own unique technical languages and thus must learn each other's language before they can communicate effectively (recall the concept of "trained communication incapacity" in Chapter 2). Informal networks must regularly be used or they will disappear. Unless two people communicate on a fairly regular basis they will forget the language and frame of reference used by the other person. Just as competence in a foreign language wears off with disuse, learning the frame of reference of other employees also wears off. Then, when a crisis occurs in which employees need to communicate, they will find it difficult to do so. Typically informal networks are maintained through **gossip**, the sharing of personal information that is irrelevant to specific tasks or organizational decisions.[22] But without gossip, informal networks dissolve.

One of the most prominent features of informal networks are **cliques**. Cliques are tightly knit groups of employees that form spontaneously as a result of informal communication. Cliques often develop in formally defined organizational units, because people who work together communicate informally as well. However, cliques made up of members of different units may also form if these employees have informal contacts. Leonard Sayles distinguished four different types of cliques, each of which develops for different reasons. *Command groups* are composed of a supervisor and his or her subordinates and they develop because these people get to know each other informally as they work together. The superior is still given a certain amount of deference in the command group, but the distance between superiors and subordinates is reduced by the informal interaction between them. The informal relationships provided by command groups enable managers and employees to discuss innovations and problems "off the record." *Task groups* are composed of members who have to collaborate or work together on a common task. As in the command group, working together tends to lead to informal interaction that may result in clique formation. Often task groups develop ways of doing work that differ from those specified by the formal organizational structure. In some cases these lead to increased productivity on the part of the group. For example, one study of radar teams in the Air Force found that they used informal communication networks that were established through off-the-job socializing to compensate for deficiencies in formal, chain of command networks.[23] Of course, in other cases, informal procedures can reduce work effectiveness, as when members work together to withhold information about customer complaints or illegal/unethical group activities from the organization.

Two other types of cliques are less dependent on the organization's formal structure. *Friendship cliques* are based on employees' off-the-job interests and associations and also based on previous work experience. Age, common activities, gender, marital status, and ethnic background are among the types of mortar that hold friendship cliques together. Friendship cliques can be beneficial to the organization. A number of studies have documented the people's need for sociability (recall Chapter 1), and friendship cliques meet this need on the job.[24] As a result, they tend to reduce turnover and in some cases may reduce the effects of unpleasant work conditions. Indeed, some advocates of relational strategies have advocated that management promote the formation of friendship cliques in order to stabilize the organization's workforce. *Interest cliques* form when a group of workers attempts to exploit opportunities to improve their relative position in the organization. Interest cliques may form to advocate a certain change, such as institution of flexible work hours. They may also form to resist changes, such as the adoption of new technologies in the organization. Interest cliques are not always workers-versus-management, though they may be. Often these cliques cut across status boundaries, uniting lower and higher level employees from a number of units.

Organizations differ greatly in the number and types of cliques that form. Some organizations, particularly those that are new or that arrange employees where they cannot easily interact (e.g. along a long assembly line), have relatively few cliques. Others have dense cliques that overlap and are interconnected. The types of cliques that form and grow in an organization exert an important influence on the type of communication that flows through the informal network system.

Generally speaking, informal networks help organizations in three ways—by *compensating for the weaknesses in formal communication,* by *improving organizational decision-making,* and by *fostering innovation.* Formal communication networks allow people to handle predictable, routine situations but they are inefficient means of meeting unanticipated communication needs, for managing crises, for dealing with complex or detailed problems, sharing personal information, or exchanging information rapidly. In one study Keith Davis found that during a quality-control crisis in a large firm, the information that was needed to solve the problem was rapidly disseminated using informal networks, not formal channels.[25] And, informal communication also may be more reliable than formal communication. Because it is less restricted by status differences and other constraints, and because it depends less on formal task requirements than formal communication, it is richer in content. Mutual give and take is less inhibited in informal communication, so communicators provide more detail in their messages and also are more willing to give and receive feedback. Even *gossip* and **rumors**, messages whose accuracy cannot immediately be determined by management, usually provide accurate information. Job-related rumors occur because employees are not adequately informed through formal channels. Although some gossip and rumors may be false, when compared to formal communication, with its inherent problems of withholding and distortion (recall Chapter 2), informal communication may be even more accurate.[26] It goes through shorter communication chains and allows people to temporarily ignore power and status differences. Informal networks also tend to be self-correcting. Once an employee is caught spreading false rumors, his or her credibility is reduced. Formal communication networks are not based on interpersonal relationships, so they tend not to be self-correcting.

Informal networks also can be used strategically. Sometimes people have access to a wealth of valuable information that they are not "officially" supposed to possess. Informal relationships with those people provide an invaluable source of information, especially information that is not supposed to be public knowledge. Employees can release "trial balloons" and monitor employees' reactions while never having to officially admit that the proposal was even being considered. Being able to talk off the record seems to improve organizational decision-making, especially when organizations are in the early stages of defining problems and searching for solutions. Through his twenty-year study of bureaucratic organizations, Peter Blau found that informal communication allowed employees to obtain advice and assistance without "really" admitting that they needed it and provided them with politically safe opportunities to "think out loud" about new ideas or experiences. As a result, informal networks foster innovation. In general, the more open, rapid, and complete an organization's communication system is, the more innovative its employees can be. Through informal networks people share innovative ideas, obtain feedback that allows them to improve those ideas, and eventually obtain support for those innovations. Informal networks allow (but do not guarantee) people to come to a shared understanding of new ideas and their importance to the organization, and thus stimulate them to take collective innovative action.[27]

RELATIONAL STRATEGIES OF MOTIVATION AND CONTROL

Traditional strategies of motivation and control are based on the assumptions that workers are motivated primarily by the promise of economic gain, and secondarily by needs for stable and predictable lives and by the self-esteem that comes from succeeding in their jobs. Relational strategies expand the concern for workers' self-esteem, and propose a number of strategies that are based on fulfilling employees' non-economic needs.

Fulfilling "Upper-level" Needs

Three of the most influential advocates of this approach to motivation and control were Abraham Maslow, Frederick Herzberg, and Chris Argyris. Maslow's model of human motivation is widely known—people have five kinds of needs that are arranged in a hierarchy: **physiological** (expressed in feelings of thirst, lust, and so on), **safety** (feeling free from danger, harm, and the fear that physiological needs will not be met), **belongingness** (a desire for meaningful relationships with other people), **esteem** or **ego** (feelings of accomplishment and recognition), and **self-actualization** (a concept that Maslow never explained clearly but that seems to be related to the feeling that one has done or is doing what one is meant to do). Once lower-level needs are fulfilled, upper-level needs become salient.

Herzberg refined Maslow's model by differentiating "lower-level" needs (which, if not fulfilled, cause people to be dissatisfied) and "higher level" needs that, if fulfilled, cause people to be satisfied. Herzberg argued **hygiene factors** (his label for things that fulfill lower-level needs) motivate people by allowing them to avoid pain. When these needs are not met, people feel discomfort; when they are met, the discomfort is reduced but once an adequate level of fulfillment is reached no additional pleasure is felt. **Motivators** (his term for higher-level needs) create pleasure when they are provided but their absence does not cause frustration or pain. Although neither of Maslow's nor Herzberg's conclusions have been supported consistently by subsequent research, their perspective became the basis of a number of strategies of increasing workers' job satisfaction by enlarging and enriching their jobs.[28]

Instead of examining the factors that motivate people at work, Argyris used Maslow's model to examine how people become alienated from their jobs and their organizations. He argued that many of the key characteristics of traditional models of organizing frustrated the needs of normal, psychologically healthy people. Jobs that are specialized or **routinized** (performed in the same way day after day), supervisors who control their employees "tightly," and highly competitive, individualistic atmospheres are especially alienating. People respond to these situations by choosing strategies that are counterproductive for the organization—becoming defensive (attacking or withdrawing from coworkers) or apathetic (for example, daydreaming), socializing with other frustrated workers instead of focusing attention on their work, leaving the organization, or attempting to advance to positions that are less frustrating.

In short, Maslow, Herzberg, and Argyris proposed a view of human beings and work that was diametrically opposed to the underlying assumptions of the traditional strategy of organizing. As Chapter 1 of this book noted, people have important needs for autonomy and creativity, needs that are frustrated by organizations' (and societies') needs for control and coordination. Advocates of traditional strategies not only overlooked that tension, they developed an implicit view of human beings that rationalized it, a perspective that Douglas McGregor has labeled "Theory X." Traditional strategies of organizing maximize that tension; relational strategies, Maslow and his successors argued, could minimize it. Doing so involved three strategies: persuading supervisors to adopt a radically different view of human beings and the role that meaningful work plays in their lives (a perspective that McGregor calls "Theory Y"; see Table 3-1), enlarging and enriching jobs, and adopting relationship-oriented leadership strategies.[29]

TABLE 3–1
McGregor's Theory X and Theory Y

THEORY X	THEORY Y
1. Workers must be supervised as closely as possible, either through direct oversight or by tight reward and/or punishment systems.	1. People usually do not require close supervision and will, if given a chance to control their own activities, be productive, satisfied, and fulfilled.
2. Work is objectionable to most people.	2. Work is natural and enjoyable unless it is made offensive by the actions of organizations.
3. Most people have little initiative, have little capacity for being creative or solving organizational problems, do not want to have responsibilites, and prefer being directed by someone else.	3. People are ambitious, desire autonomy and self-control, and can use their abilities to solve problems and help their organizations meet their goals. Creativity is distributed "normally" across the population, just as is any other characteristic.
4. People are motivated by economic factors and a need for security.	4. People are motivated by a variety of needs only some of which involve economics or security.

Job Enlargement and Enrichment

Job enlargement (giving workers more tasks to perform) and **job enrichment** (giving them more complex or challenging tasks) are relatively simple concepts. But they are a major departure from the traditional strategy. Under Taylor and his successors, managers focused on segmenting, simplifying, and routinizing jobs—making them as "impoverished" and "small" as possible. When these simple tasks are arranged sequentially, as in the "miracle" of Henry Ford's assembly line, efficiency is maximized. As an added benefit, supervisory control is enhanced. Because workers perform tasks requiring few skills, they are easy to replace. Arrayed along an assembly line, they have little or no opportunity to communicate with one another and must adjust the pace of their activities to the pace of the machines. This keeps them from sharing grievances, comparing the way management treats them, or making plans for collective action.[30] New technologies are developed that simplify and routinize jobs even further. For example, at one time the service jobs of grocery-store checker and fast-food sales clerk required at least minimal arithmetical, keyboarding, and memory skills. Today computerized cash registers—that, like all other deskilling technologies, increase output per person hour—make it possible to hire people without these skills. (The next time you visit your local McDonald's, look closely at the keyboard on the cash registers and ask yourself what skills are necessary to operate it. For a really excellent test, order something that is not represented by a button on the keyboard and see what happens.) By the mid-1960s most production workers in the United States were involved in this kind of routine, repetitive, *deskilled* activity, which failed to fulfill individual needs for creativity, autonomy, or sociability. By the mid-1980s many white-collar workers were involved in similar jobs.

Although deskilling increases productivity for a time, it also decreases job satisfaction and increases labor–management hostility. For decades organizations using traditional strategies relied on economic reward systems to offset this dissatisfaction. It is not accidental that the most routinized sectors of our economy, automobile manufacturing, for example, traditionally have paid the highest average wage rates. High wages may temporarily increase both job satisfaction and management's control (because highly paid workers face certain reductions in their standard of living if they quit or are fired and because unemployed workers see those jobs as being highly attractive).[31] But, eventually they also reduce profits, Managers using traditional strategies have two responses possible. On the one hand they can attempt to further increase productivity through further deskilling and technological advances. Eventually tasks become so routinized that productivity-based reward systems no longer make sense, because it is the speed of the assembly line (or other production technology) rather than the employees' efforts that determines output. Performance-based reward systems are replaced by hourly wage systems, which separate performance and rewards and destroy the motivational basis of traditional organizations. Wage rates continue to escalate; job satisfaction and productivity continue to decline in a vicious cycle.

On the other hand, they can hire employees who have few alternatives and thus cannot resist regardless of how alienated they are from their jobs—children, retired people, disabled people, or, most recently, residents of Third World countries (including children). Alternatively, they can attempt to influence public policy in ways that reduce the power of other groups of employees—for example, supporting increased barriers to unionization or striking by unionized workers—or both, for example revising child labor laws to allow them to hire progressively younger employees.

Or, advocates of relational strategies argue, organizations can "enlarge" or "enrich" employees' jobs. Doing so increases efficiency because it allows organizations to *decentralize* and it increases profitability by substituting rewards of enhanced creativity and autonomy for increased salaries and wage rates. But, providing assignments that allow workers to use their abilities to the fullest (enrichment) relies heavily on communication. If a job is too complex it is frustrating, not satisfying. If it is too simple it is boring. Successfully matching workers and jobs, as Taylor realized a half-century ago, requires a high level of open communication and feedback between supervisors and their subordinates. In addition, workers seem to determine how "rich" their jobs are both by monitoring what they do and by talking with other workers. Unless people believe that their tasks are stimulating they will not be. Workers develop these beliefs when other workers tell them that they envy their jobs. Successful job enrichment requires both careful job design and active and supportive informal communication.[32]

Group Influences on Motivation

While there are many programs that attempt to meet member needs through managerial attention, rewards, and job enrichment, their influence is often filtered through the cliques employees belong to.[33] Probably the most important single influence on worker behavior is the groups of fellow employees he or she belongs to. If groups interpret motivational attempts by the organization as exploitative, their members may reject these programs, no matter how attractive they may seem to those who devise them. On the other hand, if groups buy into job enrichment or other programs, it may significantly increase their motivational impact.

Attention to work group influences on motivation goes back at least as far as the original Hawthorne studies. Groups, both formal and informal, have been shown to influence the level of productivity of their members. Many cases of group influence on **ratebusters** have been documented. These employees, who produce too much or who go along with management too readily, often are punished by coworkers. Sanctions can range from explanations, to warnings, to the silent treatment, and even to physical violence. However, cases have also been documented in which groups work out shortcuts that increase production. Sayles notes that "We have many instances on record where the group has sanctioned increasingly high productivity, rejected fellow workers who could not maintain high output, and resisted threats to existing high quality standards." This line of thought is behind recent advocacy of team-based organizations: properly composed and motivated teams may create a more effective organization than more traditional forms of organizing.[34]

In any case, it is important to remember that the relational strategy does not think only in terms of isolated individuals who respond to organizational attempts to motivate them. Instead, it recognizes that individuals are suspended in networks of relationships that influence how they react to motivational attempts. What is important is not just what the individual employee thinks of the motivational attempt (or for that matter of any organizational initiative), but also what the individual's cliques think of it. This concern with relationships also extends to the topic of leadership.

RELATIONAL STRATEGIES OF LEADERSHIP

Although there are a large number of different relational strategies of leadership, they all focus on enhancing the relationship that exists between a supervisor and each of her or his immediate subordinates by creating and sustaining high levels of trust and reducing the uncertainty that exists within the relationship. These goals are achieved by fostering open and supportive communication, negotiating shared interpretive frames and interactional rules (a process often labeled **transactional leadership**), and adapting leadership strategies to situational guidelines and constraints.

Fostering Open and Supportive Supervisor–Subordinate Communication

Eventually, advocates of relational strategies of leadership recognized that relationships are two-way streets (the transactional perspective described in the next section). But, initially they focused almost wholly on supervisory communication. In two pioneering series of studies, Rensis Likert, Edwin Fleishman, and their associates examined the supervisory attitudes and communicative behaviors that fostered the development of open and supportive relationships with their subordinates. Likert found that high-producing organizations and units of organizations had supervisors who were both highly competent in the technical aspects of their jobs *and* were "employee-centered," that is, they expressed genuine concern about the human aspects of their subordinates' problems, communicated a kind of contagious enthusiasm about achieving high-but-achievable performance goals, supervised "loosely," and actively encouraged their subordinates to participate in decision-making.[35] Similarly, Fleishman found that work groups led by supervisors who communicated "consideration" to their workers were more productive, at least up to a point, than work groups with supervisors who did not do so. **Consideration** involved expressing trust and respect for workers, communicating a degree of warmth and rapport, encouraging shared decision-making and allowing consensual assignment of tasks. It did not involve superficial "pat-on-the-back" or "first-name" gimmicks but emphasized a deeper concern for the group members' needs.[36]

Considerate, employee-centered supervisor–subordinate relationships depended on avoiding defensive communication. In a classic article Jack Gibb noted that communication creates feelings of discomfort and defensiveness when either its content or the way in which it is presented makes people feel that they are constantly being *judged* (even praise creates discomfort if it is excessively strong or too public); being *manipulated* (tricked into believing that they are having an important role in the organization when they are not), or *controlled too tightly* or inappropriately; being subjected to *cold, impersonal, uncaring treatment;* or being "preached at" or otherwise treated as an *inferior,* relatively useless person.

Instead, a supervisor can create feelings of personal worth and comfort if he or she communicates in ways that are descriptive and objective rather than evaluative; focuses on working together to solve important problems; is spontaneous, open, and honest about the supervisor's true feelings; affirms the subordinates' competence; and encourages them to question or provide input into decisions, or otherwise initiate communication, even if doing so involves negative topics or information. Fifty years before Gibb, Mary Parker Follett argued that even orders could be given in a way that affirmed subordinates' self-esteem. The orders themselves need to be clear and specific, seem to be *logical* and *appropriate,* and be **legitimate** in the sense that Weber used that term (that is, accepted as normal and proper by workers). But, they also need to be communicated in a way that allows subordinates to retain a sense of personal pride, self-respect, and autonomy (to "save face," a concept that will be described in Chapter 6). In addition, workers must believe that they are making a free and open choice to obey this order. They will do so only when (1) they have been trained to make the desired choices, (2) they have made similar choices so often in the past that they have developed habits of obeying, and (3) the order comes from a supervisor with whom they have formed a good relationship and who has given orders in a way that protects their feelings. For example, even subordinates who like their supervisors and want to comply with orders also need to feel like they are in control of their lives. Wise supervisors present orders in a way that allows the subordinate to help decide what he or she should do, that expresses their liking for the subordinate, and that indicates that they are confident in the subordinate's ability to figure out how to best implement the command. In this way, supervisors create a situation in which their subordinates can resolve their internal conflict between wanting to obey and wanting to resist while fulfilling their needs for autonomy and creativity.[37]

Supportive communication increases the level of trust between a supervisor and subordinates and creates the perception that the supervisor is considerate or employee-centered. Its positive effects also depend on the supervisor's listening skills—when subordinates feel that their supervisors understand their communication, supportiveness can succeed—and his or her ability to avoid disconfirming communication.[38] Messages carry meaning at both content and relational levels—they provide information and they make a statement about the interpersonal relationship that exists between the communicators (see Chapter 6 for a more detailed discussion). **Disconfirming communication** occurs when a supervisor communicates in a way that does not acknowledge a subordinate's right to exist. For example, a young accountant waited two weeks to see her supervisor. After having meetings canceled, rescheduled, and canceled again; telephone calls cut off; and chance meetings in the hallway in which the supervisor did not even stop walking to say hello; the accountant finally got into a meeting. After explaining that she did not understand new tax laws on capital gains rates, her supervisor said, "This isn't my problem. Talk to the training department." Her long-awaited meeting lasted three minutes. Clearly, she concluded, her supervisor does not recognize that she exists, much less that she is an important part of the team. This does not mean that supervisors cannot *disagree* with their subordinates, because one can reject or question the *content* of persons' communications without rejecting their identities.[39]

Open and supportive supervisory communication has two important advantages. Maintaining an open, supportive communicative relationship helps compensate for the problems in formal communication that were described in Chapter 2. Openness creates trust, and trust reduces withholding or distorting of information. Supervisors give trusted subordinates more attention, support, and sensitivity than they do to subordinates they do not trust, and they use persuasion or information-giving instead of coercion as a means of influence. In turn, this kind of communication gives subordinates a great deal of information about their jobs, organizations, and their supervisor's needs. This knowledge allows them to know what information is important to their supervisors and enables them to better filter the information that they exchange with their supervisors.[40] Trusted subordinates provide more information and more accurate information, and thus give their supervisors incentives to trust and be open with them. Nontrusted subordinates grow to mistrust their supervisors and withdraw (withhold or distort communication), giving their supervisors "evidence" that they cannot be trusted. Through this kind of reinforcing communication cycle, openness begets openness; closed and defensive communication perpetuates closed and defensive communication.[41] Open and supportive is especially important when subordinates have complex and ambiguous jobs. In these situations subordinates often need task-related information and advice that only their supervisors can provide. It is difficult to ask for help from a closed and non-supportive supervisor, making it more difficult for us to master new or complex tasks, making it more likely that we will make more errors while learning.[42] In summary, closed communication climates are difficult to change. No one person can decide to create open and supportive relationships, even if that person realizes that he or she is trapped in a nonproductive cycle of communication.

Transactional Leadership

As the previous paragraph suggests, supervisor–subordinate communication is a two-way, interactive process. Although supervisors tend have a greater impact on communicative relationships than their subordinates because of their formal authority, relationships develop because of the *mutual* exchanges that take place between the parties. This is the primary assumption underlying *transactional* views of leadership. Leaders, according to this model, must legitimize their position—formal rank alone does not make one a leader—but legitimation is a "two-way street." Leaders and each of their followers negotiate working relationships. Both parties may communicate in ways that demonstrate that they share the same core values and are loyal to one another (and to their work group). In these exchanges, both parties grant the other a degree of status, influence, and freedom to act independently. They "align" themselves with one another—converge toward the same set of values, are able to solve complex and unprecedented problems together, and have a relaxed, mutually supportive relationship.[43] They become "**co-oriented**," they reach agreement on the rules that guide their relationship, and they both understand those rules (for example, what topics will they discuss and what topics will they avoid, must they schedule meetings or can they just "pop in" to one another's office, will they use first names or titles, will they interrupt one another or quietly wait until the other is finished talking to respond). They *negotiate* a trusting relationship, one in which their motives, intentions, openness, and integrity are *consistent,* in which they are *dependably* competent, willing, and able to help one another with job-related problems, and in which the judgment is *reliable.*[44]

In other relationships, supervisors and subordinates merely **accommodate** to one another. The supervisor tends to guide and constrain the subordinate's choices, and, although the subordinate may politely disagree with her or his supervisor, they negotiate roles that are more formal and distant than in "aligning" relationships. In still other relationships the parties engage in polarized, conflictful exchanges. The supervisor monitors the subordinate closely; the subordinate resists the supervisor and rejects his or her authority. Consequently, it is not just the supervisor's communicative action that influences the kind of relationship that is developed with each of her or his subordinates. Instead, it is the pattern of mutual *transactions* that leads to the development of different kinds of relationships.

Even supportive communication is mutual and transactional. Trust, respect, and task factors like risk-taking and support for innovative ideas have been shown to be highest when supervisors give high levels of support *and* subordinates perceive that they receive high levels of support—both the level of support and the level agreement about the level of support are important factors. Terri Albrecht and Mara Adelman found that supervisors and subordinates support *one another* in a number of ways: by talking about "how organizations work" (for example, discussing potential career moves and their likely effects); by helping develop new skills or giving one another tangible assistance when it is needed (for example, a director of programming "jumping in" to help solve a knotty language problem and doing so cheerfully without a "this will cost you later" attitude); by providing an outlet for venting anger or frustration (serving as a "sounding board"); or offering praise, acceptance, or reassurance.[45]

In short, transactional views of leadership focus on the development of particular kinds of supervisor–subordinate relationships. It recognizes that neither person is wholly in charge of the process, and that supervisors often will have different kinds of relationships with different subordinates.

Contingency Theories of Leadership

This final "relational" view of leadership recognizes that supervisor–subordinate relationships develop within a complex set of situational guidelines and constraints (recall Chapter 1). Some situations encourage supervisors and subordinates to negotiate some kinds of relationships, others encourage the development of other types of relationships. Because most of them were developed before the advent of transactional perspectives they tend to focus on supervisory communication.[46]

One of the earliest and still perhaps the best-known contingency model of leadership was developed by Fred Fiedler and his associates. The factors included in Fiedler's model are summarized in Figure 3–2. Two situational factors, "good" versus "bad" leader–group member relationships and "strong" versus "weak" formal power of the leader are self-explanatory. The third factor, which Fiedler called "task structure," is a bit more complicated. It has four dimensions: (1) the clarity of the group's goals; (2) "path multiplicity," the number of courses of action that potentially are available to the group; (3) the "effect verifiability" of the group's decisions (the extent to which group members know the effects of their decisions); and (4) the specificity of the decisions that they must make. "Structured" tasks involve clear goals, low "path multiplicity," high verifiability, and specific decisions. "Unstructured" tasks have the opposite characteristics. Fiedler's model includes eight possible combinations of these four situational factors. His research indicated work groups in combinations five through seven would perform better if their leaders adopted relational strategies, and groups in the other combinations would perform better under traditional strategies. Similar, but more successfully replicated models have been developed by Robert House and by Lyman Porter.[47] Like Fiedler, House and Porter focused on the tasks that employees perform—how intrinsically satisfying they are and how complex and ambiguous they are. House's "path–goal" theory of leadership asserts that (1) the degree of satisfaction that employees gain from performing their tasks (their "intrinsic" as opposed to their "extrinsic" rewards), (2) the ambiguity and complexity of their jobs, and (3) the communication strategies adopted by their supervisors will combine to influence their overall job satisfaction or performance. In highly complex, intrinsically satisfying jobs, supervisors who provide direction and structure (through the use of traditional strategies) will help employees clarify confusing situations, making it easier for them to do their jobs well and thus increasing both their satisfaction and performance.[48]

FIGURE 3–2
Fiedler's Contingency Model

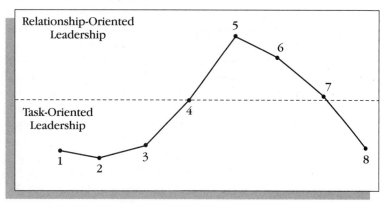

Leader-Member Relation	Good	Good	Good	Good	Poor	Poor	Poor	Poor
Task Structure	Structured		Unstructured		Structured		Unstructured	
Formal Leader-Position Power	Strong	Weak	Strong	Weak	Strong	Weak	Strong	Weak
Combinations:	1	2	3	4	5	6	7	8

Using relational strategies will have little or no effect on employees who have complex jobs, because the intrinsic satisfaction they gain from doing their tasks well is so great that they do not need the additional satisfaction gained from warm relationships with their supervisors. Conversely, in low-level, unsatisfying jobs, relational strategies will increase worker satisfaction because it can help offset the frustrations that are created by boring and repetitive tasks. However, they will not substantially influence worker performance. If supervisors use traditional strategies in this situation, their efforts will be perceived as attempts to force workers to concentrate on their dissatisfying jobs and thus will create anger, dissatisfaction, increased numbers of grievances, and increase turnover, *but* probably will *increase* performance. In effective work groups, situationally appropriate leader–follower relationships will naturally emerge.[49]

Other contingency models of leadership focus on the extent to which subordinates are prepared to perform the tasks they are assigned. For example, Paul Hersey and Kenneth Blanchard concluded that some subordinates are more self-motivated and more capable of self-direction than other. A subordinate's level of **maturity** depends in part on his or her **willingness** to do the job, which in turn depends on factors like commitment, enthusiasm, self-confidence, interest in the job, independence, and so on. Subordinates who are not "willing" to do the job are not necessarily hostile; they may be distracted by family problems, have low self-esteem, or any number of other barriers to being fully involved in the task. Other subordinates may be willing but not "*able*" to do the job, or lack the knowledge, information, or experience necessary to perform well. Thus "maturity" varies across different employees and across different situations or tasks for each employee.[50]

When subordinates are neither willing nor able, supervisors should use a ("traditional") **telling style**—giving them direction and feedback but not emotional support or autonomy. Other employees should be led with different kinds of "relational" strategies: Willing but unable employees should be led by the **selling style**—providing support *and* direction; unwilling but able subordinates should be led through a "participating" style in which the supervisor provides a great deal of support but little direction. Finally, subordinates who are both willing and able should be left alone (a **delegating style**), since directive, task-related communication would suggest that the supervisor does not trust them and actively supportive communication might be perceived as patronizing.[51]

Assessment: Relational Leadership Strategies

It is possible to evaluate a strategy of organizing or particular leadership strategies in a number of different ways—impact of employees' job satisfaction, effects on organizational performance and profitability, and contribution to society as a whole are three commonly used criteria (see Chapter 12). In the case of relational strategies of leadership one's choice of evaluative criteria will largely determine one's evaluation of the approach.

Relational Strategies and Employee Job Satisfaction.   Relational leadership strategies do lead to increased job satisfaction, although probably not because they fulfill employees' "higher-level" needs. Supervisors who are perceived as employee-centered, supportive, understanding, informative, tolerant of disagreements, willing to listen to their subordinates, and willing to involve their subordinates in salient decisions have more satisfied employees. The impact of relational strategies has been shown to be rather small from a practical standpoint, but it does seem to occur consistently regardless of the kind of organization being studied or the specific research method employed. The relationship is strongest for employees near the bottom of the organizational hierarchy, and with people who need large amounts of information to do their jobs well.[52] In short, employees in open, supportive communication climates are satisfied employees.

Creating and maintaining high levels of job satisfaction is important for a number of reasons. Perhaps most important, work groups composed of satisfied people simply are more pleasant places to work. Since most of us spend much of our lives at work, this may be sufficient justification for the use of relational strategies. There also are some more tangible benefits. Job dissatisfaction has consistently been linked to high levels of absenteeism and voluntary turnover. About 10–15 percent of voluntary turnover can be attributed to low levels of job satisfaction.[53] When employees who perform tasks that are important and cannot be easily performed by others are absent, the stress experienced by other employees increases and organizational performance declines. When the costs of searching for and training replacement personnel are high, voluntary turnover is costly. But if absences allow a worker to return rested and rejuvenated and to work more efficiently, or if employees who resign can be replaced easily, absenteeism and turnover may not reduce organizational performance. In fact, many organizations—government agencies and industries that have predictable slack periods during the year—have systems that encourage absenteeism (taking "leave without pay") during times of low workload. Assembly lines have "rovers" who fill in for absent workers. Because the rover's job is less boring, he or she may be more productive than the employee who is absent. By allowing employees to temporarily escape the pressures of work, these industries increase job satisfaction and reduce absenteeism and turnover during peak times. Thus, although satisfaction is related to absenteeism and turnover, it may or may not be related to organizational performance, depending on a number of factors.

However, high levels of job satisfaction *do not,* in general lead to high levels of individual or organizational performance. It *does* makes sense intuitively that satisfied workers will work harder and perform better than dissatisfied workers; if people are happy at work, they *should be* more committed to their organization and to their contribution to it, and thus *should want* to work harder in order to make sure their organizations succeed. Unfortunately, workers often do not respond as they "should" to satisfying work situations. They may not be motivated to work harder, and even if they want to work harder, they may not actually do so. Fifty years of research on the relationship between job satisfaction and performance has not found strong or consistent relationships between the two. In 1964, Victor Vroom summarized early research on the relationship between satisfaction and performance and found that the average correlation was 0.14, that is, about 2 percent of differences in employees' performance could be attributed to differences in job satisfaction. Twenty years later, after examining 217 additional studies involving more than 12,000 employees, Iaffaldo and Muchinsky concluded that "20 years and at least 200 satisfaction–performance correlations later, the average correlation was found to be nearly the same."[54] In sum, research on satisfaction–performance relationships indicates either that high performance leads to high job satisfaction (because workers feel pride in a "job well done") or that other factors simultaneously increase both satisfaction and performance. If, for instance, workers value hard work and high levels of performance for its own sake, or if they believe they will receive tangible rewards from high performance, they tend to be both satisfied and productive. If they do not hold these beliefs, they tend to be both dissatisfied and relatively unproductive regardless of the leadership strategies used in their organizations.[55] Or, people working in an autocratic organization with no opportunity for advancement or sense of personal fulfillment but few employment opportunities because of their race, gender, ethnic background, lack of education, disabilities, or the general economic situation, may be both dissatisfied and productive because they are afraid of losing their jobs.[56] Conversely, people whose nonwork lives meet their upper-level needs may expend only the minimum amount of effort necessary to keep their jobs and the income they provide.

As a result, Edwin Locke's extensive survey of research on job satisfaction and productivity concluded that "both logic and research suggest that it is best to view productivity and satisfaction as separate outcomes of the employee–job interaction, and to expect causal relationships between them only in special circumstances." Repeated studies since Locke's have reached the same conclusions.[57] In short, the work world seems to be relatively full of people who smile a lot and do very little and people who smile not at all and do a lot.

Relational Strategies and Individual/Organizational Performance.   As indicated earlier, there are some situations in which relational strategies do positively influence individual and organizational performance. In many situations, employees need a rapid exchange of accurate information to perform their tasks well. If the only—or most—reliable source for that information is their supervisor, relational communication strategies increase information flow, reduce rates of making errors and thus increase employees' performance.[58] This is most likely when employees perform complex and challenging tasks, as the contingency models of leadership explained, and when employees play "boundary-spanning" roles (recall Chapter 1).

As Chapter 2 explained, organizations that are immersed in highly competitive, turbulent environments operate most effectively when they have open, relatively free-flowing communication systems. This is why traditional, bureaucratic strategies tend to fail in these environments. Relational strategies of organizing, both decentralized participatory decision-making and open and supportive supervisor–subordinate communication, are especially well adapted to these environments. Boundary-spanners can obtain information from the environment and rapidly disseminate that information to other employees who will be able to draw on multiple kinds of expertise to solve complicated, unprecedented problems. In addition, boundary-spanners in organizations that employ relational strategies also tend to more effectively represent the organization to outside constituents. Employees tend to mirror their supervisors' communication with them in their own communication with clients, suppliers, and other outsiders. If their supervisors are not warm, supportive, and open with them, they will not be with their clients and customers. Alienated subordinates create alienated customers, who may take their business elsewhere.

Summary.   In general, relational strategies seem to have a consistently favorable effect on employees' job satisfaction but only a limited *direct* effect on their performance. The exceptions to this generalization involve a number of different task characteristics. If employees need to be able to exchange information rapidly and to have available a wide variety of expertise in order to do their jobs well, relational strategies enhance performance substantially. But, these positive effects result from improved information exchange and decision-making, not from increased motivation.

These comments on the *limitations* of relational strategies intended to be just that—an indication that their effects *depend* on a large number of factors. In a great many cases organizations have adopted relational strategies and found that both morale and productivity have increased significantly. But these successes occurred because steps were taken to create realistic expectations about the effects of the strategy and to offset complicating factors. Middle and upper managers were actively involved in their design and implementation. Steps were taken to assure all participants that sharing influence and responsibility would not make them more vulnerable. Groups were formed carefully to ensure a relatively even distribution of expertise, and all employees were trained in communication skills and provided problem-relevant information. Evaluations of the strategy were delayed until after a realistic period of time and were based on appropriate criteria. Relational strategies of organizing can be highly effective, but only when implemented in appropriate ways.

CONCLUSION: PRINCIPLES OF RELATIONAL COMMUNICATION STRATEGIES

The relational strategy of organizing is based on a number of principles of communication.

Principle 1. Informal communication is just as important to organizational functioning as formal channels. Whereas the traditional strategy dictates that organizations should restrict communication as much as possible, the relational strategy advocates cultivating informal as well as formal communication. Relational organizations acknowledge the fact that informal communication is going to occur whether management wants it to or not, and try to utilize informal channels for the good of the organization. This involves aligning the organization's structure, motivational strategies, and leadership so that it nurtures an informal communication system that promotes the organization. By empowering members, the relational strategy attempts to create a flexible, responsive organization that is open to innovation and change.

Principle 2. Emphasize both lateral and vertical communication. To create a communication system that helps the organization, the relational strategy emphasizes lateral communication as much as vertical communication. For groups and networks to promote flexibility and innovation, it is important that coworkers communicate openly with each other and that they make cross-unit linkages. This creates a problem-solving system that transcends the narrower perspectives of particular individuals or units and pools the best knowledge in the organization.

Rather than conceptualizing vertical communication as a chain of single superior-subordinate links, the relational strategy construes it as groups passing information to other groups through linking pins. So vertical communication is not simply a matter of one-to-one transmission; instead it is influenced by the group surrounding both sender and receiver. How messages are interpreted and the reactions they elicit depend as much on group processes as on individual predispositions, beliefs, and attitudes. The other cliques to which group members belong also influence vertical communication. For example, a receiver who is a member of a clique interested in resisting automation of an organization might distort a message about a new technology in a negative direction, rather than passing it on down the chain faithfully.

Principle 3. Do not restrict communication to task matters only; expressive and relationship-oriented communication is just as important. The traditional strategy emphasizes information related to the task. The relational strategy argues that emotional, expressive, relationship-building communication is just as important. Building rich, multiplex relationships among members is critical to opening up the flow of communication. Multiplex ties are also important because they help to build a sense of community that increases members' loyalty and willingness to remain with the organization. In the relational view the purpose of communication is not only to help the organization, but to help its members develop their skills and meet their needs.

NOTES

[1] George Cheney and Jim Brancato, "Scientific Management's Rhetorical Context and Enduring Relevance," paper presented at the Speech Communication Association Convention, Chicago, November 1990.

[2] Edwin Locke, "The Ideas of Frederick Taylor," *Academy of Management Review,* 7 (1982): 14–24; Raymond Miles, *Theories of Management* (New York: McGraw-Hill, 1975); Warren Bennis, "Beyond Bureaucracy," *Trans-action,* 2 (1965): 31–35.

[3] Quoted by Judson Gooding in *The Job Revolution* (New York: Macmillan, 1972): 119.

[4] The concept of empowerment is popular in contemporary organizational theory, and will appear repeatedly throughout this book, especially in Chapters 4, 5, and 7. One of the most important lines of research underlying the relational strategy was conducted by Arnold Tannenbaum and his associates. They found that in many kinds of organizations in both capitalist and socialist countries, employees believe that they exercise far less influence over decisions that affect them directly than does upper management. In contrast, Tannenbaum found that the most productive organizations and departments were ones in which all employees, even those at the bottom of the organizational hierarchy, perceived that they had substantial influence over decisions (see Arnold Tannenbaum, "Control in Organizations," *Administrative Science Quarterly,* 7 [1962]: 17–42). It is important to note that Tannenbaum's work retains a characteristic of the traditional strategy—organizational performance and efficiency (short-term profit maximization) as the dominant criterion for evaluating organizational strategies.

[5] As Chapters 4, 5, and 13 explain, this is the primary basis of recent efforts to "downsize" or "rightsize" U.S. firms—reducing the costs of managerial "overhead."

[6] Dennis Organ, "Linking Pins Between Organizations and Environments," *Business Horizons, 14* (1971): 73–80. For an extended critique of Likert's model, see Alfred Marrow, David Bowers, and Stanley Seashore, *Management by Participation* (New York: Harper & Row, 1967).

[7] For an excellent summary of research on communication and participation, see David Seibold and Christine Shea, "Participation and Decision-making," in L. Putnam & F. Jablin (Eds.), *The New Handbook of Organizational Communication* (Thousand Oaks, CA: Sage, 1997).

[8] Angella Michelle Chiles and Theodore Zorn, "Empowerment in Organizations: Employees' Perceptions of the Influences on Empowerment," *Journal of Applied Communication Research, 23* (1995): 1–25.

[9] Edwin Lawler, *High Involvement Management* (San Francisco: Jossey-Bass, 1986).

[10] David Jamieson and Julie O'Mara, *Managing Workforce 2000* (San Francisco: Jossey-Bass, 1991).

[11] Charles Conrad, "Power, Identity and Decision-making in Churches," *Journal for the Scientific Study for Religion, 27* (1988): 345–361.

[12] Seibold and Shea; Peter Dachler and Bernhard Wilpert, "Conceptual Boundaries and Dimensions of Participation in Organizations," *Administrative Science Quarterly, 23* (1978): 1–39.

[13] Communication apprehension and anxiety influence individual and organizational effectiveness in a number of different ways (see Virginia P. Richmond and K. David Roach, "Willingness to Communicate and Employee Success in U.S. Organizations," *Journal of Applied Communication Research, 20* [1992]: 95–115 and James McCroskey and Virginia Peck Richmond, "The Impact of Communication Apprehension of Individuals in Organizations," *Communication Quarterly, 27* [1979]: 55–61).

[14] Chris Foreman, "The Reality of Workplace Democracy: A Case Study of One Company's Employee Involvement Process," Paper presented at the International Communication Association Convention, Chicago, IL, 1996; John Ivanevich, "High and Low Task Stimulating Jobs," *Academy of Management Journal, 22* (1979): 206–222.

[15] Jeffrey Pfeffer, "Power and Resource Allocation in Organizations," in *New Directions in Organizational Behavior,* Barry Staw and Gerald Salancik (Eds.) (New York: St. Clair Press, 1977); Walter Nord and Douglas Durand, "What's Wrong with the Human Resources Approach to Management," *Organizational Dynamics* (Winter, 1978): 13–25.

[16] Supervisors also resist by structuring decision situations so tightly that subordinates make only narrow decisions. See Bernard Bass, *Bass and Stogdill's Handbook of Leadership,* 3rd. ed. (New York: The Free Press, 1990).

[17] See Mauk Mulder, "Power Equalization Through Participation?" *Academy of Management Journal, 16* (1971): 31–38; and Mauk Mulder and H. Wilke, "Participation and Power Equalization," *Organizational Behavior and Human Performance, 5* (1970): 430–448.

[18] Michael Huspek, "The Language of Powerlessness," Ph.D. Dissertation, University of Washington, 1987.

[19] Bass; Teresa Harrison, "Communication and Participative Decision-Making," *Personnel Psychology, 38* (1985): 93–116. For summaries of the relationship between organizational communication and voluntary turnover, see Myria Watkins Allen, "The Relationship Between Communication, Affect, Job Alternatives, and Voluntary Turnover Intentions," *Southern Communication Journal, 61* (1996): 198–209; J.A. Lischeron and T.D. Wall, "Employee Participation," *Human Relations, 28* (1975): 863–884; also see Lawler, *Involvement;* Kathleen Miller and Peter Monge, "The Development and Test of a System of Organizational Participation and Allocation," in *Communication Yearbook 10,* Margaret McLaughlin, ed. (Beverly Hills, CA: Sage, 1987).

[20] Bass.

[21] Terrance Albrecht, "An Overtime Analysis of Communication Patterns and Work Perceptions," in *Communication Yearbook 8,* Robert Bostrom, ed. (Beverly Hills, CA: Sage, 1984); Malcom Parks and Mara Adelman, "Communication Networks and the Development of Romantic Relationships," *Human Communication Research, 10* (1983): 55–80; Karlene Roberts and Charles O'Reilly, "Organizations as Communication Structures," *Human Communication Research, 4* (1978): 283–293; Fredric Jablin, "Task/Work Relationships," in *Handbook of Interpersonal Communication,* Gerald Miller and Mark Knapp, eds. (Beverly Hills, CA: Sage, 1985); Eric Eisenberg, Peter Monge, and Kathleen Miller, "Involvement in Communication Networks as a Predictor of Organizational Commitment," *Human Communication Research, 10* (1983): 179–201; Charles O'Reilly and David Caldwell, "Informational Influence as a Determinant of Task

Characteristics and Job Satisfaction," *Journal of Applied Psychology, 64* (1979): 157–165; and David Caldwell and Charles O'Reilly, "Task Perceptions and Job Satisfaction," *Journal of Applied Psychology, 67* (1982): 361–369.

[22] James March and Guje Sevon, "Gossip, Information, and Decision Making," in *Advances in Information Processing in Organizations,* Lee Sproull and Patrick Larkey, eds. (Greenwich, CT: JAI Press, 1982), vol. I.

[23] Leonard Sayles, "Work Group Behavior and the Larger Organization," in W.F. Whyte (Ed.), *Research in Industrial Human Relations* (New York: Harper, 1957); E. Gross, "Some Functional Consequences of Formal Controls in Formal Work Organizations," *American Sociological Review, 19* (1954): 15–24.

[24] A classic study supporting this concept is E.E. Chapple, "Applied Anthropology in Industry," in A.L. Kroeber (Ed.), *Anthropology Today* (Chicago: University of Chicago Press, 1953).

[25] Keith Davis, "Management Communication and the Grapevine," *Harvard Business Review* (September-October, 1953): 43–49; also see Noel Tichy, Michael Tushman, and Charles Fombrun, "Social Network Analysis for Organizations," *Academy of Management Review, 4* (1979): 507–519.

[26] Everett Rogers and Rekha Argawala-Rogers, *Organizational Communication* (New York: The Free Press, 1976).

[27] See Terrance Albrecht and Bradford Hall, "Facilitating Talk About New Ideas," *Communication Monographs, 58* (1991a): 273–288; Terrance Albrecht and Bradford Hall, "Relational and Content Differences Between Elites and Outsiders in Innovation Networks," *Human Communication Research, 17* (1991b): 535–561; Betsy Bach, "The Effect of Multiplex Relationships Upon Innovation Adoption," *Communication Monographs, 56* (1991): 133–148; David Bastien, "Change in Organizational Culture," *Management Communication Quarterly, 5* (1992): 403–442; Beth Ellis, "The Effects of Uncertainty and Source Credibility on Attitude About Organizational Change," *Management Communication Quarterly, 6* (1992): 34–57; Michael Papa and Karen Tracy, "Communicative Indices of Employee Performance with New Technology," *Communication Research, 15* (1988): 524–544; Ronald Rice and Carolyn Aydin, "Attitudes Toward New Organizational Technology," *Administrative Science Quarterly, 36* (1991): 219–244. And, if you're still curious about processes of innovation after reading all of these articles, see the special issue on "Technology, Organizations, and Innovation," ed. Michael Tushman and Richard Nelson, *Administrative Science Quarterly, 35* (1990): 1–222.

[28] Edwin Locke, "The Nature and Causes of Job Satisfaction," in *Handbook of Industrial and Organizational Psychology,* Marvin Dunnette, ed. (Chicago: Rand-McNally, 1976).

[29] McGregor found that supervisors really do tend to communicate to their subordinates in ways that are consistent with one of these two sets of assumptions. Also see Fred Luthans and Janet Larsen, "How Managers Really Communicate," *Human Relations, 39* (1986): 161–178 and John Courtright, Gail Fairhurst, and L. Edna Rogers, "Interaction Patterns in Organic and Mechanistic Systems," *Academy of Management Journal, 32* (1989): 773–802.

[30] Richard Edwards, *Contested Terrain* (New York: Basic Books, 1978); Ivar Berg, *Education and Jobs* (New York: Praeger, 1970); J. Greenbaum, "Division of Labor in the Computer Field," *Monthly Review, 28* (1976): 40–56; Christopher Dandeker, *Surveillance, Power and Modernity* (New York: St. Martin's Press. 1984).

[31] For example, see "The Lordstown Auto Workers" in *Life in Organizations,* Rosabeth Moss Kanter and Barry Stein, eds. (New York: Basic Books, 1979).

[32] James Shaw, "An Information-processing Approach to the Study of Job Design," *Academy of Management Review, 5* (1980): 41–48; and Edward O'Connor and Gerald Barrett, "Informational Cues and Individual Differences as Determinants of Perceptions of Task Enrichment," *Academy of Management Journal, 23* (1980): 697–716; Daniel Brass, "Structural Relationships, Job Characteristics and Worker Satisfaction and Performance," *Administrative Science Quarterly, 26* (1981): 331–348; Robert Vecchio, "Worker Satisfaction and Performance," *Academy of Management Journal, 23* (1980): 479–486; John Ivanevich, "The Performance-Satisfaction Relationship," *Organizational Behavior and Human Performance, 22* (1978): 350–365; and Dean Tjosvold, "Effects of Leader Warmth and Directiveness on Subordinate Performance on a Subsequent Task," *Journal of Applied Psychology, 69* (1984): 422–427.

[33] Elton Mayo, *Social Problems of an Industrial Civilization.* (Boston: Graduate School of Business Administration, Harvard University, 1945. Edgar H. Schein, *Organizational Psychology,* 3rd edition (Englewood Cliffs, NJ: Prentice-Hall, 1980).

[34] In *The Human Group* (New York: Harcourt Brace, 1950) George Homans gives a readable account of the information provided by the Hawthorne Studies on work group influences on members. For examples of the processes described in this paragraph, see Sayles; William Foote Whyte, *Money and Motivation: An Analysis of Incentives in Industry* (New York: Harper & Row, 1955), pp. 20–27; and Susan A. Mohrman, Susan G. Cohen, and Allan M. Mohrman, *Designing Team-Based Organizations: New Forms for Knowledge Work* (San Francisco: Jossey-Bass, 1995).

[35] See Gail Fairhurst, "Dialectical Tensions in Leadership Research," in L. Putnam & F. Jablin (Eds.), *The New Handbook of Organizational Communication* (Thousand Oaks, CA: Sage, 1997).

[36] Rensis Likert, *New Patterns of Management* (New York: McGraw-Hill, 1961); also see the articles by Edwin Fleishman and his associates in the first and second editions of *Studies in Personnel and Industrial Psychology,* Edwin Fleishman and Associates, eds. (Homewood, IL: Dorsey, 1961 and 1967). For a critique of this research see Abraham Corman, "Consideration, 'Initiating Structure,' and Organizational Criteria," *Personnel Psychology, 19* (1966): 349–361.

[37] This is the underlying assumption of the concept of "unobtrusive control" that will be described in Chapter 4.

[38] Joseph Sgro, et al., "Perceived Leader Behavior as a Function of Trust," *Academy of Management Journal, 23* (1980): 161–165. Also see Martin Remland, "Leadership Impressions and Nonverbal Communication," *Communication Quarterly, 19* (1987): 108–128; and Virginia Richmond, James McCroskey, and L.M. Davis, "Individual Differences among Employees, Management and Communication Style and Employee Satisfaction," *Human Communication Research, 8* (1982): 170–188.

[39] Fredric Jablin, "Superior-subordinate Communication," in *Communication Yearbook 2,* Brent Ruben, ed. (New Brunswick, NJ: Transaction Books, 1978).

[40] R.C. Liden and G. Graen, "Generalizability of the Vertical Dyad Linkage Model of Leadership," *Academy of Management Journal, 23* (1980): 451–465.

[41] Dennis Gioia and Henry Sims, "Cognition-Behavior Connections: Attribution and Verbal Behavior in Leader-Subordinate Interactions," *Organizational Behavior and Human Performance, 37* (1986): 197–229.

[42] Research on organizational climate is summarized in M. Scott Poole and Robert McPhee, "Bringing Intersubjectivity Back In: A Change of Climate," in *Organizational Communication: Interpretive Approaches,* Linda Putnam and Michael Pacanowsky, eds. (Beverly Hills, CA: Sage, 1983) and M. Scott Poole, "Communication and Organizational Climates," in *Organizational Communication,* in Robert McPhee and Phillip Tompkins, eds. (Beverly Hills, CA: Sage, 1985).

[43] G.B. Graen and T.A. Scandura, "Toward a Psychology of Dyadic Organizing," In B. Staw and L.L. Cummings (Eds.), *Research in Organizational Behavior,* vol. 9 (Greenwich, CT: JAI Press, 1987); Gail Fairhurst, Edna Rogers, and Robert Sarr, "Manager-subrodinate Control Patterns and Judgments about the Relationship," in *Communication Yearbook 10,* Margaret McLaughlin (Ed.) (Beverly Hills, CA: Sage, 1987); Gail Fairhurst, "Echoes of the Vision: When the Rest of the Organization Talks Total Quality," *Management Communication Quarterly, 6* (1993): 331–371; Fairhurst, "Tensions;" Gail Fairhurst and Robert Sarr, *The Art of Framing* (San Francisco: Jossey-Bass, 1996).

[44] Richard Farace, Peter Monge and Hamish Russell, *Communicating and Organizing* (New York: Random House, 1977); John Gabarro, "The Development of Trust, Influence, and Expectations," in A.G. Athos & J.J. Gabarro (Eds.), *Interpersonal Behavior* (Englewood Cliffs, NJ: Prentice-Hall, 1978).

[45] Terrance Albrecht and J. Halsey, "Mutual Support in Mixed Status Relationships," *Journal of Social and Personal Relationships, 9* (1992): 237–252; Terrance Albrecht and Mara Adelman, *Communicating Social Support* (Newbury Park, CA: Sage, 1988).

[46] For a more complete summary than I could present in this chapter, see Henry Mintzberg, *Structuring in Fives* (Englewood Cliffs, NJ: Prentice-Hall, 1983).

[47] See, for example, Robert Dewar and James Werbel, "Universalistic and Contingency Predictions of Employee Satisfaction and Conflict," *Administrative Science Quarterly, 24* (1979): 426–447; Chester Schriesheim and Mary Ann Glinow, "The Path-Goal Theory of Leadership," *Academy of Management Journal, 20* (1977): 398–405; and Robert Vecchio, "An Empirical Examination of the Validity of Fiedler's Model of Leadership Effectiveness," *Organizational Behavior and Human Performance, 19* (1977): 180–206; Bass.

[48] House uses the terminology of the Ohio State Leadership Studies: "A Path-Goal Theory of Leadership Effectiveness," *Administrative Science Quarterly, 16* (1971): 321–339.

[49] Lyman Porter, working with Edward Lawler and J. Richard Hackman, developed a model that also focused on task characteristics, but added the overall strategy of organizing used in the organization ("traditional" or "relational") and the employees' need for personal and professional growth as important situational factors. Like House, they found that task complexity is a strong situational influence on the effectiveness of different organizational and leadership strategies. This model is summarized in J. Pierce, O. Dunham, and R. Blackburn, "Social Systems Structure, Job Design, and Growth Need Strength," *Academy of Management Journal, 22* (1979): 223–240.

[50] Paul Hersey and Kenneth Blanchard, *Management of Organizational Behavior,* 3rd ed. (Englewood Cliffs, NJ: Prentice-Hall, 1977). Porter and his associates also recognized the importance of subordinates' attributes, focusing their attention on followers' needs for personal and professional growth.

[51] Of course, a supervisor's job is much easier and an organization functions most effectively if all subordinates are high in both willingness and ability. Fortunately, Hersey and Blanchard argue, supervisors can gradually move any subordinate toward this goal. When a low-ability, low-willingness subordinate begins to perform well, the supervisor should decrease his or her task-related, directive communication and be more supportive. As the subordinate increases his or her willingness and ability, the subordinate should continue to gradually increase support and reduce direction until each subordinate has reached her or his maximum point of development. Every employee will at times drop below his or her maximum point—a crisis at home reduces commitment or a new task requires a higher level of skills, and so on. When this happens the supervisor should change his or her leadership strategy and start moving the subordinate back up the curve.

[52] Michelle Iaffaldo and Paul Muchinsky, "Job Satisfaction and Job Performance," *Psychological Bulletin, 97* (1985): 251–273; Katherine Miller and Peter Monge, "The Development and Test of a System of Organizational Participation and Allocation," in *Communication Yearbook 10,* Margaret McLaughlin, ed. (Beverly Hills, CA: Sage, 1987); Ruth Guzley, "Organizational Climate and Communication Climate," *Management Communication Quarterly, 5* (1992): 379–402; and Paul Muchinsky, "Organizational Communication," *Academy of Management Journal, 20* (1977): 592–607.

[53] John Trombetta and Donald Rogers, "Communication Climate, Job Satisfaction, and Organizational Commitment," *Management Communication Quarterly, 4* (1988): 494–514; Dominic Infante and William Gordon, "How Employees See the Boss," *Western Journal of Speech Communication, 55* (1991): 294–304; and Karlene Roberts, Charles Hulin, and Denise Rousseau, *Toward an Inter-Disciplinary Science of Organizations* (San Francisco: Jossey-Bass, 1979). Of course, a number of factors influence employees' decisions about these things: obligations to employers or to people who depend on them for financial support, level of financial need, and the availability of other jobs, for example. Perhaps 80 percent of voluntary decisions to change jobs are related to workers' impressions of how strong the economy will be in the near future. Even church pastors, whose upper-level needs are salient, seem to change churches when the economy is good and stay put when it is bad.

[54] Iaffaldo and Muchinsky, 266. Also see Edwin Locke, "The Nature and Causes of Job Satisfaction," in *Handbook of Industrial and Organizational Psychology,* Marvin Dunnette, ed. (Chicago: Rand-McNally, 1976); Cynthia Fisher, "On the Dubious Wisdom of Expecting Job Satisfaction to Correlate with Performance," *Academy of Management Review, 5* (1980): 607–612; and W.J. Goode and I. Fowler, "Incentive Factors in a Low Morale Plant," *American Sociological Review, 14* (1949): 618–624.

[55] This lack of a general relationship seems to hold even when people are highly committed to their organization. In a study of an Israeli cooperative farm (kibbutz) David Macarov found neither that job satisfaction improved performance nor that people who worked hard were more satisfied than people who did not (see *Incentives to Work* [Beverly Hills, CA: Sage, 1981] and *Worker Productivity: Myths and Reality* [Beverly Hills, CA: Sage, 1982]).

[56] In fact, there is rather clear evidence that the desire for work that fulfills upper-level needs is important only to educated, middle- or upper-class people. The motivational assumptions underlying relational strategies of organizing may just be an expression of middle- to upper-class liberal academic values and beliefs. What may be intuitively acceptable to professors and

their students may be largely irrelevant to other people (see John Wagner and Richard Gooding, "Effects of Societal Trends on Participation Research," *Administrative Science Quarterly, 32* [1987]: 241–262). However, this situation may change in the near future because so many college graduates are becoming underemployed (working in unskilled or semiskilled jobs). As students who have learned these "academic" values begin to occupy positions near the bottoms of organizations the gap between academic and worker values should narrow (recall the "Generation X" case study in Chapter 1 and see K.D. Duncan, M.M. Gruneberg, and D. Wallis, *Changing Values in Working Life* (New York: John Wiley, 1980).

[57] Edwin Locke, "The Nature and Causes of Job Satisfaction," in *Handbook of Industrial and Organizational Psychology,* Marvin Dunnette, ed. (Chicago: Rand-McNally, 1976), p. 1333. More recent research is summarized in Arthur Brief and Raymond Aldag, "The 'Self' in Work Organizations," *The Academy of Management Review, 6* (1981): 75–88 and in Barnard Bass, *Bass and Stogdill's Handbook of Leadership* (Greenwich, CT: JAI Press, 1993).

[58] Bass; Charles O'Reilly, "Supervisors and Peers as Information Sources, Group Supportiveness, and Individual Decision-making Performance," *Journal of Applied Psychology, 62* (1977): 632–635.

Chapter 4

CULTURAL STRATEGIES OF ORGANIZING

The reality of the [social] world hangs on the thin thread of conversation.

—PETER BERGER AND THOMAS LUCKMANN

CENTRAL THEMES

- Cultural strategies of organizing assume both that managers can influence employees' beliefs, values, and perceptions of reality, and that employees actively create their own beliefs, values, and perceptions.
- Organizational cultures are communicative creations, embedded in a history and a set of expectations about the future. They usually are heterogeneous, composed of multiple subcultures.
- Cultural strategies of motivation rely on unobtrusive systems of control, achieved through symbolic acts—myths, metaphors, stories, and ceremonies—and the regulation of employees' emotions.
- Cultural strategies of leadership focus on "transformational" processes through which leaders communicate a vision of the organization and help employees "frame" everyday events.
- Critics of traditional, relational, and cultural strategies of organizing argue that all three disguise the contradictory interests of owners, managers, and workers through processes of "systematically distorted communication."

KEY TERMS

Culture	Ceremonies
Organizational cultures	Ceremonies of passage
Subcultures	Degradation ceremonies

Metaphors	Enhancement ceremonies
Stories	Renewal ceremonies
Story temporality	Integration ceremonies
Story grammar	Charisma
Personal relevance	Framing
Mythologies	Systematically distorted communication
Storytelling	Pacification
Rituals	Disqualification

In Chapter 1 I suggested that one of the central tensions in U.S. society is between *individuality* and *community.* Both the "traditional" and "relational" strategies of organizing focused on the individual pole of this tension. Rewarding employees for their *individual* competence and performance or meeting their *individual* "higher-order" needs would motivate them to choose to act in ways that would meet the organization's needs for *control* and *coordination* while meeting their own needs.[1] Similarly, both traditional and relational strategies of organizing recognized that employees' choices are based on their own interpretations of "reality." But, those strategies depicted employees' sense-making processes as problems to be overcome. Supervisors must persuade subordinates to believe that their reward systems are fair and equitable or negotiate shared interpretations of the transactions that take place between them. The cultural strategy of organizing reverses these foci. Employees' beliefs, values, and sense-making processes are treated as the primary basis for their strategic choices. Motivating and controlling employee behavior depends on persuading them to accept appropriate beliefs, values, and frames of reference. Creating a sense of "community" within work groups is depicted as a primary means of managing the tensions between individual and organizational needs. In cultural strategies, organizational design is less important than devising tactics of motivation and leadership.

THE CONTEXT SURROUNDING CULTURAL STRATEGIES OF ORGANIZING

Probably the hottest topic in organizations and management training during the 1980s was the concept of organizational culture.[2] An entire industry of training programs, videotapes, consulting firms, and speakers is devoted to teaching employees how to "manage" the cultures of their organizations. These activities have been valuable because they have focused attention on the intangible and human aspects of organizational life. Managers have started to realize that employees' *beliefs* about how their organization operates are important, even more important than how official documents say it does. Researchers have recognized that organizational myths, rituals, stories, and metaphors—the symbolic forms that are discussed later in this chapter—are significant because they mean important things to employees. Corporate trainers have started to encourage decision-makers to look carefully at their own values, the values espoused by their organizations, and their subordinates' values when they make organizational policy.

The sudden popularity of this "new" strategy of organizing resulted from two factors. The most important factor involved the declining fortunes of major U.S. organizations (and to a degree organizations in all of the Western economies) after 1975. The market share of many U.S. firms, both internationally and in the United States, fell steadily after the Arab oil embargo. In their place foreign firms, particularly from Japan, made major inroads into markets long dominated by traditional U.S. firms. As a result, U.S. managers and researchers started to examine Japanese firms. They found that both Japanese society and Japanese organizations were much more like communities—groups of people with shared values (including quality), beliefs, and interpretive frames—than were traditional U.S. firms. And, Japanese managers seemed to use very different strategies of leading than U.S. managers did—strategies that focused on employee involvement and on symbolism.

At about the same time organizational researchers in Western societies seemed to rediscover the idea that people, including workers, are "actors"—living, thinking, beings who make decisions about how to act based on their beliefs, values, and ways of interpreting the information and events that they encounter. And, as Max Weber and others had argued a century ago, those beliefs, values, and frames of reference were influenced significantly by the taken-for-granted assumptions characteristic of the societies from which organizations drew their members. At least on the surface, the two discoveries seemed to coincide. But, below the surface there was an important tension. The first perspective assumed that organizational "cultures" could be managed strategically, that management could inculcate desired values in their workforces, could create a sense of community that bound employees together in a coordinated (and thus controlled) group. The second assumed that, although people often have similar interpretive frames because they have had similar societal backgrounds and experiences, they also interpret their surroundings in their own, individual ways. Consequently, while managers could attempt to persuade their employees to accept certain beliefs and values, the workers might interpret and respond to management's efforts in very different ways than they intended. The *unintended consequences* of efforts to manage organizational cultures may be very different, and much more important than the consequences that were intended by management.[3]

CULTURAL STRATEGIES OF ORGANIZATIONAL DESIGN[4]

Although most advocates of cultural strategies of organizing were comfortable with relational conceptions of organizational design—decentralization, participation, and so on—issues of design were relatively unimportant to them.[5] Instead, they focused on the processes through which different cultural configurations emerge in organizations. Initially they viewed those processes as relatively simple and straightforward. They defined **culture** as the *shared* assumptions, values, beliefs, language, symbols, and meaning systems that hold the organization together. They differentiated "strong" cultures, in which employees throughout the organization—regardless of their rank, tasks, networks of interpersonal relationships, or formal roles—shared the same goals, had the same kinds of feelings about the organization, and interpreted the culture in the same way from "weak" cultures in which these things were less homogeneous. They argued that the cultural configuration that emerged in a particular organization could be managed strategically and rather simply. Upper management merely had to persuasively communicate the core values of the organization to all of its employees and provide tangible and intangible rewards to employees who act in accordance with those values. Eventually, a homogeneous and harmonious "strong" culture would emerge, and that culture in turn would be the key to managerial control, worker commitment, and organizational effectiveness.[6]

Organizations as Homogeneous Cultures

Typical of this early view was Tom Peters and Robert Waterman's conclusion that "excellent" firms—those that for long periods had exceptional productivity, profitability, and stability—differed from "non-excellent" firms in a number of ways. Some differences were rather traditional—they hired and retained competent personnel and did not take on tasks that were beyond their expertise. Others echoed relational strategies of organizing—managers respect and value all employees' skills and creativity, encourage them to be autonomous and entrepreneurial, and maintain close ties with their environment and are responsive to environmental pressures. But others involved creating "strong cultures." This combination of factors, Peters and Waterman argued, is particularly relevant to the highly competitive, turbulent economic situation faced by U.S. firms in the 1980s and 1990s.[7]

Of course, this perspective was very attractive to managers in U.S. organizations. It suggests that *they* are the key to making organizations succeed; provides some relatively simple tools that *they* can use to increase control over employees' behaviors; offers some relatively inexpensive ways of increasing employee morale, commitment, and productivity; and promises significant short-term increases in the competitiveness and profitability of their firms. Consequently, it very rapidly became the dominant view of organizational cultures among managers and scholars alike.[8] But almost as soon as the perspective was presented, critics began to question its assumption that cultures could be strategically controlled by upper management. They argued that there is little evidence that lower-level employees in "excellent" firms actually share the values and beliefs that upper management said they do and that the perspective seriously underestimates the complexity of changing an organization's culture and the unpredictability of efforts to manage cultures.[9] Organizations are composed of active, thinking human beings. As I will frequently suggest during the rest of this book, people sometimes interpret their organization's culture as offensive and manipulative (regardless of how management interprets it), sometimes desire changes that are different from those envisioned by managerial "change agents," often resist even positive changes in their organization's culture, and generally make "culture management" or "planned cultural change" exceptionally difficult. This does not mean that modifying cultures in positive ways is impossible. It does mean that successful culture change depends on understanding how all employees perceive and respond to their organization's culture and to efforts to change it.[10]

However, even critics of the perspective applauded it for recognizing that factors like beliefs, values, and taken-for-granted assumptions are important aspects of organizations and the ways in which employees interpret and respond to their experiences at work. A revised cultural perspective emerged, one that defined **organizational cultures** in terms of the intangible, "taken-for-granted shared meanings that people assign to their surroundings."[11] In this perspective, cultures are *communicative creations.* They emerge and are sustained by the communicative acts of all employees, not just the conscious persuasive strategies of upper management. Cultures do not exist separately from people communicating with one another. Members of a culture develop distinctive ways of perceiving, interpreting, and explaining the events and actions that they observe around them. Although every member perceives the world in somewhat different ways, their worldviews are similar in many ways; they are more like each other than like those of people from other cultures. Through communicating, members of cultures (and thus of organizations) learn who they are, what their roles are, and what kinds of actions are expected of them by other members of their culture. Through communicating they enact their culture. By articulating its values, paying homage to its heroes, and making decisions based on its key assumptions, they demonstrate that they are legitimate members of the culture.

By acting and communicating in appropriate and predictable ways they make other members feel comfortable with them and their presence. Communication also fills their needs for social ties. And, by enacting their organizational cultures employees fulfill their organizations' needs for control and coordination.[12]

Cultures also are *historical.* They emerge and develop over time, adapting to changes in their membership, functions, problems, and purposes. The *legacy* of past events, people, and patterns of communicating continues to be reflected in the ways in which people interpret and respond to their organizations. Similarly, the *expectation* that the culture will continue to exist influences the ways in which people act and communicate with one another.[13] The events that led to the development of a particular way of communicating may be long forgotten, but the patterns that were established in the past persist. The "permanence" of historical patterns of acting is illustrated best by rituals.

Academic departments may gather together each morning for coffee or hold weekly faculty meetings or social events at winter break. At one time there may have been purely functional reasons for these rituals. Perhaps all the professors taught sections of the same course and needed to coordinate their activities each morning. Perhaps the department involved every professor in every decision it faced, necessitating weekly meetings. Perhaps a large number of graduate students could not go home for the holidays and needed some event to make them feel like they had a surrogate family at school. For them a major winter party would fulfill an important function. But rituals and ritualized communication often continue to exist long after their functional basis has disappeared. Their sole function becomes one of maintaining the culture of the organization. Participating in them symbolizes one's membership in and commitment to the culture and its members. In a sense rituals contain the history of an organization and reflect the constraints that its history imposes on its members.[14]

The Emergence of Organizational Subcultures

Some employees may choose not to participate in an organization's key rituals, or may participate for different reasons. Some may be full participants in the culture, relish the spring picnic, and interpret it as a symbol of what the organization and their coworkers mean to them. Others may participate less completely, accepting some of the culture's taken-for-granted assumptions while rejecting others. Still others may remain part of the organization for their own reasons while cynically seeing its taken-for-granted assumptions as manipulative nonsense and its key rituals as meaningless "command performances." Even if a "strong culture" exists, not all employees will participate in it equally or in the same ways. Employees will tend to form communicative ties with people who share their view of the organizational culture. **Subcultures** emerge, groups of people whose *shared* interpretation of their organization helps bind them together and differentiate them from other groups of employees. Consequently, complex organizations are likely to be a grouping of distinct and different subcultures rather than a homogeneous culture consciously defined and guided by upper management, subcultures created and sustained through the processes of network emergence and reproduction that were described in Chapter 1.[15]

I once visited the technical writing division of a major computer firm. I entered through the front door and was examined by the security team at the front desk. Then I was led down corridor after corridor past each of the major divisions of the firm into a separate building that housed the writing staff. One of the first things I noticed was the staff's coffee room. On the wall was a poster of the firm's newest product, an exceptionally powerful portable computer that was not yet on the market. But unlike the hardware division, which had an entire wall covered with the posters, or the software group, which had arranged to have one of the posters professionally framed and displayed in the center of their workroom, the technical writing group had only one poster and displayed it in a dark corner. In front of the poster was a Norfolk pine that all but obscured it from view.

Prominently displayed in the center of the room was a poster of a penguin jumping off an ice cliff into the ocean with a long row of penguins following it. Someone had written the division head's name next to the lead penguin and the other writers' names next to the others. Significant symbols reveal a great deal about the culture (or subculture) of an organization. In this organization the poster-symbols suggested that Technical Writing was a subculture—a strong and stable one—that was separate from the other units of the organization. They perceived themselves as writers, not as employees of Computer Firm X, and proudly told me that they were in *their* isolated building because *they* had asked to be there. Subcultures may not be limited to a particular division of an organization and each formal division may be composed of more than one sub- culture. Subcultures may tend to follow divisional lines because communica- tion networks are influenced by patterns of activity (recall Chapter 1) and ac- tivities tend to be different across different divisions. But other factors—like geographical location or background and experience—also may lead people to form different kinds of communication networks, and thus create different sub- cultural arrangements.

However, thinking of organizations as collections of subcultures intro- duced the concept of tension into the perspective. In an important sense, this change made the cultural strategy be more realistic—like larger societies, orga- nizations are made of shared values and frames of reference, *as well as* tensions and characteristic means of managing them.[16] Sometimes the various subcul- tures have important differences but they coexist peacefully; in other cases their values, patterns of acting, sense-making processes, and so on are conflict- ing and irreconcilable. Complicating "culture management" further, subcul- tures, like the communication networks that underlie them, are fluid and changing. Sometimes those changes are stimulated by environmental pres- sures. For example, salespersons in high-tech firms face a unique set of pres- sures. The environment outside of their firms is constantly changing. Competi- tors suddenly develop and market new products; or unanticipated and uncontrollable fluctuations in interest rates and other economic factors lead customers to suddenly make major purchases or cancel purchasing plans.

Internal pressures also may create change. When a particular issue be- comes important, a number of employees (perhaps including everyone in one or more subcultural groups) band together and array themselves in opposition to other groups. As they communicate, a unique combination of agreements, disagreements, pockets of knowledge and ignorance, and patterns of hypocrisy become apparent. When the salient issues change, so may the alliances, values, and so on. Or, the changes may merely reproduce original networks, returning the system to a state of homeostasis. If the production and quality control divi- sions suddenly refuse to cooperate with one another, salespeople may have no products to ship, or worse yet, products with unacceptable flaws that anger long-time customers.[17] If the marketing director installs a new computerized inventory-and-control system, salespersons suddenly may find themselves swamped in new accounting procedures or unsure of the inventory. The day-by-day realities of task assignments and environmental pressures lead people and their units to develop their own flexible and individualized ways of perceiving and coping.[18]

And in some cases the subcultures may indeed be so similar that they form what is in effect a homogeneous culture. The shared values of the overall culture are so powerful and communicated so persuasively that differences in activities and environmental pressures are overwhelmed, and the company has a relatively homogeneous culture. But whatever the particular pattern of subcultures that emerges in a particular organization, the important point is that subcultures *do* emerge. They are not "designed" by upper management, or by anyone else for that matter. They are patterns of acting and interpreting that develop in ways that meet the needs of employees.

People interact with one another as if they shared culture. Through trial and error, sometimes through conversation and negotiation, they confirm whether or not their meanings are similar enough to get through social interactions appropriately. Sometimes their expectations are confirmed; at other times they break down, leading to further negotiation or even conflict. From a base of shared culture, people can negotiate new apparently shared meanings, and do, as a matter of course.[19]

CULTURAL STRATEGIES OF MOTIVATION AND CONTROL

Both the traditional and the relational strategies of organizing relied on systems of motivation and control that were "obtrusive," that is, known by and visible to workers. Reward and punishment systems, "technical" factors like assembly lines, and the policies, procedures, and promises of promotions for reliable and cooperative administrators that characterize bureaucracies all operate within the conscious awareness of workers.[20] Indeed, if workers were not consciously aware of them, they would not succeed at all. As I have indicated, employees may choose to resist these overt forms of motivation and control, and often do so, but they are aware that they are doing so. Consequently, obtrusive forms of control constantly need to be legitimized, and always require management to find ways of preventing or controlling resistance. In contrast, cultural strategies of organizing focus on "unobtrusive" forms of control, on creating situations in which employees will choose to act in ways desired by the organization while perceiving that they are freely choosing to do so.

Unobtrusive Control

The key to unobtrusive control is persuading employees to accept the core beliefs and values of the organization and to base their decisions about how to act at work on those beliefs and values.[21] Employees are persuaded to accept these values in a number of ways—through particular kinds of leadership strategies (examined later in this chapter) and through socializing newcomers into the organization (examined in Chapter 6). But, if employees can be persuaded to accept the beliefs and values of upper management, they can be counted on to make the same kinds of decisions that upper management would make. Thus employees, especially managers, can be allowed a great deal of freedom of action because they will choose to act in desired ways.

Perhaps an example will clarify this concept. In an extended study of the U.S. Forest Service during the late 1950s, Herbert Kauffman interviewed foresters in five widely separated national forests. He was struck by the similarity of their views of their organization, their roles in it, and their actions. Different rangers, who seemed to be very different people facing very different problems, shared the same values, beliefs, and attitudes. Even more striking was the similarity between the bases on which they made their decisions and the principles that upper managers used to make decisions thousands of miles away in Washington, D.C. As Kauffman examined the service more deeply he found that these similarities were far from accidental. From the days of the formation of the modern USFS under Gifford Pinchot, the service hired only those people who had graduated from approved college forestry programs. And, since the USFS was the dominant employer for graduates of those programs, Pinchot was able to persuade universities all across the country to develop curricula that both taught the technical skills that foresters needed and the beliefs and values of the USFS. Once employees were hired, they were further socialized to accept those values, and while they worked for the service they constantly were exposed to messages and activities that reinforced those values. No one from the Washington office looked over their shoulders once they were in the field, but no one had to. The foresters had come to accept a set of values, beliefs, and bases for making decisions that led them to choose to act in desirable ways.

Symbolic Action as Motivation and Control

Symbolic forms—metaphors, stories, myths, and rituals—have a dual relationship to organizational cultures—they express the taken-for-granted assumptions of the culture and, when articulated, reproduce those assumptions. Some advocates of the cultural strategy of organizing assume that upper management can motivate employees to act in desired ways by strategically managing organizational symbolism. Unfortunately, this view seriously oversimplifies the nature of symbolic acts and organizational cultures. Employees are human beings, and humans actively perceive, process, and choose to respond to messages in their own often idiosyncratic ways. They interpret stories and other symbolic forms in terms of their own needs, experiences, and frames of reference. An individual symbolic act—a story told by one's officemate, for example—*reveals* a great deal about how the storyteller interprets the culture of the organization.

Recurring symbols—metaphors, stories, and myths—told by many people in many contexts reveal shared assumptions as well as tensions among those assumptions. Different employees, or different "subcultures" of employees, may interpret the same symbolic act in different ways. They also may articulate different symbolic forms—tell different stories about management, create their own independent rituals, or describe their organization or unit through the use of different metaphors. Upper management may tell a different story to explain an organizational disaster (or success) than production employees do; employees in a subculture dominated by marketing employees may tell a story that blames the research and development division for a failed product line while research and development employees may tell the same story in a way that satirizes members of the marketing subculture. Thus some symbolic acts, and some interpretations of various symbolic acts, may create a depiction of the organizational culture that is consistent with the values and beliefs that management would prefer that employees accept. In these cases, symbolism functions as a powerful mode of organizational motivation and control. But, other acts, and other interpretations, may be irrelevant to the preferences of management; still others may oppose or resist the preferred set of values, beliefs, and patterns of action. In these cases organizational symbolism may actually reduce managerial control and may "motivate" employees to act in ways that are not preferred by management.

Metaphors.   **Metaphors** are symbolic forms in which one image is used to describe another one. They often are used to describe an entire organization. Frequent organizational metaphors are military machines ("Working here is like being in the army"), families ("These people are my closest friends, my family" or "This desk is my home away from home"), and games ("To survive here you have to play the game, pretend to be what the big shots want you to be").[22]

Of course, metaphors should not be interpreted literally. The metaphorical family is not patterned after any real family, but is a construct based on someone's idea of what a family is or should be like—the Ingallses (*Little House on the Prairie*) or Taylors (*Home Improvement*) or Huxtables (*The Cosby Show*) or Walshes (*Beverly Hills 90210*) or any other mythical family whose attributes are like those of the employee's organization. Metaphors are important because they guide and constrain our interpretations of everyday events. They also are stable because we tend to perceive reality in ways that confirm our metaphors. If we believe our organization is a family we perceive employees who behave in "unfamily-like" ways as being "bad" family members; only in rare cases do these events lead us to question the accuracy of the metaphor itself.[23]

For fifty years a large West Coast toy manufacturer has been described by its employees as an "army under siege." Although the enemy has changed many times, from "profit-hungry" East Coast companies during the 1950s to "wily" foreign importers who "keep their workers in poverty" during the 1960s and 1970s to computer firms that "care about wires and chips, not children" in the

1980s, the guiding metaphor has remained the same. Employees talk about "fighting the battle," which means constantly working hard to maintain efficiency; "taking no casualties," which means having everyone constantly monitor quality (including a company program in which samples are donated to employees provided they take them home and see how long it takes their children to destroy them); "everyone being a spy," which leads most employees to regularly take their children to toy shops just to see which of their competitors' products are popular and ought to be duplicated; and "foot soldiers in the battle," which both involves every employee in the mission of the organization and justifies a hierarchical, rule-governed style of management. But the most powerful expressions of the metaphor are borrowed from the larger culture: "Be all that you can be" is used to justify voluntary overtime, and "lean, mean fighting machine" is used to explain reductions in the number of middle managers. Almost every normal work experience is explained in language reflecting the "army under siege" metaphor; almost every behavior desired of workers can be justified by referring to the metaphor. In cases like this one, management and employees share the same metaphorical description of their organization, and define that metaphor in the same way. Motivation and control are enhanced. But, metaphors are highly ambiguous—they can be interpreted in a number of different ways.[24] And, they are not static, they emerge, change, become dominant for a time, and eventually are replaced by other metaphors. When metaphors are interpreted in different ways, or when management relies on an outdated metaphor to motivate and control their employees, the power of metaphor may lead to very different outcomes.

CASE STUDY:
TROUBLE IN THE HAPPIEST PLACE ON EARTH*

The metaphors that people use to describe their organizations can reveal a great deal about the degree of homogeneity within the organizational culture. When groups of employees use different metaphors or interpret the same metaphor in different ways, the organization is likely to be composed of multiple, sometimes conflictful, subcultures.

On the surface, Disneyland and Disney World seem to be perfect examples of a homogeneous "work hard/play hard" culture. Employees are selected to correspond to the image of "all-American" boys and girls—clones of Annette

---

*This case is adapted from John van Maanen, "The Smile Factory," in *Reframing Organizational Culture*, Peter Frost, et al., eds. (Newbury Park, CA: Sage, 1991) and Ruth C. Smith and Eric Eisenberg, "Conflict at Disneyland: A Root-Metaphor Analysis," *Communication Monographs, 54* (1987): 367–380.

(continued)

(continued from the previous page)

Funicello and Frankie Avalon. They are hired because they have exceptional "people skills," although few of them have much direct contact with customers and all of them are taught to refer all but the simplest questions to supervisors or security people (whose identities are obscured but not disguised—they are the Keystone Kops, or Town Marshals in Frontierland, or Cavalry Officers on Tom Sawyer's Island). If they understand and practice common courtesy they can fulfill the people parts of their jobs quite well.

There is a hierarchy among the clones, however. Part of the hierarchy is informal—good looks, college affiliation, career aspirations, and anything else typically valued by middle- and upper-class white college students all contribute to one's status. Among women, uniforms convey status—the "sexier" the uniforms, the greater the status. In fact, a story at Disneyland tells how the tour guides were offended by the uniforms of the ride operators in the new "It's a Small World" ride because the operators were given uniforms with shorter skirts and more revealing blouses. Eventually the guides were able to prompt changes in the ride operators' uniforms that returned tour guides to the top of the "sexiness" hierarchy. But there is a formal hierarchy, too. Bilingual tour guides are at the top of the hierarchy, followed by skilled ride operators, unskilled ride operators, sweepers, and finally, the lowly food and concession workers. No one really knows how an individual worker gets assigned to his or her place in the hierarchy ("central casting" makes these decisions in secret), but salary and perks like frequency of rest breaks go along with a higher rank. There is *very little* movement up the hierarchy, although it happens often enough for dishwashers to dream of becoming pirates in Captain Hook's band. Romances are common among Disney employees but, of course, people do not date, mate with, or marry people from the "wrong" status level.

According to management, Disney parks are strong culture organizations, in which "the customer is king" and employees are happily committed to making the parks the "happiest places on earth." Control is exercised unobtrusively, as that term is described in Chapter 2. After a lengthy acculturation process, newcomers leave Disney University with deep pride in themselves and their organization, and with an even deeper commitment to doing things "the Disney way."

But workers give a somewhat different view of the culture. The parks are filled with supervisors who are not, as management tells the students at Disney University, there only to help. They are also there to catch them when they make mistakes or violate park policies. Infractions, no matter how trivial, are met with instant and harsh discipline. Workers who supervisors decide are "malcontents," "troublemakers," or simply "jerks" are often fired. Consequently, each group in the status hierarchy coalesces into a tightly knit subculture committed to defending one another against the supervisors, although there are "finks" and "stool pigeons" among each group. Ironically, this close camaraderie

(continued)

(continued from the previous page)

among alienated employees is one of the main attractions of working at Disney and one of the main reasons that employees return year after year. But in 1984 the "strong culture" in the "happiest place on earth" began to crumble.

Early in its history Disneyland management consciously propagated a view of reality that presented the Magic Kingdom as a giant drama in which every employee played a "role" in making customers happy. Dress codes were labeled "costuming," rules about how to look, talk, and behave were depicted as "all part of the show," and the personnel department was called "casting." The drama metaphor turned even the most mundane of employees' activities into a calculated fiction designed to please customers. Although part of the metaphor stresses the "fun" of role playing, management also explicitly stressed that "each member must have a clear understanding of "the business of show business." Much of the organization's formal communication with employees quotes Walt Disney: "I don't want the public to see the real world they're living in. I want them to feel they're in another world."

Eventually the drama metaphor started to be replaced by a "family" metaphor. Disneyland was known as a "friendly place to work" where keeping everyone on a "first-name basis" was valued and teamwork was essential. Organizational stories reported that Disney had insisted that everyone call him Walt and that he was a caring family man who reserved his Saturdays for his two daughters and designed the park to give all families a safe, clean, enjoyable place to go. But, like the drama metaphor, these notions (originally meant to refer only to customer–employee relationships) soon were used by employees to refer to worker–management relationships. The friendly, family atmosphere was so appealing that most employees and many managers started to believe it uncritically, forgetting that Disneyland was a for-profit business. In good times there was little need to be clear about exactly how a term like "family" might be interpreted or about how it would influence employee behavior. The inevitable ambiguity of metaphors and stories allowed employees to develop their own preferred interpretations of what "drama" and "family" meant to them.

As the family metaphor took control, employees not only treated the public like personal guests but came to expect similar treatment from management. Management, in turn, did little to discourage this, since the close-knit feeling helped business, improved morale, and even seemed to be consistent with their dreams of what the park should be like. But, as financial problems grew, business considerations became increasingly important. Employees started to resent this new concern: "It used to be, 'Let's try to make the employees as happy as possible so that they make the public happy,' and now it's 'Let's save as much money as we can and make a buck'" (a ride operator with thirty years' experience) or "There was a time when the employee was very important to the company; now they're more of a company. It's getting more like a business, and I

(continued)

(continued from the previous page)

don't think the park should be run like a business" (service employee, twenty-five years' experience). In 1984 management cut wages and benefits for some employees. Shocked, the employees argued that management's decisions were not true to the spirit of Disneyland, to Walt's original dream. They held a candlelight vigil, printed bumper stickers that said "Disneyland—Walt's dying dream," and eventually went on strike.

Employees claimed that management was unfair, that this was not the way to treat their family: "It's just totally business. They are not worried about the family thing" (twenty-four years' experience); "It's not fun to work at Disneyland anymore. They gave us a cold slap in the face" (thirty-two years); "Walt wanted family, but it's a business now, not Walt's dream. That's shot, it's not what he wanted" (twenty-three years). Management responded with its interpretation of the family metaphor: Sometimes family life is hard, and truly close families make sacrifices if they are to survive.

Discussion Questions

1. Why did the dominant metaphors change?
2. How did these changes influence the attitudes and actions of employees and management?
3. Were the stories and metaphors under management's control? Did that control eventually dissolve? If so, why?
4. What factors allowed Disneyland to succeed in spite of the existence of a number of subcultures of alienated workers? Why did these factors not prevent a bitter strike?
5. What does the Disneyland experience imply about the stability of organizational symbols? Organizational cultures?
6. What could management do now to recreate a unified, cooperative culture?

Stories and Myths; Storytelling and Mythmaking.   Human beings are storytelling animals. From childhood fairy tales to the tales told during executives' weekend retreats, stories provide concrete, vivid images of what life is or will be like and what behaviors our culture values or prohibits.[25] **Stories** are a distinctive form of symbolism that combine **temporality**, a characteristic **grammar**, and a high level of **personal relevance**. By *temporality* I mean that stories present events in sequence rather than in a list or chart.[26] This sequencing makes the events seem to be connected in natural, inevitable ways. They seem to be the causes and effects of other events. They help us make sense of the present, which may seem to be chaotic and senseless, by connecting it with the past. Stories also have a characteristic *grammar*—they begin with a preface that explains how the story is relevant to the current situation, include a lengthy recounting of events, and conclude with a closing that in some way explains the moral or lesson of the story. Stories whose grammar is consistent with the norms of a particular society are viewed as being more credible than those that use a surprising grammar. In Western societies this means that credible stories will have a protagonist, antagonist, dramatic conflict, climax, and resolution of the conflict.[27]

Third, stories are *relevant* to the needs and experiences of members of the organization. Stories are told most often, and are most powerful, when people are confused and concerned about what is going on in their organizations (for instance, when a person is entering a new organization or when the organization is undergoing major changes).

If stories fulfill these requirements, they provide explanations of events, policies, procedures, and so on that are beyond doubt or argument. They function as social *myths* (recall Chapter 1), not in the sense that they are untrue (although they may be), but in the sense that their "truths" are taken for granted by the people who believe them. Like stories, the power of myths stems from their coherent, vivid details; their ability to help people make sense of their surroundings; and their consistency with other organizational stories and myths.[28]

Finally, stories and myths do not stand alone and usually are not interpreted alone. Instead they coalesce to form **mythologies**, groups of interconnected symbols that support one another. In short, stories and myths tell people how things are to be done in a particular group and provide a "social map" that points out potentially dangerous topics, events, or persons present in at least one of an organization's subcultures. To be credible stories must express a value, purpose, or philosophy that is consistent with the taken-for-granted assumptions of the culture or subculture and must provide employees with guidelines for acting. They often tell employees what management wants them to believe is valued and rewarded in the organization; they sometimes tell employees what management *really* rewards and who *really* has power. And, sometimes they may do both.

Some examples may help clarify these ideas. According to a frequently repeated story at 3M, a junior employee accidentally discovered Scotch tape when he spilled glue on a roll of cellophane. Unfortunately, his superiors did not believe his claims for the usefulness and potential market for the product. Frustrated, he slipped into the boardroom before an important meeting and taped all of the members' materials down to the table. The board members were so impressed they decided to give his product a chance. In another company all newcomers were warned that people making presentations to top management could expect to be verbally assaulted. Upper management delighted in destroying presenters' arguments, yelling at them, insulting their intelligence, and throwing their materials on the floor or in their faces. But if the presenter stands his or her ground and generally survives, she or he will gain their respect and be on the way up the corporate ladder. In another production firm, a recurring story involves a crisis faced during the mid-1970s that was created by a drop in orders. Instead of laying newer employees off, the company reduced everyone's—including upper management's—workweek to four days and paychecks to 80 percent of normal.

Other stories involve key individuals, often founders of the firm or people who were instrumental in its development. Employees of the Disney empire hear story after story about Walt Disney. He constantly walked around Disneyland making sure it was a clean, wholesome, family environment; he knew employees' names and talked to them about their families and so on. In these stories mundane tasks like picking up trash and cleaning rides are transformed into a noble quest to make Disneyland what Walt dreamed that it would be, the "happiest place on earth" and the best place to take a family.

It is relatively clear how management is likely to prefer that these stories be interpreted. The tape story is supposed to "say" that 3M values innovation but expects employees to fight creatively for their ideas. The presentations story warns employees to have exquisitely prepared presentations and to learn to be "tough" advocates of what they believe. The no-layoff story carries a number of "preferred" messages—that the company cares about all of its employees, that it was a team from top to bottom, and that it values keeping a "lean" staff so that it will not have to face layoffs during economic downturns. The "Uncle Walt" stories encourage the best possible customer service.

But, most organizational stories are more complex and ambiguous than these, allowing a number of possible interpretations. Many of these interpretations are negative. For example, Mary Helen Brown reported a recurring story in a nursing home:

> When I come on shift I check in with the nurse who's there and ask "is everything ok?" One night I came on and she said yes. I put my lunch away and put on my sweater—it was cold. I started my rounds. When I got to the men's end I went in a dark room and bumped into something on the floor. I had no idea there was a patient on the floor because she had told me that everything was ok. I turned on the light. He had fallen off the bed and lay there for several hours with one very thin blanket over his legs. His foldie [IV] tube was wrapped around his legs. I couldn't move him, but covered him up. About 4:30 p.m. I got him awake and back to bed. Everything was hurting. People like that shouldn't be allowed to be [live or work, the meaning was not clear] in a nursing home.[29]

This story could be interpreted in many different ways—as a plea that the home should not admit patients who were invalids, as a complaint that the home does not value high-quality patient care and does nothing about employees who ignore patients or treat them badly, or as a warning that employees can expect to encounter crises at any time of day or night and will have to deal with them alone. Some interpretations will support management's preferred beliefs and values, and thus serve to motivate and control employees; others will not.

To this point I have discussed the content of organizational stories, myths, and mythologies, indicating that they provide valuable information about how employees interpret and respond to the core beliefs, values, and taken-for-granted assumptions of their organizational cultures and subcultures. However, much of the influence of these symbolic forms comes from the *process* of enacting them, not from the *content* itself. **Storytelling** is an interactive process in which the teller presents his or her version of a story, usually leaving out many details, while others jump in and challenge, reinterpret, and revise the storyteller's version.[30] The process allows each of the storytellers to link his or her own experiences to the experiences and interpretations of other storytellers. Through this process of mutual interpretation and re-interpretation the taken-for-granted assumptions of the group are shared and reproduced. During the storytelling process differences and tensions among interpretations may be expressed and managed. Thus, through a complicated process the values and taken-for-granted assumptions of the group are produced, reproduced, and revised.[31]

Of course, the observation that processes of symbolic action can have powerful effects on the beliefs, values, and taken-for-granted assumptions of participants does not imply that those outcomes always are positive. Shared symbolic action may lead a group of employees to create a view of reality that isolates them from other employees and makes it impossible for them to recognize problems that are created by that view. Tom Hollihan and Patricia Riley's study of a "Toughlove" group provides an excellent example. Toughlove is a self-help voluntary organization composed of parents who have troubled teenagers. Toughlove meetings are like "testimonial services" in Protestant churches. Members come to tell stories about their experiences and their successes in overcoming their problems. Their individual stories combine to form a complicated mythology that unifies the members through their common experiences. The core experience is suffering brought on by the actions of their delinquent children; the common salvation is recognizing that adolescent children choose to behave as they do, realizing that parents have rights to peaceful homes and productive lives, and taking action to regain control of their lives instead of remaining victims of the tyranny of their children. Their stories are filled with villains and nostalgic images of a peaceful past. The villains are child-service professionals—teachers, social workers, therapists, and counselors who are too quick to blame the parents for their children's delinquency and who are responsible for the modern "permissive" view of child-raising that the parents believe has created the problem of delinquent children. The nostalgia is of their childhoods when "visits to the woodshed" led them to both fear and respect their parents and learn to behave in socially acceptable ways.

Their stories also provide information about how to cope with everyday experiences. Parents are advised to label their children "incorrigible" when requesting police support because it is "the right legal mumbo-jumbo" to get them arrested. Success stories of setting and enforcing rules, or ejecting children from the home as a last resort, are presented as "no-lose" actions. Even if sending the child out onto the streets did not persuade him or her to reform, it led to peace in the home, improving the lives of the parents and other children. As the Toughlove mythology develops, parents learn responses for every possible event, hear justifications for each necessary action, and gain support from people who share their experiences. In all organizations, as employees and members listen to stories they learn the values that bind the culture together and discover what they must say in order to be accepted in the culture.

Hollihan and Riley conclude that:

> Shared stories [and myths] respond to people's sense of reason and emotion, to their intellects and imagination, to the facts as they perceive them, and to their values. People search for stories that justify their efforts and resolve the tensions and problems in their lives. . . . Those who do not share in the storytelling . . . might view particular stories as mere rationalization, but this is to miss the very nature of the storytelling process.[32]

Rituals and Ceremonies.   Like storytelling, rituals and ceremonies gain their power from the *act* of participating in them, as well as from the meaning that people extract from them. Because the meaning of rituals and ceremonies is located in the "doing," they can be especially powerful symbolic acts.[33] **Rituals** are informal celebrations that may or may not be officially sanctioned by the organization, and **ceremonies** are planned, formal, and ordained by management. When a work crew gets together at a local bar on Friday evenings, it is a ritual, an informal gathering. When all of the employees of a department store are asked to appear at a media event designed to "kick off" a new line of clothes, it is a ceremony.

Participating in rituals and ceremonies helps individual employees understand the political and interpersonal nuances of their organization. If they perceive that the ritual or ceremony is meaningful, participating also may increase their commitment to the organization because it makes them feel like they are a part of the organizational community. Consequently, advocates of cultural strategies of organizing suggest that management take ceremonies very seriously. And, many do, as witnessed by Advanced Micro Devices' 1984 Christmas party, which cost $700,000 and involved 10,000 guests, and Apple Computer's expenditure of $110,000 for nineteen parties during 1984.[34] Management may use different kinds of organizational ceremonies in order to communicate different messages.

Harrison Trice and Janice Beyer have observed that there are five primary types of organizational ceremonies. **Ceremonies of passage** "tell" everyone that a person has changed organizational roles and now has a new set of responsibilities, behavioral guidelines and constraints, and interpersonal relationships. **Degradation ceremonies** assign responsibility for errors or problems, refocus attention on the kinds of performance that is expected by management, and remove the "guilty" party from the power structure of the organization (usually through demotion, reassignment, or resignation). When President Boris Yeltsin ordered that every evidence of Russia's communist past be erased—renaming Leningrad, destroying statues, removing the names of party heroes from all schoolbooks, chiseling their names off the fronts of buildings—he merely did on a giant scale what firing ceremonies do in organizations every

TABLE 4-1

Types of Organizational Ceremonies

TYPE	EXAMPLE	EFFECTS
Ceremonies of passage	Army induction and basic training; fraternity hazing	Help people change roles; reestablish comfortable role relationships.
Degradation ceremonies	Firings and demotions	Dissolve target's power; discredit him/her.
Enhancement ceremonies	Mary Kay seminars	Enhance self-esteem; increase power of exceptional performers.
Renewal ceremonies	Organizational development and "training"	Reenergize people; reemphasize culture.
Integration ceremonies	Office Christmas party	Revive bonds between employees; reinforce commitment.

day. **Enhancement ceremonies** reemphasize the goals of the organization and create instant heroes who symbolize those goals. Regular "awards ceremonies" for the top salespersons can serve this function. **Renewal ceremonies** like annual executive retreats complete with "motivational" speakers create an image of action and deflect attention from underlying organizational problems. **Integration ceremonies**—for example, giving every employee an identical Thanksgiving turkey—redefine the organization as a community and "tell" each employee that she or he is a part of that community (see Table 4-1).

The patterns of ceremonies that characterize an organizational culture or subculture may reveal much about the core values and beliefs of the people who design and enact it (usually management). Organizations dominated by ceremonies of passage may value hierarchy and structure above all else. When the most important ceremonies involve degradation, they may signal that management is primarily concerned with restricting employees' behavior and freedom of action and requiring employees to take a defensive, low-risk posture. Managers in enhancement-oriented cultures may value outcomes more than the strategies that people use to achieve those outcomes; integration ceremonies "say" that management permits approved-but-controlled emotional displays. When renewal ceremonies dominate an organization they may indicate that actual problem solving is not encouraged and open discussion of problems is prohibited, but maintaining an image of productive problem solving is valued highly. Managers who sponsor a large number of ceremonies of passage may be telling their employees that they should not desire or expect stability of work assignments, responsibilities, or coworker relationships.

But, the power of ceremonies to motivate and control employees depends on the meaning that employees extract from them, and the extent to which they are meaningful. Like all symbolic forms, ceremonies can be interpreted in many different ways. The foundry that I worked in during my undergraduate years (recall the time-motion study example in Chapter 2) had a Christmas ceremony during which hams were distributed by the owner to each worker from the back of a truck—every worker except me. After my first Christmas ceremony, the owner quietly explained that I was excluded because I was a part-time employee (summers and holidays) and he feared that giving me a ham would make the ceremony less meaningful (or might even cause resentment) for the full-time workers. Later a group of workers took me aside and told me they felt bad that I had been left out, explained that they thought the oversight was because I was not the head of a family like they were and thus didn't need the gift, and presented me with a ham that they had purchased during lunch with a pool of money they had created after the ceremony. Interestingly, although the two "meanings" were very different, they both recognized that the ceremony was *meaningful* to the owner and workers alike.

Some office holiday parties may provide an opportunity for a closely knit group of people to celebrate their commitment to a common goal and their legitimate emotional attachments to one another. Others may only be "command performances" that people attend because the plant manager takes roll. People participate only in the sense of going through the motions; they are never emotionally involved in the ceremony. The meaningfulness of key ceremonies as well as the meanings extracted from the experience may reveal the strength of the organizational culture.[35] Ceremonies that are meaningless to employees, or ceremonies that mean something very different to managers and workers may reveal a culture or subculture that is in the process of decay.

Rituals have some of the same characteristics as ceremonies. Their power stems from the emotional commitments created by the act of participating in them, and they also may vary in meaningfulness and in the meanings that are extracted from them. Some rituals provide opportunities for workers to express their independence from (or hostility toward management); others may provide a means of fulfilling sociability needs that are not met on the job; others may help people deal with job-related changes and the interpersonal changes that they require. For example, wives of major league athletes usually form a close-knit, supportive unofficial family. A key ritual for them is to sit together during home games. When it appears that a wife's husband is about to leave the team through a trade or being sent down to the minors, the unofficial family begins to dissolve. Other wives begin to spend less time with her, begin to sit away from her during games, and so on. The new ritual signals to her— and to her husband—that they must prepare themselves psychologically for a major change and a new informal family.[36]

In some cases rituals reinforce the meanings of ceremonies, as when organizations die, enhancing motivation and control.[37] In other cases they help meet employees' needs for autonomy, creativity, and sociability, thereby reducing the alienation that comes from unfulfilling jobs, also enhancing motivation and control. But, in other cases they may contradict or redefine the meanings of ceremonies, undermining managerial control, or serve as opportunities for resistance.

Emotional Regulation as Motivation and Control

The concept of unobtrusive control and the symbolic forms discussed so far in this chapter have focused on how the employees' beliefs, values, and interpretations guide and constrain their thoughts, which in turn guide and constrain their actions and decisions. But, human beings are not only thinking creatures, we also have emotions that hold implications for cultural strategies of motivation and control. Of course, the concept of emotionality is not limited to the cultural strategy of organizing. Taylor valued the enhanced self-esteem that workers would receive from successfully performing the scientifically designed tasks and the "upper-level" needs of relational strategies are emotion-laden. But, emotionality and emotion control are central parts of the cultural strategy. For example, the sequel to *In Search of Excellence* has the word "passion" in its title and focuses at length on emotions like pride and love (recall endnotes 6 and 7). In fact, John van Maanen and Gideon Kunda warned that the cultural strategy "masks managerial attempts to control not only what employees say and do but also what they feel."[38] Emotions are relevant to cultural forms of motivation and control in three ways. At the simplest level, supervisors can use their positions to manipulate employees' emotional responses. The emotions may be positive, as in ceremonies of enhancement or they may involve the negative emotions of degradation ceremonies. Often the recognition is based as much on complying with the organization's control system as on making tangible contributions; often the recognized employee is chosen because he or she has in some way enhanced or threatened the power of the supervisor. But, in any case, public recognition solidifies the supervisor's power position because *she* or *he* makes the decision about whom to recognize and how to do so. Wanting to be recognized (and wanting to avoid embarrassment) serve as potent bases for this form of cultural control.

Cultural control also is exercised when employees learn to interpret emotional responses in preferred ways. Emotional responses are highly ambiguous—fear and excitement *feel* very much the same—and must be interpreted. The core beliefs and values of an organization often "tell" employees how to interpret their emotional responses. They may learn to feel "pride" only when the organization's goals are met, not when their own objectives are fulfilled. For example, stewardesses may be successfully taught to interpret their anger at obnoxious passengers as care and concern for their helpless and dependent charges.[39] Employees also may begin to interpret their responses to organizational changes (for example, downsizing) as "excitement" about new opportunities rather than as fear that they may be the next victim.

In extreme cases employees may learn to "package" their emotions in ways that are prescribed by their organizations. For example, Arlie Hochschild's study of stewardesses found that emotions often are not just *responses* to work, but emotion control *is* the work. Like most workers in service industries, stewardesses learn to *experience* only the feelings that are required by their organizational roles and to *suppress* other feelings. They create a "package" of emotions and emotional displays in which genuinely felt emotions are transformed into organizationally acceptable emotional displays. There are ways to resist the process, of course. For example, some of the stewardesses in Hochschild's study admitted spilling hot coffee in the laps of especially obnoxious patrons. But, much more often they strived to maintain a package of artificial emotions, an exhausting task that eventually begins to take a psychological toll. Employees can minimize the psychological stresses by either becoming emotionally numb[40] or by what Hochschild calls "deep acting," actually beginning to feel only those emotions that are organizationally acceptable. Emotions are constantly being negotiated in very complicated ways, but the negotiation and the process of emotional packaging can serve as a powerful form of cultural control.

CASE STUDY:
THE HIDDEN EMOTIONS OF TOURISM*

As I have indicated throughout this book, resistance is an inevitable aspect of systems of motivation and control. This is true even of cultural forms of control, although the forms and extent of resistance may be different in different strategies or organizing. This case is about emotional control and resistance in what may be the ultimate kind of service organization, an upscale Caribbean resort.

"Pairs" (the names have been changed to protect the innocent—and guilty) is an upscale, all-inclusive resort that caters to couples from all over the world, but primarily from Europe and North America. Its marketing rhetoric, from brochures to television ads, depicts it as a place where suntanned tourists are catered to in every way, at any cost, by smiling, happy servants. As one staff member said, "a guest coming here could be a thief or a murderer, but we have to be nice to them no matter what." From the beginning of their interviews, Pairs workers are taught that "the customer is always right" and that they are to

---

*This case is based on Simone Carnegie, "The Hidden Emotions of Tourism: Communication and Power in the Caribbean," M.A. Thesis, Texas A&M University, 1996.

(continued)

(continued from the previous page)

display the "happy-go-lucky" attitude that tourists expect of Caribbean people. Both commands are reinforced at every turn.

Each guest is given an "evaluation sheet" that includes a section where she or he is asked to comment on the performance of the staff by name. Twice a month the public relations office posts the comments for all employees to see. Although cash rewards are given to employees who receive many positive comments, and punishments are given those with negative comments, the employees also reward and punish one another. When the first summary sheet was posted all of the desk staff excitedly huddled together behind the reception desk to read the results. Positive comments were read aloud for all to hear; workers with the highest points received congratulations from their peers; workers with negative comments and low points were talked about behind their backs for the rest of the week. When Ken, a bellman, walked by the desk, Simone teased him by saying "I don't see your name here." He immediately turned the pages of the report until he found a remark that included his name: "It only takes one," he said. And, the control system *seemed* to work. Most of the workers are like Trendy, about whom Ian once commented, "I've never seen Trendy get mad. I'm not telling a lie. In all the years I've been here I've just seen her smile, and then when the guest leaves, she stops smiling." But, judging from their comments, the guests never see anything but smiling, carefree, always-willing-to-serve workers.

But, behind the scenes "servanthood" is a different thing entirely. Perhaps most important, most of the workers see their act as just that, a strategic way of behaving that fulfills management's commands while making their lives easier. For instance, Trendy explained that she smiles because "I have to be nice because these people complain about every little thing. If I'm not nice and if I don't smile then tomorrow there would be complaints." Their performances are so fluid and so convincing that they seem to be scripted. One script welcomes new guests: "Hi, I'm Laura your concierge [big smile]. I am here to help. If you have any questions don't hesitate to call. If any situations arise (I won't say problems because we don't have problems at Pairs), please call. We are out of the office a lot but we have a radio, so just call the operator and he will get in touch with us."

Even the actor's voice is scripted. When the staff members talk to one another or to guests from the Caribbean they use the local patois, with its rhythmic tone and colorful metaphors. But with most guests only standard English is used. When a guest is spotted coming near, everyone switches into his or her role and voice; when the guest turns and walks away the staff just as instantly switch back to their normal selves and voices.

(continued)

(continued from the previous page)

While safely out of the hearing of guests or management Pairs staffers talk about anything and everything, but often they talk about the customers. I was working at the desk with Sandy one day and a U.S. tourist interrupted and asked Sandy if he could mail his postcards with U.S. stamps. Sandy, in his best British English, explained that the would have to use local stamps "because each country uses its own stamps and postal system." As the guest departed he immediately shifted into his local dialect and we talked at length about how little U.S. residents, including his friends at school, knew about Caribbean or West Indian culture. In fact, one of the dominant topics of conversation involved the various failings of the guests—their stupid questions ("Why is it raining?" or "What language are the staff members speaking?" (the answer is English), their arrogance (for example, one U.S. resident who repeatedly demanded that the desk clerk check his bill for unauthorized long-distance calls after seeing his maid using his phone, even after being told that the maids *always* use the room phones to notify the desk when they have finished cleaning a room), their paranoia (the German couple who would not leave their luggage for a moment lest a staff member steal the tacky palm leaf hat and the couple who demanded to know the location of the American embassy in case of civil unrest, something that had not happened on this island in almost a century), and their racism (all staff members are black; almost all guests are white). Telling these stories to one another seemed to have three purposes—they place the worker in a superior role vis-à-vis the guest, thus reversing the complete subservience demanded by their organization; they help cushion the worker from negative comments by the guests, making it less likely that they will blame themselves when they encounter rude behavior; and, paradoxically, they allow the worker to continue to play his or her assigned role while they simultaneously reject it. Of course, some staff members accepted their scripted roles more completely than others; some engaged in resistance much more often and with greater intensity than some of their peers. But, all both played their role *and* resisted in a complex web of control.

Discussion Questions

1. How do the various forms of control used at "Pairs" support one another? How would the points/bonus system work differently if there was no system of managers watching the employees? Of guests being encouraged to watch and report on the employees?

2. What functions does resistance play for the workers? What effects does it have on the functioning of the organization? On the organizational control system? Why?

CULTURAL STRATEGIES OF LEADERSHIP

I noted earlier in this chapter that there is a key tension within cultural strategies of organizing. On the one hand the perspective assumes that cultures can be managed strategically; on the other it focuses on the processes through which employees actively perceive, interpret, and strategically respond to their organizational situations. As a result, cultural strategies of organizational designs, motivations and control consistently must recognize that individual employees' strategic choices cannot be determined by an overall strategy of organizing. Cultural strategies of leadership recognize that this tension exists, and strive to deal with it through what have been labeled "transformational" processes. The most important of these processes are called *visioning* and *framing*.

Visioning and Transformational Leadership

When it was first proposed, the concept of transformational leadership was similar in many ways to the *transactional* perspective of the relational strategy of organizing. Both transformational and transactional leaders are characterized by their *consideration* for employees and their individual needs, their willingness to actively involve their subordinates in decision-making (even encouraging them to question the basic assumptions of the organization or unit), and their willingness to supervise "loosely." Both forms of leadership involve familiar communicative strategies—they clarify the challenges that the organization or unit faces while encouraging, supporting, and inspiring their subordinates to use their own abilities to meet those challenges, and they maintain close communicative ties to their subordinates, a process that Peters and Waterman called "managing by walking around." In short, they play the roles of cheerleader, enthusiast, nurturer, coach, and facilitator that seemed to characterize leadership in "excellent" firms.[41] But, transformational leaders also differ from transactional leaders. Their authority is based on what Max Weber called "**charisma**," the image that they possess some divine, supernatural, or otherwise "special" talents or attributes, not on their formal role or even their task-related achievements. At the heart of charismatic leadership is the ability to create a *vision* of where the organization or unit is going and how it is to achieve those goals and persuade others to accept that vision.[42] Visionary leadership involves communicating a mission for the organization or unit that encompasses each employee's hopes, desires and so on (even if it requires the leader to sacrifice some of her or his own gains) and skillfully managing conflicts and crises. They are able to *"transform"* their subordinates' creative ideas and action so that they further the mission of the organization or unit, and do so without embarrassing them or claiming ownership of their ideas.

Of course, not just any vision will do. A transformative vision is realistic and credible. It is consistent with the history of the organization or unit and "fits" the realities of the current situation, and it is attractive. Bennis, Parikh, and

Lessem call transformative visions "targets that beckon" and argue that the genius of transformational leadership is the ability to "assemble—out of all the variety of images, signals, forecasts, and alternatives—a clearly articulated vision of the future that is at once simple, easily understood, clearly desirable, and energizing."[43] Visions provide a picture of the future, an explanation and sense of purpose, and guidelines for acting on an everyday basis.[44] They allow each employee to find his or her own role in the organization, her or his own way to contribute to the mission, and in doing so release new energies and enthusiasm. They emerge over time, with experience, and through mutual consultation with subordinates. They are flexible and adaptive. They include long-term goals, which help define a series of short-term goals, which in turn both guide and are influenced by goals that emerge out of everyday experience. For example, when Dr. Barbara Barlow was appointed chief of pediatric surgery at Harlem Hospital Center, her goals focused on successful treatment of patients. But she and her staff noted that many patients were hospitalized because of injuries suffered from falling out of buildings, playing on unsafe playground equipment, and improperly operating their bicycles. So, her goals changed to focus on preventative care *as well as* acute care—increasing the number of window gates in apartment buildings, teaching children safety rules and street smarts, and so on. Her unit now pursues long-term, short-term, and emergent goals simultaneously, and each kind of goal influences their pursuit of the others.[45]

Finally, visions are *appropriately* ambiguous. It is somewhat ironic that transformation leadership *relies* on ambiguity, because it is *ambiguity* that allows employees to interpret situations and symbolic acts in their own idiosyncratic ways, thus complicating cultural strategies of motivation and control. But, ambiguity may be intentional. This is a somewhat strange concept for members of Western societies because we have been taught to strive for clarity in our communication.[46] But in other societies ambiguity is treated as something that should be managed strategically. Some situations call for a high level of clarity and specificity—communicating technical standards for precision equipment or delivering negative performance feedback, for example. But, in other cases, ambiguity actually can be helpful. It allows different people to interpret the same message in different ways, helping to maintain a diversity of perspectives within an organization. When the organization faces new or particularly difficult problems, or experiences important organizational changes, this diversity can lead to innovative solutions. It also may allow parties involved in conflicts to avoid having to blame anyone for an impasse or escalation, thus saving face.

Ambiguity also can allow people to take actions that are necessary but forbidden by existing policies and procedures, providing needed flexibility. A supervisor usually cannot openly tell his or her subordinates, "OK, do it that way, but if you get caught I'll never admit that we had this conversation." He or she can, however, leave instructions so ambiguous that a sensitive subordinate will "get the message." Ambiguity provides flexibility, and in highly structured organizations, flexibility may be more important than clarity (see Chapter 6).

But, judging the level of ambiguity that is appropriate in a particular situation is more an art than a science. And any message *may* be interpreted in widely varying ways by different employees. So, good visions must be *both* focused in order to direct activities and energize employees, but ambiguous enough to allow flexibility. According to cultural/transformational strategies of leadership, this dilemma is managed through processes of **framing**.

Framing and Transformational Leadership

Instead of attempting to persuade employees to accept a particular set of beliefs, values, and assumptions through messages that they may interpret in various ways, framing involves persuading employees to view their organizational "reality" in particular ways. It involves interpreting a new situation as a "challenge" rather than a "problem," or, as in the "tourism" case presented earlier in this chapter, labeling difficulties "situations" rather than "problems." All messages, events, and actions are ambiguous to some extent—it is both inevitable and necessary for employees to make sense out them. But, framing allows this ambiguity to become a "space" within which transformational leaders can act, not a barrier to motivation and control.

Framing begins when a leader develops her or his own view of "reality," when we carefully sort through our own images of how the world works, looking for a systematic frame of reference. Once our own frames of reference are solidified, we can "arrange" our past experiences in ways that make them make sense to us. In this sense, the key to framing lies in our memories. To be credible to followers, a leader's application of his or her frame of reference to everyday problems must be spontaneous and honest (recall Gibb's discussion of defensiveness-producing communication in Chapter 3). Then when we encounter a new situation, we will automatically approach it through our frame of reference, others will see how we make sense out of new situations, and begin to incorporate our frames of reference into theirs.

And, eventually we will develop a language that is consistent with our frames of reference. We will think in terms of a particular set of metaphors and categories, interpret events in accord with stories and myths that we find useful in our own efforts to make sense out of reality, and infuse some of those terms with values that are especially meaningful to us. So, the key to persuading others to accept our own frames is not to persuade them in any overt way, but to model a particular frame of reference in our everyday activities. By paying attention to some things and ignoring others, expressing honest emotions of anger in response to some things and joy in response to others, and reacting to critical incidents and crises in particular ways, we let other people know how we make sense out of life, and in the process let them know what we *really* value. Of course, leaders do communicate their frames of reference in more formal ways. During planning sessions a leader sets an agenda for a group by guiding the discussion toward a certain set of priorities or suggesting that the group view a particular event or problem in a certain way. Leaders also send powerful messages about what they *actually* value when they appraise employees' performance and distribute rewards. But, the most powerful way to communicate a frame is by everyday behavior, by seizing what Fairhurst and Sarr call "leadership moments," opportunities to suggest a particular way to view events, messages, and communication.

A RETROSPECTIVE LOOK AT THE MAJOR STRATEGIES OF ORGANIZING

Throughout Chapters 2 through 4 I have examined strategies of organizing in very instrumental terms, primarily asking, "Do they work?" This was not a particularly easy task, since they operate from different sets of assumptions about people, work and organizations; have different effects in different situations; and achieve some objectives while creating barriers to others. And it can be critiqued on at least two different grounds.

Criticism #1: Organizations Just Aren't That Simple

One criticism is that the picture of organizing presented in these chapters is a little misleading because it separates the three strategies, making them seem to be mutually exclusive alternatives. There are very few (if any) real organizations that use only one strategy of organizing. Organizations emerge and develop in their own, distinctive ways as their members collaborate (and compete) to deal with the situations they face. They develop their own "mixes" of traditional, relational, and cultural strategies. Sometimes these strategies are in tension with one another, as when retail organizations develop cultural strategies that focus on flexibility and customer service, but operate in a traditional bureaucratic structure. In other cases, the strategies are more congruent with one another, but even then the organization may have built-in problems.

Consider two examples. The W. L. Gore Company has developed a strategy of organizational design and cultural strategies that are mutually supportive. In 1969, Bill Gore founded W. L. Gore and Associates and started making a variety of products out of Dupont Teflon—everything from outdoor clothing and camping gear to vein grafts and filters for blood transfusions. Gore decided to keep his plants relatively small—never more than 250 "associates," as employees are called—and to arrange them in clusters. Gore was convinced that when organizations or units become too large it is difficult to make cultural strategies of organizing succeed. Members are so isolated from one another and from upper management that they tend not to share in the vision and values of their cultures. He also believed that the kinds of communication breakdowns described in Chapter 2 become inevitable as size increases. This concern for culture, equality, and effective communication also influences the structure of each plant. Instead of being structured like a pyramid, W. L. Gore plants look like a lattice, a crosshatch that represents unrestricted communication (no chain of command), and no formal authority. Associates communicate with whomever they need to talk with in order to get the job done. The lattice survives partly because management does not interfere with the natural emergence of informal communication networks and partly because it assists in the process. But the overall strategy works because structural and cultural choices are congruent with one another, and are based on a concern for maximizing organizational effectiveness in a competitive, turbulent environment.[47]

In other cases an organization may have created a congruent design and culture that combine to make it dysfunctional. After a number of apparently avoidable airline crashes during 1996 a number of "think tanks" examined the Federal Aviation Administration, whose missions include maintaining airline safety. The studies found that the organization, like many government agencies, had developed a highly bureaucratic structure that made it virtually impossible to affect change or help the agency learn from its mistakes. As a result, there was very little accountability in the system—one division of the organization could easily shift responsibility for errors to another division and so on. But, the FAA also "is a culture that does not recognize or serve any client other than itself."[48] The organization is adequately funded and full of capable, hard-working people, but it has chosen a structure and developed a culture that combine to make bad decision-making almost inevitable. So, the key question facing organizations and their members is *not* "Should we rely on traditional, relational, or cultural strategies of organizing?" It is "What combination of strategies can we develop that best meets our needs and the needs of the people and groups we serve?"

Criticism #2: Myths of Shared Interests and Open Communication

There is a very different way to evaluate strategies of organizing, one proposed by a number of scholars who call themselves "critical theorists." Their concern is not with the relative merits of any particular strategy of organizing or any particular combination of strategies, but with *all* such strategies. Many of their ideas are important not only for understanding the remaining chapters of this unit, but also for understanding many of the challenges that are examined in Unit II.

Two key concepts are especially relevant—*interests* and *legitimate participation.*[49] At one level, owners, managers, and workers all *seem* to have many common interests, including the long-term survival of their organization. On a closer look it becomes clear that all three groups have some self-interests that are different from, and contradictory to, the interests of the other groups. For example, workers almost always have a strong vested interest in the continued operation of their firms in a particular locale and with stable or increasing real (adjusted for inflation) wages. When plants are closed and relocated, workers usually lose their jobs and find it difficult to find comparable employment elsewhere. Even if they are offered employment in other plants, relocating is psychologically and financially costly, especially when the workers have not previously moved. Similarly, reductions in wages or benefits can be devastating for

workers, and programs to increase organizational productivity through technological innovations often lead to layoffs or a lowered standard of living.

Managers in American firms usually benefit very little from creating conditions in which their subordinates have secure jobs or from maintaining the
long-term viability of the organization. This is because today managers rarely
are owners, especially in large firms. They were not entrepreneurs whose vision, ideas, and work built an organization to which they are psychologically
and financially committed. Indeed, their careers usually involve moving from
one organization to another and they usually are rewarded annually based on
the short-term profitability of the firm (especially now that a large proportion
of managers' total income is based on year-end performance bonuses). Consequently, they may have little self-interest involved in the firm's long-term success and much interest in actions that close plants, reduce workers' wages and
benefits, and replace workers with new technologies, because each of these
steps may increase the firm's short-term profitability. Increases in short-term
profits may increase their salaries, bonuses, and job security because they meet
the financial needs of investors.[50] Similarly, successful strategies of motivation
and control tend to serve management's interests much more than workers' interests. Even if they lead to increased organizational effectiveness and profitability, the rewards of those changes are not evenly distributed to the various
stakeholders in the organization (these ideas were developed in more detail in
Chapter 3).

Owners (which means stockholders in most large firms) also are interested
in limiting worker incomes and benefits. They also have an interest in limiting
management's salaries and bonuses, because all of these limits serve to increase
stock dividends. Because it is relatively easy to sell stock on the public market
when an organization begins to decline, owners also may have very little interest in the long-term survival of the firm. A similar analysis can be developed for
organizations that are not in the private sector.

Two highly publicized cases illustrate this point. During the 1980s, Frank
Lorenzo was the CEO of Texas Air, the parent company of Continental Airlines
and Eastern Airlines. Although Continental and Eastern regularly lost $200 mil-
lion or more each year and entered bankruptcy proceedings three times,
Lorenzo regularly received annual performance bonuses of more than $1 mil-
lion. When Eastern finally went out of business, its owners (creditors) received
approximately three cents for each dollar they had invested in the airline. Similarly, during the late 1980s and early 1990s, Lee Iacocca decided to move much
of Chrysler's production operation overseas (primarily to Mexico and the Far
East). These steps cost thousands of autoworkers their jobs, but they also increased Chrysler's profits (or, initially, reduced its losses) and the value of its
stock. Iacocca was rewarded with multimillion-dollar annual performance
bonuses and one of the largest retirement bonuses in American history. Iacocca
could have taken a different approach to revitalizing Chrysler—reducing stock
dividends and reinvesting the funds in improved production technologies, as
many German automakers have done, or reducing the massive gap between

worker income and managerial salaries as Japanese automakers have done, or decentralizing the structure of the organization, or reducing overhead by restraining managerial salaries. There is little evidence that Chrysler's management (or the management of virtually any large U.S. organization) ever seriously considered these approaches.

In sum, actions that may be in management's self-interest may violate the short- and long-term interests of workers and owners and vice versa. Because workers and owners have little influence on the everyday operations of an organization, it is the interests of the managers that take precedence (critical theorists use the term "privileged").

However, the conflicting nature of these interests often are disguised by the discourse of modern organizations, a process that Jurgen Habermas has labeled "**systematically distorted communication**."[51] One way of disguising the contradictions is to treat one set of interests (for example, management's) as everyone's interests. Installing a computerized system for monitoring employees' work usually is justified in terms of its increased efficiency and the firm's enhanced ability to compete. Efficiency and increased competitiveness are presented as being in everyone's interests. In the long run they may or may not be, depending on a large number of economic considerations, but in the short term the new system increases management's control, increases workers' stress, and has no guaranteed effects on either workers' or owners' incomes because the savings may not be passed on to either group.

Another way of disguising the contradictions is to simply deny that they exist.[52] Simple forms of denial include *refusing to discuss a topic* or to deny that one's actions meant what they seemed to mean ("Of course I wasn't trying to get rid of you. I just wanted you to have the excitement of working in Mogadishu."). A more complicated mode of denial is **pacification**, in which legitimate conflicts are treated as unimportant, "mere communication breakdowns," or irresolvable differences, as when organizational discourse defines an organization as a "team" or "family" and believes that the terms means that "we're all in it together." In fact, critical theory responses suggest that many systems of decentralization, participatory decision-making, and all symbolic forms discussed in this chapter—rituals, myths, stories, and metaphors—disguise the contradictory interests of workers, managers, and owners.

Another way of disguising contradictory interests is **disqualification** of some interest groups, as in "This is a managerial problem, and you just don't have the information necessary to understand it fully."[53] Recall that part of the traditional strategy and the legacy of scientific management was the assumption that *only* managers possess the expertise and information needed to make major decisions. Another is *naturalization* and *neutralization* of policies, procedures, and other managerial decisions (recall the discussion of "hegemony" in Chapter 1). If events are defined as inevitable or unavoidable (layoffs during recessions, for example) or value-neutral ("We have to base our personnel decisions on the data, not on how we feel.") they cannot be discussed, much less challenged.[54] Whatever the specific technique, the effect of organizational discourse is to disguise or redefine the contradictory interests of workers, managers, and owners.

The second key concept of the radical critique is that systems of "empowerment," including participatory decision-making, have to have certain characteristics if they are to be legitimate. First, participation must be valued for its own sake, as a means of ensuring that the legitimate interests of all organizational groups are represented in decisions. This means that it cannot be justified because it increases organizational efficiency, because efficiency inherently fulfills the interests of managers and owners more than workers (for example, efficiency and job security for workers usually are contradictory).[55] And it must provide equal opportunities actually communicating. This sounds simple, as when women's consciousness-raising groups use "talking sticks" (an object that someone must be holding in order to be allowed to speak) to ensure that all members get an equal number of speaking turns. Legitimate empowerment programs also ensure equal opportunities to influence the group's decisions. But legitimate empowerment also involves ensuring that all participants have realistic access to the same relevant information (instead of management being able to withhold key data from owners and workers or being able to put that data in a form that the other groups cannot understand), that all conceptions of truth be accepted by the group (for example, single parents' reports of their own frustrating experiences finding adequate child care are respected as much as the results of management's surveys on child-care issues), and that conflicts within the group will not be resolved through appeals to some external "higher" authority (as in "It's a great idea, but the CEO will never buy it").

As implemented in modern organizations, radical critics argue, "empowerment" programs inevitably obscure conflicting interests and legitimate participation rarely is possible.[56] As long as participatory systems are used within traditional organizational designs, managerial interests will be privileged. The existence of the hierarchy and the right of management to make final decisions—including how, when, where, over what issues, and with what outcomes participation will occur—will be treated as natural and neutral and managerial interests will be privileged.[57] When workers are trained to participate in decision-making (or quality-control programs or quality of working life groups), they are taught to make decisions on criteria (like efficiency) and through processes that favor the interests of management.[58] When managers use supportive communication in order to increase morale and productivity and reduce absenteeism and turnover, they fulfill their own interests more than those of workers or owners. When management determines what issues will be examined by participatory groups, what range of solutions they may choose among, and what information will be made available to them, they maintain unequal levels of power in the guise of power sharing. But the discourse surrounding human relations strategies presents them as processes of meeting all groups' interests within a context of legitimate participation.

In the next chapter, Marshall Scott Poole will examine a number of new strategies of organizing that currently are emerging in response to a number of social and economic changes. The impetus for these strategies has been the rapid growth of new electronic technologies and the ways in which they influence and are influenced by the design and operation of organizations.

NOTES

[1] There are exceptions to this generalization, of course. Some traditional strategies included group-based reward systems (one of the most effective of these was called a "Scanlon Plan") and some versions of relational strategies examine work groups and group pressures.

[2] Sociologists long have debated the relationship between the terms "society" and "culture" (see, for instance, Joseph Gusfield, *Community* [New York: Harper & Row, 1975])), with the former referring to the "structural" aspects of a group of people (how is the economy organized, who controls capital, and so on) and the latter referring to "softer" factors like beliefs and values. I will treat them together because I do not believe that "structural" factors exist without a supporting pattern of beliefs and values or that beliefs and values develop in isolation of the "structural" aspects of a social situation. I chose to use the term "society" instead of "culture" in Chapter 1 solely because I anticipated using the phrase "organizational culture" in this chapter and did not want to confuse the two different senses of the term.

[3] One of the most popular of these early organizational culture perspectives was offered by William Ouchi and A. Jaeger. They argued that, as I noted in Chapter 1, U.S. workers no longer are involved in meaningful informal organizations. Consequently, U.S. firms must provide a sense of community for them at work, while maintaining the level of individuality traditionally valued in U.S. society (see "Type Z Organization," *Academy of Management Review, 3* [1978]: 305–314 and William Ouchi, *Theory Z* [Reading, MA: Addison-Wesley, 1981]). For an extended analysis of the development of the culture strategy see Eric Eisenberg and Patti Riley, "Organizational Culture," in L. Putnam and F. Jablin (Eds.), *The New Handbook of Organizational Communication* (Thousand Oaks, CA: Sage, 1997).

[4] The distinctions that I will make in this section are treated at length in Debra Meyerson and Joanne Martin, "Cultural Change: An Integration of Three Different Views," *Journal of Management Studies, 24* (1987): 623–647; Peter Frost, et al. (Eds.), *Reframing Organizational Culture,* Newbury Park, CA: Sage, 1991 and Joanne Martin, *Cultures in Organizations: Three Perspectives,* New York: Oxford University Press, 1992.

[5] Karl Weick has argued that what I will call "unobtrusive control" and decentralization are necessary to one another ("Organizational Culture and High Reliability," *California Management Review, 29* (1987): 112–127).

[6] The primary proponents of this view were Tom Peters and Robert Waterman, *In Search of Excellence* (New York: Harper & Row, 1982); Terrance Deal and Alan Kennedy *Corporate Cultures* (Reading, MA: Addison-Wesley, 1982); William Ouchi, *Theory Z,* and Pascale and Athos, *The Art of Japanese Management. In Search of Excellence* was the most popular book on organizations ever published (selling more than 5 million copies in its first three years). It generated a series of follow-up books, videotapes, and consulting programs and by 1987, three years after its publication, Peters' consulting firm was grossing about $3.5 million per year.

[7] In a sequel, Peters and Nancy Austin reduced the eight characteristics to four—*taking care of customers* (courtesy, responsiveness, and respect), constantly *supporting and rewarding innovation, faith in people,* and *leadership* (*A Passion for Excellence* [New York: Random House, 1985]).

[8] The popularity of the perspective is explained in Charles Conrad, "Review of *A Passion for Excellence,*" *Administrative Science Quarterly, 30* (1985): 426–429. The dominance of the perspective is examined by Stephen Barley, G.W. Meyer, and Debra Gash, "Cultures of Culture," *Administrative Science Quarterly, 33* (1988): 24–60. Important critiques include Daniel Carroll, "A Disappointing Search for Excellence," *Harvard Business Review* (December, 1983); "Excellence Spawns a Too-Similar Sequel," *Business Week* (June 3, 1985); "Who's Excellent Now?"

Business Week (November 5, 1984); Michael Hitt and R. Duane Ireland, "Peters and Waterman Revisited," *Academy of Management Executive, 1* (1987): 91–98; Joseph Byrnes, "Review of *In Search of Excellence*," *Personnel Administrator, 28* (1983): 14–18; Walter Kiechel, "Management Winners," *Fortune* (November 29, 1982): 159–160; Caren Siehl and Joanne Martin, "Organizational Culture: A Key to Financial Performance," in *Organizational Climate and Cultures,* B. Schneider, ed. (San Francisco: Jossey-Bass, 1990).

[9] See, for example, David Knights and Hugh Willmott, "Organizational Culture as Management Strategy: A Critique and Illustration from the Financial Service Industries," *International Studies of Management and Organization, 17* (1987): 40–63. Critics also rejected the idea that having a "strong culture" predicts organizational effectiveness. They argued that the conclusion was based on research that is questionable in methods and in the inferences that are drawn. They noted that advocates of the perspective never have been able to demonstrate (or even explain) that the factors they have isolated actually cause any positive outcomes. They observed that over a ten-year period the "excellent" firms have not been any more effective (profitable) than a randomly selected group of major U.S. organizations. (The fact that a majority of the "excellent" firms they identified are now out of business or undergoing serious problems seems to support this argument.) In addition, while the "excellence" factors are crucial to some organizations and/or parts of organizations, they are moderately important to others, and trivial for others. Furthermore, even if cultures can be easily managed (and they probably cannot be), and even if all employees can be persuaded to believe upper management's statements about the values of the organization and interpret those messages as management desires (and this is unlikely), culture management cannot provide a sustained competitive advantage. If the keys to "strong cultures" can be isolated and created by one group of managers (with or without the aid of one of the many consultants who came to be called "culture vultures"), they can be isolated and created by all competent teams of managers. Although all organizations thus could become more effective, no one would be any more effective than the others (see Jay Barney, "Organizational Culture: Can It Be a Source of Sustained Competitive Advantage?" *Academy of Management Review, 11* (1986): 656–665).

[10] Alan Wilkins, *Managing Corporate Character* (San Francisco: Jossey-Bass, 1989).

[11] These ideas are developed at length in *Organizational Culture,* Peter Frost, et al., eds. (Beverly Hills, CA: Sage, 1985) and in Frost, et al., *Reframing.*

[12] People often believe that when others communicate productively it is because they understand their organization's culture. Although it sometimes is true that employees' actions reveal a conscious awareness of their culture, this is not always the case. We often act in certain ways without being aware of it or without consciously recognizing that our actions are consistent with and guided by the expectations of our culture.

[13] Richard C. Palmer, *Hermeneutics* (Evanston, IL: Northwestern University Press, 1979).

[14] See Thomas Dandridge in Frost, et al.

[15] Sometimes distinct organizational subcultures are created intentionally, as when Apple created a separate team to develop the Macintosh and isolated it from the rest of the organization. But in most cases organizational subcultures emerge naturally.

[16] J.K. Benson, "Organizations: A Dialectical View," *Administrative Science Quarterly, 22* (1977): 1–21. For examples of subculture combinations, see Michael Rosen, "Breakfast at Spiro's," *Journal of Management, 11* (1985): 31–48; and Ed Young, "On the Naming of the Rose," *Organization Studies, 10* (1989): 187–206 and Leslie Baxter, " 'Talking Things Through' and 'Putting It In Writing'," *Journal of Applied Communication Research, 21* (1994): 313–328.

[17] Jack Meredith, *Project Management* (New York: John Wiley & Sons, 1989).

[18] William Ouchi and Alan Wilkins, "Efficient Cultures," *Administrative Science Quarterly, 28* (1983): 468–481; Kathleen Gregory, "Native-view Paradigms," *Administrative Science Quarterly, 28* (1983): 360–372.

[19] Kathleen Gregory. However, subcultural differences can lead to serious communication breakdowns and conflicts (see Chapter 11).

[20] For an excellent analysis of the development of control systems in Western organizations, see Richard Edwards, *Contested Terrain* (New York: Basic Books, 1978) and "The Social Relations of Production at the Point of production," in M. Zey-Farrell and M. Aiken (eds.), *Complex Organizations: Critical Perspectives* (Glenview, IL: Scott Foresman, 1981). The ideas that I will present in this section are similar to those of Richard D'Andrade ("Cultural Meaning Systems," in

R. Schweder & R. LeVine, eds., *Culture Theory* [Cambridge: Cambridge University Press, 1984]) and Mats Alvesson, "Cultural-Ideological Modes of Management Control: A Theory and a Case Study of a Professional Service Company," in Stanley Deetz (ed.), *Communication Yearbook 16* (Newbury Park, CA: Sage, 1994, pp. 3–42).

[21] These ideas are developed at length in a number of articles by George Cheney and Phillip Tompkins. See, for example, "Communication and Unobtrusive Control in Contemporary Organizations," in Robert McPhee and P. Tompkins (eds.), *Organizational Communication: Traditional Themes and New Directions* (Beverly Hills, CA: Sage, 1985, pp. 179–210).

[22] Stephen Coffman has provided an excellent example of the ways in which metaphors articulate the underlying assumptions of different employees ("Staff Problems with Geriatric Care in Two Types of Health Care Organizations," *Journal of Applied Communication Research, 20* (1992): 292–307.

[23] Louis Pondy, "The Role of Metaphors and Myths in the Organization and the Facilitation of Change," and Joanne Martin and Melanie Powers, "Truth or Corporate Propaganda: The Value of a Good War Story," in Pondy, et al., *Culture*.

[24] Kenwyn Smith and Valerie Simmons ("The Rumpelstiltskin Organization," *Administrative Science Quarterly, 28* [1983]: 377–392)

[25] A number of sources have investigated the relationship between stories, organizational and otherwise, and cultures. A treatment of the relationship between society and stories that has become popular among communication scholars was presented by Walter Fisher, "Narration as a Human Communication Paradigm," *Communication Monographs, 51* (1984): 1–22; an extended treatment of the relationship between stories and societal control is available in Dennis Mumby (ed)., *Narrative and Social Control: Critical Perspectives* (Newbury Park, CA: Sage, 1993). For extended analyses of organizational stories, see Harrison Trice and Janice Beyer, *The Cultures of Work Organizations* (Englewood Cliffs, NJ: Prentice-Hall, 1993); Mary Helen Brown, "Defining Stories in Organizations," in James Anderson (ed.), *Communication Yearbook 12* (Beverly Hills, CA: Sage, 1989); Alan Wilkins, "The Creation of Company Stories," *Human Resource Management, 23* (1984): 41–60 and "Organizational Stories as Symbols Which Control the Organization," in Pondy, et al., eds., *Culture;* and Joanne Martin, Marsha Feldman, Mary Hatch, and Sim Sitkin, "The Uniqueness Paradox in Organizational Stories," *Administrative Science Quarterly, 28* (1983): 438–453.

[26] Brown. For an extended distinction between lists and stories, see Larry Browning, "Lists and Stories in Organizational Communication," *Communication Theory, 2* (1992): 281–302. Also see Karl Weick and Larry Browning, "Argument and Narration in Organizational Communication," *Journal of Management, 12* (1986): 243–259; Larry Browning, J.T. Korinek, and M. Cooper, "Downplaying Formal Rules Negotiation in a Military Cultural System," paper presented at the International Communication Association Convention, Philadelphia, May 1979.

[27] Northrop Frye, *Anatomy of Criticism* (Princeton, NJ: Princeton University Press, 1957).

[28] Fisher.

[29] Brown.

[30] The distinction between stories and storytelling is developed at length in Michael Pacanowsky and Nick O'Donnell-Trujillo, "Performance," and in Michael Pacanowsky, "Creating and Narrating Organizational Realities," in *Rethinking Communication,* vol. 2, Brenda Dervin, et al., eds. (Beverly Hills, CA: Sage, 1989). Joachim Knuf has drawn similar conclusions about other symbolic forms, including ritual, a topic that will be discussed later in this chapter and in Chapter 9 ("'Ritual' in Organizational Culture Theory," in Stanley Deetz (ed.), *Communication Yearbook 16* (Newbury Park, CA: Sage, 1994, pp. 61–103).

[31] See David Boje, "The Storytelling Organization," *Administrative Science Quarterly, 36* (1991): 106–126.

[32] Thomas Hollihan and Patricia Riley, "The Rhetorical Power of a Compelling Story," *Communication Quarterly, 35* (1987), 15. The following section is based on this essay.

[33] For a thorough summary of research on organizational rituals and ceremonies, see Trice and Beyer, *Cultures ,* and "Studying Organizational Cultures Through Rites and Ceremonials," *Academy of Management Review, 9* (1984): 653–669. For analyses of the emotional power of ritual as performance, see Waldron, "Emotion" and Knuf, "Ritual".

[34] Cited in Stanley Harris and Robert Sutton, "Functions of Parting Ceremonies in Dying Organizations," *Academy of Management Journal, 29* (1986): 5–30.

[35] Kenneth Burke, *Attitudes Toward History* (Berkeley: University of California Press, 1939).

[36] Betty Webber Conrad, "The Moving Experience," *The Waiting Room, 2* (1985): 12–18.

[37] Harris and Sutton.

[38] See "Real Feelings: Emotional Expression and Organizational Culture," in L.L. Cummings & B.M. Staw, eds. *Research in Organizational Behavior,* vol. 11 (Greenwich, CT: JAI, 1989, pp. 43–104) and Waldron.

[39] Arlie Hochschild, "Emotion Work, Feeling Rules, and Social Structure," *American Journal of Sociology, 85* (1979): 45–56; and *The Managed Heart* (Berkeley: University of California Press, 1983).

[40] Social service workers often respond to the stresses of their work in this way, a dynamic that has been labeled "burnout" (see Christina Maslach, *Burnout, the Cost of Caring* [Englewood Cliffs, NJ: Prentice-Hall, 1982]).

[41] For a summary, see Barnard Bass and B.J. Avoilo, "Transformational Leadership: A Response to Critiques," in Martin Chemers and R. Ayman (eds.), *Leadership Theory and Research: Perspectives and Directions* (San Diego, CA: Academic Press, 1993, pp. 49–80) and Trice and Beyer, *Cultures.*

[42] See M.Z. Hackman and C.E. Johnson, *Leadership: A Communication Perspective* (Prospect Heights, IL: Waveland Press, 1991) and J.M. Kouzes and B.Z. Posner, *The Leadership Challenge: How to Get Extraordinary Things Done in Organizations.* (San Francisco: Jossey-Bass, 1987); and C. Pavitt, G.G. Whitchurch, H. McGlurg, and N. Peterson, "Melding the Objective and Subjective Sides of Leadership: Communication and Social Judgements in Decision-Making Groups," *Communication Monographs, 62* (1995): 243–264.

[43] Warren Bennis, Jagdish Parikh, and Ronnie Lessem, *Beyond Leadership: Balancing Economics, Ethics, and Ecology* (Cambridge, MA: Basil Blackwell, 1994, p. 58).

[44] Peter Senge, *The Fifth Discipline* (New York: Doubleday, 1990).

[45] The example and the analysis of different kinds of goals is from Gail Fairhurst and Robert Sarr, *The Art of Framing: Managing the Language of Leadership* (San Francisco: Jossey-Bass, 1996) who based their analysis on Steve Wilson and Linda Putnam, "Interaction Goals in Negotiation," in James Anderson (ed.), *Communication Yearbook 13* (Newbury Park, CA: Sage, 1990) and Pamela Hellman, "Her Push for Prevention Keeps Kids Out of ER," *Sunday Examiner and Chronicle Parade Magazine,* April 19, 1995, pp. 8–10. An excellent discussion of the need for visions/goals to be adaptive and flexible is available in Michael Hitt, B. W. Keats, H.F. Harback, and R.D. Nixon, "Rightsizing: Building and Maintaining Strategic Leadership and Long-Term Competitiveness," *Organizational Dynamics, 23* (1994): 18–32.

[46] See Robert Pascale and A.G. Athos, *The Art of Japanese Management* (New York: Warner, 1981) and Eric Eisenberg, "Ambiguity as Strategy in Organizational Communication," *Communication Monographs, 51* (1984): 227–242. Notions of rationality as a societal construction are examined at length in Chapter 9.

[47] For an extended analysis of the Gore company, see Michael Pacanowsky, "Communication in the Empowering Organization," and Terrance Albrecht, "Communication and Personal Control in Empowering Organizations," in James Anderson (Ed.), *Communication Yearbook 11,* (Beverly Hills, CA: Sage, 1987).

[48] Don Phillips, *Houston Chronicle,* July 12, 1996, 6A.

[49] Stan Deetz and Dennis Mumby have explained how difficult it is to define the term "interests" in "Power, Discourse and the Workplace," in *Communication Yearbook 13,* James Anderson, ed. (Beverly Hills, CA: Sage, 1990). In this chapter I define "interests" in terms of organizational roles—owners, managers, and workers—while recognizing that these roles are not wholly distinct. Because of space limitations I do not provide a summary of the development of critical theory or the various perspectives included in that framework. Stanley Deetz, *Democracy in an Age of Corporate Colonization* (Albany, NY: SUNY Press, 1991), and Dennis Mumby, *Communication and Power in Organizations* (Norwood, NJ: Ablex, 1988), provide summaries of the key concepts. The best analysis of the development of critical theory and its many versions is David Held, *Introduction to Critical Theory* (London: Hutchinson, 1980). A very recent, and somewhat advanced, application to organizations is Mats Alvesson and Hugh Wilmott, eds. *Critical Management Studies* (Newbury Park, CA: Sage, 1992).

[50] See Deetz, *Democracy,* especially Chapter 9.

[51] See *Knowledge and Human Interests* (London: Heinemann Educational Books, 1972) and *Communication and the Evolution of Society* (London: Heinemann Educational Books, 1979).

[52] See John Forester, *Planning in the Face of Power* (Berkeley: University of California Press, 1989); Deetz, *Democracy*, Chapter 7; and Mumby, *Power*, especially Chapter 4. The foundation of the ideas that I present in this section is Goran Therborn, *The Ideology of Power and the Power of Ideology* (London: Verso, 1980). A fine summary of issues regarding the concept of ideology is available in Astrid Kersten, "Culture, Control, and the Labor Process," in Stanley Deetz (ed.), *Communication Yearbook 16* (Newbury Park, CA: Sage, 1993, pp. 54–60).

[53] Richard Jehensen, "Effectiveness, Expertise, and Excellence as Ideological Fictions," *Human Studies, 7* (1984): 3–21.

[54] For analyses of how seemingly objective organizational "data" are manipulated symbolically to privilege management's interests, see S. Ansari and K. Euske, "Rational, Rationalizing, and Reifying Uses of Accounting Data in Organizations," *Accounting, Organizations, and Society, 12* (1987): 549–570 and David Sless, "Forms of Control," *Australian Journal of Communication, 14* (1988): 57–69.

[55] Deetz, *Democracy*.

[56] This critique applies regardless of the strategy of organizing that is in place. Even cultural strategies that on the surface seem to be highly empowering may not be (see, for example, Mats Alvesson, "Organizations, Culture and Ideology," *International Studies of Management and Organization, 17* [1987]: 4–18 and *Organization Theory and Technocratic Consciousness* [New York: Walter de Gruyter, 1987]).

[57] B. Abrahamsson, *Bureaucracy or Participation* (Beverly Hills, CA: Sage, 1977); Charles Perrow, *Complex Organizations*, 3rd ed. (New York: Random House, 1986); Mumby.

[58] Stewart Clegg, *Power, Rule and Domination* (London: Routledge and Kegan Paul, 1975); Jeffrey Pfeffer, *Power in Organizations* (Marshfield, MA: Pitman, 1981). This may be true even when workers believe they are acting in their own interests, as when the machinists in the Foodcom case sabotaged the QWL program. In maintaining their own power over the other workers they supported management's interests in making the program fail.

Chapter 5

COMMUNICATION TECHNOLOGY AND NEW STRATEGIES OF ORGANIZING

The possibilities are endless.
—ADVERTISING SLOGAN
FROM THE 1960S

To err is human; to really foul things up requires a computer.
—PROVERB FROM THE 1970S

CENTRAL THEMES

- How effective an organization's structure and communication system are depends on the nature of the organization's work, its interdependencies with other organizations, and its environment.
- Contingency design theory attempts to explain which structures are most effective under various conditions and gives advice on how to design an effective organizational communication system.
- Over the past fifty years, there has been a transition from a production economy based on physical production of goods in factories to a knowledge society, in which most value is added through information and knowledge-related activities.
- The knowledge society gives rise to different types of organizations than did the production economy, and to two new types of workers, knowledge workers and information workers.
- Along with the knowledge society came an increased rate of change in the growth of knowledge and in markets, products, and competition, much of it spurred by the globalization of the economy.
- Information technology offers one way of dealing with the complexity of the knowledge society and its increased rate.
- Information technology has evolved from centralized computing, in which information processing was carried out in large mainframe computers, to today's emphasis on distributed, decentralized computing.

- Five types of information technology are important in today's organization: electronic data processing, management information systems, decision support systems, office automation, and expert systems.
- The increased complexity and required speed of response has led organizations to emphasize flatter structures with more lateral links; a number of different types of integrating mechanisms have been developed to coordinate these organizations.
- Information technology and integrating mechanisms have given rise to novel organizational arrangements, including the dynamic network, the virtual organization, and telework.
- Information technology opens up a wide variety of communication options to organizational members; in choosing among them, they should consider information richness, fit with the organization's culture, and symbolic value of the medium.

KEY TERMS

Knowledge society	Electronic calendaring
Staff qualifications	Audio conferencing
Interorganizational relationships	Video conferencing
Technology	Computer conferencing
Routine technology	Videotex
Nonroutine technology	Imaging
Communication adequacy	Desktop publishing
Pooled interdependence	Expert systems
Sequential interdependence	Networked computing
Reciprocal interdependence	Distributed computing
Environmental complexity	Centralized computing
Environmental stability	Informate
Integrating roles	Liaison roles
Knowledge work	Task forces
Information work	Integrating teams
Information technology	Managerial linking roles
Electronic data processing	Dual authority systems
Accounting information systems	Matrix
Management information systems	Dynamic networks
Decision support systems	Virtual organizations
Group decision support systems	Telework
Office automation	Voice mail
Electronic mail	

One goal that both researchers and practitioners share is to develop ever more general theories. Describing the traditional and relational strategies of organizing raised questions about how they are interrelated. The simplest answer is that they are diametrically opposed, and that the cultural strategy represented yet a third viewpoint opposed to the first two. But simple answers often are misleading. As the philosopher Alfred North Whitehead cautioned, "Seek simplicity, and distrust it." The caution proved true in this case: Much research and theory suggests that the relationship between the traditional and relational strategies was more complicated than simple opposition. Some researchers argued that the two strategies were actually simply different ways of organizing and that each worked better under different conditions. Indeed, when it came to structuring an organization, combinations of the two strategies and even additional approaches were identified. This perspective was codified in what has come to be known as *contingency design theory.* Contingency design theory helps to explain why some organizational systems are more effective than others. It also gives very useful advice about the design of organizational structures and communication systems.

But no sooner had contingency design theory been worked out than the world began to change. The information technology revolution picked up steam in the late 1960s and has enjoyed explosive growth since. It has made possible many new organizational forms undreamed of by the older theorists. And new organizations still are needed, because beginning in the 1960s, fundamental changes in society and economy also began to show themselves. Most advanced societies have evolved into **knowledge societies** in which the most important work involves the generation and application of abstract knowledge, such as scientific theory or law. Knowledge societies operate by a very different set of rules than did the production societies in which the bureaucratic and relational organizing strategies developed. The increased pace of change in technology and markets and the globalization of the economy add further uncertainty to the situation. Driven by these circumstances, and facilitated by information technology, new types of organizations are evolving. They have been called dynamic networks, federated organizations, "cloverleaf" forms, virtual organizations, and post-bureaucracies. Most of these forms have not been described in definitive terms at this time, in part because their mechanics are still being worked out by the organizations that use them. It is truly a time of change in organizational communication systems. What this change adds up to, and whether it is not really change, but just old organizations dressed up in new clothes, is not yet clear.

This chapter begins by explaining contingency design theory and its usefulness in understanding organizational communication. Then it turns to the advent of the knowledge society and the ways in which increased rates of technological and environmental innovations pose new problems for organizations. Information technology has been the driving force behind the transformation of organizations in response to these currents. I will discuss various types of information technology, the new organizational forms it makes possible, and the effects that information technology has on organizations and their members. One of the key premises of systems theory (recall Chapter 1), the need for organizations to adapt, plays a very prominent role in this chapter.

DESIGNING EFFECTIVE ORGANIZATIONAL COMMUNICATION SYSTEMS: CONTINGENCY DESIGN THEORY

So what is the best way to set up an organization? As Chapters 2, 3, and 4 suggest, it depends. Weber, Mayo, Likert and others who first described the bureaucratic and relational strategies thought they had found *the one best way* to organize. However, much research and practical experience has shown that they were mistaken. Under some conditions, the bureaucratic strategy works best, while under other conditions, the relational strategy is superior.

Contingency Design Theory

Viewing organizations as systems suggests that to survive they must adapt. Contingency design theory attempts to specify how organizations must adapt their structures in response to situational changes in order to be effective and viable.[1] These theories suggest that the nature of organizational communication and communication systems must change to "fit" prevailing conditions for the organization to survive and thrive.

Contingency design theory suggests that organizations may alter several features of their structures and processes in order to adapt. These include:

Formalization: As defined in Chapter 2, formalization is the degree to which the organization has well-defined roles, strict division of labor into relatively small tasks, and rules and procedures that apply to most activities. Bureaucratic structures are high in formalization. An organization lower in formalization would have more flexible role definitions, adjustment and redefinition of tasks, and few codified rules and procedures. The structures associated with the relational strategy are typically low in formalization.

Centralization: This refers to the degree to which control is centralized in management. As Chapter 2 noted, bureaucratic structures tend to be highly centralized. Power is more widely distributed in the relational strategy and they are therefore less centralized.

Staff Qualifications: This is defined as the degree to which workers and staff have to obtain specialized training or degrees to carry out their work effectively. Some organizations, such as engineering firms, require a highly trained staff with a great deal of experience to function. However, other organizations do not require many special qualifications. In these organizations, which include fast food restaurants and department stores, most employees are hired with minimal screening because the organization believes it can easily train them to do an adequate job.

Span of Control: This means the number of employees who report to a single manager or supervisor. Managers with wide spans of control supervise many employees, whereas those with narrower spans supervise fewer.

Narrow spans of control are important when managers must check for details, special problems, or errors. Wider spans of control are workable when there are not many exceptions and the work is pretty much the same all the time.

Communication and Coordination: Organizations may vary the frequency, formality, and medium of communication among members. The more coordination problems there are, the more frequent communication must be. In addition, coordination problems require less formal and more immediate communication contacts. While a preset form may be sufficient for routine communication, more direct and unregulated interaction is required to solve problems and deal with exceptional circumstances. And while routine communication can be handled through written media (memos, electronic mail), communication about problems, exceptional circumstances and nonroutine matters are more effectively dealt with through face-to-face discussion, telephone calls, and meetings.

Interorganizational Relationships: Organizations may also vary the degree to which they form and maintain stable relationships with other groups or organizations. Some organizations have well-defined boundaries and remain self-contained, while others form relationships with other organizations in the form of contracts, joint ventures, or partnerships.

Contingency Design Theory and Organizational Environments

Contingency design theory builds on the observations outlined in Chapter 2 about the organization–environment relationship. This relationship was first noted in the late 1950s by two English sociologists, Burns and Stalker.[2] They found that when conditions are stable, a well-planned, efficient organization, which is epitomized by the bureaucracy, will outperform all other types because it is the most efficient organization. Other types of organizations may do well for a while, but ultimately the bureaucracy will outrace them because it will produce the optimal results with the least input. It will have superior profitability and more funds to reinvest in improving its product or service. However, when the environment is unstable and turbulent, the bureaucracy is too slow to adapt because its formal structures, standard operating procedures, and centralized decision-making render it slow to recognize the need for change and inflexible about changing. The relational form, which features decentralized decision-making and informal structures, is much better at adapting.

Contingency design theory posits that organizations are most effective when they are designed to fit their situation. It offers both an explanation for why some organizations do better than others and guidelines for designing organizational structures and communication systems. To understand contingency design theory it is important to define its key concepts in greater detail. Research has identified three characteristics that are particularly important in determining organizational design: technology, interdependence between units, and the organizational environment.

Technology.   The first variable that has been shown to influence organizational design is **technology**. Technology is construed broadly as the tools, techniques, and actions used to transform organizational inputs into outputs.[3] This definition means that technology includes more than just machinery, computers, or chemicals; technology refers to the means by which the work of the organization is done. According to this way of thinking, a social service agency has a technology just as much as an automobile plant does. The social service agency's technology are the procedures followed for patient intake and record-keeping, the service procedures (for example, such things as client counseling or therapeutic methods), and procedures for discharge and billing. This technology enables the social service agency to serve its clients, which in turn ensures a flow of funds to the agency.

In general terms, technology varies along a continuum from **routine** to **nonroutine**.[4] A *routine* technology is defined by two characteristics: The process by which the work must be done is well understood and there are few unexpected problems or exceptions in the work. When a task is routine, it can be broken down into steps and programmed. In many cases routine tasks can be automated, reducing the organization's reliance on human labor. Examples of routine tasks are work in a fast food restaurant and on the assembly line. Fast food restaurants generally offer limited menus and the procedures for preparing the food are highly standardized. Machines often do the cooking, and workers follow carefully planned recipes and portion control formulas that ensure a consistent product and good returns for the franchise. Exceptions can be easily planned for in fast food restaurants. Even "having it your way" can be broken into a relatively limited set of ingredient variations and preparation steps and planned in advance. The worker's degree of discretion and control over the work is kept to a minimum in this case. Usually engineers, operations management specialists, and other experts analyze the work and determine how it should be done.

At the other end of the scale is the *nonroutine* case in which work that cannot be analyzed, because the procedures for doing it are not well understood, because there are many exceptional cases, and because human judgment and discretion must be applied to each case. As the old phrase goes, the work is more of an "art" than a "science" for low analyzable tasks. Because the work cannot be broken into steps or dissected into a limited number of operations, skilled workers are needed to exercise finely trained judgments in doing the work. Typically a lot of problem-solving is involved in nonroutine technologies. Doing strategic planning requires planners to draw on extensive know-how and background, but they also do not always understand exactly what is the right way to respond to the situation before them, because it is unique. In addition, planners do not always know what the situation will be like in the future. Hence they must improvise and project based on their own knowledge and experience.

Generally speaking, uncertainty increases as we move from routine to non-routine technologies. As a result, traditional organizations will be most effective for routine technologies while relational organizations will be most effective for nonroutine technologies. What about intermediate cases, those between the two ends of the continuum? In such cases there is less than perfect knowledge of how to do the work and more than a few exceptions; however, these intermediate cases do not have the extremely high degrees of uncertainty that nonroutine technologies are designed for. Examples of intermediate cases are clothing design and pattern making, specialty steel manufacturing, legal work, and the performing arts. A typical intermediate strategy is to develop a repertoire of methods or techniques that can be mastered and applied to different cases. The challenge is selecting and combining the right routines to get the job done properly. So the surgical team knows many different procedures (anesthesia, opening the patient, tying off blood vessels), and combines different sets of them in different ways, depending on the type of operation being done and the particular characteristics of the patient.

Organizational communication is quite different in organizations with routine and those with nonroutine technologies. The greater the uncertainty, the greater the need for direct, intensive communication and many adjustments. However, the more direct and intense communication is, the more costly it is in terms of time spent communicating and coming to understanding, the cost of adjustments in work and plans, and conflicts that may arise during discussions. For best results, a balance must be struck between communication needs and cost: The organization should enact the least costly communication system that can adequately meet its needs for communication and coordination. I will call this the criterion of **communication adequacy**. While most people report that they may prefer face-to-face discussions, managing work through this medium is not necessarily the most adequate route. If people need to exchange only standard information, such as an order for a meal, then placing the order through a more impersonal medium, such as a checklist or computer system, is more adequate because it conveys the same information with less communication costs (of course, the computer system is costly in its own right, but for high volumes of communication the cost per message comes out to be quite low).

For *routine* technologies, vertical, formal, written communication is most adequate. For highly analyzable tasks there is usually a wealth of documented information and statistical analysis concerning how best to do the work and how to handle problems. This can be put in formal manuals or work procedures that substitute for direct communication between workers or between workers and managers. Most direct communication is vertical for routine tasks, as managers give orders to and solve problems for subordinates. Low levels of task variety suggest that few exceptions that require discussion will occur and that instructions for handling those that do can be built into procedures manuals.

For *nonroutine* technologies uncertainty reaches very high levels. There is high variety and low analyzability, so each task must be approached with a great deal of direct, often unscheduled communication. Face-to-face consultations and long, intense meetings are often the only adequate form of communication to meet the needs of nonroutine work.

For intermediate cases, there is a need for higher levels of communication than routine organization allows for, but less than the nonroutine case. The lowest cost means of increasing communication beyond formal channels is the scheduled meeting, because this can be planned into the work. When more issues and problems arise and communication is needed with more frequency than scheduled meetings allow, then planned, direct horizontal communication between those involved is the most adequate method. Several methods for establishing these links are discussed later. These coordination modes are sufficient for most intermediate cases, which do not require the fully interactive relational form.

To sum up, depending on the nature of the technology employed in a unit, it will have different levels of uncertainty and different communication needs. To remain effective and viable, the organization must develop a communication system that is adequate for the demands placed on it. Assessing a unit's technology can help us understand why its communication is effective or not and what needs to be done to improve communication.

Interdependence.   Technology influences the communication systems of intact units. However, units do not always work in isolation. They are often interdependent with other units in that their work depends on inputs from other units or in that they produce something another unit needs to do its work. As a result interdependence is the second major variable that influences organizational design, and, in particular, the design of communication systems.

Three different types of interdependence can be distinguished[5]: pooled, sequential, and reciprocal. Each imposes different communication requirements on the organization. In the case of **pooled interdependence**, units have very low degrees of dependency. Work does not flow between units, but instead the units each work on their own product or services and the total output of the organization is the pooled work of the individual units. Franchise restaurants, such as Denny's or McDonald's, are good examples of pooled interdependence. Franchises in different locations do not need to coordinate with each other; each does its own work and contributes independently (more or less) to the return of the whole chain. Other organizations with pooled interdependence include personal tax return preparation services and independent long haul trucking firms.

Communication among units or people linked in pooled interdependence can be handled through standardization, the creation of rules, and formal written plans to ensure that each of the parallel units is adequately supplied and turns out work of adequate quality. These plans and rules serve as substitutes for communication and reduce the need for other forms of communication. Managers above the pooled units provide sufficient coordination to keep them operating smoothly, and vertical communication between managers and units is the final ingredient in an effective coordination system. Units with pooled interdependence do not require strong communication links with each other; hence they do not have to be located together or linked by telecommunications.

FIGURE 5–1

Three Types of Interdependence among Organizations or Units

Type of Interdependence	Communication Requirements
POOLED 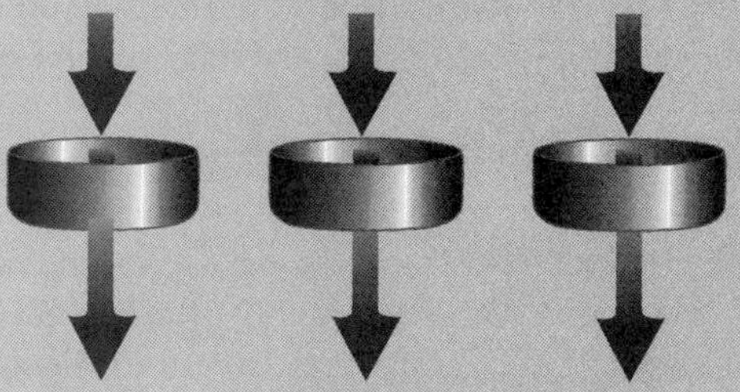 Work in Work Out	Low
SEQUENTIAL  Work in Work Out	Moderate
RECIPROCAL 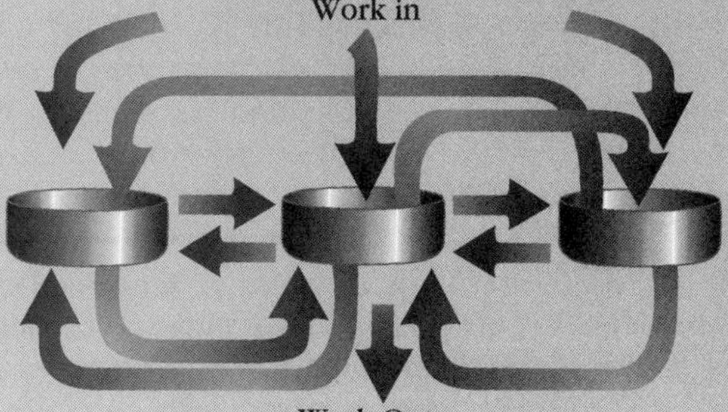 Work in Work Out	High

Sequential interdependence is the case when units are in a series and the output of one department is the input to another, the output of the second is the input to the third, and so on. In this case, how well each successive unit can perform depends on how well the previous units have done their work. Sequential interdependence increases coordination needs. Since one-way flow of materials, people, or information occurs, extensive planning and scheduling is required and feedback concerning problems is needed to ensure earlier steps have been done properly. The classic example of sequential interdependence is the assembly line. Other examples include college admissions offices, financial institutions, and unemployment offices.

As Figure 5-1 indicates, sequential interdependence requires higher levels of communication than pooled interdependence. Sequential interdependence is most adequately coordinated by active planning among participants, guided by management. Managers use vertical communication channels to do a great deal of the coordination work for sequential units. Under the auspices of management, representatives of these units also come together in scheduled meetings to form plans that will ensure smooth operation and minimize problems. Problems that arise are dealt with either by management or through horizontal communication among units.

The highest level of interdependence is **reciprocal interdependence**. In this case all units are involved together in the work; the outputs of each unit become the inputs of the others, and vice-versa. Units work together intensively when there is reciprocal interdependence, so a great deal of communication and coordination is needed. It is not always possible to predict beforehand the types of operations or problems that will occur under reciprocal interdependence, so it falls to the units to manage coordination through direct interaction as the need arises.

Reciprocal interdependence requires extensive coordination and is best handled through mutual adjustment of the units, though the modes of coordination employed for pooled and sequential cases, standardization and planning, can help as well. Coordination needs for reciprocal interdependence tend to arise "on the fly" and must be handled by horizontal communication via unscheduled meetings, face-to-face communication and electronic channels. While managers can help resolve coordination problems for reciprocally linked units, the units themselves are in the best position to actually suggest and try out solutions.

To sum up, at low levels of interdependence, substitutes for communication are sufficient; as interdependence increases plans, scheduled communication, and vertical communication are needed, until at high levels of interdependence horizontal, unscheduled and continuous communication is required. Organizations that want to coordinate their units adequately (sufficient communication with minimum cost) would do well to follow these guidelines.

Environment.   The third variable affecting organizational design and communication structures is the organization's *environment*. The notion of organizational environment has already been introduced in Chapter 1 and discussed in Chapter 2. In this section, I will define environment in more detail, and connect it to the design of organizations and their communication systems.

Literally, environment refers to everything outside the organization's boundaries. However, for purposes of analysis it can be defined as those institutions, organizations, groups, and people outside the organization that affect it. Environments are made up of many elements, including domestic and foreign competitors, customers and clients, government agencies and regulators, general economic conditions, technological developments relevant to the organization, financial resources, the labor market, raw materials suppliers, and the general culture surrounding the organization. Not all of these elements are similar or equally important for every organization; depending on its purpose and location, each organization has a particular mix of these elements as its environment.

Organizational environments can be described in terms of two basic dimensions, **complexity** and **stability**.[6] The *complexity* of an organization's environment refers to the number of elements in the environment that the organization has to deal with. An organization with a simple environment may have only a few elements to deal with, whereas one in a complex environment may deal with dozens or hundreds of elements. For example, a university library has a relatively simple environment; it has to deal with university administration, with student and faculty clientele, with publishers and other publication sources, and with other libraries. Many of the library's dealings with other agencies, such as the Occupational Safety and Health Administration and the Social Security Administration, are handled for it by the university administration, greatly reducing the complexity of its communication demands. On the other hand, a publishing house has to deal with a much more complex environment. It has to deal with stockholders or owners, with competing publishers, with authors, with customers, with an assortment of government agencies, with the financial institutions that provide its capital and operating monies, with unions, and with new technologies that compete with published books, magazines, and journals. Clearly their environments place different demands on university libraries and publishing houses.

The other dimension of organizational environment, *stability,* can be defined as the rate of change in the elements of the environment and their relationships. In some instances the environment remains relatively stable or changes in a predictable fashion. The organization can set itself up to deal with this stable situation and can manage needed adaptations fairly easily. Before deregulation, the telephone company had a stable environment. Its environment—regulators, suppliers, customers—was very predictable. Its monopoly status gave the phone company a guaranteed market and its relations with the regulators ensured it would make a reasonable profit. Change came mainly in the form of new technologies and services that the phone company developed itself. On the other end of the continuum are organizations whose environments are changing rapidly and continuously. These organizations must adapt constantly, and unpredictability is expected and factored into their operation. To deal with instability, these organizations develop special positions and units to monitor and to plan reactions to the environment. Firms in the information technology field offer a good example of life in an unstable environment. Driven by the fast pace of technological change and cutthroat international competition, they often change their products, their markets, and their own structures in order to survive and remain competitive.

Together the complexity and stability dimensions define four basic situations that can be arranged in order of increasing uncertainty. Simple, stable environments create relatively low levels of uncertainty. Organizations in these environments can focus mostly on optimizing how they deal with their situation in terms of setting up the most effective and efficient organizations. Examples of organizations in this cell include soft drink distribution companies and law offices. Complex, stable environments offer medium levels of uncertainty. As a result, the organization must evolve special units or procedures for dealing with uncertainty and anticipate a certain amount of change. Examples of organizations with complex, stable environments include universities and chemical companies.

Moderate to high uncertainty is experienced by organizations in unstable, simple environments. Whereas these environments are relatively simple, they undergo continuous change, and organizations must change to survive in them. Examples of organizations with unstable, simple environments include firms in the clothing industry and manufacturers of personal computers who supply the big retail outlets. Finally, the unstable, complex environment creates the highest level of uncertainty. In this environment, the organization must constantly plan for change and react to circumstances beyond its control. To do this, special positions and units are created to monitor and guide reactions to environmental change and a flexible organizational structure is needed to promote adaptation. Examples of organizations in this quadrant are software, telecommunications, and airline firms.

To be effective, organizations in stable environments should adopt the traditional strategy, while those in unstable environments should adopt the relational strategy.[7] The traditional form is the most effective when the organization can plan its structure and procedures carefully, because of its advantage in efficiency. However, when the environment is changing, the flatter, more interconnected relational form is preferred, because of its adaptability.

As environmental complexity increases, the number of departments in the organization generally increases. Organizations typically have units to deal with critical aspects of their environments, and the more of these there are, the greater the number of units there must be. The only bank in a small rural town has a relatively simple internal structure, officers to deal with regulators and make major decisions, accountants and auditors to keep track of the money, tellers to deal with customers, and janitors to keep the place clean. However, if another bank moves into town, the first one may add a marketing unit to compete for customers; if a large plant relocates to the town, the bank may add a commercial lending unit. As the number and interrelationship of environmental elements increases, the structure of the organization becomes more complex. In the same vein, organizations facing complex environments may add "boundary spanning" personnel who directly relate to various organizations or groups in the environment. The small-town bank, for example, may add a special position dedicated to contacting and serving the relocated plant.

As instability and complexity increase, organizations will become more complex and also have less stable structures. This increases the need for communication and **integrating roles** in the organization. Integrating roles are those that help different units coordinate their efforts and resolve actual and potential conflicts. Organizations with high levels of instability and complexity in particular will have many integrating roles.

Interrelationships Among the Variables.   Each of the three variables affects somewhat different features of organizations and their communication systems. Technology influences the communication system within units, interdependence the communication between units within the organization, and environment the communication system that crosses the boundaries of the organization. If we can assess the values of these variables for a given organization, we can know what an effective communication system should be like. Contingency theory can also help pinpoint possible problems in an organization's communication system and suggest ways in which it can be made more effective.

These variables also suggest a key problem: What if the variables are inconsistent with each other? An organization might, for example, have a nonroutine technology, but confront a simple, stable environment. The technology suggests that the relational strategy should be used, but its environment suggests the traditional strategy. Two possible outcomes have been suggested for organizations in this situation. First, some scholars suggest that the organization should adopt the most complex organization indicated by the three variables. At the cost of some inefficiency, the organization would be able to deal with its toughest challenge. Second, other scholars suggest that cases when the variables are inconsistent represent instances when the organization must "suboptimize" or underperform, because it is faced with contradictions.

The Limits of Contingency Theory.   Contingency theory was developed largely between 1960 and 1985. Beginning in the early 1980s, the world economy began undergoing major transformations that have introduced new challenges for organizations. Part of this change has been the transformation of many of the more developed societies into what Peter Drucker has termed "knowledge societies." With this transformation—facilitated by the explosive advances in information technology—have come new organizational imperatives and forms that stretch the bounds of traditional contingency design theory. The insights and advice contingency theory yields are still valid and useful, but they may not apply to some of the new organizations currently evolving.

CASE STUDY:
STEELING AWAY INTO A DIFFERENT STRUCTURE*

From the days of Andrew Carnegie and the other steel barons to the late 1960s, the steel industry was dominated by large, vertically integrated companies. The industry existed in a stable environment and the rate of technological advance was steady and gradual. If steel manufacturers could produce steel of good quality at a reasonable price, it could be sold.

Excelsior Steel is 125 years old, employs 2,200 and makes 250,000 tons of steel a year. Located in Northern Indiana, it is housed in a huge plant that consolidated all operations under one roof. Excelsior had a centralized, hierarchical structure. From its offices in downtown Gary, top management made decisions regarding the products Excelsior would manufacture and the level produced, with the aid of engineering. Separate departments handled manufacturing, marketing, metallurgy, field sales, and support for these units. Over the years top managers had forged close contacts with unions and the unions often worked with Excelsior to determine work rates and how the work should be done.

But all that changed starting in the late 1970s. The inflation of that period, coupled with the recession that followed it and fierce competition from Germany, Japan, and Brazil, brought Excelsior to the edge of bankruptcy. Excelsior was in danger of following many of the other steel giants that lined the southern edge of Lake Michigan out of the steel business. But Excelsior did not become another of those huge abandoned buildings north of Hammond, Indiana. Instead it took aggressive steps to solve problems.

After extensive diagnosis, Excelsior's managers found that their products were no longer keeping pace with the market, 60 percent of the firm's orders ran behind schedule, and profits were eaten up by materials, energy, and labor costs. In this more turbulent environment, the stable, hierarchical structure was not nimble enough. Moreover, technological advances had rendered much of Excelsior's plant outdated. Smaller furnaces equipped with the latest computer-assisted manufacturing devices could turn out many of Excelsior's products at much lower cost.

In consultation with outside experts and the union, management at Excelsior concocted a strategy to save the plant. The strategy hinged on shifting production to high-value products tailored for separate markets, while upgrading technology and research.

To get started, Excelsior set up three product task forces: sheet metal, special alloys, and open-die forgings. These task forces had representatives from

---

*This case is a composite of several cases describing companies both inside and outside the steel industry. It was inspired by Richard Daft, *Organization Theory and Design*, pp. 244–245.

(continued)

(continued from the previous page)

all departments involved in the products and their charge was to determine how each product could be produced in an independent product group. These task forces formed the basis for permanent integrating teams headed by product managers, each of which was responsible for all aspects of one of the three product areas, including sales. Each product area was also responsible for introducing new products and trimming products that were not successful.

Over time, there were so many orders for different types of specialty steel that the special alloys group subdivided into multiple project teams, instituting a "mini-matrix" structure within the group. Since it was important to keep the personnel in the special alloys groups trained in the latest technology and metallurgical research, the functional departments assumed increased importance. Functional managers, such as the manger of metallurgy, were responsible for keeping abreast of the latest technical developments and for keeping personnel trained. These personnel were then assigned to one or more projects, under the supervision of the project manager. This structure greatly enhanced communication both within and between specialties.

Excelsior installed electronic mail and voice mail when it implemented an order and inventory tracking system. These greatly increased the ability of Excelsior's employees to keep in touch with each other and increased the flow of ideas. Along with this Excelsior created a program to cultivate new ideas in which employees who had brainstorms could set up project teams to develop them, provided they could make a good case with the management team. From this program came several new product lines.

Implementation of this new structure was not painless. The company had to lay off workers because the three product lines did not require as many employees as Excelsior had in its heyday. By the end of the reorganization, Excelsior had only 1,300 employees; however, as production increased it hired back about 300 more. Many of the laid-off employees were replaced by technology. The union still hung on, but union and management were much less adversarial than in the past. Union and management worked together to reorganize the plant. Middle managers and foremen were especially confused by the transition to product units and the matrix-based structure. Not used to dealing with ambiguity, they initially resisted the increased number of meetings and negotiation required. Over time the most disgruntled managers and foremen retired, and the new structure, which emphasized horizontal and integrative links as well as vertical communication took over. Many of the managers who initially resisted this shift have found it to be a "growth" experience; they try to involve younger employees in new product development and problem-solving to develop them for the future.

Excelsior Steel is now back on track. Deliveries are on time better than 95 percent of the time. An average of twenty new products are introduced each

(continued)

(continued from the previous page)

year and profits are up. Market share has recovered as well. Excelsior employees gladly embrace their new motto, "Change or Die."

Discussion Questions
1. How did Excelsior respond to changes in its environment and technology? Which of the integrating methods did Excelsior use?
2. It is not clear that a company in Excelsior's position can ever stop changing. What are some of the disadvantages of continuous change? How could Excelsior minimize them?
3. What communication problems would you expect to occur as Excelsior moved from its old structure and culture to the new one?

THE RULES OF THE GAME ARE CHANGING

Peter Drucker, an astute observer of society and of organizations, wrote in 1994:

> No century in recorded history has experienced so many social transformations and such radical ones as the twentieth century. . . . In the developed free-market countries—which contain less than a fifth of the earth's population but are the model for the rest—work and work force, society and polity, are all, in the last decade of this century *qualitatively* and *quantitatively* different not only from what they were in the first years of this century, but also from what has existed at any other time in history: in their configurations, in their processes, in their problems, and in their structures.[8]

Some of the changes that have occurred include:

The transformation to a knowledge society. For most of this century and the last, the economy focused largely on production, on the laborious work in farm and factory that resulted in tangible products. Before World War I, farmers were the largest single group of workers in most countries. From 1920 to 1950 the farm population declined, though the production of food increased. In the 1950s, blue-collar workers accounted for 40 percent of the American workforce, representing the emphasis on factory production through manual labor of that period. However by 1990, blue-collar workers accounted for less than 20 percent of American workers and farmers less than 5 percent. The largest classes of workers in 1990 were those employed in what Drucker terms "knowledge work" and what has been called "information work."

Knowledge work involves creating and applying knowledge. Examples range from research scientists, engineers, attorneys, and financial analysts on the high end of the scale to teachers and X-ray technicians on the low end. Several things differentiate knowledge work from production work. Knowledge is intangible; working with knowledge involves performing abstract operations and results in more intangible products. Indeed, the only tangible outcome of much knowledge work is a document. However, despite its intangible nature, knowledge is the critical factor in the development of new products and the delivery of services such as legal and financial advice. Knowledge work organizes other forms of work, including production work. Knowledge work adds value to materials and to information, making them more useful or desirable or effective. An engineer's designs turn sand, copper, and aluminum into computer chips; an attorney's interpretive and negotiation skills create business partnerships from indecipherable (to any ordinary person) legal tomes and discussions among the parties involved. Knowledge-based work requires formal education (as opposed to apprenticeships or trade school) and an ability to acquire and apply abstract theoretical and analytical knowledge. It also requires a commitment to continuous learning; the knowledge worker's best and only asset is his or her expertise, which must be developed constantly through experience and further schooling.

Information work supports knowledge work. It involves gathering, entering, formatting, and processing information. Examples of information workers include clerical jobs, data entry, and telemarketing. These jobs are generally lower paying than the lowest rungs of knowledge work. They have been called "pink-collar" work, because they are often office positions staffed largely by women.

Together knowledge and information workers comprise about 40 percent of the workers in manufacturing firms and up to 80 percent in service organizations. They have become the largest class of workers in our society. This does not mean that production work is no longer important. It is, after all, what actually creates the products that knowledge workers design and that information workers catalog and sell. However, production work has become subsidiary to knowledge work in the new social arrangements. Advances depend far more on increases in knowledge than on production per se.

Increased instability, complexity, and turbulence of organizational environments. The growth of knowledge in recent years has resulted in an increased pace of change. Products now change much more quickly. Product life cycles, the time from introduction to the point at which the product is outmoded or dated, have grown increasingly shorter. The life cycle of a computer chip has decreased from five years to one. Even refrigerators have product life cycles of only three years now, as opposed to ten or more years ago. Services are also changing rapidly. The difference in the number of options for telephone or banking service now and ten years ago is striking.

The pace of change in products and services is driven in part by the rapidly increasing pace of technological advance. Technology—driven by advances in basic and applied research—is changing at an ever-increasing rate. To keep up with their competition organizations have to consider upgrading and updating their technology constantly. Rapid technological change makes the continuous learning characteristic of knowledge work particularly important.

Along with increased instability has come increased complexity of organizational environments. The globalization of the economy has introduced many new competitors into the United States and, in turn, made opportunities available in many more places than was previously envisioned by most U.S. organizations. The rapid change and growth in knowledge and technology has increased competition as well, as companies strive for advantage. The public, too, has become more aware of the impacts of organizations on the quality of life in general. As a result, organizations have to deal with increasing regulation, lawsuits from disgruntled parties, and consumer protests. As time goes by the environment of many organizations becomes more crowded with stakeholders who are more tightly interconnected.

The result of this is that many organizations must deal with extremely uncertain conditions. They employ nonroutine technologies, face high levels of interdependence, and environments that are unstable and highly complex. Traditionally, this has been the least well understood case in contingency theory. But it is becoming very common, and there is a need for better analysis of how organizations can deal with nonroutine, high interdependence, and highly turbulent situations.

In the "good old days" organizations would have had to throw up their hands and cope as best they could. However, now there is a wild card—information technology.[9] It opens many options to organizations that were previously simply too time-consuming or costly. The advent of information technology is also one of the enabling forces behind the emergence of the knowledge society. It facilitates both the management of existing knowledge and the growth of knowledge.

INFORMATION TECHNOLOGY: EXPANDING THE HORIZONS OF ORGANIZATIONAL STRATEGIES

Often **information technology** (IT) is regarded simply as another variable that influences organizational communication. However, I believe this is misleading, because in most U.S. organizations IT has become so much a part of everyday operations that it is an integral part of the organization. It plays just as important a role in the organization and its communication system as a face-to-face conversation or a telephone call.

I use the term information technology to refer both to computerized systems and to advanced telecommunication systems. Relevant computerized systems include those used to manage databases containing budget, order, or inventory information, to provide communication through electronic mail and conferencing, and to coordinate work processes. Advanced telecommunication systems include voice mail systems, fax technology, proprietary telephone systems (e.g. PBX systems), teleconferencing, and videoconferencing. All of these systems enable organizations to operate much more rapidly and (sometimes) adapt more quickly than they could if human communicators and traditional modes of communication (memos, letters, phone calls) made up the entire communication system. The speed, thoroughness, and reliability of IT in gathering and transmitting information has the potential to enable human links in the communication system to focus more on quality thinking, reasoning, and service, the job for which they are best suited.

There is much concern about the impacts of information technology on organizations and organizational communication. Some scholars argue that information technology does not really change organizations.[10] They perceive its main impacts to stem from increased speed, efficiency, and integration. Other scholars argue that information technologies alter the ways in which we communicate, and that this results in fundamental change in organizations.[11] I will return to this issue later.

A Quick Tour of Organizational Information Systems

When the first computers were developed in the late 1940s, many scientists predicted that the world would only need a dozen or so computing machines. They could not imagine the vast array of applications that would develop over the next fifty years and the ubiquitous spread of the computer throughout society. In the early years, computers were large boxes that had to be housed in special rooms to guard against overheating and other environmental stresses. The sale of "Big Iron"—large mainframe computers—catapulted IBM, Burroughs, Control Data, and other companies into the forefront of technological innovation. The first applications of mainframe computers centered around **electronic data processing**, the tabulation and analysis of large amounts of data into meaningful form.[12] Applications of computers to process data include their use by the Census Bureau, by scientists, and by organizations for accounting purposes. The term **accounting information system**, mentioned in Chapter 2, refers to the use of information systems to manage data such as sales figures, customer accounts, client records, and budgets for firms. These data management functions can be integrated so that, for example, changes in customer orders can trigger changes in sales figures, updates inventory records, and orders for stock to replenish depleted inventory. Integrated accounting information systems enable firms to coordinate their functions by managing the large amounts of data involved. Accounting information systems produce some meaningful information for the organization through summary analysis of the data.

Prior to 1964 most computers were constructed with vacuum tubes, which burned out easily and created a great deal of heat. In 1964 a new generation of mainframe computers based on silicon chips was introduced. They were promoted with the concept of **management information systems**, the idea that in addition to data processing, computers could be used to actively support the work of managers.[13] A management information system (MIS) is a system that makes information available to management to help it plan, control, and evaluate the activities of the organization. The information describes the organization or one of its major units in terms of what has happened in the past, present performance, and what is likely to happen in the future. MISs use various models to analyze organizational databases and develop reports for managerial use. For example, an MIS might perform an analysis of the financial potential of a division of an organization based on its sales and costs and on information about markets and competitors. The analysis would be based on a formal mathematical model built into the MIS (and would only be as valuable as the model was accurate). This report would help managers make decisions about whether the division should expand, and if so what financing to seek and on what terms. Various types of MISs include executive information systems (which create special analyses for top management), marketing information systems, manufacturing information systems, financial information systems, and human resource information systems.

The value of all these MISs depends on the accuracy of the data in the databases and the validity of the models used to analyze the data. If the models make unrealistic assumptions or do not take important factors into account, the advice they give will be poor. Launched with much fanfare in the mid-1960s, early MISs often did not live up to expectations. One mistake that was often made was to try to integrate all the organization's information and analysis into one giant MIS, which most often collapsed due to overcomplexity. But many organizations, IT personnel and researchers persisted, and today MISs are widely used with a great deal of success.

One response to the problems with large-scale MISs was to design more limited **decision support systems**, "information-producing systems aimed at a particular problem that a manager must solve and decisions the manager must make."[14] The decision support system (DSS) is designed to help individual managers make special types of decisions. It differs from the MIS in that the MIS is designed for use by a group of managers to manage a whole organization or its unit, whereas the DSS is aimed at helping an individual decision-maker with specific, localized decisions. DSSs also typically help the manager through all the steps of the decision process, whereas MISs are best for more restricted problem or opportunity identification. DSSs help managers and other members structure problems, gather data to understand and analyze the problem, and make decisions about the best course of action. Examples of DSSs include systems designed to assist in product pricing decisions and plant investment decisions by managers, patient referral decisions by social service intake workers, and analysis of potential contributors by a charitable fund-raiser.[15] **Group decision support systems** (GDSSs), described later, offer support for decision-making by groups of people.

Like the MIS, the DSS is helpful only if the data is accurate and the model built into the DSS is accurate and applicable to the situation. Force-fitting a decision about ethical issues into a DSS designed for economic decision-making would not lead to good outcomes.

In the late 1960s, about the time DSSs were evolving, a different application of computers emerged. **Office automation** (OA) includes "all of the formal and informal electronic systems primarily concerned with the communication of information to and from persons both inside and outside the firm."[16]

People at all levels of the organization, as well as those outside the organization, utilize office automation. The application that drove office automation originally was word processing, introduced by IBM in 1964. Computers were used to enter, store, move, and print documents throughout the firm. As time passed, a number of other OA applications have been developed, including electronic mail, voice mail, electronic calendaring, audio conferencing, video conferencing, computer conferencing, fax, videotex, imaging, and desktop publishing.[17]

Electronic mail (e-mail) is the use of networked computers to allow users to send, receive, store, and forward messages in electronic formats. Users type in messages and send them to others' electronic mailboxes. Most e-mail systems allow for automatic reply addressing, forwarding, and sending copies of messages to additional parties. E-mail greatly reduces the time spent in trying to contact others. Studies have shown that as many as 75 percent of business telephone calls do not reach the desired person; often two parties end up playing telephone tag, when each tries to call the other repeatedly, only to find the party out or busy.[18] E-mail eliminates this, enabling parties to have messages waiting for each other and to reply rapidly. **Voice mail** is like e-mail except that messages are sent by voice and people use their telephones to retrieve messages instead of a computer. Voice mail messages can be stored and forwarded, just like e-mail messages.[19]

Electronic calendaring is the use of a networked computer to keep and retrieve calendars for members of the organization. The person or a secretary can enter appointments on the calendar. Often members are allowed to call up each other's calendars to determine when they are free to meet. In principle, electronic calendaring enables the entire organization to coordinate scheduling. In practice it has met with less success, because it is difficult to get people to take the effort to keep their calendars current.

Audio conferencing is the use of voice communication equipment to establish a link among a set of people. The conference call enables a group to meet even when its members are in different locations. **Video conferencing** is the use of video technology to link geographically dispersed people or groups. Unlike audio conferencing, which requires only telephone equipment and special linking software, video conferencing requires cameras and video transmission channels. Many video conferencing facilities are similar to television broadcast studios, but recent advances have made desktop videoconferencing through PCs possible. Videoconferencing has been tried and failed to get off the ground many times in the past due to problems of high cost and technological shortcomings.[20] For example, videoconferences used to yield only jerky pictures and the screen often went blank due to inability to transmit the images rapidly enough. However, recent advances have brought the price of teleconferencing units down considerably, and the availability of sufficient transmission bandwidth to carry good images has encouraged many organizations to implement videoconferencing.[21]

Computer conferencing is similar to electronic mail, but it facilitates communication among dispersed teams and organizes their discussion around specific topics.[22] A conference enables members to enter comments about various topics in a sequence, indicating which prior comment they are responding to. Members can sign on at any time to participate and comments are kept permanently so that new members can catch up easily. The slower pace of conferencing, which allows team members to reflect on comments prior to entering them, often results in more thoughtful, deeper discussions. However, a key challenge for the conference is making decisions and coordinating activities; the slower pace of conferences makes them better for deliberation than for action. Newer conference tools incorporate workflow tools, action tracking, and automated reminders to "pick up the pace" of group work. An advantage of computer conferences over audio and video conferencing is that they can include very large numbers of members. One of the largest computer conferences on record was formed at IBM to discuss the IBM PC; it included over 40,000 members and there were over 4,000 separate topic areas.[23] However, many users find computer conferences less personal and immediate than audio and video conferences and some are reluctant to use them.

Several office automation technologies allow users to work with graphics as well as text. **Fax** transmits document images from one place to another. This technology, perfected in Japan to transmit ideographic writing, has proven to be very useful to organizations. **Videotex** uses computers to access and display stored text and graphic material. Some organizations use videotex internally to make documents accessible to all members. However, a more common use is for organizations to purchase videotex services from firms that maintain large databases of useful information. Examples of these firms include Lexis, which provides legal research and documents, and Lotus One Source, which provides financial and other information on a wide variety of firms. Sometimes this material is accessed over a network and sometimes provided on CD-ROM. **Imaging** is the use of optical character recognition to create digital files of text and graphics that can be accessed and worked with on computers.[24] Organizations that have large volumes of graphical material, such as maps or oil field diagrams, find imaging and document management systems very useful. Applications of imaging are spreading rapidly as its technology becomes more workable and affordable. **Desktop publishing** is the use of computers to prepare output that is very close in quality to that produced by typesetters and publishing houses. Many organizations are using desktop publishing to prepare documents for presentations and public relations purposes.

The original vision for office automation was integration of all these applications. For example, an oil exploration company in Houston would use imaging to store diagrams of geological formations, move these images into a videoconference with a client half the world away in Nigeria, process a contract negotiated in the videoconference and attach the geological images, send it via e-mail or fax to the client, then get the signed and authenticated contract back via e-mail, and finally store it in the contract database, which has special links to various work notification messages sent via e-mail that would inform exploration employees of the new job, who would then e-mail back to verify assignments, call up the images to help plan drilling, and so on. The ideal office automation system would link all the information processing and "paperwork" of the firm into a seamless whole. It would enable the organization to move information easily and quickly from one tool to another. And it would greatly reduce paper consumption and filing problems, because all this work is done in the so-called "paperless" office. This vision is still unrealized, for the most part, but various vendors continue to work on it. The closest most of us have come to the paperless office is probably those advertisements for computer networks where happy employees are sitting at desks without a single slip of paper on them, keyboarding away. When integration can be achieved, it will offer great potential for organizational communication. Raymond McLeod calls office automation the "sleeping giant" of information systems applications.[25]

The first four types of information systems move from an emphasis on processing data (electronic data processing) to providing information from that data (management information systems) to using that information to provide support for decision-making (decision support systems) to communication in general (office automation). The final type of information system goes beyond passive information presentation or communication support to provide active counseling to organizational members. **Expert systems**, first developed in the 1960s, attempt to capture expert knowledge in a computer model that can be used to "think through" problems just as the expert would. Typically this involves finding one or more outstanding experts in a specific area and studying their thought processes to build a rule-based model of how they reason and make decisions under different circumstances. If this is done effectively, every member of the organization can have on his or her desk the best advice possible on a given subject. Expert systems have been constructed to help brokers make investment decisions, to aid medical diagnosis, and to construct legal cases.

A different approach to modeling, neural networks, creates an expert system that can learn the optimal approach for various problems. Basically, neural networks simulate the structure of the brain and learn by building up patterns and testing to see if the outputs those patterns produce yield good results. So it is necessary to have a task for which there is plentiful, readily available feedback. Given this type of task, the network can take a set of input variables associated with the task and work out a pattern of associations between those variables that yields good outcomes. Neural networks have been used, for example, to deduce optimal operating conditions for oil refineries. They "learn" the proper temperatures, pressures, catalysts and conversion rates to produce good products. Then they can play a major role in maintaining a smoothly running refinery.

Other approaches to the development of expert systems are being tried as well. This growing area promises to turn information technology from conduit and enabler to adviser, making it a much more active participant in the organization. As with all modeling efforts, the resulting system is only as good as the data it is based on and as the model that is utilized.

Data processing, management information systems, decision support systems, office automation, and expert systems all germinated as applications during the age of mainframe computers. However, since the early 1980s a revolution has occurred in information technology that changed forever how it is used in organizations. As personal computers, microcomputers, and computer networks developed a new paradigm for computing emerged—**networked computing**.[26] In networked computing, also called **distributed computing**, processing is no longer conducted in one large central processing unit, but instead is spread out among many machines dispersed in a network. For example, in the older computing paradigm a decision support system would be located in a large mainframe computer along with all the data it required. Input would come from terminals scattered around the organization and output could be displayed on these terminals, but the computing was done in the mainframe computer located in the information systems department. In the new paradigm, there would be a network, with perhaps a mainframe for storing data and many other types of personal computers and workstations located in the departments that use them. In this case the decision support system software might be located on the executive manager's PC. When an analysis is conducted, it would draw data from databases in the mainframe and also on two other minicomputers located in different departments. It might route its output to several other managers' PCs via e-mail messages.

The differences between centralized and distributed (networked) information systems are significant for organizational communication. **Centralized computing** tended to keep information technology the preserve of a few highly skilled technicians in the information systems department. Maintaining and working with mainframes requires special skills and training, and so this arrangement gave power and control to the information systems people. As distributed computing spread it became possible to locate computers out in departments where the work was done and not just in the information systems preserve. In order to do this it was necessary to develop computer programs that could be understood, configured, and operated by the end user. This has taken a while to accomplish, but programs and even programming are much easier now than they were ten or even five years ago. Scholars in the information technology area look forward to the time in the near future when programming can be done automatically in response to "natural language" descriptions by the user (indeed there are fairly good "code generators" right now, but they still require some specialized training in programming to operate). The advent of networked computing and the user-friendly interfaces of personal computers made many communication applications such as electronic mail, word processing, database management, desktop publishing, and even videoconferencing much easier and more accessible to all members of the organization. The result has been a significant opening of communication channels in many organizations.

Distributed computing also may contribute to significant shifts in the nature of work. Once applications are in the office or on the workfloor, employees can begin to master computers themselves. They can use the computers to analyze their work and improve it. Shoshanna Zuboff[27] argued that the preferred strategy for organizations is not simply to use computers to automate work and replace employees with machines. Instead she advocated using information technology to **informate** work, to enable workers to learn which processes are effective and which are not. Information is possible because computers—properly programmed and utilized—can generate informating on how the work is done and the output associated with different configurations of steps or methods. This makes workers smarter about their work and also better able to suggest and to make improvements.

For informating to work, those at the top of the organization must be willing to share power with those lower down. Those at lower levels must feel some control over their work and some power to make changes for them to take the initiative to change how they work based on the new information. While management often initiates the empowerment of workers, distributed technologies themselves may also shift the balance of power downward. Enhanced communication via electronic mail and other telecommunications facilities make it possible for lower level employees to form coalitions and share information that increases their power in the organization. For example, a number of years ago, the electronic mail system in IBM, V-Net, also became known as "Gripe-Net" because lower level employees used its open architecture to engage in discussions about problematic managers and management practices; this consciousness raising can be the beginning of resistance at lower levels.[28]

In general, moving to distributed computing has opened up organizations and societies. It moves the control over information technology into all parts of the organization and society. The Internet, which has fascinated everyone with its explosive growth and spread, is probably the best example of the impact of distributed computing. And as information technology becomes easier for non-experts—"more transparent" in the terminology of the computing industry—the number of networks and the dispersion of computing through society will continue. Computer networks and the communication links based on them grow organically, rather than only through formal planning as had to be the case when central processors were the only option for design.

Distributed computing makes much more complex and flexible organizational structures possible. It is no longer necessary to take months or years to painstakingly design and build formal structures for information storage and processing, as it was in the days when paper or centralized processors were used to manage organizational information flows. Distributed information systems make rerouting information flows relatively easy; it is a matter of reconfiguring or expanding the arrangement of computers and telecommunications in the network. Communication can be managed quickly and with relatively low overhead, so altering the organization's structure is not likely to block the flow of command and coordination communication. Information systems also make it possible to monitor employees and work processes, so there is no longer the need to have employees or work done where supervisors can oversee it directly. Organizations can be dispersed over many locales and their members linked with high-speed information systems.

Distributed information systems are well-suited for the demands placed on organizations by the knowledge society, turbulent environments, and rapid change. Their flexibility and speed facilitates organizational adaptation. Most of today's organizations must develop complex structures to deal with their environments, but this complexity cannot be purchased at the price of building up an inflexible structure. Organizations must also be able to change quickly to meet new challenges and opportunities. For this reason, many organizations are moving away from the traditional, "tall" structures that are fine for routine, stable situations to "flatter" structures that emphasize networks of links between units rather than simpler hierarchies. The key problem is integrating the many disparate functions and units developed to help the organization cope with instability and change. For this reason, more recent strategies for organizing have emphasized integration of units with different functions and perspectives.

Methods for Integrating Organizations

One commonality across all three contingency variables is that they are all related to uncertainty. The organization's uncertainty increases as technology becomes nonroutine and as interdependence, complexity, and instability increase. Jay Galbraith discussed a number of methods organizations use to cope with uncertainty, and based on recent developments in information technology we can add several others.[29] Galbraith, too, was concerned with *adequacy*, with implementing methods sufficient to reduce uncertainty to manageable levels while maintaining as low cost in money and time spent communicating as possible. Of particular interest to us are methods for creating lateral relationships, relationships that facilitate communication and coordination across different units. Here are some of the most popular methods for creating lateral linkages in organizations:

Liaison roles: Personnel are assigned specifically to link two units. This may be a part-time or full-time assignment. For example, the assistant to the director of a local social service agency was asked to be liaison to the County Health Department. This assignment took one day a week, and involved keeping contact with the Department to ensure that the social service agency's soup kitchen and homeless shelter complied with codes and to represent the agency to the Health Department. By having a "person on the spot," the social service agency ensured that it had some input on the writing and enforcement of regulations. Filling the liaison role usually has beneficial career development consequences, because it broadens the liaison's outlook and sharpens his or her communication skills. The major disadvantage is that the liaison may come to identify more with the unit he or she visits than with the home unit or organization.

Task forces: A short-term team set up to deal with a specific problem or project. Members are drawn from several different units based on their special knowledge about the issue and the interests their units have in it. Task forces typically dissolve after a set time or when the project is finished. A key challenge for the team is to overcome communication barriers posed by the fact that its members come from different units (and sometimes different organizations) and have to overcome differences in experiences, terminology, and interests. If this problem can be surmounted, task forces often outperform other teams. When Texaco, Inc. faced charges that it systematically discriminated against black managers, it formed a blue-ribbon task force to find the roots of this problem and work out a solution. The task force went to work, quickly made some recommendations, and was dissolved.

Integrating teams: Sometimes a problem or project continues indefinitely or recurs regularly. In this case, a dedicated team is formed on a permanent basis. Assignments to this team become a permanent part of the members' jobs. Many universities have ongoing committees dedicated to increasing the number of women and minorities they hire. These integrating teams have representatives from all parts of the university.

Managerial linking roles: Often the integrating team has a special "in-between" status. Everyone agrees it is dealing with an important problem and upper management agrees to back up its recommendations and actions, but the team itself is still not regarded as a legitimate unit on a par with long-established departments or units. To give the integrating team more legitimacy and power, a formal manager may be added to this team. This managerial integrator is directly connected into the hierarchy of authority and has a budget. He or she represents the team to the organization and serves as a symbol. Having an integrating manager gives the team more legitimacy and resources to work on its own.

One company that designed integrated computer hardware and software systems had several teams working on different parts of its new System Alpha. To deliver System Alpha on time and in shape, it was vital that each team's work be compatible with that of the others. The company created an Alpha Management Team whose assignment was to coordinate the work of the System Alpha teams. An engineer who had informally worked on coordinating the teams involved in System Alpha was appointed manager of the Management Team. She was given a budget for personnel to test the compatibility of products that the different teams were creating and to provide extra help to "fight fires" that broke out in teams having problems. This extra "heft" that the manager had enabled her to stimulate the teams to action, and System Alpha was delivered on schedule.

Dual authority systems: Sometimes organizations face tasks of very high complexity that require them to constantly adjust and coordinate the activities of a great many specialties and departments. In these cases it is useful to shift to a "dual" authority system in which members of specialized departments are assigned to one or more projects and report both to the integrating manager of their project team and to their department manager. The most common type of dual authority structure is called the **matrix**.[30] As Figure 5–2 illustrates, the matrix literally is a matrix structure in which members of project teams report to two managers, the project manager and their department manager.

To accomplish the incredibly complex and daring feat of landing a person on the moon, NASA developed one of the first matrix organizational forms. Members of various departments were assigned to one or more special projects. For example, a materials engineer specializing in forming parts from metal alloys might be assigned to the Nosecone Team for 50 percent of his time and to the Booster Team for 30 percent of his time, and spend the remaining 20 percent back in the Materials Engineering Laboratory. On both teams, the engineer would lend his special expertise in materials to creating the best possible nosecone or booster, working closely with other engineers and scientists with different specialties. Back at his "home" lab, the engineer could consult with other materials engineers about problems that needed solving on his teams and catch up on the latest knowledge in materials engineering.

The advantage of dual structures like the matrix for the organization is that teams keep the work focused on tangible products and outcomes (nosecones and boosters), while reporting back to their home department helps members keep their skills sharp and up to date on the latest developments in their fields. So our engineer is kept focused on nosecones by the project emphasis of the Nosecone Team; other members of this team will keep him from applying only his materials perspective to the problem and he will keep them "honest" by making sure that materials issues are considered in each decision the team makes. But as he goes back to the Materials department the engineer is able to consult with other knowledgeable materials people about materials problems on the project that he does not know much about. This sharpens his own expertise and makes him more valuable to the project team.

The matrix structure as a whole helps ensure that the various project teams and departments are coordinated. The project managers meet as a team and with their integrating managers to ensure that the various projects come together into an effective whole. Using a structure like this, NASA succeeded in putting a man on the moon by 1969, after starting almost from scratch in 1961. No one, even NASA managers, thought it could be done, but the matrix organization was up to the task. Giant corporations like Dow-Corning have put permanent matrix structures into operation to integrate their international operations.

The matrix attempts to ensure effective performance on complex tasks by dividing them among highly focused project teams. However, to ensure that the personnel on these teams are highly qualified and current in their fields, they are drawn from specialized departments that they keep in

Diagram of a Dual-Authority Matrix Structure

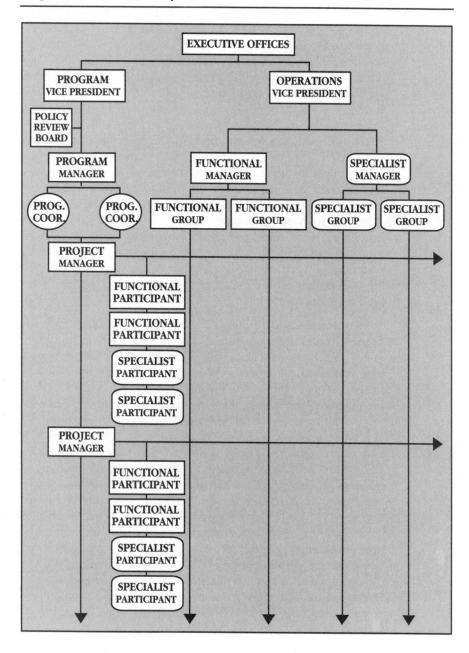

touch with. The overall structure of the matrix coordinates the work of the various project teams. The glue that holds the matrix together is intensive communication. Through many team meetings, liaisons between teams, integrating teams across projects, and communication back with functional departments, members of the matrix create a deep and complicated flow of information and ideas throughout the organization. For the matrix to work, communication within project teams and in specialized departments must create team and organizational cultures that promote open communication, innovation, constructive criticism, and high standards of excellence.

This communication-intensive organization has costs as well. Serving more than one supervisor can create ambiguities in the chain of command and tensions for workers who are torn between the mandates of two or more bosses. The requirement of continuous open communication can cause overloads and stress in its own right. Meetings, meetings, meetings can drive workers to distraction. And the solution to these problems is often even more communication. The matrix keeps all workers on their toes, but can be exhausting as well. In addition, this form works only as well as the integrating managers can coordinate the various projects, bringing to completion on schedule so that one project will not hold up other interdependent ones.

Telecommunications: Simple forms of telecommunications, such as telephones, voice mail, conference calls, and fax have become standard integrating mechanisms. They enable people in different locations to coordinate work and make decisions much more rapidly than they could have thirty years ago. Previously, organizations would assign people who were highly interdependent to the same location to allow for face-to-face contact. The advent of reliable telecommunications eliminated this necessity, and today people commonly coordinate complex work, such as sales of high ticket items with complex specifications, over fax and phone.[31] Many insurance firms have done away with central offices, assigning agents and underwriters to the field, where they work out of cars and hotel rooms via telecommunications and electronic mail. At AT&T, about 5 percent of the company's 373,000 employees do their work from cars or hotels. These "road warriors" save their companies millions in overhead each year. But they also complain of the lack of a feeling of belonging to their organizations and of the stress of living on the road many weeks a year.

As the telecommunications infrastructure improves and technology advances, more and more firms are turning to videoconferencing. High-quality videoconferencing can replace much face-to-face contact for work purposes.

Electronic mail: E-mail is a fast and effective linking mechanism, for several reasons. Electronic mail enables communication between people who are on different schedules because it can be read and answered whenever convenient for the receiver. It is also less intrusive than a phone call or face-to-face contact; the recipient can reply on her or his own schedule. Hence, e-mail encourages communication between people who do not know each other well, who differ in status, or who are in different units that do not have formal relationships. Electronic mail also allows the sending of "broadcast" messages, requests or memos sent to a large group of recipients, even to the whole organization. This enables people who do not know whom to ask to gather information and create links.

When e-mail systems are implemented, the total amount of communication within an organization or work group increases and the use of the telephone and written memos does seem to decrease, although the use of face-to-face communication *increases.* Thus the electronic media seem to supplement, rather than replace, traditional media.[32] The information exchanged via electronic media does not seem to be any more or less accurate than information exchanged through other media, although people tend to be less confident of its accuracy. In face-to-face communication we rely on vocal cues (pitch, rate of speech, loudness) and nonverbal cues to confirm our interpretations of the meanings of the words that people use. Because these cues are less readily available or are absent in mediated communication, we feel less secure in our interpretations.

Studies show that electronic mail often increases lateral communication, contacts across organizational levels, and the flow of ideas compared to more traditional communication media. Sara Kiesler[33] reports a case in which a broadcast request for ideas to solve a problem received over 100 replies in two days, several of which solved or significantly improved the problem.

There are also costs to electronic mail, notably message overload. In e-mail intensive organizations it is not unusual to receive more than fifty messages a day (One manager in an information technology firm came back from a two-week vacation to find over a thousand messages waiting!). Sorting through this to separate the junk mail from the important messages can take much time and energy. Some have worried about the impersonal nature of computer-mediated communication. However, studies have generally shown that this medium can be as personal as any once users master it.[34] The style of electronic messages often is less formal than in written messages, and people seem to think less about social norms and hierarchical relationships when constructing electronic messages than when constructing messages for other media. Their communication may be less inhibited—they may express extreme emotions overtly (a process called "flaming") and swear more often. Of course, groups of people develop and enforce cultural expectations that require users to refrain from flaming or to engage in other patterns of communicating like reading and responding to electronic mail messages within a specified period of time.[35]

The availability of electronic message networks also allows people to address messages by topic rather than by the name of the recipient.

Employees who are unhappy about a recent management decision can instantaneously locate other people who also are unhappy, share their gripes, circulate resumes, and help one another look for new jobs, as Emmett observed in a large computer organization.[36] Of course, this highly efficient means of letting angry employees know that other people share their sentiments was probably not what upper management had in mind when they purchased the systems.

Electronic Workflow Linkage: Several types of information technology help organizations integrate work processes. *Electronic data integration* (EDI) systems enable the management of data exchange among units, divisions, and companies that have to coordinate their work. Organizations use EDIs to set up automated exchanges of information needed to coordinate key tasks. For example, Chrysler Corporation has an EDI linking its suppliers and plants.[37] This EDI keeps track of inventory and is used for parts requests by managers; as parts are needed, suppliers are informed and orders arrive at the factory just in time to be installed. This "Just In Time" parts system eliminates the cost of keeping large inventories and helps avoid purchase of unneeded parts; as a direct link between suppliers and Chrysler, the EDI also helps the suppliers avoid manufacturing parts that go unsold and increases production quality through immediate feedback. Customers may also be included in EDI systems. American Hospital Supply was a leader in utilizing information technology for customer orders. It placed terminals into health care organizations to enable them to order supplies directly from AHS, resulting in huge sales growth. A second type of workflow integration, *Computer Aided Design/Computer Aided Manufacturing* (CAD/CAM) systems, integrate the design of parts and products with their manufacturing. In an integrated system, design and manufacturing are done in a seamless process mediated by the information technology. This enables much easier redesign and correction of problems than do traditional methods. *Office automation systems*, discussed above, are another type of electronic workflow linkage.

The monetary cost of electronic workflow linkage is substantial, since it typically involves design of complex hardware configurations and integrating software across many applications. Even with substantial investment, problem-free integration of the various parts of a system is difficult. Many office automation projects, for example, remain unfinished because incompatible software and hardware make it impossible to link the various subsystems together. There may also be human resistance to workflow integration. Automating integrating functions may eliminate jobs. It also tightens up surveillance, which may cause resentment, even as it increases quality and control. However, the gains from electronic workflow integration can be substantial, in terms of effectiveness and efficiency. So long as the process being integrated constitutes a substantial part of the organization's critical work and the implementation of the integration is competent, the gains will outweigh the costs.

Groupware: This refers to various technologies that support the work of groups or teams. From an integration point of view groupware is useful to help dispersed groups.

To help groups make better decisions, some groupware incorporates formal decision tools, such as problem-solving sequences, analysis methods, and evaluation tools (such as voting and rating). These systems, called Group Decision Support Systems (GDSSs), have enjoyed increasing use over the past ten years. GDSSs are often used to help groups meeting face to face make important decisions or resolve conflicts, but they can also be used to help coordinate dispersed groups. Figure 5.3 shows a typical GDSS for relatively small face-to-face groups. Each member has his or her own computer and the group can view the results of activities such as brainstorming or a vote on a public screen. The menu for this GDSS gives the group a number of decision procedures to work with, including idea generation, idea evaluation, and decision procedures such as multiattribute decision analysis (which enables groups to evaluate options on many criteria), stakeholder analysis (which enables groups to conduct analysis of the political climate surrounding a decision), and problem formulation. GDSSs have been shown to increase the number and quality of ideas considered by groups, to enable more effective conflict management, and in many cases, to promote more effective decision-making.[38]

Which Integration Mechanism to Use? How does one choose among and combine these integration mechanisms. Research suggests that organizations should use several criteria to select among the different integration methods.

One thing to consider is the communication adequacy of a method, its benefit-cost ratio. Benefits depend on the method's effectiveness in handling the level of uncertainty the organization experiences. Liaisons, task forces, telecommunications, and electronic mail are effective for moderate to moderately high levels of uncertainty. Organizations facing high levels of uncertainty need to apply methods such as integrating teams, managerial linking roles, the matrix, electronic workflow integration, and groupware.

Costs include hardware and personnel expenses, time spent learning to use the method and getting it to work smoothly, information load imposed by the method, and amount of stress involved. The five nonelectronic mechanisms—liaisons, task forces, integrating teams, integrating managers, and the matrix—are arranged in order of increasing cost. The cost of the four electronic methods depends on whether the organization already has the appropriate technological infrastructure; for example, electronic mail requires the organization to have networked computers and support staff. If the expense of infrastructure is counted, then the cost of the four electronic modes is on the order of the matrix. However, if infrastructure already exists, then telecommunications and electronic mail are very low-cost coordination mechanisms. Workflow integration and groupware still have substantial costs, because they require the organization to learn new ways of working.

FIGURE 5–3

Small Decision Room with Group Decision Support System

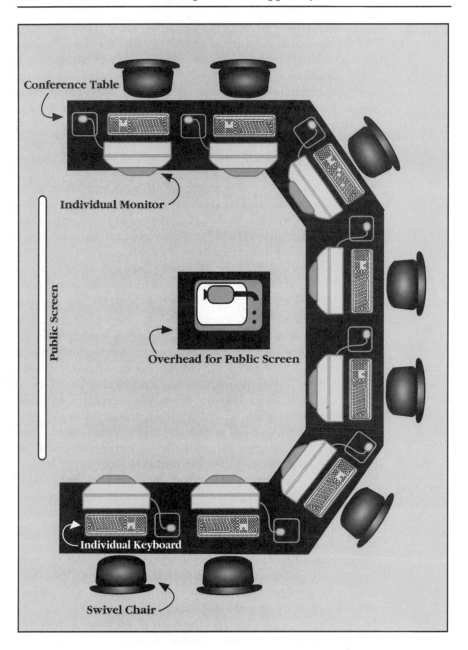

From a cost-benefit standpoint, an organization should select the least costly mechanism that meets its needs for uncertainty reduction. For example, an organization in a very complex, unstable environment with a highly difficult task may have to choose a highly flexible, yet costly form such as the matrix or electronic workflow integration. On the other hand, an organization in a more stable situation that has one difficult problem may be able to handle things with a task force or via e-mail.

Another factor to consider in choosing integration mechanisms is *geographical dispersion.* Organizations whose members are highly interdependent, yet spread around a number of locations must utilize one of the electronic forms of integration. Before the advent of electronic modes of linking, organizations either had to situate employees working on highly interdependent tasks in the same place or allow for delays due to the time taken to manage interdependence via letter, memo, or phone. However, electronic linkages are so fast, reliable, and provide such rich interaction that organizations can now plan to have work dispersed to the locations where it can be done most effectively and integrate via electronic communication. For example, a sales team working with a firm purchasing industrial equipment can work directly with engineers back at the home office to determine if alterations desired by the customer are feasible and to price the changes. Where this may have taken a week or more in "the old days," electronic linkages make it fast and relatively easy.

A third variable to consider in choosing a linking mechanism is the *cultural strategy in place* within the organization. The values, traditions, and history of an organization may predispose it to be more comfortable with some integration methods than others. Selecting a method the organization is not accustomed to requires a period of learning and change. For example, implementing e-mail is not just a matter of installing the software. More important is getting members who are not accustomed to electronic communication to try it out. Many will be quite uncomfortable with such a rapid form of communication that does not involve face-to-face, or at least verbal, contact. Electronic mail and other technologies that connect people are only attractive to users insofar as they can communicate with the people they want to reach, and for this to be possible the others must also be "on" the technology. So it is important to attain a *critical mass* of users to attract people to the technology. This critical mass may be a substantial number of people—so many that nonusers will want to join in to show they are "with it"—or it may be a smaller number of "important" people whom everyone wants to talk to. Achieving a critical mass in an organization whose culture is not compatible with new technologies is a difficult proposition.

No single integration method will work under all circumstances or for all organizations. The balance among cost-benefit considerations, geographical dispersion, and culture depends on which is more important to the organization or the task at hand. In many cases, organizations settle on integration modes after a period of experimentation in which different methods are tried and rejected.

After examining virtually every published case study of introducing new communication technologies into organizations (and surveying their own consulting experiences), Noshir Contractor and Eric Eisenberg* created a "hypothetical" typical case that explains the complexities of this kind of organizational change process.

The Chief Executive Officer (CEO) of a manufacturing company returned from a convention having been convinced that his firm needed a voice mail system, although this technology was rare in his city or industry. He had learned that voice mail was a prompt, personal, and accurate way for people (like himself) who were often away from their offices to keep in touch. At first the system was installed only for upper management, but it was an immediate success. Everyone used this tool that had been blessed by their boss, and everyone reported that the CEO had again come up with a brilliant idea. The CEO then announced that the system would be added throughout the company because it was so personal, fast, and accurate. These attributes quickly became the criteria that the employees would use to evaluate the new system.

As expected, many employees quickly started to use the system. Salespersons found that it was a wonderful way to keep from feeling so isolated when they were away. Assembly line workers also used it, but not in the way the CEO anticipated. Instead of using it to keep in touch with their supervisors they used it as a way to *avoid* talking to them face to face. Their primary use was to make contact with workers on other shifts. The engineers and accountants also surprised the CEO by resisting the new system. Engineers refused to use a system that precluded the use of visual aids (try sometime to describe the inside of your telephone to someone over the telephone); accountants were unable to adapt their usual ways of communicating numbers and texts to the new medium.

As a result, the sales department improved their contacts with upper management, while the relationships between upper management and the accounting and engineering divisions deteriorated. After noticing that their political standing in the organization was declining, the accountants started a campaign to discredit the system. They argued that the system was much more expensive than it had been projected to be, and claimed that people had been passing private messages on to upper management. For both reasons, people reduced their use of the system, and management responded by restricting access to the system. Engineering reacted to their isolation by proposing that the organization

---

*See "Communication Networks and New Media in Organizations," in *Organizations and Communication Technology* (Newbury Park, CA: Sage, 1991).

(continued)

(continued from the previous page)

purchase more technology—a LAN (local area network) system that would allow the transmission of both audio and visual information. Upper management, who was still enamored with the new technology, approved the purchase, which allowed engineering to again have direct access to them, and led to additional changes in the way the various groups communicated with one another.

Discussion Questions
1. Could the CEO have anticipated all of the different uses that the employees made of the voice mail system? Would the organization have benefited from the CEO's being able to anticipate these uses?
2. What effects did the installation of these systems have on the role that middle managers (the supervisors of the various divisions) played in the organization? Were they more important before or after the installation of the system?

New Organizational Forms

The knowledge society and the changing environment couples unusual demands with unusual opportunities for growth and innovation. This has resulted in a number of new organizational strategies. We will briefly discuss several, including the dynamic network, the virtual organization, and telework. Some scholars believe these forms represent the future of organizations and organizational communication.[39]

The Dynamic Network

The **dynamic network** is an organization whose component units are assembled to meet a particular set of demands and disassembled when the need for it is done. In some cases the units are from the same organization, while in others they are different organizations temporarily integrated for a specific project. Miles and Snow[40] were among the first to describe the networked organization, and they outlined four key characteristics. First, dynamic networks are *disaggregated* organizations. The functions required to carry out the project are not combined in a single organization. In older forms, design, production, inventory, marketing, and accounting would all be departments configured to work together over a long period of time. In the dynamic network, these functions would be spread across separate units brought together for the duration of the project. For example, in a large firm, a dynamic network to produce a new product and bring it to market might be put together by an integrating project manager who would assemble units for the project: Design might be carried out by a team assigned from engineering, production would be from a particular plant with excess capacity, inventory would be handled by suppliers on a just-in-time basis, marketing would be the responsibility of a sales team reassigned from a downsizing division, and the accounting department would handle bookkeeping. The project manager would start with no organization and through negotiation and competitive bidding get units together to bring the product out. When the product was out and sales had begun, it might be transferred to an existing functional unit of the organization and the dynamic network disbanded. Alternatively the dynamic network might become a more settled division in the company.

A second characteristic of the dynamic network is that it is assembled by a *broker,* a manager or firm that locates appropriate units and builds them into a temporary organization. The broker may be an integrating project manager, as in our previous example. Alternatively, the broker may be an independent agent or organization. Building contractors, who coordinate the work of carpenters, plumbers, electricians, and others, are one of the most familiar examples of brokers.

Third, dynamic networks use *market mechanisms* to manage relationships among their constituent units. The broker puts together a set of units by having them enter into contractual relationships with each other. Payments go to each unit for their part of the work, based on the income the broker realizes for the whole. This is quite different from older forms in which each department did the work it was responsible for with no thought of direct payment; in the older forms compensation came from the organization as a whole.

Units join the dynamic network through a process of competitive bidding, in which each indicates what it can do and its fee and the broker selects based on quality, price, and compatibility with the emerging network. Communication in market-based organizational situations is different from communication in established organizations. Whereas previously the problem was how to relate to another set of units one is more or less "stuck with," in the market, the problem is how to project an image of competence, efficiency, and quality. In a real sense each unit—even those within intact organizations—becomes an independent small business vying for business with many potential competitors. This requires a very different strategy for communicating with other units than do the three strategies discussed in Chapters 2, 3, and 4.

Communication in the dynamic network is managed through their fourth characteristic, *full disclosure information systems.* A critical issue in dynamic networks (and other new organizational forms) is trust: If you come together with other people and units you will work with only temporarily, how can you trust them to be fair with you and to uphold their part of the contract? Any unit not fulfilling its contract can, of course, be sued, but going through the courts can take years. Far better is to maintain open communication among parties in order to create and build trust and the ability to work together. A full disclosure information system is composed of an accounting information system and electronic communication systems. The accounting information system is a set of open databases that shows participating units whether other units are meeting their responsibilities and the level of return obtained by the organization. For example, units in the new product venture described earlier could determine from this data whether suppliers are on time with their deliveries and the amount of product marketing has "moved" this month. This accounting information system reassures units that others are holding up their end of the bargain and puts pressure on them to hold up their own end. As units see that others are faithfully fulfilling their obligations, they come to trust them and trust builds over time. Also important in this trust building process are timely and effective use of electronic communication systems such as e-mail, teleconferencing, and groupware. Direct, rapid communication and response help the network coordinate work and iron out problems. Both the accounting and communication systems help to build trust, and trust is a self-reinforcing cycle: Open communication builds trust, which leads to more open communication and to more trust, in an ever-increasing spiral.[41]

Many textbook publishers now operate as dynamic networks. Older publishing companies have traditionally consolidated the acquisition of new books, their design and layout, printing, and sales in a single organization. More recently publishers have been farming out some, and in some cases all, of these functions. The publisher may acquire the book, then hire a graphics firm to handle layout, an independent printer to produce the books, and several firms, including the publisher's own staff, to market the book. Special types of books are produced for the publisher by smaller independent firms, themselves dynamic networks, often founded by former employees of the publisher who have gone out on their own. Publishing is a very different game today than it was thirty years ago.

The dynamic network is a novel form for at least two reasons. First, it combines units from different organizations or from very different parts of the same organization into an ad hoc, project-related network. No longer is it necessary to think of organizations as self-contained entities with definitive structures. Instead they can be composed and rearranged, stuck together by various integrating mechanisms, as the occasion demands. Organizations become "mix-and-match" systems. The dynamic network is a very good description of the various joint ventures, cross-firm alliances, and consortia that are becoming increasingly prevalent today. A good example of this type of venture network is Sematech, the Austin, Texas-based research and development consortium put together by more than ten leading information technology companies. Typically firms assign researchers to Sematech, where they work with employees of other companies to develop cutting edge products and share insights into solving production problems. The rationale behind such a consortium, which is seen as a temporary venture (even though Sematech has now been in existence more than ten years), is that the United States needs a prosperous, technically advanced group of information technology companies if it is to remain among world leaders in this area.

The second reason for the novelty of the dynamic network is that it makes "temporariness" permanent. No longer can employees assume they'll be working for the same company for thirty or forty years. By their very nature, dynamic networks force their employees to think of a future when they'll have to find new contracts and new positions in a new organization. This implies that building a reputation in the field is very important for small units and individuals who make up the dynamic network.

Dynamic networks—and other new organizational forms—present problems for theory and research as well. Can a dynamic network have an organizational culture? How does a temporary aggregation of independent units develop values and a distinctive approach? Can such an organization be said to have a formal communication structure? Typically formal relations among units are set up by the contracts, but interchanges among the units occur whenever needed, and new linkages and integration methods may be used to address new problems or demands. Many concepts useful in the analysis of older forms come into question when new forms are considered.

Virtual Organizations

A **virtual organization** is one that has no physical existence.[42] It has no building, no campus, no office. Instead it exists across a computer network. Some dynamic networks are virtual organizations, but other types of organizations are as well. Many catalog companies' sales divisions are virtual organizations, with independent individual sales agents operating out of their homes. The catalog companies link them via high-speed computer lines to a central database that handles order delivery and other functions. Compaq Computer Corporation moved its sales force into home offices and reported a 50 percent reduction in sales expenses as a result.

The California flower company Calyx & Corolla is a good example of a virtual organization. The organization is really a virtual network composed of a negotiated agreement between three organizations. Calyx & Corolla mails catalogs showing flower arrangements out to potential customers and takes orders using a 1–800–number order center located in a suburb of San Francisco. The orders are then forwarded via computer network or fax to flower growers who have also agreed to package the flowers in arrangements prior to shipping them. Calyx & Corolla has a negotiated agreement with Federal Express that picks up and delivers the arrangements the next morning any place in the continental United States. Orders are tracked and monitored via a computer system that also handles accounting and distribution of payments to the various components of the organization. Calyx & Corolla itself is relatively small, but the virtual organization it has put together is much larger, composed of the growers and Federal Express. Consumers cannot differentiate the different organizations that make up Calyx & Corolla; from the point of view of the customer, Calyx & Corolla looks like a traditional florist who delivers.

One characteristic of virtual organizations is that to outsiders they appear to be just like older self-contained organizations. They deliver the same or better product or service with the same or better efficiency. Information technology and telecommunications enables these dispersed organizations to coordinate their activities and to maintain coherent work processes. Each part of the virtual organization is able to focus on its particular function, resulting in competent and even excellent performance. By staying small, the component organizations keep their costs for management and overhead down, enhancing efficiency. Smallness also makes communication easier within the components, opening them up for fast development and testing of new ideas.

Like the dynamic network, the virtual organization requires the development of a great deal of trust among members. However, unlike the dynamic network, in many virtual organizations trust is often cultivated by forming long-term relationships among component organizations. Kingston Technology, one of the most successful firms in Silicon Valley, has only 220 employees, with the rest of the organization spread out over a network of subcontractors.[43] However, unlike many subcontractors who are hired for short jobs, Kingston maintains long-term, solid ties with its partner companies. Kingston designs systems that speed up PCs and data transfer. These are assembled by Express Manufacturing, which works closely with Kingston, and then they are shipped by Federal Express. When Kingston needed more manufacturing capacity, Express Manufacturing built more because it knew it could depend on the business from Kingston. While Express has other customers, Kingston always comes first. When Kingston needed more advertising material shipped, it worked with its printer to expand that business, again guaranteeing work. As the companies work together and develop stronger and stronger communication ties, trust grows. Kingston often does business without contracts and pays ahead of time on its orders so its small affiliates will have the money to do their work. It also maintains totally open books, so that all its employees maintain trust in management. Kingston has built a virtual organization by building a family of firms and a family of its own employees. It has developed an enduring culture that spans a number of companies.

Telework

Telework refers to a wide range of working arrangements in which employees work outside the traditional office and conduct a large portion of their work via computer or telecommunications linkages.[44] The nature of telework varies widely. Some teleworkers conduct all their business from home; the telephone salespersons for the catalog companies mentioned in the previous section are one example, but many other professional employees work out of their homes as well. Some employees telecommute only part-time, working at home a few days a week or month, and going into a regular office the rest of the time. Another type of teleworker is the "road warrior" mentioned earlier, who is on the road almost all the time, working out of a car or hotel room. The number of teleworkers has been growing steadily from 4 million in 1990 to over 15 million in 1996.

Telework is feasible for any job that centers around paperwork and information processing. There are a number of incentives for telework. For organizations, the attraction stems from lower overhead since they don't have to maintain office buildings and, for the many teleworkers who work on a part-time basis, don't have to pay benefits. For the worker, advantages include closer contact with home and family (except for the road warrior), a more relaxed lifestyle away from the formality of the office, avoidance of office politics, and fewer long commutes. There are also advantages for the public, since less commuting means less expense for highways and other infrastructure and less automobile pollution. Evaluations of telework support its advantages. The majority of studies suggest that teleworkers are more productive and less costly than those based in the office.

There are several prerequisites for teleworking arrangements to succeed. First and foremost, the technological infrastructure must be developed. Often this means that high-speed transmission lines must be installed by the phone companies or other communication carriers. The organization must also purchase the proper technology (computers and high-speed modems) for processing and moving the information. Second, all involved must have developed "communication discipline," that is, they must be in the habit of using their e-mail, groupware, and other communication technologies to stay in contact. These new media require users to develop new patterns of behavior based on different communication modes (usually written) than the verbal channels most people are accustomed to. Managers must be able to trust that commands issued via communication technology will be followed; employees must learn to understand what managers mean over media such as e-mail that do not offer the direct personal contact that often provides extra information and detail. A final prerequisite for effective telecommuting is that home workers must create a work environment in their homes. Provisions must be made so that family matters do not constantly intervene in work. Some employees take on considerable expenses in setting up and equipping home offices. Since some office equipment is too expensive to be installed in the homes of all workers, many companies have set up satellite offices where employees can come when they need office facilities. Satellite offices are also places where employees can work with information too sensitive to transmit over public media.

A major barrier to effective telework arrangements is the discomfort of managers who can no longer see what their employees are doing. Before they get used to electronic media, many middle and upper managers are wary of supervising employees whom they cannot see. "Management by walking around" is premised on visual contact and face-to-face communication. The manager does not know what she or he will find, but walks around to see what is happening; in the process he or she sees things that work and should be done more and problems that have to be addressed. This must be done very differently with teleworkers. The information technology provides ways to monitor work, but understanding and working with the information requires managers to learn new procedures and skills. Managers who do not have these, or who are uncomfortable with new technologies in general, are likely to perceive a loss of control due to telework.

Telework may also present some problems for the employee. The line between work and private or family time often blurs for teleworkers. Telework may be convenient in the sense that it gives the employee a more informal and flexible work environment, but it also makes it more convenient for others to reach the employee. Most teleworkers—and almost all road warriors—report that they work more hours. When work intrudes into the family space, there is nowhere for employees to escape work-related stress and get a break from the pressure. Teleworkers must exert considerable effort to keep their nonwork lives intact.

Despite these disadvantages, telework is here to stay. It is simply too attractive to both organizations and employees. Some futurists predict that telework will reverse the growth of cities and suburbs. If a travel agent can work as easily from her farm 100 miles from Minneapolis as she could in the city, there is nothing to keep her in the city. A corporation that can locate satellite offices around the country in cheaper rural locales could be sorely tempted to vacate its high-priced suburban campus. It is possible that telework will encourage dispersion of the population and a general move away from the cities. The result may be further deterioration of cities and, eventually, suburbs, as those holding the highest paying jobs disperse more evenly around the country.

Summary

Dynamic networks, virtual organizations, and telework are just three of the more prominent new organizations. Many other new forms are springing up and no end appears to be in sight. While many of these new forms appear novel at first sight, they also exhibit many of the same structures and processes discussed in the traditional, relational, and cultural strategies and they face many of the same challenges. The relational strategy in particular has much in common with the new organizational forms. And some scholars maintain that so-called "new" forms actually are similar to existing forms, particularly to the types of organizations that were common prior to the 1850s, when the bureaucracy began to emerge, and to alternative and international organizational forms that have sprung up since 1950.[45] Currently it is hard to decide this point, because new forms are still evolving and have not stabilized into specific "types" yet.

CONCLUSION

Organizations have always had a wide range of options for organizing themselves, and new technologies have broadened this range still further. This chapter began by discussing contingency design theory, which attempts to explain what makes different organizational structures effective. Contingency design theory gives advice on how an effective organization and its communication system can be designed based on three variables: its technology, its interdependence with other organizations or units, and its environment. Contingency design theory worked very well to explain how organizations and their communication structures should be designed during the 1950–1980 period, but developing trends in society and economy have introduced new complexity.

The gradual evolution of the knowledge society in the last half of this century set the stage for the explosive rate at which the emphasis on knowledge and information work has developed over the past twenty years. Along with this came the globalization of the economy, rapid growth in knowledge and technology, and increased environmental turbulence. The rapid development of information technology has facilitated and fed on these changes. Computer and telecommunications technologies have permeated organizations and made many types of structures and communication systems possible that were only visions before 1980.

To deal with the increased pace of change and adapt to turbulent environments, organizations must move more toward flatter, network structures that rely on integrating communication mechanisms for coordination. We discussed a number of different methods for integrating organizations and suggested that they be evaluated on the basis of benefits and costs to the organization, the degree of geographical dispersion of the organization, and the organization's culture. Ideally the least costly method that can adequately meet the organization's needs should be chosen. In practice this is not always possible due to limitations in member knowledge and willingness to use a given method and due to lack of fit with the organization's culture.

Information technology has promoted the emergence of new strategies for organizing, including the dynamic network, the virtual organization, and telework. These new forms are very communication intensive and provide some features of control that the traditional strategy offered, but the flexibility, adaptability, and empowerment offered by the relational strategy. What is less clear is whether these forms can evolve coherent organizational cultures.

NOTES

[1] A very accessible discussion of contingency design theory can be found in R. Daft, *Organization Theory and Design,* 3rd edition (St. Paul: West, 1989), Chs. 2 and 4. The research on contingency theory is summarized in Henri Mintzberg, *The Structuring of Organizations* (Englewood Cliffs, NJ: Prentice-Hall, 1979).

[2] Tom Burns and G.M. Stalker, *The Management of Innovation* (London: Tavistock, 1961).

[3] Charles Perrow, "A Framework for the Comparative Analysis of Organizations", *American Sociological Review, 32* (1967), pp. 194–208.

[4] Perrow divides technology into two dimensions: analyzability and variety. *Analyzability* refers to the degree to which the process the technology is designed to carry out is known and understood. The second dimension of technology is its *variety,* the number of exceptions encountered in the course of doing the work. In some work, exceptional cases are very rare; there are only small differences from case to case and the "inputs" to the organizational systems are pretty uniform. This defines four types of technology. Two are covered in detail in the main text:

low analyzability coupled with high variety (nonroutine technologies apply) and high analyzability coupled with low variety (routine technologies apply). The other two cases are:

(3) *Engineering technologies,* with high analyzability, but also high variety, are complicated, because many exceptions are encountered. However, because cause-effect relationships are well understood for these tasks, it is possible to develop a set of formulas that can then be applied to the different cases. For engineering technologies, uncertainty is somewhat higher. Manuals and standard procedures describe the various programs the unit can carry out, but members of the unit may need to consult regarding the specific programs that will be used, how they will be coordinated with each other, and what to do if problems arise. Hence, engineering technologies will be most adequately served by a combination of written, standardized communication and verbal communication directed to coordinating work and problem resolution.

(4) *Craft technologies,* with low analyzability and low variety, have a stable set of activities, but the transformation process is not well understood. Extensive training and experience is required to master work techniques and judgment necessary for applying them. For example, a group of performing artists putting on a play, knows the script, but turning that script into a performance requires them to draw on years of slowly accumulated know-how that they cannot put into words. For craft technologies uncertainty is still higher than for engineering technologies. Because these technologies deal with low analyzable work, the use of manuals and standard procedures is less feasible. The most adequate way of coordinating craft work is through horizontal verbal communication among those who have to work together. This can often be scheduled. For example, a specialty steel fabricating plant might have a scheduled weekly meeting to discuss formulations for new orders.

[5] This important distinction was developed by James Thompson, *Organizations in Action* (New York: McGraw-Hill, 1967).

[6] Robert B. Duncan, "Characteristics of Perceived Environments and Perceived Environmental Uncertainty," *Administrative Science Quarterly, 17* (1972): 313–327.

[7] Daft, especially Chapter 2; Howard E. Aldrich, *Organizations and environments* (Englewood Cliffs: Prentice-Hall, 1979).

[8] Peter Drucker, "The Age of Transformation," *Atlantic Monthly* (September, 1994): p. 53.

[9] Scores of books have been written about the options information technology makes available to organizations. One of the most readable is Henry Lucas, *The T-Form Organization* (San Francisco: Jossey-Bass, 1995).

[10] This opinion is expressed by Susan J. Winter and S. Lynne Taylor, who argue that new IT-supported organizational forms resemble those found in the pre-industrial era. See their article in *Information Systems Research, 7* (1996): 5–21.

[11] Lucas, *T-Form;* Mowshowitz, "Virtual Organization: A Vision of Management in the Information Age," *Information Society, 10* (1994): 267–288; J. Fulk and G. DeSanctis, (Eds.), *Information Technology and New Organizational Forms* (Newbury Park, CA: Sage, in press).

[12] This section owes a debt to an excellent book by Raymond McLeod, Jr., *Management Information Systems,* 6th ed. The various types of information systems defined here are discussed in more detail by McLeod in Chs. 2, and pp. 12–21.

[13] McLeod, Chapter 13.

[14] McLeod, p. 19.

[15] The concept of decision support system was originated by G. Anthony Gorry and Michael S. Scott-Morton, "A Framework for Management Information Systems," *Sloan Management Review, 13* (Fall 1971): 55–70. In that article they define the various functions of decision support systems. An updated account can be found in McLeod, Ch. 14. Dozens of examples of decision support systems are described in the journal *Interfaces.*

[16] McLeod, p. 436.

[17] McLeod, p. 439.

[18] Ron Rice, *New Communication Technologies* (Beverly Hills: Sage, 1984).

[19] Good descriptions of the development and state of voice mail and most other office technologies can be found in August Grant and Jennifer Harmon Meadows (Eds.), *Communication Technology Update IV* (Boston: Focus Press, 1996). This series of books gives readable, up-to-date descriptions of many communication technologies.

[20] Grant and Meadows, *Update IV.*

[21] Grant and Meadows. See also, Bob Francis, "Tune in to Cheaper Videoconferencing", *Datamation, 39* (October 1, 1993): 48–51.

[22] The classic book about computer conferencing is by Starr Roxanne Hiltz and Murray Turoff, *The Network Nation: Human Communication via Computer* (Reading, MA: Addison-Wesley, 1978). Computer conferencing is also discussed in Ron Rice, *The New Media;* Robert Johansen, Jacques Vallee, and Kenneth Spangler, *Electronic Meetings: Technological Alternatives and Social Choices* (Reading, MA: Addison-Wesley, 1979); Elaine Kerr and Starr Roxanne Hiltz, *Computer-mediated Communication Systems* (New York: Academic Press, 1982).

[23] McLeod, p. 446.

[24] For an interesting account of facsimile (fax) development, see Jonathan Coopersmith, "Facsimile's false starts," *IEEE Spectrum* (February, 1993): pp. 46–49. Rice, *The New Media,* discusses various uses of videotex; and McLeod, pp. 448–449 discusses imaging.

[25] McLeod, p. 453.

[26] McLeod, Chapter 1.

[27] Shoshanna Zuboff, *In the Age of the Smart Machine* (New York: Free Press, 1988).

[28] Lee Sproull and Sara Kiesler, *Connections: New Ways of Working in the Networked World.* (Cambridge, MA: MIT Press, 1992).

[29] Jay Galbraith, "Organizational Design," in *Handbook of Organizational Behavior,* J. Lorsch (Ed.) (Englewood Cliffs: Prentice-Hall, 1987).

[30] A readable account of the matrix organization can be found in Robert Youker, "Organization Alternatives for Project Managers," *Project Management Journal, VIII* (March, 1977): 18–24. Also see Galbraith.

[31] Kirk Johnson, "Many Companies Turn Workers Into High-Tech Nomads", *Minneapolis Star-Tribune* (April 3, 1994), 1J.

[32] R. Johansen, *Teleconferencing and Beyond* (New York: McGraw-Hill, 1984).

[33] Sproull and Kiesler, *Connections;* Sara Kiesler, Jane Siegel, and Timothy W. McGuire, "Social psychological aspects of computer-mediated communication," *American Psychologist, 39* (1984): 1123–1134.

[34] Sproull and Kiesler, op. cit.; Lee Sproull and Sara Kiesler "Reducing social context cues," *Management Science, 32* (1986): 1492–1512; Tom Finholt and Lee Sproull, "Electronic groups at work," *Organization Science, 1* (1990): 41–64; Ron Rice, R. and G. Love "Electronic emotion," *Communication Research, 14* (1987): 85–108; Joe B. Walther, "Interpersonal effects in computer-mediated interaction," *Communication Research, 19* (1992): 52–90.

[35] Joanne Yates and Wanda J. Orlikowski, "Genres of Organizational Communication," *The Academy of Management Review, 17* (1992): 299–326. Also see Lee Sproull and Sara Kiesler, "Reducing social context cues," *Management Science, 32* (1986): 1492–1512 and S. Rafaeli, *Electronic Message to Computer-mediated Hotline* (Comserve Electronic Information Service, April 26, 1990); and Charles Steinfeld, "Computer-mediated Communication in the Organizations," in *Cases in Organizational Communication,* Beverly Sypher, ed. (New York: Guilford, 1991).

[36] R. Emmett, "Vnet or Gripenet," *Datamation, 27* (1981): 48–58. This capacity sometimes can cause problems for new users of the systems. When I was first learning to use e-mail I sent a relatively personal note to a colleague whose work I often cite in this book congratulating him on his promotion to associate professor. I accidentally told my computer to send the message to everyone who is on the organizational communication network, which, of course, includes him. I know this because some kind people recognized what I had done and sent me instructions about how to keep from doing it, but I have never admitted my error to him. He may never know unless he reads this footnote.

[37] Lucas, *T-Form,* pp. 144–146.

[38] Gerry DeSanctis and Brent Gallupe, "A foundation for the study of group decision support systems," *Management Science, 33* (1987), 589–609; Brent Gallupe, Laura Bastianutti, and W.H. Cooper, "Unblocking Brainstorms," *Journal of Applied Psychology, 76* (1991), 137–142; Jay F. Nunamaker, Alan R. Dennis, Joe Valacich, Doug Vogel, and Joey George, "Electronic Meeting Systems to Support Group Work," *Communications of the ACM, 34* (1991): 40–61; V. Sambamurthy and Marshall Scott Poole, "The effects of variations in capabilities of gdss designs on management of cognitive conflict in groups," *Information Systems Research, 3* (1993): 224–251.

[39] Lucas, *T-Form*, makes such an argument, as do Sirkka Jarvenpaa and Blake Ives, "The Global Network Organization of the Future: Information Management Opportunities and Challenges," *Journal of Management Information Systems, 10* (1994): pp. 25–57.

[40] Robert E. Miles and Charles C. Snow, "Organizations: New Concepts for New Forms," *California Management Review, 28,* 3 (1986): 62–73.

[41] Dale E. Zand, "Trust and managerial problem-solving," *Administrative Science Quarterly,* 17: 229–239.

[42] Lucas, *T-Form,* describes virtual organizations in some detail.

[43] Michael Meyer, "Here's a 'Virtual' Model for America's Industrial Giants," *Newsweek* (August 13, 1993): p. 40.

[44] Peter Leyden, "Teleworking Could Turn Our Cities Inside Out," *Minneapolis Star-Tribune,* (September 5, 1993): 15A-16A.

[45] Susan J. Winter and S. Lynne Taylor, "The Role of IT in the Transformation of Work: A Comparison of Post-industrial, Industrial, and Proto-Industrial Organizations," *Information Systems Research, 7* (1996): 5–21.

UNIT 2

Strategies of Organizational Communication

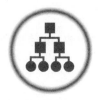

Chapter 6

MANAGING MEMBERSHIP
IN ORGANIZATIONS

CENTRAL THEMES

- Organizations and newcomers must negotiate mutually acceptable roles for the employees to play.
- Entering organizations consists of three stages—anticipation, encounter, and arrival.
- Emotional responses and changes in morale complicate the newcomer's experience.
- Sometimes socialization is so complete that newcomers "identify" with their organization.
- The key to "encountering" a new organization is making sense of it; the key to arriving in a new organization is developing appropriate image-management and influence strategies.

KEY TERMS

culture shock
generalized self-concept
indirect questions
self-disclosure
testing limits
cognitive complexity
empathy
role taking
rhetorical sensitivity
morale
identification
public self
private self

quasi-theories
excuses
justify
counterclaims
open persuasion
manipulative persuasion
wearing a target down
ingratiation
manipulation
justifications
rationalizations
topoi
strategic ambiguity

rationality   media richness
professionalism   symbol-carrying capacity
loyalty   instrumental purposes
denial

In Chapter 1, I explained that this book is organized around the concept "strategic organizational communication." The chapters of Unit I explain one sense in which organizational communication is "strategic"—the notion that every organization is "organized" through a set of choices. Sometimes these strategic choices are conscious; sometimes they are not. Sometimes they are efficient adaptations to the environments surrounding an organization; sometimes they are not. Sometimes they are productive for *all* of the organization's members, managers and workers alike; sometimes they are not. And, as Chapter 12 will explain in detail, sometimes a particular strategy of organizing *also* meets the needs of outsiders who have a stake in what the organization does and does not do. Sometimes it does not meet stakeholders' needs.

The chapters in this unit examine the second sense in which organizational communication is "strategic." Every strategy of organizing creates particular kinds of organizational situations that employees must manage. Each of the chapters in this unit examines a situation that employees are likely to face in modern organizations. Each chapter will explain how employees can make sense out of those situations and will discuss the communicative strategies that are available for dealing with them. This chapter focuses on the experience of entering a new organization and managing membership in it. Subsequent chapters will deal with other common situations and challenges encountered in contemporary organizations.

ENTERING ORGANIZATIONS: STAGES, PRESSURES, AND COPING PROCESSES[1]

When people enter a new organization or a new division of their existing organization, they bring with them a lengthy and complex history. They have learned to perceive their organizational worlds in highly individual ways and have developed patterns of acting and communicating that have succeeded in the past. They enter an organization (or unit) that also has a complex history and a group of employees who have developed their own successful, stable, predictable, and comfortable ways of perceiving and acting. Since both newcomers and old-timers understandably want to change as little as possible while adjusting to one another, they must negotiate a new relationship. Old-timers want to socialize newcomers to accept a preexisting role. But, to some extent, newcomers need to resist the socialization process, to retain a separate identity and "individualize" their organizational roles.[2] In short, the entry experience is a time during which the tension between an organization's needs for control and coordination and an individual's needs for autonomy, creativity, and sociability (recall Chapter 1) is most clear. If the negotiation fails, the newcomer typically leaves the organization, usually within six months to a year. If a "match" between the newcomer's goals, values, and styles of working can be negotiated, he or she will stay in the organization and tend to be satisfied and productive.

Some newcomers are better able to cope with new situations than others. Newcomers who have had many and varied work experiences deal with the "reality shock" of the entry experience more easily than people with few work experiences.[3]

Some personality characteristics also may make it easier for people to cope. For example, people who are "inner-directed," that is, who rely on their own beliefs, values, and analytical skills, cope more easily than people who are "outer-directed," who usually rely on the opinions and interpretations of others.[4] But all newcomers experience some degree of **culture shock**—the sudden realization that what was taken for granted in their previous organization is not the same as what is taken for granted in their new one.

The entry experience usually occurs in three stages, which I will label *anticipation, encounter,* and *arrival* (see Table 6–1).[5] The stages are not discreet—people do not wake up one morning and suddenly realize "I'm now in encounter"—but there often are key "turning points" that, in retrospect, signaled one's move from one stage to another. But it is helpful to think of the experience as made of stages because each stage has its own cognitive, emotional, and behavioral dimensions.

STAGE ONE: ANTICIPATION

"Anticipation" involves three processes—coping with expectations, managing self-concept, and "letting go" of the past. Expectations are influenced by the taken-for-granted assumptions of our society, and by the dynamics of selection processes. Some of the taken-for-granted assumptions of a society involve work and life in organizations (recall the "Generation X" case study in Chapter 1, for example). These assumptions create expectations that may or may not be fulfilled by a person's new organization. For example, students in U.S. universities seem to expect to someday get a "real" job, one that "pays well" (the "realest" ones have six-figure salaries), is full-time, involves managerial tasks, "perks" (independence and a large private office), includes the possibility of advancement, and is with a reputable company.[6] In "real" jobs supervisors are capable and do not mistreat their subordinates. Of course, these expectations are elitist, and they are stereotypically masculine because the "realness" of a job depends on traditionally male considerations like financial gain and upward mobility. Stereotypically feminine attributes like nurturing and caring for others are characteristic of jobs that are not "really" even jobs. But students' definitions of a "real" job include a particular set of expectations about organizational life and a specific set of criteria for evaluating their organizations, their jobs, and their selves.

TABLE 6–1

Stages in the Entry Experience

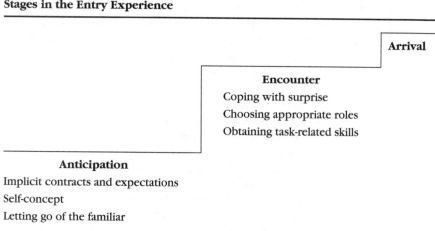

Arrival

Encounter

Coping with surprise

Choosing appropriate roles

Obtaining task-related skills

Anticipation

Implicit contracts and expectations

Self-concept

Letting go of the familiar

Anticipation also occurs at a more specific level. Once an individual has accepted a new position, he or she begins to anticipate what the new job will be like and to develop expectations about the new situation. For some people these expectations will be relatively accurate; for others they will not be. Interestingly, the difference does not seem to depend on the amount of information that the newcomer has available. It does depend on the procedures through which people are selected and hired. Interviews give applicants and hiring agents opportunities to create the most favorable (as opposed to the most accurate) images of themselves and their organizations. When the job market is tight, applicants tend to inflate their credentials even more than usual; when it is "loose," recruiters tend to create more inflated expectations than normal.[7] Negotiations over terms of employment also may create inaccurate expectations. Both the firm and the applicant engage in communication that is much like romantic courtship, with each party striving to present the best possible image. But, as in many marriages, the realities of the first six months may be quite different from the expectations created during courtship.[8] This is not to imply that either party intentionally misleads the other (although either of them sometimes may do so). It is to suggest that the selection process itself can generate expectations that may not be fully met.

For example, a new psychiatrist entered an international competition for a postdoctoral research fellowship at a major medical center in the southeastern United States. After being flown at the agency's expense to New York, Boston, and Washington for three rounds of extensive interviews, she learned that she had won the competition. Filled with justifiable pride and the expectation that she would arrive at the medical school as a respected colleague of an established research team, she was met by a secretary who escorted her to a hidden-away corner of the center where she joined five other "postdocs." Because of an error by the purchasing department, her desk and chair were not scheduled to arrive for two weeks. Three years later she angrily described her postdoc experience in a single phrase: "I didn't even have a chair." The most memorable experiences often involve employees' first few weeks at work.[9] Like the postdoc's, these remembered experiences often involve finding that one's expectations are violated, that the organization failed to fulfill a contract that the newcomer assumed was in force.

Old-timers' expectations about their newly hired colleagues also may not be met. When expectations are violated, people feel betrayed, and their trust in the other parties is reduced. As Chapter 3 explained, low levels of trust reduce the amount of and accuracy of communication. As the quality of communication between newcomers and old-timers is reduced, it becomes progressively more difficult for either side to understand the other. New expectations are formed, based on patterns of withholding or distorting information. Since these expectations are unrealistic they are easily violated. As employees become less predictable to one another they tend to withdraw, making it even more difficult for them to communicate effectively. Their expectations become less realistic, their orientations toward one another less trusting, open, or cooperative. Their access to the information they need to perform their assigned tasks effectively is reduced. Fortunately, this cycle of unfulfilled expectations, reduced trust, and isolation is not an inevitable part of the anticipation stage. Organizations can prevent it to some degree by attempting to create accurate expectations among new employees and old-timers. Newcomers can reduce it if they understand that their anticipation of a new job distorts their perceptions and if they adopt communication strategies that help them cope with reality shock.

The second important process in the anticipation stage is managing conflicts between one's generalized self-concept and one's organization-specific self-concept.[10] Every person has a **generalized self-concept**, a view of himself or herself that develops from childhood on through communication with others. We acquire complicated sets of beliefs about our *competencies,* the extent to which we should be allowed to be *independent* and *autonomous,* and the level of respect that others should show us. When people enter new organizational roles they receive messages that will, to one degree or another, fulfill or conflict with these beliefs. They may be assigned tasks that exceed newcomers' perceptions of their abilities, leading to reduced self-respect, or are so simple that they are insulting, undermining the newcomers' perceptions of their competence. In either case, they feel frustration and alienation. Their generalized self-concepts are not consistent with the messages they receive from their new organization. In similar ways, newcomers' preferences for autonomy and independence may be exceeded, frustrated, or appropriately met by their organization.[11] Over time the newcomer may adapt his or her generalized self-concept to "fit" her or his organizational specific self-concept. Since it is natural for newcomers to want to fit in, it is difficult to resist pressures to redefine one's self-concept. But since it also is difficult to accept a role that violates a person's general self-concept, fitting in can be frustrating.

CASE STUDY:
JULIE'S EXPERIENCE, PART I

Julie was a project manager in an important support division of a major international firm. She had started as a temporary employee and was hired as a full-time project assistant when she received her degree. Although she did not have the title or salary of a "project manager," she had so impressed her supervisor that she had been given many of the project manager's responsibilities. Her job was exciting and challenging. She had to understand the firm's entire line of products and have exceptional written and oral communication skills. Her advancement resulted from her willingness to work hard to improve her technical expertise and from her ability to take on and complete tasks that required sixty to eighty hours per week of complex work under severe time pressures. She very much enjoyed the communication element of her job, but she never really felt excited about the sophisticated computerized machinery that she was communicating about.

So she started to look for other jobs. Her workload had started to interfere in her family life, and the high stress and low morale of her department had started to make her dread going to work. She felt that she could do nothing about the workload, because in her company's culture working a sixty-hour week was normal and expected. In fact it was seen as evidence of loyalty to the firm. This was especially frustrating because the extra load often was avoidable—it almost always resulted from poor organization, jumping into projects before thinking through the details, or changes in design because of communication breakdowns between units.

She also was concerned about her ability to move up in the firm. Although she did not need to move immediately, she soon would be promoted to an official project manager position. After she was promoted, her salary would be high enough that it would be difficult to leave Widgets, Inc., without taking a major pay cut. Since other firms would be suspicious about why she was willing to sacrifice $10,000 a year to move, her promotion easily could trap her at Widgets. And her next promotion would probably be her last. There just were not many positions above the next level, and a large number of people would be competing for the few higher-level openings.

One afternoon a friend told Julie of an upcoming opening at nearby firm whose products were similar. All she knew about Family, Inc., was that it was a major competitor of Widgets and was reputed to be "a good place to work." Founded by an entrepreneur who still was the top manager, it had an exceptional number of perks—exercise room and indoor pool, gourmet food in the cafeteria, private offices, and comparable salaries to those at Widgets. When she first talked with people at Family she was impressed. Everyone seemed to have both technical and professional skills and worked as a team. The description

(continued)

(continued from previous page)

of the new job was very much like her favorite assignment at Widgets. In the end she was not offered that position, but Family had been so impressed with her that they offered her a project leader position for a product that sounded interesting but somewhat outside of her expertise.

Impressed with the close, collegial relationships among her potential coworkers, the obvious concern for employees—everyone was virtually required to work no more than a forty-hour week, and Family was one of the few firms in the area with high-quality on-site day care—and the large number of women in upper-management positions, she decided to make the move.

Discussion Questions

1. How did Julie's situation at Widgets influence her priorities when she started looking around?
2. How did the situation influence her perceptions of Family? What factors were more important than they otherwise would have been? What might she have overlooked because of her frustrations with Widgets?
3. In what ways did her priorities shift during the selection process? (Focus particularly on the differences between the two jobs at Family.)

The final process in the anticipation stage is letting go of the past, of accepting the fact that what made sense and was appropriate in one's previous organization(s) may not in the new organization. "Tried and true" means of perceiving, analyzing, and coping with organizational situations provide a sense of stability and predictability, but they may not work in one's new organization.[12] Newcomers also may try to maintain relational ties to coworkers in their old organizations. Ironically, people tend to strengthen their relationships with coworkers during the weeks between their decision to leave an organization and the time that they actually do so. Their coworkers reciprocate, strengthening their relational ties and making it even more difficult to leave and to "let go" of the past.[13]

But sometimes the newcomer's old organization helps with the letting-go process. An exceptionally productive and valuable researcher announced that after thirteen years she was leaving her firm to join a competitor. She made the announcement two months ahead of time in order to give the firm ample time to locate a replacement. Within two days her security clearance was canceled, leaving her with little to do and no access to the files, information, or support systems needed to do her job. During the following month she felt more and more isolated from her coworkers, who could not include her in work-related discussions and tended to exclude her from social events. She was already an outsider, and she acutely felt the stress and pain that accompanies exclusion. By the end of the month she no longer felt a part of the firm.

When she arrived at her new firm she was welcomed with open arms and whisked away to a week of training in the "way things are done here." There, isolated from other sources of information, and immersed in a group of other newcomers, she arrived at a clear, comfortable definition of her new role and found an instant support group of people who were undergoing the same kind of experiences. Her dominant feeling was relief and stability.[14] For her, leaving her old organization was traumatic. But letting go once she arrived was quick and relatively painless.

STAGE TWO: ENCOUNTER

Soon after their first days in a new job, newcomers move from anticipating the new world to confronting it. Some aspects of the new job fulfill the newcomer's expectations; others are surprising.[15] Newcomers may be surprised to learn that some parts of their jobs are less stimulating than they expected them to be. They may find that the *experience* itself is not what they thought it would be. Medical students know at an intellectual level that they will work sixty to eighty hours a week while in residency; mental health professionals know that they will be overloaded with complicated cases and buried in unnecessary administrative red tape. But they do not—indeed, they cannot—know what it will *feel* like until they actually do it. New employees also may surprise themselves. They may have chosen a position, or even a career, because they thought they wanted independence, a sense of achievement, feelings of contributing to society, or some other goal. Once they are given an opportunity to achieve that goal, they discover that it was not what they wanted after all. Most of the college students of my generation thought they wanted to "make the world a better place to live." Many of them have discovered that what they really want is to be able to afford to buy a house.

Making Sense of Organizational Situations

The key to coping with surprise is to make sense out of it. But sense-making is a complicated process. It begins when someone *acts*.[16] Trying to make sense out of an action helps a newcomer begin to make sense out of the situation she or he faces. But sense-making also involves *interaction*. When we are surprised we seek out information and perspectives from other people—we interact with them in order to manage our ambiguity and uncertainty. Through *interacting* with others the surprises that a newcomer experiences begin to make some sense, enough sense that she or he can begin to seek out additional information about how his or her new organization works.[17]

Newcomers *should* be given information about the formal requirements of their job by their supervisor—the nature and relative importance of assigned tasks, key deadlines, and the newcomer's interdependencies with other employees or units of the organization. But some supervisors are isolated from their subordinates or do not encourage communication with them. They are less useful sources of information than supervisors who are open and who serve as liaisons with different parts of the organization. Fortunately, newcomers will know within a month or so what kind of communicative relationship they will have with their supervisors. Relationships that are close and collegial at one month tend to be close and collegial long into the future; relationships that are cooperative but distant tend to stay that way.

When their supervisors are not effective communicators, newcomers may have to rely on their peers for formal information. Since peers have only indirect insight into the supervisor's expectations for the newcomer, this information may be unreliable or it may contradict other available information, creating stress and uncertainty. Fortunately, peers *are* good sources of information about behavioral expectations. Newcomers never are given an official script, and usually go through a "honeymoon period" when they are not overtly pressured to conform by old-timers. But they still learn how to play their parts. New managers often learn never to say anything negative about the firm or its products in public; officers (supervisors) usually learn that they do not fraternize with enlisted personnel (subordinates); employees sometimes learn to maintain the public images of their roles and their firms. They use its products, live in its neighborhoods, and subscribe to its dress code. Employees learn that their job descriptions exclude some responsibilities that actually are mandatory and include others that actually are forbidden. Job descriptions for secretaries rarely include making coffee for their bosses, buying presents for their bosses' relatives, or lying to their spouses about their location or activities. But these behaviors sometimes are expected. Employees who have accepted a job because its official job description includes some desirable "perk"—representing the firm at trade conventions held in exotic ports of call, for example—may find that their bosses prefer to perform that task themselves.

Peers also help newcomers learn about organizational power relationships. They explain when subordinates are expected to defer to their superiors; when they should remain quiet and let their supervisors accept credit for their work or blame them for their own errors; and when they should invite superior-grade personnel to dinner parties, show concern for their spouses and families, note their birthdays and anniversaries, and so on. They learn to at least pretend that they have cooperative, friendly, and professional relationships with their associates. "Team spirit" is demanded by almost all organizations, and acting like a member of the team is expected of every employee. In many cases these expectations will be easy to fulfill. Newcomers soon feel that they actually are part of a team. In other cases they will have to pretend that they do. And because fulfilling expectations is important, the most successful new employees often are the most consummate pretenders.

Just as there are a number of potential sources of information, there are a number of strategies that newcomers can use to obtain it. Asking overt questions is the most *efficient* way to obtain information, but asking questions is awkward because doing so reveals one's ignorance. Doing so is especially difficult for newcomers who have been transferred from other parts of the organization because they are *supposed* to know what is going on. Asking overt questions also is complicated because old-timers tend not to answer direct questions about sensitive topics until they feel comfortable with the newcomer.[18]

So, newcomers tend to avoid overt strategies of obtaining information until they perceive that the risks, including the possibility of being embarrassed, are small (see Table 6–2). Instead, they may devour all of the written information that is available to them. Or they may ask **indirect questions** about a harmless topic that is related to what they really want to know. They may hint or ask other employees about *their* histories with the firm as a way of finding out about how people advance through the organizational hierarchy.[19] *Joking* about key characteristics of the new organization or **self-disclosing** (revealing a relatively private aspect of one's experiences or identity) may generate informative responses from other employees. For example, a newcomer might tell his or her supervisor that she or he prefers "all-nighters" to missing deadlines in the hope that the supervisor will respond by revealing preferences about deadlines and work styles.[20] Newcomers also may simply *observe* other employees completing specific tasks and model their actions, a process that has been labeled *surveillance.*

Or, as Chapter 4 pointed out, newcomers can obtain a great deal of insight into the beliefs and values of the organization by closely monitoring key symbolic forms—stories, myths, metaphors, rites, and rituals. Of course, they must be careful to remember that the "official" meaning of a symbol may be very different from the "real" meaning that employees attribute to it. The primary function of an oft-repeated story may be to make an unfair reward system seem acceptable, or the purpose of the annual picnic may be to gloss over serious conflicts between management and labor. But even indirect strategies sometimes are risky. *Asking third parties* may produce incorrect or misleading information, or may lead a newcomer to view the organization in ways that conflict with his or her supervisor's views.[21] An even more risky covert strategy involves **testing limits**, when newcomers intentionally violate the rules of the organizational culture and interpret other employees' responses.

However, the most effective way to learn to make sense out of an organization may be to engage in normal processes of building interpersonal relationships—talking with people about the community, their families, their outside interests and finding common grounds with at least some of the old-timers. As newcomers establish interpersonal relationships, they begin to be accepted as part of the work group. Coworkers withhold less information and respond more positively to even very specific, overt questions than they did earlier in the relationship. Eventually they feel safe enough to reveal even sensitive information.[22] In general, the information that newcomers receive during these informal, face-to-face conversations provide the most valuable clues for making sense out of their new situation.

TABLE 6–2
Types of Information-Seeking Behavior

	OVERT QUESTIONS	DIRECT QUESTIONS (HINTING)	THIRD PARTY	TESTING LIMITS	DISGUISING CONVERSATIONS	OBSERVING	SURVEILLANCE
Newcomer comfort level	High	Low	Low with supervisors Medium with peers	High	Low	Low	Low
Fear of being embarrassed	Low	High	High	Low	High	High	High
Source availability/ competence	High	High	Low	High	High	High	High
When used	"Honeymoon" Period and Late in Encounter or in Arrival	Encounter after Honeymoon Period	Encounter	Late Encounter/ Arrival	All phases, depending on topic	All phases	All phases
Risks	High	Medium	Low	High	High	Moderate to High (depending on degree of culture shock)	Moderate (because relies on newcomers' perceptions)

Analyzing Organizational Situations

Most of organizational life—including organizational communication—is habitual.[23] In fact, one of the best indicators that a newcomer is successfully managing the "encounter" stage is that she or he has started to act out of habit. He or she knows the routines of the new organizational context well enough that she or he can treat them as routines. But the most important organizational situations are ones that call for people to abandon habitual behaviors, to analyze a particular situation and make sense of it.[24] Some people are more capable of making sense out of situations than others. But all people can enhance their ability to do so by learning some basic principles of listening.

Variations in Analytical Abilities.   As indicated earlier in this chapter, some people just seem to be more adept at analyzing organizational situations than others. Some people are **cognitively complex**, which means that they are able to interpret other people's actions and communication from a number of different perspectives and are able to accurately interpret ambiguous or contradictory information. Some people seem to be more **empathic** than others, more able to experience the emotions that another person is experiencing. Some are more able to engage in **role taking**, that is, constructing a mental image of what it is like to "be in another person's shoes." Some people are more **rhetorically sensitive** than others. They believe that (1) people are complex beings who can legitimately play a large number of different roles, (2) people should be conscious of the needs of others and express their own feelings when it is appropriate and productive to do so, but not sacrifice their own ideas and feelings in the process, and (3) communication should be flexible, even if adjusting to different situations sometimes violates social norms and conventions, or makes it seem that a communicator is inconsistent. People who are cognitively complex, empathic, and rhetorically sensitive seem to be more adept at analyzing organizational situations than people who are not. Fortunately, situational sensitivity can be increased by learning to listen.[25]

Developing Listening Skills.   Listening is a complex and difficult process. Effective listening depends on understanding the nature of messages and on developing a specific set of skills. Every message includes multiple levels of meaning.[26] Messages "mean" on a *cognitive* level—they convey bits of information. They also "mean" at *emotional* and *relational* levels. It is possible to detect a speaker's emotional tone and intensity during face-to-face communication, even though communicators often attempt to hide their emotions, especially in organizations where rationality is valued and emotional displays are frowned on. It is more difficult to assess emotional tone when messages are communicated in modes that do not include nonverbal cues, for example, in written memos. Finally, messages "say" something about the sender's interpersonal relationship with the receivers, with other members of the organization, and with the organization itself.

Simultaneously listening for cognitive, emotional, and relational dimensions of meaning is important for two reasons. First, it gives employees more complete and more accurate information about the purposes that underlie communication from others. For example, when an old-timer tells a newcomer, "That's a pretty good idea, for a rookie," the comment may reflect a variety of purposes. It could be intended to focus attention on a good idea (primarily a content purpose), to express a tutor's pride in the accomplishments of a mentoree (an emotional purpose), to remind the newcomer that he or she is a subordinate (rookie, a relational purpose), or any combination of the three. The rookie can accurately understand the comment and its purposes only by thinking "What does it mean at content, emotional, and relational levels?"

Second, listening for multiple levels of meaning also gives employees a sense of what responses are appropriate to different messages. For example, the effects of the rookie's responding "Yep. . . . Gee, I'm smart, aren't I?" will depend on the old-timer's purpose(s). If it was content, the response would have little impact. If it was emotional, the response could deny the old-timer's right to feel pride in the mentoree. If it was relational, it could challenge the hierarchical relationship that existed between them. In either case, the response would alienate the mentor.

Just as employees must listen for multiple levels of meaning, they also must listen for the *organizational functions* and *personal implications* that messages contain.[27] Some messages serve a decision-making function. They call for a rational analysis of problems and give permissions to disagree with one another to some extent. Other messages only *seem* to serve a decision-making function, but really are organizational ceremonies (see Chapters 4 and 7). For example, when upper-level personnel resign or retire, messages like "What can we ever do to replace Andy?" abound. They may sound like a call for analysis, but responses like "Well, Fred, Jennie, or Stanley could easily move up and do quite well" or "Ah, come on . . . anyone could handle Andy's job" would miss the point entirely. Messages also function to negotiate organizational roles, especially when newcomers are involved.

Messages also include *personal implications.* Every message can influence employees' "public" images and their private conceptions of themselves. The challenge that newcomers face is to understand that the organizational functions and personal implications of messages often do not coincide. The difficulty of constructing messages that meet both goals simultaneously is illustrated by research on organizational friendships. Work fosters the development of friendships because it places people in sustained contact with one another, because it makes it easier to find common interests, backgrounds, and so on, and because it creates opportunities for people to demonstrate their loyalty to and concern for one another. Contact, similarity, and emotional commitment are the bases of strong interpersonal relationships, in part because they foster high levels of trust.[28]

But work also creates tensions within friendships. One tension is between autonomy and connectedness. Friends enjoy contact and interaction, but too much contact can "smother" the relationships and create tension. Other tensions involve organizational roles. Friendships are most stable if both parties are open, honest, and nonjudgmental. But organizational roles often require people to evaluate one another's work, especially in supervisor–subordinate relationships and in work teams, and organizational situations usually limit the kinds of information that coworkers can share with one another.[29]

When working relationships involve organizational romance, the situation is even more complicated. Most romances involve supervisors and their subordinates (about 70 percent), often married male supervisors and single female subordinates. Most seem to be based on "true love" rather than on job- or advancement-related motives (about 80 percent). In general, research indicates that romances do not harm organizational performance, unless they generate such a high level of gossip that it interferes with task performance. In fact, romances may increase the performance of the couple because it makes them more approachable and may encourage them to perform at their best because they know they are being watched closely by their coworkers. But, obviously, perceptions of favoritism are more likely if a person is involved in a romantic relationship with her or his supervisors.[30] Even if no romance is involved, work relationships are complicated "blends" of friendships and task activities.

Coping with Emotions and Communication

To this point I have focused on the cognitive aspects of the entry experience. But all experiences have emotional dimensions and they are important both in themselves and because of how they influence our thoughts and perceptions. Emotions are triggered when a person's normal processes of making sense out of her or his surroundings are upset or interrupted, and emotional responses last until a new sense-making system is constructed. Newcomers usually enter an organization with an abnormally high level of **morale**—a term that encompasses feelings of satisfaction, excitement, and confidence.[31] They also have ambivalent feelings about the new situation (job). The key emotional problem newcomers face when they arrive is *fear of the unknown.* Newcomers are apprehensive about what will happen to them and anxious about how they will perform. But they also are enthusiastic and highly motivated. Energy and activity levels are high.

During this time of high morale and anxiety newcomers need communication that provides emotional support, a stable and predictable work environment, and a sense of direction about how to complete their assigned tasks. However, sometimes organizations fail to provide sufficient support and direction, and sometimes newcomers complicate the situation by seeming to be self-satisfied and overconfident. Old-timers find their communication to be offensive and become less willing to provide supportive feedback or the information that newcomers need to cope with their new roles. Sense-making processes are short-circuited or delayed, leading to increased numbers of surprises, reduced morale, and increased interpersonal tension with the old-timers.

For almost all newcomers, morale eventually falls to an abnormally low level. Newcomers begin to question their decision to enter the organization. Their dominant emotion is a *feeling of loss.* Their activity level is artificially lowered; their error rates are artificially elevated. They are frustrated and begin to feel depressed. They need supportive performance feedback and information that helps them prioritize their responsibilities and efficiently structure their tasks. But their frustration and depression may lead them to either withdraw from others or to project their hostilities onto them. Withdrawn or hostile people receive little support, often misperceive positive feedback as criticism, and obtain little information to help them cope with the cognitive demands of organizational entry. At this point many leave the organization, or remain in it but operate at a minimal level of competence.

Other newcomers respond to lowered morale by seeking out support. Eventually their morale level begins to recover, although not to the artificially high level that it had been. They become active, productive employees. Their view of their organization is in balance, allowing them to realistically criticize themselves and to speak out about the organization and needed changes. They are able to realistically reassess their situation, recognizing both the strengths and weaknesses of their organization and their previous situations. Their morale may continue to fluctuate as they feel new anxieties and new satisfactions. But the large emotional swings of the earlier stages have been confronted successfully.

CASE STUDY:
JULIE'S EXPERIENCE, PART II

Julie: "Within a month of joining Family I knew I had made a mistake. It probably was the kick in the pants I needed to switch to do what I wanted to do. The project was even more boring than what I'd been doing at Widgets. Now I realize that I had much better tools to work with there. Our support equipment is antiquated and slow, something that took me completely by surprise because Family is internationally known for making precisely the kind of support equipment that we need but don't have—I didn't even bother to ask. And I made some errors. Although everyone seemed to be open and supportive, I once compared Family to Widgets and found that 'loyalty' in this corporate culture means that you don't criticize, not even in private. When it comes down to it, because Family gives you all of these benefits, they want your soul, they *really* want your soul. And I'm not willing to give it!

"There's also this feeling (assumed and verbalized) that you must become part of the family. You feel these pressures to be sucked into the group and react by trying to stay apart and separate. It wasn't until then that I realized that

(continued)

(continued from the previous page)

I identified with Widgets more than I had known. It's frustrating—at Widgets you got the equipment we needed to do the job but not the people, here we get the people but no support equipment, even things that we make upstairs. Family is much more efficient and you waste so much less time. But it's all so informal. Basically it's a mismatch. I really shouldn't have made a move until I knew definitely what I wanted to do, or had it more focused, I guess.

"One of the good things about Family is that is has a much stronger commitment and flexibility to families. It got to a point [at Widgets] where you got to see your son for half an hour in the morning and ten minutes at night if you're lucky. And they really do seem to promote people on the basis of ability, not gender. I've never, ever heard a comment by anybody about somebody's competence based on gender. I knew that before I made the move. They're so flexible in some areas, but so very rigid in others. There are just some parts of the culture that are fixed in stone. You're expected to be there at 9:00 a.m. regardless of how late you work the night before, and sometimes everyone has to work over. But 'teamdom' means that by God you're there as early as everyone else."

Discussion Questions

1. What surprised Julie about Family? Why was she surprised?
2. What are her priorities now? How do they differ from her priorities while she was looking to leave Widgets?
3. What information should she obtain about new firms before she makes a decision to move again?
4. Pretend that you are in Julie's position. Will she/you stay with Family, Inc.? Why or why not?

STAGE THREE: ARRIVAL

By the end of the encounter stage newcomers will have learned the expectations and taken-for-granted assumptions of their organizations and will have mastered the cognitive and emotional challenges of being a newcomer. During the arrival stage some employees also will move beyond developing a comfortable relationship with their organization to actually "identify" with it and successful employees will learn to use the influence strategies that are appropriate to their new situations. It is difficult to predict how long it will take a newcomer to reach the "arrival" stage of entering an organization—three to twelve months is typical. Newcomers will "know" they have arrived when they (1) can make sense out of events and messages without having to consciously analyze them, (2) understand their role in the organization, and (3) no longer experience stress because of being uncertain about how to act.[32]

The Nature and Processes of Identification

The best way to explain **identification** is with an example. Chapter 4 described Herbert Kauffman's study of the U.S. Forest Service. Rangers scattered all across the country encountering very different problems based their decisions on the same premises. Kauffman also noticed that the rangers also had come to view the service as part of who they were as people. Just as employees of IBM long said "I am an IBMer" and meant it literally, the foresters might say "I am a USFSer."[33] They had reached what sociologist Peter Berger called the "internalization" (Chapter 1) phase of becoming part of a society. Their *self-image* depended on their membership in the organization and on the prestige that other people held for the USFS; their *self-esteem* depended on their ability to act in ways that are consistent with the taken-for-granted assumptions of the organization. In essence, they had undergone a metamorphosis—changed from individuals with independent identities to members of a tightly knit organization. The organization had become part of their identities.

Organizations encourage employees to "identify" through a variety of strategies communicated via a number of different sources. Many identification messages laud a *team atmosphere* between workers and the organization. In 1983 General Motors attributed its sudden increase in profits to "working together, and we must continue to exert our best efforts, working together."[34] Ford reported that its 1983 turnaround also resulted from "a new spirit of teamwork." Evidence of this "team" attitude was management's commitment to new programs of improving the quality of workers' lives. Other identification strategies involve *expressing concern for individual employees* and *recognizing individual contributions* to the organization through enhancement ceremonies. Organizational newsletters may include praise for the firm, either by outsiders or by employees. Conoco reported that it had received awards from the Whooping Crane Conservation Association and the Audubon Society for its efforts to protect the environment. The Bank of America newsletter includes a regular feature in which employees talk about their contributions to the company.

Or, employees may be encouraged to identify with their organizations by messages that identify a common enemy. When Steve Jobs was head of Apple Computer, he expressed respect for IBM as a "national treasure" but galvanized Apple's employees by telling them that he was "concerned" that Apple was the only thing that kept IBM from "total industry domination." Throughout the 1970s and early 1980s the Big Three automakers unified their employees by accenting the threat of unfair foreign competition and unnecessary government intrusion into the marketplace. The specter of the Japanese menace

TABLE 6-3

Identification Strategies in Formal Communiques

Concern for individuals	Recognizing individual contributions
Espousing team values	Advocating benefits and activities
Praise by outsiders	Testimonials by employees
	Fighting a common enemy

worked so well that during a recent temporary closing of a General Motors plant for renovation, UAW employees voted to ban from the plant parking lot all construction workers who drove foreign-made cars. The ban was lifted when autoworkers noted that because about 40 percent of Big Three automakers' cars were either foreign-made or had major foreign-made components, the ban would be impossible to enforce. Each of these communicative strategies (see Table 6–3) create a corporate "we" between workers and the organization, a feeling that "we" are inextricably tied together, teammates in the struggle against common enemies. Through overt persuasive efforts, organizations attempt to move employees toward identifying with it. Newly hired employees are suddenly immersed in this rhetoric precisely when they are most vulnerable to it—while they are searching for a sensible way to interpret their new surroundings.

Newcomers also may help persuade themselves to identify with their organizations. When newcomers enter an organization their friends, former coworkers, and relatives will ask them about their new jobs and organizations. These questions tend to make newcomers feel that they must justify their decision, so they tend to construct positive responses. They hear themselves saying positive things about their new organizations, and may begin to believe their own rhetoric. Psychologist Daryl Bem developed a "self-perception" theory that concludes that people first observe their actions and communication and then discover that they hold the beliefs and values that make their actions seem rational.[35] If we hear ourselves telling others that our new organization has a wonderful family atmosphere where "quality is job 1," we may begin to believe it, may begin to make work-related decisions based on that belief, and may begin to perceive ourselves as persons who are committed to quality. Slowly, through our own communicative acts, the organization, with its goals and values, becomes part of us.

However, some employees will choose to resist these pressures to identify. They may stay in their organization solely for functional reasons. Members of the United Automobile Workers who work for General Motors may do so only because "I can't get anywhere near $18 an hour anywhere else." They have a vested interest in seeing that the organization succeeds but because it is in their self-interest to do so, not because they define themselves in terms of the organization. Other employees may identify only in part. Their own beliefs, values, and interests happen to coincide with those of the organization. They understand where they fit in the organization, take pride in their contributions to its success, and feel commitment to its continuation. They may accept some of the taken-for-granted assumptions of the organization, but they do so because they actually believe in those values, not because the organization tells them they should. They may believe and proudly say "I am an IBMer" in a way that suggests that they have identified completely with the organization, while realizing that their commitment is primarily based on coinciding goals and functional ties. Even true-blue IBMers call their generous retirement programs and benefits packages "golden handcuffs" (because they would lose so much money by moving to another firm that they are effectively tied to IBM). They learn the taken-for-granted assumptions of the organization but do not accept them uncritically.

They are able to resist identification pressures because people have complex and multifaceted identities. For example, I simultaneously am a husband, father, researcher, teacher, organizational communication scholar, member of a rather unique communication department, part of a College of Liberal Arts and a university with a distinctive "culture" and tradition, and a number of other "people." My "self" is constantly being created and recreated as I receive and interpret messages from people who see only one or two of my many identities.[36] As a result, it is unlikely that I would ever identify completely with any of the organizations or groups of which I am a member. I do tend to identify most closely with those organizations in which I am most directly involved because I communicate most with the people who are most central in my communication networks—my immediate family and my immediate work group (my department). And I identify most closely with organizations that I have been involved with for a long time, because I have developed closer communicative relationships within them.[37]

An employee's level of identification also will vary across time and with different organizational experiences. A handsome reward or especially moving integration ceremony may lead an employee to temporarily identify more strongly with the organization; a negative performance evaluation or conflict with a coworker may reduce such identification. But even during those times, identification is a powerful mode of organizational control. In George Cheney's study of identification, a number of employees felt estranged from the organization, usually as the result of an unresolved conflict. Even alienated employees reported feeling a degree of emptiness because of the separation and a hope that they soon would feel as much a part of the organization as they once did. Our organizational identities give us a sense of self and of self-esteem. During the arrival stage we start the process of identifying with our organizations. But it is a process that continues as long as we are members of them.

CASE STUDY:
IDENTIFICATION AT INTERFACE PRECISION BENCHWORKS*

In many ways IPB is a unique company. From its inception it has been an employee-owned firm that is committed both to financial success and to creating a workplace in which any worker—especially workers who are profoundly mentally and/or physically retarded—can succeed. In 1984 IPB was funded primarily by the state of Massachusetts, but a new management team decided to transform it into a profitable, independent company, one which still retained its "people first, profits second" mission. By 1989 the company was such a successful producer of components for the electronics industry that Hewlett-Packard recognized IPB as one of its top ten suppliers and only 12 percent of the firm's operating funds came from the state. And, during the entire period IPB retained its commitment to providing meaningful work for its disabled employees, providing many of them with their first real job opportunities. It has done so through a "Total Quality Management" system that places "target" (disabled) and "alternative" (non-disabled) workers on the same work teams.

When employees are asked to describe the organization, it becomes clear that they—management and workers—share the vision of "people first, profits second." The office area and shop floor are separated by a wall, but it does not function as a barrier. One manager noted that when s/he** is having a bad day he finds a room with an office overlooking the shop and watches the teams in action; one "alternative" worker reported that when assembly work begins to get especially boring s/he focuses on the impact that the work is having on the "target" workers—"it makes you feel good . . . especially if they can end up doing it on their own."

Management described identification as a two-stage process, gradually integrating the target workers into a work environment and gradually integrating the alternative workers into teams that rely on coordination between alternative and target workers. Part of the process involves being persuaded to accept the values and vision of the organization, but an equally important part is learning to "talk IPB." Everyday talk reinforces the vision and values; confusion in everyday talk undermines them. Eventually, employees realize how unique IPB is, and begin to view themselves as people who are the "kind of people" who fit into its vision

---

*This fictional company name and the case study that follows are based on Claire Ferraris, Rod Carveth, and John Parrish-Sprowl, "Interface Precision Benchworks: A Case Study in Organizational Identification," *Journal of Applied Communication Research, 21*(1993): 343–357.

**Ferraris, et al. do not identify the gender of the workers they interviewed.

(continued)

(continued from the previous page)

and operations. They become emotionally tied to the organization, and to its ways of doing things. People who don't share the vision don't stay at IPB.

However, some of the changes that IPB underwent during the late 1980s management created tensions that needed to be managed. For example, at one point management decided that IPB needed to have more of a formal, bureaucratic structure. IPB traditionally had very flexible job descriptions—"We don't have job descriptions. We do whatever you got to do. From cleaning the floors, to sweeping the floors, to whatever." For some new employees this level of flexibility was alienating:

When they hired me, I was told I was hired to be an assembler and now it's gone further down the line, we could accept the trainer job, if we wanted to and get a pay raise with it, but now it's "we're asking you to do the bathrooms and if you don't do it you get written up"—because I spoke up she said "I don't know what your problem is"—I said "The problem is that I wasn't hired to be a janitor."

So, management tried to establish formal job descriptions, and to enforce them through bureaucratic procedures like "writing people up." Both changes created a great deal of confusion about work responsibilities and were inconsistent with the team vision of the firm. Trying to make these changes met a great deal of resistance from the established workers, and started to undermine the sense of vision that workers identified with. Identification depends on employees having consistent and clear communication throughout the organization. Confusion and uncertainty undermine the process.

Discussion Questions

1. IPB clearly is a unique organization. In what ways is it easier to facilitate "identification" at IPB than in other firms? In what ways is it more difficult? Why?
2. Many of IPB's employees are concerned about what would happen to the organization if it was purchased by a different management group? What would you predict would happen? Why?

Choosing and Using Appropriate Influence Strategies

As newcomers "arrive" in their organizations they learn to make sense out of the situations they face. Eventually, they learn how to manage those situations communicatively. They develop an image that is positive and accepted and they learn how to construct messages that influence others. By learning to communicate strategically, they become effectively parts of their organizations.

Image-Management Strategies.   For millennia communication scholars have recognized the impact that a communicator's image has on her or his messages. As early as 330 B.C., Aristotle observed that the images speakers create of themselves are their strongest persuasive tools. Images are created though communication and can be altered by subsequent communication. The content of organizational communicators' messages, the justifications they provide for their recommendations, and the beliefs and values they espouse, all influence their images. Conversely, the images they create influence the way other employees interpret, evaluate, and respond to their messages.[38] Employees cannot choose between creating an image and not creating one. They *can* choose between creating an image by chance or doing so by design. They can manage the images they present without being dishonest. Every person has a number of traits, abilities, and personality characteristics. Impression management means choosing to communicate in ways that make other people more aware of some of those characteristics and less cognizant of others. It involves putting on one's "best face" but not putting on a false face.[39]

Consequently, one employee rarely can know the "real" person of another employee. Erving Goffman, a sociologist whose research provides the most thorough analysis of image management, has differentiated a person's **public self**—the image that the people around us have of us—and our **private self**—the image that we have of ourselves. In order to feel comfortable in relationships with others, Goffman argues, people need to be able to keep some of their self private. In organizational relationships the barriers to self-disclosure are even greater. Consequently, one employee can know only the surface person, the public image created by other employees.[40] Hiring decisions are based largely on selection agents' conclusions about the extent to which candidates fit their images of the kind of person needed for a particular job and promotions are granted or withheld primarily on the basis of how well an employee's image conforms to decision-makers' preferred images. Employees live in fishbowls (or given the size of most organizations, in aquariums) in which they are constantly observed and their actions analyzed and interpreted.

Once employees learn what attributes are valued by members of their organizations, they can begin to create situationally appropriate images. Although cultures vary widely in what they value, most Western societies and the organizations that exist within them seem to value the images of being **rational**, **professional,** and **loyal**. "Rational" employees limit and control their emotional responses and are able to create justifications for their ideas that are organized, relevant, based on seemingly "objective" data, and are acceptable to more powerful employees. Being "professional" involves adopting the values, beliefs, and language of one's unit or profession, and limiting one's interpersonal relationships to persons of equal or superior rank in the organization. Being "loyal" often involves demonstrating a willingness to sacrifice time and commitments to outside relationships in order to meet organizational goals. But any attributes are an important part of an employee's image if they are consistent with the values of the organization.

However, if the gap between one's public and private images is too great, the employee will be required to engage in a great deal of exhausting pretending. In these cases employees might be wiser to either change their aspirations or move to an organization in which their private image would be valued. Professors who enjoy performing in the spotlight probably should gravitate toward institutions that value undergraduate teaching; those who are most comfortable working alone or with small groups may be more successful and more comfortable in major graduate research universities.

Once an image is created it must be maintained. Doing so is made difficult by the dynamics of nonverbal communication. Some nonverbal cues are easy to manage; others are not. Personal appearance can be consciously managed and has been related to career success, although the size of the effect is small. In general, people who fulfill cultural assumptions about what constitutes attractiveness may be preferred over people who do not. For example, men who are tall (over 6 feet) and trim have been shown to have higher salaries than men who are short (5 feet, 5 inches) and overweight, and having long hair or beards is negatively related to getting an initial job offer, especially in organizational cultures in which having a particular kind of appearance is a strong taken-for-granted assumption. For women, the dynamic is more complicated. Hair that is too short may seem to be "unfeminine" and violate traditional cultural assumptions about sex roles, but hair that is too long (or blonde) may be interpreted as sexy and contribute to perceptions of incompetence or low intelligence.[41]

Other nonverbal cues are more difficult to manage consciously. Maintaining direct eye contact, active gesturing, a relaxed and open body position, responsive nonverbal cues (e.g., nodding in agreement), and leaning forward while talking all are perceived positively and can be consciously controlled. For example, in job interviews, interviewers' perceptions of an applicant's social skills seem to be more positive if she or he is animated (gestures actively for a period of time during the interview), responsive (provides extended and relevant responses to questions), and conforms to expectations regarding attire and appearance (is moderately formally dressed).[42]

Fortunately, "presenting an appropriate self" (as Goffman labels the image-maintenance process) is made easier by two elements of interpersonal communication. First, people usually establish working agreements to support one another's public images. If any participants violate the implied agreement they risk having others retaliate by undermining their images. Image maintenance also is aided by the availability of "front stages" and "back stages." Even in organizational fishbowls there are times and places in which people can rehearse and perfect the communication patterns they are trying to establish. The need for back stages is one of the reasons that employees have resisted "open office" arrangements: Walls and doors create back stages. Removing these physical barriers to communication robs employees of the vital process of rehearsing their images.[43]

Image-maintenance strategies also can be used to defend one's image after making errors.[44] Of course, one can offer a legitimate apology—admitting error, accepting responsibility, and suggesting remedies or reparations. Doing so may assuage one's guilt and save one's face, but it also invites sanctions. Consequently, in organizational discourse legitimate apologies are relatively rare. It is more likely that an employee will simply **deny** having made the error. One also may offer a "**quasi-theory**," that is used to explain away errors. In our culture commonly used quasi-theories include "boys will be boys," or "we had a falling out." Or, one may offer an **excuse** in which one acknowledges making an error but denies any harmful intent or claims that she or he had no choice in the matter ("the devil made me do it"). Or, one may **justify** one's actions by blaming them on some socially accepted rule or conduct, on organizational policies, or a higher authority. For example, during the 1980s and 1990s the upper managers of many American firms have argued that their decisions to close relatively inefficient plants involved two issues: concern for the relatively small number of workers hurt by the plant closing balanced against a more important concern for staying solvent and thus protecting the jobs of thousands more employees.[45]

Or, one can offer **counterclaims**, in which one denies intentions to influence or hurt anyone or asserts that he or she really had the other person's interests at heart ("I really wasn't trying to sell you more life insurance, I was just telling you what I do for a living" or "This policy is such a wonderful deal that I really had to share it with you"). Another strategy is **bolstering**, in which the accused person (or company) accepts the charges but attempts to overcome them by linking himself or herself to relationships, concepts, or objects that the audience values. An employee who states, "Of course, I made a mistake, but you know I've always been a loyal supervisor who has your best interests at heart" adopts a bolstering strategy. And, of course, one can combine many of the more complex strategies.[46]

For example, during 1996 the Texaco Oil Company became involved in a highly publicized case of racial discrimination. A suit filed in 1994 claimed that Texaco systematically discriminated against minority employees in favor of less qualified whites in hiring and promotion decisions, and fostered a racially hostile environment. Plaintiffs complained of being called "uppity" for asking questions about policies and procedures, and were called "orangutans" and "porch monkeys." Texaco *denied* that any discrimination had taken place. Federal law requires plaintiffs to produce hard evidence that their treatment was both discriminatory and that the discrimination was because of their race. There are many ways for a company to hide evidence of discrimination—obscuring discriminatory decisions in larger downsizing moves, changing job descriptions to make a qualified minority applicant seem unqualified, or (as Texaco did) simply keeping one set of records for private use and another for government agencies, courts, and the public. As a result, it is almost impossible to obtain direct evidence of discrimination, so denial is a very effective strategy. Without direct evidence, the 1994 suit had languished, although in early 1996 the Equal Employment Opportunity Commission issued a preliminary decision in favor of the plaintiffs. This decision triggered what was to become a fateful meeting among Texaco executives.

It was a frank and wide-ranging discussion of issues related to Texaco's affirmative actions programs. Worried about the suit, David Keough (senior assistant treasurer) discussed ways to *carefully* destroy company documents so that evidence of discrimination was eliminated but evidence supporting Texaco's case was retained. The secret appraisal documents and minutes of meetings during which they were discussed were the biggest concern. Robert Ulrich, the company treasurer, concluded that "you know, there is no point in even keeping the restricted version anymore. All it could do is get us in trouble." After reviewing Texaco's promotion history, Ulrich noted that "all the black jelly beans seem to be glued to the bottom of the bag." Eventually the executives discussed their feelings about the suit and the employees who had filed it. Ulrich complained that those "niggers" were causing difficulties for them.

None of this would ever have been known except for two events. Richard Lundwall, the coordinator of personnel in Texaco's finance department, had been assigned to keep minutes on the meeting and had tape-recorded it in order to have an accurate record. In August 1996 Texaco fired Lundwall in a downsizing move and he turned his tapes over to the plaintiffs' attorneys, who released them to the *New York Times.* They broke the story on November 4.

Denial no longer was a viable response; and there simply were no quasi-theories, excuses, or justifications readily available. Texaco immediately shifted strategies to a barrage of *bolstering.* Texaco attorney Andrea Christiansen was "shocked and dismayed" by the tapes; CEO Peter Bijur announced that "the rank insensitivity demonstrated in the taped remarks . . . offends me deeply. . . . This alleged behavior does not represent the way the company feels about any of our employees. This alleged behavior violates our code of conduct, our core values, and the law. . . . Wherever the truth leads, we'll go." He also announced that Texaco would hire an outside attorney to assist the authorities with the investigation, would spend $35 million on outside evaluations and enhancement of Texaco's affirmative action and diversity management programs, and had hired an outside expert to evaluate the tape. On November 14 Texaco announced a new scholarship program for minority students, but said that "the program has nothing to do with recent negative publicity concerning published reports of racial slurs used by company executives." Faced with a boycott of its products by civil rights groups, Texaco settled the two-year-old suit within two months, and accepted external oversight of their hiring and promotion programs as part of the settlement. Virtually everything that a company and its spokespersons can say or do to bolster its image as a nondiscriminatory employer was done between November 1996 and January 1997.

In addition, the company briefly offered a *counterclaim.* The independent specialist hired and paid by Texaco to analyze the tape reported that the word that had initially been translated as "nigger" really was "St. Nicholas." But this strategy was short-lived, because, as CEO Bijur admitted when the finding was announced, "these preliminary findings merely set the record straight as to the exact words spoken in the conversations, but they do not change the categorically unacceptable context and tone of these conversations."[47]

Similar strategies can be used to maintain individual employees' images in the face of adverse events or errors. Shifting responsibility and changing perspectives allows employees to maintain images of rationality, expertise, and competence in the face of the errors they inevitably will make. But all image-management strategies involve presenting information to others that alters their interpretations of events. To maintain their images, employees must have access to and control of valuable information, and they must understand the strategies that can be used to maintain images. It is inevitable that employees develop images. The decision they must make is whether to allow their images to emerge through accident or as the result of careful strategic communication.

Choosing Appropriate Influence Strategies.   Analyzing organizational situations provides guidelines about what communicative strategies to use and how to turn those strategies into messages. Of course, one aspect of the situations an employee faces is his or her image. A communicator's image influences the credibility of any message that she or he might construct, just as the credibility of his or her messages influence image.

Fortunately, employees have a wide variety of message strategies available to them.[48] These strategies can be grouped into three categories. **Open persuasion** occurs when make their goals and methods clear to their target(s). Some open persuasion strategies are *cooperative,* as when an influencer bases appeals on rational arguments grounded in the available information. Bargaining also may be an open, cooperative strategy if both parties are interested in achieving a mutually beneficial outcome.

Other open persuasion strategies are *competitive,* as when an influencer simply orders someone to do something or threatens or promises sanctions. Threats, promises, and self-centered bargaining are available to all employees; even workers at the bottom of the organization can threaten to quit working or promise to work harder. As one might expect, subordinates rarely use competitive strategies to influence their supervisors; rational strategies are used instead. However, when resources are tight, and competition for them is intense, competitive strategies are more common.[49]

A second type of influence strategies involve **manipulative persuasion**, when influencers disguise their strategies but not their goals. "Going over someone's head," seeking support from coworkers, and manipulating interpersonal relationships are competitive versions of this strategy. **"Wearing a target down"** with repetitive influence attempts is another. **Ingratiation**, making others feel important or humbling oneself, is a common cooperative form. Although ingratiation rarely influences decisions or outcomes, it does seem to make targets like influencers more, which may benefit the influencers in the long run.[50]

The final category involves **manipulation**, disguising one's goals and one's strategies. A complex version of manipulation involves overloading a target person with information until the target is confused. The influencer then offers a solution that she or he prefers. There is a substantial amount of evidence that manipulation is the most common organizational influence strategy. The reason is simple—the potential costs of failing to influence are smallest when one's intention to influence is hidden. If the influencer fails, he or she can merely claim not to have been trying to influence. Retribution then would be seen by others as arbitrary and capricious behavior.[51]

Concern for retribution also seems to influence organizational persuaders' choices of *targets* for their efforts. The optimal target is someone who is sufficiently powerful in the organization to actually influence the outcome of an issue, but who cannot retaliate against an employee who tries to influence him or her but fails. Trying to influence one's immediate supervisor carries risks because she or he can retaliate if the attempt is found offensive. It is safer to choose a target who can impose smaller costs—a peer, group of peers, or employee in another unit of the organization. Thus, two supply sergeants at different bases will bargain with one another for desired materials more than they will bargain with their base commandants. If the negotiations go awry, neither one can punish the other. Thus, the optimal target for influence attempts is the weakest person in the organization who can give the influencer what she or he wants. But, regardless of the target choice, in general, the "softer" influence strategies (open persuasion or ingratiation) seem to be more effective in persuading other employees to change their beliefs or actions than "harder" strategies.[52]

Other factors that influence employees' choices of strategies include *cultural backgrounds, goals,* the *status of their target,* and the *point in the influence effort.* For example, Anglo managers in U.S. firms seem to use different strategies depending on the issue. When the issue clearly is within an Anglo U.S. manager's formal authority (for example, a subordinate not coming to work on time), they tend to use highly individualistic and dominating strategies—issuing ultimatums or threatening the subordinate with punishment. When the issue is less clearly within the manager's range of formal authority, Anglo U.S. managers tend to use softer individualistic strategies—requests ("I want you to feel free to ask me for help"), promises ("I reward people who have good ideas"), and ingratiation ("I really trust your judgment"). In contrast, Japanese managers seem to use community-related strategies regardless of the issue—altruism and appeals to duty ("For the good of the company, please do it") or counseling ("Can I help you get here on time?"). Of course, Anglo U.S. managers also occasionally use community-related strategies, Japanese managers also sometimes use individualistic strategies, and there is no evidence that all Japanese (or all Anglo U.S.) managers are alike in their selection of influence strategies. But the tendencies of the two groups seem to be quite clear regardless of the kind of organization they work in, and clearly related to their cultures of origin.[53]

Communicators' goals and the status of their targets also seem to influence strategy selection, at least among Anglo U.S. employees. When the goal is to improve performance or meet organizational objectives, cooperative strategies are more common; when the objective is to get personal assistance or rewards, ingratiation is most common. When the target has high formal status, rational argument is most common; when the target is of low status, competitive and manipulative strategies seem to dominate. Supervisors' personal preferences seem to be a more important influence on their choices of influence strategies than strategic considerations: They use friendly and attractive compliance strategies with subordinates whose communication is friendly and attractive, and they use unattractive strategies with subordinates who communicate in unattractive ways.[54]

Finally, communicators seem to use different influence strategies at different *"points in the influence effort."* Organizational communicators are like modern politicians, who do not try to sway voters with a single brilliant speech or television ad but instead hope to influence them through a lengthy persuasive campaign. Organizational "politicians" usually begin influence efforts with open and cooperative strategies, and shift to competitive or manipulative communication when they encounter resistance or discover that more cooperative strategies have failed.[55]

Two conclusions can be drawn about research on choices of influence tactics. The first is that supervisors really do engage in preferential treatment—they communicate differently with those they like than with those they do not like. The second is that, like virtually everything else about organizational communication, the choice of influence strategies is reciprocal. Supervisors mirror the influence styles of their subordinates, who in turn mirror the supervisors' influence styles.

Developing Effective Messages.   Employees inevitably need to explain their recommendations, proposals, and positions on issues. Some explanations are **justifications** (reasons presented in public before an action is taken, a policy is implemented, or an issue is resolved); others are **rationalizations** (reasons presented after a decision or action). Both forms of explanation are essentially the same—they are presented by an image to an audience through some medium of communication and consist of reasons arranged in some order. In the best of times employees carefully choose the reasons, structure, medium, and image. In the worst of times they do not.

The construction of effective messages begins with a search for acceptable reasons. Communication theorists since Aristotle have observed that there are two "places" in which acceptable reasons can be found—the assumptions that are accepted by all people within a culture and the preferences of the particular group of people who will serve as the audience of a message. (Aristotle called these places *"topoi."*) Employees can discover the reasons that can be used effectively in their organizations by monitoring the justifications used successfully by other employees.[56] If they notice that in their organizations rationalizations often are based on statistical data of a certain type, they can conclude that this kind of data is a "place" from which they can draw reasons for policies and actions.

Conversely, if they find that statistical data *never* are offered successfully as reasons, they can eliminate this kind of information from their list of valuable *topoi.* Of course, some of the items in the "acceptable" list will be more powerful than others in a particular situation. Moral arguments like fairness, equity, and honesty may be used successfully in personnel decisions but not in budget decisions. In other situations, none of the usually acceptable reasons are viable, forcing the employee to employ a usually unacceptable reason and create some plausible explanation of why is it appropriate "in this case and only in this case." For example, during the 1980s American firms often argued "we *never* want to eliminate American jobs, but in this case union greed has forced us to move our operation overseas. But we'll never do it again and wouldn't have done it this time except for . . ." My point is that the actions of employees determine which reasons are acceptable; employees sometimes change their minds; and naive employees can get caught in the middle of the shift if they are not careful.

Once employees choose a set of situationally appropriate reasons to support their ideas, they still have to express those reasons in a message. In Western societies and organizations, messages are more influential if they are clear, organized, include extensive supportive evidence, and generally create an impression of rationality. Creating effective messages involves a great deal of editing. In general, messages that offer simple, straightforward *expressions* of one's feelings or thoughts tend to be minimally effective.[57] Most organizational situations are complex and multidimensional, requiring people to pursue multiple goals simultaneously. For example, subordinates almost always want to construct messages that *both* preserve or strengthen their relationships with their supervisors and achieve one or more tangible goals. Even when a supervisor-subordinate relationship is hostile or otherwise negative, subordinates want to maintain at least the minimum level of civility needed to perform his or her assigned tasks.[58] Expressive messages tend to be too simple and blunt to achieve multiple goals simultaneously. And, they tend to lock relationships into us-against-them patterns, polarize positions on the issue(s) being discussed, and create ill feelings. If reciprocated they tend to create rapidly escalating conflicts (see Chapter 10).

Messages that draw on the *conventions* of a society or organization tend to be more effective than expressive messages. But by using the rules and resources that exist in a particular situation of a group, conventional messages reproduce situational rules and tend to create rigid, emotionally distant, formal work relationships. *Rhetorical messages* allow employees to pursue multiple objectives simultaneously—express feelings, create harmony, foster relational development, demonstrate sensitivity to others, and generate productive outcomes. They recognize the unique circumstances faced by the other person or the unique complications that exist in a particular situation. And, they also tend to be **strategically ambiguous**.[59]

Students and employees often are told that clarity is a virtue. But in organizational situations ambiguity can be strategic. It allows someone to speak without being held accountable for what he or she says. Employees sometimes may want to say, "Making a good decision on this issue is more important to this organization than pretending that we all get along." But they realize that the message must be presented in a way that ensures that only insiders will know its real meaning. One of the marvelous features of communication is that people can exchange a great deal of information without ever saying anything explicit. Items that are omitted often say more than items that are included. Messages can *imply* many things without ever saying them.

Strategic ambiguity also allows people to violate expectations—to say things that are not supposed to be said—without overtly doing so. For example, in contemporary organizations, recommendation letters often are left ambiguous for two reasons. Legal factors may make it impossible to keep recommendation letters confidential. If a recommender prefers not to spend time in court, she or he has three options: refuse to write a recommendation (which also may be cause for legal action), write only "factual" information (telling when a person worked at the organization, what jobs he or she held, and so on), or write a highly ambiguous letter. The second reason involves the circumstances surrounding a worker's termination. It often is in the best interests of the organization to persuade an employee to resign rather than be fired (the organization may be able to avoid paying unemployment compensation or fulfilling contractual obligations regarding severance pay).[60] Typically, part of the arrangement that is negotiated involves giving future employers positive, or at least neutral, recommendations. Ambiguous messages allow these negotiations to succeed. But it works only when both sender and receiver understand its value and are willing to tolerate its use.

Ambiguity also allows different people to interpret the same message in different ways, helping to maintain a diversity of perspectives within an organization. When the organization faces new or particularly difficult problems, diversity of interpretations can lead to innovative solutions. Interpretations differing from what was intended often reveal problems in the organization and can eventually lead to organizational change. If goals and procedures set in the past are clear, they also are constraining. If they are ambiguous, they can be changed without anyone having to admit that they have abandoned the past.

Finally, ambiguity also may allow people to take actions that are necessary but forbidden by existing policies and procedures. A supervisor usually cannot openly tell his or her subordinates, "OK, do it that way, but if you get caught I'll never admit that we had this conversation." He or she can, however, leave instructions so ambiguous that a sensitive subordinate will "get the message." Ambiguity provides flexibility, and in highly structured organizations, flexibility may be more important than clarity. However, ambiguity also can be used to manipulate employees. People are led to believe that commitments have been made that later are not carried out. They take risks and exert time and effort for promised rewards that do not materialize.[61] They become angry and defensive, resorting to the destructive bureaucratic behaviors that were described in Chapter 2. Cycles of distorting and withholding information are established, and people become more concerned with creating a protective "paper trail" documenting their activities than in maintaining effective work groups.

In general, rhetorical messages are more effective than expressive or conventional ones. They are quite common in good working relationships, and uncommon in poor ones. This seems to largely be because of supervisors' biases. They seem to allow their preferred subordinates a great deal of latitude about the kinds of messages they can use. Preferred subordinates can pursue many objectives simultaneously—they can engage in "small talk" and informal discussions of a wide range of personal and non-work-related topics. Preferred subordinates may even construct messages designed to negotiate a better relationship or to establish informal "contracts" about how the two parties will act toward one another. In contrast, supervisors seem to require their non-preferred subordinates to use expressive or conventional messages. Non-preferred subordinates respond in kind, often by using "protective" strategies like withholding or distorting information (recall Chapter 2), further locking the relationship into a distant and tense pattern. In a complex cycle, relational factors guide and constrain message production and message effectiveness, and the types and effectiveness of the messages that people produce create and sustain relational factors.

Choosing an Appropriate Message Medium

As Chapter 5 explained, members of modern organizations have a plethora of media available. However, what medium should one choose? Several theories offer some advice about choosing an appropriate medium for different messages.

Trevino, Lengel, and Daft developed a framework for media choice based on the relative **richness** of the media.[62] Media richness depends on the number of cues the medium can carry, the timeliness of feedback via the medium, the variety of language that can be used in the medium, and the degree to which the medium allows the message to be personalized. A highly rich medium would carry many cues, allow immediate feedback, a wide variety of language, and a high degree of personalization of messages. Less rich media are deficient in one or more of these respects. Based on this definition, media can be ranked according to their richness. The richest medium is face-to-face conversation, because it allows people to exchange a wide range of vocal, nonverbal, and verbal cues. Telephones screen out nonverbal cues and thus are less rich than face-to-face conversation. Electronic mail also screens out vocal cues. Personal written messages are even less rich, and written messages sent to a number of people are the leanest medium of all.

Simple, routine messages like requests for information ("lunch at Fred's at 1:15?") can be communicated in either rich or lean media, and complex messages or sensitive processes like negotiating or managing disagreements and conflicts need to be done face to face.[63] If the parties are unfamiliar with electronic media, people should use richer media than they would with people who are experienced and comfortable with the new technology. Of course, this assumes that the communicator wants to be understood as fully as possible. Employees who wish to be purposefully ambiguous may want to choose leaner media.[64] But, *in general,* when communicators want immediate feedback, need to monitor emotional responses or determine how a message influences their interpersonal relationships with the other person, or are communicating equivocal or ambiguous information, they should rely on rich media.[65]

However, media richness theory fails to take into account the ways in which organizational situations guide and constrain choices of communicative media. Like everything else, perceptions of what are appropriate media for different kinds of messages and different communication processes are socially constructed. Employees learn the taken-for-granted assumptions of their cultures or subcultures about media use the same way that they learn other assumptions—indirectly, by observing what other people do, and directly, through conversations with others, particularly those in their immediate groups.[66] After an advertising account representative lost an important account because she was offended by the brevity and impersonality of an electronic mail message, all of the executives started using the telephone or face-to-face meetings with their clients. An engineer asked his associates how to deliver bad news to the manager of another division of the organization. One colleague advised using "lean" media for this message, another recommended using a written memo sent through the normal chain of command in order to signal respect for the other division, and still another told a story about what happened the last time an engineer communicated with the other division through a memo. Together, the engineers established a set of their own "rules" for choosing appropriate media. Although considerations like the inherent "richness" of a medium are important, those considerations must be interpreted within the cultural context of the organization.

A final consideration is raised by Sitkin, Sutcliffe, and Barrios-Choplin: One should also consider the symbolic impact of media choice.[67] They note that immediate goals and norms are not the only influences on communicators' media choices. Instead, communicators also consider the **symbol-carrying capacity** of the medium. Symbol-carrying capacity manifests itself in at least two ways. First, media vary in their ability to transmit the core values of the organization. For example, an organization that values efficiency will find electronic mail, which can deliver a message almost instantaneously, a better device for signaling this value than "snail mail": regular postal delivery that could take several days for the same message. Symbol-carrying capacity is also evident in the symbolic value that the medium itself comes to hold. During World War II, parents of a soldier serving at the front shuddered when they saw the Western Union delivery person, because the news of deaths was announced in telegrams; telegrams came to symbolize death and mourning. For many of today's communicators being "on" e-mail symbolizes being technologically savvy and innovative, whereas sending the same message in a handwritten note indicates backwardness. Because the form of a message is often as important as its content, symbol-carrying capacity is an important criterion to consider in choosing a medium. Of course, organizational cultures and coworker attitudes also shape what a medium symbolizes. Symbol-carrying capacity may vary a great deal from organization to organization.

Together, richness, cultural norms, and symbol-carrying capacity provide a useful set of criteria to guide media choice. As was the case for the contingency design variables described at the beginning of this chapter, the only problem arises when the "recommendations" made by different criteria conflict with each other. Probably the most basic criteria is the organization's culture. There are indications that it shapes both perceptions of richness and symbol-carrying capacity.

CONCLUSION

Organizational communication has an **instrumental purpose**; it is oriented toward achieving goals as well as expressing emotions or transmitting information. It may involve objectives as personal as creating a desired image of oneself in the minds of others, or as broad as improving the organization's market share. Of course, employees sometimes do communicate primarily in order to express emotions or disseminate information. They may lock themselves in restrooms and scream just for the thrill of it. Or they may mechanically pass information on to others just for the sake of doing so. But it is *purposive communication* that allows organizations and their members to succeed and that helps them fail.

Organizational communication also is *strategic;* it involves making sense out of the situations that are created by a particular strategy and it involves choosing communicative strategies for managing those situations. However, it is important to always keep in mind that strategically managing organizational situations is not the same thing as *accommodating* oneself to organizational constraints. One of the recurring themes of this book is that while communication strategies often serve to *reproduce* the guidelines and constraints that are present in a particular organizational situation, they do not have to do so. The *rules* and *resources* that exist in a particular situation also can be used to *resist* and potentially to *transform* situational constraints.

I have included this cautionary reminder because many published discussions of "communication competence" tend to equate "competent" communication with "compliant" or "accommodationist" communication. An entire industry of publications, consultants, and trainers has developed whose goal is to teach managers (and *only* managers) how to be "effective" communicators.[68] Like all forms of "systematically distorted communication" (recall Chapter 4), the rhetoric of communication competence *seems* to be equitable and neutral. But the goal of many programs of developing "communication competency" is to increase managerial control of employees, to meet the organization's goals by motivating workers to sacrifice for the organization when doing so promises few rewards for them, to successfully discipline workers who have legitimate complaints, or to prevent "wrongful dismissal" suits or other corrective legal actions. Competent *subordinates* would upset the system. For example, in a study of communication between nurses and their supervisors, Peterson and Albrecht found that when supervisors were "rhetorical" communicators (as the concept was described earlier in this chapter) people in their work groups had high levels of trust, strong feelings that their supervisor-subordinate relationships were stable and predictable, and low levels of stress and burnout. The next most productive relationships were ones in which subordinates were rhetorical communicators, but their supervisors were less competent—using expressive or conventional "design logics." However, when *both* supervisors and subordinates were rhetorical communicators there were lower levels of trust and predictability, and higher levels of stress and burnout. So, in the organizations that Peterson and Albrecht studied, communication "competence" seems to be valued only when it is used by supervisors to influence their subordinates, *or* when subordinates use it to compensate for the relative communicative incompetence of their supervisors. In both of these cases the definition of "competence" supports the supervisors' dominance. But when subordinates display communicative competence that is comparable to that of their supervisors, it is not accepted, perhaps because it challenges the supervisors' dominance and thereby creates a more tense working relationship.[69] Supervisors may say that they want their subordinates to be competent communicators, but mean that they want compliant subordinates.

Communication competence need not mean *accommodation*. It can involve the effective use of communicative strategies by all employees to create more meaningful and more fulfilling work situations and working relationships. But it will do so only if the knowledge and skills associated with strategic organizational communication is available to all employees regardless of rank or function.

NOTES

[1] I will not attempt to list all of the relevant sources, but summaries of research on the entry experience include: Daniel Feldman, "The Multiple Socialization of Organization Members," *The Academy of Management Review, 6* (1981), 309–318; Fredric Jablin, "Assimilating New Members into Organizations," in *Communication Yearbook 8,* Robert Bostrom, ed. (Beverly Hills, CA: Sage, 1984), pp. 594–626; Fredric Jablin, "Organizational Entry, Assimilation and Exit," in *The New Handbook of Organizational Communication,* Fredric Jablin and Linda Putnam, eds. (Newbury Park, CA: Sage, in press); Fredric Jablin and Kathy Krone, "Organizational Assimilation," in *Handbook of Communication Science,* Charles Berger and Steve Chaffee, eds. (Newbury Park, CA: Sage, 1987); Meryl Reis Louis, "Surprise and Sense-making in Organizations," *Administrative Science Quarterly, 25* (1980): 226–251; and John van Maanen and Edgar Schein, "Toward a Theory of Socialization," in *Research in Organizational Behavior,* Barry Staw, ed. (Greenwich, CT: JAI Press, 1979), vol I.; Vernon Miller and Fredric Jablin, "Information Seeking during Organizational Entry," *Academy of Management Review 16* (1991): 92–120.

[2] Jennifer Chatman, "Matching Person and Organization: Selection and Socialization in Public Accounting Firms," *Administrative Science Quarterly, 36* (1991): 459–484; Jon Hess, "Assimilating Newcomers Into an Organization: A Cultural Perspective," *Journal of Applied Communication Research, 21* (1993): 189–210.

[3] Gareth Jones, "Psychological Orientation and the Process of Organizational Socialization," *Academy of Management Review, 8* (1983): 464–474.

⁴ A summary of these personality variables is available in Terrance Albrecht and Betsy Bach, *Organizational Communication: A Relational Perspective* (Fort Worth, TX: Harcourt Brace, 1996, especially Chapter 7); Renee Edwards, "Sensitivity to Feedback and the Development of Self," *Communication Quarterly, 38* (1990): 101–111; Also see G. Graen, "Role-making Processes Within Complex Organizations," in *Handbook of Industrial and Organizational Psychology,* Marvin Dunnette, ed. (Chicago: Rand McNally, 1976) and Meryl Reis Louis, "Acculturation in the Workplace," in *Organizational Climate and Culture,* B. Schneider, ed. (San Francisco: Jossey-Bass, 1990).

⁵ These labels are taken from Louis. Other authors have different labels, but the concepts are essentially the same. (J. Kevin Barge and G.W. Musambria, "Turning Points in Chair-Faculty Relationships," *Journal of Applied Communication Research, 20* [1992]: 54–77; Connie Bullis and Betsy Wackernagel Bach, "Socialization Turning Points," *Western Journal of Speech Communication, 53* [1989]: 273–293 and "Are Mentoring Relationships Helping Organizations?" *Communication Quarterly, 37* [1989]: 199–213.)

⁶ Robin Patric Clair, "The Political Nature of the Colloquialism, 'A Real Job,'" *Communication Monographs, 63* (1966): 249–267.

⁷ Steven Ralston & William Kirkwood, "Overcoming Managerial Bias in Employment Interviewing," *Journal of Applied Communication Research, 23* (1995): 75–92; Fredric Jablin and K.B. McComb, "The Employment Screening Interview," in *Communication Yearbook 8,* Robert Bostrom, ed. (Beverly Hills, CA: Sage, 1984); Jablin and Krone; J. Wanous, *Organizational Entry* (Reading, MA: Addison-Wesley, 1980); Louis. It's just as disorienting when the organization changes around the employee, as during mergers. In these cases, providing accurate information also is important (see David Schweiger and Angelo Denisi, "Communication with Employees Following a Merger," *Academy of Management Journal, 34* [1991]: 110–135).

⁸ The courtship process may be just as misleading for average as for excellent applicants. If, for example, the firm has interviewed four finalists and has been turned down by the top three, it has even more incentive to hire the fourth than it had to hire the first. If it fails to land that person, it will be forced to expend extra time and energy conducting another search. If a unit of an organization fails to hire the fourth candidate, it risks losing the position to other units of the organization. However, because the candidate is fourth, the firm has little incentive to make actual changes in the autonomy granted the newcomer or the "richness" of the job. But since the newcomer has been courted so vigorously by the firm, she or he may have come to expect a substantial degree of freedom, responsibility, and so on. See Jablin, "Entry, Assimilation and Exit."

⁹ Cynthia Stohl, "The Role of Memorable Messages in the Process of Organization Socialization," *Communication Quarterly, 34* (1983): 231–249.

¹⁰ A concept similar to the one I present in this section is developed and confirmed in Hess and in Jon Pierce, Donald G. Gardner, Larry Cummings, and Randall Dunham, "Organization-based Self-Esteem," *Academy of Management Journal, 32* (1989): 622–648.

¹¹ The concepts of job enrichment and job enlargement were discussed at length in Chapter 3.

¹² E.C. Hughes, *Men and Their Work* (New York: Free Press, 1958).

¹³ For excellent analyses of communication surrounding job transfers, see Michael Kramer, "Communication and Uncertainty Reduction During Job Transfers: Leaving and Joining Processes," *Communication Monographs, 60* (1993): 178–198 and "Communication After Job Transfers: Social Exchange Processes in Learning New Roles," *Human Communication Research, 20* (1993): 147–174).

¹⁴ van Maanen and Schein.

¹⁵ Meryl Reis Louis, "Surprise"; for an analysis of the effects of socializing newcomers on organizational old-timers, see Robert L. Sutton and Meryl Reis Louis, "How Selecting and Socializing Newcomers Influences Insiders," *Human Resource Management, 26* (1987): 347–361.

¹⁶ The perspective on sense-making that I will develop in this section is based on Karl Weick, *Sensemaking in Organizations* (Thousand Oaks, CA: Sage, 1995). Also see Barbara Czarniawska-Joerges, *Exploring Complex Organizations* (Newbury Park, CA: Sage, 1992).

¹⁷ Jones; Graen; van Maanen and Schein. For fine summaries of newcomers' information-seeking tactics, see Vernon Miller and Fredric Jablin, "Information-seeking During Organizational Entry," *Academy of Management Review, 16* (1991): 92–120 and Debra Comer, "Organizational Newcomers' Acquisition of Information from Peers," *Management Communication Quarterly, 5* (1991): 64–89.

[18] Kramer, "Exchange"; and Michael Kramer, "Communication During Intraorganizational Job Transfers," *Management Communication Quarterly, 3* (1989): 213–248.

[19] Patrice Buzzanell, "An Information Acquisition and Use Approach to Perceived Career Uncertainty, Transitional Events and Career Tracks." Unpublished doctoral dissertation, Purdue University, West Lafayette, IN, 1987.

[20] Charles Berger and James Bradac, *Language and Social Knowledge* (London: Edward Arnold, 1982); the example is taken from Miller and Jablin.

[21] Hewes, et al.; T.M. Lodahl and S.M. Mitchell, "Drift in the Development of Innovative Organizations," in *The Organizational Life Cycle,* John R. Kimberly and Robert H. Miles, eds. (San Francisco: Jossey-Bass, 1980).

[22] Charles Berger & Kathy Kellerman, "To Ask or Not to Ask," in *Communication Yearbook 7,* Robert Bostrom, ed. (Beverly Hills, CA: Sage); Dean Hewes, et al., "Second Guessing," *Human Communication Research, 11* (1985): 299–334; Jablin and Krone.

[23] Frances Westley, "Middle Managers and Strategy," *Strategic Management Journal, 11* (1990): 339. Also see Barbara Czarniawska-Joerges, *Exploring Complex Organizations* (Newbury Park, CA: Sage, 1992).

[24] Weick, *Sensemaking.*

[25] For key analyses of the role of cognitive complexity, see Beverly Davenport Sypher and Theodore Zorn, "Communication-related Abilities and Upward Mobility," *Human Communication Research, 12* (1986): 420–431; and B.D. Sypher, "The Importance of Social Cognitive Abilities in Organizations," in *Competence in Communication,* Robert Bostrom, ed. (Beverly Hills, CA: Sage, 1984). Rhetorical sensitivity is explained in Roderick Hart and Don Burks, "Rhetorical Sensitivity and Social Interaction," *Speech Monographs, 39* (1972): 75–91; Roderick Hart, Robert Carlson, and William Eadie, "Attitudes Toward Communication and the Assessment of Rhetorical Sensitivity," *Communication Monographs, 47* (1980): 1–22. For an analysis of the relationships between listening skills and managerial effectiveness, see Elmore Alexander, Larry Penley, and I. Edward Jernigan, "The Relationship of Basic Decoding Skills to Managerial Effectiveness," *Management Communication Quarterly, 8* (1992): 58–73.

[26] Northrop Frye, *Anatomy of Criticism* (Princeton, NJ: Princeton University Press, 1957); Paul Watzlawick, Janet Beavin, and Don Jackson, *Pragmatics of Human Communication* (New York: W.W. Norton, 1967).

[27] For example, many stories are corporate stories, and express the official values, beliefs, and assumptions of the organization (see Teresa Harrison, "Frameworks for the Study of Writing in Organizational Contexts," *Written Communication, 4* [1987]: 3–23.) Other stories are personal stories and the *process* of *telling stories* fulfills employees' personal needs, primarily those of the storyteller(s). Many stories are accounts in which the storyteller is the central character. Telling personal stories helps people enhance or clarify their identities, both in their own minds and for their coworkers.

[28] This section is based largely on Karen Bridge and Leslie Baxter, "Blended Relationships: Friends as Work Associates," *Western Journal of Communication, 56* (1992): 200–225. For a summary of dimensions of trust in supervisor-subordinate relationships, see Chapter 3; for an application to peer relationships, see D.J. McAllister, "Affect- and Cognition-Based Trust as Foundations for Interpersonal Cooperation in Organizations," *Academy of Management Journal, 38* (1995): 24–59. For an analysis of the difficulty of achieving multiple goals simultaneously in cases of sexual harassment, see Shereen Bingham and Brant Burleson, "Multiple Effects of Messages With Multiple Goals," *Journal of Applied Communication Research, 16* (1989): 184–216.

[29] Bridge and Baxter; Michael Kramer, "A Longitudinal Study of Superior-Subordinate Communication During Job Transfers," *Human Communication Research, 22* (1995): 39–64; Patricia Sias and Fredric Jablin, "Differential Superior-Subordinate Relations, Perceptions of Fairness, and Coworker Communication," *Human Communication Research, 22* (1995): 5–38; Patricia Sias, "Constructing Perceptions of Differential Treatment," *Communication Monographs, 63* (1996): 171–187.

[30] See James Dillard and Katherine Miller, "Intimate Relationships in Task Environments," in Steve Duck (Ed.), *Handbook of Personal Relationships* (pp. 449–465); James Dillard, J.L. Hale, and Chris Segrin, "Close Relationships in Task Environments," *Management Communication Quarterly, 7:* 227–255; Sue DeWine, Judy Pearson, and Carol Yost, "Intimate Office Relationships and Their Impact on Work Group Communication," in Cynthia Berryman-Fink, D. Ballard-Reisch,

and L.H. Newman (Eds.), *Communication and Sex Role Socialization* (pp. 139–165) (New York: Garland Publishing Company, 1993).

[31] For analysis of the relationship between emotions and sense-making, see Weick, *Sensemaking,* pp. 45–50. The analysis presented in the following section is based on "Towards Understanding Morale," working paper, The Wil Menninger Center, Topeka, KS. In research that started with Peace Corps volunteers and later involved executives in government and business, Walter Menninger found that like sense making, emotional responses to the entry experience develop in predictable ways. The comments on communication processes in this section are my extension of Menninger's work. For an extensive summary of emotions and organizations, see Vincent Waldron, "Once More with *Feeling:* A Reconceptualization of Emotion in Organizations," and Kim Witte and Charles Conrad, "Some Emotional Roads not Taken," in *Communication Yearbook 17,* Stanley Deetz, ed. (Thousand Oaks, CA: Sage, 1994, pp. 388–430).

[32] Kramer, "Uncertainty."

[33] Herbert Kauffman, *The Forest Ranger* (Baltimore: Johns Hopkins University Press, 1960). The concept of identification has been treated by a number of organizational theorists, including Michael Brown, "Identification and Some Conditions of Organizational Involvement," *Administrative Science Quarterly, 14* (1969): 346–355; Thomas Rotondi, Jr., "Organizational Identification and Group Involvement," *Academy of Management Journal, 18* (1975): 892–897 and "Organizational Identification," *Organizational Behavior and Human Performance, 13* (1975): 95–109. The most extensive treatment, and the one on which this section is based, is George Cheney, "Organizational Identification as Process and Product," Master's thesis, Purdue University, 1982, much of which is available in "The Rhetoric of Identification," in *The Quarterly Journal of Speech, 69* (1983): 143–158, "On the Various and Changing Meanings of Organizational Membership," *Communication Monographs, 50* (1985): 342–363; and Philip Tompkins and George Cheney, "Communication and Unobtrusive Control in Contemporary Organizations," in *Organizational Communication,* Robert McPhee and Philip Tompkins, eds. (Beverly Hills, CA: Sage, 1985); George Cheney and Greg Frennette, "Persuasion and Organization," in *The Ethical Nexus,* Charles Conrad, ed. (Norwood, NJ: Ablex, 1993). Complex relationships between identification (process) and commitment (outcome) are examined in George Cheney and Phil Tompkins, "Coming to Terms with Organizational Identification and Commitment," *Central States Speech Journal, 38* (1987): 1–15 and James Sass and Daniel Canary, "Organizational Commitment and Identification," *Western Journal of Speech Communication, 55* (1991): 275–293.

[34] Examples from automakers' reports are from Charles Conrad, "Corporate Communication and Control," *Rhetorical and Critical Approaches to Public Relations,* Elizabeth Toth and Robert Heath, eds. (New York: Praeger, 1992). The other examples are from George Cheney, 1983, and Cheney, "The Corporate Person [Re]Presents Itself," in Toth and Heath. When organizations also adopt team-based production systems, identification and "unobtrusive" processes can combine to create a very powerful form of organizational control (see James Barker, "Tightening the Iron Cage: Concertive Control in Self-Managing Teams," *Administrative Science Quarterly, 38* [1993]: 408–437 and James Barker, Craig Melville, and Michael Pacanowsky, "Self-Directed Teams at Xel," *Journal of Applied Communication Research, 21* [1993]: 297–312). Interestingly, corporate rhetors evidently use the same strategies to create ties with other organizations (C. Marlene Fiol, "A Semiotic Analysis of Corporate Language," *Administrative Science Quarterly, 34* [1989]: 277–303).

[35] Daryl Bem, *Beliefs, Attitudes and Human Affairs* (Belmont, CA: Wadsworth, 1972).

[36] I am not alone in this respect. See George Cheney, *Rhetoric in an Organizational Society: Managing Multiple Identities* (Columbia, SC: University of South Carolina Press, 1991); Linda Larkey and Calvin Morrill, "Organizational Commitment as Symbolic Process," *Western Journal of Communication, 59* (1995): 193–213.

[37] See Craig Scott, "Identification with Multiple Targets in a Geographically Dispersed Organization," paper presented at the International Communication Association Convention, Chicago, 1996; and James Barker and Phillip Tompkins, "Identification in the Self-Managing Organization: Characteristics of Target and Tenure," *Human Communication Research, 21* (1994): 223–240.

[38] Cathy Enz, *Power and Shared Values in the Corporate Culture* (Ann Arbor: UMI Research Press, 1986). The concepts of power and organizational culture are examined at length in Chapter 7. In a follow-up study Enz found that, when organizations are not homogeneous and instead are made of multiple subcultures, those departments whose members expressed the values of upper management had the greatest influence in the organization (Enz, "The Role of Value Congruity in Intraorganizational Power," *Administrative Science Quarterly, 33* [1988]: 284–304).

[39] Erving Goffman, *The Presentation of Self in Everyday Life* (New York: Doubleday, 1959); Goffman, "On Face Work," *Psychiatry, 18* (1955): 213–231; Thompson. For a valuable organizational study, see Gail Fairhurst, Stephen Graen, and Kay Snavely, "Face Support in Controlling Poor Performance," *Human Communication Research, 11* (1984): 272–295.

[40] Victor Thompson, *Modern Organizations* (New York: Knopf, 1963). Giddens integrates Goffman's work with his model of rules and resources in *The Constitution of Society* (Berkeley: University of California Press, 1984). For a discussion, see Steve Banks and Patricia Riley, "Structuration as an Ontology for Communication Research," in *Communication Yearbook 16,* Stanley Deetz, ed. (Newbury Park, CA: Sage, 1993)

[41] Judee Burgoon and T.J. Saine, *The Unspoken Dialogue: An Introduction to Nonverbal Communication* (Boston: Houghton Mifflin, 1978); Virginia Peck Richmond, James McCroskey, and S.K. Payne, *Nonverbal Behavior in Interpersonal Relationships* (Englewood Cliffs, NJ: Prentice-Hall, 1987).

[42] R. Gifford, C.F. Ng, and M. Wilkinson, "Nonverbal Cues in the Employment Interview," *Journal of Applied Psychology, 70* (1985): 729–736. For an excellent discussion of the role that nonverbal cues play in image management, see Judee Burgoon, David Buller, and W. Gill Woodall, *Nonverbal Communication: The Unspoken Dialogue* (New York: Harper & Row, 1989), especially Chapter 7. Complications regarding race, gender, and ethnicity are described in Chapter 11 of this book.

[43] Jeffrey Pfeffer, *Organizations and Organization Theory* (Marshfield, MA: Pitman Publishers), 1983.

[44] The key source for the following section is William Cupach and Sandra Metts, *Facework* (Newbury Park, CA: Sage, 1994). For detailed analyses of what I will label counterclaims, see Randall Stuttman, "Denying Persuasive Intent," paper presented at the Western Speech Communication Association Convention, San Diego, 1988, and Joe Folger, Marshall Scott Poole, and Randall Stuttman, *Working Through Conflict,* 3rd ed. (New York: Addison-Wesley, 1997) and for "conversational repairs," see Michael McLaughlin, *Conversation* (Beverly Hills, CA: Sage, 1984). For an application to the communication of public figures, see B.L. Ware and W.A. Linkugel, "They Spoke in Defense of Themselves," *The Quarterly Journal of Speech, 59* (1973): 273–283.

[45] For an interesting study of how Union Carbide used these strategies in response to the disaster in Bhopal, India, see Richard Ice, "Corporate Publics and Rhetorical Strategies," *Management Communication Quarterly, 4* (1991): 341–362.

[46] For a number of case studies in the strategies that organizational rhetors use to maintain the images of their firms, see Elizabeth Lance Toth and Robert Heath (eds.), *Rhetorical and Critical Approaches to Public Relations* (New York: Praeger, 1992) and George Cheney and Steve Vibbert, "Corporate Discourse," in *Handbook of Organizational Communication,* Fred Jablin, et al., eds. (Beverly Hills, CA: Sage, 1987).

[47] This example is based on Kurt Eichenwald, *New York Times,* November 4, 1966, A1, C4 and "Texaco Reeling from Racial Scandal," *Houston Chronicle,* November 5, 1996, 1C; Sharon Walsh, "Plaintiffs Say Texaco Tough in Bias Cases," *Houston Chronicle,* November 14, 1996, 1C; L.M. Sixel, "Workplace Racism Cases Hard to Win," *Houston Chronicle,* November 13, 1996, 1C; and Salatheia Bryant, "Texaco Initiates Scholarship Program to Help Minorities," *Houston Chronicle,* November 12, 1996, 17A.

[48] This research is summarized quite effectively in David Seibold, James Cantrill, and Renee Meyers, "Communication and Interpersonal Influence," in *Handbook of Interpersonal Communication,* Gerald Miller and Mark Knapp, eds. (Beverly Hills, CA: Sage, 1985).

[49] For a summary of subordinates' influence strategies, see Kevin Lamude, Tom Daniels, and Kim White, "Managing the Boss," *Management Communication Quarterly, 1* (1987): 232–259. Also see Nancy Roberts, "Organizational Power Styles," *The Journal of Applied Behavioral Science, 22* (1986): 443–455; and Seibold, et al.

[50] Dean Tjosvold, "Affirmation of the High-power Person and His Position," *Journal of Applied Social Psychology, 8* (1978): 230–243.

[51] Madison, et al.; Porter, Allen, and Angle. Also see Frost, pp. 28–29.

[52] Cecilia Falbe and Gary Yukl, "Consequences of Managers' Using Single Influence Tactics and Combinations of Tactics," *Academy of Management Journal, 32* (1992): 638–652.

[53] Randy Hirokawa and A. Miyahara, "A Comparison of Influence Strategies Used by Managers in American and Japanese Organizations," *Communication Quarterly, 34* (1986): 250–265.

[54] The explanation of strategy selection presented in the remainder of this section is based on research that includes only Anglo U.S. employees. Anglo U.S. supervisors seem not to be very strategic in their selection of influence strategies. Their goals seem to dictate their choices, regardless of what factors are likely to have caused the problems they are trying to correct (Young Yong Kim and Katherine Miller, "The Effects of Attributions and Feedback Goals on the Generation of Supervisor Feedback Message Strategies," *Management Communication Quarterly, 4* [1990]: 6–29). For an analysis of relational effects on supervisor strategies, see Michael Garko, "Persuading Subordinates Who Communicate in Attractive and Unattractive Styles," *Management Communication Quarterly, 5* (1992): 289–315.

[55] G.H. Morris et al., "Aligning Actions at Work," *Management Communication Quarterly, 3* (1990): 303–333; Gail Fairhurst, Stephen Green, and B. Kay Snavely, "Managerial Control and Discipline," in *Communication Yearbook 8,* ed. Robert Bostrom (Beverly Hills, CA: Sage, 1984).

[56] A more recent version of Aristotle's model was developed by Chaim Perelman and L. Olbrechts-Tyteca, *New Rhetoric* (South Bend, IN: Notre Dame University Press, 1970); C. Perelman, *The Idea of Justice and the Problem of Argument* (London: Routledge and Kegan Paul, 1963). This brief description is imprecise at one point. When Perelman and Olbrechts-Tyteca discuss *loci* (their word for *topoi*) that are "universally" acceptable they do not really mean "to everyone." Their "universal audience" is a fictional entity, not the summation of every living human. It is a speaker's perception of what "everybody knows to be true" and thus reflects his or her internalization of the values of his or her culture.

[57] Barbara O'Keefe, "The Logic of Message Design," *Communication Monographs, 55* (1988): 80–103 and "Variation, Adaptation, and Functional Explanation in the Study of Message Design," in G. Philipsen and T.L. Albrecht (Eds.), *Developing Communication Theories* (Albany, NY: SUNY Press), In Press.

[58] See Vince Waldron and Kathy Krone, "The Experience and Expression of Emotion in the Workplace," *Management Communication Quarterly, 4* (1991): 287–309, and Vince Waldron, "Achieving Communication Goals in Supervisor-Subordinate Relationships, *Communication Monographs, 58* (1991): 289–306.

[59] The best single treatment of organizational ambiguity is Eric Eisenberg, "Ambiguity as Strategy in Organizational Communication," *Communication Monographs, 51* (1984): 227–242. Also see Eisenberg and Steven Phillips, "Miscommunication in Organizations," in *"Miscommunication" and Problematic Talk,* N. Coupland, H. Giles, and J. Wieman, eds. (Newbury Park, CA: Sage, 1991).

[60] Forcing employees to resign in order to save these monies also is illegal, but it is very difficult to prove that the organization's motives were to do so.

[61] See Amatai Etzioni, *The Moral Dimension* (New York: The Free Press, 1988) and Stanley Deetz, *Democracy in an Age of Corporate Colonization* (Albany, NY: SUNY Press, 1992), pp. 194–195.

[62] Linda Trevinio, Ralph Lengel, and Richard Daft, "Media Symbolism, Media Richness, and Media Choices in Organizations," *Communication Research, 14* [1987]: 553–574

[63] When messages are not complex, personal preferences seem to determine which media people use (Trevino, Daft, and Lengel). For example, people with high levels of oral communication anxiety seem to avoid face-to-face media unless the complexity of the message absolutely requires them to use it (Elmore Alexander, Larry Penley, and I. Edward Hernigan, "The Effect of Individual Difference on Managerial Media Choice," *Management Communication Quarterly, 5*[1991]: 155–173).

[64] Contractor and Eisenberg. There also is evidence that people quickly learn to manipulate the "richness" of a medium. Olgren and Parker found that employees who regularly use video-conferencing learn to control vocal and nonverbal cues, so that they "put on a performance" rather than communicate the substance of their ideas (*Teleconferencing Technology and Applications,* Dedham, MA: Artech House, 1983).

[65] Ron Rice, "Evaluating New Media Systems," in *Evaluating the New Information Technologies,* J. Johnstone, ed. (San Francisco: Jossey-Bass, 1984); Richard Daft and R.H. Lengel, "Information Richness," in *Research in Organizational Behavior,* vol. 6, Larry Cummings and Barry Staw, eds. (Greenwich, CT: JAI Press, 1984).

[66] Janet Fulk, Charles W. Steinfield, Joseph Schmitz, and J.G. Power, "A Social Information Processing Model of Media Use in Organizations," *Communication Research, 14* (1987), 529–552.

[67] Sim B. Sitkin, Kathleen M. Sutcliffe, and J.R. Barrios-Choplin, "A Dual-Capacity Model of Communication Medium Choice in Organizations," *Human Communication Research, 18* (1992), 563–598.

[68] For an extended presentation of these ideas, see Stephanie Baron and Robin P. Clair, "From Coercion to Manipulation: Communication Competence as Disciplinary Discourse in the Organization," paper presented at the International Communication Association Convention, Chicago, 1996. For a similar analysis, see Stanley Deetz, *Democracy in an Age of Corporate Colonization* (Albany, NY: SUNY Press, 1992). Baron and Clair apply their analysis to "accommodationist" perspectives on gender relationships in organizations, a topic that I discuss at length in Chapter 11. For examples of traditional/managerial treatments of communicative competence, see Pamela Shockley-Zalabak, *Fundamentals of Organizational Communication: Knowledge, Sensitivity, Skills, Values* (3rd ed.) New York: Longman, and Terrance Albrecht and Betsy Bach, *Organizational Communication: A Relational Perspective* (Fort Worth, TX: Harcourt Brace, 1996).

[69] L. Peterson and Terrance Albrecht, "Message Design Logics and Mixed Status Relationships," paper presented at the Speech Communication Association Convention, Chicago, 1992. This is my interpretation of Peterson and Albrecht's results, although I believe that it is consistent with their interpretation, with Bacon and Clair's analysis, and with the analysis of resistance that is presented in John Jermier and Terrance Albrecht, "New Directions in the Study of Communication, Power, and Domination," paper presented at the International Communication Association Convention, Sydney, Australia, 1994.

Chapter 7

COMMUNICATION, POWER, AND POLITICS IN ORGANIZATIONS

Whatever else organizations may be . . . they are political struc-
tures. This means that organizations operate by distributing au-
thority and setting a stage for the exercise of power.

—ABRAHAM ZALZENIK

Insofar as knowledge is power, communication systems are power
systems.

—DAVID BARBER[1]

CENTRAL THEMES

- Power usually is thought of as the "ability to dominate" other people. Not only does this perspective ignore the "accomplishment" aspect of power, but it also seriously oversimplifies its multifaceted nature.
- Power is perceptual and thus is created and sustained through communicative interactions.
- Power has two components: a "surface structure," which consists of overt displays of power and conscious but unspoken decisions about who, when, and how to challenge power relationships; and a "deep structure," which consists of unconscious elements of power relationships.
- Whenever people are able to control resources that others perceive they need, they have a potential base of power.
- Resource control can be transformed into power only if the resource is perceived as scarce, significant, and irreplaceable.
- Employees can develop power through developing personal characteristics (expertise, interpersonal skills, and access to symbols of power) and through controlling key resources (information, rewards and punishments, roles in coalitions)

- The "hidden face" of power has the effect of suppressing dissent by encouraging employees to never openly challenge powerholders. As a result, employees tend to be politically active only when the deep structure and hidden face of power are ambiguous or in transition.
- One of the effects of social and organizational power relationships is to silence the voices of dissenting individuals and "different" groups. One of the most important sources of resistance to power relationships is raising those voices.

KEY TERMS

Surface structure of power	Significant resources
Gag rules	Irreplaceable resources
Hidden face of power	Practical questions
Deep structure of power	Deconstruction
Organizational politics	Technical questions
Scarce resources	Whistle-blowers

The words *power* and *politics* are used every day by almost everyone to explain much of what happens in life and at work. Consumers complain about their powerlessness in the face of big business. Students explain that they are victimized by arbitrary professors and administrators, but can do nothing in response. Subordinates vow to change their organizations for the better as soon as they advance to positions of power (but they rarely do). Power influences employees' choices about which audiences to address (and which to avoid) and how to communicate to them. Political considerations tell people what actions must be taken in particular situations and what actions and emotions should be suppressed.

If subordinates see their supervisors as powerful members of their organizations, their job satisfaction may increase and their tendency to withhold or distort may decrease. Similarly, if subordinates perceive that their supervisors are actively involved in organizational politics, they may trust them less and be more likely to withhold information.[2] Employees base their choices about how to communicate on their assessment of organizational power relationships and politics, and their choices about how to communicate reproduce power relationships.

A PERSPECTIVE ON ORGANIZATIONAL POWER

Many discussions of organizational power and politics are based on a misconception about what power is and how it functions in organizations. Usually the term "power" is used in conjunction with the phrase "abuse of." In Anglo-Western societies "power" tends to be defined as "ability to dominate." In fact, best-selling books like Michael Korda's *Power: How to Get It and How to Use It* and Betty Harragan's *Games Mother Never Taught You* "make it seem that the only issue alive in organizations is in getting power over others. No one seems to do any work anymore!"[3]

There are a number of problems with this "power over" view. One is that abuse stems from *imbalances* of power, not from power itself. The accent in Lord Acton's dictum that "absolute power corrupts absolutely" should be on absolutism, not power. David Kipnis has observed that when high power people "control other people's behavior and thoughts [it] encourages the belief that those we control are less worthy than ourselves."[4] Moreover, high power persons tend to perceive that low power persons go along with their wishes because they want to win favor, not because they have decided that the high power person was correct. As a result high power people are less trusting of others than the situation warrants. Powerlessness also is damaging. People need to feel that they have influence over their lives to one degree or another. Those of us who feel that we have control over our lives and relationships are more satisfied with ourselves and our lives, and are more productive, than people who do not.[5] People who do not believe that they have influence over their lives often become depressed and helpless, have higher levels of felt stress, develop physical symptoms like headaches and hypertension, and impede valuable organizational change and innovation.[6] Powerlessness creates feelings of vulnerability, and vulnerability leads to abuse. Understanding how communication generates power can lead to *empowerment,* and increasing the degree of balance in power relationships reduces the potential for abuse.

An "ability to dominate" view of power also makes us overlook the positive role that power plays in mobilizing people and resources to get things done.[7] Power is necessary to accomplish goals, both individual and organizational. If members of an organization define power as accomplishment, the nonproductive and personally destructive power games described in the popular press are less likely. But because the "domination" view of power is a taken-for-granted assumption in our culture, we find it difficult to shift our focus to an "accomplishment" perspective. The shift can happen, but only through understanding how communication, power, and politics are interrelated.

The final problem with "power over" views is that they seriously oversimplify the nature of power by focusing only on its overt, conscious level. I call this level the **surface structure of power**.[8] It has two dimensions. One involves overt displays of power—threats, promises, negotiations, orders, coalitions, **gag rules** that forbid employees to discuss organizational concerns with people outside of their units or firms (see the sexual harassment case in Chapter 10), and so on. But there is a second dimension of the *surface structure* of power, its **hidden face**.[9] This *face* of power works in two ways. First, it forms the parameters within which employees decide about when and how to challenge powerholders. Old-timers recount stories of battles in which low power employees won and lost. They also tell newcomers how to get ahead in the organization, and getting ahead usually involves winning some battles, playing some political games successfully. Armed with this knowledge the newcomer learns when to acquiesce and when to confront.

The hidden face of power also works by regulating public and private issues. Newcomers soon learn that some issues are not to be discussed in public, some potential solutions are not to be considered openly, and some arguments are not to be made. Open discussions are limited to "safe" topics (those that powerholders are willing to have discussed in public), acceptable alternatives, and unofficially sanctioned premises for making decisions. Consensus in open discussions is the rule, not the exception. Disagreements tend to be over minor issues and serve the purpose of perpetuating the myth that open, rational, and objective decision-making exists in the organization. If individuals violate these constraints they may either be ignored or attacked by the rest of the group. If they persist they will be "educated" by an unofficial tutor. If they cannot be educated, they may be removed.

But, as I have suggested about much of organizational life, there is another aspect of power, a **deep structure** that operates below employees' conscious awareness. Unit I examined the processes through which the taken-for-granted assumptions of a society guide and constrain employees' actions. We act in ways that we have learned are *normal* and *natural,* and we usually do so without being aware that we are. Our society's taken-for-granted assumptions tell people who they are, what their role is in society, and where they fit in the formal and informal hierarchies that constitute that society. It is through these nonconscious parameters of action that power is normally exercised. Persons act in certain ways, not because of overt threats, promises, or appeals, but because doing so is consistent with their nonconscious assumptions about who they are and what actions are normal and natural in their societies and organizations. More important, we rarely if ever realize that those societal assumptions are part of organizational power relationships or that they are important influences on how we act.[10]

For example, in Western societies we tend to take it for granted that people who seem to possess the greatest expertise on an issue should have the greatest influence over decisions. This assumption ensures that people who control access to information or who have had training in argumentation will have the greatest degree of power in a decision-making situation. This is true even if the decision is one for which information and argument are largely irrelevant, for example, on highly value-laden issues. Deciding when to terminate life support for a terminally ill patient is a matter of values and emotion much more than one of information and expertise. But the assumptions of our society lead us to treat it as an information-based decision. So, we typically defer to the "expert" opinion of medical professionals.[11] By doing so we support our culture's assumptions and in doing so reproduce the deep structure of power.

In this chapter I will first examine the potential *bases* of power that generally are available to people in the organizations of Western societies. Second, I will discuss the ways in which power is overtly exercised in organizations, a process that I will label **organizational politics**.

SOCIETAL ASSUMPTIONS AND THE BASES
OF ORGANIZATIONAL POWER

Power is in the eye of the beholder.[12] It is the belief by some members of a society or organization that they should obey the requests or commands and seek the favor and support of other members. Power is not possessed by a person. It is granted to that person by others. One person may order another to act in a certain way. But the person giving the command has no power over the other until she or he accepts the first person's right to dominate. In this sense power is a feature of interactions and interpersonal relationships, not of individuals or organizational roles.[13] People have power only when other people perceive that they do and act accordingly.

Creating perceptions of power is important to every employee. But having power is particularly important for people who depend on other people to help them do their jobs. Even employees located near the bottom of an organization can have power if other employees depend on them. For example, in a group of tobacco processing plants the mechanics who repaired machines realized that they had a great degree of power; without their cooperation the plant would come to a grinding halt. Over time they trained new mechanics orally, making sure that there were no written diagrams of equipment or repair instructions around. They modified the equipment in ways that would make it very difficult, if not impossible, for outsiders to repair it. As a result, as long as they cooperated with one another, they could virtually force management to act as they wanted. Although their power was fragile, it could be maintained as long as management depended on them to keep the equipment running.[14] If an employee is relatively autonomous and independent, creating and maintaining power is less important. But only completely self-sufficient workers need not be concerned with developing power.

The traditional strategy of organizing assumed that power and power relationships could be built into the formal structures of organizations. But formal position alone rarely provides sufficient power because employees always have access to non-formal sources of power.[15] For example, a few years ago an employee of the U.S. Government Printing Office in Pueblo, Colorado, was suspected of destroying, rather than processing, citizens' requests for booklets. His supervisors devised an ingenious scheme for gaining evidence of his malfeasance. They secretly marked a number of order forms and then searched all of the employees' wastebaskets at the end of the day. Soon they located a large number of discarded requests, which they could prove were the suspected employee's responsibility. The employee was dismissed, but an appeals board reinstated him on the grounds that he had been unfairly "entrapped" by the supervisors. As a result of the board's decision, the supervisors were left with virtually no formal power to discipline the employee, even for as clear an action as refusing to do his job. In order to influence his—or any other employee's—actions in the future, they had no choice but to rely on non-formal sources of power. Of course, this is an atypical example. But there are gaps in all formal systems of power. If there were not, employees would never act in ways that their managers did not anticipate and desire.

Employees soon learn that they must compensate for these gaps by acquiring power on their own, independent of their formal position in their organizations. They do so by demonstrating that they possess one or more valued *personal characteristics* or that they have the ability to control the distribution of resources valued by other people. But resources cannot be transformed into power unless they are **scarce** (available in supplies that are smaller than the existing demand), **significant** (employees depend on them to do their jobs), and **irreplaceable** (depletable and not easily replaced).

Gaining Power through Personal Characteristics

In Western societies two kinds of personal characteristics are assumed to be a legitimate basis on which some people can exercise power over others: their *expertise* and their *interpersonal relationships.*

Expertise as a Source of Power.   In our culture expertise has at least two dimensions. The first is a person's *actual knowledge* of a job. But task-related knowledge provides power only if other people depend on it and it is scarce, significant, and irreplaceable—something that the tobacco machine mechanics immediately understood. This explains why people sometimes do not want to hire (or promote) the most competent applicant. If the newcomer has the same expertise that an old-timer has used to gain power, the newcomer is very threatening. When you are the only person who can operate the computer system, you have almost complete power. When you are one of two people who knows how to do so, you have little power unless you can form and sustain an alliance with the other person. It also explains why employees sometimes develop equipment or procedures that only they understand. Secretaries have known for millennia that if they devise filing systems that only they understand, they may be irreplaceable. Recently, middle managers who feared that the installation of computerized management information systems would eliminate their jobs have used similar strategies to increase their organizationally relevant expertise. They may create files that only they can locate, design systems that only they can operate, or enter data in forms that only they can interpret.

Communication also is necessary to transform expertise into power. Sometimes other employees are not aware of a person's expertise or they do not understand why a particular employee's expertise is important to them and to the organization. This is one of the reasons why it is more difficult for staff personnel to be rewarded for their contributions than it is for line personnel. The upper managers of chemical firms usually are chemists, not human resource specialists. Engineering firms usually are controlled by engineers, not former directors of personnel. They can understand the value of being able to develop new chemicals or design new equipment. They may find it more difficult to understand why the ability to design and administer a new appraisal system is significant. Expertise itself does not give a person power. Perceptions do that.

The second dimension of expertise is an employee's ability to *articulate* positions effectively, to argue successfully in favor of preferred courses of action. Anyone can find facts and arguments to support a position on complex issues. But, as Chapter 6 explained, influence depends on articulating situationally appropriate reasons. In addition, choosing *appropriate* arguments creates an image of expertise.[16]

Being able to present masterful, logical arguments in support of a proposal is a wonderful skill. But if the proposal is rejected, the advocate's credibility will be reduced. It will matter little that the expert employee is always "right" in an objective sense. She or he eventually will be perceived as a failure, not as an expert. Good proposals often are rejected solely for political reasons. They may involve scuttling a powerful member's pet (but failing) project or shifting the staff and budget of a powerful department to a less powerful one. Or if well conceived and articulated, good proposals may even provide evidence that a subordinate is more expert than a supervisor. In any of these cases, the proposal may threaten powerholders and may be resisted and, ultimately, rejected.

To summarize, people can create the perception that they are expert (powerful) by advocating measures that are both cogent and accepted. Creating this perception depends both on one's technical expertise and on one's ability to understand and adapt to the constraints of an organizational situation, including existing power relationships. In what may seem to be a kind of perverse logic, expert people are those whose ideas are accepted, and people whose ideas are accepted are perceived as experts. And, as I will explain later in this chapter, it is a logic that gives artificial advantages to some individuals and groups while disadvantaging others.

Interpersonal Relationships as a Source of Power.   The second primary base of personal power in our culture is the creation of *interpersonal relationships.* People have learned that it is natural and normal to comply with the wishes of people with whom they have good relationships. We have learned to value relationships for their own sake. If we believe that refusing to comply with a friend's request may threaten the relationship, we are more likely to comply. Maintaining effective interpersonal relationships also increases a person's power in less direct ways. People view those with whom they have good relationships as being more expert, powerful, and trustworthy than others. They communicate more freely with friends and give them information they can use productively. An employee who has many friends in the organization eventually knows more about what is going on and can use that information to create an impression of expertise and power. Because we are attracted to expert, powerful people, we form friendships and share information with them. Our sharing provides them with additional information and expertise. In a complex cycle, creating and sustaining interpersonal relationships also enhances an individual's access to other bases of power.

Interpersonal relationships with groups of people also can provide power.[17] Coalitions are particularly important for employees or departments that lack other bases of power. Having allies includes the additional benefits of increasing employees' self-confidence and reducing their stress. Alliances are based on common interests—policies that each party wants to see enacted, threats that each party has received and cannot overcome alone, resources that each party wants to obtain and is willing to share. But coalitions are flexible and ever-changing. When the conditions that created the common interests change, the coalition becomes temporarily inactive or dissolves. Coalitions are inherently unstable because issues and interests change and because every member has the option of defecting and joining a different alliance. It also takes time and communication to build or revive coalitions. This is why less powerful employees often try to delay decisions. They hope that they will be able to build a winning coalition before any final decision is made. It also explains why powerholders also sometimes try to force issues to a quick decision. What may seem to be innocuous motions to refer an issue to a committee or take a straw vote may be symbols of important underlying struggles for power. Because of the dynamics of coalitions, relatively powerless employees suddenly may find that they have substantial influence because their support is being wooed by a number of competing coalitions—for once in their lives they have the tie-breaking vote. After the vote is taken, they will just as suddenly become powerless again unless they are wise enough to use their temporary power to extract long-term concessions from powerful people.

Coalitions also are unstable because of the dynamics of size. Alliances are based on the expectation that some form of "spoils" will be divided up if the coalition is victorious. Each member's reward will be increased and obligations to the other members decreased if the alliance is of the "smallest winning size." But employees also must think about the future and the need to implement the decision once it is made. Implementation often requires the cooperation of a large number of people. Their support will be stronger if they are part of the alliance that got it enacted. To gain their support, coalition members must give up some of their potential rewards to these persons. Each member of the coalition thus may be ambivalent about the presence of each other member. Coalitions are unstable, although for many people they may be the only available base of power.

Gaining Power through the Control of Key Resources

People control resources when they (1) are *key communicators* or *gatekeepers* in communication networks, (2) occupy formal positions that allow them to distribute *legitimate rewards* and *punishments,* or (3) can obtain access to the *symbols* of power.

Controlling Information.[18]   In societies that value rational decision-making (see Chapter 8), knowledge can be a potent source of power. It allows people to anticipate organizational problems and either prevent them or be ready with solutions when they do occur. It enables employees to assess the needs and biases of other employees and to meet their needs and not activate their biases. It helps them locate and exploit weaknesses in potential adversaries and to discover employees with whom they have common interests. But knowledge can be acquired only from other employees, usually through informal communication networks. Employees who occupy a central role in these networks (the key communicators described in Unit I) have access to more information than people who occupy peripheral roles.

Being a key communicator and possessing information reinforce one another. When people are confused they seek out people who are reputed to be "in the know." In conversations the seeker tells the key communicator that "I have observed such and such" and "I think it means . . ." These messages provide the sought-out person with information about what is going on and insight into the values, biases, and sense-making processes of the seeker. As long as the key communicator reinforces the seeker by listening, confirming interpretations, or providing information, the communication link will continue to exist. The key communicator will gain even more information, which will attract others and solidify a central position in the communication network.

Key communicators also send messages strategically. Information is a significant resource in all organizations. But it gives people power only if it is scarce. If it is disseminated selectively, it can enhance an individual's image as an expert and increase his or her ability to act in appropriate ways. For example, in a classic study of how an organization chose between two computer systems, Andrew Pettigrew revealed the strategies a middle manager used to see that his preference was purchased. The manager gathered information about both systems from his subordinates, passed little information about the system he opposed on to his supervisors (unless that information was negative), and sent on favorable information about the system he favored. In effect, he created uncertainty about one system, and then provided the information needed to resolve that uncertainty. Since he was in a central position in the formal communication network and was able to prevent his subordinates from "going over his head," he was able to control communication.[19] This control gave him influence over both the computer decision and subsequent decisions. Of course, in an organization with an active informal communication network, controlling information flow is very difficult. But since key communicators in formal networks also tend to play central roles in informal networks, it may not be impossible.

Employees also can gain power by processing information about an organization's environment. As the chapters in Unit I indicate, organizations must adapt to the pressures imposed on them by their environments. They must obtain accurate and timely information, but in obtaining information they create ambiguities and uncertainties for their decision-makers. Boundary spanners obtain and interpret this information. They create a dependency relationship between themselves and their organizations. One's place in overall communication networks provides a basis of influence. In fact, it may be the most potent source.[20] Power is perception. What appear to others to be personal characteristics—expertise, relational skills, and so on—often, perhaps most often, are the result of using information skillfully.

Formal Control of Resources.   Some positions in formal hierarchies involve officially sanctioned control of scarce assets. Of course, formal control of assets leads to power only if other people accept the assumption that someone's formal position is a legitimate reason to allow him or her to control the distribution of assets. The television series *M*A*S*H* featured a number of episodes in which a supply sergeant withheld equipment from the doctors, who complained loudly but rarely rejected the sergeant's right to control access to medical equipment. Secretaries in universities have a surprising amount of power because professors accept their right to control access to stamps, stationery, duplicating paper, printer cartridges, and long-distance telephone connections—assets vital to everyday activities. In both cases, the duties of the employee involve the control and distribution of scarce, valuable, and irreplaceable resources.

Resource control gives people power by enabling them to reward or punish (promise gains or threaten losses to) other employees. As long as they threaten subtly or promise tactfully, they will be able to exercise power.[21] Resource control also allows employees to persuade others to share some of the assets that they control. Our society has ingrained norms of reciprocity. When people give us something voluntarily, we feel pressure to reciprocate.

Although any scarce resource can be used to threaten or promise, the most important is money. Employees and committees that control funds invariably are the most powerful parts of an organization. In all organizations a substantial proportion of the budget is fixed. The allocation of the remainder (usually less than 10 percent) is flexible and can be distributed at someone's discretion. Once it is distributed, recipients begin to depend on it. They start payments on new equipment, hire new staff, or expand sales territories. If the discretionary funds suddenly are withdrawn, the person or unit will face serious problems. Payments will not be met, new staff will have to be fired, and new clients will have to be abandoned. Controlling discretionary funds is a potent source of power, and it provides an exceptionally strong basis for making threats, promises, or bribes. It's a golden rule: "The one who has the discretionary gold makes the rules."

Obtaining Access to the Symbols of Power.   At first glance it may seem strange to think of symbols as a resource. But power depends on perceptions, and symbols are powerful influences on our perceptions. In all societies tangible materials symbolize power: large offices, large desks, royal blue carpets, the keys to the executive washroom, invitations to social events that include high-status people, and even office windows.[22] Symbols create the impression that the person who possesses them should be honored and obeyed. They take on meaning disproportionate to their "real" value.

Some of the most intense and humorous battles ever observed involved an office with a large window or office space that neither combatant really needed. While I was an undergraduate I worked in a foundry. The key symbol of power there was a hard hat—lower-level workers had none, foremen had blue ones, supervisors white ones. One day one of my friends and I started wearing yellow plastic, nonprotective hard hats that we had borrowed from one of my neighbor's children. For two weeks the foremen and supervisors puzzled over what to do about our toy hats, although they agreed from the out-set that *something* must be done. Since there was no official rule about wear-ing toy hard hats, we were violating no policy, but we were upsetting the power relationship by violating (and making fun of) its most important symbol. Finally, after a one-hour high-level meeting, a new policy was enacted that for-bade the wearing of "unapproved" hats, "because they provided no added safety for workers," of course. Possessing symbols of power creates the percep-tion of power, but only if some people are denied access to them.

Communication and the Bases of Power.   Table 7–1 summarizes the bases of power and the communicative processes related to those bases. "Referent" power means power that is based on the quality of one's interpersonal relation-ships with others. "Legitimate" power means the influence granted people be-cause of their formal roles in their organizations—the "awe" and status that ac-companies being Chairperson of the Board as well as the official ability to control resources that accompanies formal rank. The remaining bases are self-explanatory.

In an interesting study, Wheeles, Barraclough, and Stewart examined the communicative strategies that employees use to obtain and exercise power. Although they found that many strategies were used, three were most com-mon. The first essentially involved making threats and offering promises. The second relied on referent power or on an employee's identification with the firm (recall Chapter 6). The final group of strategies involved persuasion based on shared values or on a sense of obligation. Sometimes the obligation is personal—return of a favor—and sometimes it involves a person's role in the organization, for example, trying to influence one's supervisor by argu-ing that "good supervisors help their subordinates out." The key message of Table 7–1, and of this section, is that employees have a wide range of power sources, but their ability to obtain and use power depends on their commu-nicative skills.

Summary.   Power is in the eye of the beholder, and what we behold as legit-imate sources of power depends on the taken-for-granted assumptions of our culture. Individual employees can create the perception that they are powerful by developing a particular kind of personal image or the impression that they control resources or a place in a powerful coalition. Although these bases have been discussed as if they were independent of one another, in real organiza-tions they are interrelated. People who occupy central network roles also tend

TABLE 7–1

Communication and Bases of Power

I. French and Raven's Traditional View of Power Bases*
   A. Major Bases:
      —Referent Power (based on liking or identification with other people)
      —Expert Power
   B. Secondary Bases:
      —Punishment Power
      —Reward Power
      —Legitimate (or formal) Power (based on people's formal roles in their organizations)
II. Wheeles, Barraclough, and Stewart's Communication-centered Bases of Power**
   A. Preview or Predict Expectations and Consequences (communicating reward and punishment power)
   B. Invoke Relationships and/or Identification (communicating expert and referent power)
   C. Summon Values or Obligations (communicating legitimate power and/or the values of the organizational culture)

* Based on Daniel Katz and Robert Kahn, *The Social Psychology of Organizations*, 2nd ed. (New York: John Wiley, 1978).

** Based on "Compliance Gaining and Power in Persuasion," in *Communication Yearbook* 7, Robert Bostrom, ed. (Beverly Hills, CA: Sage, 1983). Also see Virginia Richmond, et al., "Power Strategies in Organizations," *Human Communication Research* 11 (1984), 85–108.

to be perceived as experts and generally are involved in many interpersonal relationships. Individuals who are supposed to have powerful allies often are seen as being more expert and having access to more information than other people. Our perceptions of others are not separate and discrete. They merge together and overlap into complicated overall images. The communication strategies that employees can use to establish one base of power also influence other bases. Individuals or units of organizations are seen as being powerful or powerless depending on the *composite image* that their communicative acts establish in the minds of other members of their organization.[23]

David Mechanic once observed that theories about organization power usually focus on the rare occasions when relatively powerless employees refuse to obey more powerful employees or speak out against them. The common pattern in which the hidden face of power leads less powerful people to quietly carry out instructions and seek the support of powerful people has largely been ignored. Typically, employees assume that existing power relationships cannot be challenged successfully, and their assumptions so constrain their actions that instances of overt disagreement or overt exercise of power are really quite rare. In an important sense, when employees do openly challenge powerful people, or powerholders are forced to make overt threats or promises, both the deep structure and the hidden face of power have failed. They can be reinstituted, but only through the overt exercise of power, which risks raising nonconscious assumptions to a conscious level, and unmasking the hidden face of power.

ORGANIZATIONAL POLITICS: OVERT POWER IN COMMUNICATIVE PROCESS

Politics is power in communicative action.[24] In its simplest form organizational politics involves individuals or groups using the image management and influence strategies described in Chapter 6 to pursue what they perceive to be their own interests. Political action often depends on organizational actors' abilities to disguise their intentions. Employees must appear to be cooperative members of their organizations or units, lest they be perceived as untrustworthy, thus destroying their credibility and undermining their ability to gain consent from others. Politics depends on power, but power often depends on not seeming to be political.

Organizational Politics as Strategic Communication

Because of the power of the *deep structure* and *hidden face* of power, open political activity is relatively rare. When it does occur, it usually is in situations in which the deep structure and hidden face of power have been challenged or are ambiguous. This is why managers are involved in political activities more often than lower-level employees. Their jobs involve dealing with ambiguous or uncertain situations and topics. Uncertainty and ambiguity create power vacuums that invite political activity. It also explains why organizations are more political when certain issues are involved—reorganization, personnel assignment (hirings, firings, and promotions), and budget allocation. These issues are directly related to organizational power, partly because they are important to the organization and salient to individual employees, and partly because they involve high levels of uncertainty.[25] Hence, uncertainty invites political action and managing organizational politics involves managing uncertainty and ambiguity.

Managing Power Relationships

Power relationships are a central element of all organizational situations. Managing power relationships involves the same processes that were outlined in Chapter 6—interpreting situations and strategically adapting to them, including the challenging processes of managing working *relationships*. Managing power relationships also is complicated by two of the concepts discussed earlier in this chapter—the hidden face of power and the fact that not all bases of power are available to all employees. Power's hidden face limits the range of goals that are realistic in a particular situation and influences the range of communication strategies that might be successful. The nature of bases of power means that only people who are perceived as experts can draw on expertise as a basis of power; only people who are "known" to be part of powerful coalitions can employ coalition-related strategies, and so on. But the greatest complication in managing power relationships is the game-like nature of organizational politics.[26]

In some ways "game" is an unfortunate metaphor. When used in the two popular texts mentioned at the beginning of this chapter, it tends to trivialize political action. It also suggests that there are stable "rules" that govern organizational politics. Neither notion is accurate. Even what seem to be incredibly trivial political games—fights over corner offices, the largest cubicle, and so on—often are serious processes of negotiating organizational power relationships. Similarly, while organizational political games seem to have rules, the rules always are negotiable. In this sense, organizational games are more like childrens' games, in which the rules are flexible and constantly being negotiated, than like the rules of the National Football League, whose rules change only once a year.

Sociologist Peter Frost has argued that organizational politics is game-playing, and he has developed a model of political games that is very much like the perspective on organizational power that is developed in this chapter. Some games involve the "surface structure" of power. The goal of these games may be assertive, as when employees attempt to influence the beliefs and actions of other members of their organization, or defensive, when the individual or coalition seeks to maintain their own freedom of action. The political strategies may be relatively transparent uses of the persuasive strategies that were discussed in Chapter 6. Or political strategies may be more covert, as when employees *appear* to simply be trying to make sense out of ambiguous events or action. As Chapter 6 explained, sense-making is an inherently political process.[27] When employees interpret events or actions, they label them as either legitimate or illegitimate. Actors who act in ways that are perceived to be legitimate tend to garner acquiescence or support from others, and because they act "legitimately" tend to maintain or increase their power. Conversely, actions that are defined as "illegitimate" tend to generate resistance, and reduce an actor's power. Making sense out of events does not *seem* to involve pursuit of self-interest, at least not to the extent that more overt strategies do. As a result, much of organizational politics is covert and subtle, as the following case study will illustrate.

CASE STUDY:
IT'S MY PARTY AND I'LL DO WHAT I WANT TO*

Subtle and covert political games often take place in settings that on the surface do not seem to be political settings at all. Chapter 4 explained that organizational ceremonies function to maintain the "culture" of an organization. Since the core of an organization's culture is the view of "reality" that its members take for granted, and since power relationships are grounded in employees' views of reality, maintaining an organization's culture necessarily involves maintaining its

*This case is based on Michael Rosen, "You Asked for It: Christmas at the Bosses' Expense," *Journal of Management Studies, 25* (1988): 463–480 and "Breakfast at Sprio's," in Peter Frost, et al. (eds.), *Reframing Organizational Culture* (pp. 77–89) Newbury Park, CA: Sage, 1991.

(continued)

(continued from the previous page)

power relationships. In a study of annual ceremonies at a Philadelphia-area advertising agency—a Christmas party and an annual breakfast—Michael Rosen has shown the subtle and powerful ways in which ceremonial events serve as covert power games.

Organizational ceremonies are part "party" (a celebration of a sense of "community" that binds people together) and part "work" (a reminder of the status and power hierarchy that separates people from one another). Shoenman and Associates' annual Christmas party had characteristics of both. Although it was held after hours on the Friday before Christmas, attendance was required, no spouses or family members were allowed to attend (except the boss's family), and a formal program—a four-page list of the evening's activities printed on heavy yellow paper—was provided. But it also is a party. It was held at a rustic bar away from work, where people seem to eat, drink, and "make merry" with one another as "equals" regardless of their formal rank, and where the boss acts more like a host than like a supervisor—wearing casual clothes and circulating from table to table making "small talk" at each stop. But the tension between the two identities also is quite clear. As one married member put it, the structure of the event tells employees that "your work is your life, and these are your friends. It's so f——— weird. There's dancing later. I don't want to dance with people that I work with." The "party" *did* require employees to be away from their families for an extended period during the most family-oriented time of the year. But, perhaps because of the timing—the holiday season—or the location, most of the employees seemed to think of the event as more party than work.

After dinner was over, the program began—a series of jokes and skits that are carefully prepared and professionally executed. All of them were funny; all were ambiguous; most made fun of the higher-ups in the firm. Together they created a "joking relationship" that seemed to help "bridge" or "flatten" the hierarchy of the firm. They celebrated the bosses' problems. All three top managers were going through divorces. The employees joked about the divorces and presented a skit entitled "The Mating Game" (a take-off of the TV series "The Dating Game") that included a voluptuous blonde asking pointed questions about the sexual appetites and exploits of the three contestants (the three divorcing upper managers). Other jokes and skits made fun of the managers' status symbols and of one manager's inability to keep secretaries because of his obnoxiousness. The humor also commented on the crazed pace and work hours of the agency—one skit raffled off a coupon for electroshock psychotherapy treatments and many of the jokes were about the "craziness" of the work environment. They also made fun of other workers. One skit spoofed the large number of female employees who dyed their hair blonde; another made fun of the different

(continued)

(continued from the previous page)

attire of the "business" side of operation (dark blue suits and ties) and the "creative" side (almost anything else).

At one level, the humor made it seem that the organization's hierarchy had disappeared and it was a community of equals. After the program ended, the participants adjourned to the bar and dance floor. During this very informal part of the ceremony bosses and subordinates "buddied around" the bar, arms on shoulders, joking and laughing. Workers commented on how the humor had skewered the bosses. Some were even honest with management. The obnoxious manager asked the office manager what people thought of him. Thinking "what the h——," she told him that he was considered to be a bastard and is the most disliked person in the agency, something she admitted that she never would have said at work. She could "get by" with saying it, because they were at a party. In Western societies eating "signals" community, and drinking alcohol symbolizes freedom, especially from the "drudgery" of work. Parties are times of unusual license, and frictions encountered in the presence of alcohol tend to be forgiven. It *seemed* that the rules of the game were very different at the party than they were at work.

But, behind the scenes things were different. Hierarchy and formal power/authority relationships were subtle, but still in place. People seemed to dance with one another as equals, but even during the most informal part of the party, the women (most of whom are secretaries) danced with males who were their own age or older and who occupied higher positions in the organization. The skits that "skewered" upper management were written by a "skits committee" only after a lengthy negotiation process, and were revised many times before being approved by the committee chair. As one member put it, "we really had to watch our asses, but we had a f—— ball putting this thing together." A skit at the previous year's party had superimposed a picture of the boss over a picture of a farmer in overalls, boots, and pitchfork, with the title "Big Wally (boss) Sells B——s—— (advertising) Cheaper." Walter had made it very clear that the picture was out-of-bounds, primarily because it was a "permanent" record that could leave the party, not a joke or skit that could be remembered but not reproduced. Through censorship, the "rules" of the "work game" invaded the "party game," and actions that were permitted under the party rules were not allowed to be carried back to the work game. In addition, much of the party celebrated and legitimized the rules of the work game. One of the most important work rules was that work comes before anything else—that all employees were expected to sacrifice their personal and family lives in order to meet deadlines and satisfy clients' every whim. Much of the humor at the party focused on the frenetic pace of the organization—even divorces could be celebrated because everyone knew that they resulted, at least in part, from the demands of the

(continued)

(continued from the previous page)

workplace. Even the party itself required employees to sacrifice time that could be spent with outside relationships.

Interactional rules were constantly being negotiated, but negotiated in a way that maintained the underlying power relationships. Subordinates *could* make fun of their supervisors, but only in "approved" ways; supervisors *could* fraternize with their subordinates, but only in ways that maintained the hierarchy of the firm; supervisors *could* ask for frank reports on how they were perceived by others, but they alone could decide what to do with that information; subordinates *could* give frank responses, but only in private and only when asked. Some kinds of communication were "out-of-bounds" and other kinds were permitted. Although the "bounds" were different at the party than they were at work, boundaries did exist, and in negotiating them everyone was reminded that underneath it all was a power relationship that could not be challenged.

While the Christmas ceremony was a party that retained vestiges of the power and authority relationships at "work," the breakfast ceremony was work with some of the trappings of a party. Held at one of Philadelphia's most posh hotels, everyone—even the servers—were dressed in formal attire. In one way everyone was alike—even the lowliest employee could experience opulence at least once a year just by being part of the team. For a moment, even they were being served instead of serving. But in other ways the opulence focused attention on hierarchy—most of the employees could never have afforded this place on their salaries, and for a short time everyone was looking and consuming *as if they were managers*, not as if they were "regular" employees. But, it also and the differences between the "business" and "artistic" sides of the organization were obscured.

After breakfast, the speeches started. Unlike the Christmas party, the boss (Walter) was in control of the "entertainment" part of this ritual. Walter congratulated everyone for the firm's success and noted that it occurred in spite of the recession, in spite of "problems" in the public relations division, and because of their hard work and sacrifice (late hours and frenetic work pace). Walter gave gifts to retirees and recognized their loyalty to the firm. Walter talked about the "things the agency does for *us*," like funding the pension program (not mentioning that the "agency" [that is, Walter] has a legal obligation to do so, that "it" did so instead of giving year-end bonuses that were customary in other advertising agencies and had been customary in their firm, or that it could do so because of the work and skills of the workers). After a slide show that made fun of the "creative" side of the firm, Walter announced that the money that would have gone to bonuses reluctantly had to be retained "for the good of the firm." Although managers would benefit from the decision because it would increase the value of their stock in the firm, it meant that the workers' incomes actually fell because of the effects of inflation. And, raises and bonuses would occur only when management decided that they should be given, and no one

(continued)

(continued from the previous page)

knew when that might happen. One accountant referred to this tendency to leave potentially troubling details out of his announcements about the munificence of management as a "Walterism."

Finally, the vice-president of public relations spoke. He talked about how important the division was, admitted that it had problems and failures, and confessed that all of those problems were his fault. After the confessional, Walter returned to the podium and led the celebrants in a "pep rally," focusing on "telling" versus "listening" ("If everyone in this agency told and listened, we'd have fifteen percent more revenue"); "me" versus "we" ("If we can get all of the ambitions of the Me under the We, Shoenman and Associates could add another 15 to 20 percent to our revenues"); and "drive/win" ("Laid-back people have no place in this agency. . . drive is what it takes to win . . . let's get back to work").

Although still subtle, the discourse at breakfast enacted the organization's power relationships in a much more overt form than the Christmas party. *Walter* decided who would be rewarded, who would be chastised, who would be allowed to talk. *Walter* defined and celebrated the values of the organization, and legitimized them in terms of increased revenues. And *Walter* decided how those revenues would be distributed. Although at least some of the employees understood all of these things, they said nothing, for saying nothing is how *they* play the Walter game.

Discussion Questions

1. Rosen argues that the power of these political rituals is that they obscure the organizational power relationships while enforcing them. How would the employees' interpretations and responses have been different if Walter had been overt and direct about his expectations about employee performance and his evaluations of their work? Why?

2. What would have happened if an employee who understood what was going on had spoken up? How would the other employees have responded? Why?

The Biggest Game of All: Taking and Silencing Voices

Recently, organizational communication theorists have started to focus on the concept of "voice," recognizing that a crucial element of social and organizational power relationships is regulating who gets to speak (and who does not), what they may speak about, and how they must speak in order to be heard. The process of regulating voice occurs at an individual level when organizations suppress dissent, but it also occurs at a broader level. Organizational discourse tends to be discourse by and for a particular group of people—almost exclusively educated white male managers—and tends to exclude the voices of other groups—women, non-management workers, and members of racial and ethnic minority groups. Since these concepts will be developed in more detail in Chapters 10 and 11, I will introduce them only briefly in this chapter. But since processes of privileging some voices and muting others are essentially political processes, it is important to think about them in terms of organizational power relationships.

Muting Individuals' Voices.   Almost a decade ago, W. Charles Redding, generally viewed as the "father" of organizational communication, summarized a speech given to his class by a high-ranking officer of a *Fortune* 500 firm:

> A single dominant theme emerged from the speaker's lecture. . . . "Although the company needs people who, of course, are intelligent and competent, our over-riding objective is to find people who will *'fit in.'* . . . "Will this applicant become a Company Man or a Company Woman?" (a "loyal" employee who internalizes corporate goals and values). . . . To be sure we heard the conventional wisdom that the company needed college graduates with "ideas," with "creativity and imagination." However class questions elicited the caveat that generating innovative ideas did *not* extend to challenging "basic corporate policies" or "managerial prerogatives." I wrote down at one point the speaker's exact words, which he emphasized with appropriately vigorous gestures: *"We don't particularly need boat-rockers."*[28]

Redding's point was that in most contemporary U.S. organizations, dissent, regardless of how principled or correct it might be, is forbidden. Employees are expected to speak in the "organization's" (that is, upper management's) voice, both inside and outside of the organization.

Of course, in most organizations, most of the time, dissent is not even an issue. Every strategy of organizing (recall Unit I) has its own system of controlling employees. Every system of control covers what employees do *and* what they say. But no control system is perfect; the hidden face of power always provides some space for resistance, and dissent is a potent form of resistance. When resisting voices are raised, surface-level power strategies come into play. These overt strategies of suppressing dissent typically take place in graduated phases. Initially, organizational powerholders attempt to persuade the dissenter that he or she is wrong, mistaken about the facts, and so on (a process sometimes called "nullification"). If that fails, the dissenter is isolated from her or his coworkers—disconnecting telephones or revoking computer access codes, removing the dissenter's name from invitation lists for social events, or transferring him or her to the corporate version of Stalin's Siberia. If isolation fails (and it rarely does because most people decide that dissent is not worth the costs) direct sanctions are applied—defaming the dissenter or expelling him or her from the organization.

The processes through which organizations suppress dissent is illustrated clearly by the situation faced by **whistle-blowers**, people who report unethical or illegal activities within their organizations to the authorities or the press.[29] When John Kartak reported fraudulent activities in a Minneapolis Army recruiting office, he was ordered to report to a Veterans Administration hospital for psychological evaluation. After being declared "fit for duty," he returned to his unit. He was constantly watched by his supervisors and ostracized, threatened, and intimidated by his coworkers (many of whom were later proven guilty of fraud). Then he was ordered back to a military hospital for another psychological evaluation, which also declared him fit for duty. (For other examples, see the case study that follows this section or watch your daily newspaper; even illegal suppression of dissent is really quite common.)

The risks to a whistle-blower's advancement, relationships with coworkers, and personal safety often are quite large and the potential gains quite small. But the personal costs of not doing so—reduced self-esteem, guilt, and fear that someone else will report it, leaving the employee in the role of an accomplice—also may be quite large. For potential whistle-blowers merely deciding whether to communicate is in itself a complicated problem. Most people do not speak up even when doing so promises equivalent gains and risks; very few do so when speaking involves substantial risks with little opportunity for gain. As a result, whistle-blowing is relatively rare, and whistle-blowers' complaints often are withdrawn before any corrective action is taken.

CASE STUDY:
SUPPRESSING DISSENT IN THE NUCLEAR INDUSTRY*

Because of the obvious risks to public health and safety, the nuclear industry has one of the strongest whistle-blower protection systems in U.S. industry. Since 1974, if a nuclear organization is convicted of discriminating against an employee for raising safety concerns, the U.S. Department of Labor can order reinstatement, back pay, promotion, and other compensation and the Nuclear Regulatory Commission (NRC) can fine the company and refer the matter to the Justice Department for criminal prosecution. But the power relationships between nuclear organizations and their employees mean that "the system is stacked against you . . . if you've got the law and the facts and God on your side, you've got a 50 percent chance of winning," says Larry Simmons, a former contact welder who blew the whistle at Florida Power Company's Crystal River plant in 1988. The results of the many complaints filed against nuclear firms seem to support Simmons' conclusion. (In January 1993, 142 such cases were pending nationwide, a figure that almost certainly underestimates the number

---

*The primary source for this case study is a series of articles published by the *Houston Chronicle* during March and September 1993. For a broad analysis of issues regarding the release of low-level radioactivity, see Jay Gould, *Deadly Deceit: Low Level Radiation, High Level Coverup* (New York: Four Walls Eight Windows, 1990) and Jay Gould and Ernest Sternglass, *The Enemy Within: The High Cost of Living Near Nuclear Power,* forthcoming.

(continued)

(continued from the previous page)

of violations, since most people do not blow the whistle on their employers.) It is nearly impossible to win against a multimillion-dollar firm with a battery of skilled attorneys who can drag a case out for years while the plaintiffs' savings and resolve are depleted and their careers ended. Even in the relatively rare cases when plaintiffs receive a settlement, the vast majority of the money goes to cover their legal expenses, and fines levied against the organizations are small relative to the firm's size (fines of $25,000 to $250,000 are common for violations at plants that generate $1 million a day in revenues).

Three cases are illustrative of the experiences of nuclear industry whistleblowers. In March 1989, Len Trimmer (who had worked for the University of California division at Los Alamos National Laboratory since 1962, receiving numerous promotions) was assigned to inspect drums of radioactive material to see that they met safety standards. He complained that his test equipment was malfunctioning and later discovered about 20 leaking drums. The drums tested with the flawed equipment were labeled "certifiable" and the leaking drums were left to leak. He complained to the NRC and subsequently experienced a number of events that he believed were in retaliation—one coworker kicked a chair out from under him, and he was ordered to move heavy drums, aggravating an old back injury. While he was on disability leave his desk and locker were broken into, and on the day that the local newspaper ran a story about him a large rock bounced off his parked car. He was never called back to work.

Martin Marietta Energy Systems, the primary contractor at Oak Ridge National Laboratory, transferred Charles Varnadore to a high radiation chemistry lab and assigned the task of manipulating radioactive materials with mechanical arms, something he couldn't do well because he had been blind in one eye since birth and didn't have the depth perception necessary to operate the equipment properly. After he made a number of "messes," he complained. From then on he was a *persona non grata,* being transferred so often that he earned the nickname "technician on roller skates." He returned to work in July 1989 after surgery for colon cancer to find that his job had been filled by a younger man, and his new office was a room "with mercury all over it" where drums of radioactive waste were stored. In June 1993, Judge Theodor Von Brand ruled in Varnadore's favor and wrote a blistering criticism of Martin Marietta that concluded that "they intentionally put him under stress with full knowledge that he was a cancer patient . . . particularly vulnerable to the workplace stresses to which he was subjected." Since the court decision, Varnadore has filed additional complaints, one of which accuses a company labor relations officer of saying during a training session that "someone should get a gun and take him out and shoot him."

One of the longest and most complicated case involves Vera English, whose eight-year battle against General Electric's nuclear fuel plant in Wilmington, North

(continued)

(continued from the previous page)

Carolina, has included favorable rulings by the U.S. Supreme Court, NRC, Department of Labor, and a number of other judges; $250,000 in lost wages and legal fees; no financial gain; and a $20,000 fine paid by GE. In March 1984, after two years of complaining to GE management about safety-related violations, English charged GE with violations of company policy regarding safety. In April, GE told her that she would lose her job unless she applied to be transferred to the non-nuclear section of the plant. In July she was fired, in August she filed a complaint with the Department of Labor, which found evidence of discrimination in October. GE appealed the verdict. A year later an administrative law judge ordered GE to reinstate her to her original position and pay her $73,007 in damages plus back pay. GE appealed. In January 1987, the Secretary of Labor reversed the decision on the grounds that English had not filed the complaint within 30 days of being warned of the layoff. She appealed, arguing that she did complain within 30 days of being fired. After a number of other re-hearings and appeals within the Labor Department, the secretary again dismissed her complaint.

But English also had sued GE in federal court. In February 1988, a federal district judge found that she had a valid claim, but dismissed it on a technicality. In June 1990, after two additional appeals, the U.S. Supreme Court ruled in her favor and returned the case to the lower court. In October her case was dismissed because she had not proven GE's actions to be "outrageous," a decision that was upheld on appeal. Amount of time spent fighting the case: 7 1/2 years with the Department of Labor; 5 1/2 years in court. Outcome: no damages recovered. A Tennessee Valley Authority whistle-blower concluded: "We all discovered that the process doesn't do anything but put a big bull's-eye on your back."

However, the outcome sometimes is different. David Lamb and James Dean, who raised safety concerns about a south Texas nuclear power plant run by Houston Lighting and Power (HLP), were fired in 1992. In late 1993 an administrative law judge in the Department of Labor ruled that they had been harassed and fired because of their whistle-blowing activities, but the company appealed the ruling to the Secretary of Labor. In November 1996, HLP paid a $160,000 fine to the NRC as a result of the allegations, and on November 19, 1996—the day before the Secretary of Labor was to announce his decision—the company reached an out-of-court settlement with the two for an undisclosed amount of money. Neither man has been able to find employment in the nuclear power industry, but Lamb concludes that "[the settlement takes] a big load off our backs. No amount of money will every pay for what they did to us or what I believe they have done to other personnel. But it sure goes a long way."**

**Jim Morris, "Whistle-blower Claims Settled," Houston Chronicle, Nov. 20, 1996, A24–25.

(continued)

(continued from the previous page)

Discussion Questions

1. Pretend that you are the manager of a nuclear plant and are not especially constrained by ethical considerations. Also pretend that an employee keeps making complaints about safety problems at the plant. The likelihood of these problems becoming public knowledge are quite slim, but they could be very expensive and embarrassing if they ever were made public. But solving the problems would be very expensive, and your supervisors already are pressuring you to reduce costs. So, the "rational" strategy seems to be to silence the dissenter. What strategies are available that would allow you to do so? What are the likely costs and effects of each of those strategies?

2. Now pretend that your efforts to suppress dissent failed, and the employee reported the problems to the Nuclear Regulatory Commission. What strategies now are available to you to deal with the problem? What are the likely costs and effects of each of those strategies?

Muting Groups' Voices.   One of the recurring themes of this chapter, indeed of this book, is that power and control in organizations depends on the processes of perceiving and attributing meaning. Sense-making is guided by social and organizational power relationships; strategic communication manages power relationships largely through creating shared sense-making. In turn, sense-making and strategic communication creates, reproduces, and sometimes transforms power relationships. At first glance, the interrelationships among meaning-creation, communication strategies, and power relationships seem to be the same for all people and all groups of people. But a number of contemporary views of social and organizational power suggest that taking a closer look will reveal that there are important power inequalities embedded in meaning-creation and communication.

In short, in most U.S. organizations, what an act "means" is determined by the beliefs, values, and frames of reference of educated, white, male upper-level managers. Although employees who are non-white, lower-level, less educated, or female may make sense of an event or action in very different ways, the discourse of organizations tends to privilege the interpretive frames of the dominant group. For example, the meaning that typically is attached to the job cuts that have accompanied organizational "downsizing" during the 1980s and 1990s is that they are unavoidable adaptations to the pressures of a global economy. They will increase efficiency and productivity, thus making U.S. firms more competitive in the long term and protecting Americans' jobs. Of course, many other interpretations are possible. For example, one could argue that downsizing primarily benefits upper management (recall Chapter 1), not workers, stockholders, or society as a whole; or that downsizing has had little positive effect on efficiency or productivity. Twenty-six percent of downsized firms report efficiency increases while 19 percent report decreases and 39 percent report no change, in part because of resulting increases in absenteeism, voluntary turnover, and stress (11 percent report increased absenteeism, 62 percent report lower morale, and 39 percent report increased voluntary turnover). So, for workers and middle managers—more of whom tend to be female, nonwhite, less well educated, and less wealthy than upper management— "downsizing" means lost income, reduced self-esteem, and increased stress and insecurity, not increased profits or a rosy future. But the discourse about downsizing that takes place within organizations, and by organizations in the popular media, focuses almost completely on the managerial interpretation and almost completely ignores or "mutes" other interpretations.[30]

Another alternative interpretation involves the criteria of "efficiency" and "effectiveness" themselves. Roger Jehensen has called these concepts "ideological fictions" that foster the interests of some groups over the interests of others.[31] "Efficiency" is not itself a goal or outcome, it is a means of reaching some other goal or outcome. Driving fast, or driving in a fuel-efficient manner (two possible definitions of "efficient" travel), are meaningless unless doing so gets us somewhere, and gets us somewhere that we want to be. Presumably, organizational efficiency is important because it produces something else of value— profits or the continued existence of the organization, for example. If we define "efficiency" in this way, as a *means* to an end, then we immediately ask questions about the value of the ends themselves. We will ask what communication theorist Jurgen Habermas has called **practical questions**, questions like "What level of environmental damage are we willing to accept in order to increase profits?" or "What proportion of a firm's profits should be reinvested in the publicly funded infrastructure (roads, education systems, and so on) that the organization uses to produce those profits?"[32] But if we instead define efficiency as an *end* in itself, we tend to ask only **technical questions** about how to achieve the highest levels of efficiency that are possible. We no longer ask *practical* questions about where our efficient organizations are taking us. In effect we transform value-laden questions about goals and social costs into seemingly value-neutral questions about techniques. In the process we privilege narrow, technical kinds of expertise—the expertise that managers are presumed to have—and silence the voices of people who ask *practical* questions that are based on their expertise, experiences, and values—workers and members of the communities in which our organizations exist (see Chapter 12).

Focusing on *technical* questions instead of *practical* ones privileges the interests of some groups over others. The definitions that make up the questions themselves have the same effect. For example, the usual "technical" definition of "efficiency" is "output per person hour." But what if "efficiency" was defined in terms of "output per dollar of supervisory overhead"? Both definitions are justifiable on economic grounds, but the former definition focuses attention on workers, places the burden for organizational success on controlling and motivating *them,* legitimizes management's efforts to do so, and suggests that the rewards gained for increased efficiency should be given largely to management because it was *their* skill at motivating and controlling workers that created "efficiency." Similarly, the usual definition justifies blaming workers for negative outcomes because it could only have been *their* lack of effort, ability, and productivity (in spite of management's best efforts) that caused the losses, thereby further legitimizing management's efforts to motivate and control workers in the future. In contrast, the second definition of "efficiency" focuses attention on managerial overhead, places the burden for organizational success on management's shoulders, suggests that the number of managers and their compensation should be kept as small as possible, and tends to assume that non-managerial personnel do the *real* work of the organization. The former definition elevates the interests and "voice" of managers over workers; the latter elevates the interests and voice of workers.

A number of feminist scholars have extended this concept of silencing the voices of powerless groups, to examine the ways in which organizational discourse privileges the meaning systems of males. The three underlying assumptions of the perspective are that:

1. The structure of Western economies divides labor into different categories by gender (men have tended to work for pay in public while women have tended to work without pay in private settings like the home), which means that men and women have different experiences and thus perceive the world differently;
2. Men dominate the public realm (politics and organizations), so their perceptions dominate the public realm, preventing alternative meanings from being expressed or accepted;
3. When women enter the public realm they are expected and pressured into adapting their meaning systems to "fit" the dominant (male) system.

As a result, women have more difficulty expressing themselves in the public realm than men do, sometimes because men simply do not have a term for many of women's experiences; women find it easier to understand men than men find it to understand women (because women have been required to learn men's language, but men have not been required to learn women's language); women often try to change the dominant rules of communicating or systems of meaning in order to better express their experience, but find it more difficult to do so than men do; and men and women interpret symbolism differently (for example, men and women have different senses of humor—they laugh at different things and for different reasons).

But masculine constructions of reality permeate the way we think as well as the way we communicate; language and thought are two sides of the same coin. For example, men (at least in Western societies) learn to think of interpersonal relationships in terms of hierarchy ("Who *is* the captain of this team, anyway?") while women tend to think in terms of "webs" of interconnected people.[33] Each of these metaphors suggests different definitions of achievement, ethics, power, effectiveness, and so on. For example, the hierarchy metaphor suggests that achievement means moving above others, power means being dominant *over* others, effectiveness means obtaining goals in the face of resistance, and "ethics" is defined in terms of the legal acceptability or success of an action. "Reality" is perceived in terms of discrete categories—policies are *either* good *or* bad, organizational issues are "line" concerns *or* "staff" concerns, decisions are rational *or* irrational.[34] Once one metaphor is accepted as dominant within a society or social group, it is treated as *normal* and *natural*. It no longer needs to be justified, and any other metaphor is automatically defined as inferior and must constantly be justified. People who speak in the language of hierarchy automatically are heard; people who speak in the language of connectedness constantly need to explain and legitimize themselves and their ideas.

In Western organizations, the hierarchy metaphor is both dominant and exaggerated. In fact, hierarchy has become accepted as the defining characteristic of the public realm of experience, and connectedness largely has been relegated to the private realm of families and intimate relationships.[35] People who think and communicate in different terms or who are *assumed* to do so upset the taken-for-granted construction of "reality" of hierarchical, male-oriented organizations. Their presence alone is threatening because it calls into question the entire set of "ideological fictions" that define Western organizations. It is especially disruptive when different people begin to enter the upper levels of organizations, because the essence of upper management is faith in hierarchy. Unless people believe that managers should be obeyed because they are managers, or because they are rational or expert, the power relationships that underlie bureaucratic organizations disappear. Stability can be maintained only if the threat to "hierarchy" is reduced. The most direct way to do that is to remove the threat, to suppress, ignore, or eliminate any "different" voices.

One means of muting these voices is to persuade potentially "disruptive" people to adopt the language and thought of the dominant members—to persuade women, members of minority groups, non-managerial employees—to become as "normal" (that is, as "managerial") as possible. This is the essence of the accommodationist advice that often is given to women and minority managers (discussed in more detail in Chapter 11). Adopting the language of hierarchy, the values of upward mobility, the "power over" definition of power, and even the dress and mannerisms of middle- and upper-class white males, are depicted as the most direct avenue to organizational "success" (with "success" defined in terms of hierarchy) for "different" employees. In short, in order to have influence, employees must adapt their communication to the dominant power relationships of the organization. But adapting to those power relationships means communicating in the language of masculinity, which reproduces the dominance of masculine conceptions of reality and silences differing voices.

When people *do* speak in the language of connectedness and emotionality, their speech can be ignored or devalued ("Don't be so emotional," or "Of course it's important to consider the effects that our decision will have on the lives of our workers, but we really have to make a 'bottom-line' decision and we have to make it today," or "That's not a bad idea for a woman/African American/Latino/production worker/etc.") Different voices also are suppressed by treating people with professional credentials as if they were lower-level workers, as when women managers are assumed to be secretaries and treated as if they are, or African American and Latino managers are assumed to be and treated as it they were custodians. The voices of people who might deviate from the language of hierarchy also can be muted by placing them where they are easy to ignore—outside of informal communication networks, in small offices that are hidden from public view, or in divisions of the organization that have little influence (for example, human resources or public relations). Issues that are particularly important to marginalized groups (for example, equity or sexual harassment) can be ignored, referred to a committee, or localized in powerless departments.

Claiming a Voice for Marginalized Groups.[36]   Three approaches have been suggested as means of claiming a voice for marginalized groups. One approach is the creation of alternative organizations that are grounded in collectivist metaphors, practices, and modes of thought. A number of these alternative organizations were described in Chapter 5; feminist organizations will be discussed in Chapter 11. But, as Chapters 5 and 11 explain, creating and sustaining truly alternative organizations is difficult, in part because all members of Western societies have been acculturated to take masculine assumptions for granted. For example, even in organizations in which the elite group of power-holders is primarily composed of women, there still is a tendency for the elites to use their positions in communication networks to reinforce their own positions of privilege.[37] In addition, alternative organizations typically have to interact with traditional hierarchical organizations, and those external pressures make it difficult to operate in a truly non-hierarchical way. One way of managing these pressures is to create unique organizational systems that retain a degree of hierarchical structure (with a single person identified as the "top manager") in order to fulfill the expectations of outside organizations, while organizing everyday activities around shared leadership that rotates among organizational members. In this way, the patterns of acting in the organization affirm values of flexibility and provide a means for every member to achieve her (or his) own goals.[38]

Another approach to creating a voice for marginalized groups involves creating collective groups within hierarchical organizations. A number of studies have found that women faculty members are able to create and sustain collectivist informal groups within large, bureaucratic, masculine-dominated universities. Similarly, programs of legitimate participation in decision-making serve to empower members of organizations whose voices have been muted. But internal strategies are difficult to implement. As Chapter 3 explained, formal programs of empowerment generate resistance from precisely those persons who have the greatest degree of organizational power, resistance that can take on a variety of subtle forms. Overcoming that resistance seems to require employees to rely on the power relationships and political strategies of hierarchical organizations in an effort to change those relationships and strategies.[39] Like much of organizational life, affecting change is a paradoxical activity.

A final approach to creating multiple voices involves the critical analysis of organizational discourse. One of the recurring themes of this book is that the taken-for-granted assumptions of a society or organization are potent largely because they are taken for granted. Consequently, resistance often is as simple as raising those assumptions to a conscious level and examining them directly. One approach to doing this is called **deconstructing** organizational discourse. The concept originated in what often is labeled "postmodernist" literary criticism. Deconstruction begins with the recognition that *all* organizational discourse, like all strategies of organizing, is strategic. It privileges some people and groups while it disadvantages others. Claims to truth, knowledge, expertise, and ethicality are legitimate only within particular views of reality, and those views of reality are strategic choices. So, deconstructing an organizational text means to ask what it takes for granted, what it says, what it does not say, and how all of that influences power relationships. I provided one example of deconstructing an organizational text earlier in this chapter when I discussed the different ways in which organizational "efficiency" could be defined. Another example was provided by organizational theorist JoAnne Martin. While conducting research at OZCO (her pseudonym for a Silicon Valley firm), Martin observed the CEO's response to a question about how the company helps women workers who have children. Initially he responded "I'm not sure." When asked why the company had not made any provisions for day care, unlike many firms in the industry, he responded "Well, I think we are, of course, concerned about family values. I think they are on the decline, and I think that is a problem." When pressed further he told a story:

> We have a young woman who is extraordinarily important to the launching of a major new [product]. We will be talking about it next Tuesday in its first worldwide introduction. She arranged to have her [baby born by a] Caesarean [operation] yesterday in order to be prepared for the event, so you—we have insisted that she stay home and this is going to be televised in a closed circuit television, so we're having this done by TV for her, and she is staying home three months.

The CEO interpreted the story as evidence of OZCO's commitment to helping mothers with managerial duties, and he expressed pride in the company's willingness to incur the costs of granting her a three-month maternity leave, and paying for a closed circuit TV to her bedroom so she could perform her duties. Of course, a number of other interpretations of the story are possible.

For example, when Martin told the story to a group of employees, many hissed, and retorted that the story demonstrated how low the company would go to extract work from their employees ("That baby deserved to be born when it was ready, not when OZCO scheduled it to be"). Others said that the organization's purported humanitarian policies were merely a cover for their low pay scale and lack of sensitivity to gender issues. There were no women in senior positions at OZCO, those in managerial positions were not supportive of lower-level women, and one of the dominant themes of the organization was that of "the midwestern Mommy and Daddy: Daddy makes the decisions and takes care of the family and Mommy does the supplementary stuff." Others interpreted it as showing how out of touch upper management was with the needs of workers, or how confused they were about the policies that actually existed in the firm.

Martin's "deconstruction" of the story accepts the observation that there are a number of different ways in which one can interpret what the story says. But she goes even further to examine what was not said. For example, the first line of the story says "we *have* a young woman," not "we *employ* a young woman." The choice of the verb "have" suggests an exceptionally high degree of organizational control, and carries sexual implications. She suggests that the gender-related dimension of the story becomes clear if one substitutes a male manager having a coronary bypass operation for the pregnant manager. Interpretations of a firm arranging for *him* to have a closed-circuit TV system brought into his room the day after he returns home from surgery tend to be very different from the interpretations that are offered of the Caesarean story.[40] Organizational power relationships are grounded in deep structure, assumptions that are taken for granted. Deconstructing those assumptions in itself serves as resistance to hierarchical power, and can serve as the basis of the many kinds of resisting discourse that have been discussed throughout this book.

CONCLUSION

Traditional models of organizational power focus on only one dimension of power relationships—overt displays like orders, threats, promises, and political strategizing. But power has additional, equally important dimensions. The "surface" structure of power also has a "hidden face," the conscious processes through which employees decide which battles to fight and how to fight them. And power has a deeper structure. Power is perception; it exists in the minds of social and organizational actors, not in a realm independent of our activities. It is inextricably linked to the taken-for-granted assumptions of our culture, both in general and in particular organizational cultures. All three dimensions of power must be considered if any one dimension is to be understood. Overt displays are influenced by the hidden face of power and its deep structure, *and* both of these dimensions are influenced by overt displays.

Similarly, the hidden face is influenced by employees' perceptions of what actions are *normal* and *natural* in their cultures, and employees' decisions about which battles to fight and how to fight them influence the overt displays of power as well as what we perceive are normal and natural ways of dealing with organizations. Finally, the assumptions of a society are created, reproduced, and transformed by its members' overt actions and hidden decisions about power relationships. One dimension of power simply cannot be understood without simultaneously considering the others.

NOTES

[1] Abraham Zalzenik, "Power and Politics in Organizational Life," *Harvard Business Review* (May-June 1970): 47–60; David Barber, *Power in Committees* (Chicago: Rand-McNally, 1966): 65. The literature on social and organizational power is almost overwhelmingly large, so much so that it would be impossible to list even a small proportion of the important works here. Instead of trying to do the impossible, I will cite a number of sources that summarize the main ideas presented in the chapter. Particularly valuable are Henry Mintzberg, *Power In and Around Organizations* (Englewood Cliffs, NJ: Prentice-Hall, 1983); Ian Mitroff, *Stakeholders of the Organizational Mind* (San Francisco: Jossey-Bass, 1983); and Jeffrey Pfeffer, *Power in Organizations* (Marshfield, MA: Pitman, 1981) and *Managing With Power* (Boston: Harvard Business School Press, 1992). More complete listings of key sources are available in Charles Conrad, "Organizational Power: Faces and Symbolic Forms," in *Communication and Organizations,* Linda Putnam and Michael Pacanowsky, eds. (Beverly Hills: Sage, 1983), Charles Conrad and Mary Ryan, "Power, Praxis and Person in Social and Organizational Theory," in *Organizational Communication,* Phillip Tompkins and Robert McPhee, eds. (Beverly Hills, CA: Sage, 1985), and Dennis Mumby, "Power in Organizations," in *The New Handbook of Organizational Communication,* Linda Putnam and Fredric Jablin, eds. (Thousand Oaks, CA: Sage, In Press.)

[2] Fred Jablin, "An Exploratory Study of Subordinates' Perceptions of Supervisory Politics," *Communication Quarterly, 29* (1981): 269–275.

[3] Michael Pacanowsky, "Communication in the Empowering Organization," in *Communication Yearbook 11,* James Anderson, ed. (Beverly Hills, CA: Sage, 1987).

[4] David Kipnis, *Technology and Power* (New York: Springer-Verlag, 1990): 38. Also see E.E. Jones, K.J. Gergen, and R.G. Jones, "Tactics of Ingratiation Among Leaders and Subordinates in a Status Hierarchy," *Psychological Monographs, 77* (1963): 119–128; and D.G. Pruitt and J. Rubin, *Social Conflict* (New York: Random House, 1986).

[5] Malcolm Parks, "Interpersonal Communication and the Quest for Personal Competence," in *Handbook of Interpersonal Communication,* Mark Knapp and Gerald Miller, eds. (Beverly Hills, CA: Sage, 1985).

[6] Terrance Albrecht, "Communication and Personal Control in Empowering Organizations," in *Communication Yearbook 11,* James Anderson, ed. (Beverly Hills, CA: Sage).

[7] Rosabeth Moss Kanter, *Men and Women of the Corporation* (New York: Basic, 1979).

[8] Multilevel models of power are developed in a large number of contemporary writings. Two of the most important are the works of Anthony Giddens, cited throughout this book, and Steven Lukes, *Power, a Radical View* (London: Macmillan, 1974). For summaries of these models, see Stewart Clegg, *Frameworks of Power* (Newbury Park, CA: Sage, 1989) and Charles Conrad, "Was Pogo Right?" in *Communication Research in the Twenty-first Century,* Julia Wood and Richard Gregg, eds. (Cresskill, NJ: Hampton Press, 1995).

[9] See Calvin Morrill, "The Private Ordering of Professional Relationships," in *Hidden Conflict in Organizations,* Deborah Kolb and Jean Bartunek, eds. (Newbury Park, CA: Sage, 1992); Robyn Clair, "The Use of Framing Devices to Sequester Organizational Narratives," *Communication Monographs, 60* (1993): 113–136; and Mintzberg.

[10] Recall the discussions of organizational identification in Chapter 6 and the concept of "unobtrusive control" discussed in Chapter 4. An excellent case study of how the multiple dimensions and levels of power are interrelated is available in J.P. Gaventa, *Power and Powerlessness: Quiescence and Rebellion in an Appalachian Valley* (Urbana, IL: University of Illinois Press, 1980).

[11] David Smith, "Stories, Values, and Patient Care Decisions," in *The Ethical Nexus,* Charles Conrad, ed. (Norwood, NJ: Ablex, 1992) and Marsha Vanderford, David Smith, and Willard Harris, "Value Identification in Narrative Discourse," *Journal of Applied Communication Research, 20* (1992): 123–161.

[12] Charles Berger, "Power, Dominance, and Social Interaction," in *Handbook of Interpersonal Communication,* Mark Knapp and Gerald Miller, eds. (Beverly Hills, CA: Sage, 1994). Also see William Gamson, *Power and Discontent* (Homewood, IL: Dorsey, 1968). Many of the ideas that are developed in this chapter are grounded in the research summarized by Jeffrey Pfeffer, *Power;* Samuel Bacharach and Edward Lawler, *Power and Politics in Organizations* (San Francisco: Jossey-Bass, 1980); and John Kotter, *Power in Management* (New York: AMACOM,

1979). Research on the bases of power can be traced to an article by J.R.P. French and Bertram Raven, "The Bases of Social Power," in *Studies in Social Power,* Dorwin Cartwright, ed. (Ann Arbor: University of Michigan Press, 1959).

[13] Edna Rogers-Millar and Frank Millar, "Domineering and Dominance," *Human Communication Research, 5* (1979): 238–246; Elizabeth Janeway, *Powers of the Weak* (New York: Random House, 1981); P.B. Kritek, *Negotiating at an Uneven Table* (San Francisco: Jossey-Bass, 1994).

[14] M. Crozier, *The Bureaucratic Phenomenon* (Chicago: University of Chicago Press, 1964).

[15] There is some evidence that upper-level managers and especially CEOs rely almost exclusively on formal, position-related power (Sydney Finkelstein, "Power in Top Management Teams," *Academy of Management Journal, 35* [1992]: 505–538).

[16] Peter Drucker, *The Changing World of the Executive* (New York: Times Books, 1982); Cathy Enz, *Power and Shared Values in the Corporate Culture* (Ann Arbor: UMI Research Press, 1986) and "The Role of Value Congruity in Intraorganizational Power," *Administrative Science Quarterly, 33* (1988): 284–304.

[17] Bacharach and Lawler; Linda Putnam, "Conflict in Group Decision Making," in *Communication and Group Decision Making,* Randy Hirokawa and M. Scott Poole, eds. (Newbury Park, CA: Sage, 1986).

[18] See, for instance, Edward Lawler and John Rhodes, *Information and Control in Organizations* (Pacific Palisades, CA: Goodyear, 1976); Andrew Pettigrew, "Information Control as a Power Resource," *Sociology, 6* (1972): 187–204. Richard M. Emerson, "Power-Dependence Relations," *American Sociological Review, 27* (1962): 31–41, provides a classic discussion of how interdependencies influence power. Pfeffer (*Power*) suggested many of the examples used in this section.

[19] Andrew Pettigrew, *The Politics of Organizational Decision-Making* (London: Tavistock, 1973); Bertram Raven and Arie Kruglanski, "Power and Conflict," in *The Structure of Conflict,* Paul Swingle, ed. (New York: Academic Press, 1970).

[20] Peter Monge and Noshir Contractor, "Emergent Communication Networks," in *New Handbook of Organizational Communication,* Linda Putnam and Fred Jablin, eds. (Thousand Oaks, CA: Sage, in press). Also see Peter Blau and R. Alba, "Empowering Nets of Participation," *Administrative Science Quarterly, 27* (1982): 363–379; Cynthia Stohl, *Organizational Communication: Connectedness in Action* (Thousand Oaks, CA: Sage, 1995); Charles Fombrun, "Structural Dynamics Between and Within Organizations," *Administrative Science Quarterly, 31* (1986): 403–421; David Hickson, W. Graham Astley, Richard Butler, and David Wilson, "Organization as Power," in *Research in Organizational Behavior,* v. 3 (Greenwich, CT, JAI Press, 1981); and Mintzberg.

[21] For a discussion of the complexities of threats and promises, see James Tedeschi, "Threats and Promises," in *The Structure of Conflict,* Paul Swingle, ed. (New York: Academic Press, 1970). These strategies are discussed more fully in Chapter 11.

[22] Jeffrey Pfeffer argues that an outsider can tell how much power the departments in a large West Coast university have by noting how far down the hill their buildings are from the main administration building (Pfeffer, *Power*).

[23] Putnam, "Group."

[24] Excellent summaries of research on organizational politics are available in Don Madison, et al., "Organizational Politics," *Human Relations, 33* (1980): 79–100, Dennis Mumby, "Power, Politics, and Organizational Communication," in L. Putnam and F. Jablin, eds. *New Handbook of Organizational Communication* (Thousand Oaks, CA: Sage, in press), and Patricia Riley, "A Structurationist Account of Political Culture," *Administrative Science Quarterly, 28* (1983): 414–437.

[25] Victor Thompson, *Modern Organizations* (New York: Knopf, 1967); Lyman Porter, Robert Allen, and Harold Angle, "The Politics of Upward Influence in Organizations," in *Research in Organizational Behavior,* v. 3 (Greenwich, CT, JAI Press, 1981); and Madison, et al.

[26] Karl Weick, *Sense-Making in Organizations* (Thousand Oaks, CA: Sage, 1995, p. 160). Readers who are interested in more complete summaries should consult Jeffrey Pfeffer, *Organizations and Organization Theory* (Marshfield, MA: Pitman, 1982) and "The Bases and Uses of Power in Organizational Decision-making," *Administrative Science Quarterly, 19* (1974): 453–473; and Richard Cyert and James March, *A Behavioral Theory of the Firm* (Englewood Cliffs, NJ: Prentice-Hall, 1963).

[27] For an example, see Gail Fairhurst, L. Edna Rogers, and Robert Sarr, "Manager-subordinate Control Patterns and Judgments about Relationship," in *Communication Yearbook 10,* Margaret McLaughlin, ed. (Beverly Hills, CA: Sage, 1987).

[28] Charles Redding, "Rocking Boats, Blowing Whistles, and Teaching Speech Communication," *Communication Education, 34* (1985): 245–258.

[29] See Marcia Miceli and Janet Near, *Blowing the Whistle: The Organizational and Legal Implications for Companies and Employees* (New York: Lexington Books, 1992) and Sissela Bok, *Secrets: On the Ethics of Concealment and Revelation* (New York: Random House, 1982).

[30] The data presented above is based on a September, 1996, survey of 5,000 companies by the Society for Human Resource Management. A summary was published in the October 1, 1996 *Houston Chronicle,* B1.

[31] For an analysis of the mythology of "efficiency" and "effectiveness," see Roger Jehensen, "Effectiveness, Expertise, and Excellence as Ideological Fictions," *Human Studies, 7* (1984): 3–21.

[32] Habermas' work is treated at length in a number of sources. Two communication theorists have done an especially thorough job of developing the ideas that I will summarize in this section: Dennis Mumby, *Communication and Power in Organizations* (Norwood, NJ: Ablex, 1988) and Stanley Deetz, *Democracy in an Age of Corporate Colonization* (Albany, NY: SUNY Press, 1992). Two valuable related works are John Thompson, *Studies in the Theory of Ideology* (Berkeley: University of California Press, 1984) and Jehensen.

[33] See Jane Flax, "Postmodern and Gender Relations in Feminist Theory," *Signs, 12* (1987): 621–643; Carol Gilligan, *In a Different Voice* (Cambridge: Harvard University Press, 1982); Cheris Kramerae, *Women and Men Speaking* (Rowley, MA: Newbury House, 1981). For applications to organizational discourse, see Kathy E. Ferguson, *The Feminist Case Against Bureaucracy* (Philadelphia, PA: Temple University Press, 1984), especially Chapter 5, and Judi Marshall, "Viewing Organizational Communication from a Feminist Perspective: A Critique and Some Offerings," in S. Deetz, ed., *Communication Yearbook 16* (Newbury Park, CA: Sage, 1993).

[34] Julia Penelope, *Speaking Freely* (New York: Pergamon, 1990).

[35] See R.W. Connell, "Theorizing Gender," *Sociology, 19* (1985): 260–272 and *Gender and Power: Society, the Person, and Sexual Politics* (Stanford, CA: Stanford University Press, 1987; and Ann Douglas, *The Feminization of American Culture* (New York: Anchor Press, 1988).

[36] For an excellent summary of the issues raised in this section, see Patrice Buzzanell, "Gaining a Voice: Feminist Organizational Communication Theorizing," *Management Communication Quarterly, 7* (1994): 339–383.

[37] Terrance Albrecht and Bradford Hall, "Relational and Content Differences Between Elites and Outsiders in Innovation Networks," *Human Communication Research, 17* (1991): 535–561.

[38] Dennis Mumby and Linda Putnam, "Bounded Emotionality." *Academy of Management Review, 17* (1992): 465–486; Nancy Wyatt, "Shared Leadership in the Weavers' Guild," in Barbara Bate and Anita Taylor, eds., *Women Communicating: Studies of Women's Talk* (Norwood, NJ: Ablex, 1988).

[39] For examples of participatory processes, see Eric Eisenberg, "Dialogue as Democratic Process," in Stanley Deetz (Ed.), *Communication Yearbook 17* (pp. 275–284), Thousand Oaks, CA: Sage, 1994, and K.P. Ianello, *Decisions Without Hierarchy* (New York: Routledge, 1992). For examples from academic organizations, see H. Gottfried and P. Weiss, "A Compound Feminist Organization; Purdue University's Council on the Status of Women," *Women and Politics, 14* (1994): 23–44, and Betsy Bach, "Making a Difference by Doing Differently: A Response to Putnam," paper presented at the Arizona State University Conference on Organizational Communication, Tempe, AZ, 1990. And, for an analysis of resistance to voicing strategies, see H. Eisenstein, *Gender Shock* (Boston: Beacon, 1991).

[40] Joanne Martin, *Cultures in Organizations* (New York: Oxford University Press, 1992). For additional examples, see Dennis Mumby and Cynthia Stohl, "Power and Discourse in Organization Studies," *Discourse and Society, 2* (1991): 313–332.

Chapter 8

COMMUNICATION AND DECISION-MAKING: INDIVIDUAL, GROUP, AND ORGANIZATIONAL CONSIDERATIONS

Plans are important in organizations, but not for the reasons people think.

—KARL WEICK

CENTRAL THEMES

- Both Western culture and traditional models of organizing view individual employees and organizations as rational actors. In contrast, many contemporary perspectives suggest that these assumptions are cultural myths and that actual decision-making processes often are not rational.

- Because our rationality is "bounded" and our choices are "intransitive," we cannot be rational actors. Consequently, we use communication to make choices that are acceptable and not necessarily rational.

- Because we often make decisions first and then seek information to support (rationalize) them, we often make nonrational choices.

- Groups also deviate from the rational model because of a number of internal and external pressures.

- To make effective decisions groups must exchange and analyze information in a critical fashion, maintain a balance between group cohesion and conflict, and counteract hidden agendas.

- Group decisions are not made in a vacuum, but are influenced by the surrounding organization, its hierarchy, and political system.

- Organizational decision-making is more often "intuitive" than rational.

- Political pressures, power relationships, and the complexities of decision situations create ambiguity and uncertainty for employees. Through nonrational processes they are able to manage these uncertainties, to *act* when action is required.

- Plans and planning serve a number of objectives in organizations, only one of which is actually solving problems.

- A number of situational and interactional factors influence the extent to which a particular organizational decision can or should be made through strictly rational processes.
- Because rationality is a core value of Western cultures, people need to rationalize their nonrationality. However, doing so tends to privilege the interests of managers over those of workers.

KEY TERMS

Bounded rationality

Intransitivity

Loosely coupled systems

Complex interactions

Consensus

Cohesion

Substantive conflict

Egocentric influences

Hierarchical structure

Irrationality

Oversight

Resolution

Satisficing

Tightly coupled systems

Linear interactions

Standard agenda

Negotiation

Norms of concurrence

Affective conflict

Connectivity

Intuition

Burnout

Flight

Enactment-selection-retention

Most views of organizations *assume* that they are rational, cooperative enterprises. According to this perspective, organizations exist so that people can pursue their goals through the most efficient means, and they will be efficient only if the people who comprise them are trained to and rewarded for making "rational" decisions. Rational employees encounter problems or challenges, systematically seek out the information and expertise needed to choose among courses of action, and make careful, objective decisions based on the available information.

Organizations function in a similar way. Rational employees collaborate in making rational decisions for their organizations (see Figure 8–1). Both employees and organizations sometimes make unwise decisions, but these errors result from a lack of adequate information, the perversities of group pressures, momentary slips in thinking, or some other aberration. Even when bad decisions are made, the decision-making process still is seen as an essentially rational and objective enterprise.

In this chapter I take a somewhat different position about individual, group, and organizational decision-making. I first present what has been labeled the "rational actor" model of individual and organizational decision-making. I then contrast that *theoretical* model with research on how individuals, groups, and organizations *actually do* make decisions. I conclude that, except in the simplest decision situations, people are not and cannot be

FIGURE 8–1

The Rational Actor Model of Organizational Decision Making

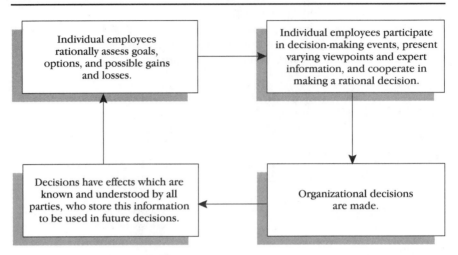

strictly "rational" actors. My goal is not to disparage the decision-makers. Instead my objective is to suggest that strictly rational theories of decision-making simply do not reflect the complex maze of personal, interpersonal, political, and ethical considerations that employees incorporate into their decision-making. In short, it is the "rational actor" model that is in error, not the employees. In general, employees make the best decisions they can given the nature of the situations they face. They deviate from the dictates of the "rational actor" model in a number of ways, and in doing so they cope with the situations they face.

Of course, I realize that the notion that "good" decisions need not be strictly rational decisions may seem counter to common sense. But, as I have suggested throughout this book, the "common sense" notions of a society are strategic, symbolic creations. And the notion that decision-makers must be as "rational" as possible is a core assumption in Western societies. In a provocative article aptly entitled "The Technology of Foolishness," James March explained that our culture embraces three primary articles of faith:

1. *The Preexistence of Purpose:* We begin with goals, make choices based on these goals, and can offer adequate explanations of our actions only in terms of our goals;
2. *The Necessity of Consistency:* We choose to act in ways that are consistent with our beliefs and with our roles in our social groups (families, organizations, communities, and so on); and
3. *The Primacy of Rationality:* We make decisions by carefully projecting the probable effects of different courses of action, *not by intuition* (in which we act without fully understanding why we do what we do) or

by tradition or faith (in which we do things because they always have been done that way).[1]

A major part of our acculturation involves learning these three commandments. We learn that children act impulsively, irrationally, and playfully. Adults act calmly and rationally, making decisions by carefully considering of a number of complicated factors, and are spontaneous only when they have calmly and rationally decided to be spontaneous. Because we are products of our societies, our individual identities and self-esteem are linked to the belief that we are rational people. Even when we do behave in ways that are not strictly rational, we need to pretend that we have not. Because we all need to "save face" (recall Chapter 6), we usually cooperate in maintaining the image that we are all rational adults, even if we sometimes doubt that we, our peers, or our organizations really are. Understanding the processes through which people make effective decisions at work requires us to (1) view the rational actor model as a symbolic (and thus artificial) creation, and (2) relax our taken-for-granted assumption that decision-making can and should be strictly rational.

COMMUNICATION AND INDIVIDUAL DECISION-MAKING

In contrast to traditional rational views of individual and organizational decision-making, contemporary models operate from a different set of assumptions. Instead of assuming that individuals and organizations should be rational actors, they examine the ways in which people manage complicated decision situations.

Communication and Traditional Models of Individual Decision-Making[2]

According to "rational actor" models of decision-making, people choose among all of the available courses of action in a particular situation by comparing the probable outcomes of each alternative and selecting for the one that promises the greatest return. For example, if we are trying to choose among three proposals of marriage (made by persons X, Y, and Z), we will select a set of criteria we believe are relevant to making a matrimonial decision (for the purposes of this example I have chosen wealth, passion, excitement, and the probable permanence of the relationships) and attach a "weight" to each criterion reflecting its relative salience to us. We estimate the likelihood that accepting each proposal will fulfill the criteria that we have chosen. Then we multiply each weight by its associated probability, add the products, and *voilà,* we have our mate (see Table 8–1). But in order to use this system successfully, we must have (1) a complete list of potential options (mates) and weighted criteria, (2) accurate and complete information about the outcomes and probabilities, (3) knowledge of all options, outcomes, and probabilities at the same time or the ability

TABLE 8–1
A Marriage Decision: A Rational Model

CAREER OF LOVER	WEALTH		PERMANENCE/ STABILITY		PASSION		EXCITEMENT		TOTAL
X (Surgeon)	.9(7)	+	.8(2)	+	.1(9)	+	.2(11)	=	11
Y (Professor)	.1(7)	+	.5(2)	+	.1(9)	+	.1(11)	=	3.7
Z (Baseball shortstop)	.4(7)	+	.1(2)	+	.3(9)	+	.9(11)	=	15.6

In this example excitement is highly salient to the person making the decision, so she or he gives it a weight of 11; passion is a bit less salient (9); wealth a bit less (7); and permanence/stability is relatively unimportant (2). He or she estimates that the probability of a surgeon mate being wealthy is quite high (and attaches a probability of .9), of a shortstop is moderate (the shortstop evidently wants to stay with the lowest-paying team for an entire career, so he or she attaches a probability of .4), and a professor quite low (probability = .1). The person also believes that shortstops are exciting both during and between seasons (probability = .9), and passionate at least during the off-season (.3); professors and surgeons are too tired or preoccupied to be either exciting or passionate at any time (probability of .1), and so on.

to use the same estimates during each of a series of decisions, and (4) sufficient time and computational skill. In the most simple life (and organizational) decision situations, these requirements may be met. But most of the choices we face are more complicated, and in those situations one or more of the requirements will be violated.

Contemporary Models of Individual Decision-Making

Studies of individuals' actions during decision-making situations indicate both that humans cannot act in accordance with this "rational actor" model and that we do not do so.[3] At most we appear to act in ways consistent with the model.

Why Humans Cannot Be Rational Actors.   People cannot be rational actors because our decision-making is limited (the research says that our rationality is **bounded**) by our analytical skills and by a variety of situational factors.[4] In real-world situations, we rarely have complete information about our options, criteria, weightings, and probabilities. Even if we had all of this information available, we do not possess unlimited computational time or ability. In short, we are not the completely informed, unlimitedly competent beings envisioned in the rational actor model. We do make decisions, however, and they usually meet at least minimal criteria of acceptability. We may not make the best possible decision in every case, but we do "get by" by making satisfactory choices.

We search through a haystack of complicated options looking for a needle that is sharp enough to sew with, not for the sharpest needle available. Herbert Simon and James March have labeled this process **satisficing**, that is, searching for a decision that is satisfactory, but not necessarily optimal (the best possible).[5] Although the rationality of some people seems to be more tightly bounded than others, and although some decision situations are more complex than others, we rarely can rely on strictly rational processes to make choices in real situations, and we rarely need to.

Our rationality also is bounded by our inability to separate the weight we attach to an event from the probability of its occurrence. Like Pollyanna, we overestimate the likelihood of "good" outcomes and underestimate the probability of "bad" ones. For example, no matter how much information students are given about past patterns of grading in a course and about their own academic records, they invariably seem to overestimate their chances of receiving A's and B's and underestimate their chances of getting C's, D's or F's.

We also tend to make different choices in different situations (the rational actor model labels this tendency **intransitivity**). This is partly because we shift our preferences, criteria, weightings, and probability estimates around between decisions. If our mythical decision-maker had received his or her marriage proposals in a sequence, or even two at a time, he or she probably would have arrived at different scores for each proposal than he or she did when they were received all at once. His or her perceptions of the outcomes, weights, and probabilities would have changed. (George/Judy may've looked pretty impressive until Fred/Jane came along.)

The criteria that we use also vary across different situations.[6] In the marriage example, the relative salience of the criteria of wealth, security and stability, passion, and excitement is likely to change over time. Passion may be exceptionally salient for decision-makers aged 13–29, but less salient for other age groups. Although "changing our minds" may reflect our ability to be flexible more than our lack of intellectual discipline, it violates the strict assumptions of the rational actor model.

Finally, the degree to which people are emotionally involved in decision-making also varies. When decisions are important to people and they have high levels of energy available, they tend to be very much involved in the process. They will search actively for information, use their information-processing abilities to the greatest extent possible, and consider as wide a range of outcomes, criteria, and probabilities as they can. They will come as close as personally possible to being a rational actor. But when the decision is less emotionally involving or they have less energy available, their choice-making will deviate from the rational actor model even more than is usual. If X, Y, and Z's marriage proposals are the fifteenth, sixteenth, and seventeenth that our decision-maker has received, and she or he is trying to choose her or his thirteenth mate, both the perceived significance of the decision and the energy that he or she has left for marital decision-making (or anything else, for that matter) could be quite low. His or her decision-making in this situation would be even less strictly "rational" than usual.

For a variety of reasons, then, individuals cannot behave as "rational actors." But we still have to make choices. To do so we must simplify the complicated situations that we face. We can do so largely because we are able to communicate. Once two of my students (an engaged couple) sought advice about purchasing a new automobile. They said their goal was noble, to shift from their old "gas guzzler" to a fuel-efficient model in order to do their part to forestall a worldwide energy crisis. I suggested that this goal would be best achieved if they kept their old car. The amount of fuel they would save during the lifetime of their new car would be far less than the amount of energy and nonrenewable minerals that would be used in the manufacture of their new car. Besides, there was no guarantee that the person who purchased their old car would use it to replace an even less fuel-efficient vehicle. Thus the net effect of their buying a new car, regardless of how fuel-efficient it might be, would be to increase the depletion of nonrenewable resources, bringing the world even closer to eco-catastrophe.

Now, the rational actor model does not predict that the students would discover that I was correct. But it does suggest that they should respond to my argument by seeking out information about (1) the resources used in fabricating new automobiles, (2) means of controlling the energy use of potential purchasers of their old car, and (3) the relative scarcity of petroleum compared to the scarcity of the other resources used in the fabrication of cars. The model predicts that they would use their communicative and intellectual skills to obtain the information needed to find out whether I was right or not. But it does not recognize that some of the needed information may either not exist or be so difficult to locate that it would not be worth the effort, or that they could not care less about the effects that their actions might have on other people's actions, or that their friends all are committed to energy conservation, or that a host of other intangible factors may be involved in their decision-making.

Eventually they chose a course of action that did incorporate some of these considerations. They returned after a lengthy discussion produced the following changes in their position: (1) We are going to be concerned only about gasoline (because it is too much work to determine the net effect of our purchase will have on other resources); (2) we are going to ignore the effects that our decision has on anyone else's energy use; and (3) we are going to buy a new fuel-efficient car because it will symbolize our commitment to conservation whether it has that effect or not. So, in retrospect our discussion (and theirs) did not lead to a strictly rational decision, at least not as the rational actor model defines that term. But their communication with one another did allow them to (1) simplify their decision situation and make it more manageable, (2) provide mutual validation of their new view of the situation, and (3) provide social and emotional support for one another's decision-making processes. They were, in the end, able to make a decision and to make it with conviction. Communicating usually helps people make decisions, not make strictly "rational" decisions.

Why Humans Are Not Rational Actors.   The rational actor model presumes that we determine desired outcomes, values, and decision-making processes and seek out relevant information before we actually make decisions. Observations of human decision-making, and especially of organizational decision-making, suggest that we often may reverse the sequence, first making choices and acting on them and then seeking out the information and beliefs that support our decision. We discover, for instance, that we have married a professional baseball player and then determine that we "weigh" excitement and passion more than security. We make a decision that seems to be correct and then construct a picture of our decision-making process that makes us seem to be rational actors. This kind of "backward thinking" seems to occur in almost all kinds of human decision-making. *Rationalizing* decisions that we have already made seems to be more common than creating *justifications* for choices that we will make.[7]

CASE STUDY:
NORMAL ACCIDENTS*

In some organizational situations it is not possible to approximate rational decision-making. Time pressures may be too intense, information too limited or too ambiguous, and decisions too complex. In a few situations the pressures are so extreme that intuition also is useless. And in a few cases the costs of making the wrong decision may be catastrophic.

In 1984 Charles Perrow, professor of sociology at Yale University and former member of the President's Commission to Investigate the Three Mile Island Incident, published *Normal Accidents*. In it Perrow argued that the structure of modern high-technology organizations combines with the dynamics of decision-making in a way that virtually guarantees that disasters like Three Mile Island (and Chernobyl, USSR; Bhopal, India; and the Exxon Valdez since 1984) will recur. The basis of his analysis is quite simple—"elegant" is the usual social science term. Organizational decision-makers must cope with two "facts" of life—the degree to which organizational subsystems are "tightly" or "loosely" coupled and the "complexity" of interactions among those systems. In **tightly coupled systems** the events that occur in one subsystem rapidly and directly influence events in other systems. The subsystems of a tightly coupled system are like each member of a row of dominoes. Events in one part of the system immediately influence the other systems, just as pushing over the first domino rapidly leads the rest to fall down. In **loosely coupled systems** there is a great

---

*Based on Charles Perrow, *Normal Accidents* (New York: Basic Books, 1984). For related analyses see Karl Weick, "The Vulnerable System: An Analysis of the Tenerife Air Disaster," *Journal of Management, 16* (1990): 571–593 and "The Collapse of Sense-Making in Organizations: The Mann Gulch Disaster," *Administrative Science Quarterly, 38* (1993): 628–652. For an excellent analysis of how we attribute blame to accidents see R. P. Gephart, Jr., "The Textual Approach: Risk and Blame in Disaster Sensemaking," *Academy of Management Journal, 36* (1993): 1465–1514.

(continued)

(continued from the previous page)

deal of buffering between subsystems. An event in one subsystem influences others only indirectly, and only after a large number of people interpret the event and decide how to respond to it. For example, universities are loosely coupled systems. Entire departments can be eliminated (and in today's era of budget cuts are being eliminated) without anyone in the other departments being affected. If there is any impact, it can take years to be felt.

Linear interactions involve routine, expected, planned, and visible processes. In them people can see something go wrong in one part of the system and intervene to keep the event from damaging other parts. A traditional automobile assembly line is a linear interaction. If one part breaks down, any number of people can stop the line or compensate for the breakdown by taking steps that they understand.

In contrast, **complex interactions** are composed of unfamiliar, unplanned, unexpected, invisible, or not fully understood processes. For example, nuclear power plants involve complex interactions. Once fission begins it continues rapidly, invisibly, and in ways not yet fully understood. If something unexpected happens in a nuclear plant, other parts of the system are affected in ways that cannot be observed directly, may not be fully understood, and may not allow human beings to intervene to stop the process.

Decision-making is most difficult in the organizations in quadrant 2 of Figure 8.2 (tight coupling plus complex interactions). If something goes awry in a chemical plant or space mission, other systems are damaged instantly (tight coupling) and with little possibility of effective intervention (complexity). If these organizations also produce potentially hazardous products (radioactivity in the case of nuclear weapons and nuclear power, and wars in the case of faulty military early-warning systems), errors in decision-making may have potentially catastrophic results.

The 1979 accident at Three Mile Island is typical of quadrant 2 accidents. It started when about a cup of water leaked out of a backup cooling system into an air system controlling a number of instruments. The instruments triggered a safety system, which told the pumps circulating cooling water to stop because something was wrong (it wasn't). The same instruments told the operators that there was a problem and that it had been taken care of. Soon, the emergency cooling pumps came on, but the valves between the pumps and the cooling pipes had been left closed during routine maintenance two days earlier. Two indicators on the control panel showed this, but one was covered by a tag. Because the other instruments told the operators that the problem had been solved, they did not check the dial under the tag. Eight minutes later, after a number of other steps had been taken, the readings had become terribly confusing and the operators did stop to look at the dial under the tag, but by then it was too late to prevent the initial damage.

(continued)

(continued from the previous page)

FIGURE 8–2
Interaction/Coupling Chart

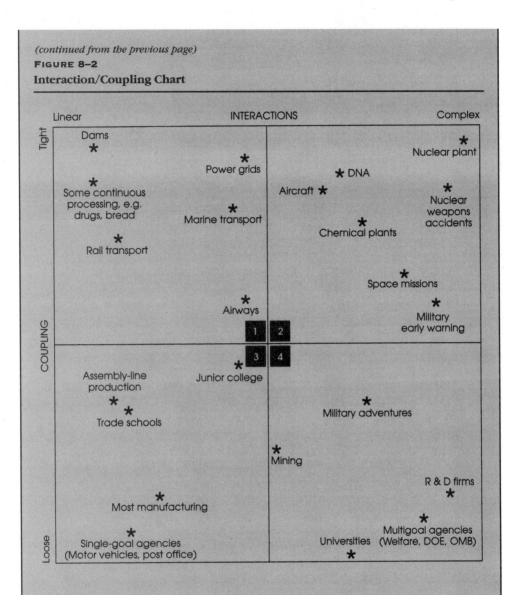

The electricity-producing generator had boiled dry. The rods that control the nuclear reaction immediately dropped into the core, stopping it. But it took time for the superheated core to cool. During that time massive amounts of heat were produced, enough to generate electricity for 18,000 homes. Normally the cooling system speeds the cool-down process, but it was not working. The next safety system is a pressure relief valve that is supposed to close, divert built-up pressure, and keep the radioactive cooling water within the plant. It is rarely

(continued)

(continued from the previous page)

used and on the average fails one time in fifty. This was one of those times, and it dumped 32,000 gallons of superheated radioactive water into the cooling vessel around the core. The valve had activated a light that (incorrectly) told the operators that the valve had performed properly. Consequently, the information available to the operators was either confusing (the contradictory dials) or inaccurate. Because there is no way to observe the inside of a reactor chamber directly (remember, that is one of the characteristics of complex systems), they could not have known exactly what was going on inside of the reactor (p. 22).

Other warning systems detected the radioactive water and alerted the operators. But because the light connected to the pressure-relief valve told the operators that it was working properly, they concluded that the radioactive water must be coming from a broken pipe. There simply was no other rational explanation. Eventually another safety system—a high-pressure water-injection process—came on. It is a very risky system because it injects cold water into a superheated containment vessel, and the temperature difference can crack the core or containment vessel (just as an ice cube cracks if you pour boiling water on it). After two minutes the operators turned it down, because leaving it on and being wrong would cause more damage than turning it down and being wrong. As a result more water was leaving the core than coming in, further uncovering the core and creating the real risk of a core meltdown.

The majority of the president's investigating commission focused on this decision as the key example of "operator error." That conclusion was unrealistic—it was based on the assumption that the operators could and should have been strictly rational actors, when the situation was so complex and confusing that strictly rational decision-making was impossible. The operators had looked at two dials, one saying that pressure was decreasing and one saying it was increasing. Because there was a more immediate danger if the second dial was correct, they decided to turn the system down. Immediately the other dials and gauges started returning to normal, confirming the operators' view that they had made the correct decision. But the "reality" they had constructed from the available information was incorrect—the core still was becoming uncovered. Suddenly the cooling pumps started shaking violently. Because the problem evidently had been solved, the operators decided to shut the pumps down. Fortunately, a new shift—people who had not been involved in making sense out of the confusing and contradictory information that the original operators had made sense out of—came on in the control room. One of the newcomers checked the pressure-relief valve that had started the accident and reversed the original group's decision, shutting off the water flowing to it. Perrow notes:

> The operator testified . . . at the president's commission hearings that it was more of an act of desperation to shut the block valve than an act of understanding.

(continued)

(continued from the previous page)

After all, he said, you do not casually block off a safety system. It was fortunate that it occurred when it did; incredible damage had been done, with substantial parts of the core melting, but had it remained open for another thirty minutes or so, and the HPI [high-pressure injection system] remained throttled back, there would probably have been a complete meltdown with the fissionable material threatening to breach containment (p. 29).

Luck, more than technical skill, safety systems, or informed decision-making, stopped the accident and prevented the destruction of much of the northeastern United States for thousands of years to come.

Normal Accidents describes a series of additional factors that make rational (or even intuitional) decision-making in high-technology organizations difficult. The airline and air traffic systems are handicapped by overconfidence because of years of success and, ironically, by the presence of modern safety systems. The overconfidence is misplaced because (1) airline disasters tend to be idiosyncratic, making it virtually impossible to acquire lessons from one disaster that can be used to prevent disasters (recall the effects of twenty-five successful flights on the decision to launch the shuttle *Challenger*); and (2) safety systems fail and cause airplane accidents, just like a breakdown in safety systems contributed to the accident at Three Mile Island.

Structural factors like bonuses for speed and insurance rates that are not based on safety records plague the maritime industry. For example, the wreck of the Torrey Canyon, which produced the largest oil spill in history prior to the wreck of the Exxon Valdez, occurred when the captain took a shortcut in order to make a bonus deadline. The channel he chose was so shallow that he had only a few inches of clearance. He missed by about a foot. Unanticipated considerations influence other organizational decisions. When the Corps of Engineers determines how strong a dam should be, it always carefully estimates the pressure that the water in the lake will place on the dam. But they consistently underestimate the effect that the weight of the water contained behind dams has on the stability of the bedrock underlying the dam. The dam will probably never collapse, but it may be swept downstream intact when the rock under it crumbles. When combined, these elements of organizational decision-making suggest that accidents like Three Mile Island will recur frequently enough to become normal.

Discussion Questions

1. What should be done? Perrow concludes that accident-prone industries with high catastrophic potential or available alternatives (like nuclear power) should be abandoned and safety procedures (as opposed to systems) be strengthened in all others (see Figure 8–3). Is this a viable proposal?

(continued)

(continued from the previous page)

(continued from the previous page)

FIGURE 8–3

Policy Recommendations

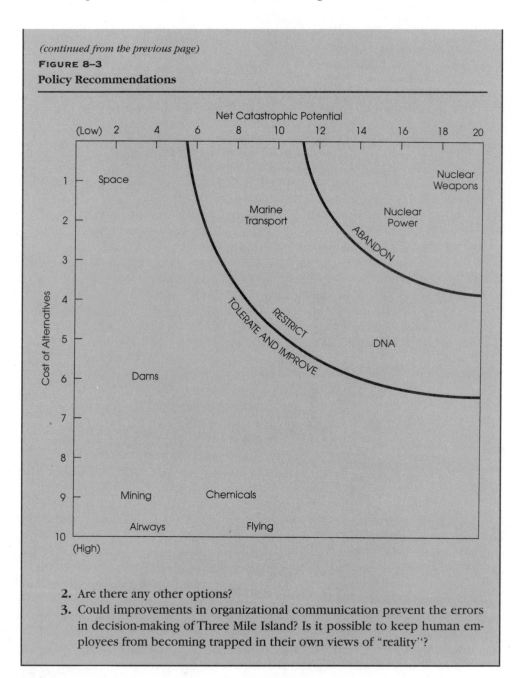

2. Are there any other options?
3. Could improvements in organizational communication prevent the errors in decision-making of Three Mile Island? Is it possible to keep human employees from becoming trapped in their own views of "reality"?

COMMUNICATION AND MODELS OF GROUP DECISION-MAKING[8]

People form groups for a number of reasons, both inside and outside of organizations. Many of these reasons have been discussed in earlier chapters—to get social and emotional support or stimulate creativity (Chapter 3), to exchange task-related information (Chapter 2), or for specific purposes like improving the quality of what they produce (Chapter 3). But a primary purpose of forming organizational groups is to make decisions.

Traditional Views of Group Decision-Making Processes

Traditional models of group decision-making are based on traditional (rational actor) models of individual decision-making. The nineteenth-century philosopher John Dewey argued that people confront personal problems through a five-step process: (1) a problem or general feeling of uneasiness is recognized, (2) the problem is located and defined, (3) the person sets standards by which to test a solution, (4) several response options are identified and tested, and (5) a solution is selected and implemented. From this individual model developed a "standard agenda" model of group decision-making. To make an effective decision, groups should begin by

1. Defining the task facing the group, making sure each member understands why the task is important, what its final product will look like, and what that product will be used for; then
2. Reach agreement on group and individual responsibilities ("who is to do what about what"); then
3. Seek out all of the information needed by the group, arrange it for easy access, and evaluate its accuracy; then
4. Establish criteria for evaluating possible courses of action, including recognizing what options and outcomes are realistic; then
5. Discover and evaluate options; and finally
6. Prepare to persuasively present and defend its choice to people who will be involved in implementing it.

Each phase has characteristic goals, tasks that must be performed, and obligations for members and leaders.

Determining the Form of a Decision. Early during the process the group must make decisions about how the decision should be made. One form of decision-making assumes decisions are best made by **consensus**, unanimous agreement of all members. Consensus is a valuable goal, because it can create unified support for the group's final decision. But it is time-consuming and may lead to weak decisions because it takes so many compromises by every member in order to find an outcome that is acceptable to everyone. A second form is **negotiation**, which involves bargaining to create a decision that honors each member's position on key issues. Unlike consensus, which leads to unanimous agreement on both a decision and its rationale, negotiation culminates in a decision that is acceptable without requiring agreement on goals and rationales. As the final sections of this chapter will indicate, this kind of outcome is common in organizational decision-making. Employees often have incompatible goals, but interdependent roles. Thus they are able to agree on outcomes, but not reasons for accepting them.

Negotiating takes less time than consensus and does not "water down" solutions, but can lead to piecemeal outcomes that are less coherent. Often in organizations, differing political interests make it virtually impossible for members to agree on group goals. "Smooth production" and "satisfying customers" may be impossible to achieve simultaneously. So the group decides to meet one goal at a time, cycling between the them in different decision-making episodes.[9] A third method is *voting.* As well as being consistent with our culture's acceptance of majority rule, voting is quick, efficient, and decisive. But it also reduces the information exchange necessary for good decisions, may allow high-power members to force weaker members into accepting a decision they oppose, and can polarize winner and losers, creating frustration and resentment. When it is imperative that every member actively support the group's decision after it is made, voting may be the least preferred decision form.

Determining Leadership.   In Western societies people are taught to assume that groups must have a designated leader or leaders.[10] In most organizational decision-making groups the leader is identified before the group begins its work, either explicitly when person X is ordained as chairperson, or implicitly when members realize that person X is the group member who has the highest status in the organization. If no leader is selected for the group, it has three options: designate one person as leader from the outset, take a chance that a leader will emerge, or hope that the different members of the group will share leadership tasks efficiently and smoothly. The second and third options have their advantages, but they are also risky. When the group allows a leader to emerge naturally, the person best suited to the task and group often rises to the occasion. Emergent leaders generally are more effective than leaders appointed by management.[11] However, the danger in the emergence option is that no one may emerge as a leader, keeping the group from maintaining a sense of direction and purpose, or constant power plays between candidates may split the group. Sharing among all members develops every member's skills and commitment to the group. However, unless members are very conscientious, no one may feel responsible for managing the group's interactions, and progress may be slow and frustrations high.

Groups with clearly identified leaders are often more efficient, have fewer interpersonal problems, and produce better decisions, provided the leader is competent and effective at organizing the group.[12] This does not mean that "leaderless" groups are doomed to failure. It just means that they will have problems unless members have the right mix of leadership skills and exercise them effectively. Another strategy for a leaderless group or self-managed team is to rotate leadership; this builds all members' skills and also gives the team one clear point of responsibility without giving power to one person on a permanent basis.[13]

Regardless of how leadership is determined, the leader role must fulfill three functions. Leadership means influencing members' *perceptions of themselves*—motivating them to contribute to the group and to feel committed to it and its task. Leadership also involves influencing members' *perceptions of the group*. It means focusing the group's attention on the group's goals and the role that each step has in the group's meeting those goals. Making members feel that the group is an autonomous entity by minimizing references to outside pressures, involving members in decisions about tasks and procedures, and asking questions of and responding seriously to each member's comments all help focus attention on the group.

Finally, leadership means influencing the *pace* and *direction* of the discussion and the *decisions* made by the group. In general, leaders should avoid acting like advocates, especially early in the group's history. If they "jump in" too early or too forcefully, members are discouraged from sharing their ideas and expertise, and the advantages of group decision-making are reduced. But leaders were selected because of their perspective or expertise and there are times when the group needs to have that information made available.

Members who are not identified as leaders also play important roles. Group tasks are too large or complex to be performed by individuals. Consequently, the group needs the expertise and efforts of all members. But commitment rarely is high or equal among all members. Economist Mancur Olson concluded that

> Though all of the members of a group have a common interest in obtaining (some) collective benefit, they have no common interest in paying the cost of providing that collective good. Each would prefer that the others pay the entire cost, and ordinarily would get any benefit provided whether he (sic) had borne part of the cost or not.[14]

Olson's conclusion, based on research with labor, agricultural, medical, and educational groups, probably is consistent with your own experience with classroom group projects. When I ask my own students to list each project that was a good experience, I rarely have more than 1 percent respond positively. Usually they report that wide differences in the group members' commitment to the group and willingness to work hard to achieve its goals made the experience a frustrating one. Whatever else group projects teach students, they teach them that Olson is right about the motivations and rewards of group members. When groups are large—beyond five to seven members—the problem of low commitment to group *work* is increased.[15]

The opposite extreme, when members are excessively committed to the group, is equally damaging. Groups benefit from disagreement, from constructive conflict. When members agree for the sake of agreeing, the group does not benefit from their expertise or from the careful testing of ideas and evidence that comes from positive confrontation. In sum, the primary obligation of group members is to act like valuable members of a cooperative activity. For groups to function, both leadership and member roles must be successfully fulfilled.

Contemporary Models of Group Decision-Making

Traditional models of group decision-making are based on the assumption that groups both should and do follow a **standard agenda** model of group process. This implies that the group's decision process evolves in a simple, consistent, and straightforward manner and that model leaders and followers should adapt to the phase of decision-making the group is in. Contemporary research indicates that these assumptions are only partly correct. Groups are systems in the sense that the concept was defined in Chapter 1. As such they are constantly dealing with pressures from their subsystems and suprasystems. Some of these pressures are constant throughout the decision-making process. For instance, the group's assigned task is a continual pressure. Other pressures are intermittent. They occur only at certain points during the process and pressure the group to change its direction, at least temporarily. Some are external, as when members discover and introduce new information from outside of the group. In organizational groups external pressures often are political, and they often slow, sidetrack, or reverse decision-making processes.[16]

Other pressures are internal, developing out of the group discussion. Groups seem to participate in "reach testing," where they propose, develop, modify, drop, and then restart testing of ideas. As a result, the linear, step-by-step "standard agenda" rarely is—and rarely should be—implemented in the way that the traditional model envisioned.[17] Instead, group processes are idiosyncratic and cyclical. Different phases overlap, members move from one phase to another and back again, roles change with the flow of the conversation. The key to effective participation is not adapting to the "phase" of group development, but adapting to the specific situations that emerge as the process continues. Participation is "strategic," in the sense that this book uses the term. It involves monitoring and interpreting the communication of the group, choosing productive ways of responding to that situation, and communicating effective strategic responses, while recognizing that each member's actions transform the situation and communication of the other members.[18]

Each of the tasks envisioned in the traditional model—establishing criteria, evaluating alternatives, seeking and presenting information, and so on—still must be fulfilled, but are fulfilled only when doing so is appropriate to the communicative process. Fortunately, although almost everyone has been taught to follow the standard agenda, people are willing to deviate from its procedural norms when it is appropriate to do so.[19] In the case of group decision-making, we tend to be strategic communicators in spite of our training.

Information Exchange.   Regardless of the specific process that a decision-making group follows it faces three problems: achieving effective information exchange, managing conflicts, and counteracting egocentric influences on the decision. Five information-related factors can lead a group to accept poor decisions:

1. The improper assessment of a situation,
2. The establishment of inappropriate goals and objectives,
3. The improper assessment of the strengths and weaknesses of various alternatives,
4. The establishment of a flawed information base, and
5. Faulty reasoning based on the group's information base.[20]

Improper information use sometimes results from errors in scanning. In complicated and ambiguous situations—the kind in which groups are better decision-makers than individuals—members often do not know what kinds of information are useful or when they have sufficient amounts to make the choice. Thus, they often unknowingly collect too little information, the wrong information, or so much information that they cannot process it adequately.[21] In other cases they may not evaluate the information they obtain accurately. Organizational power relationships and political considerations also may lead members to withhold or distort the information they provide the group. In still other cases, groups may have to make a decision very quickly, without sufficient time to properly understand the problem or the situation. This was the case for President Gerald Ford's response to the swine flu epidemic of the mid-1970s. Feeling intense pressure from what seemed to be an impending disaster, the Ford administration set up an inoculation program on an emergency basis. However, not only did it turn out that the inoculation program was unnecessary (the epidemic was overstated and did not materialize), but the vaccine led to illnesses among some of those who were inoculated.

In addition, the communication processes that occur within the group may create distortions. Groups collaborate in creating "realities" based on the information they have gathered (recall Chapter 1).[22] Once these realities begin to be shared they influence subsequent interpretations of information. Citing Irving Janis, Dennis Gouran noted that this kind of process seemed to influence American policy during the Korean War:

> The Chinese were seen by President Truman and his advisors as weak puppets of the Soviet Union. . . . The puppetlike image created in presidential discussions, coupled with the belief that the Soviets were reluctant to become involved in a ground war, laid the foundation for predicting success in the contemplated action (crossing the border into North Korea). In reality, the decision proved to be one of the president's most costly. Something of the same mentality has been attributed to those in the Johnson administration who recommended increased military involvement (in Vietnam).[23]

Group Cohesion.   In order to function as a group, **cohesion** (the feeling that the group members are unified about goals, values, and means and are mutually supportive and respectful) is necessary. Without it members are not satisfied with the group, do not participate actively in its activities, and are not committed to its outcomes. But the value of cohesion is curvilinear; that is, it is valuable up to a point, but beyond that point it begins to do harm. In an important way "cohesion" is like "identification" as that term was explained in Chapter 6. When people identify fully with their organizations they make decisions through the processes and based on the taken-for-granted premises of their organizations. If those processes are inappropriate or if the premises are incorrect or irrelevant in specific situations, they will make choices that also are inappropriate. When group members identify fully with one another, that is, when the group is highly cohesive, they may make the same kinds of errors.

In all groups, but especially in highly cohesive groups, pressures develop that may reduce the range and quality of information presented and thus eliminate the advantage of having decisions made by groups rather than by individuals. Often these pressures are not deliberate. Groups may develop **"norms of concurrence,"** which pressure members into agreeing with other members rather than seeking the best solutions. If an individual member dissents from the group's position or questions the assumptions the other members seem to share, others respond by arguing with, ignoring, or in extreme cases (or if the deviant persists) expelling the dissenter from the group. As the discussion continues the group shifts to the position initially taken by the majority or by its most vocal members. These "choice shifts" depend not on the information available to the group, but on in-group communicative pressures. As a result groups may make "extreme" decisions—ones that unquestioningly continue precedents and existing policies or that are inordinately risky. Since cohesion generates high levels of commitment to decisions and the high levels of motivation necessary to implement them, excessive cohesion may also lead groups to do everything they can to implement foolish decisions and to ignore or distort feedback indicating that their decision was unwise.[24] The communicative processes that *should* lead to the generation of creative ideas, sharing of accurate and relevant information, and the critical analysis of options begin to support what often may be unwarranted and unwise decisions.

Irving Janis and his associates have argued that these processes often dominate political decision-making. Classic examples of "groupthink" include the 1941 decision to ignore warnings that Japan might attack Pearl Harbor, the 1961 decision to invade Cuba at the Bay of Pigs, and the Committee to Reelect the President's 1974 decision to break into the Democratic Party's headquarters in the Watergate Hotel. In each case extensive group deliberations preceded the decision, and ample information was available that suggested that the outcome was unwise. But as Wood, Phillips, and Peterson conclude: "the transcripts of these committees' discussion[s] clearly demonstrate that some members knuckled under to group opinion, others rationalized going along with the majority, and still others could not see beyond the 'party line.' "[25] The intelligence, extensive experience, and power of these groups did little to compensate for the communicative pressures that prevented constructive dissent.

Cohesive groups also may develop an illusion of invulnerability. Not only does this illusion hamper decision-making, in organizational settings, it leads members to see themselves as separate from and better than other work groups. The competitive orientation that develops increases intergroup conflict. In time, the errors that highly cohesive groups make and the conflicts they have with other groups may create dissension with the group. Members may respond by even more intensely suppressing disagreement, which increases cohesion and its disadvantages. In a continuing cycle, highly cohesive permanent groups may become less and less capable of making good choices. As these comments suggest, conflict can be a positive element of group communication. (Because the dynamics of conflict will be examined at length in Chapter 9, it will be discussed only briefly here.)

Like cohesion, some conflict is valuable, excessive conflict is damaging. In fact, a group's search for a mutually acceptable decision requires conflict if it is to succeed.[26] Comparing and evaluating ideas—classifying, narrowing, refocusing, selecting, eliminating and synthesizing—depend on the expression of divergent points of view. Properly managed, **substantive** conflict (over issues) aids group processes. When it is transformed into **affective** conflict (over emotions), productive conflict management becomes quite difficult.[27]

Counteracting Egocentric Influences on Decision-Making.
In some cases one or more members of a group have high need for control or are otherwise driven by a "hidden agenda" to push for a particular decision. Gouran and Hirokawa illustrate this **egocentric influence**:

> As more than one observer has noted, former President Richard Nixon was ultimately responsible for his own political undoing in the Watergate case because of his inability to permit normal investigative processes to move forward in regard to the break-in at Democratic National Headquarters. Instead his need for control dominated discussions among members of his inner circle and culminated in the fateful decision to engage in a cover-up.[28]

Signs of egocentric influences on group decision-making include (1) members adopting a win-lose orientation and appearing to be preoccupied with getting the group to adopt their particular solutions; (2) highly defensive members; and (3) statements like "Please, don't question me, I know what I'm talking about," "I have been dealing with this kind of problem for over ten years," or "It's the principle of the thing."

To counteract egocentric influences, groups should adopt procedures that force it to approach the problem systematically and that do not give one member's viewpoint too much weight.[29] It is also important that other members clearly indicate to the egocentric member that they are not going to knuckle under to him or her. Working out creative decisions that meet the member's needs, but also guard against problems in the hidden agenda is another way of handling egocentric influences without creating serious fractures in the group.

Group Decision-Making in Organizational Settings

A key tenet of this book is that people adapt their communication to the situations they face. The situations faced by organizational decision-making groups often are very different from those of the isolated, laboratory groups involved in the research underlying the preceding sections.[30] For instance, the types of tasks used in laboratory groups may not even exist in real organizations. In addition, the communication that takes place in laboratory groups usually is private, rarely being overheard by anyone outside of the group. In organizational groups, communication rarely is private and generally is influenced by the presence of other people, either physically or "in the heads" of the participants. The size of groups usually is smaller in laboratory groups, and being assigned to an organizational group often depends as much on political considerations as on expertise or interest in the topic. Perhaps most important, laboratory groups tend to be "zero-history" groups, ones made up of people who have not been together previously and who probably never will be again. Since employees base decisions about how to communicate partially on their past experiences with other members of their groups and with work groups in general, and partially on their expectations of future contact, they may communicate very differently in organizational groups than in laboratory groups.[31]

In summary, three elements of organizations limit the applicability of group communication research to organizational groups—**connectivity**, **hierarchical structure**, and political considerations.[32]

Group Connectivity. As Unit I pointed out, employees and units of organizations differ in terms of their "interdependence;" some employees/groups work independently of other employees/groups while others are highly dependent. This means that some units are "tightly coupled." Each decision they make depends on information and expertise obtained from other groups, and in turn influences the decisions of groups with which they are interdependent. Other groups are "loosely coupled." Their decisions either do not influence other groups or do so only after considerable time and a number of intervening decisions.[33] Loosely coupled groups make decisions independently, relying primarily on information and expertise from within the work group. When units are interdependent, their effectiveness depends on their "linking pins," members who actively communicate with outside people and units (see Chapter 3). In effective tightly coupled groups linking pins talk more and have more impact on the group's decisions than other members. For these groups, centralized networks and leadership may be more productive than laboratory research would suggest. For loosely coupled groups, the general lessons of group communication may be more relevant.

Hierarchical Structure. Organizational group communication also is influenced by the hierarchical structure of the organization. Some work groups are ongoing while others are temporary—ad hoc committees formed to solve specific problems and project teams. Usually involvement in temporary groups is added to employees' normal responsibilities, making it difficult for them to be committed to those groups. Since they are outside of the normal organizational hierarchy, they have little formal power to implement the decisions they reach. Leaders of temporary groups face formidable problems creating and sustaining motivation and the impact the group has may depend more on its members' being able to gain informal support outside of the group than on the quality of its own communication and decision-making. If the issue is important to the organization, rapid and effective decisions may be reached by temporary groups.

But if it is not important, or if the issue threatens any established interests, the discussions may drag on forever, making morale and motivation even greater problems. A major university faced serious shortages of classroom space. The administration decided to help solve the problem by encouraging departments to schedule more evening classes. Eventually the administration took control of scheduling and started offering night classes without consulting the departments. Unfortunately, the daytime regulation of parking was not enforced after 5 p.m. and the city's bus service stopped running at 9 p.m., before evening classes were dismissed. Suddenly there was a serious shortage of night parking. A task force was appointed to find a solution to the problem. Even before their first meeting complaints started to be made—faculty members who were not teaching night classes were "concerned" that they would not have access to lots near the library and computer center if the committee voted to restrict evening parking. The theater and music departments complained that limiting parking would make their performances and concerts inconvenient to important patrons and their budgets would suffer.

As the committee's meetings continued it seemed that every conceivable group had a vested interest in maintaining the chaos in night parking. They also learned that it was difficult to convince the upper administration that the problem was serious, in part because administrators had reserved spaces and "had never noticed any problems parking at night." Eventually, they found a way to reserve only a few lots for students and faculty who were involved in night classes, leaving the rest of the lots open to the interest groups. After two years of work they implemented the new plan at the beginning of the spring semester. The system worked beautifully until January 13, the night of the first home basketball game. At this university, men's basketball is a very serious—and very lucrative—business, and the administration suddenly received an avalanche of hostile calls from wealthy alumni who had driven all over campus searching for parking spaces. The new policy was canceled, by the same administrator who formed the committee in the first place, and the committee sent "back to the drawing board." For some reason attendance has dropped off at recent committee meetings. For this and most ad hoc groups, the character and effectiveness of its internal communication is less important than its external communication. And, external pressures are so constraining that even superhuman leadership would do little to make the group ever again function as a cohesive, committed unit.

Organizational Groups and Political Considerations.   A third reason
why organizational groups differ from laboratory groups also involves considerations of organizational power and politics. Members may be appointed to the
group as representatives of some other group or interests. Their communication reflects their out-group allegiances as much as it does their commitment to
the group. Regardless of what happens within the group, members may have
strong incentives to withhold or distort information or advice in order to protect their outside interests. The adverse effects of these pressures seem to be
smaller when members represent highly interdependent groups because they
know that misleading or alienating other groups eventually will hurt them.[34] In
sum, whether external or internal, political considerations provide a powerful
impetus for groups to move away from the traditional model of group decision-
making.

COMMUNICATION AND ORGANIZATIONAL DECISION-MAKING

When it is applied to organizations, the rational actor model depicts decision-
making as a systematic process through which:

1. An employee recognizes that a problem exists and that it is caused by
   some unexpected or as-yet-untreated change in the organization's environment or by the actions of some of its members;
2. Each member of the organization who, because of his or her formal position, expertise, or available information, has an interest in the problem is told about it and invited to help solve it;
3. Alternative courses of action are compared through open, problem-
   solving communication;
4. The optimal solution is chosen and implemented; and
5. Its impact is monitored and information about its effects is gathered and
   stored for use in similar situations in the future.

Through this feedback process the rational decision process is able to correct itself.[35] As in the case of individual decision-making, there are cases in
which employees can and do make decisions in this way. But in many others
they deviate from the rational actor model, either by making decisions through
"intuition" or through not fully rational processes.

Making Decisions through Intuition.[36]   Fifty years ago Chester Barnard
and Mary Parker Follett (see Chapter 3) examined the way executives make decisions. They noted, much to the dismay of executives reading their books, that
most decisions were made through the kind of "backward thinking" described
early in this chapter. Recent research labeled these processes "decision by **intuition**." Managers often are required to act quickly. Seeking out adequate and
accurate information and devising and considering alternatives simply cannot

be done. Instead, managers "play hunches," usually are quite confident in the quality of those hunches, and often make "intuitive" decisions that are quite successful.

Experience in any endeavor teaches people to recognize meaningful patterns. Without that experience, the events and conditions that make up a decision situation are just random bits of information. For example, present a chess champion and a chess novice a board with twenty-five pieces arranged at random. Remove the pieces and ask the players to replace the pieces in their correct positions. Both players will be able to replace about six pieces accurately. Later on, play a game of chess until there are about twenty-five pieces left on the board. Repeat the experiment. The novice will still be able to replace about six pieces, but the champion will correctly reposition twenty-three or twenty-four pieces. The difference lies in the champion's experience and the way it allows him or her to recognize meaningful patterns. When the pieces are randomly arranged, there are no patterns and the champion's experience does not help. Playing a game creates familiar patterns, which the champion can recognize instantly and intuitively. Managers' experience has the same effect. When confronted with a problem, they draw on experience, recognize the pattern, and recall solutions that had worked before. Of course, intuition is not foolproof—many situations only appear to be like past situations, and rapid recognition can be wrong recognition. There is substantial evidence that organizational decision-makers tend to "remember" history as being much more like current situations, and much less ambiguous, than it actually was.[37]

But in a great many situations, it is more important to *act* than to take the *best* action—accurate perceptions and decisions are nice, but often they simply are not necessary.[38] Weick tells a story about a small Hungarian military unit that became lost during maneuvers in the Swiss Alps. Snowbound for two days, one of them finally found a map in his pocket, and using it, they found their way back to camp. Eventually, they discovered to their astonishment that the map was of the Pyrenees mountains, not the Alps. He concludes:

> this incident raises the intriguing possibility that when you are lost, any old map will do. . . . [Maps and plans] animate and orient people. Once people begin to act (enactment), they generate tangible outcomes (cues) in some context (social), and this helps them discover (retrospect) what is occurring (ongoing), what needs to be explained (plausibility), and what should be done next (identity enhancement).[39]

In short, intuition generates effective solutions, especially when "rational deliberations" are impossible.

Making Decisions through Not Strictly Rational Processes

The rational actor model assumes that making the best possible choice always is the best organizational strategy. In contrast, "nonrationality" models suggest that this kind of situation is quite rare in organizations. This perspective does not advocate **irrational** decision-making—ignoring the realities of a situation—but neither does it exclude emotional aspects of the situation. Instead, it proposes that organizational decision situations are complex and multidimensional and that decision-making processes should be adapted to the complexities of those situations. "Nonrationality" models are difficult to accept because they violate many of the taken-for-granted assumptions of modern Western societies. Consequently, fully understanding nonrational organizational decision-making needs to involve an analysis of key societal myths.

The Myth of Understanding.   According to "nonrationality" models of organizational decision-making, organizations are to some degree self-monitoring anarchies. They are composed of people who have a number of goals that constantly are changing, frequently are inconsistent, and often are not clear to anyone. Employees can discover their goals and those of their peers only by observing one another's actions. The "intelligence" of an organization is more a loose and transient collection of impressions than a systematic and logical group of tightly interlocked preferences and procedures. As explained earlier in this chapter, each employee is a set of preferred "solutions" looking for problems, a decision-maker looking for work.[40] These nonrational processes work because employees' creativity often overcomes the boundedness of their rationality.

In normal organizational decision situations, employees make organizational decisions and then begin to construct, share, and publicize a seemingly rational explanation and justification of their choices. Often decision-makers search more actively for relevant information after they make decisions than before they do so. Even when their information searches precede their decisions, they may use information as much because it is readily available as because it is accurate or relevant. Not only does it take time and effort to obtain information, seeking information usually involves admitting one's ignorance. In organizations in which appearing to be uninformed is punished, it may be wiser to rely on information that is easily accessible than to search for better information that cannot be obtained without publicly admitting one's ignorance.[41]

Rational actor models assume that the more uncertainty employees face, the more they will seek out relevant information. Similarly, the more threatening a situation is (and therefore the more serious the consequences of the decision for the person or organization), the more decision-makers will seek out accurate and relevant information. However, neither assumption seems to be accurate. Information seeking has a curvilinear relationship to both uncertainty and threat; that is, when situations are simple and unimportant, people seek out little information. Decisions are "routinized" as that term was described in Chapter 2. In situations that are somewhat more confusing or threatening, they seek more information, but only to a point. In conditions of high uncertainty or threat, obtaining information may only create more confusion and almost certainly will create increased anxiety. So, in highly ambiguous or threatening situations, decision-makers reduce their information search.[42]

The rational actor model also depicts communication as a process through which people obtain information in order to reduce uncertainty and ambiguity

FIGURE 8–4

Acting, Coping, and the Management of Ambiguity

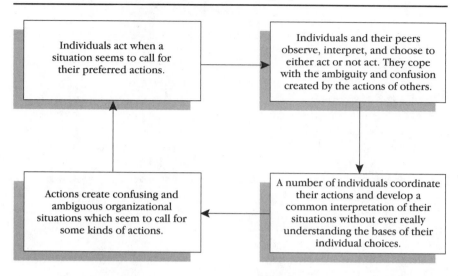

Individuals act when a situation seems to call for their preferred actions.	Individuals and their peers observe, interpret, and choose to either act or not act. They cope with the ambiguity and confusion created by the actions of others.
Actions create confusing and ambiguous organizational situations which seem to call for some kinds of actions.	A number of individuals coordinate their actions and develop a common interpretation of their situations without ever really understanding the bases of their individual choices.

(recall Chapter 6). Nonrationality models suggest that communication is a process through which people *manage* confusion and ambiguity. Employees encounter nonsensical situations and act in response to them. But in acting they change those situations.[43] These changes create confusion and ambiguity for other members of their organizations, and probably for themselves as well. Their actions also lead others to act in ways that also change the situation. In time these cycles of acting and interacting transform the situation, creating new ambiguities and confusion and so on in a continuous cycle of acting, confusing, and coping (see Figure 8-4). The situation never really becomes clear; ambiguity never is eliminated and often is not even reduced. But ambiguity is managed—people are able to make choices and take actions that satisfy their needs and the needs of their organizations. Because the underlying causes of the problems are not eliminated, problems that employees thought they had solved long ago crop up over and over again. But for people who are paid to "solve" problems, having a never-ending supply of problems to be solved may not be all that bad a thing.

As well as gathering information in nonrational ways, employees often manage the information they obtain in ways that violate the assumptions of the rational actor model. After all, organizational decision-makers are people, often acting in groups, and thus are subject to all of the pressures and nonrational processes described in the first parts of this chapter. They rationalize decisions already made, engage in groupthink, and persist in failing policies long after the available evidence makes it clear that they should be abandoned.[44]

CASE STUDY:
MANAGING THE AMBIGUITY*

One of the key assumptions of "nonrationality" models of organizational decision-making is that ambiguities cannot be reduced or eliminated, but can only be managed. One of the most ambiguous roles played in a hospital is that of the social worker. Usually hospital social workers work with terminally ill patients and their families. But what they do with their clients is multidimensional and ambiguous. Some social workers say they "get families to communicate better when someone is dying;" others "help people live better when they are under stress;" still others "prepare people to leave the hospital as quickly as possible." And, although almost all say that their primary concern is with providing the best possible care for their patients, the meaning of "quality care" depends on a number of factors. Sometimes "quality care" means playing the role of a bureaucrat—getting people out of the hospital as quickly as possible (or at least before their insurance or HMO coverage ends) or helping the family move their loved one to a nursing home and deal with the mountains of paperwork that are part of this process. Sometimes it involves providing psychotherapy, either for the family members or for the dying patient. And sometimes it involves helping people work through religious issues regarding death and afterlife. But always, there is a great deal of ambiguity about what a hospital social worker "does."

A social worker's role in the medical organization also creates ambiguity. Most hospitals operate on the basis of a "medical model," the view that medicine is "about" curing people—fixing what's broken, treating a disease through objective, emotionally detached, scientific methods, sending the patient home when she or he is "cured." In this view of medical care everyone with the same condition should receive the same treatment, and only outcomes—getting the patient well—matter. But sometimes social workers operate on the basis of a very different view, a "psychosocial" model that calls for treating each individual patient as a whole person who has psychological, medical, social, and economic needs. It values empowering the patient, giving him or her as much control over what happens as possible. It treats emotions and emotional responses as central to the healing process. It tells social workers to be empathic and focus on both the treatment process and its outcomes. But since hospital social workers practice in hospitals that are dominated by the medical model they often are "caught in the middle" between two different views of patient care and must find ways to manage the ambiguities and tensions that result.

---

*This case is based on Debra Meyerson, "'Normal' Ambiguity?" in Peter Frost, et al., *Reframing Organizational Culture* (Newbury Park, CA: Sage, 1991 and "Interpretations of Stress in Institutions," *Administrative Science Quarterly, 39* (1994): 628–653.

(continued)

(continued from the previous page)

Finally, authority relationships create ambiguities. Social workers are taught to value egalitarian relationships, but they work in bureaucratic, authoritarian organizations. An egalitarian supervisor might be more comfortable to work with, but may not have the credibility with the upper administration that is needed to get the resources necessary for improving patient care. None of these ambiguities and tensions can be eliminated, because they are inherent in the nature of social work as a discipline and in hospitals as bureaucratic organizations. But managing them adds stress to an already stressful occupation. This does not mean that they cannot be managed. But the ways in which the tensions and ambiguities are managed have important implications, both for patients and for the social workers themselves.

One mode of ambiguity management is through controlled chaos. In some social work units people talked at the same time, came and went as they pleased, communicated as if no one else were in the room, and held meetings that were unstructured free-for-alls. They described life at work as "like you're trying to find a place to stand in the middle of a kaleidoscope;" another said that "life is gray, not black and white. If you want black and white go to Macy's, not to a social work unit." But not only did their confusing, chaotic madness allow them to manage incongruities, it even contributed to their satisfaction with work and with their careers.

Another way of coping was less chaotic, but still not traditional. The social workers accepted the fact that they were part of a bureaucracy, but felt that their role was to keep "an elbow in the system's side," to constantly advocate for individual patients and their unique needs in a context designed to treat everyone alike. But because they have little formal power within the hospital bureaucracy, they could best change the system by acting within its rules. For them, life was composed of constantly looking for opportunities to change the system from the inside, to rebel against the system while accepting their role in it. They coped with this contradiction by developing a "healthy cynicism," by using humor to diffuse the most frustrating situations, or by expressing the group's shared emotions about unjustifiable policies that they knew could never be changed. Neither chaos nor cynicism eliminated the ambiguities or resolved the contradictions that hospital social workers faced, but they did allow them to manage their situations.

Social workers also seemed to adopt one of two approaches to making sense out of their own experiences. Social work is a stressful occupation; stress that is sustained over long periods of time often leads to **burnout**, feelings of emotional exhaustion and psychological withdrawal from their jobs. Stress and burnout also are ambiguous experiences, they can be interpreted as either an individual employee's problem or as a symptom of the organizational situation. In most hospitals social workers seem to use the medical model to make sense

(continued)

(continued from the previous page)

out of their own stress and burnout—they are abnormal responses, caused by individuals' inability to manage stress properly, that need to be treated and controlled. One social worker said, "I think that they [people that burn out] will have the same problem wherever they go. They probably had the problem before they came here. I see it as an internal problem. I don't see it as job-situated at all." Another concluded, "Yeah that's my professional job [to fight off burnout]. See, I would consider that if somebody said to me, 'I'm burned out' then I would call them a very nonprofessional person. I wouldn't deal with them anymore because they should quit." (1994: 643). Stress and burnout are understandable during times of crisis, organizational change, or when someone is new to a job. But it is something that can and should be cured. In the words of The Eagles, "get over it."

But sometimes stress and burnout are interpreted through a sociopsychological model. It is a normal condition, a healthy response to stressful situations: "there is no way not to have occasional bouts of burnout when you do this kind of work. . . . Burnout is the need to detach and I think that there's something healthy about needing to detach sometimes. . . . And just like stress, it's not a bad thing when you start to feel the signs and symptoms of stress, it's a warning signal to take care of yourself, and it can be a positive thing." It is an organizational and situational problem, not an individual pathology.

It should be addressed by the organization, by providing time off for people who are burned out, by offering retreats that provide training in stress management, and so on. One social worker noted that "I read something somewhere that hospice has the lowest turnover rate in social work because it's a place that honors that [stress and burnout]. If you get really depressed you can honor that, take a few days off for mental health days. That saves you in the long run" (1994: 648).

Discussion Questions

1. Try to recall the most ambiguous or confusing experience you have ever had in an organization. Briefly describe the actions taken by members of the organization that caused your confusion. How did you manage the frustrations that you experienced? How did the other members of the organization manage the confusion that you caused them?

2. Now try to recall the most confusing experience that you have had with an organization in which you were not a member. How did members of that organization deal with you (and thus with the confusion, ambiguity, and frustration that you caused them)? Why might they have chosen those ways of dealing with you instead of others?

The Myth of "Solving" Problems.   The rational actor model also presumes that the focus of decision-making activities is on solving problems. Observations of decision-makers indicate that sometimes it is more important to take action, a notion that some organizational theorists have labeled "actional rationality." Decisions, James March has noted, can be made through any of three "styles:"

1. **Oversight**: making quick choices when it appears that waiting may allow the problems to become more complicated. Once the decision-maker acts he or she no longer is responsible for the problem. She or he will have completed her assigned responsibility.
2. **Flight**: delaying a choice until the problem becomes less complex because other people have acted. Because complicated organizational problems usually involve a number of people, all of whom feel pressure to act, delaying a decision may both simplify the problem and allow the decision-maker to shift responsibility for errors to others. For example, an employee may leave town on the day before a crisis erupts. If other people handle the situation well at that time, the problem may almost be solved when the person returns. Then she or he can intervene, make the choices that still need to be made, and claim at least partial credit for resolving the crisis. If the others perform poorly before the person returns, he or she can make decisions that appear to "pick up the pieces." In either case, delaying action will have served the person's purposes.
3. **Resolution**: working through problems in a way that approximates the rational actor model.[45]

Neither oversight nor flight fulfills the requirements of the rational actor model, but both styles make complex problems more manageable. In some organizations, decisions seem to be made through resolution only when it is impossible to use the other approaches. Because oversight and flight do little to solve the underlying causes of problems, the same problems occur over and over again, providing decision-makers with frequent opportunities to act (make decisions) and thus legitimize their roles as decision-makers. In this sense, meetings are political rituals, not decision-making episodes.[46] Like the mythical Sisyphus, sentenced to repeatedly push a rock up a hill only to have it roll down over and over throughout eternity, organizational decision-makers repeatedly face the same choices. The focus of choice making is not as much on solving problems as on being visibly involved in choice-making activities.

Like initiation rites in fraternities, sororities, and other primitive cultures, decision-making events are rituals through which members of organizations demonstrate their competence, power, and commitment to the organization by participating in the ritual.

Of course, decision-making events are a special kind of ritual. Not only do they fulfill important symbolic functions, they also often generate *satisfactory* decisions. Many complex problems should be avoided; many situations can be changed in important ways by making minor changes. To an outside observer, especially one who believes that decision-making should conform to the dictates of the rational actor model, it will seem that "nothing ever gets done" in these decision-making events. If the observer is an anthropologist or sociologist, he or she soon will realize that what "gets done" is the "doing," the act of making choices. If the observer is a recently hired college graduate who has been trained in strategic decision-making, it may take years to realize that what goes on in meetings is meeting. When former students return to their alma maters and complain to their mentors that "I'm always going to meetings where nothing ever gets decided" (as they invariably seem to do), they provide testimony to the ritualized nature of organizational decision-making.

Viewing decision-making events as rituals also helps explain the otherwise mystifying processes through which employees decide when and how to become involved in decision-making events. Employees have a variety of personal goals, favored actions, and "pet" plans. They move along during the day-to-day activities of their organizations until they discover a decision-making event relevant to one of their concerns. They then choose to participate in that event. Other members participate in the same event for different reasons. If they eventually do agree on a course of action, their consensus may be based on a long list of individual and often inconsistent goals. One supervisor may support a building plan because it will give his subordinates more overtime. A department head may support it because it will give her an opportunity to transfer two troublesome workers to another section. Other employees may agree because it will divert upper management's attention away from the large equipment purchases that they plan to make next week. Of course, it is quite unlikely that any of these "real" motives will be expressed openly during the decision-making episodes. Instead, the participants will search for a rationale for the building project that is acceptable to everyone and that can be stated in public. Thus, communication obscures the participants' real motivations rather than reveals them, but in the process it also allows the participants to make a "rational" decision. When an agreement is reached in organizations, it sometimes is an agreement over decisions and public justifications of them, not over the reasons or goals that lie behind the choice (see Figure 8–5).

James March and his associates have captured the essence of ritualized decision-making processes in their description of organizational decision-making events as "garbage cans."[47] When a number of employees decide to become involved in an event, they use it like a garbage can, dumping into the discussion a plethora of concerns, only some of which are "logically" related to the problems being discussed. Although some organizations have more garbage-can decisions than others, the existence of these processes means that all organizations have some problems that rarely are "solved."

Some issues are "dropped into" the can more regularly than others. Ones that are important to the organization and that help managers manage uncertainty appear most frequently. Once they are dropped in, some issues are scrutinized more thoroughly and with greater precision than others. The decision process itself

FIGURE 8–5

Coping with Multiple Aims and Multiple Decision Events*

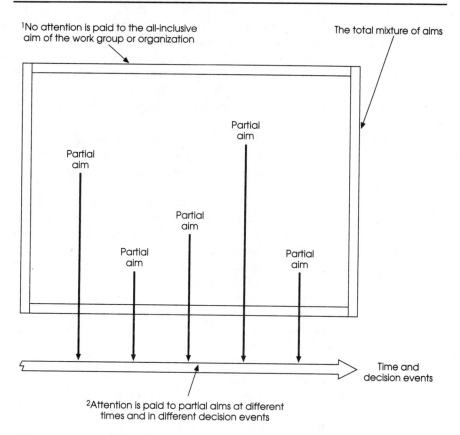

¹No attention is paid to the all-inclusive aim of the work group or organization

The total mixture of aims

Partial aim

Partial aim

Partial aim

Partial aim

Partial aim

Time and decision events

²Attention is paid to partial aims at different times and in different decision events

* Adapted from Gunnar Westerlund and Sven-Erik Sjostrand, *Organizational Myths* (Harper & Row, 1979).

also varies. Powerful employees can push an issue through the process rapidly or can interrupt the process by pressuring for a longer information search, demanding that other "interested" parties be involved in the process, tabling the issue or referring it to a subcommittee. Political considerations and power relationships may influence the decision-making process far more than does the goal of making the best decision.[48] For example, the president of a subsidiary of a large multinational corporation chairs an eleven-person committee which includes the vice-presidents and department heads (remember, organizational groups tend to be larger than the optimal five to seven members because of political considerations). The group must decide between the terms of an existing contract and a new pricing system. After a half-hour it is clear that the president and executive vice-president disagree on the proposal. One senior vice-president adds information about international market conditions, but no other members speak up because they realize that doing so may alienate one of the two top-ranking people in the organization. No action is taken, but another meeting is scheduled to discuss the issue further (and then another, and another . . .).[49] In many organizations, employees attend meeting after meeting, year after year, where the same issues are discussed and the same arguments and information are presented. This repetitiveness is irritating primarily to employees who believe our cultural myths that problem-solving rituals should solve problems once and for all. For employees who realize that the purpose of meeting is meeting, repetitive problem-solving is easy to understand.

The Myth of Plans as Solutions.   Karl Weick has suggested that "plans are important in organizations, but not for the reasons people think."[50] The first four of these reasons are related directly to organizational communication. Plans serve as:

1. *Symbols:* signals to outsiders that the organization really does know what it is doing. For example, when small Japanese-built automobiles took more than 20 percent of the American market, it would have helped American manufacturers to unveil a new line of competitive cars. But because no cars were available, unveiling plans for competing cars was the next best thing (so they did).

2. *Advertisements:* tools with which to attract investors or mobilize workers.

3. *Games:* ways to see how serious people are about their ideas. Planning takes time and energy. If a group of employees presents an idea that a supervisor dislikes but does not want to oppose in public, the supervisor can create a committee to work out the details of the proposal and place each of the employees on it. Unless the group is committed to the idea, they will not expend the effort needed to plan. In the long term, employees learn that the best ways to stay off planning committees are not to present new ideas and to support only those that they are willing to work for. The 3M Company is famous for cutting off the funding for its new projects at least six times, in order to cut their advocates back to the real fanatics.[51]

4. *Excuses for Further Planning:* because many decisions are too complex to be sorted out completely in a single decision-making episode, they need to be simplified in some way. Complexity can be managed by reducing the number of options being considered seriously. Ambiguity will be even less if the options differ only slightly from existing policies or programs. Information about existing conditions is more reliable than predictions about the effects of radical changes. So if decision-makers limit their considerations to a small number of relatively conservative changes, they can manage even very complex situations. They do not eliminate the sources of ambiguity, but they do simplify their task. Once one of these conservative options is implemented the situation is changed, allowing further consideration of a group of minor alterations.

In a provocative series of publications, Charles Lindblom has argued that governmental organizations make choices through this procedure of making "successive limited comparisons." Organizations "muddle through" (Lindblom's phrase) problems, making decisions and taking actions that help them simplify complex situations. Plans help decision-makers make sense out of complicated problems and convince others that the decision-makers really do understand those problems.[52]

Organizational decision-makers do learn, but they do not do so through strictly rational processes. Karl Weick has described organizational learning as a process in which people first act (he calls this phase **enactment**), then observe their actions and the effects of their actions (he calls this phase **selection**), and then construct explanations of their actions (a **retention** phase) (see Figure 8–6). Later, organizational decision-makers remember the "solutions" (actions) that succeeded in the past, and a rough outline of the situations in which they seemed to work. This list gives them guidelines about when not to act and how and when to act. In fact, organizational "learning" and "sense-making" is largely a process of constructing a link between the present and the past.[53]

A Contingency Model of Organizational Rationality.   The goal of the preceding pages has been to suggest that people often do not act in ways that conform to the "rational actor" model, either in everyday decision-making or during organizational decisions. My goal was not to disparage employees. On the contrary, I hoped to suggest that people violate societal myths of strict rationality for a number of understandable reasons.

Some of these reasons involve the nature of the decision itself. It is possible to array organizational decision situations along a continuum. At one pole of the continuum are simple problems for which the effects of different courses of action can be quantified; where the information needed to make the decision is finite, well-defined, and readily available; where only a limited number of options are possible; and where the relevant communication networks are simple. At the other pole are decision situations that are so ambiguous, problems so complex, and information so inaccessible that rational decision-making

FIGURE 8–6
Weick's Model of Organizational "Learning"

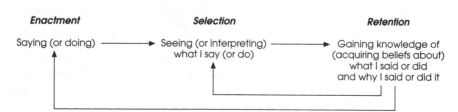

TABLE 8–2

A Continuum of Forms of Decision Making

"RATIONAL DECISION MAKING"—BOTH POSSIBLE AND PREFERABLE	"RATIONAL DECISION MAKING"—EITHER IMPOSSIBLE OR INAPPROPRIATE
Quantifiable outcomes	Ambiguous outcomes
Clear decision-effect links	Ambiguous decision-effect links
"Finite" communication	Unknown or ill-defined parameters
Redundant available sources	"Infinite" communication
Defined information needs	Unknown or indefinite information
Limited communication networks	needs
Minimal organizational and	Diverse or undefined
environmental change	communication networks
Precedented and/or simple problems	Constant organizational and/or
	environmental change
	Unprecedented and/or complex
	problems

is impossible (see Table 8–2). Using strictly rational decision-making processes is both possible and preferable at the simple extreme; it is either inappropriate or impossible at the other. In other situations a combination of rational and nonrational processes is appropriate.

A second continuum reflects the need to implement organizational decisions once they are made. It *is* important for organizational decision-makers to make decisions of at least satisfactory quality. But it often is just as important to arrive at decisions that people will support actively. For example, in a six-year study of how hospitals make decisions about purchasing CAT scanners and other equipment costing millions of dollars, Alan Meyer uncovered a recurring decision-making process that combined rational and ritual processes in a complicated maze.[54] In general, the decision-making episodes started with careful consideration of program needs, equipment costs, projected payoff periods, and other objective factors. Necessary information was gathered before the decisions were made, important people were involved in the process, and so on. In short, the early phase of the decision-making process approximated the rational actor model.

But eventually, in most of the episodes, the process deviated from the rational model. Communication among participants became more vague and started to focus on abstract topics like the parties' shared beliefs, values, goals for the hospital, and vision of its future. Later the decision-makers started to restructure and redefine what actually had taken place during the deliberations so that the events seemed to fit the myth of rational decision-making. The later, nonrational (ritual) phase of the process served two important purposes for the hospitals' personnel. It allowed them to emerge from what often had been highly competitive, heated discussions with a revised image of themselves as

FIGURE 8–7

Continua of Organizational Decision Contexts

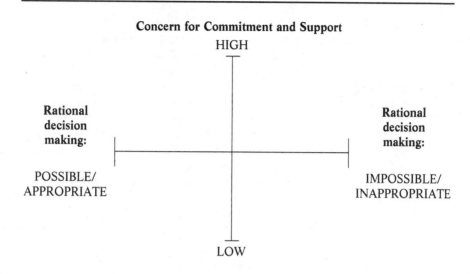

tough but cooperative members of a functioning team. In addition, their symbolic strategies allowed them to gain a sense of psychological closure on the process—to feel that the decision had been made, the battle was over, and their attention could now turn toward using the new equipment effectively. In effect these groups had used the communication strategies that bind cultures together—myths, rituals, and ceremonies—to reunify themselves into a cohesive minisociety.

In hospitals where the decision-makers used rational communication strategies throughout the process, the groups seldom reunified. Dissension continued, debates proliferated, and in some cases key staff members resigned and expensive new equipment was left sitting in the basement. Meyer's research suggests that rational communication strategies are neither always superior to nor always inferior to less rational processes. Making "rational" decisions and making decisions that people will support are separate but interrelated elements of decision-making processes. Thus, as Figure 8–7 suggests, organizational decision situations can be described by two interrelated continua. One continuum reflects the extent to which "rational" decision-making is possible and appropriate. The second involves the extent to which gaining commitment to and support for a decision is important. Different combinations of concern for rationality and concern for commitment call for different combinations of communication processes. What is important is that the mixture of these two factors be appropriate to a particular context, not that decision-makers try to conform to social myths about how people "ought" to act or how organizational decisions "ought" to be made.

RATIONALIZING ORGANIZATIONAL NONRATIONALITY

Hopefully this chapter has led readers to conclude that there are a number of good reasons why people sometimes do (and should) rely on not strictly rational processes for making decisions, both inside and outside of organizations. But this conclusion raises an additional question: "*Why do people persist in pretending that they do make decisions rationally?* The simplest answer involves the taken-for-granted assumptions of our society. Just as we need to believe that we are rational individuals, we need to believe that the organizations to which we devote so much of our lives also are rational creations. Rationalizing organizational nonrationality allows us to create and maintain the illusion that we live in a stable, predictable, "rational" world.

However, the assumptions of a society do much more than provide members with a stable and predictable perceptual world. Within each assumption and set of assumptions are hidden dimensions of social and organizational power relationships. One of the primary functions of processes of rationalizing nonrationality is to perpetuate those power relationships.

Chapter 7 introduced social theorist Jurgen Habermas' distinction between "practical" and "technical" reasoning. All societies can be defined by the kind of balance they maintain between "technical" and "practical" reason. In "traditional" societies (some people use the more pejorative term "primitive"), practical reason dominates technical reason. The experience of living is valued in itself; the meaning of an act lies more in the act itself than in what it might allow people to obtain. In industrial societies, technical reason dominates practical reason. For example, when I teach time-management skills, I begin by asking people to play a simple "priority clarification" game: "Pretend that you just learned that you will live only one more year. Your situation will not change markedly—you will not become richer or poorer, smarter or dumber, and so on. What would you begin to do that you now do not do and what would you quit doing that you now are doing?" When I ask students this question, at least 80 percent say, "I'd quit school and start to travel or spend time with my family." Now, it is possible that they could be in college primarily for practical reasons, for what school gives them in and of itself—because college piques and fulfills their curiosity about life or because it meets their natural craving for knowledge (remember, Habermas' definition of "practical" is *not* the usual definition). My students tell me, however, that they *really* are going to school for technical reasons—because getting a degree is a means for obtaining other goals like getting a "real" job (recall Chapter 7), increasing their social status, or buying a BMW. Only when these technical goals become irrelevant because of their impending death do their practical interests become salient. In Habermas' terms, technical reason dominates practical reason in their lives, just as it does in the lives of everyone in "modern" societies.

But like other societal assumptions, the particular balance of technical and practical reason that exists in a society privileges some people and groups of people over others. In "traditional" societies those people who control symbolism—priests or shamans—are granted more power than other members of the culture. In technical societies people who control "rational" decision-making are granted a privileged position. In the organizations of modern societies the bias in favor of rational decision-making favors managers, and especially upper-level managers, over other employees. Because the formal positions held by managers give them superior access to information, and because their background and training give them greater facility with the language of rational decision-making, they *seem* to have a superior ability to decide what should be done, when, where, and by whom.

In this way the circular relationship between the social myth of rational decision-making and management's privileged position is closed. As long as modern societies privilege technical reason (rationality, efficiency, effectiveness, and so on) and as long as managers are able to *appear* to be rational actors, their superior power positions will be protected. Low-power people will perceive that their lack of power results from their "natural" and "normal" limitations. In short, rationalizing nonrationality helps preserve the deep structure of power in modern organizations and modern societies.

SUMMARY AND CONCLUSIONS: COMMUNICATIONS AND DECISION-MAKING

Analyzing the social and organizational myths discussed in this chapter reveals processes of organizational choice making that are quite different from those depicted in the rational actor model. Contemporary models of decision-making teach us two important lessons about the function of communication in organizations. They indicate that both the *processes* of communicating and the *products* of communication (decisions, plans, deals, and so on) allow members of organizations to *manage* ambiguous and confusing situations. If one embraces the cultural assumption of the rational actor model without questioning it, or if one accepts the assumptions of the traditional and human relations models of organizing, the ambiguity-management function of communication will seem inefficient and perhaps a little bit perverse. But blending rational and not strictly rational elements of decision-making together in the same decision-making episodes may be neither strange nor ineffective. Doing so allows employees to *act,* and acting often is more important than reaching *optimal* decisions.

The danger facing organizational decision-makers is not that they will make decisions that are not strictly rational. Incorporating the ethical, political, personal, and interpersonal considerations that are excluded from the rational actor model often—perhaps usually—will lead to more productive outcomes than blindly following the dictates of rationality. The danger is that decision-makers may become trapped in their patterns of communicating and making decisions, and becoming trapped is possible in both rational and not strictly rational decision processes. Our patterns of acting provide us with a great degree of stability. But, as Karl Weick has noted, the stability and predictability that come from "tried and true" ways of acting may themselves prevent us from adapting to new needs and demands. Adaptation to past needs may prevent adaptability to future ones.

In order to avoid both of these problems—inappropriately imposing rational actor models of communication and decision-making and becoming trapped in patterns of acting—employees constantly must monitor their communication and the communication patterns of their organizations, searching for strategies that can improve their ability to adapt. Employees must be able to ask themselves, "Does strategy X work? Should I use it?" rather than asserting, "I know X works. We should use it." They must be able to obtain and accurately process information that casts doubts on their perceptions, beliefs, and interpretations. And they must be able to suspend their views of the "realities" of their organizations in order to understand how they can best respond to the situations they face.

NOTES

[1] James March, "The Technology of Foolishness," in *Ambiguity and Choice in Organizations,* James March and Johann Olson, eds. (Bergen: Universitetsforlaget, 1970). Also see Michael Cohen and James March, *Leadership and Ambiguity,* 2nd ed. (Boston: Harvard Business School Press, 1974). Harrison Trice and Janice Beyer take an even more direct position, arguing that rationality is *the* core assumption of organizations in Western cultures, including our own (see *The Cultures of Work Organizations,* Englewood Cliffs, NJ: Prentice-Hall, 1993, especially Chapter 2).

[2] See the articles summarized by Paul Slovic, Baruch Fischoff, and Sarah Lichtenstein, "Behavioral Decision Theory," *Annual Review of Psychology, 28* (1977): 1–39. The model was proposed by John von Neumann and Oskar Morganstern, *Theory of Games and Economic Behavior* (New York: John Wiley, 1947).

[3] See J. Robert Cox, "Symbolic Action and Satisfactory Choices," paper presented at the Speech Communication Association Convention, New York, 1980); Leonard Hawes and David Smith, "A Critique of the Assumptions Underlying the Study of Communication and Conflict," *Quarterly Journal of Speech, 59* (1973): 423–435; and David H. Smith, "Theoretical and Research Problems with the Concept of Utility" paper presented at the International Communication Association Convention, Acapulco, 1980). The distinction between cannot and *do not* is important; the rational actor model has been defended on the grounds that although people do not consciously use the system, they behave as if they do. See Ward Edwards, "Subjective Probabilities Inferred from Decisions," *Psychological Review, 69* (1962): 109–135, and "Utility, Subjective Probability, Their Interaction and Variance Preferences," *Journal of Conflict Resolution, 6* (1962): 42–50.

[4] Dennis Mumby and Linda Putnam have argued that the usual interpretation of the concept of bounded rationality inappropriately privileges "rational" conceptions of decision-making while simultaneously devaluing decisions based on intuition or emotional experience ("The Politics of Emotion: A Feminist Reading of Bounded Rationality," *The Academy of Management Review, 17* [1992]: 465–487). The ideas that I present in this chapter are consistent with their conclusion, although the rationale I present is somewhat different.

[5] James March and Herbert Simon, "The Concept of Rationality," in *Human Behavior and International Politics,* David Singer, ed. (Chicago: Rand-McNally, 1965), p. 343. For a critique of this concept, see Mumby and Putnam, "Rationality."

[6] Kenneth May, "Intransitivity, Utility and Aggregation of Preference Patterns," *Econometrica, 22* (1956): 1–36; and T. Dolbear and L. Lave, "Inconsistent Behavior in Lottery Choice Experiments," *Behavioral Science, 12* (1967): 14–23.

[7] Karl Weick, *The Social Psychology of Organizing* (Reading, MA: Addison-Wesley, 1979); James March and Johann Olson, *Ambiguity and Choice in Organizations* (Bergen, Norway: Universitetsforlaget, 1970); and G. Westerlund and S. Sjostrand, *Organizational Myths* (New York: Harper & Row, 1979). These three works are important sources for the ideas presented in the remainder of this chapter.

[8] This survey is based largely on Julia Wood, Gerald Phillips, and Douglas Pederson, *Group Discussion,* 2nd. ed. (New York: Harper & Row) and Randy Hirokawa and M.S. Poole (Eds.), *Communication and Group Decision Making,* 2nd ed. (Thousand Oaks, CA: Sage, 1996). For more extensive summaries of research, see Dennis Gouran and B. Aubrey Fisher, "The Functions of Communication in the Formation, Manintenance and Performance of Small Groups," in *Handbook of Rhetorical and Communication Theory,* C.C. Arnold and J.W. Bowers, eds. (Boston: Allyn and Bacon, 1985); and Dennis Gouran, "The Paradigm of Unfulfilled Promise," in *Speech Communication in the Twentieth Century,* T.W. Benson, ed. (Carbondale, IL: Southern Illinois University Press, 1984).

[9] David Hickson, W. Graham Astley, Richard Butler, and David Wilson, "Organizations as Power," in *Research in Organizational Behavior,* v. 3 (Greenwich, NJ: JAI Press, 1981) and Peter Abell, *Organizations as Bargaining and Influence Systems* (London: Heinemann, 1975).

[10] Martin Chemers, "Culture and Assumptions about Leadership," in *Small Group Communication,* Robert Cathcart and Larry Samovar, eds. (Dubuque, IA: William C. Brown, 1984).

[11] Ernest Bormann discusses the dynamics of leadership emergence very insightfully in *Small Group Communication: Theory and Practice,* 3rd ed (New York: HarperCollins, 1990). Also see Bernard M. Bass, *Bass & Stogdill's Handbook of Leadership: Theory, Research, and Managerial Applications,* 3rd edition (New York: Free Press, 1990), pp. 106–107.

[12] E.P. Hollander, *Leadership Dynamics* (New York: Free Press, 1978)

[13] Bass, pp. 685–686.

[14] Cited in Thomas Schiedel, "Divergent and Convergent Thinking in Group Decision-making," in Randy Hirokawa and M. Scott Poole, *Communication and Group Decision-Making* (Beverly Hills, CA: Sage, 1986).

[15] *Ibid.*

[16] M. Scott Poole and Carolyn Baldwin, "Developmental Processes in Group Decision-making," in Hirokawa and Poole, *Groups,* 2nd ed. Also see M. Scott Poole, "Decision Development in Small Groups," Parts I, II and III in *Communication Monographs 48* (1981): 1–24; *50* (1983): 206–232; and *50* (1983): 321–341; and Henry Mintzberg, Duru Raisinghani, and Andre Theoret, "The Structure of 'Unstructured' Decision Processes," *Administrative Science Quarterly,* 21 (1976), 246–275.

[17] B. Aubrey Fisher, "The Process of Decision Modification in Small Discussion Groups," *Journal of Communication, 20* (1970), 51–64; also see Poole and Baldwin in Hirokawa and Poole, 2nd ed.

[18] Wood., et al.

[19] Linda Putnam, "Preference for Procedural Order in Task-oriented Small Groups," *Communication Monographs, 46* (1979), 193–218. Randy Hirokawa conducted a study which compared the relative effectiveness of groups which carried out the basic decision functions of problem definition, criteria development, thorough evaluation of options, and careful selection of an option, but did not do them in any particular order with groups which followed the standard agenda. The more of these functions groups carried out, the more effective their decision was, but the order in which they were carried out did not influence effectiveness. See R.Y. Hirokawa, "Discussion Procedures and Decision-Making Performance: A Test of a Functional Perspective," *Human Communication Research, 12* (19): 203–224.

[20] Dennis Gouran and Randy Hirokawa, "Functional Theory and Communication in Decision-Making and Problem-Solving Groups: An Expanded Perspective," in Hirokawa and Poole, 2nd ed.

[21] Thomas Schiedel and Laura Crowell, *Discussing and Deciding* (New York: Macmillan, 1979).

[22] Ernest Bormann, "Symbolic Convergence Theory and Communication in Group Decision-making," in Hirokawa and Poole, 2nd ed.

[23] Hirokawa and Poole, 2nd ed., p. 105.

[24] David Seibold and Renee Meyers, "Communication and Influence in Group Decision-making," in Hirokawa and Poole. Also see Tim Cline and Rebecca Cline, "Risky and Cautious Decision Shifts in Small Groups," *Southern Speech Communication Journal, 44* (1979), 252–263; S.M. Alderton and Larry Frey, "Effects of Reactions to Arguments on Group Outcomes," *Central States Speech Journal, 34* (1983), 88–95; and Frank Boster and Michael Mayer, "Differential Argument Quality Mediates the Impact of Social Comparison Process of the Choice Shift," paper presented at the International Communication Association Convention, San Francisco, 1984; Irving Janis, *Victims of Groupthink* (Boston: Houghton Mifflin, 1972); "Sources of Error in Strategic

Decision-making," in *Organizational Strategy and Change,* Johannes Pennings and Associates, eds. (San Francisco: Jossey-Bass, 1985); and Irving Janis and L. Mann, *Decision Making* (New York: Free Press, 1977).

[25] Wood, et al, p. 103.

[26] Nancy Harper and L. Askling, "Group Communication and Quality of Task Solution in a Media Production Organization," *Communication Monographs,* 47 (1980), 77–100; Schiedel in Hirokawa and Poole, 1st ed.

[27] Hirokawa and Scheerhorn; Harold Guetzkow and J. Gyr, "An Analysis of Conflict in Decision-making Groups," *Human Relations,* 7 (1954), 367–381.

[28] Gouran and Hirokawa, "Functional Theory," p. 61.

[29] Many such procedures are available, including brainstorming, Nominal Group Technique, and Multi-Attribute Decision Making. See Susan Jarboe, "Procedures for Enhancing Group Decision Making," in Hirokawa and Poole, 2nd ed., for a good introduction and references to various group decision-making procedures.

[30] An excellent argument in favor of studying "bona fide" groups rather than laboratory groups is featured in Linda Putnam and Cynthia Stohl, "Bona Fide Groups: An Alternative Perspective for Communication and Small Group Decision Making", in Hirokawa and Poole, *Communication and Group Decision-Making,* 2nd ed.

[31] Richard Farace, Peter Monge, and Hamish Russell, *Communicating and Organizing* (Reading, MA: Addison-Wesley, 1977).

[32] This section is based on Linda Putnam, "Understanding the Unique Characteristics of Groups within Organizations," in *Small Group Communication,* Robert Cathcart and Larry Samovar, eds. (Dubuque, IA: William C. Brown, 1984). Also see Fred Jablin and David Seibold, "Implications for Problem-solving Groups of Empirical Research on 'Brainstorming,'" *Southern Speech Communication Journal,* 43 (1978), 327–356; Fred Jablin and Lyle Sussman, "An Exploration of Communication and Productivity in Real Brainstorming Groups," *Human Communication Research, 4* (1978), 329–337; Fred Jablin and Lyle Sussman, "Organizational Group Communication," in *Organizational Communication Abstracts,* vol. 8, ed. Howard Greenbaum, Ray Falcione, and Susan Hellweg (Beverly Hills, CA: Sage, 1981); Larry Browning, "Diagnosing Teams in Organizational Settings," *Group and Organization Studies, 2* (1977), 187–197; J.S. Heinen and E. Jacobson, "A Model of Task Group Development in Complex Organizations," *Academy of Management Review, 1* (1976), 98–111; L.R. Hoffman, "Applying Experimental Research on Group Problem Solving to Organizations," *Journal of Applied Behavioral Science, 15* (1979), 375–391.

[33] This is Karl Weick's distinction (see *Organizing).* It was an important concept in the "Normal Accidents" case study earlier in this chapter.

[34] Jeffrey Pfeffer and Gerald Salancik, *The External Control of Organizations* (New York: Harper & Row, 1978).

[35] Karl Weick and Larry Browning, "Argument and Narration in Organizational Communication," *Yearly Review of Management of the Journal of Management, 12* (1986): 243–259.

[36] This section is based on Chester Barnard, *The Functions of the Executive* (Cambridge, MA: Harvard University Press, 1938); Mary Parker Follett, *Creative Experience* (New York: Longmans, Green, 1924); Herbert Simon, "Making Management Decisions," *Academy of Management Executive, 1* (1987): 57–64; Warren Thorngate, "Must We Always Think Before We Act?," *Personality and Social Psychology Bulletin, 2* (1976): 31–35; and William Starbuck, "Acting First and Thinking Later," in *Organizational Strategy and Change,* Johannes Pennings and Associates, eds. (San Francisco: Jossey-Bass, 1985).

[37] Parker Follett, *Creative;* also see William Starbuck and E.J. Milliken, "Executives' Perceptual Filters," in D.C. Hambrick, ed., *The Executive Effect* (Greenwich, CT: JAI, 1988) and H.W. Brands, "Fractile History, or Clio and the Chaotics," *Diplomatic History,* 1992: pp. 495–510. It is important to differentiate "ambiguity" and "uncertainty." An ambiguous situation in one in which any number of plausible interpretations are available while an uncertain situation is one in which no plausible interpretation is available. Consequently, obtaining information may reduce uncertainty, but it will not remedy ambiguity (see Weick, *Sensemaking,* pp. 91–100.)

[38] Weick, *Sensemaking,* p. 60.

[39] Weick, *Sensemaking,* pp. 54–55.

[40] M. Cohen, J. March, and J. Olson, "A Garbage-can Model of Organizational Choice," *Administrative Science Quarterly, 17* (1972): p. 2.

[41] Weick, *Psychology*. Detailed studies of how people manage ambiguity have been completed by Charles Bantz and David Smith, "A Critique and Experimental Test of Weick's Model of Organizing," *Communication Monographs, 44* (1977): 171–184; Gary Kreps, "A Field Experimental Test of Weick's Model of Organizing," in *Communication Yearbook 4,* Dan Nimmo, ed. (New Brunswick, NJ: Transaction, 1980); and Linda Putnam and Ritch Sorenson, "Equivocal Messages in Organizations," *Human Communication Research, 8* (1982): 114–132.

[42] Richard Daft and N. Macintosh, "A Tentative Exploration into the Amount and Equivocality of Information Processing in Organizational Work Units," *Administrative Science Quarterly, 26* (1981): 207–224; Bart Victor and Richard Blackburn, "Determinants and Consequences of Task Uncertainty," *Journal of Management Studies, 18* (1987): 108–132; Barry Staw, L. Sandelands, and J. Dutton, "Threat-rigidity Effects in Organizational Behavior," *Administrative Science Quarterly, 26* (1981): 501–524; and R.M. Cyert and James March, *A Behavioral Theory of the Firm* (Englewood Cliffs, NJ: Prentice-Hall, 1963).

[43] Charles O'Reilly, "Variations in Decision-makers' Use of Information Sources," *Academy of Management Journal, 25* (1982): 756–771; and T.J. Allen, *Managing the Flow of Technology* (Cambridge, MA: M.I.T. Press, 1977). Analyses of how acting changes situations are available in N. Brunnson, *The Irrational Organization* (Chichester, UK: Wiley, 1982); G. Astley and Andrew Van de Ven, "Central Perspectives and Debates in Organizational Theory," *Administrative Science Quarterly, 28* (1983): 245–273; and Marshall Scott Poole and Andrew Van de Ven, "Using Paradox to Build Management and Organization Theories." *Academy of Management Review, 14:* 562–578 and Andrew Van de Ven and M.S. Poole, "Explaining Development and Change in Organizations," *Academy of Management Review, 20* (1995): 510–540.

[44] Joel Brockner, Robert House, Kathy Lloyd, Sinaia Nathanson, Gregg Birnbaum, Janet Deitcher, and Jeffrey Rubin, "Escalation of Commitment to an Ineffective Course of Action," *Administrative Science Quarterly, 31* (1986): 109–126; J. March and M. Feldman, "Information in Organizations as Signal and Symbol," *Administrative Science Quarterly, 26* (1981): 171–186; D. Caldwell and C. O'Reilly, "Responses to Failure," *Academy of Management Journal, 25* (1962): 121–136; Gerald Salancik, "Commitment and the Control of Organizational Behavior and Belief," in B.M. Staw and G.R. Salancik, eds., *New Directions in Organizational Behavior* (Chicago: St. Clair, 1977); B. Staw, "Counterforces to Change," in P.S. Goodman & Associates, eds., *Change in Organizations* (San Francisco: Jossey-Bass, 1982); B. Staw, "Knee Deep in the Big Muddy," *Organizational Behavior and Human Performance, 16* (1976): 27–44; B. Staw and J. Ross, "Commitment to a Policy Decision," *Administrative Science Quarterly, 23* (1978): 40–52; and F. Fox and B. Staw, "The Trapped Administrator," *Administrative Science Quarterly, 24* (1979): 449–456.

[45] March.

[46] Anne Huff, "Politics and Argument as a Means of Coping with Ambiguity and Change," in L.R. Pondy, et al., eds., *Managing Ambiguity and Change* (New York: John Wiley, 1988).

[47] Cohen, March, and Olson; O'Reilly; and Richard Butler, David Hickson, David Wilson, and R. Axelsson, "Organizational Power, Politicking and Paralysis," *Organizational and Administrative Sciences, 8* (1977): 44–59. For a revision of the original garbage-can model, see Michael Masuch and Perry LaPotin, "Beyond Garbage Cans," *Administrative Science Quarterly, 34* (1989): 38–68.

[48] Richard Butler, Graham Astley, David Hickson, Geoffrey Mallory, and David Wilson, "Strategic Decision Making in Organizations," *International Studies of Management and Organization, 23* (1980): 234–249.

[49] This example is based on George Farris, "Groups and the Informal Organization," in *Groups at Work,* Roy Payne and Cary Cooper, eds. (New York: John Wiley, 1981).

[50] Weick, *Psychology:* p. 10. The first four of these functions are discussed by Weick; the fifth is drawn from C. Lindblom, "The Science of Muddling Through," *Public Administration Review, 19* (1959): 412–421.

[51] Tom Peters and Nancy Austin, *A Passion for Excellence* (New York: Random House, 1985).

[52] Lindblom. Henry Mintzberg and Alexandra McHugh, "Strategy Formation in an Adhocracy," *Administrative Science Quarterly, 30* (1985): 160–197 provide an excellent example of a successful "muddling through" organization.

[53] Weick, *Sensemaking*.

[54] Of course, my brief summary oversimplifies Meyer's research. See "Mingling Decision-Making Metaphors," *Academy of Management Review, 9* (1984): 231–246. Karl Weick takes an even more explicit position, concluding that a search for "accurate" conclusions sacrifices commitment and motivation (*Sensemaking,* p. 60).

Chapter 9

COMMUNICATION AND THE MANAGEMENT OF ORGANIZATIONAL CONFLICT

Not only do members of organizations use communication to "work through" conflicts, they are able to "work" through managing conflicts effectively.

—ANNE MAYDAN NICOTERA

CENTRAL THEMES

- Conflicts are an inevitable part of relationships characterized by interdependence and interaction. People may perceive that a conflict exists when there is no realistic basis for one and vice versa.
- The ways in which people "frame" conflicts and the choices they make during the early phases of conflicts create parameters that guide and constrain the communication during overt conflicts.
- Overt conflicts are composed of interactive cycles of communication, which tend to be self-perpetuating and self-reinforcing.
- Structuring strategies can be used to define an issue or guide a discussion in ways that favor a particular employee's position.
- The greatest barrier to productive conflict management is the tendency for conflict cycles to escalate.
- Destructive escalation occurs when major power imbalances exist. They can be prevented or controlled if all parties understand the communication strategies available to them.
- In productive conflicts many kinds of communication strategies are used; in destructive ones only a few strategies are employed.
- Conflicts escalate in three ways—expansion of issues, involvement of self, and dominance of emotion and symbol.

KEY TERMS

Conflict resolution	Conflict
Latent conflict	Mixed-motive interactions
Conflict frames	Perceived conflict
Avoidant orientations	Accommodative orientations
Compromising orientations	Competitive orientations
Collaborative orientations	Felt conflict
Reflexive communication	Punctuation

This chapter examines another practical reality of organizational life: *Disagreement and conflict are inevitable aspects of working relationships, and the need to manage conflicts is always with each of us.* For many years researchers and managers viewed organizational conflict as an inherent evil. Conflicts revealed a weakness in the organization, a flaw in its design, operation, or communication.[1] Conflicts needed to be **resolved**; that is, their sources had to be discovered and eliminated. Peace and stability had to be returned to the organization. The word *conflict* conjured up images of otherwise fair and equitable societies and rational organizations "gone bad."

However, contemporary views of conflict present a different view. Organizational conflicts are inevitable and potentially valuable, both for individuals and for cultures. Conflicts provide employees with opportunities to publicize, test, and refine their ideas and to demonstrate their competence and value to the organization. Conflicts also help organizations adapt to changes, foster innovation, and integrate their diverse constituent groups into a functioning whole.[2] They are neither inherently good nor intrinsically bad, although they do vary in their *productiveness* and *destructiveness*. Conflicts that are relatively productive for the organization as a whole may be highly destructive for some of the individuals who are involved and highly productive for other participants. Similarly, episodes that are disruptive and damaging to the organization may be productive for many of the participants.

THE BASES AND EARLY PHASES OF ORGANIZATIONAL CONFLICT

Typically when people hear the term *organizational conflict* they imagine executives shouting at one another in a boardroom, giant oligopolies bidding for a majority share of a competitor's stock, or, for the more fanciful of us, secret meetings on foggy nights in which technological secrets are exchanged for chalets on the Riviera. Although overt and sometimes hostile confrontations are part of organizational conflict, they are only one part. I will define **conflict** more broadly, as *communication between people who are interdependent and who perceive that other people stand between them and the realization* *of their goals, aims, values, and so on.*[3]   This definition encompasses each of the examples listed earlier in this paragraph, as well as everyday discussions of organizational policies and projects, negotiations between employees or groups of employees (for instance, labor–management negotiations), and cooperative attempts to find mutually acceptable solutions to problems. In short, **conflicts** are communicative *interactions* among people who are *interdependent* and who perceive that their interests are *incompatible, inconsistent,* or *in tension.*

Theorist Louis Pondy has developed one of a number of similar depictions of the *bases* and *phases* of organizational conflict.[4]   Conflicts move through five phases: *latent, perceived, felt, overt,* and *aftermath.* This chapter focuses on the *overt* phase, for it is in that phase that communication is most important and complex. The earlier phases also are important, for they establish the parameters within which the conflict will be played out, and parameters guide and constrain communication in important ways.

Latent Conflict.   Phase 1 is **latent conflict**, a situation in which there are grounds for conflict but the parties have not yet realized that the grounds exist. Potential grounds for conflict exist whenever people are involved in *interactive* and *interdependent* relationships. Conflicts are "episodes" within enduring organizational relationships. Parties usually have both a legacy of interacting with one another in the past and the expectation that they will encounter one another in the future. Unresolved grievances may suddenly reappear in the guise of issues completely unrelated to the original complaint. Trust developed during past interactions will make it easier to manage the current conflict productively.[5]   The anticipation of conflicts may lead parties to either "get the battle over with today" or to "let this issue go by and save my ammunition for tomorrow." Conflicts also occur within a particular organizational climate that may encourage the parties either to be cooperative or competitive with one another. Each of these factors is a latent (present but not clearly within the parties' conscious awareness) aspect of the overall context that surrounds a particular conflict.[6]

Organizational conflicts usually involve employees whose organizational roles are interdependent, because interdependency means that there are many topics over which conflicts can arise—tangible objects like awards and resources or intangible factors like status and power. When people rarely interact with one another they have few reasons or opportunities to fight. In organizational settings, the vast majority of conflicts are what theorists call **mixed-motive interactions**. This means that the parties have incentives both to cooperate and to compete. Even if employees have little incentive to cooperate during the discussion of a single issue, the fact that they will have to depend on one another in the future means that they always have incentives to reach a cooperative outcome to conflicts.

Traditional research on organizational conflict has assumed that a number of personality variables predict how people communicate during conflicts. A "variable" that often has been studied is a party's gender. However, the results of this research have been quite mixed. Many studies have found that personality variables, including gender, do influence parties' initial orientations toward conflict—women prefer cooperative and passive orientations, for example. But other studies have found that women view conflicts as "wars," thus adopting a stereotypically male perspective, especially when the situation leaves no other option. Studies that have examined actual communicative strategies have found that the influence of gender changes as conflicts progress. For example, although supervisors tend to eventually shift from cooperative to competitive strategies when their subordinates do not comply with their wishes, male supervisors make the shift more quickly than do female supervisors.[7]

Consequently, relatively stable "personality" variables like gender seem to only weakly predict the conflict strategies that people will use or the outcomes of their conflicts. What *does* seem to matter are the "**frames**" of reference that employees bring with them into conflict situations. Through past experiences, both in their organizations and in their outside lives, people develop certain ways of making sense out of situations and issues.[8]   Conflict frames include preferences about how conflicts should be managed, what I will label "orientations" to conflict. But conflict frames also include assumptions about what a conflict or issue is about, interpretations of the risks and benefits associated with different outcomes, definitions of one's position on a particular issue or group of issues, and a complex set of expectations—about how the parties in a conflict will and should act, what kinds of evidence and arguments can legitimately be used to influence the outcome of the conflict, and how the conflict episode will unfold.[9]   For example, employees' perceptions of how well they handled past conflicts seem to influence the way they will handle future conflicts. People who expect to handle a conflict well tend to employ more open and cooperative orientations and communication strategies while people who expect that they will not handle conflicts well tend to adopt coercive orientations and strategies.[10]

The frames that employees bring with them to a conflict also seem to have important effects on their actions during conflicts. Conflict situations are confusing and ambiguous, and frames help parties identify the overall themes and define the issues that make up the conflict, help them differentiate important arguments and information from secondary arguments and information, help them decide when to use risky communication strategies and when to "play it safe," and "tell" them when they should reciprocate the conflict strategies used by other parties in the conflict and when they should "go their own way." For example, when people "frame" a conflict as an opportunity to achieve some kind of gain, they tend to use more risky communicative strategies; when they "frame" it as an event that may lead to losses, their communicative strategies tend to be less flexible and the likelihood of the conflict reaching an impasse is increased.[11]

However, this does not mean that the frames automatically determine the communication strategies that people use in conflicts. Instead, they provide parameters within which people initially make sense out of a conflict situation. As conflicts proceed, the ambiguities change. As new issues are raised and old ones are abandoned, different aspects of one's past experiences become salient and others disappear from one's view. As other parties act in unexpected ways, people adjust their assumptions and expectations. Frames guide and constrain communicative acts, and communicative action leads to new frames. Framing is a *process* through which situations are reframed over and over and new guidelines and constraints are constantly being created.[12]   Nonetheless, some frames constrain parties' actions more tightly than others, making it more difficult to productively manage conflict.

CASE STUDY:
DARNED BIRD HUGGERS*

This chapter focuses on conflicts that take place within organizations. However, conflicts also occur between organizations and outsiders and among organizations. "Framing" processes often have an even more pronounced effect on these conflicts than they do on intraorganizational conflicts.** And, they often illustrate the ways in which conflict frames influence perceptions of risks, potential solutions, and the relevance of different kinds of information.***

One such conflict has pitted the U.S. Fish and Wildlife Service and the Environmental Protection Agency against the farmers and ranchers of central Texas for the past decade. The Golden Cheeked Warbler is an endangered species that inhabits the cedar (really juniper) and oak woodlands of central Texas. For ranchers and farmers, juniper is a nuisance—it grows so thickly that it chokes out grass and spreads rapidly, so rapidly that it cannot really be eliminated. But efforts to control its spread by burning or bulldozing reduce the amount of habitat available to the warbler, and thus threaten its continued existence. To complicate the situation further, most of its habitat is on privately owned land, in a state in which private property rights are taken very seriously. The Republic of Texas agreed to enter the Union only if no lands were owned by the federal government, and, with the exception of some land that has been purchased in west Texas, the stipulation has been honored for a century and a half. The law

---

*This case is based on Tarla Rai Peterson and Christi Choat Horton, "Rooted in the Soil," *The Quarterly Journal of Speech, 81* (1995): 139–166.

**See J. Chase and I. Panagopoulous, "Environmental Values and Social Psychology," in Y. Gurrier, M. Alexander, J. Chase, and M. O'Brien (eds.), *Values and the Environment* (Chichester, UK: John Wiley, 1995) and E. Vaughn and M. Siefert, "Variability in the Framing of Risk Issues," *Journal of Social Issues, 48* (1992): 119–135.

***See Michael Papa and Wendy Papa, "Competence in Organizational Conflicts," in W. R. Cupach and D. J. Canary, eds. *Competence in Interpersonal Conflict* (New York: McGraw-Hill, 1996).

(continued)

(continued from the previous page)

allows the federal government to force landowners to sell land in the warbler's range, but the government does not have the money to buy it. At the time of the study the Nature Conservancy was negotiating to purchase a small proportion of the habitat, probably not enough to maintain a viable warbler population. Those negotiations were successful. In short, it is a classic environmental conflict.

Government organizations (primarily the USFWS) have "framed" the conflict in familiar terms: The endangered species is the property of all Americans and the government's obligation is to protect it by representing the interests of all Americans, not just the local landowners who are directly affected by its presence. Doing so requires them to base their decisions on a broad, "cosmopolitan" knowledge base grounded in the best "scientific" information available. One USFWS manager noted: "We got real good reasons and we got real good laws that tell us how we will operate the refuge system . . . (unlike the ranchers who make) decisions based on what you've seen within 15 miles of your home for all your life" (p. 162).

In contrast, the farmers and ranchers frame the conflict as a battle between outsiders and "good stewards" of the land. Ranchers (the "stewards") make decisions by "common sense," grounded in their individual experiences and the experiences of previous generations of their families who lived on the land. Common sense is contrasted with "scientific" knowledge, based on supposedly "objective" research conducted by or imposed on them by city-dwelling outsiders. Their identity is linked to *living* on the land, and their ability to independently act to protect and preserve it. They take a holistic view of ecosystems, but also see meeting the needs of human beings as a central part of ecosystem management. They talk about nature in what they believe is a *realistic* way—including its constant and sometimes violent change, its disease, birth, death, and predation: "When you're from the country, you understand the normal things that happen through life, but people in the cities don't see those things, and when they see . . . animals that are sick or dying or dead, they become overly emotional" (p. 153). They see themselves as good stewards of the land—"managers" who voluntarily restrain their actions in order to preserve the land for the future, who are actively present, daily walking the land, and who accept accountability for their actions. But they believe that to be fully accountable, they also have to be independent of government regulation. And they admit that some ranchers and farmers are bad stewards of the land—they often are absentee owners; do not accept accountability for their actions because they have not been on and of the land for generations and are not concerned about the effects of their action on future generations; and they see the land as something that should be conquered or subdued, not cared for.

(continued)

(continued from the previous page)

But theirs is a voice that rarely is heard. They believe "that the broader culture no longer accommodates their interests" (p. 141) and rarely participate in the political arena directly, although many do support politically active organizations such as the Texas Farm Bureau. As a result, "public" hearings about the issue tend to involve only representatives of formal organizations—government agencies, environmental organizations, and associations that claim to speak for them.

Discussion Questions

1. Peterson and Horton seem to believe that conflicts like the Golden Cheeked Warbler controversy can be managed through open, collaborative discourse: "Exchanges between (opposing groups) are necessary for moving beyond factionalism to the potential for convergence across perspectives. . . . Dialogue holds great potential for U.S. environmentalism" (pp. 142, 163). Given what you know about the controversy and about the role that framing plays in conflict management, do you agree or disagree? Why or why not?

2. At the time of the study many of the ranchers in the warbler's habitat obtained substantial income from a federal mohair subsidy program that was started during World War II to ensure an adequate supply of fiber for military clothing (the subsidy program ended in April 1996). Would introducing evidence of their "dependence" on the government make the conflict more or less manageable? Why or why not?

Perceived Conflict. Phase 2 in Pondy's model is **perceived conflict.** This stage exists when one or more parties believe that a situation has the characteristics of *interdependence* and *incompatibility.* This perception can be created in a number of ways. Sometimes an outsider explicitly tells an employee that his or her interests are incompatible with someone else's. More often the perception stems from a "precipitating event." One employee criticizes another or makes a demand that the second person perceives is not legitimate. Or an employee makes what she or he perceives is a legitimate request and is rebuffed. Or a long period of annoyance builds up until the employee realizes that a conflict exists.[13] *Perceived* conflict can exist when *latent* conflict does not, as when siblings fight over a serving of rapidly melting ice cream so large that they cannot possibly eat all of it. There is no objective reason for conflict in this situation, although the children *believe* that their interests are incompatible. Also, *latent* conflict can exist without *perceived* conflict, as when siblings are given a seemingly (but not actually) inconsumable mound of ice cream.

This distinction becomes important when the role of communication in conflict is considered. In situations of perceived conflict without latent conflict,

TABLE 9-1
Defining Conflict

DEFINITIONS THAT MAKE CONFLICTS EASIER TO MANAGE PRODUCTIVELY	DEFINITIONS THAT MAKE CONFLICTS DIFFICULT TO MANAGE PRODUCTIVELY
1. "Mixed motive" (or nonzero-sum) definitions: Each party perceives that it can obtain desired outcomes without the others losing the same amount of reward.	1. Zero-sum: Parties perceive that whatever one gains the other loses. The outcome will either grant them complete success or complete failure.
2. Empathic definition of the issue: Parties perceive the issue from both their own and the other parties' perspectives.	2. Egocentric definition of the issue: Parties perceive the issue only from their own frame of reference.
3. Broad contextualization of the issue: Parties search for underlying concerns that place the overt issue in a broad, organizational context.	3. Narrow focus on a single issue and its immediate effects.
4. "Commercial" issue: The issue defined as problem-centered.	4. "Ideological" issue: The conflict is defined as a moral struggle between forces of good and evil.
5. Large number of possible solutions are available.	5. Small number of alternatives are available.

"improving communication" would help the children understand one another's needs and goals, making the conflict manageable (as in "I can't possibly eat half of this. Can you?"). In the situations of latent but not perceived conflict, improved communication could transform what is at least a temporarily cooperative situation into a competitive, conflictful one (as in "I'm gonna want more than half of this. Are you?"). While still in graduate school I was asked to mediate between a university administration (not my own) and the African American Students' Association. The more I talked with both sides the clearer it became that they had almost no objective reason to cooperate and many reasons to compete with each other. They still were talking largely because they did not know how they really felt about each other. The situation was exceptionally volatile, because "getting them to talk to one another"—the task I had been called in to perform—almost certainly would have transformed a latent conflict into a perceived one.

In organizations, perceived conflict exists without latent conflict if employees believe that someone else is their enemy even when their interests really do coincide. Conflicts between "line" personnel (the people who actually produce the products or deliver the services that a firm sells) and "staff" personnel (the people who support the line's activities by marketing and selling its

TABLE 9–2
Orientations to Conflict: Continuum

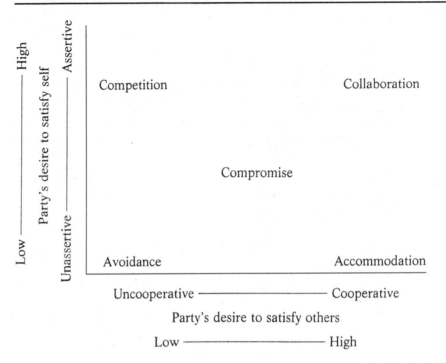

SOURCE: Adapted from Kenneth Thomas, "Conflict and Conflict Management," in *Handbook of Industrial and Organizational Psychology,* Marvin Dunnette, ed. (Chicago: Rand-McNally, 1976).

products or services, buying and delivering raw materials, and hiring and firing employees) are quite common in all kinds of organizations. Often they exist because both groups ignore or de-emphasize their need to cooperate and instead focus their attention on their incentives to compete. Latent conflict also exists without perceived conflict if people overlook minor day-to-day frictions or if they concentrate so completely on routine or easily resolved disagreements that they suppress major problems.

Perhaps more than any other factor, employees' perceptions influence what happens during conflicts and what effects conflicts have on organizations. Table 9–1 summarizes a number of ways in which employees may perceive a conflict. If they define the situation as "all or nothing," see only a small range of alternatives as acceptable solutions, believe that in order for them to "win" the other parties must "lose," or believe that the difference of opinion has a strong moral or ethical dimension, they will tend to try to impose their wills on others, perceive others as hostile and untrustworthy, and adopt a narrow and inflexible course of action during any overt conflicts.[14]

In addition to perceiving conflicts in different ways, employees also differ in their perceptions of how conflicts ought to be managed. Kenneth Thomas developed a model of five "typical" *orientations* to conflict, although he recognized that an infinite number of possible orientations exists (see Table 9–2). These "orientations" describe the approaches that people *intend* to pursue if and when a conflict begins.[15]

1. **Avoidance**: believing that unassertive and uncooperative behavior is the best approach, either because the issues are not worth fighting about, the potential costs of open confrontation are greater than the potential gains, or the issue will "go away" if it is left alone. Requires little communication.

2. **Accommodation**: acquiescing to the perceived goals of the other(s). Requires little communication.

3. **Compromise**: searching for a resolution that partly satisfies both parties. In our society compromise generally means "splitting the difference" fifty-fifty. Requires some degree of willingness to sacrifice individual goals, some communication, and some degree of assertiveness.

4. **Competition**: seeking to dominate others and impose one's preferences on them. Involves some communication, though not as much as compromise.

5. **Collaboration**: all parties believe they should assertively seek a mutually acceptable solution and are willing to spend large amounts of time and effort to reach such an outcome.[16]

The orientation an employee takes depends on a number of factors, including his or her rank compared to other parties and her or his tolerance for communicating with others (see Table 9–3). Employees high in the organizational hierarchy avoid conflicts less than people lower in the hierarchy.[17] Supervisors tend to use competition more often than the other orientations with their subordinates, especially when *their* supervisors have made it clear that they prefer a certain outcome to the conflict. They adopt nonassertive orientations (accommodation or avoidance) with their supervisors.[18] Both the anticipation of communication and the act of communicating are stressful, especially for some people. For them, the less assertive orientations—avoidance, accommodation, and compromise—are the most attractive because they promise to minimize tense or prolonged communication. The quality of interpersonal relationships between parties—the legacy of past interactions, current feelings toward one another, and anticipation of future interactions—also seems to influence orientations.[19] These interpersonal factors may operate implicitly, as when one party accommodates a favored coworker without realizing it or even telling the other person. Or they may be quite explicit, as when one party decides to support the other on a current issue in order to make it easier to gain that person's support

TABLE 9–3
Orientations to Conflict: Characteristics

ORIENTATION	DEFINITION	STRENGTHS	WEAKNESSES
Collaboration (also known as problem solving)	Seeking resolution through face-to-face confrontation to find a mutually acceptable definition of and solution to the problem; most appropriate when there are common goals that cannot be achieved without the cooperation of all parties	Effective when the conflict stems from communication breakdowns or misunderstanding; when used repeatedly, establishes norms that support collaborative problem solving	Time-consuming and inappropriate when there are legitimate differences among the parties or when they have different goals or values
Avoidance	Includes withdrawal and suppression; sometimes can be coupled with expansion of the rewards available	Natural, simple response to conflict; avoids labeling parties as winner and loser, thus reducing the negative legacy that sometimes accompanies conflicts	Usually provides no productive resolution of differences, a temporary expedient, even when combined with expansion of available rewards
Accommodation (also known as smoothing)	Plays down differences while emphasizing common features; responds to emotions that accompany conflicts while ignoring the base; includes compromise	Exploits cooperative elements that exist in all conflicts	Temporary expedient; leaves legacy of unresolved issues, unmanaged emotions, outcome depends more on relative power of the parties than on the legitimacy of their complaints or wisdom of the solution
Competition (also called forcing or autocratic)	Solution imposed by most powerful party	Effective when members recognize and accept power relationships; time efficient	Fails to treat base of conflict; temporary, with residue of unmanaged emotions; fails to address real problems

for a more important issue that will come up later. Of course, the orientation that a person takes to a particular conflict should (and usually does) change as a conflict progresses, because the parties obtain more information about the other person, their own goals, and their own priorities.[20]

Parties' orientations are important because they influence the ease with which conflicts can be managed. When the parties are oriented in complementary ways, conflicts tend to be more productive. For instance, if two parties have misunderstood each other's communication or goals, really do have good reasons to cooperate, and intend to cooperate, collaboration is an appropriate orientation for both of them. By collaborating they will discover mutual, important goals; learn to understand each other better; and resolve their differences. In other situations, collaboration may lead them to suppress legitimate differences of opinion or to spend much time and energy searching for a mutually acceptable solution when one simply does not exist.

Each orientation also has characteristic strengths and weaknesses (see Table 9-3). Because the potential effectiveness of different orientations depends so much on the importance of the issue to the participants, the importance of maintaining their interpersonal relationship, the level of trust between them, the time pressure they face, and a number of other situational characteristics, the most recent focus of research has been on developing contingency theories of conflict management.[21] Perhaps most important, orientations toward conflict seem to be only loosely related to the actual communicative acts of people in conflict. Orientations are just that—intentions about how one will communicate—and may be abandoned immediately after the conflict begins.[22] Human beings are social animals; we are influenced as much by the characteristics of immediate interactions with others as by our generalized beliefs about how conflicts should be handled. Although some orientations seem to be more stable than others, there is little reason to believe that communication in conflict situations will merely enact the parties' intended orientations.[23]

Parties are especially prone to deviate from their intended orientations when the conflict involves an emotionally "hot" topic. For example, after much delay and the gathering of a great deal of evidence, Elias decided to confront one of his subordinates about his use of illegal drugs. Elias' orientation was collaborative—he wanted to help the man get professional help for what seemed to be a serious addiction and was willing to go to great lengths to see that he could keep his job during and after the treatment. Elias called the worker in and explained his concerns. The worker denied using drugs, which made Elias a little angry, but Elias' emotions were tempered by his knowledge that drug and alcohol addicts almost always deny their dependence. He presented all of the evidence that he had collected, assuming that doing so would help facilitate an open and honest discussion of the problem. Suddenly the worker blew up, shouting about Elias' dual standard. Everyone knew, he said, that Elias had taken a three-month leave of absence in 1982 to enter a treatment program for alcoholism after the company had tolerated his tardiness, absenteeism, and excuses for three years.

Elias, he said, had a "lot of gall" confronting him. As suddenly, Elias lost his temper. He had been promised that the referral would be kept secret and to that minute believed his problem and his treatment were known only to him and his supervisor. He felt betrayed, and he projected his quite justifiable anger on the employee. He started screaming too, and ended the episode by firing the worker and throwing him out of the office. His intention to be cooperative and collaborative had disappeared in the face of a communicative interaction that he could never have predicted. Few organizational conflicts are over as serious an issue as drug dependency, and relatively few involve as radical a shift between intention and communication as this example involved. But often, communication in conflicts only vaguely reflects the generalized intentions of the parties.

Felt Conflict.   Phase 3 of Pondy's model is **felt conflict**, the point at which the parties begin to personalize perceived conflict. Differences of opinion and interests that once were only vaguely perceived begin to be focused and defined. People start to see their situations as "me against them." Internal tensions and frustrations begin to crystallize around specific issues, which take on exaggerated importance because they symbolize the parties' feelings about their relationship with one another. During this phase employees start to make choices about how they will *define* the conflict, how they will *orient* themselves toward it, what *communication strategies* they will use to confront it, and what *range of possible solutions* they are willing to accept. In short, they establish *plot lines,* expectations about how the conflict will be played out. They may even construct complicated step-by-step imaginary scenarios of what they will say, how the other parties will respond, and so on.

This process of rehearsing arguments and responses can lead to a productive outcome, but only under certain circumstances. First, parties' strategic plans must not be so *constraining* that they keep the parties from listening to one another and adapting to the information they gain.[24]   Second, they must not lead a party to confuse what she or he imagines will happen during the episode with what actually does. Conflicts are a little like poker games, in which no one *knows* what choices the other players have made and can only make educated guesses. Often these guesses are incorrect, making it even more difficult to manage conflicts productively. More important, the act of guessing tends to make the guesser become more competitive and defensive as she or he imagines offensive responses from the other parties.[25] (This, by the way, is why the optimal approach to playing poker is to simply remember the cards that have been played, constantly compute probabilities regarding the makeup of your hand and those of the other players, and play a dispassionate game based on these computations. Because it is the optimal strategy, and every other approach increases the likelihood of making incorrect guesses, it is banned by most casinos.) Third, parties must realize that their rehearsed plot lines are always capable of being *altered without loss of face.* Because the parties' choices have not yet been communicated openly to one another, no one has taken positions to which they feel they must remain committed. This is the final point before patterns of communication begin to be the dominant influence on conflicts and decision-making. Consequently, it often is the final opportunity for the parties to use cooperative strategies.

The felt conflict phase also is the point at which the different faces of organizational power are most important. Chapter 7 explained why overt conflicts reveal only part of organizational power relationships. The most potent face of power is made of the hidden processes through which employees choose whom to challenge openly and when, where, and over what issues to do so. This choice-making is the key characteristic of the felt conflict phase. Employees first choose between *openly* confronting the situation, *accepting* it, or resorting to *covert resistance.* These decisions are influenced by their general orientations to conflict and the quality of the interpersonal relationships they have with the other people who might become involved. But their choices also depend on the power relationship perceived by the employees.[26]

Open confrontation is a risky choice. It can alienate powerful people and, if the employees lose the battle, may reduce their status in the eyes of others. Both of these effects reduce their organizational power. Confrontation also may have productive results. Winning battles or arguing positions effectively can enhance employees' power and self-esteem, lead the organization to make good decisions, and dissipate destructive emotions and pent-up hostilities. But provoking open confrontations or actively participating in them is wise only when the potential gains outweigh the probable risks (unless ethical or other personal considerations make it imperative that an employee oppose offensive policies or actions). It is for these reasons that confronting a difference in an open and productive way seems to occur only when power relationships are in balance. When there are major power differences, high power employees tend to autocratically impose an outcome on the other parties and low power employees fear retaliation and thus choose not to deal with the issue openly.

Accepting a situation is a viable approach when the risks of confrontation are far greater than the potential benefits and when employees have not so completely personalized the issue that acquiescing will damage their self-esteem. When the issue is so personally involving that acquiescence is unacceptable, low power employees may resort to *covert resistance*—malicious gossip, theft, sabotage, filing grievances, whistle-blowing, or any of the other resistance strategies that have been described in this book. Consequently, many experts believe that equalizing power relationships is necessary for productive conflict management to occur.[27]

Employees make two more specific decisions during the felt conflict phase. They adopt *goals* for the conflict (decide on the range of outcomes they are willing to accept) and *make preliminary decisions about the communicative strategies they will use.* Of course, the goals, their relative importance, and strategic choices change as conflicts progress.[28]   But participants' initial choices are important because they guide and constrain subsequent choices. If the employee accepts only total victory or decides to be aggressive from the outset, the probability that the conflict will escalate is increased. For example, historians' analyses of U.S. strategy in World War II indicate that once President Franklin D. Roosevelt announced that we would accept only the complete surrender of Japan, we were committed to use every weapon at our disposal to obtain that outcome. Consequently, once the atomic bomb was developed, it was almost inevitable that it would be used against Japan.

To summarize, the three preliminary stages of organizational conflict are important because they establish the plot lines within which the conflict will be played out. *Definitions, orientations,* and *choices* influence the course the conflict will take, the communicative strategies that will be used to manage it, and, eventually, the degree to which the conflict is productive or destructive.

COMMUNICATION AND OVERT CONFLICT

Sometimes all the potential parties to a conflict accept the situation as it is and never raise the issue in public. When these choices are made, communication will have little immediate effect. Its role in these conflicts stems from its impact on employees' perceptions that a certain set of risks, potential gains, and power relationships exist. But when one or more parties express openly their felt conflict, the fourth phase has begun and the parties' communication skills become crucial. The purpose of this section is to survey research and suggest guidelines for managing overt conflicts through strategic communication.

The study of conflict in general and organizational conflict in particular has had a long and detailed history, but a relatively small proportion of this research has examined the communication strategies that participants use during overt conflicts. This gap is somewhat surprising because it long has been recognized that conflict episodes must be understood as communicative processes. Conflict frames—orientations, definitions, and strategic preferences—are significant because they create the parameters that limit and guide communication during conflicts. But conflicts are made up of communication, of *interactive* cycles of message, response, and counterresponse. Once these cycles begin, their development and outcomes are not within the control of any one participant.[29] A conflict tends to have a *momentum* all its own; it is a co-creation of the parties, their interpretations, arguments, definitions, and strategies. Parties make choices about how they will respond (communicate) based in part on their interpretations of the communicative strategies used by the other parties. They look to the other parties' communication for clues about how they are likely to respond to available communicative strategies. Conflicts are *interactions, self-perpetuating* and *self-reinforcing* cycles of strategy, interpretation, anticipation, response, reinterpretation, and so on. Understanding these strategies and the dynamics of communication in conflict is an important first step in being able to adapt productively to conflict interactions.

Communication Strategies in Conflict

In conflicts that have productive outcomes, communication is both flexible and strategic. Parties begin with a wide range of acceptable outcomes and believe that everyone will be able to get something out of the discussion (a "win-win" orientation). Initially, all parties do (and should) make lengthy statements that clearly state their positions on the key issues and the reasons for those positions (in the jargon of conflict research they "differentiate" their positions from those of the other parties). In some cases this clarification of positions leads to rapid destructive escalation of the conflict. In other cases it leads to avoidance, as one or more parties decide that their immediate interests are better served by avoiding the issue than by dealing with it. In still others the parties recognize that they have made their positions clear and shift to more cooperative communication strategies.[30]

Afterward, in *productive conflicts,* the parties engage in short cycles of different kinds of communication. Periods of coercion, cooperation, joking, relaxation, threats, and promises are mixed together as the parties move toward a solution that will be mutually acceptable. Of course, the movement is not smooth. Tension between the parties' incentives to cooperate and to compete lasts throughout the interaction. As a result, the balance shifts back and forth, and the parties' communication also shifts from cooperative strategies to competitive strategies and back again. As long as it seems that progress is being made, the positive interchange will continue. When the interaction turns in a positive direction, parties respond with supportive statements or tension-reducing strategies like jokes, which in turn move the interaction in productive directions. It does not seem to be necessary for parties to develop a mutual understanding of the conflict for the conflict to move in productive directions. As the discussion of "garbage can" decision-making in Chapter 8 indicated, as long as the frames that parties develop are productive and congruent with one another, progress is possible. But if one party seems to be excessively stubborn or noncompliant, the other party is likely to shift to more competitive communication strategies, especially if it has more power in the organization.[31] If the other parties reciprocate, they all suddenly may become trapped in escalating cycles of competitive communication, transforming a productive interaction into a destructive one.[32] It is this fear of uncontrolled escalation that encourages people to try to avoid conflicts. Ironically, avoiding conflicts tends to make uncontrolled escalation more likely, because it allows people to develop a deeply held anger that may "explode" once a conflict does occur. The same thing may happen if two parties have accommodative orientations and real differences. They will tend to repeatedly ignore their problems and over time build up a large reservoir of unexpressed hostility.

In contrast, in conflicts that have *destructive* outcomes the parties begin with a win-lose orientation and view only a small number of outcomes as acceptable. Their communication is rigid and **reflexive** (mirroring the other parties' communication) rather than flexible and strategic.[33] Long periods of competitive strategies dominate the interaction, with few if any diversions to joking, relaxation, or cooperation. The communication strategies perpetuate the competitive dimensions of the situation and tend to perpetuate themselves. For example, a labor union that used *Robert's Rules of Order* called a meeting to decide whether to stop work in support of a grievance against the plant's management. Although most of the members favored the proposal, a minority used parliamentary tactics long past the point where the outcome was in any doubt. The longer they argued against the proposal, the more polarized the group became and the more committed the majority became to winning the battle. The dispute left such a bitter legacy that the minority group eventually left the organization. Although the parties' orientations to the conflict set the stage for a destructive escalation, it was their way of communicating that led to a negative outcome.

Avoidant Strategies.   Table 9–4 summarizes the communicative strategies that most often have been observed in interpersonal, marital, group, and organizational conflicts.[34] The first group of strategies allows parties to *avoid* a divisive issue. Delaying or procrastinating can be overt ("I don't have time to talk about it now") or subtle. Employees can manipulate procedural rules to delay or avoid sustained confrontations. For instance, they can refer an issue to a committee or manipulate agendas so that it is either excluded from the discussion or considered so late in a session that time constraints force a superficial judgment. Or they can focus the discussion so completely on establishing proper rules of interaction that the issue itself is never addressed. American and Vietnamese negotiators argued for months about the shape of the bargaining table, proper display of flags, and rules for speaking times and turns. Although these topics were important for symbolic reasons (round tables symbolize that the participants are of equal status; rectangular tables do not), discussion of them delayed the consideration of key differences.

Often one or more parties avoid conflicts by refusing to admit that there is an issue between them, either through statements like "I really think we basically are in agreement on this" or transcend to a level at which agreement does exist: "I know we both have the welfare of the students at heart." Sometimes parties regress to childlike tactics or quietly make commitments to "let this one go by but get him/her in the end." Some of these regressive tactics are relatively rare in organizations, but others are quite typical. Commitments to get revenge, silently obsessing about felt conflicts, running away, unproductively worrying, begging, and pouting all are far too common among adults and children alike.[35]

Southern High School is a rural school led by a principal who makes virtually every decision and watches teachers and students "like a hawk." Like many small, service-oriented organizations, it had a "family" atmosphere. However, an issue arose over a failing grade given an all-state fullback in a required history course. The principal, who also was the football coach, asked the teacher to let the student do some remedial work. When she refused, he quietly

TABLE 9–4

Communication Strategies in Conflicts

STRUCTURING STRATEGIES	CONFRONTIVE STRATEGIES	AVOIDANT STRATEGIES

1. Definition of Issue
   Initiating focal or
   new issues
   Focusing issues
   through repetition
   or clarification
   Modifying the scope
   of the issue
   (enlarging,
   narrowing, or
   fogging)
   Attaching emotional
   labels to the
   conflict or to the
   positions taken
2. Establishment of
   Evaluative Criteria
   Overt
   Exclusion of
   alternative criteria
3. Manipulation of
   Relationships
   Bribery
   Altercasting
   Predicting self-
   feelings
   Altruism
   Appeals to guilt
	1. Coercion: Overt
	   Displays of Power
	   Formal rank
	   Coalitions
	   Expertise
	2. Coercion: Threats or
	   Promises
	3. Personalization
	   Moral accusations
	   Ad hominem
	   Revelation of secrets
	4. Toughness
	   Pure form
	   Reformed sinner
		1. Delay/Procrastination
		   Manipulating
		   procedures
		   "Putting off"
		   communication
		   Focusing on rules of
		   interaction
		2. Regression
		3. Commitments to
		   Revenge
		4. Refusing to Admit
		   Existence of Conflict

changed the student's grade in the main office. Eventually the faculty member discovered the change (on Friday night, when she saw the fullback start an important game) and confronted the principal in private. The principal minimized the event, arguing that the fullback would drop out of school if he could not play, and that his dropping out would weaken the teachers' negotiating position in upcoming contract talks. He apologized, but argued that for the good of the student, and for the good of the "family," he had little choice.

The teacher, not convinced, brought the issue up at the next meeting of the history department. Many of them agreed with the teacher, feeling that all of them had been insulted when the principal went over the teacher's head. They also were concerned about the contract talks, however, and encouraged her to forget the matter. But the anger didn't go away. Eventually the history teachers started to take sides over the issue and fight among themselves over what really were trivial issues. Others became quietly dissatisfied and started to disengage from their work. Morale dropped, as did the quality of teaching. But they did win the state football championship.

The moral of this story is really quite simple. There are cases in which avoidant strategies are productive. Avoidance may be the best response if issues really are trivial, if organizational power relationships make successful resistance impossible, if the parties lack the communication skills necessary to prevent destructive escalation, if the circumstances surrounding the issue are likely to change in ways that will eliminate the bases of the conflict, or if there is insufficient time to work through the issue adequately. Usually avoidant strategies merely delay confrontations; they do not manage or resolve differences. When people use avoidant strategies, the people who raised the issue are frustrated. They have taken risks without having an opportunity to realize any gains. Consequently, avoidant strategies may only generate hostilities that will come out in conflicts over other issues, making it more difficult to manage them productively.

Structuring Strategies.   The second group of strategies serves to *structure* conflicts.[36] Because conflict situations are so ambiguous and complicated and because people often become uncertain about how to act in stressful situations, employees may become defensive and begin to communicate in ways that lead to escalation. Consequently, structuring communication can reduce ambiguity and help the parties move toward a productive solution while avoiding destructive escalation. There are three major forms of structuring. First, some strategies *define* the issues that will be discussed. By initiating discussions of some issues and not others, by focusing the group's attention on a particular issue by repeating or clarifying it, or by fogging an issue (commenting on part of a complex issue in order to divert attention away from other parts), parties give structure to the conflict. Theoretically, any party can use structuring strategies. They are strategic because they limit the range of responses that the other parties perceive are legitimate and appropriate. Thus, they indirectly influence employees' choices.

A university department became very concerned about "grade inflation" in its graduate courses and planned to discuss the problem at the next faculty meeting, to which the president of the graduate student association would be invited. Somehow, the president realized, her constituents could not be helped by efforts to "correct" grade inflation. However, she could not think of any good arguments to justify the current situation. Instead, she decided to try to structure the discussion in a way that would help her achieve her goal (stopping action on the problem). She quickly took a poll of graduate students' perceptions of the problem in order to have "tangible" evidence to support her position. Soon after the discussion started, she produced the results of her poll, which indicated that the students felt that the problem was isolated in one unit of the department, which was widely known to give very high grades. She reported that the students also were concerned about the problem, but wanted the faculty to conduct a unit-by-unit examination of grading policies before taking any action. In effect she had redefined the issue from a question of grading to a question of equity and professional responsibility across units. Because it was impolitic for any faculty member to question, much less attack, the grading of any other (identified) members, the faculty members were left with little response. The question was tabled, which meant that no action has been taken.

However, structuring strategies are used most successfully by powerful employees. The extra credibility given to powerholders affords them an exceptional opportunity to define and redefine issues. People *listen* to powerful people and generally act as if they perceive the situation in the same way that the powerholders do.[37] When situations are complex and ambiguous, as is the case in almost all organizational conflicts, it is difficult to provide a "rational" reason for rejecting a powerful person's use of a clarifying strategy. If the vice-president of a firm declares that an issue is "about" efficient allocation of resources, it may be hard to argue successfully that it really is about fairness in the assignment of work across units of the organization.

Power is related to structuring strategies in a second way. If a person adopts strategies congruent with that person's sources or bases of power, the likelihood that the strategy will succeed is enhanced. People whose power is based on their financial expertise can define issues in financial terms; participants with high levels of "position power" can broaden issues by taking an organization-wide perspective or narrow them by asserting that "this is a purchasing problem." The rest of the parties probably will accept that structuring and discuss the issue on grounds that favor the parties with the greatest influence.[38]

Power also is related to the second kind of structuring strategy, *establishing evaluative criteria*. Criteria for decisions are not imposed on a conflict; they emerge through the use of structuring strategies. Consider a promotion decision: Jim has an excellent record. Three supervisors—Ellen, Allen, and Edna—like him and want to see him promoted. But Bill, with whom Jim would work most closely if promoted, recognizes that Jim is very competent, feels threatened by him, and wants to block the promotion. Bill must find a way to get the group to base its decision on criteria that will reduce Jim's chance of being promoted. To do so, he must eliminate past performance as a criterion because Jim's record is very good. This can be done rather easily, by highlighting his few errors and defining the new position as one that *absolutely* demands the attribute(s) that Jim's errors indicate he lacks. Bill could argue also that the new position is so fundamentally different from Jim's current job that his record is irrelevant.

But Bill still needs to create a reason for rejecting Jim. Because "personality" criteria generally are seen as legitimate for all upper-level positions, they may give Bill the key he needs. But because Ellen, Allen, and Edna like Jim, not just any personality characteristic will do. Bill decides to argue that being "a team player" is the most important characteristic for this particular position. Because "being a team player" is a legitimate criterion and an important value in almost all organizational cultures, and because Bill has a more important reason to be concerned about it than do the other supervisors (if promoted Jim would join Bill's team), and because the concept is almost impossible to define, Bill can argue that Jim does not meet this most important criterion. To support his argument, all Bill has to do is recount an instance or two when Jim disagreed with some other employee. Once the criterion is accepted and the example is produced, Ellen, Allen, and Edna have few responses available. If they disagree with any of Bill's arguments, *they* violate the team player criterion in the most offensive way by trying to force Bill to add a player to his team whom he does not want. The point of this example is that structuring strategies *work* because they leave opponents few legitimate overt responses. They may not lead to optimal outcomes, but they often do lead to the outcomes preferred by powerholders.

The third and final group of structuring strategies involves *redefining relationships*. Bribery, "altercasting" (asserting that "good" or "wise" or "evil" or "stupid" people would agree or disagree with the speaker on this issue), predicting others' responses to certain actions ("You will feel good / feel guilty / respect yourself in the morning"), and appealing to interpersonal relationships ("Remember, this is *me,* your friend, talking") all define a conflict in personal and relational rather than issue-oriented terms.

Confrontative Strategies.   If neither avoidant nor structuring strategies are available, parties in conflicts can resort to direct *confrontative* strategies. Probably *personalization* and *coercion* are best known, more because they are so often used than because they are the strategically wisest or most productive. Attacking the *person* of one's opponent(s), especially when the attack impugns morals, reveals secrets, or makes accusations of assorted "-isms" (racism, sexism, fascism, communism, and so on), denies that person any defense except counterattack or acquiescence.[39]   *Coercion* comes in at least two forms. One is the overt display of formal, expert-based, or coalition-based power. These elicit compliance only when all parties grant the attacker this kind of power and see its use as legitimate. If they do not, the strategy will fail and the attacker's power will be reduced. The second form of coercion involves *threats or promises.*[40] These function in essentially the same way, depend on the same conditions for their success, and are, in effect, two sides of the same coin. Three conditions must be present for threats and promises to succeed. First, the *sources* must be credible. They must be perceived as being capable of controlling the reward or punishment they threaten or promise to provide and must be willing to carry out their statement. Creating these perceptions is especially important when the parties have a competitive interpersonal relationship. If their relationship is cooperative, promises also depend on the target perceiving that the promiser is trustworthy, knows what is best for both of them, and has good intentions.

Second, the threat or promise must be communicated in a way that makes the *desired responses clear and specific* and the *consequences of compliance or noncompliance "vivid."* Both "I'm gonna cover you with honey and tie you to a hill of biting red ants in a glaring Arizona sun" and "I'm gonna cover you with whipped cream and . . ." are vivid threats or promises. Third, the consequence must be *perceived as being fair, equitable, and appropriate to the magnitude of the action that is requested.* Consequences that are either trivial or horrendous compared to the request will not be taken seriously.

Threats always insult the other party (although if they are worded as promises the insult is reduced), but they do help the other party understand the threatener's priorities and thus may increase the potential to avoid misunderstandings.[41] The difficulty with using threats and promises is that people's perceptions about what is credible, equitable, fair, and appropriate differ widely. Making predictions about another person's perceptions is a risky proposition, especially because the *act* of threatening or promising may influence those perceptions in unpredictable ways. The tendency to wrongly estimate perceptions is less when the parties have similar backgrounds and experiences or have observed one another's responses to threats and promises in the past. To complicate their use further, threats and promises tend to provoke counterthreats and promises, creating a sometimes comical ("My mommy will beat up your daddy") and rarely productive cycle of escalation.

A final competitive strategy is "taking a tough stance." In its pure form, where everyone initially refuses to concede their positions, taking a tough stance can lead to productive results. Because no party appears to be willing to acquiesce or be intimidated, all parties eventually are forced to search for a mutually acceptable resolution of their differences. The key is knowing when to make an initial concession. If it is made too early the other parties will see it as a sign of weakness and become more intransigent. If made too late, the conflict already may have escalated to a destructive level. One "solution" to this problem is the use of a "matching" strategy (also called "tit for tat"), in which each party matches the other party's concessions with a comparable concession. If the parties are careful not to fall into a cycle of escalation, for example, by pausing and thinking strategically for a while before matching the other party's offer, matching can allow both parties to simultaneously appear to be both tough and reasonable.[42]

In a variant of this strategy, often called "playing the reformed sinner," one party takes a tough stance until it appears to the other that no mutual solution is possible, and then makes a significant concession. However, the issue on which the party concedes was only made to *appear* to be important to him or her. Because our culture includes strong norms of reciprocity, the act of conceding creates pressures for the other parties to concede. In 1982, during the worst housing market in recent memory (mortgage interest rates were around 21 percent), my wife's career required us to move. Fortunately, she had purchased a nice, middle-priced, brick ranch house that had appreciated a bit, thanks primarily to her renovation work. She also had negotiated a 6.5 percent loan that was assumable by any buyer. In short, as long as we asked a somewhat reasonable price, we had a strong negotiating position. Our first potential buyer was a newly hired assistant professor in the psychology department of a major private southeastern university whose primary research area was conflict management. This situation created a wonderful opportunity to watch conflict strategies in action.

He and his wife said they were delighted with the house, but somewhat concerned with the deterioration of an exterior brick staircase into the basement. But they would go home and talk about it and give us a call the next day.

Because this concern was over what could be perceived as a major problem, but actually was not, it provided an excellent opportunity for him to use the reformed sinner strategy—taking a tough stance and then conceding on the staircase in order to force a reciprocal concession on a more important issue, like price. The next day I had two contractors come by and give me written estimates for repairing the stairs ($200 and $800, which should tell you something about why you should always get multiple bids on construction and home repair projects). That night the assistant professor called, explained that they were excited about the house but very concerned about the stairs and what they might suggest about the structural integrity of the foundation. They had talked about the problem with his father-in-law, who "knew a lot about construction," and learned that it could cost $4,000 or $5,000 to repair it. So, they would be happy to buy the house for $3,000 below our asking price. After telling him about the written estimates, we quickly agreed that they would love to move in next week (after paying the asking price, of course).

I provide this example for two reasons. One is to explain the "reformed sinner" strategy. The other is to suggest that, although I have discussed communication strategies only in terms of their active use, it is equally important to be able to recognize when they are being used by others. There is substantial evidence that conflicts become destructive when there is a major power imbalance between the parties. Understanding communication strategies in conflicts provides a potent source of power, which can lead to unfair domination of powerless people. Empowerment, the creation of the power balances that generate productive outcomes in conflicts, begins with training all parties in the use of strategic communication.

This rather lengthy summary of communication strategies used during conflicts has been provided primarily to suggest that a wide range of strategies is available. Conflicts are not made up of one party using one strategy. They are made of interactions, of patterns of communication, response, and counterresponse. In *productive conflicts* these patterns consist of a number of brief episodes during which the parties adopt a wide range of strategies. Coercion, threats, promises, redefinition, relational comments, digressions, joking, and relaxing are intermixed in a variety of proportions. No single strategy takes over; no sustained cycle of threat and counterthreat, coercion and regression distorts parties' perceptions or clouds their analysis of the situation. In *destructive conflicts* a narrow range of communicative strategies is used. Escalating cycles of threat, coercion, expansion of issues, and personalization lock parties into competitive, zero-sum patterns of interaction. Sometimes—perhaps often—destructive cycles are accidentally initiated by more powerful employees. They misperceive less powerful people as jealous, resentful, or hostile and overreact, adopting confrontative, competitive strategies when other approaches would have been more appropriate. Or they inadvertently place weaker people in positions where they feel they must either fight or be humiliated.[43]   But conflict cycles are never under any one member's control. It is the participants' ability to manage and control tendencies for escalation that determines whether a conflict will be productive or destructive.

One final note: Rarely are any of these communication strategies used alone. More often, each employee uses a complicated combination of strategies. Even in the case of negotiating about purchase prices, the potential buyer might expand the scope of the issue by nit-picking about the age of the object, small dents in the fenders, the pattern of the wallpaper, and so on while simultaneously threatening to terminate the negotiations and creating the "reality" that she or he cannot spend more than a certain amount. An almost infinite number of possible combinations of strategies exists. The effects of each depends on an even larger number of relational factors and on the combination of strategies adopted by the other parties. An adequate summary of these combinations would take an additional book (at least) and a significant amount of careful research that has not yet been completed.[44] But a common thread running through most analyses of conflict is the importance of not becoming trapped in escalating cycles of interaction.

CASE STUDY:
THE BARGAINING CASE

Bargaining is a special kind of conflict management. It looks like compromise, but involves negotiating shared rules and cooperation within these rules to gain a competitive advantage. It focuses on the exchange of formal offers, but making offers is only one kind of communicative interaction in bargaining sessions. As Chapter 1 explains, a major function of communication is the creation of "realities" that guide and constrain further communication. But "realities" are constantly changing throughout processes of communicative interaction. These processes—and the way in which "history" is defined and redefined through communication—is illustrated nicely in the following case study of bargaining between teachers and the school board in a small rural, midwestern district. It is based on the research of Linda Putnam and her associates.*

---

*See similar analyses in the following papers and publications: Linda Putnam and Shirley Van Hoeven, "Teacher Bargaining as a Cultural Rite of Conflict Reduction," paper presented at the Central States Speech Association Convention, Cincinnati, 1986; Linda Putnam and Shirley Van Hoeven, "The Role of Narrative in Teachers' Bargaining," paper presented at the Temple University Discourse Conference on Conflict Intervention, Philadelphia, 1987; Linda Putnam, Shirley Van Hoeven, and Connie Bullis, "The Role of Rituals and Fantasy Themes in Teachers' Bargaining," *Western Journal of Speech Communication, 55* (1991): 85–103; and Linda Putnam, "Negotiation of Intergroup Conflict in Organizations," Hallie Mande Neff Wilcox Published Lecture. Waco, TX: Baylor University, 1987.

(continued)

(continued from the previous page)

The state teachers association provided the 133 teachers with a professional bargainer, Doug. The school board hired its own pro. Usually teacher bargaining (and most formal labor–management negotiation) is limited to an exchange of money (salaries and fringe benefits) versus teacher control over their working conditions. The teachers' "reality-creation" process involved three stories (see Chapter 4). One story was about "the bad old days" of bargaining. For years the two sides had experienced hostile bargaining: long and heated arguments over rules of negotiation, making threats, fist-pounding, name-calling, and refusals to settle had dominated yearly discussions. One year the two sides' initial offers were thinly veiled insults: The board offered a $1 raise; the teachers demanded a 25 percent increase. Four years ago the hostility erupted into a strike.

The townspeople supported the teachers—telephoning the board members at home and insulting and haranguing them as they walked down the streets. But the story the teachers told one another was about the immaturity that they had shown during the strike. They prided themselves in their newfound maturity, which essentially meant that they would cooperate with the board and do everything possible to avoid another strike. Their reasoning was simple and self-fulfilling: We must avoid antagonistic bargaining because it could result in a strike, which is unacceptable because it would show that we are immature bargainers. Because we have matured we will not strike. Of course, accepting this story eliminated the only threat the teachers had, but it created a comfortable reality that would guide and constrain their communication. The second story was about Doug. He had started working with the teachers during the strike, and although no one remembered exactly what he did to achieve it, he negotiated an acceptable settlement. Telling this story reinforced the teachers' trust for Doug and led them to accept his goals, strategies, and decisions throughout the negotiation.

Doug told the third story. He had faced Jim, the board's pro, many times in the past and found him to be "a bear" on power issues—he just would not give in on these issues. The teachers adapted the story and applied it to their board. One said, "It'll be a cold day in hell before that board will give us any policy issues (control)." The fact that Doug failed to tell them that their district was far behind the other districts in the state in terms of teacher control of working conditions added to the power of the story. So the teachers decided to introduce power issues but drop them early during the bargaining. Unfortunately, the "reality" they had created was inaccurate. Jim had advised the board to be ready to give up some policy issues in order to minimize financial costs in the new contract. In fact, the board was surprised when Doug dropped these items, but of course it had no reason to say so.

The teachers told and retold these three stories throughout the bargaining session. They asked for, and thus received, less than they could have gotten.

(continued)

(continued from the previous page)

But they communicated in a way that maintained the reality that they had created—they behaved "maturely," reached an acceptable settlement (70–75 percent of the teachers supported the final contract), and avoided a strike. Of course, if you consider only the offers they made and accepted, they took a very soft bargaining position. But they compensated for that kind of softness through a ritual that "proved" they were tough negotiators. Negotiations regularly continued for night after night, extending into the early morning hours. The bargaining team even enjoyed going to breakfast together after a long night of negotiations, arriving at school just in time to go to class. This ritual, repeated every year, "proved" to the negotiators and the other teachers that their representatives were tough bargainers. (Sometimes late-night negotiations are more than ritual. I once was on a teacher bargaining committee that stayed late in order to exhaust the opposition. We enlarged the teachers' committee so that no one member had to attend more than one late-night meeting, knowing that the school board did not have this flexibility. After five weeks of negotiating, when rumor had it that four board members were on the verge of divorce, we obtained what we wanted: the transfer of a much-hated principal, and the largest salary increase in the district's history. But that was a different situation, a very different "reality.")

Discussion Questions

1. How did the parties' definitions of "reality" influence communication? The relative power of the bargainers?
2. In this situation, could an individual teacher or member have argued successfully for taking a tougher negotiating position?
3. What functions did the "staying all night" ritual play in addition to "demonstrating toughness"?
4. What long-term effects is this negotiation likely to have on (a) the teachers' perceptions of reality, (b) Doug's image and role, (c) the board's negotiating strategies, and (d) the outcomes of subsequent negotiations?

Communication and Conflict Escalation

Forms of Escalation. Conflicts escalate in three ways—*expansion of issues, involvement of self and "face,"* and *dominance of emotion and symbol.*[45] The first is self-explanatory. When episodes of conflict begin, they revolve around a small number of issues that immediately concern the participants. Sometimes the nature of these issues leads the parties to consider other, more basic issues. In fact, a number of models of conflict management recommend careful, systematic broadening of the issue being discussed. As long as the parties continue to focus on the central problem while taking new and different perspectives on it, this approach may lead to the considera-tion of a wider range of potential solutions. For instance, an academic depart-ment needs to keep its enrollment high despite reductions in the size of its faculty. This problem has within it the seeds of a highly destructive escalating conflict. It could lead to angry arguments over the fairness and equity of cur-rent teaching loads, alienation among faculty because of differences in rank and power, and attacks based on subjective judgments about educational phi-losophy and quality of teaching. But the group also could develop the follow-ing sequence:

> The problem is defined and its importance accepted.
>
> Faculty member 1 asserts that the key question is how to maintain or im-prove the quality of the education provided by the department.
>
> Faculty member 2 argues that the existing undergraduate internship pro-gram causes part of the problem because it exhausts so much faculty time for so few students.
>
> Faculty member 3 argues that using graduate students as teaching assis-tants in large lecture courses causes part of the problem because faculty members still must spend time lecturing and training the assistants.
>
> Faculty member 4 suggests that because most of the department's interns are looking toward careers in training and development, some of them could be used as teaching assistants in lecture courses, releasing graduate students to teach their own classes.
>
> Discussion continues, focused on the optimal ways of using the three re-sources available to the department. As this episode continues, the issues expand, but so does the range of available solutions.

However, issues in conflicts often expand in a very different way. The ar-chetypal example of destructive escalation is a standard fare of television sit-coms. The cycle begins when the husband complains about a burned pot roast. The wife responds that if he doesn't like it he can get off his butt and cook it himself. Before the interchange ends with one of the two storming out of the room (usually after walking into a closet by mistake), they will have discussed each spouse's parents (who are lazy, bad cooks, or whatever), stereotypical sex roles, housecleaning and repair needs, their relative incomes, and their sex lives. In these conflicts the expansion of issues obscures the initial problem, reveals no possible solutions, and redefines the problem in ways that make it impossible to arrive at any productive resolution of the initial (pot roast) disagreement.[46]

Conflicts also escalate when they begin to involve the *self-esteem or self-images* ("faces") of the participants. Had any of the professors in the previous example said, "We wouldn't have this problem if all of us were good enough teachers that our courses were filled with students," the issue suddenly would have become personal (and emotional), not substantive (issue-oriented). Peo-ple typically respond to a particular communication strategy with a similar one.

In addition, as explained earlier in this book, personalizing strategies create a need for others to defend themselves, to save face. It is very easy for negotiators to perceive that criticisms of the ideas they present are personal attacks. To complicate face saving even more, in Western cultures negotiators must appear to be tough, fair, and competent if they are to save face. Because it is difficult to simultaneously do all of these things, face management is especially complicated. If one party communicates in a way that threatens the face of the others (for instance, by making nonnegotiable demands), the others tend to reciprocate.[47] Typically they do so by adopting their own personalizing strategies ("I have low enrollments because I make demands of my students" or "You have high enrollments because you give away A's"), which create pressure for others to save face, and an escalating cycle of personalization begins.

The final form of escalation involves breakdowns in *situational sensitivity*—the balanced consideration of situations, self-interests, and others' interests (discussed in Chapter 6). Once conflict episodes begin, they create their own realities. Participants often begin to base their choices only on the immediate conflictful situation—on the communication taking place during the episode. Parties perceive that the other person's communication strategies parallel their own—if they are hostile they see the other person as hostile. As the conflict continues they begin to mirror the other person's communication rather than focusing on the situation and choosing strategies appropriately.[48] Dimensions of the larger organizational situation—the parties' organizational roles, the importance of the issue and reaching a productive resolution of it, the need to maintain effective working relationships—may become lost in the more immediate conflict. In other words, winning the *conflict* takes on a *symbolic* importance that transcends the other dimensions of the situation. In trying to win, actors lose sight of their desires to arrive at a satisfactory solution. They begin to focus wholly on their incentives to compete and forget their incentives to cooperate.

Although these three forms of escalation differ in some respects, they are similar in two important ways. First, they tend to go unnoticed by the participants. Communication strategies generate counterstrategies in a seemingly natural and appropriate sequence. Conflicts begin to become more destructive than productive; parties begin to make choices about how to communicate without realizing how their choices contribute to the escalation; and they become progressively more immersed in escalating cycles. They perceive that their increasingly hostile actions are merely responses; that if anyone is responsible for the escalation, it is someone else. Paul Watzlawick and his colleagues call this process **punctuation**.

Think of childhood conflicts that end in both children defending their actions by claiming that the other child "started it." Regardless of which one struck the first blow in the current battle, the other can recall an earlier insult, an earlier fight, or some proof that they were only defending themselves. In conflicts between adults, the parties also each choose a different "starting point" for the sequence of communication and response. By perceiving that someone else "started it," they can blame the conflict on others and justify their own contributions to the escalation as just and proper. They begin to employ nonproductive avoidant or aggressive strategies and ignore potentially productive collaborative approaches. They may withhold or distort information relevant to the issue being discussed.[49]   Communication becomes a weapon with which they can win the battle, not a process through which differences can be managed productively.

Second, the three forms of escalation can be recognized by the same cues, the most important of which are:

1. Parties argue emotionally for their preferred outcome rather than calmly explaining it and its implications.
2. Parties use individual or coalition-related pronouns rather than group or organization-oriented ones—"*we* (a coalition) think."
3. The time and emotional energy devoted to a topic is much greater than its importance (parties may begin to ask themselves "Why is this so important?" and not be able to produce sensible answers).
4. Parties cannot (or can only vaguely) remember the issue that started the discussion or the links between it and the topic currently being debated.
5. Parties find themselves thinking more about persons, positions, and strategies than about problems and solutions.

When any of these cues is present, participants should conceptually "step back" from the interaction and consciously search for and use appropriate de-escalating strategies. Sometimes this withdrawal may be physical, as when formal cooling-off periods are imposed on labor–management negotiations. At other times the withdrawal may be purely cognitive. But unless the parties are able to separate themselves from the cycle of communication, the escalation will continue.

The Bases of Escalation.   Unfortunately, the previous comments about escalation processes make them sound aberrant, almost perverse. The potential for escalation, however, exists in all conflicts and for understandable reasons. Some bases of escalation are related to the nature of organizations. In our culture people are conditioned to compete and achieve, and the cultures that develop within formal organizations often exaggerate this trait. In addition, every organizational conflict carries a legacy of past conflicts and the anticipation of future conflicts. The perfectly managed organizational conflict—in which every participant and the organization find an acceptable solution and relationships are strengthened by the interaction—is quite rare, perhaps nonexistent. Each conflict leaves its own legacy. When organizations adopt norms that suppress or repress overt conflicts, or when parties inappropriately use avoidant orientations or strategies, this legacy of hidden dissatisfaction is intense. When overt conflicts do occur, the legacy provides impetus to "win this one because I may never get another chance" or "win this one because I lost the last one."

Escalation also is supported by the two faces of organizational power (see Chapter 7). Overt conflicts occur when some employees confront existing power relationships. Whatever risks are involved in doing so are incurred at the moment the conflict becomes overt. These risks can be offset only if the employees gain power or rewards from its outcome. For this reason they have an absolute incentive to push the conflict to a point where they "win." Similarly, for powerholders, the existence of an open conflict threatens them and their position in the power structure. Once an overt conflict begins, the hidden face of power is being attacked. Because this face allows powerholders to maintain their dominance, they must defend it. "Winning" the conflict will allow them to reestablish their superior position. Losing the battle, or compromising on the issues, diminishes their power. The interrelationships between conflict and power relationships establish a motive for employees to adopt a win-lose orientation, increasing the potential for escalation.

Still another base of escalation is the nature of human communication. Chapter 6 explained that all messages have both content and relational dimensions. If the parties in a conflict focus on the relational dimension of one another's communication, the conflict will be personalized and escalation becomes quite probable. Perceptual processes also contribute. If an interaction is tense, as conflicts are, parties focus their attention on the "evidence" of hostility and competition present in other parties' communication. People perceive their opponents as more competitive than they really are and perceive themselves as being more cooperative than they really are.[50] As conflicts escalate, parties begin to see themselves, their allies, and their ideas as wholly good and their opponents and their ideas as wholly evil. Trust begins to dissolve and participants begin to listen less and argue more. Eventually communication breaks down, little information is exchanged, more information is distorted, and hostility and distrust grow. Parties begin to narrow the range of communication strategies they use and the number of outcomes they will accept. Escalation continues.

For example, workers at one plant became so angry about what they perceived as arbitrary and inflexible management and intolerable working conditions that they launched a "wildcat" strike (a local strike not sanctioned by the national union). Management perceived that the strike was an attempt to take over the organization, not a response to grievances. They responded defensively, becoming more intransigent, less flexible, and more hostile. Management's communication convinced the workers that their initial perceptions had been correct, which led them to become even more hostile and to make stronger demands for control of working conditions, which supported management's perceptions that the "real" issue was power, and so on.[51] When combined, *cultural, organizational,* and *communicational* factors make escalation an inevitable problem in overt conflicts.

THE AFTERMATH OF CONFLICTS

This chapter began with a summary of Pondy's three preliminary phases of conflict—*latent, perceived,* and *felt.* The fourth phase in his model, *overt conflict,* has been examined at length. The final phase is the *aftermath* of the conflict.

Two criteria are appropriate for evaluating the short-term effects of conflicts—the quality of the final decision and the effect of the conflict on working relationships. If a sensible solution emerges and meets the needs of every party or is supported by a legitimate consensus, the short-term effects will be positive. However, such integrative solutions are infrequent, and consensus is an elusive state. In fact, it is more likely that a conflict will move from issue to issue with no real resolution. When new issues arise, the same patterns of communicative interaction recur.[52] The more probable modes of managing conflicts—compromise, majority vote, or acquiescence by one or more parties—leave residual frustrations that will prompt future conflicts and complicate their management. Similarly, the dynamics of conflict episodes may leave behind changed perceptions of each party, unmanaged emotions, and commitments to get revenge, all of which will influence working relationships. If they are repeated often, escalating conflicts may lead employees to view their relationships with one another as competitive rather than cooperative. Because their tasks are interdependent, competitive relationships may undermine the participants' performance and the organization's success.[53]

This potential for long-term negative effects on working relationships has led many organizations to use formal procedures and make structural changes in order to minimize the impact of unproductive conflicts. Some have tried to reduce unit or employee interdependence, both to minimize the number of issues over which differences might occur and to decrease the adverse effects of long-term relational problems. But interdependence cannot be reduced beyond a certain point, and when it is reduced, the parties' incentives to cooperate with one another also are reduced. Other organizations create formal "conflict managers" or formal procedures for handling even minor disagreements. Third-party interventions *can* prevent escalation, as long as the third party is skilled in conflict management and has sufficient formal power.[54] Formal rules and procedures can structure conflicts in ways that reduce ambiguity and prevent the use of the communication strategies that prompt escalation. Although there are limits to the effectiveness of structural changes, their use accents the need to evaluate the productiveness of each episode within the long-term perspective of the organization's operation.

Conflicts can be valuable and productive for organizations and employees alike. For organizations, conflict can stimulate creative problem solving, generate or publicize superior ideas, and adjust perceived power relationships to better fit the skills and abilities of employees. For individual employees, conflict can provide opportunities to test, expand, and demonstrate their skills; better understand their organizations; and develop their self-esteem and confidence. If conflicts are limited and controlled and if satisfactory solutions to problems can be found, the total impact of each conflict can be positive. If not, conflicts can be destructive.

Two implications emerge from this comment. First, organizational conflicts must be evaluated in terms of many considerations. Open conflicts invariably are disruptive and leave behind negative legacies. But their impact on the long-term effectiveness of the organization may on balance be favorable. Attempting to suppress or repress conflicts often damages an organization more than allowing them to surface and be managed. Second, controlling processes of escalation is the key to productive conflict management. The aftermath of organizational conflicts depends on maintaining patterns of communication that simultaneously allow people to demonstrate their competencies and solve problems. Escalation robs the participants of these opportunities and establishes the bases of nonproductive legacies. The strategic use of communication is the key to productive conflict management.

CONCLUSION

Conflicts are inevitable parts of organizational life. Whenever people depend on one another and interact with one another, grounds for cooperating and competing exist. Although there is substantial evidence that it is counterproductive to try to avoid or suppress conflicts, especially in the long term, our fear of conflict escalation and the taken-for-granted assumptions of some organizational cultures make it difficult to deal with conflicts openly and productively. Fortunately, there is a wide variety of communicative strategies available to employees before and during overt conflicts. Understanding those strategies and using them *strategically* determines whether a particular conflict will be productive or destructive.

NOTES

[1] This section is based primarily on four sources: Louis Pondy, "Organizational Conflict: Concepts and Models," *Administrative Science Quarterly, 12* (1967):296–320; Morton Deutsch, "Conflicts: Productive or Destructive," *Journal of Social Issues, 25* (1969): 7–41 and *The Resolution of Conflict* (New Haven: Yale University Press, 1973); and Stephen Robbins, "Conflict Management and Conflict Resolution Are Not Synonymous Terms," *California Management Review, 21* (1978): 67–75. There is an almost infinite number of additional important citations. They are summarized effectively by Kenneth Thomas in "Conflict and Conflict Management," in *Handbook of Industrial and Organizational Psychology,* Marvin Dunnette, ed. (Chicago: Rand-McNally, 1976) and by Linda Putnam, "Conflict and Dispute Management," in *New Handbook of Organizational Communication,* Linda Putnam and Fredric Jablin (Eds.) (Thousand Oaks, CA: Sage, 1997). The most complete and most readable treatment of research on communication and conflict is Joseph Folger, M. Scott Poole, and Randall Stuttman, *Working Through Conflict,* 3rd ed. (New York: Longman, 1997).

[2] Stella Ting-Toomey, "Toward a Theory of Conflict and Culture," in William Gudykunst, ed., *Communication and Culture* (Beverly Hills, CA: Sage, 1985).

[3] Putnam, *Handbook;* Charles Franz and K. Gregory Jin, "The Structure of Group Conflict in a Collaborative Work Group During Information Systems Development," *Journal of Applied Communication Research, 23* (1995): 108–127.

[4] Pondy. For an excellent summary of phase models and their strengths and weaknesses, see Linda Putnam, "Reframing Integrative and Distributive Bargaining," in Blair Shepard, M. Bazerman, and R. Lewicki, eds., *Research on Negotiation in Organizations,* vol. 2 (Greenwich, CT: JAI Press, 1990); Michael Holmes, "Phase Structure in Negotiation," in L. Putnam and M. Roloff, eds., *Communication and Negotiation* (Newbury Park, CA: Sage, 1993).

[5] Psychological models of conflict call this process "displacement" (see Folger, Poole, and Stuttman). It is examined at length in the School Board case study and the Aftermath section of this chapter. Steven R. Wilson, "Face and Facework in Negotiation," in L. Putnam and M. Roloff, eds., *Communication and Negotiation* (Newbury Park, CA: Sage, 1993).

[6] Folger, Poole, and Stuttman.

[7] See Nancy Burrell, Patrice Buzzanell, and J.J. McMillan, "Feminine Tensions in Conflict Situations as Revealed by Metaphoric Analysis," *Management Communication Quarterly, 6* (1992): 115–149; Charles Conrad, "Communication in Conflict: Style-Strategy Relationships, *Communication Monographs, 58* (1991): 135–155; Barbara Mae Gayle, "Sex Equity in Workplace Conflict Management," *Journal of Applied Communication Research, 19* (1991): 152–169; Michael Papa and E.J. Natalle, "Gender, Strategy Selection and Satisfaction in Interpersonal Conflict," *Western Journal of Speech Communication, 53* (1989): 260–272; L.H. Turner and S.A. Henzl, "Influence attempts in Organizational Conflicts: The Effects of Biological Sex, Psychological Gender, and Power Position," *Management Communication Quarterly, 1* (1987): 32–57.

[8] Max Bazerman and J.S. Carroll, "Negotiator Cognition," in L.L. Cummings and B. Staw, eds., *Research in Organizational Behavior* (Greenwich, CT: JAI Press, 1987); M. Neale and M. Bazerman, *Cognition and Rationality in Negotiations* (New York: The Free Press, 1991).

[9] Barbara Gray, J. Prudy, and R. Bouwen, "Comparing Dispositional and Interactional Approaches to Negotiation," paper presented at the International Association for Conflict Management Convention, Vancouver, 1990. An excellent summary of frame-oriented conflict research is available in Linda Putnam and Majia Holmer, "Framing and Reframing," in L. Putnam and M. Roloff, *Communication and Negotiation* (Newberry Park, CA: Sage, 1992). For summaries of the impact that frames have on conflict behavior, see R. Fisher and W. Ury, *Getting to Yes* (Boston: Houghton Mifflin, 1981); R. Kahneman and A. Tversky, "Prospect Theory," *Econometrica, 47* (1981): 263–269; C. DeDreu, "Gain and Loss Frames in Bilateral Negotiations," Dissertation, 1994; Linda Putnam, S. Wilson and D. Turner, "The Evolution of Policy Arguments in Teachers' Bargaining, *Argumentation, 4* (1990): 129–152.

[10] Daniel Canary and Brian Spitzberg, "A Model of the Perceived Competence of Conflict Strategies," *Human Communication Research, 15* (1990): 630–649.

[11] T. Simons, "Speech Patterns and the Concept of Utility in Cognitive Maps," *Academy of Management Journal, 36* (1993): 139–156.

[12] W.L. Felsteiner, R.L. Abel, and A Sarat, "The Emergence and Transformation of Disputes," *Law and Society Review, 33* (1980/1981): 631–654; Linda Putnam, "Reframing Integrative and Distributive Bargaining," in R.J. Lewicki, B.H. Sheppard, and M.H. Bazerman, eds., *Research on Negotiation in Organizations,* vol. 2 (Greenwich, CT: JAI Press, 1990).

[13] D.R. Peterson, "Assessing Interpersonal Relationships by Means of Interaction Records," *Behavioral Assessment, 1* (1979): 221–236; H.H. Kelley, E. Berscheid, A. Christensen, J. Harvey, T. Huston, G. Levinger, E. McClintock, L. Peplan, and D. Peterson, eds., *Close Relationships* (New York: Freeman and Company, 1983).

[14] Harold Guetzkow and James Gyr, "An Analysis of Decision-making Groups," *Human Relations, 7* (1954): 367–381. Also see Folger, Poole, and Stuttman.

[15] Kenneth Thomas, "Where Do We Go from Here?" *Management Communication Quarterly, 1* (1988): 301–305.

[16] Thomas, "Conflict." A number of scales have been developed to measure orientations toward conflict. See the special issue of *Management Communication Quarterly, 2* (1988) edited by Linda Putnam.

[17] Phillip Tompkins, J. Fisher, D. Infante, and E. Tompkins, "Conflict and Communication within the University," in *Perspectives on Communication and Social Conflict,* G. Miller and H. Simons, eds. (Englewood Cliffs, NJ: Prentice-Hall, 1974); R. Ross and Susan Dewine, "Interpersonal Conflict," paper presented at the Speech Communication Association convention, Washington, D.C., 1982; R. Ross and Susan Dewine, "Interpersonal Needs and Communication in Conflict," paper presented at the Speech Communication Association convention, Chicago, 1984.

[18] S.P. Robbins, "'Conflict Management' and Conflict Resolution' Are Not Synonymous Terms," *California Management Review, 21* (1978): 67–75; Dean Morely and Pamela Shockley-Zalabak, "Conflict Avoiders and Compromisers," *Group and Organizational Behavior, 11* (1986): 387–402; and M. Rahim, "Referent Role and Styles of Handling Interpersonal Conflict," *Journal of Social Psychology, 126* (1986): 79–86.

[19] Charles Conrad, "Power, Performance and Supervisors' Choices of Strategies of Conflict Management," *Western Journal of Speech Communication, 47* (1983): 218–228.

[20] Linda Putnam, "Reframing."

[21] See the special issue of *California Management Review,* Winter 1978, and the extended analysis in Folger, Poole, and Stuttman.

[22] Kenneth Thomas, "Where Do We Go?"; also see Putnam, *Handbook.* This is especially true if we conceive of orientations as stable "personality traits" or "usual" responses to conflicts. Because people also adapt to one another's communication, our actual behaviors tend to deviate further and further away from our orientations as conflicts progress (Folger, Poole, and Stuttman); Conrad, "Conflict."

[23] Conrad, "Style-Strategy."

[24] Michael Roloff and Jerry M. Jordan, "Achieving Negotiation Goals," in L. Putnam and M. Roloff, eds., *Communication and Negotiation* (Newbury Park, CA: Sage, 1993).

[25] Folger, Poole, and Stuttman.

[26] Folger, Poole, and Stuttman provide an extended analysis of the relationship between power and conflict. See especially Chapter 4.

[27] See Berger; Deutsch; J. Folberg and A. Taylor, *Mediation* (San Francisco: Jossey-Bass, 1984); D.G. Pruitt, J. Rubin, and S. Kim, *Social Conflict* (New York: McGraw Hill, 1994); and J. Tucker, "Some Everyday Forms of Employee Resistance," *Sociological Forum, 8* (1993): 25–45.

[28] Roloff and Jordan.

[29] L. Kriegsberg, *The Sociology of Social Conflicts* (Englewood Cliffs, NJ: Prentice-Hall, 1973); Folger, Poole, and Stuttman.

[30] See Folger, Poole, and Stuttman. Of course, the parties must synchronize this shift. If one side becomes cooperative and the other fails to reciprocate, the first side will feel betrayed and shift back to competitive communication strategies (M. Scott Poole, Dale Shannon, and Gerardine DeSanctis, "Communication Media and Negotiation Processes," in *Communication and Negotiation,* Linda Putnam and Michael Roloff, eds. [Newbury Park, CA: Sage, 1993]).

[31] Donnellon and Gray; Putnam and Holmer; Conrad, "Style-Strategy"; also see William Donohue, M.E. Diez, and M. Hamilton, "Coding Naturalistic Negotiation Interaction," *Human Communication Research, 10* (1984): 403–425; Papa and Natalle; Linda Putnam and Tricia Jones, "The Role of Communication in Bargaining," *Human Communication Research, 8* (1982): 262–290 and "Reciprocity in Negotiations," *Communication Monographs, 49* (1982): 171–191; Roloff and Jordan; V. Sambamurthy and M.S. Poole, "The Effects of Level of Sophistication of Computer Support on Conflict Management in Groups," Information Systems Research, 1991.

[32] Folger, Poole, and Stuttman label this process "trained incapacity," and define the concept much as it was defined in Chapter 2 of this book. Also see Putnam, "Reframing"; M. Scott Poole, "Decision Development in Small Groups I," *Communication Monographs, 48* (1981):1–24; and M. Scott Poole and Jonelle Roth, "Decision Development in Small Groups IV," *Human Communication Research, 15* (1989): 323–356.

[33] Timothy Leary, *Interpersonal Diagnosis of Personality* (New York: Ronald, 1957); Kenneth Thomas and Richard Walton, *Conflict-handling Behavior in Interdepartmental Relations* (Los Angeles: UCLA Graduate School of Business Administration, 1971).

[34] This summary is based on a number of sources. The most important are Alan Sillars, "Stranger and Spouse as Target Persons for Compliance-gaining Strategies," *Human Communication Research, 6* (1980): 265–279; Richard Walton, *Interpersonal Peacemaking* (Reading, MA: Addison-Wesley, 1969); George Marwell and D. Schmidt, "Dimensions of Compliance-gaining Behavior," *Sociometry, 30* (1967): 350–364; Steven Lukes, *Power: A Radical View* (London: Macmillan, 1974); Peter Bacharach and Morton Baratz, "Two Faces of Power," *American Political Science Review, 56* (1962): 947–952; Morton Baratz, *Power and Poverty* (New York: Oxford, 1970); Bertram Raven and Arie Kruglanski, "Power and Conflict," in *The Structure of Conflict,* Paul Swingle, ed. (New York: Academic Press, 1970); Dean Tjosvold, "Effects of Approach to Controversy on Supervisors' Incorporation of Subordinates' Information in Decision Making," *Journal of Applied Psychology, 67* (1982): 189–191; and "Effects of Supervisor's Influence Orientation on Their Decision-Making Controversy," *Journal of Psychology, 113* (1983): 175–182.

[35] David F. Bush, "Passive-aggressive Behavior in the Business Setting," in *Passive-Aggressiveness,* Richard Parsons and Robert Wicks, eds. (New York: Brunner-Mazel, 1983). Also

see Deborah Kolb, ed., *Hidden Conflict in Organizations* (Newbury Park, CA: Sage, 1991). The list of regressive strategies is taken from Michael Roloff, "Roloff's Modes of Conflict Resolution and Their Items," in *Explorations in Interpersonal Communication,* Gerald Miller, ed. (Beverly Hills, CA: Sage, 1976).

[36] Charles Smart and I. Veritsky, "Designs for Crisis Decision Units," *Administrative Science Quarterly, 22* (1977): 640–657. Having power is both an advantage and a constraint. Our society negatively values coercion. This value makes it difficult for powerful people to overtly impose their wills on less powerful people, unless, of course, others perceive that the powerful have been provoked. The hidden face of power, however, usually leads less powerful employees to act in ways that do not provoke the powerful. If powerholders are to achieve their goals, they must be able to exercise their power subtly. They can do so, as Bacharach and Baratz argued, by using communicative strategies that structure conflict situations.

[37] Elizabeth Janeway, *Powers of the Weak* (New York: Morrow-Quill, 1980).

[38] H. Meyers, E. Kay, and J.R.P. French, "Split Roles in Performance Appraisals," *Harvard Business Review* (1965), 21–19.

[39] Julia Wood and Barnett Pearce, "Sexists, Racists and Other Classes of Classifiers," *Quarterly Journal of Speech, 66* (1980): 239–250.

[40] Wilson; James Tedeschi, "Threats and Promises," in *The Structure of Conflict,* Paul Swingle, ed. (New York: Academic Press, 1970); J. Murdock, J. Bradac, and J. Bowers, "Effects of Power on the Perception of Explicit and Implicit Threats, Promises and Thromises," *Western Journal of Speech Communication, 48* (1984): 344–361; and W. Schenck-Hamlin and G. Georgacarakos, "Response to Murdock, Bradac, and Bowers," *Western Journal of Speech Communication, 50* (1986): 200–207.

[41] Wilson.

[42] R. Axelrod, *The Evolution of Cooperation* (New York: Basic Books, 1984). Also see Folger, Poole, and Stuttman.

[43] Raven and Kruglanski; S.S. Komorita, "Negotiating from Strength and the Concept of Bargaining," *Journal of the Theory of Social Behavior, 7* (1977): 56–79.

[44] Of course, a number of such books have been written. See especially Folger, Poole, and Stuttman; Samuel Bacharach and Edward Lawler, *Negotiation* (San Francisco: Jossey-Bass, 1980); Daniel Druckman, ed., *Negotiation* (Beverly Hills: Sage, 1977); Max Bazerman and Roy Lewicki, *Negotiating in Organizations* (Beverly Hills: Sage, 1983); and Putnam and Roloff.

[45] Morton Deutsch and Robert Krauss, "Studies in Interpersonal Bargaining," *Journal of Conflict Resolution, 61* (1962): 52–76; Folger, Poole, and Stuttman; Linda Putnam and T. Jones, "Reciprocity in Negotiations," *Communication Monographs, 49* (1982): 171–191; and William Donohue, M. Diez, and M. Hamilton, "Coding Naturalistic Negotiation Interaction," *Human Communication Research, 10* (1984): 403–425.

[46] Margaret Neale and Max Bazerman have observed that organizational negotiators often engage in the same kinds of not strictly rational processes that are described in the discussion of decision-making in Chapter 8. In particular they are (1) overly influenced by the form/presentation of information rather than its content, (2) remain stubbornly committed to their initial positions when it is inappropriate, (3) assume a zero-sum posture when the situation is mixed motive, (4) make decisions on irrelevant information, (5) rely on readily available information rather than high-quality information to make strategic decisions, (6) don't take the perspective of the other party, and (7) are overconfident about ease of obtaining favorable outcomes (see "Negotiating Rationally," *Academy of Management Executive, 6* [1992]: 42–65). As conflicts escalate, the degree of irrationality also increases.

[47] Wilson; also see T. Lim and J.W. Bowers, "Face-work: Solidarity, Approbation, and Face," *Human Communication Research, 17* (1990): 415–450 and Roloff and Jordan. In non-Western cultures saving face is even more important. Stella Ting-Toomey has described the complicated saving face system that characterizes Japanese approaches to conflict management. One principle of this system is the concept of *Nemawashi,* the subtle process of achieving consensus and support for a proposal. Extensive informal communication eventually involves every relevant member of the organization, but never includes a "group confrontation" in which everyone meets in a formal negotiating session. The second principle is the Ringi System, a way of preventing open conflicts by circulating a document widely and getting everyone's seals of approval. This system diffuses responsibility and saves face for those people who initially may oppose the

proposal, and it saves face for everyone should the proposal fail. The third principle is the Go-between System, in which people with different opinions seek out a third party to mediate. This complex, time-consuming, indirect system of conflict management is appropriate for Japanese organizations because the demands and constraints of Japanese culture make it more important to prevent conflicts than to manage them in the open. Confrontation is characteristic of more open, democratic cultures like the United States ("Theory of Conflict and Culture"; also see Wilson).

[48] Patricia Renwick, "Perception and Management of Superior-subordinate Conflict," *Organizational Behavior and Human Performance, 13* (1975): 444–456; T. Ruble and R. Cosier, "A Laboratory Study of Five Conflict-handling Modes," in *Conflict Management and Industrial Relations,* Bomers and R. Peterson, eds. (Boston: Kluwer-Nijhoff, 1982).

[49] Paul Watzlawick, Janet Beavin, and Don Jackson, *Pragmatics of Human Communication* (New York: W.W. Norton, 1967); Linda Putnam and Charmaine Wilson, "Communicative Strategies in Organizational Conflicts," in *Communication Yearbook 6,* M. Burgoon, ed. (Newbury Park, CA: Sage, 1982); Sillars, "Stranger"; Roy Lewicki, "Lying and Deception," in *Negotiating in Organizations,* Max Bazerman and R. Lewicki, eds. (Newbury Park, CA: Sage, 1983).

[50] Deutsch, "Conflicts;" Robert Stagner and H. Rosen, *Psychology of Union-management Relationships* (Belmont, CA: Brooks-Cole, 1965).

[51] A. Gouldner, *Wildcat Strike* (Yellow Springs, OH: Antioch Press, 1954).

[52] For an excellent explanation of this process and case study, see Kenwyn Smith, "The Movement of Conflict in Organizations," *Administrative Science Quarterly, 34* (1989): 1–20.

[53] William Donohue, M.E. Diez, and R.B. Stahle, "New Directions in Negotiation Research," in R.W. Bostrom, ed. *Communication Yearbook 7* (Beverly Hills, CA: Sage, 1983); William Donohue and R. Kolt, *Managing Interpersonal Conflict* (Newbury Park, CA: Sage, 1992).

[54] E. Rhenman, L. Stromberg, and G. Westerlund, *Conflict and Cooperation in Business Organizations* (New York: John Wiley, 1970); Paul Lawrence and Jay Lorsch, *Organizations and Environment* (Homewood, IL: Richard D. Irwin, 1969); Putnam, *Handbook.*

Chapter 10

COMMUNICATION, GENDER, RACE, AND ETHNICITY: STRATEGIES OF ACCOMMODATION?

It (the glass ceiling) is not a natural phenomenon; it is an intentional barrier. Therefore, it must be intentionally dismantled.

—FORMER U.S. REPRESENTATIVE SUSAN MOLINARI

The dominant mood today is that enough has been done—for blacks and Hispanics, for women and children, for the poor and the sick. It is an attitude born of economic and spiritual deprivation in what was once the land of plenty. And it reflects what has always been the national character of America—its short attention span. If we as a nation cannot solve a problem quickly, we lose patience, move on, place blame on the shortcomings of others, rather than on our own lack of national resolve.

—AUDREY EDWARDS AND CRAIG POLITE

CENTRAL THEMES

- Issues regarding race, gender, and ethnicity can be fully understood only if an organization's strategy of organizing, the taken-for-granted assumptions of Western societies, and the inter-relationships between these factors are considered simultaneously.
- During the 1960s and 1970s the opportunities available to women, African American men, and Latinos increased substantially. Attitudes toward a diverse workforce also improved. But during the 1980s and 1990s the rate of improvement in opportunities and attitudes leveled off, and may even have fallen.
- Originally women were advised to accommodate to patterns of action assumed to be characteristic of white males in traditional, bureaucratic organizations. More recently the accommodationist perspective has been criticized on two grounds: (1) it has had limited success, and (2) it ignores the institutional bases of unequal opportunity.

KEY TERMS

Glass ceiling   Staff positions
Line positions   Glass walls

Chapter 1 of this book introduced the concept of *hegemony,* the idea that the hierarchical relationships that exist in a society come to be treated as if they are *natural* (that is, inevitable) and *normal* (that is, expected and morally correct). As people *internalize* the values and assumptions of their societies they also internalize its class, race, gender, and ethnicity-based hierarchical relationships. In contemporary Western societies educated Anglo, middle- and upper-class men traditionally have been (and often still are) assumed to be superior to everyone else, at least in the "public" venues of organizations. But societal assumptions are only part of the story. The other part involves the strategies of organizing that are employed in modern (primarily bureaucratic) organizations, the central concept that was developed in Unit I. As those chapters explained, organizations do not *have* to be centralized, tasks do not *have* to be segmented or *deskilled,* and reward systems do not *have* to focus on individual achievement rather than group performance. But members of contemporary Western organizations tend to choose these strategies of organizing because they are consistent with the values and assumptions of the people who hold power in their societies—primarily educated middle- and upper-class white males. Different strategies of organizing create organizational structures and practices that create greater opportunities for some employees and groups of employees than for other individuals and groups. Because we tend to forget that strategies of organizing are *choices* among a variety of options, we also tend to forget that differences in opportunity are not natural or normal, but instead are embedded in our choice of organizational strategies. As a result, success or failure in an organization (or society) *seems* to be linked solely to individual competence and performance, which also *seems* to be linked to one's class, race, sex, ability/disability, or ethnicity.[1] As I have explained throughout this book, understanding organizational processes requires an analysis of social and cultural assumptions, characteristics of different strategies of organizing, *and* the ways in which assumptions and strategies influence one another.

As if that did not make matters difficult enough, issues regarding gender, race, and ethnicity are complicated further by three factors. First, compared to the vast amount of research on the organizational experiences of white men, we know relatively little about the experiences of anyone else. What we do know is both ambiguous and complicated. The vast majority of organizational research either has involved only white men or has ignored the gender, race, and ethnicity of employees.[2] Since the early 1970s a growing amount of research has been conducted on the organizational experiences of Anglo women.

In comparison, little research has been done on the experiences of African American men, even less on the experiences of Latinos, and almost nothing on the experiences of Latinas, African American women, Native Americans, or

Asian Americans. What we do know is that the experiences of persons within each of these groups is in some ways similar—members of each group are numerical minorities in American organizations, especially among organizational powerholders; each group faces negative stereotypes about their work-related competence, especially in professional and managerial roles; and members of each group have lower status in Western societies than Anglo males do. But in other ways the experiences of Anglo women, African Americans, Native Americans, Asian Americans, Latinos, and Latinas are quite different. As a result, my summary of this research also will be uneven, with more space devoted to Anglo women, less to African-American men, and even less to members of other groups.

The organizational structure of this chapter reflects these complications. The first section examines the "realities" of contemporary American organizations and concludes that while substantial improvement has occurred in the status of Anglo women, African Americans, Latinos, and Latinas, major limitations still exist. It also will suggest that the rate of progress made since 1970 slowed after 1985 and may actually have been reversed since 1988, so that achieving "diversity" or "equality" now is becoming less likely. The second section presents the "accommodation" perspective and summarizes critiques of it. Chapter 11 develops the "diversity management" view, provides a brief critique of it, and suggests an alternative.

THE "REALITIES" OF RACE, GENDER, AND ETHNICITY IN CONTEMPORARY AMERICAN ORGANIZATIONS

As the quotation by Edwards and Polite at the beginning of this chapter suggests, many Americans today believe that issues regarding gender, race, and ethnicity are part of America's past, not its present. This perception persists, especially among Anglo Americans, in spite of almost daily disclosures of blatant examples of sexual or racial discrimination, harassment, or assault in U.S. organizations—Mitsubishi Motors, Texaco, Denny's Restaurants, U.S. Army training centers, and Circuit City stores were among the most publicized cases during 1996.

On the one hand, substantial progress has been made. Today there are far more women, African Americans, and Latinos in entry-level professional and managerial positions than was true twenty years ago. Between 1970 and 1985 the proportion of female managers in the American economy as a whole increased from 15 percent to 36 percent, and the number of female managers grew 400 percent. Two-thirds of all managers hired between 1965 and 1985 were women. In 1992 55 percent of the people earning bachelor's degrees were women, as were 35 percent of new M.D.s and 42 percent of new attorneys, suggesting that there are sufficient numbers of women receiving advanced training to continue these trends. The percentage of women in upper management grew from 3.5 in 1970 to 6.8 in 1980 to 10 percent in 1996.

The bad news is that even within managerial and professional jobs, people who are not Anglo males still are concentrated at the lower levels of organizations and in sectors with lower salaries and mobility opportunities. In 1991, 25 percent of officers and managers in small firms were Anglo women, 5 percent were African Americans, 3 percent were Latinos or Latinas, and 2 percent were Asian Americans. In very large (*Fortune* 100) firms, fewer officers and managers are women (about 18 percent), and only 7 percent are African Americans, Latinos, or Asian Americans. Upper management still is almost exclusively the province of Anglo males—90 percent of *Fortune* 500 firms do not have a woman among the five most compensated officers.[3]

Salaries for all women in the labor force have hovered around 69 percent of men's salaries for decades, but in 1992 reached a high of 72 percent, a gap that is even smaller for women aged 25–34 (82 percent), and smaller still for women aged 27–33 who have never had children (98 percent). Among professional occupations the gap is smallest in finance, law, and computers. African American men earn approximately 50 percent of Anglo men's salaries; African American women earn approximately 30 percent of Anglo men's incomes and approximately 60 percent of the income of Anglo women. Overall, Latinos earned two-thirds of the salaries of Anglo men. Of course, many of these gaps still are significant, even if the data are corrected for education, experience, or seniority within the firm.[4]

Like workforce participation and salaries, attitudes about a diverse workforce also have improved, but still serve as barriers to advancement. In 1965 the *Harvard Business Review* surveyed managers about their attitudes about women managers. Almost half of their responses (41 percent) were unfavorable; another 6 percent were strongly opposed. The opposition is strongest among young men, who see women as competitors, and weakest among older men and men who had been supervisors or colleagues of female managers. Fortunately, resistance decreases as Anglo men become accustomed to the newcomer (although this is much less true if the newcomer is African American, Asian, or Latino than if she is an Anglo woman), but increases rapidly after the percentage of "different" employees reaches 10 to 15 percent of the work group. When *HBR* repeated the study in 1985, only 5 percent of male executives then viewed female managers unfavorably, and none was strongly opposed. In addition, the percentage who felt that businesspersons would never fully accept women dropped from 61 percent to 20 percent. But there are significant differences in the attitudes and beliefs of male and female managers. For example, a survey by Catalyst, Inc., a consulting company that focuses on issues involving women and the workplace, found that male executives believed that women had made substantial progress during the past five years (49 percent) and attributed the slow progress of women into upper management to their lack of general management experience (82 percent) and "insufficient time in the pipeline" (64 percent). Far fewer women executives felt that substantial progress had been made since 1990 (23 percent) and attributed the rate to a lack of managerial opportunities in "line" positions (47 percent), to stereotyping and preconceptions (42 percent), and being excluded from informal communication networks (49 percent). Anglo males still perceive that discrimination is far less widespread than do members of all other groups. Catalyst explained the different perceptions rather simply: Since males have not experienced the problems that women cite, they do not recognize that those problems exist.[5] Similarly, executives still seem to assume that African American and Latino managers are less professional and less competent than Anglos, regardless of actual performance data.[6]

And, as the U.S. workforce becomes more diverse, other groups of employees confront the traditional assumptions and organizational strategies. For example, age discrimination has become an increasing problem during the 1990s and is likely to grow in importance as the "baby boomers" age. Like other forms of differential treatment, ageism is both pervasive and subtle. It is grounded in the cultural assumption that older people are inherently less capable than younger workers. For example, when managers described 30–year-old and 60–year-old workers, they used the terms "more productive, capable of working under pressure, flexible, able to learn, and decisive" for the younger workers and "reliable, honest, committed to quality, have good attendance records, and use good judgment" for the older ones in spite of consistent research evidence indicating that intellectual skills do not decline substantially with age. They also tend to assume that younger workers will stay with the company for twenty-five to thirty years, in spite of substantial evidence that long-term connections to a single organization no longer can be assumed of *any* group of employees (recall the "Generation X" case study in Chapter 1).[7]

Negative attitudes about gay and lesbian employees persist even though a number of organizations have taken steps to reduce differential treatment. In 1996, IBM announced that it would extend health benefits to partners of its homosexual employees, joining 470 other companies (up from 250 in 1995 and including Apple Computer, Ben and Jerry's, Dayton Hudson, Eastman Kodak, Fox Broadcasting, Glaxo-Wellcome, Hewlett-Packard, Seagram and Sons, Levi Strauss, Microsoft, NYNEX, Time Warner, Walt Disney, Wells Fargo, and Xerox). IBM's management said that their decision was based on a commitment to nondiscrimination, equity, and fairness, and because the highly competitive environment the organization now faces requires it to seek out and retain the most talented people available.[8]

Finally, there is evidence that some of the improvements in workforce participation, salaries, and discriminatory attitudes made during the 1970s and 1980s has been reversed. For example, female managers' pay increased an average of 54 percent between 1985 and 1990, while male managers' pay increased an average of 65 percent (and Mexican American men's real wages fell). This shift results in part from societal attitudes and in part from structural factors. Resistance to diversity by Anglo men tends to be strong when the first woman, African American, or Latino enters a workgroup. This is both because people generally fear change and because the newcomers also are new competitors. Now that women and minority persons have begun to approach upper levels of some organizations, upper-level managers' attitudes have started to shift. They have more positive attitudes about women *until* women begin to approach *their* level in the organizational hierarchy.[9] Only 16 percent of the respondents in a 1992 survey of chief executive officers of *Fortune* 500 firms thought that it is very or somewhat likely that a woman would be CEO of their firm within ten years, and only 18 percent think it is very likely within twenty years. Interestingly, these figures are almost identical to those found in a similar survey conducted twenty years earlier. Seventy-nine percent of the CEOs admitted that their projections were based on the existence of real organizational barriers to the progress of women managers, not to weaknesses in the managers' background, training, or competence.[10]

Interestingly, many women seem to have recognized that these barriers continue to exist and have responded by starting organizations of their own. During the 1980s a much larger number of women—one of three MBAs in one study—have left large organizations to start their own businesses. These decisions were motivated in part by anticipation of the freedom, excitement, and feelings of achievement that accompany succeeding in running one's own business in a highly competitive environment. But they also stemmed from frustration with gender-related barriers in their old firms that kept them from being rewarded adequately and equitably for their contributions, and from moving into positions of greater challenge and creativity.

For example, in 1980 there were two million women-owned businesses with $25 billion in sales or receipts; in 1992 there were eight million with $2.25 trillion in sales or receipts. And women entrepreneurs are just as successful as male entrepreneurs.[11] Consequently, as a result of their inability or unwillingness to meet the personal and career needs of professional women, large, complex organizations have lost a great deal of talent and expertise and in the process created a large number of effective competitors. Unfortunately, relatively few women or persons of color have the financial resources necessary to take this step, in part because lending agencies tend to discriminate against them.

Consequently, even politically conservative commentators admit that the progress has been slow and mixed. The so-called **glass ceiling**, beyond which women, African Americans, and Latinos can see but not reach upper management, once was assumed to be located at the level of middle management. Above that point in an organization's hierarchy the number of openings falls rapidly, and performance evaluation becomes much more subjective.[12] However, recent research has found that the ceiling is even lower than middle management for Anglo women, and lower still for African Americans and Latinos/Latinas. And, as the following section of this chapter explains, subjective performance evaluations tend to disadvantage employees who are not Anglo men. Consequently, the Department of Labor in the Bush administration concluded that:

> This report (on the glass ceiling) is also a good news, bad news document. The good news is that the participation rates of minorities and women in corporate management has improved. The bad news is that surveys in the corporate world do not point to an optimistic future unless commitments to positive change are sustained and enhanced.[13]

This does not mean that the ceiling cannot be penetrated—there are a number of noted successes—but it does suggest that the combination of differences in opportunity and cultural attitudes make it difficult to do so. And "the barriers to the upper rungs of the corporate ladder for minority women appear to be nearly impenetrable."[14]

Aspects of the U.S. economic situation also have mitigated against further progress. As large organizations have downsized they have permanently eliminated many of the middle-management positions to which women and persons of color might have been promoted and have increased the competition for the remaining managerial positions. Downsizing also has led to disproportionately large numbers of women, African Americans, and Latinos being laid off or fired. Recent recessions were felt most strongly by small and medium-sized firms, precisely those organizations that have provided the best opportunities for people who are not Anglo males. This combination of attitudinal and structural trends means that it is unlikely that the upward mobility of Anglo women, African Americans, or Latinos during the next twenty years will approach that of the last twenty.[15]

Broader societal trends also serve as barriers. The backlash against affirmative action and feminism during the 1980s, culminating in the passage of California's Proposition 209 in 1996, combined with increasingly overt hostility in the workplace—racist, sexist, and homophobic slurs in conversations, hate mail/graffiti/faxes, sabotage of work projects and computer files, and physical assaults—suggests that attitudinal barriers to diversity are on the upswing.[16]

So, the situations that women, African American men, and Latinos face today seem to be very similar to those faced a generation ago. But the demographic realities of contemporary America make it inevitable that the vast majority of employees entering our labor force during the next generation will not be Anglo males. Understanding the barriers faced by African American males, Latinos, and women and developing strategies for confronting those barriers is even more important now than it was twenty years ago.

WOMEN, COMMUNICATION, AND ACCOMMODATION

A number of the earlier chapters in this book suggested employees tend to develop individual orientations to their organizations that in some ways involve accommodating one's self and one's behaviors to the control processes of their organizations and in other ways resist those processes. From 1975 to approximately 1985 virtually all of the "advice" given women in organizations was to adopt a custodial orientation and try to "fit in"; much of it still does. But persons from lower socioeconomic classes, as well as African Americans, Latinos, and women all encounter immense difficulties breaking into the administrative ranks because they are identifiably different, they clearly do not "fit in," and their efforts to fit in are stymied by their lack of familiarity with the communication style of bureaucratic discourse. Their lack of familiarity . . . is seen by the organization's representatives as evidence of lack of "management potential."[17]

The solution, according to the accommodationist perspective, is for women, African Americans, and Latinos to learn and use the strategies of Anglo men. While this approach will tend to perpetuate stereotypical views of members of these groups, it may allow individual employees to be perceived as exceptions to those stereotypes, and thus succeed in predominantly Anglo male organizations.[18]

Strategy #1: "Fitting In"

Because of the role that perceptions and visibility play in organizational success, Anglo women were taught ways of "fitting in" to the Anglo male bureaucratic culture. One means of doing so is to *use the language of the organization*. Because cultural myths portray both managers and organizations as "rational," a key part of the language of most organizations is to justify decisions or proposals in data-based terms (recall Chapter 8) or in terms of the dominant values of the organizational culture. Because cultural myths also depict women (and African American men and Latinos) as nonrational, it is particularly important for them to use highly rational (that is, unemotional) forms of communication.[19]

A second way of "fitting in" is to demonstrate one's loyalty to the organization. Loyalty is a nebulous concept, but one that is required by almost all organizations. It cannot be demonstrated directly, but is a symbolic creation. The most common way of creating perceptions of loyalty is to repeatedly signal that the organization is one's highest priority. Although the symbols of loyalty differ in various organizations, there seems to be one common component: sublimating all other activities and relationships to one's career and one's working relationships. Consistently taking work home, seeking and accepting promotions or transfers even when they would be disadvantageous to one's family, and limiting social ties to business contacts all seem to be widely accepted indices of loyalty. Of course, there is little evidence that these activities are either a reliable sign of loyalty or necessary to the successful operation of organizations. But they are part of the symbolic reality that guides perceptions. In traditionally structured families (Ward and June Cleaver of *Leave It to Beaver*), creating these impressions is possible. The professional's wife is available to serve as hostess, secretary, child-care specialist, and therapist. But for unmarried professionals or married women professionals, there often is no one available to play this "wifely" role.[20]

Presumably the husbands of women professionals could assist in home activities. However, studies of time allocation have found that husbands of wives who have full-time jobs outside of the home spend no more time doing home-related work than husbands whose wives do not work outside of the home. In fact the total number of nonleisure hours worked by women employed full-time is almost double the total for traditional housewives.[21] As a result, the Center for Creative Leadership found that 20 percent of the women they interviewed said that balancing work and family concerns was one of the greatest challenges they had faced, while only 3 percent of the men shared this concern.

The accommodation perspective recommends that women adapt to these definitions of loyalty by seeking promotions that involve relocation and assignments that involve travel, staying with the same firm for long periods of time, and making decisions about their nonorganizational life that put their careers and organizations first—choosing not to marry, to delay marriage, or to wait to begin a family until after they are well established in their careers.[22] Women who do marry or form long-term partnerships should negotiate a lifestyle with their partners that allows them to simultaneously pursue their careers and participate in a fulfilling family life. Evidently, women largely have followed this advice. Today, executive women change jobs for career, not family, reasons; are as likely or more likely to relocate in order to further their careers than are male executives; and take the same number of vacation days. But, in spite of this evidence, upper managers still *perceive* that women put family before career, *believe* they will turn down assignments involving travel or relocation, and so on. So, when women *do* experience career interruptions, they have a disproportionately negative effect on their careers—women lose seniority, opportunities for training, and salary: "The first year back your wages are 33 percent lower than women who didn't leave. Over time, that difference diminishes (to 20 percent over 3–5 years and 10 percent after 11–20 years) but it never disappears."[23]

Strategy #2: Exceptional Performance

Virtually all studies of the upward mobility of successful women and African Americans and Latinos have found that their performance has had to be better and more consistent than the performance of Anglo men with similar backgrounds. This pattern is explained only in part by overt discrimination. As the discussions of organizational reward systems throughout this book have indicated, there is no simple and direct relationship between an employee's performance and her or his upward mobility regardless of race, gender, or ethnicity. Excellent performance is rewarded only if it also is *visible* to the organization's powerholders and only if they *perceive* that it provides evidence of exceptional competence.[24]

The Problems of Visibility and Perceptions.   For women, and for members of minority groups, visibility is paradoxical in other ways. In organizations or units that have small numbers of women, African Americans, or Latinos (Rosabeth Moss Kanter has suggested that 15 percent is a crucial level), the ones who are there often live in "glass houses." As one woman executive explained, "There is an element of derailment built into the system for women—the pressure created by having to be a role model and a 'first' along with personal competency. Men don't have to deal with this added pressure." Another admitted that "I feel that if I fail, it will be a long time before they hire another woman for the job. . . . Carrying that burden can lead women to play it safe, to be ultraconservative, to opt out if a situation looks chancy." Everyone makes mistakes. If powerholders focus on an employee's mistakes instead of her or his successes, or if they attribute an occasional error to a person's race or sex, visibility becomes a barrier, not an advantage.[25]

The visibility paradox is complicated further by perceptual and attributional processes. Cultural myths about race, gender, and ethnicity create perceptual sets through which people (1) *attend* to events and actions that confirm their predispositions and (2) *interpret* the events and actions in ways that support their perceptual sets. Three examples illustrate the role of cultural myths in perceptions.

First, the simplest way to make one's performance visible is to tell others about it. But even simple concepts are complicated by cultural assumptions and organizational structures. The effects of two specific kinds of communication illustrate these differences. One is bragging. Men have learned to be relatively comfortable bragging about their exploits. Men's bragging tends to exaggerate their successes ("I caught a fish/made a sale/won a case that was *this* big") and to express them in comparative and competitive terms. Women brag less frequently, tend to understate their accomplishments, and attribute their successes to other members of their team. As a result, males' bragging creates impressions of competence, confidence, pride, and success (all positively valued in managerial settings) while females' bragging makes people like them more and praise them for being sensitive. These impressions are consistent with social stereotypes about women, but not with stereotypes about what managers are like.[26]

A second example of how perceptions influence the effects of different ways of communicating involve what has been labeled "powerful/powerless speech." In general, people who speak a bit more rapidly and loudly than normal, present organized messages, speak in words the audience uses, and do not speak in a monotone seem to have more influence than people who do not have these attributes. Conversely, some communication patterns create impressions of weakness, insecurity, passivity, and limited competence (see Table 10-1). However, these "powerful" strategies also are stereotypically male strategies; the "powerless" ones are stereotypically female. When people use the powerful strategies, their perceived influence is increased, but the effect is greater for men than for women. However, when men use the powerless strategies it has little effect on their perceived influence; but when women use them their perceived influence falls.[27] Similarly, men who adopt human relations-oriented leadership strategies are perceived as analytical and forceful, whereas women who use these approaches are seen as open-minded and nurturing.

Perceptual processes are even more complex for African American men and Latinos, and more complex still for African American women and Latinas. Researchers long have recognized that, in general, subordinates receive significantly higher ratings from persons of their own race and sex, even when objective performance standards are used. This results in part from the continuation of overtly racist attitudes and behaviors, as the 1996 Texaco case (recall Chapter 7)

TABLE 10-1

"Powerful" and "Powerless" Modes of Speech

I. Powerful Speech
  Controlling substantial amounts of conversational time
  High rate of initiating communication
  Longer statements/messages
  Many talkovers/interruptions of others
  Many questions asked of others
  Use of strong expletives
  Simple (as vs. complex) requests

II. Powerless Speech
  Many uncertainty cues
  —Hedges ("If I'm right about"; "In the right circumstances")
  —Tag questions (". . . don't you think?")
  —Disclaimers ("The data are not all in yet"; "I know I'm out of my area of
    expertise, but . . .")
  Excessive gestures
  Overly formal grammar
  Polite forms ("please" and "thank you")

and others so clearly indicate. But differential evaluation also seems to occur even when overt racial biases are not evident. Both the criteria used to evaluate African Americans' performance and the evaluations themselves are influenced by the race of the supervisor. Anglo supervisors tend to rate all African American subordinates as average regardless of their actual performance or to rate them in less positive terms than their Anglo counterparts.[28] For example, in recent studies of performance appraisals, African Americans were not described in more negative terms than Anglos, but Anglos' positive ratings were higher than African Americans' (for example, African Americans were perceived as being ambitious, but Anglos were seen as *more* ambitious):

> when the (job or promotion) applicant had weak qualifications, discrimination did not occur between black and Anglo applicants: both were rated low. When the applicant had moderate qualifications, Anglos were evaluated slightly, but not significantly, more positively than blacks. When the applicant had strong qualifications, both blacks and Anglos were evaluated well, but blacks were evaluated less positively than Anglos who had the same qualifications. . . . (B)ias did not occur at all levels; it occurred only at the positive end. It was not that blacks were (perceived to be) worse than Anglos, it was just that blacks were not as good as Anglos.[29]

Latinas and African American women face both gender and race/ethnicity perceptual biases. Cultural assumptions also influence the relative weight that supervisors attach to the various criteria they use to evaluate their employees. They tend to base their evaluations of African American and Latino/Latina subordinates more on the extent to which they *conform* to the organization's norms of behavior than on their performance (the reverse is true for Anglo subordinates). In general, Anglo male supervisors and employers feel more comfortable with people who they perceive are like them and tend to promote similar people. Because Latinas and African American women are most dissimilar, they are least likely to be promoted. To complicate matters further, Anglo male supervisors often are not aware of their perceptions or the role that those perceptions play in their actions toward and evaluations of women and African Americans and Latinos.[30]

Differences in Attributions.   Perceptions are the bases of attributions. Even when excellent performance by women or African American men or Latinos is recognized, it often is attributed to factors outside of the employee's control—luck, special advantages, the help of other employees, the effectiveness of the organization as a whole, or high motivation and effort (which cannot be sustained over the long term)—rather than to skill and expertise. Men tend to be promoted on the basis of their potential for future positions; women because of their past accomplishments. Since predictions of future success are necessarily ambiguous, stereotypes enter into the decision-making process. In addition, successful performance by Anglo men is attributed to their intrinsic skills.

Two examples of differential attribution may help explain this process. First, if a man's success is attributed to "hard work" it usually helps his career because evaluators assume that he also is competent. But when a woman's success is attributed to hard work, evaluators tend to assume that it disguises limits to her competence, so it does little to help her advance in the organization.[31] Second, as women demonstrate expertise in their jobs, the definition of "expertise" tends to shift because of the cultural assumption that "if women can do it, it must not be all that difficult or important after all." As the proportion of women in a particular occupation or profession increases, the prestige afforded that occupation falls (and, as Chapter 1 explained, so do wage rates). In addition, supervisors also seem to feel and express less confidence in their evaluations of women subordinates than of their male subordinates.[32] When evaluators express a lack of confidence in their judgments about an employee's performance, it creates less positive perceptions than the performance merits. In organizations, as in the rest of life, perceptual "realities" are more important than actual performance.

CASE STUDY:
THE RIVER RUNNERS

Because their attitudes are part of the taken-for-granted assumptions of our culture, people often are not consciously aware that they hold many of the attitudes that place Anglo women and persons of color at a disadvantage. A number of organizations recently have started to conduct training programs in team building designed in part to help people become aware of their attitudes about gender, race, and ethnicity and how those attitudes subtly influence their actions.

(continued)

(continued from the previous page)

This case study summarizes the key events in one such program offered by Outward Bound.*

One of Outward Bound's most popular programs is a week-long white-water rafting trip. Participants, who usually know very little about the wilderness and even less about piloting a five-person raft through swirling rapids and bone-chilling water, suddenly find themselves in the middle of the woods with a group of people they have never before seen. Each raft has a leader, who tells the participants what tasks will need to be performed during their week on the river and teaches them the basics of paddling and steering their 4–foot by 10–foot inflated rubber rafts. When the trip begins, participants are filled with anxiety (people do die while white-water rafting) and ambiguity, because none of them knows exactly what the experience will be like. As one participant asked another, "Are we out here with a bunch of bored rich guys playing around, or can we really learn something in this godforsaken wilderness?" On first glance the situation seems to be one in which race, gender, and power are largely irrelevant. There is no formal hierarchy among the participants, everyone has roughly equal task-related expertise, and the climate surrounding the trip is one of equality, team building, and cooperation. The participants know they will take turns doing every task—cooking, cleaning, pitching tents, captaining the raft, and so on. Nevertheless, power relationships do emerge, and do so subtly through communication.

Raft number 4 had five passengers—John, the leader, who usually stayed separated from the others; and Marlene, Helen, Bill, and Bob. All were successful professionals in their mid-fifties. Initially, the team worked well together. Individually they were warm, friendly, outgoing people who knew how to create a supportive atmosphere. They had a number of successes—navigating small rapids and paddling in calm water. Also, they were enduring misery together: The raft was small and cramped, there was almost always a few inches of cold water in the bottom, and paddling was hard work. Very quickly this group of strangers became a "band of fellow sufferers." After a long stretch of hard paddling, trying to catch up with raft 3, Helen began to complain to Bob that she was getting tired, explaining, "I'm just not used to pushing a paddle, but I'm damn good at pushing a pencil." Bob and Bill, who also were getting tired, were less honest. Bob retorted, "Why, this is nothing, you should canoe the St. John in Maine," and Bill echoed him with "Yeah, this is nothing compared to climbing Pikes Peak" (p. 104).

Eventually, taking turns on each task made very little sense to tired paddlers trying to put their camp together in the muted light of dusk. Instead they

---

*Based on Robert Schrank, "Two Women, Three Men on a Raft," *Harvard Business Review* (May-June 1977): 100–108.

(continued)

(continued from the previous page)

claimed the tasks they were most adept at performing—Bill and Bob pitched the tents and hauled water, while Marlene and Helen made the beds, cleaned the grounds, and arranged the sleeping bags like the spokes of a wheel, with the participants' heads in the middle. (This arrangement discourages rattlesnakes from climbing into a warm bag during the night.)

As they entered more difficult rapids, it became clear that Helen and, especially, Marlene had trouble captaining the raft. At one point, Marlene shouted for a hard right turn, when the raft needed to go left. Bill and Bob looked at one another with disgust, and Bill asked, "What's the matter, honey?" She said, "I don't know right from left. You be the helmsperson." Bill suggested writing on the back of Marlene's hands. He was kidding, but they did it. Helen was angry and asked Bob, "Is it really necessary to make a baby out of her?" At first whenever Marlene said "I can't do it," someone expressed confidence in her while thinking "Ye gods! When is she going to give up?" (p. 106). As time went on Bill and Bob started to take charge subtly by trying to steer the raft from the front; this is not only virtually impossible, but it also makes the captain's job almost impossible because the raft responds so unpredictably.

On the fifth day, with Marlene as captain and Bill and Bob covertly trying to guide the raft, the group went through a very fast rapid. Instead of yelling for a hard right, Marlene froze and the raft flipped over a rock, spilling all five passengers into the chilly water. While they dried out in front of an impromptu fire, the myth of equal power was abandoned. Marlene asked to no longer captain the raft, and even Helen was happy to say, "Yeah, I just want to stay dry. You guys take the helm" (p. 106).

Marlene's "failure" had been coming for some time. Even before Bill and Bob started covertly to sabotage her leadership, they had obeyed her orders only half-heartedly. As a result, the raft did not respond as well when Marlene was in command as when the men were in the captain's role. Because she could see no overt resistance to her orders, she had no reason to believe that anything other than her errors were causing the problems. She started to blame herself, unfairly, and to lose the confidence she needed to perform well in the hard rapids. Bob commented:

(During the trip home) it became clear to me that not only had I been unhappy with a woman as helmsperson, but also that Bill and I had subconsciously, by habit, proceeded to undermine the women. . . . The effect of our male, sabotaging behavior was to increase Helen's and Marlene's doubts about themselves as leaders. For each of them, their lifelong conditioning that a woman ought to be a passive sweet thing came into play, and they gave up the helm because men "do it better." . . . Judging from firsthand experience and others' reports I believe that what happened on Raft No. 4, Inc. occurs in most organizations when women enter positions of leadership. An exception might be organizations that have

(continued)

(continued from the previous page)

been run by women from their inception. Because organizations are usually designed as pyramids, the moving-up process involves squeezing someone else out. The higher up the pyramid, the more the squeeze. As women enter the squeezing, men are doubly threatened; first the number of pyramid squeeze players is increasing; second, because the new players are women, our masculinity is on the block. The resentment of men toward women managers is also exacerbated by the shrunken job market (p. 107).

Discussion Questions

1. Had you been in Bill and Bob's position, how would you have interpreted Marlene's admission that she no longer wanted to be captain? How would you have interpreted the events that took place while Marlene was captain?
2. As far as we know all four of the main participants were Anglo. Would the interactions had been different if Bob had been Hispanic or African American? If Marlene had been? Why or why not?
3. Were there any clues that Marlene could have used to know that the men were sabotaging her leadership? If so, what are they? Are there ways in which Marlene could have acted differently that would have allowed her to maintain her role as an equally powerful member of the group? If so, what? Are there ways that Helen could have been more helpful? If so, in what ways? Bob? Bill?
4. This case is now two decades old. If the trip was repeated today would the outcome be different? Why or why not?

Strategy #3: Cultivating Mentors

There seems to be widespread agreement that successful employees, regardless of gender, race, or ethnicity, have been able to establish close, personal relationships with one or more senior employees early in their careers.[33] From these *mentors* newcomers obtain information about the behavioral expectations of the organization's culture, the dynamics of organizational power and politics, the organization's expectations about how conflicts should be handled, and nonrational aspects of decision-making. They also may gain task-related expertise or learn to deal with racism, language problems, and the values held by Anglo men that may differ from their own. Without accurate information about these subtleties of organizational life, new employees can make accidental errors that have serious consequences. Once newcomers are perceived as error-prone or politically insensitive, it becomes progressively more difficult for them to gain access to the available sources of power.

However, like all interpersonal relationships, mentor–mentoree relationships are difficult to form and maintain, especially when mentorees are of a different gender, race, or ethnic background than their mentors.[34] Both parties may feel awkward, especially at first, and once the relationship is established it may be difficult to avoid creating an actual or perceived dependency relationship. Of course, these comments about mentoring relationships hold true for all employees, regardless of their race, gender, or ethnicity. However, pervasive cultural stereotypes complicate the mentoring relationship for women mentorees, especially Latinas and African American women. Because so few women occupy positions near the top of organizations, the vast majority of mentors will be Anglo men. Typically, Anglo supervisors are willing to sponsor or assist Anglo subordinates based on their level of competence—they help highly competent Anglo men regardless of their rank in the organization but are unwilling to help less competent ones. However, Anglo male supervisors seem to be willing to mentor Anglo women, Latinos, and African American men only if they are near the bottom of the organizational hierarchy and, somewhat paradoxically, only after they have demonstrated their competence. Once they are promoted and begin to become potential threats to the Anglo male supervisors, the supervisors are unwilling to help, even if they espouse egalitarian attitudes.[35]

Traditional sex-role stereotypes also complicate mentoring relationships by making it difficult for the parties to know how to act toward one another or interpret one another's actions. The relationship may be strained and communication may be less open and spontaneous than in male–male relationships. Cross-sex (or cross-race/ethnicity) mentoring relationships also seem to be weaker, less stable, and more limited to discussions of task issues than are same-sex (and same-race/ethnicity) relationships. Anglo male mentorees also seem to obtain access to other relationships through their mentors, while this is much less true for women, African American men, and Latinos. As a result, establishing and maintaining positive mentoring relationships is more difficult for women and African American men and Latinos than it is for Anglo men, and the mentoring relationships that they do establish seem to be less beneficial to their career advancement.[36] As a result of these complications, many organizations have chosen to formally assign a mentor to every newcomer. But in a society that values individuality and choice, formal mentor arrangements also are difficult to establish.[37]

Strategy #4: Networking

Most major cities and many smaller ones now have active networks for women, African American, and Latino managers and professionals. External networks have proven to be valuable to all three groups. Being linked to *external* networks also may be necessary for Latinos, women, and African American men because it is so difficult for them to become integrated into informal networks within their own organizations. Eighty percent of executives get their jobs through informal networks and 85 percent of upper-level jobs never are advertised in public. Being excluded from internal networks limits a person's ability to know what is going on in his or her organization, and makes it difficult to form alliances with influential people. Contacts made in networks provide a wide variety of information about how organizations "work" as well as social and emotional support. Employees who have experienced overt discrimination or racial or sexual harassment gain support from persons who have had similar experiences, obtain insight that prevents them from blaming themselves for unavoidable errors, and learn how others have handled problems like those they are facing.[38]

Networks share information about which firms have good records of advancing Latinos, African American men, and women and which have poor records. They provide advice about handling everyday work-related problems and exchange information about when and where vacancies are anticipated. At times, networks can become elitist, shifting their focus from aiding all of their members to assisting a selected few.[39] When they work effectively they can provide members with all of the information that men traditionally have gained through informal "good old boy" networks and help compensate for the fact that Latinos, Latinas, Anglo women, and African Americans often are excluded from informal networks.

Strategy #5: Obtaining High-Power Positions and Assignments

Chapter 7 explained that there are a number of bases of power available to employees. Some of these are related directly to an employee's formal role in the organization. Some positions involve control of scarce resources; others do not. Seeming to be highly expert often depends as much on one's place in formal communication networks as on one's actual competence.

Latinos, African Americans, and Anglo women often are in industries that provide little opportunity to move into positions with significant formal power. In 1981, 53 percent of all women managers were employed in finance, real estate, retail trade, and communications. Not only are salaries relatively low in these sectors of the economy, but the organizations within them also tend to be decentralized, providing relatively few upper-level positions to which people can advance. Less than 10 percent of women (and a somewhat higher but comparable percentage of African American males and Latinos) were employed in wholesale trade, transportation, machinery, and manufacturing, sectors that have higher salaries and greater mobility opportunities. By 1991 the percentages had increased in all sectors, but the relative proportions were stable.[40]

These imbalances result both from broad acculturational processes and from organizational pressures. From preschool through graduate school women are encouraged to enter "nurturing" or "people-oriented" fields, and African Americans are encouraged to pursue "applied" or "practical" (as opposed to theoretical or managerial) careers.[41] As a result women, Latinos, and African American men usually are located in relatively powerless units or divisions— **staff positions** like human resources or personnel administration. Even when African American men, Latinos, and women do not "choose" staff-related careers, organizations tend to shunt them in those directions anyway. For example, there are so few women in line positions that 86 percent of all women managers would have to be transferred into other divisions to eliminate these imbalances.[42] Because virtually all organizations require upper managers to have experience managing the sectors of the organization that produce the products or services that it markets (these are called **line positions**), being limited to staff positions precludes one's being promoted. Staff positions seem to be surrounded by "**glass walls**" and these walls may be the greatest barrier to upward mobility for women and minority managers.[43]

Staff managers also tend to not receive significant assignments or advanced training. For example, although there are substantial numbers of African American men, women, and Latinos in schools of business (which the students pay for themselves), very few are enrolled in "the prestigious programs paid for by corporations that round out a manager's credentials at a key career point, usually at age 40 or 45. Companies are making only a token investment in developing female and minority executives." For example, only about 3 percent of the participants in Stanford University's Executive Development Program have been women; even fewer have been African Americans or Latinos.[44]

Interestingly, creating racially and gender-segregated sectors of an organization also reduces organizational effectiveness. People who have the same backgrounds and experiences are more prone to problems of "trained incapacity," "groupthink," and communication breakdowns. Organizations with one unit or subculture composed of all upper-class Anglo males and other units or subcultures made up of people with widely differing attributes and experiences tend to have low levels of cross-sector cooperation and high levels of cross-unit communication breakdowns.[45] But upper-managers' preferences for coworkers with whom they are comfortable seem to be more important in promotion decisions than concerns about efficient communication or "objective" decision-making.

The solution to these problems, according to the accommodationist perspective, is for women and members of racial/ethnic minority groups to actively prepare for, seek out, and accept assignments in traditionally Anglo male occupations, industries, and specializations. They should do so even if it means that they will suffer temporary financial losses or personal dislocation and will have to deal with more extensive sexism/racism and sexual/racial harassment than they would experience in more traditional organizations/specialties.[46] Of course, advocates of the accommodationist perspective recognize that career choices that lead people into low power positions are not in themselves a problem. People choose careers for many reasons other than potential financial gain or potential formal rank. A person may choose to be a beautician because it provides an opportunity to be creative, to have flexible hours to spend with family or in volunteer work, or to be her or his own boss. The problem is that our economy in effect requires people to accept a financial penalty for pursuing nonmonetary goals, even when the underrewarded careers, for example, in child care and elementary education, themselves are absolutely necessary to the continuation of our society.[47] But for Anglo women, African Americans, Latinos, or Latinas whose life goals *do* include upward mobility, making power-oriented career choices is presented as a valuable strategy.

A Critique of the Accommodationist Perspective

Since the early to mid-1980s a number of criticisms of the accommodationist perspective have been proposed. The most obvious criticism is that the perspective places virtually all of the burden for effecting change on women and members of minority groups and very little of it on organizations. It becomes very easy to "blame the victim" for her or his lack of success, attributing it to his or her lack of education, training, language skills, or mastery of Anglo male values especially in a culture like ours, which celebrates the Horatio Alger myth that anyone can be a success if he or she works hard enough.[48] Because it is unlikely that major organizational changes will be stimulated by employees with low rank and power, the perspective is simply unrealistic.

A related criticism suggests that accommodation simply has not succeeded as a strategy. Although it may have allowed a very small number of women to move into positions with significant power and responsibility, the vast majority of persons who have adopted the approach have not moved above the glass ceiling. The research on perceptual and attributional processes surveyed earlier in this chapter makes it clear that African Americans, Latinos/Latinas, and Anglo women will never fit in the same way that Anglo men do—equivalent competence and identical behavior simply are not perceived or treated in the same way.[49] As the layoffs of the late 1980s indicated, being just below the glass ceiling provides little more job security or opportunity for further advancement than being far below it does. In fact, widespread faith in the accommodationist perspective has generated a degree of optimism about the situations faced by women that both exaggerates the progress that has been made and obscures the need for attitudinal and institutional reforms that must be made before additional progress can occur.[50]

Kathy Ferguson notes that popular accommodationist books like Margaret Hennig and Ann Jardim's *The Managerial Woman,* Betty Harragan's *Games Your Mother Never Taught You,* and Marilyn Moats Kennedy's *Office Politics,* as well as "outfits like Career Track Seminars" discourage any display of individualism and place great emphasis on uncritical deference to authority, loving money at all costs, defining success solely in terms of upward mobility, and engaging in "lawful deception" as a leadership strategy. Above all else, they tell women to conform, to view their careers in individualistic terms (ignore interpersonal processes, concentrate solely on outcomes, and treat others as objects; in other words, to abandon feminist or feminine values). People who choose to accommodate may succeed in bureaucratic organizations but they do so because accommodationist strategies pose "absolutely no threat to the dominance of bureaucracies over both private and public life."[51]

AN ASSESSMENT OF ACCOMMODATION AND ITS CRITIQUE

A number of scholars have responded to criticisms of the accommodationist perspective. One response is that the critique is relevant only to an extreme version of the accommodationist view. There is substantial evidence that women who break through the glass ceiling have found ways to balance the conformity demands of organizations while maintaining a distinctive style of leading and managing that does not involve abandoning their preferred ways of acting. This seems to be even more true of Latinos and African American men who have moved beyond middle management. They may accept the overall constraints imposed by their organizations, but find ways to create cohesive, high-performing work groups within those constraints. For example, they may maintain a highly structured, unemotional mode of communicating with people outside of their units, but encourage openness and honest communication with their subordinates while providing them with support for creative risk taking.

So, even though the advice given by advocates of the accommodationist perspective recommends almost complete conformity, successful women, African American men and Latinos seem to employ the strategies of accommodation when they are useful while also maintaining their individuality. Of course, it is difficult to maintain this kind of balance between accommodation and innovation, but it is possible. In the short term, for *some* African American men, women, and Latinos, a strategy of accommodating on some issues while resisting on others may allow them to meet their career goals even in large, bureaucratic organizations.[52]

In the long term, balanced innovation has the potential for effecting significant change. It is sufficiently subtle to generate little resistance, while making "small" changes that over the long term will have major "unintended consequences." Eventually, those subtle changes may actually change the power structure of bureaucratic organizations.[53] For example, if the supervisor of one division of an organization successfully implements structural changes like flextime or flexplace, it may serve as a model for other divisions and eventually for the organization as a whole. When significant numbers of women and African American men and Latinos enter organizations they *will* be different, and their organizations eventually and *inevitably will* have to make fundamental changes. When the upper levels of organizational hierarchies begin to include some people who are not Anglo men, new perspectives, values, and ideas will become part of the discourse of upper management. When substantial numbers of Anglo men who have worked successfully with women and persons of color as peers below the glass ceiling, they will bring more positive attitudes with them when *they* move into upper management.[54]

Finally, general economic factors facing American organizations during the 1990s seem promising. Global competition has created a context in which large, bureaucratic, conformity-oriented organizations are failing and are likely to continue to decline in importance. In order to survive, large firms will need to abandon their traditional modes of operating and shift toward systems and procedures that encourage creativity, commitment, and satisfaction. They also will be forced to reward employees based on their contributions and competencies, not on irrelevant factors like race, gender, or ethnicity. Some firms will resist the movement away from bureaucratic forms of organizing and toward an increasingly diverse workforce. They will intensify efforts to get all employees to conform completely to the bureaucratic culture. But if they do not change, they will die.

In their place, small and medium-sized firms will grow and will generate the vast majority of new jobs in the years to come. It is in precisely these kinds of firms that women and African American men, and Latinos found the greatest opportunities during the 1970s and 1980s. And, as Anglo men become a progressively smaller proportion of new employees that are available to firms of all sizes, the opportunities available to other groups will inevitably increase. This final response is the basis of the "managing diversity" perspective, which is examined at length in Chapter 11.

CASE STUDY:
THE HARASSMENT CASE

The 1990s have provided substantial, repeated evidence of how pervasive sexual and racial discrimination and harassment are in U.S. organizations. Professor Anita Hill's testimony during the U.S. Senate confirmation hearings for Supreme Court Justice Clarence Thomas brought the problem into the living rooms of everyone who owns a television set; the U.S. Navy's Tailhook scandal, in which a number of female officers were shoved down a crowded Las Vegas hotel hallway and molested by a large group of Navy aviators; and the forced resignation of Senator Robert Packwood for repeatedly harassing female staff members over more than a decade provided compelling evidence of the extent of the problem for those people who had doubted the veracity of Professor Hill's testimony. By the middle of the decade media reports of allegations of sexual harassment, out-of-court settlements, or convictions became commonplace. In August 1995, Del Labs of Farmingdale, New York, agreed to pay $1.2 million to settle a lawsuit in which CEO Dan Wasong was charged by fifteen employees with touching their breasts and buttocks, asking for oral sex, and using abusive sexual language. In April 1996, the U.S. Equal Employment Opportunity Commission filed a lawsuit against Mitsubishi Motors Corporation for allowing sexual harassment to continue at its Normal, Illinois, assembly plants. In November 1996, charges of rape, coerced sex, and sexual harassment of women trainees at the U.S. Army's Aberdeen (Maryland) Proving Ground led to the publication of past or ongoing sexual harassment cases at Fort Leonard Wood (Missouri) and Fort Hood (Texas). A toll-free hotline set up by the Army after the Aberdeen case became public received more than 4,000 calls reporting cases of harassment during its first ten days of existence. In January 1997, the Publix Grocery store chain announced an out-of-court settlement of a sexual discrimination and harassment case that dwarfs the Del Labs settlement, and, in turn, will be dwarfed by the Mitsubishi case should the plaintiffs eventually be awarded only a fraction of their $150 million claim.

(continued)

(continued from the previous page)

However, my purpose in this case study is not to examine the frequency of racial or sexual harassment. The available evidence suggests that virtually all women and persons of color work in a hostile environment much of their lives. Surveys indicated that at least one-third of female students and employees experience overt sexual harassment; the figure increases to 70–90 percent if researchers explain the legal definition of sexual harassment to their respondents (Wagner, 1992). The legal term "sexual harassment" includes a continuum of behaviors. At one extreme is sexual assault, rape, and "quid pro quo" harassment, where employees are covertly or overtly promised rewards for engaging in sexual activities or threatened to be punished for not doing so. Less extreme activities include touching, groping, or pinching. At the other end of the continuum are symbolic actions—written or oral comments including sexual jokes or lewd comments, or displays like nude pinups or obscene/pornographic displays in electronic media. The less extreme activities are illegal only if (1) they are sufficiently extreme and pervasive that a "reasonable person" would conclude that they create a *hostile and intimidating work environment,* (2) they were unwanted, and (3) they were known by the plaintiff's supervisors, or reasonably could be expected to have been known by them. Consequently, what constitutes a hostile environment varies across different courts and different cases. Some courts have substituted a "reasonable woman" standard for the "reasonable person" standard because there is clear research evidence indicating that women generally perceive a wider range of symbols and behaviors to be unwanted, hostile, or intimidating than do men. Others have ruled that "harassment" must involve men and women while others have ruled that same-sex harassment is illegal.

The Mitsubishi Motors case provides an excellent example of the range of activities that may be illegal. The suit alleges that male workers called their female peers "sluts, whores and bitches;" placed drawing of genitals and breasts and various sexual acts labeled with female employees' names on car fenders and cardboard signs along the assembly lines; explicit sexual graffiti such as "kill the slut Mary" were scrawled on rest-area and bathroom walls and one supervisor declared "I don't want any bitches on my line. Women don't belong in the plant;" anonymous callers made threats like "You better watch your back, bitch" or "Die bitch, you'll be sorry;" women were subjected to groping, forced sex play, and male flashing, one complainant found her car defaced, another was forced off the road as she drove home from work, and in another case a worker put an air gun between a woman worker's legs and pulled the trigger. However, only one of these actions—the supervisor's comment—is *in itself* illegal. Peer harassment is actionable only if supervisors are directly involved, know about, or could be expected to know about, the harassment. The allegations at Mitsubishi also claim that plant management was repeatedly told of the actions and failed to take corrective measures.

(continued)

(continued from the previous page)

Because of the threat of retaliation and intimidation if they complain, and because of the low likelihood of winning harassment cases (it is *very* difficult to produce sufficient evidence to meet the legal requirements) only about 10 percent of targets of harassment actually report the incidents. Fewer still file formal complaints. But my goal is not to examine the legal barriers that exist when women or persons of color attempt to find redress for their grievances, although those barriers are significant and important. The sources listed at the end of this case study provide excellent analyses of both of these issues. Instead, my goal is to briefly summarize the ways in which organizations hide harassment and suppress complaints of harassment.

Not all cases of organizational efforts to suppress complaints are as blatant as Rear Admiral John Snyder's response to helicopter pilot Paula Coughlin's complaints about behavior at the Tailhook convention: "That's what you get when you go to a hotel party with a bunch of drunk aviators." Once Coughlin told her story to the press, the Navy conducted an investigation that was so sloppy that a year later the Navy was not even certain which of its pilots were among the seventy or so involved in the incident. In the end, the Navy investigation recommended punishment for only two aviators, one Australian and one U.S. Marine. Eventually, and again in response to public reports about the sloppiness of the investigation and resulting pressure from the House Armed Services Committee, a number of officers (including Admiral Snyder) were dismissed and the Pentagon took over the investigation (Violanti, 1996).

Because few readers of this case are autoworkers or ever will be naval officers, these examples of harassment may not seem terribly relevant. But there is substantial evidence that college and university students are frequent targets of racial and sexual abuse, and that their experiences and their university's responses are very much like those faced by career women. In all kinds of organizations, harassment is most likely when (1) the organization is dominated by an ideology that defines the "normal" employee as male and encourages strong collegial relationships, (2) the number of Anglo women or persons of color is small and people who are not Anglo men have few sources of support, (3) the organization is loosely coupled (recall Chapter 8), making it difficult to obtain timely corrective action, and (4) the power relationships between supervisors and their subordinates are highly unequal. Of course, each of these factors is present in most colleges and universities. Recently, the *Journal of Applied Communication* (Eadie & Wood, 1992) published a special issue on sexual harassment that included twenty extended verbatim narratives written by people in the discipline of communication who have been sexually harassed. These stories are quite typical of instances of harassment in the academic (and organizational) world. Some of the cases provided summaries of the responses of the survivors' peers and of university administrations that are not unlike the response of the Navy or Mitsubishi's management; three are illustrative.

(continued)

(continued from the previous page)

One new graduate student experienced three instances of unwanted sexual advances by professors. Soon after the third event, she confided in a senior Ph.D. student. Unknown to her, he called a meeting of the other doctoral students to discuss sexual harassment in the department. Although he protected the names of the professors, he revealed her identity. The doctoral students took no action, because many of them were working closely with a professor who had a reputation for harassment, and they did not want to make him uncomfortable (he was not one of the three). Because she could not even count on support from her peers, she decided not to pursue the matter any further (p. 367).

In a second case, the chair of a department told about a case that still is in progress. A woman student complained about actions by a professor that were both improper and illegal, although she did not file criminal charges. When the department chair first heard about the charge, she did not believe it. After all, the professor projected the image of an innocent choirboy and had recently published an essay in the school newspaper that provided a "feminist" analysis of sexual harassment. His outspoken support of women's issues had earned him strong support among women faculty. After a lengthy hearing, during which the professor received a leave of absence with pay (in most universities, these are highly sought-after awards, not punishments), he signed a statement admitting guilt and was allowed to return to normal duties provided he had no further contact with the student, would do nothing else to create an intimidating environment for women students, and would not socialize with students for a year. Although he has already violated the latter two terms, the administration has taken no action. His department chair has been "gagged" by the university's administration. If she were to warn any potential employers about his history she could lose her job, although she now knows he has been guilty of similar behavior at other universities. He was even dismissed from graduate school for sexual harassment, but that case too was kept confidential. Soon he will be looking for a new professorship. She concludes: "He will do a wonderful interview. You (other professors) will like him. Chances are you will hire him."

In a third case, a new assistant professor accepted a job in a department with a department chair who was reputed to be politically liberal. After two years on the job she felt secure enough to complain about her chair's repeated sexist comments and jokes:

Once, when I was advising a senior major, he stopped by my opened door, looked at me, and then turned and asked the student, "Are there any cute girls in your (sorority) house?" She blushed and turned to me. "You shouldn't say that!" I retorted. "Oh, I'm sorry. Are there any cute tarts? Are there any cute wenches?" he quipped. I yelled his name emphatically, "You know that's inappropriate." "I guess you think it's harassment (it is) and you're writing it down," he responded as he smiled and walked away. The professor complained about the event in a private meeting with the affirmative action officer and asked

(continued)

(continued from the previous page)

specifically that her identity not be revealed. Less than an hour later the officer revealed her identity to the department chair.

Eventually she was not reappointed to her position, although her performance had been excellent, and was refused access to written evaluations of her work. The university administration alerted the professor to irregularities in her case, but it did not want to overrule the department and granted her a probationary contract. Shortly before her final tenure review, one of her female colleagues filed a sexual harassment complaint against the chair. The female provost (a position equivalent to vice president in private-sector organizations) advised the professor not to support her colleague. With no support, her colleague resigned. The following year the professor was denied tenure. But in this case, the university administration overruled the department's decision and appointed the professor chair of her department.

As these cases suggest, successful complaints against professors for sexual harassment are quite rare. By the time action is taken, students often have completed their coursework with the harasser or have graduated. Universities often conduct harassment investigations in private, do not notify victims of the date and times of hearings or allow them to testify, and fail to inform the students of any actions taken against the harasser. The rationale for maintaining secrecy typically is that the matter is a personnel action and that the accused harasser deserves the protection of academic due process. If the university is a public institution, the professor also may be protected by the free speech considerations. But given the unequal power relationship that exists between harassers and targets, this conspiracy of silence primarily protects the university and the harasser from public embarrassment. More important, it lulls people into complacency that harassment is not a problem, creates skepticism and mistrust of the system among students (which mitigates against victims filing complaints), and leads victims to believe that they are alone in having been harassed, thus encouraging them (and others) to blame themselves. And the cult of secrecy ensures that the university will never face any organized pressure to eliminate harassment of students.

Consequently in the landmark *Meritor* case, the U.S. Supreme Court ruled that targets of harassment can take legal action against their employers (or universities, in later rulings) without following internal procedures, although not doing so makes it more difficult to demonstrate that supervisors knew or should have known about the harassment. The reason for the court's decision is simple: it realized that those procedures rarely work.

Discussion Questions

1. At a number of points in this book I have suggested that bureaucratic organizations typically suppress dissent, avoid conflicts, and restrict the flow

(continued)

(continued from the previous page)

of negative information. To what extent is the silence surrounding sexual or racial harassment simply another example of communication breakdowns in organizations? To what extent is it a function of racist or sexist attitudes? How might the two be interrelated?

2. Recently the U.S. Supreme Court has ruled that sexual harassment of students violates Title IX of the Civil Rights Act and that women can now collect monetary damages from universities if they are harassed. What impact is this ruling likely to have on universities and their handling of sexual harassment cases?

General Sources:

S. Bingham (Ed.), *Conceptualizing Sexual Harassment as Discursive Practice* (Westport, CT: Praeger, 1994).

Robin Clair, "The Use of Framing Devices to Sequester Organizational Narratives," *Communication Monographs, 60* (1993): 113-136.

William Eadie and Julia Wood (Eds.), *Journal of Applied Communication Research, 20* (1992): v-418.

G. Kreps (Ed.), *Sexual Harassment: Communication Implications* (Cresskill, NJ: Hampton Press, 1993).

David Terpstra and Douglas Baker, "Outcomes of Sexual Harassment Charges," *Academy of Management Journal, 31* (1988): 185-194.

Specific Cases:

*Michelle Violanti, "Hooked on Expectations: An Analysis of Influence and Relationships in the Tailhook Reports," *Journal of Applied Communication Research, 24* (1996): 67-82.

Colleges and Universities:

Robin Clair, "The Bureaucratization, Commodification, and Privatization of Sexual Harassment Through Institutional Discourse," *Management Communication Quarterly, 7* (1993): 12-157.

Charles Conrad and Bryan Taylor, "The Contexts of Sexual Harassment: Power, Silences and Academe," in *Conceptualizing Sexual Harassment as Discursive Practice,* Shereen Bingham, ed. (Westport, CT: Praeger, 1994).

B.W. Dziech, and L. Weiner, *The Lecherous Professor,* 2nd ed. (Urbana, IL: University of Illinois Press, 1990).

Paul Mongeau and Jennifer Blalock, "Student Evaluations of Instructor Immediacy and Sexually Harassing Behaviors: An Experimental Investigation," *Journal of Applied Communication Research, 22* (1994): 256-272.

M.A. Paludi and R.B. Barickman, *Academic and Workplace Sexual Harassment* Albany, NY: SUNY, 1991).

NOTES

[1] In fact, some studies indicate that organizational structures and differences in opportunities have an even greater effect on the experiences of different groups of employees than do societal assumptions. See R. Downey and M.S. Lahey, "Women in Management," in *Career Growth and Human Resource Strategies,* M. London and E.M. Mone, eds. (New York: Quorum Books, 1988); G. Moore, "Structural Determinants of Men's and Women's Personal Networks," *American Sociological Review, 55* (1990): 726–735; Sonia Ospina, *Illusions of Opportunity* (Ithaca, NY: Cornell University Press, 1996); S. Riger and P. Galligan, "Women in Management," *American Psychologist, 10* (1989): 902–910; and L. Smith-Lovin and M.J. McPherson, "You Are Who You Know," in *Theory on Gender/Feminism on Theory,* Paula England, ed. (New York: Aldine, 1993).

[2] See Linda Blum and Vicki Smith, "Women's Mobility in the Corporation," *Signs, 13* (1988): 528–545; and Linda Smircich, Marta Calas, and Gareth Morgan (eds.), *Academy of Management Review, 17* (1992): 404–611.

[3] See a survey by Catalyst, Inc., *Houston Chronicle,* 10/18/96, 3c; Stephen B. Knouse, Paul Rosenfeld, and Amy L. Culbertson, "Hispanics and Work"; Arthur Cresce, "Hispanic Work Force Characteristics"; and Cordelia W. Reimers, "Hispanic Earnings and Employment in the 1980s," all in *Hispanics in the Workplace,* P. Knouse, P. Rosenfeld, and A. Culbertson, eds. (Newbury Park, CA: Sage, 1992); and D.L. Munoz, "Myths, Facts, Reality on "The Hispanic Decade of the '80's," *La Prensa San Diego,* January 19, 1990, pp. 1–2.

[4] G.W. Bowman, N.B. Worthy, and S.A. Greyser, "Are Women Executives People," *Harvard Business Review 43* (July-August 1965): 15–28, 164–178; and C.D. Sutton and K.K. Moore, "Executive Women—20 Years Later," *Harvard Business Review, 63* (September-October 1985), 43–66; Patricia Aburdene and John Naisbitt, *Megatrends for Women* (New York: Villard Books, 19920: Laura Mansnerus, "Why Women are Leaving the Law," *Working Woman,* April 1993. The employment rates, incomes, and mobility of Latinos who have immigrated from Central or South America or from Cuba during the late 1950s and 1960s (or whose parents did so) are much greater than for Mexican American males. In general, those immigrants were educated, successful, English-speaking members of the middle or upper class in their own countries, and had matured in a cultural context in which they were treated as normal, capable individuals. As a result, they had both the positive self-esteem and the skills necessary to succeed in an Anglo-dominated society.

In contrast, Mexican Americans and recent Cuban immigrants are a much more representative sample of their home country's populations, and a much larger percentage of Mexican American and of young Cuban American employees were born and educated in the United States. Maturing in an Anglo-dominated society reduces self-esteem. The limited educational opportunities provided African American and Latino/Latina children in U.S. schools reduces achievement levels.

[5] Catalyst, *Catalyst's Study of Women in Corporate America,* New York, 1991. See Gary Powell, *Women and Men in Management,* 2nd ed. (Newbury Park, CA: Sage, 1993) for pre-1992 data and Lynn Martin, *Pipelines of Progress* (Washington, DC: U.S. Department of Labor, August 1992, pp. 13, 17); and *Hearings* for more recent data. Also see Anne Harlan and Carol Weiss, "Sex Differences in Factors Affecting Managerial Career Advancement, in *Women in the Workplace,* Phyllis Wallace, ed. (Boston: Auburn House, 1982); William Bielby and James Baron, "Men and Women at Work," *American Journal of Sociology, 91* (1986): 87–90; and Barbara Reskin and Patricia Roos, "Status Hierarchies and Sex Segregation," in *Ingredients for Women's Employment Policy,* C. Bose and G. Spitze, eds. (New York: SUNY Press, 1987). For more extensive summaries of perceptual data, see Judi Pearson, R.L. West and L.H. Turner, *Gender and Communication* (Dubuque, IA: Brown and Benchmark, 1995).

[6] See Taylor Cox, Jr., and Stella Nkomo, "Differential Performance Appraisal Criteria," *Group and Organization Studies, 11* (1986): 101–117; Fernandez, *Life; Hearings,* p. 29; and M.N. Vamos, ed., Business Week/Harris Exceecutive Poll," *Business Week* (June 8, 1992): 77; R. Scherer, "First National Survey of Minority Views Shows Deep Racial Polarization in the US," *Christian Science Monitor,* (March, 1994); and D. Brown, and D.A. Jepsen, "The Opinions of Minorities about Preparing for Work," *The Career Development Quarterly, 40* (1991): 5–19. Sheri Prasso, "Study: Stereotypes Hinder Female Executives," *Houston Chronicle,* 2/29/96, B1 and Cose, 1993.

[7] L.M. Sixel, *Houston Chronicle*, 7/19/96, C1; L.J. Bradford and C. Raines, *Twentysomething: Managing and Motivating Today's New Work Force* (New York: Master Media, Ltd., 1992).

[8] Competitive pressures seem to explain why acceptance of gay and lesbian employees seems to be taking place most rapidly in high-tech and entertainment firms (Evan Ramstad [AP], *Bryan/College Station Eagle*, 9/22/96, E6.)

[9] Kathleen Kelley Reardon, *They Don't Get It, Do They?* (Boston: Little, Brown and Co., 1995), p. 10; also see O.C. Brenner, Joseph Tomkiewicva, and Virginia Schein, "The Relationship Between Sex Role Stereotypes and Requisite Management Characteristics Revisited," *Academy of Management Journal*, (1989): 668. Unfortunately, the higher he is, the more likely it is that he holds negative attitudes about African Americans (Fernandez, *Racism and Sexism*), evidently because older persons are more likely to have internalized racist attitudes.

[10] Catalyst. A similar conclusion was drawn by Secretary of Labor Martin (*Glass*, p. 18).

[11] Anita Blair, *Houston Chronicle*, 7/8/96, 15A; Charles Boisseau, "Ranks of Female Businesses Soar," *Houston Chronicle*, 1/30/96, 1c); Arne Kalleberg and Kevin Leicht, "Gender and Organizational Performance," *Academy of Management Journal*, (1991): 157.

[12] U.S. Representative Susan Molinari explained that women succeed at lower and middle management because of their technical expertise. "The barrier appears at the higher levels, when women must exercise leadership power. Then apprehension among male seniors arises, and women are prevented from moving up the corporate ladder by male attitudes and stereotypical roles for professional women" *Hearings*, p. 27). For insightful analyses of the glass ceiling, see Patrice Buzzanell, "Reframing the Glass Ceiling as a Socially Constructed Process," *Communication Monographs, 62* (1995): 327–354; Peter T. Kilborn, "For Many in Work Force, Glass Ceiling Still Exists," *New York Times*, 16 March, 1995; Pan Suk Kim and Gregory Lewis, "Asian Americans in the Public Service," *Public Administration Review, 54* (1994): 285–290; Paul Page, "African Americans in Executive Branch Agencies," *Review of Public Personnel Administration, 14* (1994): 24–51.

[13] Martin, *Pipeline*, p. 4. Also see U.S. Department of Labor, *The American Workforce: 1992–2005* (Washington, D.C.: Government Printing Office, USDL Bulletin N. 2452, 1994.

[14] Gary Powell and D.A. Butterfield, "Investigating the 'Glass Ceiling' Phenomenon," *Academy of Management Journal, 37* (1994): 68–86; J. H. Greenhaus, S. Parasuraman, and W. M. Wormley, "Effects of Race on Organizational Experiences, Job Performance Evaluations, and Career Outcomes," *Academy of Management Journal, 33* (1990): 64–86. M. F. Karsten has noted that eight explanations have been proposed for the glass ceiling: (1) women have not been in the managerial "pipeline" long enough; (2) upper-level managers prefer to be surrounded by people like themselves, and thus tend to promote other middle- and upper-class white males; (3) women prefer to be self-employed and tend to opt out of long career paths; (4) sex segregation (what I later will label "*glass walls*"); (5) career interruptions; (6) the interactional climate that exists in most organizations combined with the scarcity of same-sex and/or same-race mentors and role models); (7) complications regarding balancing work and family; and (8) discrimination (*Management and Gender* [Westport, CT: Quorum Books, 1994]). Because the numbers of women in the management pipeline have reached a "critical mass," explanations other than discrimination will be confirmed or disconfirmed during the 1990s (Tom Daniels, Barry Spiker, and Micahel Papa, *Perspectives on Organizational Communication* [Dubuque, IA: Brown and Benchmark, 1997]. For analyses of glass ceilings for non-Anglo women, see Martin, *Pipeline*, p. 28; and Martin, *Glass*, p. 7.

[15] Reardon; Michele Galen and Ann Therese Palmer, "White, Male and Worried," *Business Week* (January 31, 1994): 50–55; Edwards and Polite; Calvin O. Pressley, "Preface," in Randolph W. Cameron, *The Minority Executive's Handbook* (New York: Warner Books, 1989); and Anne Fisher, "When Will Women Get to the Top," *Fortune* (Sept. 21, 1992): 44–56; Jamieson and O'Mara.

[16] Boslego Carter, "Women's Recent Progress in the Professions, or Women Get a Ticket to Ride After the Gravy Train Has Left the Station," *Feminist Studies, 7* (Fall 1981): 477–518; Susan Faludi, *Backlash: The Undeclared War Against American Women* (New York: Crown, 1991); John Fernandez, "Racism and Sexism in Corporate America," in *Ensuring Minority Success in Corporate Management*, Donna Thompson and Nancy DiTomaso, eds. (New York: Plenum, 1988); and Martin, *Pipeline*, p. 21. Based on her studies of workplace violence, Charlene Solomon has concluded that "the workplace probably is going to be the major site of ethnoviolent conflict throughout the 1990s" ("Keeping Hate Out of the Workplace," *Personnel Journal*

(July, 1992): 30–35; also see M.W. Zak, "It's Like a Prison in There," *Journal of Business and Technical Communication, 8* (1994): 282–298.

[17] Reardon; Kathy Ferguson, "Feminism and Bureaucratic Discourse," *New Political Science, 11* (Spring, 1983): 61–62. For a more extensive analysis, see Ferguson, *The Feminist Case Against Bureaucracy* (Philadelphia: Temple University Press, 1984), especially pp. 61–62. This book is the single best critique of the accommodationist perspective. A more recent but similar analysis is presented by Blum and Smith. Although the vast majority of the background material that I use in the remainder of this chapter involves research on (primarily Anglo) women, research on specific strategies (for example, networking or mentoring) does exist for African Americans and Latino/Latina persons. I include this latter research at appropriate points in the analysis, although it is important to remember that the overall "accommodationist" perspective was developed with women managers and professionals in mind.

[18] Edwards and Polite; A. Rizzo and C. Mendez, *The Integration of Women in Management* (New York: Quorum Books, 1990).

[19] See Dennis Mumby and Linda Putnam, "The Politics of Emotion: A Feminist Reading of Bounded Rationality," *Academy of Management Review, 17* (1992): 465–486; and Arlie Hochshild, *The Managed Heart* (Berkeley: University of California Press, 1983). The magazine *Savvy* regularly provides advice on emotion control and image management, as does Betty Harragan's column in *Working Woman*.

[20] See Rosabeth Moss Kanter, *Men and Women of the Corporation* (New York: Harper & Row, 1977), especially Chapter 7.

[21] See Uma Sekaran, *Dual Career Families* (San Francisco: Jossey-Bass, 1986), especially Chapter 4. Also see Arlie Hochschild, *The Second Shift* (New York: Viking, 1989); Rosabeth Moss Kanter, *Work and Family in the United States* (New York: Russell Sage, 1977); Robert Seidenberg, *Corporate Wives, Corporate Casualties?* (Reading, MA: Addison-Wesley, 1979); D. Hall and F. Hall, "Stress and the Two-Career Couple," in *Current Concerns in Occupational Stress,* Cary Cooper and Roy Payne, eds. (New York: John Wiley, 1980); Katherine Walker and Margaret Woods, *Time Use* (Washington, D.C.: The American Home Economic Association, 1976); and Smith, p. 194. Also see Michael Geerken and Walter Gove, *At Home and at Work* (Beverly Hills, CA: Sage, 1983); Basia Hellwig, "The Breakthrough Generation," *Working Woman,* April 1985; R. Berk and S. F. Berk, *Labor and Leisure at Home* (Newbury Park, CA: Sage, 1979).

[22] See, for example, Ann Morrison, Randall White, and Ellen Van Velsor, *Breaking the Glass Ceiling* (Reading, MA: Addison-Wesley, 1987).

[23] Korn/Ferry International, "The Decade of the Executive Woman," New York: 1993); *Houston Chronicle,* 2/19/96, B1.

[24] Kanter, *Corporation;* Martin, *Glass*.

[25] Morrison, White, and Van Velsor. For extended analyses of the visibility paradox, see Daniels, et al.; L. C. Hackamach and A. B. Solid, "The Woman Executive—There Is Still Ample Room for Progress," *Business Horizons* (April 1972): 89–93; Katherine Miller, *Organizational Communication,* (Belmont, CA: Wadsworth, 1994); Morrison and von Glinow; Powell; E.B. Schwartz and J.J. Rago, "Beyond Tokenism," *Business Horizons* (December 1973): 69–76; and Virginia Schein, "The Relationship Between Sex-Role Stereotypes and Requisite Managerial Characteristics," *Journal of Applied Psychology, 57* (1973): 95–100. Similar conclusions are supported regarding persons of color in Knouse, et al., eds., *Hispanics;* Philomena Essed, "Understanding Verbal Accounts of Racism," *Text, 8* (1988): 5–40 and *Everyday Racism,* trans. Cynthia Jaffe, (Claremont, CA: Hunter House, 1990). A more recent version of this book was published as *Understanding Everyday Racism* (Newbury Park, CA: Sage, 1991).

[26] Lynn Miller, Linda Cooke, Jennifer Tsang, and Faith Morgan, "Should I Brag," *Human Communication Research,* (1992): 364–399.

[27] William O'Barr and B. Atkins, "Women's Language or 'Powerless Language," in S. McConnell-Ginet, R. Borker and N. Furnam (Eds.), *Women and Language in Literature and Society* (New York: Praeger, 1980; Cheris Kramarae, *Men and Women Speaking* (Rowley, MA: Newbury House, 1984); Charles Berger, "Social Power and Interpersonal Communication," in *Handbook of Interpersonal Communication,* Mark Knapp and Gerald Miller, (eds.) (Beverly Hills, CA: Sage, 1985).

[28] This is likely to also be true for Latinos/Latinas, but there is little directly relevant research. See John Dovidio, Samuel Gaertner, Phyllis Anastasio, and Rasyid Sanitioso, "Cogni-

tive and Motivational Bases of Bias," in Knouse, et al., eds., *Hispanics;* and Essed, *Everyday.* For evidence of continuing overt racism, see Robert Vecchio, "Worker Alienation as a Moderator of the Job Quality-Job Satisfaction Relationship," *Academy of Management Journal, 23* (1980): 479–486; and E. Konar, "Explain Racial Differences in Job Satisfaction," *Journal of Applied Psychology, 66* (1981): 522–534; also see Cox and Nkomo; Clay Hamner, J.S. Kim, L. Baird, and W.J. Bigoness, "Race and Sex as Determinants of Ratings by Potential Employers in a Simulated Work-Sampling Task," *Journal of Applied Psychology, 59* (1974): 705–711; R.W. Beatty, "Blacks as Supervisors," *Academy of Management Journal, 16* (1973): 196–206; Fernandez, *Life;* and Huck and Bray, 1976. For an excellent case study of these processes in action, see Clayton Alderfer, Charleen Alderfer, Leota Tucker, and Robert Tucker, "Diagnosing Race Relations in Management," *Journal of Applied Behavioral Science, 16* (1980): 135–166.

[29] Dovidio, et al., p. 85. For additional evidence of covert bias in performance appraisals, particularly in real organizations, see K. Kraiger and J. Ford, "A Meta-Analysis of Ratee Race Effects in Performance Ratings," *Journal of Applied Psychology, 70* (1985): 56–65.

[30] Martin, *Hearings,* p. 29. For summaries of perceptions of women and persons of color, see Denise Segura, "Walking on Eggshells: Chicanas in the Labor Force," and Dovidio, et al., both in Knouse, et al., eds., *Hispanics;* L. Benjamin, "Black Women Achievers," *Sociological Inquiry, 52* (1982): 141–151; and A. Smith and A. Stewart, "Approaches to Studying Racism and Sexism in Black Women's Lives," *Journal of Social Issues, 39* (1983): 1–15. Sociologists long have debated the extent to which the cumulative effects of racism and sexism are additive or even more constraining than the additive model suggests. Stella Nkomo has provided a thorough but brief summary of this debate in "The Black Female Manager," in *Women's Careers: Pathways and Pitfalls,* Suzanna Rose and Laurie Larwood, eds. (New York: Praeger, 1988). Her conclusion is that the effects are more than additive. Segura provides a similar analysis of the situations faced by Chicanas. Rosabeth Moss Kanter, *A Tale of "O": On Being Different in an Organization* (New York: Harper & Row, 1980) provides an excellent analysis of the effects of being "different," as do Harlan and Weiss and Dovidio, et al.

[31] Karsten.

[32] Clare Burton, "Merit and Gender," in Mills and Tancred, eds.; V. O'Leary and R. Hansen, "Trying Hurts Women, Helps Men: The Meaning of Effort," in *Women in the Workforce,* H.J. Bernardin, ed. (New York: Praeger, 1982); and S. Kessler, D.J. Ashenden, R.W. Connell, and G.W. Dowsett, "Gender Relations in Secondary Schooling," *Sociology of Education, 58* (1985): 42–58; Marjorie Nadler and Larry Nadler, "Feminization of Public Relations," in Cynthia Berryman-Fink, D. Ballard-Reich, and L.H. Newman, eds., *Communication and Sex-role Socialization* (New York: Garland Publishing Company, 1993). Supervisors' confidence in their evaluations is examined in Stella Nkomo, "The Emperor Has No Clothes: Rewriting Race in Organizations," *Academy of Management Review, 17* (1992): 487–512; Thomas Pettigrew, "New Black-White Patterns," *Annual Review of Sociology, 11* (1985): 329–346; G. Green and T.R. Mitchell, "Attributional Processes of Leaders in Leader-Member Interactions," *Organizational Behavior and Human Performance, 23* (1979): 429–458; K. Deaux and T. Emswiller, "Explanations of Successful Performance on Sex-linked Tasks," *Journal of Personality and Social Psychology, 29* (1974): 80–85; and J. Feldman-Summers and J.B. Kiesler, "Those Who Are Number Two Try Harder," *Journal of Personality and Social Psychology, 62* (1977): 29–33. Problems related to perceptions and explanations of success are the bases of advice often given women to enter careers in sales or merchandising. The assumption is that these occupations provide employees with quantifiable and easily communicated evidence of their success. To the extent that objective data are available, differential attribution of success is a less serious problem.

[33] For related research on women, see Morrison, White, and Van Velsor; Margaret Hennig and Ann Jardim, *The Managerial Woman* (New York: Pocket Books, 1976); Kathryn Ring, "Behind Every Successful Woman . . . There's a Mentor," *Women in Business* (July-August 1978): 9–11; Jacqueline Thompson, "Corporate Survival," *Essence* (August 1978): 82, 122–123; Raymond Noe, "Women and Mentoring," *Academy of Management Review, 13* (1988): 65–78; and Kathy Kram, *Mentoring* (Chicago: Scott, Foresman, 1986). For work on African Americans, see David Thomas and Clayton Alderfer, "The Influence of Race on Career Dynamics," in *Handbook of Career Theory* (New York: McGraw-Hill, 1989), and on Hispanics, see Stephen Knouse, "The Mentoring Process for Hispanics," in Knouse, et al., eds. This essay provides an extensive summary of the complications and values of mentor relationships for Hispanic employees, as does Dickens and Dickens for African Americans.

[34] Linda Hill and Nancy Kamprath, "Beyond the Myth of the Perfect Mentor," Teaching Note 9–491–096, Harvard Business School, 1991. Informal mentoring systems tend to exclude African Americans and Latinos/Latinas, and to a somewhat lesser degree, white women (David Thomas, "The Impact of Race on Managers' Experiences of Developmental Relationships (Mentoring and Sponsorship)," *Journal of Organizational Behavior, 2* (1990): 479–492; Assistant Secretary of Labor Vartanian, *Hearings,* p. 13.

[35] Dovidio, et al.; L.W. Fitt and D.A. Newton, "When the Mentor Is a Man and the Protege Is a Woman," *Harvard Business Review, 59* (March-April 1981): 3–4.

[36] Nkomo, "The Black Female Manager;" Herminia Ibarra, "Personal Networks of Women and Minorities in Management," *Academy of Management Review, 18* (1993): 56–87; Also see B.R. Ragins and D.B. McFarlin, "Perceptions of Mentor Roles in Cross-Gender Mentoring Relationships," *Journal of Vocational Behavior, 37* (1990): 321–339; G.F. Dreeher and R.A. Ash, "A Comparative Study of Mentoring Among Men and Women in Managerial, Professional, and Technical Positions," *Journal of Applied Psychology, 75* (1990): 539–546; R. Keele, "Mentoring or Networking?" in *Not as Far as You Think,* Linda L. Moore, ed. (Lexington, MA: Lexington Books, 1986); A.K. Missirian, *The Corporate Connection* (Englewood Cliffs, NJ: Prentice-Hall, 1982); Noe; B.R. Ragins, "Barriers to Mentoring," *Human Relations, 42* (1989): 1–22; and Thomas and Alderfer.

[37] Jamieson and O'Mara.

[38] A.A. Blumrosen, *Affirmative Action Programs and Claims of Reverse Discrimination* (New York: American Civil Liberties Union, 1995); Hennig and Jardim; Ibarra, "Networks." This is the primary reason why the federal courts (including the U.S. Supreme Court) recently ruled that the Virginia Military Institute and the Citadel could no longer be all-male universities. Both universities embed their students in communication networks that give them career advantages in their states. Consequently, even universities with identical curricula and so on would not provide women students with the career opportunities that male students at VMI and the Citadel receive. Edwards and Polite discuss the positive impact that networks have had on the careers of successful African American employees and summarize the key features of successful networks (*Children of the Dream: The Psychology of Black Success* ([New York: Doubleday, 1992]). Randolph Cameron provides a list of major formal networking organizations for African American and Latino/Latina employees (*The Minority Executive's Handbook* [New York: Warner, 1989]).

[39] Karen Sacks, "Networking: When Potluck is Political," *MS, 11* (April 1983): 97–98.

[40] Martin, *Pipeline,* p. 16. Also see U.S. Bureau of the Census, *Population Reports* (Washington, D.C.: Government Printing Office, 1987, 1992).

[41] Powell; John H. Stanfield, II, "Commentary: The Race Politics of Knowledge Production," *Research in Social Policy, 2* (1990): 177–194 and "Racism in America and in Other Race-Centered Nation-States," *International Journal of Comparative Sociology, XXXII* (1991): 243–260. In an extensive study, M.M. Marini and M.C. Brinton found that 86 percent of male high school students aspired to traditionally male occupations, while only 4 percent wanted to enter traditionally female careers. In contrast, 53 percent of the female high school students aspired to feminine careers, while 35 percent wanted to enter traditionally male fields. Almost all of the boys *expected* to enter the careers they wanted, but one-third of the girls anticipated that they would not be able to do so. High school girls seem to realize that there are greater constraints on their aspirations than there are on those of men ("Sex Typing in Occupational Socialization," in *Sex Segregation in the Workplace,* B.F. Reskin, ed. (Washington, D.C.: National Academy Press, 198); M.M. Marini and E. Greenberger, "Sex Differences in Occupational Aspirations and Expectations," *Sociology of Work and Occupations, 5* (1968): 147–178; and Louse Kapp Howe, *Pink Collar Workers* (New York: Putnam's, 1977).

Even within high-income occupations such as medicine, a disproportionate number of women specialize in psychiatry or pediatrics, whereas relatively few concentrate on surgery or gynecology. The group of "women's specialties" has lower salaries than the group of "male" concentrations, even though they require comparable education, training, and skills. Overall, approximately one-fourth of the income difference between men and women can be attributed to occupational differences, although it is a far more important factor for college graduates than for other employees.

[42] Bielby and Baron; Reskin and Roos; Martin, *Glass,* p. 16. Also see "Race in the Workplace," *Business Week,* July 8, 1991; and *Hearings,* p. 46. This dynamic often leads women to play "wifely" roles—handling details, performing tasks that carry no rewards, serving as cheer-

leaders—in their organizations (Anne Huff, "Wives of the Organization," paper presented at the Women and Work Conference, Arlington, TX, May 11, 1990). It is especially problematic for African American women and Latinas (Denise Segura, in Knouse, et al.)

[43] Ironically, men who enter stereotypically female occupations seem to advance more rapidly than they would in traditionally male fields. Their coworkers seem to realize that having a male supervisor would provide their unit with more influence among upper managers and so support their being promoted. So, instead of facing a glass ceiling, they encounter a glass escalator up the hierarchy. Of course, they also face significant cultural biases against their being involved in nontraditional occupations, perhaps even more so than women do. See R.A. Zaldivar, "Men Tiptoeing Their Way into Women's Work," *Houston Chronicle,* January 26, 1997, 1E.

[44] *Business Week,* October 1991; and Martin, *Pipeline,* p. 8.

[45] Jorge Chapa, "Creating and Improving Linkages Between the Tops and Bottoms," paper presented at the Organizational Innovation Conference, Humphrey Institute of Public Affairs, University of Minnesota, Minneapolis, September, 1992; Ospina; B. Schneider, S. Gunnarson, and J. Wheeler, "The Role of Opportunity in the Conceptualization and Measurement of Job Satisfaction," in C.J. Crannay, et al., eds. *Job Satisfaction* (New York: Lexington Books, 1992); *Houston Chronicle,* 10/18/96, 3C; Korn/Ferry; Julie Lopez Amparano, "Study Says Women Face Glass Walls as Well as Glass Ceilings," *Wall Street Journal,* 3 March, 1992.

[46] Morrison, White, and Van Velsor.

[47] Carol Gilligan, *In a Different Voice* (Cambridge, MA: Harvard University Press, 1982).

[48] Nkomo, "Emperor." See John Cawelti, *Disciples of the Self-Made Man* (Cambridge: Harvard University Press, 1974) for a discussion of the Horatio Alger myth in American culture. Many advocates of the accommodationist model have recognized this weakness. For example, the Center for Creative Leadership recently published a sequel to *Breaking the Glass Ceiling* that focuses on changes that organizations must make to remove barriers to the advancement of women and persons of color (see Ann M. Morrison, *The New Leaders: Guidelines of Leadership Diversity in America* [San Francisco: Jossey-Bass, 1992]). A second edition of the original book, which addresses this issue, is in preparation.

[49] Burton.

[50] Blum and Smith, p. 529. Also see Calas and Smircich, "Liaisons"; Marta Calas, S. Jacobson, R. Jacques, and L. Smirich, "Is a Woman-Centered Theory of Management Dangerous?," paper presented at the Academy of Management Convention, Miami, August 1991; and J. Fletcher, "Feminist Standpoint Research and Management Science," unpublished manuscript, Northeastern University, June 1992.

[51] Ferguson, "Discourse," p. 69, also see Ferguson, *Case,* pp. 182–195; and Blum and Smith.

[52] The specific strategies for maintaining an appropriate balance are complex. Because "self-help" books for African Americans and Latinos/Latinas were written after the accommodationist perspective declined in popularity, they provide extensive advice on how manage the innovator role. For example, Dickens and Dickens argue that eventually all African American employees will need to confront their supervisors over issues of racism and provide extended advice about when, how, and over what specific issues to do so. Many of the other sources cited in this chapter provide similar advice. Interestingly, self-help books oriented toward white women rarely provide advice about how subordinates should confront their supervisors over issues of sexism, except perhaps in cases of overt sexual harassment, perhaps because they are written from a more completely accommodationist perspective. For an analysis of how African American women implement the "balancing act," see Ella Louise Bell, "The Bicultural Life Experience of Career-Oriented Black Women," *Journal of Organizational Behavior, 11* (1990): 459–477.

[53] See Linda Putnam, "Feminist Theories, Dispute Processes, and Organizational Communication" and Betsy Bach, "Making a Difference by Doing Differently," papers presented at the Arizona State University Conference on Organizational Communication: Perspectives for the 1990s, Tempe, AZ, April 1990; and Connie Bullis, "At Least It's a Start," in *Communication Yearbook 16,* Stanley Deetz, ed. (Newbury Park, CA: Sage, 1993).

[54] Critics of the accommodationist perspective might respond to this somewhat optimistic prediction by arguing that there is little evidence that white women maintain a sense of solidarity with other women, and particularly with African American or Latino women once they break through the glass ceiling. The same kind of dynamic has been observed of successful neoconservative African American men. Accommodation encourages people to identify with organizational

powerholders. To the extent that they do so, they distance themselves from employees who are not white men (recall the discussion of identification in Chapter 6). If their organizations also artificially limit the number of nonwhite men who move into upper-level positions, successful women and minority candidates are encouraged to compete more intensely with other women and minority men than with all employees, thus making it even less likely that they will maintain a high level of solidarity with people who are similar to themselves. And, if organizational powerholders choose to fulfill their commitments to diversity by promoting members of only one group—and typically the one group is white women—it drives a further wedge between disadvantaged groups. These concerns are developed in most detail in work related to women. See, for example, Essed, *Racism;* Audre Lorde, "Nobody Said It Was Simple," in *Common Differences: Conflicts in Black and White Feminist Perspectives,* Gloria Joseph and Jill Lewis, eds. (New York: Anchor, 1981); bell hooks, *Ain't I a Woman? Black Women and Feminism* (Boston: South End Press, 1981) and *Feminist Theory: From Margin to Center* (Boston: South End Press, 1984); and Patricia Hill Collins, "Learning from the Outsider Within: The Sociological Significance of Black Feminist Thought," *Social Problems, 33* (1986): S14–S32.

Chapter 11

COMMUNICATION, GENDER, RACE, AND ETHNICITY: MANAGING DIVERSITY?

Eighty-five percent of the net growth in the workforce between today and the year 2000 will be women and members of minority groups. By 2005 more than half of California's population will be people of color who speak more than 80 languages. (Every year since 1992 less than 50 percent of Texas' first graders have been Anglo.) We have moved from an era in which large portions of the workforce were assumed to be similar, and those who were different were expected to adapt, to an era when the workforce is composed of many different individuals, each of whom wants to be supported and valued. In the past, there was a dominant majority in the workforce. Attention, policies, and management practices were all focused on the "average" worker—the white male with a homemaker wife and children. Today, as the sheer numbers of nontraditional workers grow, so does their impact and influence. While concern about workforce diversity is high, it has generally not been matched by action. The number of companies with specific programs to address diversity issues is relatively small. Few report involvement in support groups, mentoring programs, or English as a second language training, and only slightly over 25 percent are training supervisors to effectively manage a diverse group of employees.

—DAVID JAMIESON AND JULIE O'MARA[1]

CENTRAL THEMES

- Two arguments underlie the diversity-management perspective: Demographic realities mean that U.S. organizations will have to adapt to the needs of a diverse workforce; and a diversity of experiences and perspectives is a resource that organizations can use strategically.
- Women, African American men, and Latinos have distinctive leadership preferences that are especially appropriate in a global, competitive environment.

- Diversity management involves four overall strategies: (1) managing and rewarding *performance;* (2) matching *people* and jobs; (3) informing and involving employees in decision-making; and (4) supporting diverse work styles and life needs.
- The diversity management perspective has been criticized for (1) ignoring lessons from history; (2) underestimating the level of resistance that exists in organizations, and, in some cases, increasing it; and (3) unintentionally increasing differential treatment of employees in the guise of flexibility and adaptability.
- A number of alternatives to diversity management have been proposed, including "civility management" and new forms of organizing. But, like diversity management, each of these alternatives must deal with the tension between individuality and community described in Chapter 1.

KEY TERMS

Familialism	Machismo
Simpatía	Plateaued
Flextime	Flexplace
Total quality management (TQM)	Cafeteria benefits plans

As the quotation at the beginning of this chapter indicates, the "diversity" perspective rests on the assumption that demographic realities soon will require organizations to hire, promote, and empower Anglo women, Native Americans, Asian Americans, Latinos/Latinas, African Americans, older workers, and persons with disabilities whether they want to or not. Proponents of the perspective also believe that a more diverse workforce will bring the kinds of values, work habits, and "people skills" that are absolutely necessary for American firms to compete successfully in a global economy. They predict that different organizations will respond in different ways to today's economic climate. The upper management of some firms will celebrate the increasing diversity of their workforce and will welcome and support their new employees, leading to a more satisfied and productive workforce. Organizations in which upper management chooses to celebrate diversity will thrive because they do so.

In other organizations managers will resist pressures to diversity or will take a minimalist approach. They will grudgingly accept the realities they face, and spend their efforts trying to make only those changes that are absolutely necessary for them to manage the pressures for change that come with diversity. Their employees will continue to be alienated by traditional strategies of organizing and their firms will find it difficult to hire and retain highly skilled employees, especially those in scarce technical specialties. Some of these organizations may survive but not prosper; others will die. Unlike the accommodation perspective, which focused on changing women, African American men, Latinos, and others to "fit" into bureaucratic organizations, the diversity perspective focuses on changing bureaucracies to better utilize the talents and abilities of all employees.

THE RESOURCES PROVIDED BY A DIVERSE WORKFORCE

David Jamieson and Julie O'Mara, two of the most popular proponents of the diversity perspective, have noted that today's diverse workforce has a different set of core values than those of Anglo male "organization men." Virtually absent are an unquestioning loyalty to the organization and an obsession with the pursuit of money.[2] Instead, today's workers value recognition, feelings of accomplishment, being treated with respect and dignity, psychological involvement and pride in meaningful work (recall Chapter 3), and quality of life, including opportunities for self-development and health and wellness. These values are inconsistent with traditional, bureaucratic strategies of organizing and are consistent with the more flexible, culture- and relationship-oriented strategies that were described in Unit I.

Women's Ways of Leading

A number of researchers argue that the leadership strategies Anglo women, African Americans, Latinos, and Latinas use are especially appropriate to the turbulent and globally competitive environments faced by modern organizations. For example, Tom Peters has concluded that

> it's perfectly obvious that women should be better managers than men in today's topsy-turvy business environment. As we rush into the '90s, there is little disagreement about what business must become: less hierarchical, more flexible and team-oriented, faster and more fluid. In my opinion, one group of people has an enormous advantage in realizing this necessary new vision: women[3]

Sally Helgessen compared the day-by-day work activities of (primarily Anglo) male managers to those of (primarily Anglo) female managers. She found that males tend to work at an unrelenting pace, with no scheduled breaks during the day. Their days are characterized by interruptions, discontinuity, and fragmentation. They spare little time for activities not directly related to work, maintain a complex set of relationships with people outside of their organizations, *identify* strongly with their jobs and organizations, immerse themselves in a day-to-day need to keep the company going, spend little time in long-term planning or reflecting on their goals or the effectiveness of the strategies they use, and feel positive about themselves only when they complete tasks or achieve goals, not through the act of working itself. They prefer face-to-face communication to written messages but have difficulty sharing information with coworkers and subordinates.

Women, Helgessen observed, also have extensive networks outside of work and prefer face-to-face interactions, although they do use and pay attention to written communication. But they work at a steady pace and schedule small breaks during the day, complete unscheduled tasks but see them as normal parts of the job rather than as frustrating interruptions, make time for non-work-related activities, take a broader and long-term perspective instead of focusing solely on day-to-day activities, actively share information with others (even going so far as scheduling time to do so), and have complex and multidimensional personal identities that allow them to gain satisfaction from *both* the process of working *and* its results.[4]

These differences are grounded in the distinctively female "ways of knowing and acting" described by Carol Gilligan and others. According to this research women tend to see themselves as connected to other people, rather than being opposed to them, or above or below them in a hierarchy. Women's developmental experiences lead them to develop a particular kind of interpersonal relationship. Those relationships are not based on pure self-interest; nor are they based on altruism and self-sacrifice. Rather, both parties are psychologically connected to one another and their interpersonal relationships are a fundamental component of their individual identities. Women tend to assume responsibility for taking care of others as a moral obligation, rather than as a responsibility that accompanies a task or formal role or as a manipulative strategy. Their evaluations of people's behavior recognize the influence that situational constraints have on people, and they focus on the process of doing things rather than on abstract outcome-related criteria.

Power is defined as the ability to *act with* others in order to accomplish goals that could not be achieved by individuals acting alone rather than as *power over* others (recall Chapter 7). Leadership becomes a form of empowerment, for leadership involves being at the *center* of a group rather than in front of it. Leaders' claims that they deserve authority because of "rational" considerations like their "greater expertise" are not accepted without reflection. Instead, claims of authority must be justified continually. Assertions of greater expertise cannot be transformed into power unless the leader can explain his or her expert knowledge clearly and persuasively to subordinates in terms they can readily understand.[5]

Latino and African American Ways of Leading

Latin cultures are grounded in the concepts of familialism, machismo, and simpatia. **Familialism** involves strong values attached to family and community, and a commitment to hard work and achievement as a way of honoring one's family. It also involves aiding others who are in need. It is for this reason that having a job that pays low wages is even more stressful for Latinos than for other males. **Machismo**, a concept that is widely misunderstood by non-Latinos/Latinas, embraces a strong sense of loyalty and duty to other members of the community and a sense of honor and duty, not to an impersonal organization, but to other people. **Simpatía** is a complex concept that involves engaging in positive, agreeing behaviors whenever possible, showing respect for one's superiors by conforming to their wishes, and avoiding conflict and confrontation *in public settings*. But it does not mean conformity and blind obedience because it also requires superiors to show respect to their subordinates, especially in public. Consequently, when Latinos and Latinas do confront their supervisors it usually is over a lack of respect shown to them or others.

These values lead to a high level of concern for interpersonal relationships and the feelings of other people, a participatory, open-door leadership style, and a preference for face-to-face communication. They also generate a desire for fair treatment and high levels of freedom and autonomy. Latino/Latina supervisors tend to feel a responsibility for developing their subordinates' skills and abilities. Latin culture also encourages a high level of flexibility in leadership strategies, including a willingness to ignore the formal chain of command when it is inefficient.[6] African American managers also seem to lead by developing cooperative work teams, openly sharing information, encouraging participation in decision-making, and helping to develop all employees' expertise.[7]

In sum, Anglo men use what Chapter 2 called "transactional leadership." Women, Latinos, and African American men prefer what Chapter 4 called "transformational leadership," an approach that is particularly well suited to the turbulent environment of a competitive, global economy. However, most organizations create strong pressures for women to adapt stereotypically male leadership styles. Women accommodate to these pressures so often that overall there is no meaningful difference in the behavior of male and female managers when time and organizational experience are included in the equation. Latino and male African American leaders tend to adopt more "innovative" roles, in part because they have less often been advised to accommodate to traditional organizational practices than Anglo women have been. But, by pressuring people to adopt accommodationist strategies, organizations sacrifice many of the advantages of "diverse" styles of leadership.[8]

IMPLEMENTING DIVERSITY MANAGEMENT

In order to capitalize on the skills and leadership abilities of a diverse workforce, organizations need to stop requiring people to conform to traditional bureaucratic norms of behavior and develop a new set of attitudes, policies, systems, and practices.[9] Like all efforts to make major changes in the nature of organizations, diversity management involves both a new set of attitudes and a new set of policies, systems, and practices.

Fostering Attitudes that Support Diversity

Three beliefs underlie the diversity management perspective. The first is accepting the virtues of *flexibility*. It has two components: (1) *recognizing* that achieving goals of equity and effectiveness does not mean treating everyone in the same way, but means treating them all fairly; and (2) *believing* that organizations should be adapted to fit the needs and develop the talents of every *individual* employee, instead of *demanding* that every employee adapt to the organization. An organization needs to make very different adjustments in order to fully utilize the talents of a single mother of two preschoolers, a computer programmer who is confined to a wheelchair, a deaf investment counselor, a group of Latina production workers, or a middle-aged Anglo male who has **plateaued** (reached the highest level in the organization that he will ever reach). On-site or subsidized day care or **flextime** (allowing employees to work schedules that fit their needs) may be invaluable for the mother; working at home with a specially equipped terminal three days a week may solve the programmer's transportation problems (a **"flexplace"** arrangement); a specialized marketing campaign to put the investment counselor in touch with hearing-impaired clients could maximize her or his performance; a lateral transfer into a new and exciting division could revitalize the plateaued male; and on-site education programs could help production workers develop their skills and discover new areas of expertise and interest.

For example, the Aluminum Company of America (ALCOA) hired Kevin Kennedy, an operations engineer who had a degenerative eye condition that restricted his peripheral vision and would eventually lead to blindness. From the beginning, ALCOA assigned an assistant to help him when his job involved operating large industrial machinery or visiting plants he was not familiar with. When his vision deteriorated, Kennedy expressed concern about being able to do his job safely and about his future with the company. The organization responded by redefining his duties so that they focused on computer modeling, provided special lighting for his workspace and a large magnifying glass to help him read, and is considering purchasing a large-screen computer and software for converting written texts to Braille when his circumstances warrant doing so. In this way the company is able to retain a highly competent employee at a cost far below what it would take to hire and train a replacement.[10] In the process, they discovered what researchers have known for some time—meeting the needs of disabled workers is far less expensive than managers believe that it will be.

The second attitudinal change involves focusing on *outcomes* instead of constraints. Different employees will produce the best outcomes if they are enabled to do their jobs in their own ways. For example, Jim James, a research engineer, had promised his wife that he would retire in two months. He knew he would not be able to finish the project that he was working on in that amount of time. His supervisor decided that his expertise on the project was too valuable to lose, so he arranged to have James spend twenty hours a week as a consultant to the firm and to be assigned a co-op student from the local university as a research assistant. He was able to arrange his own working schedule, keep his commitment to his wife, and offer his firm expertise on specified projects that only he could provide.

Finally, all employees, but especially supervisors, need to develop a high level of awareness of cultural differences and a positive view of multiculturalism. Achieving this change in attitudes will be difficult in an overall culture that still resists racial integration of schools, still maintains largely segregated housing patterns, and still demands that non-Anglos adopt the language and mores of the "majority" culture.

Capitalizing on the Resources of Diversity:
New Policies, Practices, and Procedures

Advocates of the diversity management perspective offer a wide variety of specific techniques for implementing the "mental revolution" that underlies the perspective. Although there are some differences in their recommendations, they all seem to share a commitment to three strategies.

***Strategy #1: Managing and Rewarding* Performance.** In organizations that focus on getting employees to conform to the existing organizational arrangement or that subjectively reward people for attributes not directly related to performance, it is unlikely that diversity management will succeed. Instead, organizations should design reward systems that focus on performance, even for complex and ambiguous jobs. Performance-based systems involve collecting data on the number and proportion of people who are promoted, breaking that data down by gender, race, and ethnicity, and *publicizing* that data throughout the firm. This is because upper managers tend to *overestimate* the success of diversity programs, leading to complacency, and Anglo males who are competing with newcomers tend to *underestimate* the opportunities that they have, leading to unnecessary hostility and backlash.[11]

Like all organizational change efforts, diversity management will succeed only if it is strongly, honestly, and openly supported by upper management.[12] *They* must establish policies and procedures that target women, African American men, and Latinos for recruitment, professional development, and advancement. *They* must support the development of internal advocacy groups and task forces to provide emotional support for diverse groups of employees and *they* must keep the organization's diversification goals at the forefront of everyday activities.

Part of the effort involves training and education that is designed to create positive attitudes about diversity among all of their employees. Sensitivity training for managers helps them become aware of their own biases and helps them accurately interpret their subordinates' actions. For example, an Anglo male supervisor may misinterpret an Asian American's (or Latino/Latina's) respect for modesty and deference to authority as evidence of lack of leadership skills or managerial competence. The goal of these programs is to get managers not to define "differences" as "deficiencies" and to recognize that meaningful change requires *the supervisors* to adapt.[13] For example, one of my friends who runs a consulting firm in California says that a good sign that a company is *really* committed to diversity is that they spend as much energy teaching the Spanish language to Anglo supervisors as they spend teaching English to their Latino/Latina workers. But, regardless of the specific programs that are instituted, successful flexibility requires "management to tune in to people and their needs, create options that give people choices, and balance diverse individual needs with the needs of the organization."[14]

But policies, procedures, and training will fail unless they are supported by very tangible changes in the organization's reward system. To make diversity management credible, upper management must create a *system to measure progress* toward diversity goals, provide *financial awards and advancement* for managers who effectively implement diversity programs, and *punish* those who do not—with *no exceptions.*[15] After all, Texaco (recall Chapter 7) had a number of diversity management and fair employment practices policies and procedures on the books, and had even won a number of awards for them. Although their existence provided a basis for Texaco management's claims that the organization *really* is committed to diversity, they clearly had done very little to change either racist attitudes or discriminatory practices in the organization. As a result of this gap between policies and organizational performance, pointing to the existence of policies no longer seems to be a viable defense in discrimination and harassment suits. For example, in 1994 San Diego Gas and Electric Company was ordered to pay $3 million to a former worker who had been repeatedly called a "nigger," "coon," or "boy," and subjected to threats and racial and sexual graffiti about him. Walmart recently lost a $50 million sexual harassment suit (later reduced to $5 million on appeal) in spite of the company's "strong" commitments, policies, and procedures. In both cases there was no evidence that the commitments and policies had ever been translated into action—no one had been disciplined for any of the activities included in the cases. The courts' message was really very simple—when it comes to diversity management, "talking the talk" is not sufficient.

The same message is supported by management consultants. For example, Peter Robertson recently noted, "I know an executive vice-president who got fired for sexual harassment. . . . (The company) didn't have to do a lot of training after that."[16] The question is credibility. If the organization's reward system does not support its commitments, or if the only advocates of diversity are managers in relatively powerless divisions of the organization like human resources, people will not take them seriously. Even though these requirements are quite stringent, a number of U.S. organizations have met them. For example, Hoechst Celanese ties bonuses and profit-sharing payments to measures of diversity. They have even told universities to provide a more diverse pool of qualified graduates or the company will stop recruiting on their campuses. Since taking these steps the company has consistently exceeded its goals. In 1986 Ortho Pharmaceutical Corporation established a "Managing Diversity Committee," which serves as an independent observer of what goes on in and outside of Ortho with respect to diversity management: "Each member serves as a 'champion' to his or her own organizational unit in looking for ways to remove barriers to the full participation of women and people of color."[17]

Success in workforce diversification should become a requirement for organizational advancement for *all* supervisors and managers. In short, the organization should make every employee accountable for contributing to diversity management and should enforce that accountability through the organization's reward system.

Strategy #2: Matching* People *and Jobs.   Organizations will benefit most from its employees' talents if it individualizes career paths and opportunities.

For example, Hallmark Corporation no longer encourages members of its artistic staff to specialize. Instead it rotates new employees through a number of different assignments in order to give them a wide range of actual job experiences. If potential candidates for a promotion lack a specific set of skills, the organization may assign them to a different department for six months or so in order to give them a chance to develop the skills necessary to move up. In some cases the employee may discover that he or she is better suited for the division to which she or he is temporarily assigned, and the organization does everything possible to facilitate a move to that division.

Traditionally, "promotion" has meant abandoning one's technical specialty and becoming a manager. But many people who have exceptional technical skills do not have the interests or abilities necessary for them to be successful managers. So, they are forced to either remain in the same no longer challenging positions or move into a role with which they are not comfortable. Diversity management proposes that organizations create "alternative career paths," in which people stay within their specialties but receive promotions and increasingly complex technical assignments, or which allow people to cycle in and out of management positions.

Strategy #3: Supporting Diverse Work Styles and Life Needs.   One of the easiest ways to get a sense of the kinds of programs and policies that can be valuable to a diverse workforce is to peruse the annual copy of *Working Mother* magazine that lists the 100 best firms to work for. Firms are evaluated in part on the fairness of their salary schedules and their record of promoting women. But they also gain points for having programs like multiple child care arrangements, flextime, flexplace, and flexible benefits plans. But *Working Mother* also warns readers about surveys that look *only* at a company's policies, because they often are either not implemented or implemented in a way that penalizes employees who use them. For example, the woman who helped the Dupont company institute their diversity management program, as well as almost every woman on Dupont's managerial "fast track," eventually left the company because the company's culture continued to privilege Anglo males. New Jersey's Merck and Company, Inc. also has been identified as a company with excellent policies that the company fails to live up to. Even well-intentioned programs create problems if they are not administered in a fair and flexible way. For example, many firms are experiencing increasing tensions between parents and childless workers because the firms do not find ways of coping with the increased workload that traditional employees experience when their colleagues use family leave or other family-friendly policies.[18]

There are many examples of programs and policies that seem to have been implemented successfully. Ben and Jerry's Homemade (Ice Cream), Inc., pays health club fees and reimburses parents for adoption fees (up to the cost of a hospital delivery of a baby); Beth Israel Hospital in Boston provides breast pumping stations for returning mothers who are nursing their babies; Arthur Andersen and Company provides on-site day care for employees during the peak tax preparation season; Barnett Bank in Florida provides round-trip transportation for employees' children to summer day camp at the local YMCA; Lincoln National Insurance has trained 300 family day care providers to be employed by their workers; and Colgate-Palmolive pays the full cost of in-home emergency care for ill children for its employees. At the Bureau of National Affairs, Inc., employees with ten years of service are eligible for six-month sabbaticals at half-pay, and Consolidated Edison of New York has a new training program to attract women to higher-paying jobs traditionally held by men (such as utility repair work).[19]

The list could be extended almost endlessly. Of course, some of the preceding benefits are irrelevant to the needs of all but a small number of employees. But that is the point of diversity management. The organization consults with employees about what *their* needs are, then designs flexible programs that, within broad constraints imposed by budgets and concerns for fairness, *individualizes* policies, procedures, and benefits.

Criticisms of the Diversity Management Perspective

Three primary criticisms of the diversity management perspective have been proposed. The first involves the justification of the program itself—adapting to the competitive and demographic realities of the world economy. Historically, whenever organizations have opened their doors to women (or members of racial or ethnic minority groups) because it is economically beneficial for them to do so, the positive effects have been short-lived. When women entered the textile mills in and around Lowell, Massachusetts, early in the Industrial Revolution, and when the United States needed "Rosie the Riveters" during World War II, managers generally celebrated their presence and contributions. Their working conditions and opportunities were quite good, and they performed at levels comparable to or better than those of the men they replaced. But when new technologies or a ready supply of alternative labor became available—European immigrants for the textile mills, returning veterans for "Rosies"—women were forced out of organizations, their opportunities were eliminated, and the working conditions of their replacements rapidly deteriorated.

Unfortunately, critics argue, the diversity perspective ignores this history, and ignores a number of present realities that indicate that the new global economy may not provide women, Latinos, or African American men with either increased opportunities or increased organizational power. Downsizing of organizations will continue to reduce promotion opportunities, and global competition will continue to depress the wages of newcomers to the U.S. labor force. Consequently, critics argue, the likely result of "diversification" will be to benefit the upper management and owners of bureaucratic organizations by providing low-cost workers.

A second criticism of diversity management programs is that they underestimate the level of resistance that is likely to occur. The concept of resistance to organizational control systems and to change has been examined throughout this book. Resistance is especially likely when new ideas, policies, and practices promise to change organizational power relationships. The nature of the system has mattered little—the consultation and shared responsibility of scientific management, the supportiveness and power sharing of relational strategies of organizing, the consultation and mutual respect of QCC (quality control circles), QWL (quality of working life), and TQM (**total quality management**) programs all have been sabotaged or abandoned as soon as they seemed to be effecting significant organizational change.[20] But diversity management programs face a different level of resistance. Efforts to promote equality of opportunity for everyone regardless of their sex, race, or ethnic background have met with intense, often violent opposition in U.S. society. The furor over the extension of the Civil Rights Act during 1988 and over immigration and "affirmative action" programs during the 1990s all are evidence of the extent of this backlash. Because diversity management confronts both sets of societal biases—against power sharing and against racial, ethnic, and sexual equality—it is likely to generate very intense resistance. Instead of dealing effectively with resistance, some diversity management programs may exacerbate these tensions.

Training programs often encourage employees to be open and honest about their attitudes and feelings about employees who are different than they are. The assumption is that increased understanding will lead to improved attitudes and behaviors. But by focusing on *differences* among employees, *common* values, beliefs, and experiences may be obscured. Instead of facilitating the management of workplace conflicts, focusing on differences may further polarize a workforce. In fact, a number of successful harassment lawsuits have focused on diversity management training programs as a key element of a hostile work environment—"open and honest" but flagrantly negative and sexist comments made by male managers of Lucky Stores supermarkets and racially charged comments made by a diversity management trainer at U.S. West Communications, Inc. ignited volatile situations and exacerbated tensions.

Unless carefully conducted, training programs also may reproduce negative stereotypes, making resistance more likely:

> A male manager may learn in diversity training, for example, that women generally tend to use a more tactful style of communication than men and prefer to work by building consensus rather than through confrontation. If the manager already believes that women are not "tough enough" or "competitive enough" to succeed in business, and thus shouldn't be given major responsibilities, he can easily conclude that his negative stereotypes have been validated by the training.[21]

In addition, when people talk about their attitudes and feelings during diversity training, they often are perceived as speaking for their gender, race, or ethnic group. Others are invited to see them and subsequently to treat them as a member of that group, not as individuals, with unique experiences, attitudes, and skills. If people entered into diversity training programs with no preconceived notions, these perceptual problems would not be as important. But they do not, and as a result, diversity training may encourage the beliefs and perceptual processes that they are designed to change.

A third criticism of diversity management programs is that efforts to make organizations more flexible and responsive may lead to increased discrimination.[22] Advocates of diversity management typically assume that once management accepts the demographic and economic realities of the 1990s and beyond, and once employees begin to successfully work side by side with a diverse group of people, new attitudes will develop. There is some evidence that, in general, people's attitudes do tend to shift in ways that are consistent with their behaviors and that Anglo males' attitudes about working with or being managed by women or members of minority groups do become more positive as they become accustomed to doing so. But other evidence indicates that managers often use new policies, procedures, and so on to unfairly manipulate workers in the guise of improving their organizational lives. A similar caution has been offered for the "managing diversity" perspective. "Diversity" programs focus on flexibility and individualization.[23] But "individualized" programs can easily be transformed into discriminatory programs, especially in an atmosphere of covert racism or sexism. For example, Jamieson and O'Mara applaud Security Pacific Corporation's "Career Opps" program in which current and retired employees are given bounties for finding applicants who eventually are hired. But the U.S. Department of Labor's "glass ceiling" study found that using word-of-mouth or employee referral systems for hiring often led to a *less* diverse workforce or to a preference for members of one "diversity" group (usually Anglo women) at the expense of others.[24]

Similarly, individualizing performance criteria and evaluation processes may increase their subjectivity, thus making covert or unrecognized biases more of a problem. Of course, if organizational decisions were not influenced by biased perceptions and attributions, none of this would be a problem. But, if perceptions and attributions were not influenced by biases related to race, gender, or ethnicity, there would be little need to implement diversification strategies in the first place.

CASE STUDY:
MANAGING DIVERSITY?*

In many ways SCIENCETECH, Inc.'s (a pseudonym for a *Fortune* 500 company) diversity management program is a model of what "should" be done. The firm has been dealing with the issue for twenty years, but increased its

---

*This case is based on Sandra Fish, "Preparation for the Year 2000: One Corporation's Attempt to Address the Issues of Gender and Race," *Howard Journal of Communication, 3*(1991): 61–72.

(continued)

(continued from the previous page)

efforts substantially in 1986 in response to predicted demographics of their workforce in the year 2000 and the results of an in-house survey that found high attrition rates for African American and women managers. Its program has four components:

1. **numerical goals for promotion and attrition of African American and women managers**
2. **a series of training programs for all 3,000 employees that focus on developing positive attitudes toward diversity**
3. **structural changes designed to create a formal mentoring system, a career development process for women and African Americans, and including accountability for diversity goals in all employees' appraisals**
4. **an expansion of support services like day care and quality of working life programs to make the organization more attractive to women and African Americans.**

Each of these components has been communicated to all interested audiences through a variety of media, including speeches and publications by the CEO, upper management, and outside consultants and trainers. Professor Sandra Fish concluded:

> Overall SCIENCETECH is seeking to be thorough and exhaustive in its efforts to reduce attrition of women and blacks, increase its attractiveness in recruiting, and develop and promote its employees more equitably. Their goals are, of course, designed to enhance its financial status as well as to "do the right thing" (p. 65).

What impact has the program had? The positive outcomes include an increased awareness of diversity issues, which has led to increased communication among different gender, racial, and ethnic groups, a sense that people are more accountable for dealing with diversity issues, and a belief that conflicts are avoided less and managed more effectively. Some women and African Americans now believe that some Anglo males can become allies as they come to understand the adverse impact that traditional modes of operating have on their wives and daughters. In addition, African Americans' and women's groups feel that they are more visible within the organization, that it is becoming safer for them to take risks, and that it now is easier for all employees—including Anglo males—to attempt to balance family and work life. Finally, managerial practices really have improved. The diversity goals are being met, and supervisors are better able to deal with diversity issues.

But problems remain. Some employees believe that the program's *real* goal is to give "lip service" to diversity. Others feel that the corporate culture still is

(continued)

(continued from the previous page)

dominated by "old boys," still requires employees to sacrifice their family to their careers, and still is very resistant to changes of any kind. Members of all racial and gender groups feel that backlash among Anglo males is a problem, one that is manifested in hostility, fear, resentment, and withdrawal. Women and African Americans are concerned that the program puts an uncomfortable spotlight on them, by allowing others to perceive that their success is based on the organization's desire to fulfill quotas rather than on their individual competencies. But they are concerned that the program will not be sustained for the long term—that upper management may not be sufficiently committed. For the program to succeed, they say, management must spend time talking with employees at all levels of the firm, must deal with the backlash problem directly, and must make all managers accountable for the program's success.

Discussion Questions

1. According to the diversity management perspective, what new steps should SCIENCETECH now take to ensure the continued success of the program? What aspects of the current program should be continued and strengthened?

2. Diversity programs inevitably threaten to change the power relationships that exist within an organization. Given what you know about resistance to programs of power sharing (a brief review of Unit I might be helpful), at what points and for what reasons is it likely that SCIENCETECH will abandon or weaken its program? Why?

ALTERNATIVE APPROACHES TO MANAGING ISSUES OF DIVERSITY

A number of alternative approaches to diversity management have been proposed. Although the two that I will discuss in the remainder of this chapter are very different from one another on the surface, they are similar in many respects. Both assume that attitudes about race, gender, and ethnicity are such a fundamental part of a society's taken-for-granted assumptions that they are virtually impossible to change, at least in the short term. But they also differ in one fundamental respect. One relies on the motivation and control dimensions of existing strategies of organizing and focuses on changing behaviors within existing organizational contexts. The other argues that existing strategies of organizing form significant barriers to creating equal opportunity. Those barriers can be overcome and the advantages of diversity can be realized only within a truly alternative form of organizing.

Diversity through Civility

According to the civility perspective, organizations have had relatively little success in changing workers' attitudes and beliefs—the taken-for-granted assumptions of a society simply provide too great a barrier. What organizations can do is change behaviors. Of course, as the chapters in Unit I pointed out, behavior control is not a simple task and resistance is an inevitable part of any control strategy. But it is employees' *behaviors* that create discriminatory or hostile work environments, and the first step to changing those environments is to influence behaviors.

Proponents of civility-oriented programs argue that, unlike attitude-oriented diversity management programs, their approach is simple and relatively easy to administer. Upper management makes it clear that they expect all of their employees to treat one another in a fair and equitable way. They use a variety of strategies to communicate that commitment, and they make necessary changes in the organization's policies, procedures, and operations to enforce that commitment. Managerial discourse focuses on the goals and interests that employees have in *common*, goals like maintaining smooth and effective working relationships and avoiding unnecessary tensions and conflict. Training programs focus on encouraging civil behaviors and preventing uncivil ones. Employees should be taught that statements or conduct that denigrates coworkers because of the race, gender, or ethnicity will not be tolerated. The guidelines are simple and concrete: do not refer to fellow employees by ethnic-, disability, racial-, or gender-related nicknames; don't make disparaging statements or jokes about gender, race, disability, or ethnicity; do not engage in acts that make coworkers uncomfortable or that in any way distracts the team from its tasks. Since "pin-up" calendars may offend one's peers, do not put them up; if celebrating one religious holiday in exclusion of others may make some people not feel part of the work group, do not do it (or celebrate all of the holidays that are important to any members of the work group). People who engage in uncivil behaviors should not be defined as "insensitive" or "racist" or "sexist," they should be defined as people who cannot follow the rules of conduct of their organizations and should be treated exactly as people are who violate rules about punctuality or theft.[25] Promotions and rewards should be based on performance alone.

The advantage of "civility management" lies in what it does not do. As Unit I explained, employees grant their organizations a wide range of latitude to control their behaviors. They tend to see efforts to influence their attitudes as less "legitimate," and tend to resist them much more stringently than they resist efforts to control behaviors at work. And, because everyone is expected to obey the same set of concrete rules, it is less likely that employees will see the program as granting preferential treatment to other workers or groups of workers. Since the program does not foster artificial "openness" or involve activities that inadvertently reinforce stereotypes or stereotype-based behavior, it will not make the situation worse.

Ironically, the disadvantages of the "civility management" perspective also are based on what it does not do. As Chapter 10 explained, there are two primary barriers to the "success" of diverse employees in U.S. organizations—*structural factors* that create different opportunities for members of different gender, racial, and ethnic groups, and *attitudinal* barriers. Like the accommodation perspective, civility management does nothing to change the societal bases of differential career choices or the opportunity structures of different careers and specialties. Although civility management easily can be accompanied by structural modifications that allow individual employees to maximize their contributions to the organization without creating backlash—for example, **cafeteria benefits plans** that provide each employee with a fixed dollar amount for benefits but allow them to decide how to allocate those monies among child care, vacation time, retirement expenses, and so on—it does not inevitably involve those changes. Since it defines "the problem" solely as a lack of civil behaviors it tends to focus attention away from structural differences in opportunity and the need for more flexible organizational policies and practices.

Perhaps more important, civility management ignores the role that attitudinal and perceptual factors play in differential opportunity. Even if discriminatory and hostile behavior are eliminated, the nonconscious processes that were outlined in Chapter 10 still will exist. Upper managers still will *feel more comfortable with* similar others, still will *perceive* the subordinates' performance in terms of socially sanctioned stereotypes, and still will *attribute* their success or failure to different factors. While conflicts over issues that are directly related to diversity will be limited (suppressed or "smoothed over"), resulting tensions are likely to be played out in conflicts over other issues (recall Chapter 9). In short, bringing civility to the workplace clearly is an important part of the solution to issues surrounding workplace diversity, but it is only one part.

Alternative Forms of Organizing

The most common types of truly alternative forms of organizing have emerged at the intersection of feminist theories of organizing (discussed in Chapter 7) and research on "women's ways of leading" described earlier in this chapter. Feminist theorists argue that masculine conceptions of reality, modes of organizing, and ways of communicating dominate the "public realm" in Western societies. Masculine organizations are dominated by metaphors suggesting hierarchy, rely on "power over" views of interpersonal influence, define "effectiveness" as achieving goals in spite of resistance by others, and privilege centralized expertise and decision-making. In contrast, feminine (as well as feminist) organizations are defined by metaphors that describe "webs" of interconnected interpersonal relationships, define effectiveness in terms of achieving consensus among organizational members, and focus on systems of shared leadership and diffuse expertise. The distinction between "feminine" and "feminist" organizations is important because many alternative organizations, while composed primarily or exclusively of women, are not based on feminist goals regarding social change and their members may not espouse feminist values at all.

For example, Nancy Wyatt described a women's organization that was composed primarily of middle-class conservative women who were unified by their common interest in sewing and weaving, but never expressed an interest in feminist politics. But they created and sustained an organization that was fundamentally different from any of the strategies of organizing discussed in this book. The women provided one another with mutual support and opportunities to learn new skills from one another; they saw failure as an equally important part of learning as success; were avidly noncompetitive; and maintained diffuse and nonhierarchical power relationships and modes of decision-making. Leadership was shared by eight members of the weavers' guild, some of whom were leaders because they were uniquely able to articulate a shared vision for the organization, and some of whom were leaders because of their ability to organize the group's activities. But all eight were very much concerned that they not dominate the others—they provided advice and direction only when asked, for example. This was in part because of the history of the group. At one time it had a strong, centralized leader, and when that woman left the guild it almost fell apart. But it also was because of their focus on maintaining a supportive community within the group. So, formal roles rotated among the group's members so that a variety of talents and interests were represented in decision-making, and the guild's activities were orchestrated so that each member's goals were met. There were tensions within the group, usually over the organization's unique form of organizing. One member once had been a weaver by profession, and tended to withhold her expertise from the other members because doing so had been a successful political strategy in her previous organizations. Members who wished to use the guild as a stepping-stone for a future career in "typical" weaving organizations were frustrated by the shared responsibility and shared credit characteristic of the guild. In spite of these tensions, the weavers' guild was able to create and sustain a fundamentally different kind of organization, one that was able to simultaneously be a community and address the needs and desires of its individual members.[26]

Other feminist organizations have found it more difficult to maintain that kind of balance. Frequently, feminist organizations begin with an emphasis on consensus, equality, collectivity, and legitimate participatory decision-making, but emerge toward more traditional, hierarchical strategies of organizing in which representative democracy replaces participation. This shift seems to stem from environmental pressures on the organization (recall Unit I). Feminist organizations face an important dilemma: How can an alternative organization maintain a collective, nonhierarchical, participatory, egalitarian strategy of organizing while simultaneously pursuing other goals like profitability? Some external pressures are overt and direct. In Western societies, organizations need funds in order to survive and especially to grow. A major donation or grassroots political campaign may provide sufficient funding for an organization to be created and even to succeed at a relatively small size. But if it is to grow, other sources of funds become necessary, and significant funds usually are available only from traditional, bureaucratic organizations—government agencies, banks, and the financial markets. Decision-makers in traditional bureaucracies are comfortable with organizations that operate on the basis of similar strategies of organizing. So they pressure alternative organizations to be less "alternative," or at least to appear to be. Alternative strategies of organizing become less "alternative," and, if the organization is involved in social change efforts, those efforts are moderated or made less visible. For example, *MS* magazine faced a central tension from the day it was created—it drew its content from feminist publications but designed its format and marketing to be like mainline women's magazines. Its funding came from readers, who were attracted to the magazine because of its feminist ideology, and from advertisers who saw it as an opportunity to reach women readers. Advertisers pressured the editorship to focus content on "career feminists," who had the disposable income that they coveted. But career feminists were only part of *MS*' readership, and many of them were attracted to its feminist ideology. As competition and costs increased during the 1980s, advertising revenues became more necessary, and the advertisers' influence over content increased. Readers found many of the ads to be offensive and resisted the shift. The opposition crystallized around a 1987 issue on women and addiction, which included none of the tobacco and alcohol company ads that had become common. Readers were irate about what they saw as blatant hypocrisy, and the editors' argument that *MS*' policies had led to improvements in advertising directed toward women fell on deaf ears. Although the magazine's content had become progressively less political as the advertisers exerted increased control, advertisers abandoned the magazine during the highly conservative political climate of the late 1980s. In 1989 the magazine folded, only to be reborn the following year with no advertising.[27]

Environmental pressures also may be subtle. People bring the dominant assumptions of their societies with them into their organizations, regardless of their gender and regardless of the strategy of organizing that is in place. Thus, people in Western societies tend to value "efficiency," "expertise," and "experience." Consensus decision-making and participation consume a great deal of time and energy (recall Chapter 3), and thus *seem* to be inefficient, especially in the short term; differences in expertise and experience *seem* to warrant hierarchical power relationships. Members of alternative organizations are pressured by the many different traditional organizations in which they also are involved—churches, schools, clubs, and so on. These competing organizations work on a schedule and through a process that contradicts the flexibility and adaptability of the alternative organization. Consequently, it is difficult for members to continue to support forms of organizing that seem to be so *nonnormal*, so *unnatural*. A number of factors do help offset these pressures—small organizational size, common goals, relatively equal knowledge and experience, and a benign environment. As a result, there are a number of flourishing cooperatives and collectives that operate on the basis of alternative strategies, but sustaining them involves a constant process of managing tensions.[28]

Alternative organizations face a second dilemma: can alternative strategies of organizing successfully include people from diverse racial, ethnic, class, and gender groups? Alternative organizations tend to begin with local, grass-roots organizing. These groups tend to have common interests and homogeneous backgrounds and experiences. For example, in the United States, feminist groups have primarily involved educated middle- and upper-middle-class Anglo women. Unless they actively reach out to men and to people of other classes, races, and ethnic origins, they tend to remain homogeneous. Since an alternative form of organizing does not in itself bridge racial, class, or ethnic differences, and since the concerns that bring middle-class Anglo women together in alternative organizations may not be salient to anyone else (and vice versa), diversifying alternative organizations is quite difficult. Doing so is more likely when the organization emerged in a multiclass, multiethnic community, but even then it takes a great deal of time and energy to sustain a truly diverse organization. Consequently, pressures for efficiency may be especially acute for these organizations, making factors like small size and common goals even more important.[29]

CASE STUDY:
EVOLUTION AT REDWOOD RECORDS*

Redwood Records began as a "mom and pop" (literally) operation designed to produce and market records by Holly Near. Although she had a sizable and stable following, major record companies refused to contract with Near because her anti-Vietnam War message was controversial and because her music was not as "submissive" as women's music was "supposed" to be. By the mid-1970s Near's parents tired of running the company, creating a need for a new organization. Near restructured Redwood Records into a feminist alternative organization: an all-woman, worker-run, nonhierarchical, social change-oriented organization. All employees performed all of the necessary tasks—from licking stamps to making strategic decisions. Their ideology was explicitly anti-profit, and their goals focused on helping create a women's music industry designed to foster social change. Communication among members was excellent, information flow was good, and power really was shared among members, creating high levels of morale, effort, and commitment. But, like many alternative feminist

---

*This case is based on Cynthia Lott, "Redwood Records: Principles and Profit in Women's Music," in Barbara Bate and Anita Taylor, *Women Communicating* (Norwood, NJ: Ablex, 1988).

(continued)

(continued from the previous page)

organizations founded during the 1970s, Redwood's combination of participatory, consensus decision-making and lack of formal structure created problems: Service was inconsistent, salaries and job security were low, burnout and turnover among staff members was high, and financial problems were almost constant.** In short, Redwood Records was a social movement that happened to be a business.

After 1980, Redwood evolved to become a business that had an alternative strategy of organizing and a vision of social change. It signed a number of other women artists, and as Near's role in the organization declined, it began to rely more and more on profits to sustain itself. Redwood maintained an atmosphere of informality and support as well as its commitment to consensual decision-making and open confrontation as a primary mode of conflict management (recall Chapter 9). But it began to focus more on efficiency in order to keep up with growing demand for its products. Eventually a management team was formed, and day-to-day communication became more formal and bureaucratic—meetings involved the minimum number of people necessary rather than all employees and meeting times were set in advance instead of being spontaneous, for example. After 1985, Redwood decided to quit limiting its selections to music designed for a women's audience, but continued to have an all-woman staff.

Throughout its existence, Redwood has had to manage a tension between economic demands and its political change ideology and commitment to an alternative strategy of organizing. It maintains a balance by being very strategic about the projects it takes on. Money and profits were redefined to be means to a social change end. Profits gained from some products allow Redwood to support social change activities that do not in themselves make money. Some members focus more on profits than politics; others more on politics than profits; and most are in the middle, trying to simultaneously maintain both. Its continued openness and commitment to consensus policy-making allows it to manage this central tension successfully. It has found a middle ground between bureaucratic structures and modes of operating and a fluid and structureless mode of operating.

Discussion Questions

1. Some critics of Redwood Records complain that the organization has "sold out" its political commitments to obtain profitability. Has it? How can an organization like Redwood "know" when it has tipped the balance between politics and profits too far in one direction?
2. What does Redwood's experience predict for the new (non-advertising) *MS* magazine? What is likely to happen to *MS* over the long term? Why?

**See Jo Freeman, "The Tyranny of Structurelessness," *MS* (July, 1976).

CONCLUSION

In Chapter 1, I argued that one of the characteristic tensions of U.S. culture is between individuality and community. This tension is most clear, and most problematic, around issues of diversity. One of the dominant myths of U.S. society is that of the "melting pot," the notion that all of the differing beliefs, values, and experiences that people bring with them to the United States can somehow blend together into a seamless, homogeneous hybrid. Tensions created by gender, racial, and ethnic differences will somehow disappear if everyone identifies with one another and with their common citizenship or residency and only secondarily with other dimensions of their identities. But, like all social myths, the melting pot construct is a goal, at most, rather than a description of experience. Differences in opportunity, educational institutions, and housing patterns that perpetuate segregation by race, class, and ethnicity, and organizational processes that create and reproduce preferences for working with "similar" others, all mitigate against the creation of a truly homogeneous culture. As Chapter 6 explained, people simultaneously manage multiple, competing identifications. Although they may be able to construct a coherent, integrated identity for themselves (and many theorists argue that even this is impossible in our fragmented, "postmodern" society), doing so requires a constant process of negotiating competing pressures. Developing a coherent, homogeneous societal "self" is impossible, and would be counterproductive even if it was feasible.

Efforts to manage the increasing diversity of the U.S. workforce confront the tension between individuality and community directly. Some approaches choose to suppress individual needs and differences in processes of conformity. In fact, all of the strategies of organizing discussed in Unit I of this book seek to create homogeneous patterns of acting or thinking—all organizational control strategies seek to reduce or manage differences among employees.[30] This preference for homogeneity may be clearest in traditional strategies of organizing, but it also is true of relational and cultural strategies (recall the critiques of each of these approaches). The most popular approach to diversity management—accommodation—also seeks, and often achieves, homogeneity. A coherent "community" is created, but only through the suppression of individuality. But programs that focus on flexible adaptation to the needs of individual employees often undermine concepts of community—as when diversity training perpetuates racial, ethnic, or gender stereotypes and exaggerates differences at the expense of commonalities. Creating organizational "melting pots" is just as difficult as creating societal melting pots, and for the same reasons. The tension between individuality and community that permeates U.S. society also permeates U.S. organizations.

NOTES

[1] David Jamieson and Julie O'Mara, *Managing Workforce 2000* (San Francisco: Jossey-Bass, 1991), pp. 6, 23. Also see Susan Molinari, *Women and the Workplace: The Glass Ceiling,*

Hearing before the Subcommittee on Employment and Productivity, Committee on Labor and Human Resources, U.S. Senate, October 23, 1991, p. 23; and Audrey Edwards and Craig K. Polite, *Children of the Dream: The Psychology of Black Success* (New York: Doubleday, 1992), p. 2. Many commentators note that by 1986 less than 10 percent of U.S. families were of traditional form (a married couple with children in which only the husband works outside of the home), thus removing any economic basis for preferential treatment of male employees. However, some commentators add census data figures differently, and conclude that as much as 34 percent of American households are "traditional" (using 1986–87 data; see, for example, David Blakenhorn, Steven Bayme, and Jean Bethke Elshtain, *Rebuilding the Nest* [Milwaukee, WI: Family Service America, 1990]). My own reading of census data leads me to conclude that 15 percent is the most accurate figure. But, regardless of the exact figure, it is clear that the "traditional" household no longer is the norm in American society, and that the percentage of people in that kind of household has declined steadily for the past fifteen years.

[2] The phrase "organization men" refers to William Whyte's classic study of men who conform totally to the dictates of traditional bureaucracies (*The Organization Man* [New York: Simon and Schuster, 1956]).

[3] Tom Peters, "The Best New Managers Will Listen, Motivate, Support: Isn't That Just Like a Woman?," *Working Woman*, Sept. 1990, p. 216.

[4] Sally Helgessen, *The Female Advantage: Women's Ways of Leadership* (New York: Doubleday, 1990). Her summary of male styles is based on Henry Mintzberg's *The Nature of Managerial Work* (New York: Harper & Row, 1973). For similar conclusions, see Marilyn Loden, *Feminine Leadership: How to Succeed Without Being One of the Boys* (New York: Times Books, 1985); Jan Grant, "Women as Managers: What They Can Offer to Organizations," *Organizational Dynamics* (Spring, 1988), pp. 56–63; and Judith Rosener, "Ways Women Lead," *Harvard Business Review* (Nov.-Dec., 1990): 119–125.

[5] Carol Gilligan, *In a Different Voice* (Cambridge, MA: Harvard University Press, 1982). For a summary, see Katherine Ferguson, *The Feminist Case Against Bureaucracy* (Philadelphia: Temple University Press, 1984). Also see Nancy Hartsock, *Money, Sex and Power* (New York: Longman, 1983).

[6] For a summary of Latino/Latina leadership styles, see Bernardo Ferdman and Angelica Cortes, "Culture and Identity Among Hispanic Managers in an Anglo Business," in *Hispanics in the Workplace*, S. Knouse, P. Rosenfeld, and A. Culbertson, eds. (Newbury Park, CA: Sage, 1992), especially p. 265. Also see G. Marin and B.V. Marin, *Research with Hispanic Populations* (Newbury Park, CA: Sage, 1991); H.C. Triandis, Y. Kashima, C.H. Hui, J. Lisansky, and G. Marin, "Acculturation and Biculturalism Indices Among Relatively Acculturated Hispanic Young Adults," *Inter-American Journal of Psychology, 16* (1982): 140–149; Richard Cervantes, "Occupational and Economic Stressors Among Immigrant and United States-Born Hispanics," in Knouse, et al.

[7] Floyd Dickens and Jacqueline B. Dickens, *The Black Manager* (New York: AMACOM, 1991); Jamieson and O'Mara.

[8] B.M. Wilkins and P.A. Anderson, "Gender Differences and Similarities in Management Communication," *Management Communication Quarterly, 5* (1991): p. 27. Also see Gary Powell, *Women and Men in Management* (Newbury Park, CA: Sage, 1993). Pressures to conform seem to be greater in U.S. firms than in Europe because of a greater appreciation of the value of "women's" styles in European societies (Frederica Olivares, "Ways Men and Women Lead" *Harvard Business Review* [January-February, 1991]).

[9] Unfortunately, even very recent research focuses on selecting individuals who conform to the existing organizational culture or helping them adapt to that culture. For example, see Charles O'Reilly, Jennifer Chatman, and David Caldwell, "People and Organizational Culture: A Profile Comparison Approach to Assessing Person-Organization Fit," *Academy of Management Journal, 34* (1991): 487–516.

[10] This example is abstracted from Jamieson and O'Mara, p. 89; also see John Dovidio, Samuel Gaertner, Phyllis Anastasio, and Rasyid Sanitioso, "Cognitive and Motivational Bases of Bias," in Knouse, et al. The diversity perspective does suggest that individual employees also adapt, but it does *not* counsel them to conform. For example, like accommodationist manuals for women managers, Dickens and Dickens suggest that African Americans find mentors and external networks and make careful career plans because the organization will not do it for them. But they also warn against oversocialization and provide extensive advice about how to recog-

nize overt and covert racism among supervisors and coworkers and how to confront and "manage the racist behavior of others" (pp. 280–350).

[11] Jamieson and O'Mara; Morrison, *The New Leaders: Guidelines on Leadership Diversity in America* (San Francisco: Jossey-Bass, 1992); Lynn Martin, *A Report on the Glass Ceiling Initiative* (Washington, D.C.: U.S. Department of Labor, July, 1991). Edwin Lawler and his associates found that the only significant predictor of the success of appraisal systems is the extent to which they are customized for individual workers (A.M. Mohrman, S. Resnick-West, and Edwin Lawler, *Designing Performance Appraisal Systems.* [San Francisco: Jossey-Bass, 1989]). Unfortunately, gender and racial bias have been shown to influence the results of even highly objective appraisal systems (William Bigoness, "Effect of applicant's sex, race, and performance on employers' performance ratings," *Journal of Applied Psychology, 61* [1976]: 80–84; William C. Hamner, J.S. Kim, L. Baird, and W.G. Bigoness, "Race and Sex as Determinants of Ratings by Potential Employers in a Simulated Work Situation," *Journal of Applied Psychology, 59* [1974]: 705–711).

[12] This summary is taken from Ann Morrison, *Leaders,* which is in turn based on the Center for Creative Leadership's study of firms with successful diversity management programs.

[13] Dovidio, et al.; Martin, *Pipeline.* Jamieson and O'Mara list Hewlett-Packard and Hallmark as organizations with successful training programs; Morrison, *Leaders* provides additional examples. Unfortunately, little evidence exists to show that education in itself can overcome racism or sexism, either in general [see, for example, Talcott Parsons and Kenneth Clark, eds. *The Negro American*. Boston: Beacon, 1965; Ulf Hannerz, *Soulside* (Columbia University Press, 1969); and William McCord, Joun Howard, Bernard Friedberg, and Edwin Harwood, *Lifestyles in the Black Ghetto* (New York: Norton, 1969)] or in terms of appraisal processes [K. Kraiger and J. Ford, "A Meta-Analysis of Ratee Race Effects in Performance Ratings," *Journal of Applied Psychology, 70* (1985): 56–65].

[14] Jamieson and O'Mara, p. 38.

[15] Martin, *Pipelines;* "Sincerity Needed for Diversity," *Houston Chronicle,* Dec. 17, 1996, 1C." Jeffrey Kerr and John Slocum, Jr. examine the role that reward systems play in all organizational change programs in "Managing Corporate Culture Through Reward Systems," *Academy of Management Executive, 1* (1987): 99–108.

[16] Cited in L.M. Sixel, "Sincerity."

[17] Jamieson and O'Mara, p. 85.

[18] *Bryan-College Station (TX) Eagle,* 9/22/96, E2. The top ten firms in the 1996 survey were Barnett Banks (Jacksonville, FL); MBNA America Bank (Wilmington, DL); NationsBank (Charlotte, NC); Hewlett-Packard (Palo Alto); IBM; Eli Lily (Indianapolis); Merck & Co. (Whitehouse Station, NJ); Johnson and Johnson (New Brunswick); Patagonia (Ventura, CA); and Xerox, whose lengthy efforts to implement an effective *flextime* program in spite of opposition by many of its managers recently was chronicled in a Ford Foundation-sponsored study. The Ford Foundation study of Xerox and the examples of "pseudo" programs are from William Bole, "'Family Friendly:' Some Firms Make Slogan a Reality," *Houston Chronicle,* 10/20/96: 8A. Also see Rochelle Sharp, "The Waiting Game," *Wall Street Journal,* March 29, 1994, A1, and Ann Morrison, *Leaders.* Frictions between parents and childless/childfree employees are described by Mildred Culp, "Child Care Issue Can Affect Work," *Houston Chronicle,* 5/19/96, EE1.

[19] Interestingly, many of these steps have been mandated by law for decades in most of the countries with which American firms compete. In Ecuador, for example, firms must provide women with three months of paid maternity leave and schedule them for only six hours of work at a time during the next three months (so that they can nurse their babies). Most firms have on-site day care for their employees' children and provide special breaks so that nursing mothers can feed their babies during the day. Canada and European countries and firms have similar provisions.

[20] For a summary of managerial resistance to TQM programs, see G. Sewell and B. Wilkinson, "Something to Watch Over Me: Surveillance, Discipline, and the Just-in-time Labor Process," *Sociology, 26* (1992): 271–289.

[21] Stephen Paskoff, "Ending the Workplace Diversity Wars," *Training: The Human Side of Business* (August, 1996), p. 3.

[22] The most comprehensive statement of this position that I have found is in Marta Calas and Linda Smircich, "Dangerous Liaisons: The 'Feminine in Management' Meets 'Globalization,'"

Business Horizons (March/April, 1993: 106–132). Also see Marta Calas and R. Jacques, "Diversity or Conformity?" Paper presented at the Annual Conference on Women and Organizations, Long Beach, CA, August 1988, and Linda Smircich and Marta Calas, "Using the 'F' Word: Feminist Theories and the Social Consequences of Organizational Research," in *Gendering Organizational Analysis,* A. Mills and P. Tancred, eds. (Newbury Park, CA: Sage, 1992).

[23] Jamieson and O'Mara, p. 81.

[24] Martin, *Pipeline* and *Glass.* Stella Nkomo, "The Forgotten Case of the Black Female Manager," in *Women's Careers: Pathways and Pitfalls,* S. Rose and L. Larwood, eds. (New York: Praeger, 1988) discusses the ways in which diversification policies create and exploit tensions among white women, African Americans and Latinos/Latinas.

[25] One of the foremost proponents of this position is Steven Paskoff. For summaries of his views, see Paskoff, "Wars," and Barbara Presley Noble, "An Employee Rights Minefield," *New York Times,* May 30, 1993, E1.

[26] Nancy Wyatt, "Shared Leadership in a Weavers' Guild," in B. Bate and Anita Taylor (Eds.), *Women Communicating* (Norwood, NJ: Ablex, 1988). An excellent, in-depth treatment of feminist organizations is Myra Marx Ferree and Patricia Yancey Martin, *Feminist Organizations* (Philadelphia: Temple University Press, 1995).

[27] Amy Farrell, "Like a Tarantula on a Banana Boat," in Marx Ferree and Yancy Martin (Eds.) *Feminist Organizations.*

[28] See Joan Acker, "The Gender Regime in Swedish Banks," *Scandanavian Journal of Management* (1994) and "Feminist Goals and Organizing Processes," in Marx Ferree and Yancy Martin (Eds.) *Feminist Organizations;* Joyce Rothschild-Whitt and J. A. Whitt, *The Cooperative Workplace* (Cambridge: Cambridge University Press, 1986); George Cheney, "Democracy in the Workplace," *Journal of Applied Communication Research, 23* (1995): 167–200.

[29] Acker, "Organizing;" Mary Pardo, "Doing it for the Kids," in Marx Ferree and Yancey Martin (Eds.) *Feminist Organizations.*

[30] H. Sussman, "Is Diversity Training Worth Maintaining?" *Business and Society Review, 89* (1994): 48–49.

Chapter 12

ETHICS AND ORGANIZATIONAL COMMUNICATION

What I found was really disappointing. Before undertaking this re-search I believed that people's personal values made a big differ-ence in how they behave (ethically) in the workplace. But now I'm convinced they don't.

—ARTHUR BRIEF

Our conversations about corporations need to change for us to truly create the good society.

—R. EDWARD FREEMAN AND JEANNE LIEDTKA[1]

CENTRAL THEMES

- There is a great deal of evidence that issues of unethical and illegal behav-ior are important questions facing contemporary U.S. organizations.
- Treatments of organizational ethics in the United States have focused on "micro-ethical" questions that assume the legitimacy of *laissez-faire capi-talism* and *traditional strategies of organizing.*
- Ethical systems are social constructions. The dominant systems discussed in U.S. society tend to treat ethics as an *individual* issue, when the bases of ethical dilemmas more often are *organizational* practices. Conse-quently, applying standard ethical systems to organizational actions is very difficult.
- Recently, some U.S. managers and researchers have raised "macro-ethical" questions about our economic system and dominant strategies of organiz-ing. Long common in Europe and Latin America, these questions focus on issues of "corporate social responsibility," "corporate social responsive-ness," and the need to represent the interests of *multiple stakeholders* in democratic societies.
- U.S. society is changing, especially in terms of people's work-related values and expectations. These changes place U.S. organizations at a crossroads, one

that will lead to either increased competition among different interest groups or to enhanced cooperation. The choices made by "baby boomers" and members of "Generation X" will determine which road U.S. organizations take.

KEY TERMS

Macro-ethical questions

Micro-ethical questions

Altruism

Regressive tax systems

Charity principle

Corporate social responsibility

Laissez-faire capitalism

Hedonism

Progressive tax systems

Casuistry

Stewardship principle

Corporate social responsiveness

Clearly, ethics is an important issue facing modern organizations and their employees. During the 1980s and 1990s repeated revelations of misconduct by employees have raised serious questions about the values that seemed to guide their actions. Highly publicized cases of fraud, embezzlement, and other illegal activities (for instance, "insider trading" of stocks) created the impression that many members of the business community had abandoned the values of honesty and fair play that are so important to our society. But repeated reports that *organizations* had systematically and strategically planned to act in illegal or unethical ways suggested that moral decay was much more than the result of isolated activities by "ethically challenged" individuals. In fact, between 1975 and 1985 two-thirds of the *Fortune* 500 firms were *convicted* of serious crimes ranging from price fixing to illegal dumping of hazardous wastes. In late 1996 Archer Daniels Midland was fined a record $100 million by the U.S. Justice Department for illegally fixing prices of citric acid and lysine (an additive in animal feeds). Many other organizations reached out-of-court settlements or were convicted of misdemeanors. In some sectors of the economy (for example, financial fraud in defense contracting, sexism in the military, and racism in the petroleum/petrochemical industry), pressures to engage in illegal or unethical actions are so intense and the actions are so frequent that they have come to be seen as the normal way of doing business.[2]

In addition, many studies find that managers believe that their jobs require them to compromise their own values. In a typical study, Posner and Schmidt found that 72 percent of employees face pressure to engage in actions *that they perceive are unethical,* and that 41 percent admit that they have succumbed to those pressures. A 1995 study of thirty Harvard MBAs revealed that twenty-nine of them had been ordered to violate their own personal ethical standards at least once during the previous five years. Consequently, the key ethical question is "What organizational factors encourage people to decide to act in illegal or unethical ways and how do those processes operate?", rather than "What kinds of people act in unethical or illegal ways and what has happened to their individual sense of integrity?"

As a result of adverse publicity regarding unethical and illegal activities, many organizations have created "codes of ethics" for their employees. Unfortunately, these codes typically are very narrow in scope, focusing on activities in which the organization is the *victim* of unethical or illegal activities and largely ignoring cases in which members of organizations *victimize* other employees or outside groups. But, even with this narrow focus, U.S. organizations spend $100 billion per year investigating fraud, solving ethical problems, and attempting to see that they do not happen again.[3] In short, dealing with ethical dilemmas is one of the most important challenges that employees will encounter.

TRADITIONAL PERSPECTIVES ON ORGANIZATIONAL ETHICS

The study of organizational ethics historically has involved two different sets of issues. **Macro-ethical questions** deal with the desirability of the overall economic system and typical strategies of organizing that are used in a society. In the United States the overall economic system is characterized by *laissez-faire* capitalism and some version of the traditional strategy of organizing (recall Chapter 2) is most common. *Laissez-faire* **capitalism** is based on the assumption that a free-market economic system has sufficient checks and balances in place to ensure that the interests of all members of a society will be met. Individuals compete with other individuals and organizations compete with other organizations in pursuit of their own self-interests. The competitive dynamics of a free marketplace will ensure that no individuals or organizations will be able to unfairly impose their own wills on others. Government has only a very limited role in the economy. It sometimes may need to take steps to ensure that economic markets remain competitive (through antitrust laws, for example) or that the rights of different property holders are protected. But, with these few exceptions, government is best when it does the least. Of course, many people have argued that capitalism rarely operates as a free market, that pursuit of individual self-interest inevitably leads to distortions of competition and unfair returns, and so on. These *macro-ethical* questions long have been and still are important issues in Europe and Latin America. But because U.S. citizens long have taken the value and fairness of *laissez-faire* capitalism for granted, they have been de-emphasized in U.S. discussions of organizational ethics. This has changed somewhat during the 1990s with the development of "corporate social responsibility" and "multiple interest group" perspectives that will be described later in this chapter. As a result, discussions of organizational ethics in the United States have focused on **micro-ethical** issues that assume the existence (and goodness) of the current economic and business systems.[4] Micro-ethical issues involve the problems that confront individual employees on an everyday basis. Typically, micro-level ethics programs propose that the "solution" to illegal or unethical behavior is to teach employees how to make sense of organizational situations and choose ethical courses of action. They presume that ethics is a matter of individual integrity, not an aspect of organizational decision-making. People with good moral codes act ethically and those who lack them do not. William Frederick has called this model of organizational ethics the "bootstrap" theory. According to the bootstrap perspective, everyone faces temptations to act in unethical ways, both at work and elsewhere. To resist those temptations employees need only "pull themselves up by their bootstraps" and act in morally acceptable ways.[5]

But is organizational "ethics" really an issue about the morality of individual employees? In this section I argue that individual moral codes are an important part of ethical decision-making. In the following section I will suggest that a more important influence on ethical action is the set of pressures that are present in a particular organizational situation. These pressures are created by the strategy of organizing that dominates a particular organization. In the final section of the chapter I will return to the concept of macro-ethical issues.

The Social Construction of Ethical Systems[6]

Throughout this book I have argued that the taken-for-granted assumptions of societies and organizations are social constructions—choices that groups of people make and subsequently treat as unquestioned and unquestionable truths. This observation is just as accurate regarding ethical assumptions as it is about anything else—strategies of organizing, theories of motivation, assumptions about class, race, gender, and ethnicity, and so on. In Western societies the dominant ethical systems are grounded in *utilitarianism*, which in turn is a response to ethical theories that are based on conceptions of natural law.

Perhaps the oldest Western natural law-based theory was proposed by St. Thomas Aquinas, who argued that there is a component of God's laws of the universe that govern moral life. This aspect of God's law is "engraved" on the heart of persons and is immediately known through reason. A less religious natural law-based system was developed by Immanuel Kant, who argued actions are inherently good or bad, regardless of the interests (or "ends") that it served. Determining whether an action is "good" (or "evil") involves asking oneself "what would happen if everyone in a society acted in this way?" For example, making false promises (one that the promiser does not intend to keep, but makes in order to gain some benefit) is unethical because doing so denies the ultimate value of people and, if adopted as a standard of conduct by everyone in a society, would destroy interpersonal relationships and the trust necessary for stable societies.

Utilitarian perspectives reject universal constructs like Aquinas' or Kant's because they fail to consider the specific situations surrounding a particular act. There are a number of different versions of utilitarianism, but they share an assumption that actions are ethical if they benefit everyone involved in a particular situation (the work of philosophers Jeremy Bentham, John Stuart Mill, and G. E. Moore represent three different versions of utilitarianism). Utilitarianism should not be confused with **hedonism**—the pursuit of one's own pleasure—because the interests of other people and society as a whole are as important as the interests of any individual. Utilitarianism also should not be confused with **altruism** because it does not require a person to sacrifice his or her own needs to meet others' needs.

A third group of perspectives extend the concept that ethics are grounded in social and interpersonal relationships. A number of theories assert that all members of a society have certain **inalienable rights**—to be regarded as a person who deserves to be left alone (a right to liberty) and is equal to other persons (a right to equality). Societies and the interpersonal relationships that comprise them are based on contracts, not on any ambiguous notion of natural law. Some contracts are explicit; others are implicit in the taken-for-granted assumptions of a society. Actions are ethical to the extent that they fulfill these mutual obligations (proponents of this perspective include Thomas Hobbes, John Locke, Jean Jacques Rousseau, and John Rawls). Social policies are ethical to the extent that they give the greatest benefit to the least advantaged people, thereby facilitating social equality. For example, **progressive** systems of taxation that require upper-income people to pay a larger percentage of their income than lower-income people (most income tax systems are supposed to be "progressive" in this sense) are preferable to **regressive** tax systems that do the opposite (for example, sales taxes and the U.S. FICA [social security] tax).

Thus, three different but interrelated ethical theories have been proposed, legitimized, and implemented (at least in part) in Western societies. Evaluating the ethics of a particular action or decision depends on which system is used.

Applying Ethical Systems to Organizational Decisions

In some cases it is not difficult to apply these ethical systems to organizational actions. For example, one of the most common questionable practices in organizations involves unfulfilled promises made by managers to their subordinates. Often these promises involve the organization's formal reward system—bonuses that are earned but never paid, or commitments to promote or otherwise reward employees who take certain actions that are never fulfilled. For example, employees often exert substantial time, money, and energy earning an advanced degree because they have been led to believe that doing so will be rewarded, only to find that the rewards never materialize. Promise-breaking (or any form of lying in order to obtain individual gain) would be judged to be unethical under any of the systems described in this section.[7]

But in other cases, the situation creates complex ethical dilemmas. One kind of dilemma involves "drawing lines." In theory, one can array a series of ethical decisions along a continuum, from actions that are obviously "good" to ones that are clearly "bad," and draw a line at the point where actions become unethical. Determining whether an action is ethical is a simple process of locating it on the continuum—if it is on the "unethical" side of the line, it is objectionable, if it is on the "ethical" side, it is not.

But is it really that simple? For example, one might use monetary value as a continuum for evaluating the ethicality of employee theft. The "bad" end of the continuum might be embezzling hundreds of thousands of dollars from a church.

The "good" extreme might involve taking a fire extinguisher out of a hallway without obtaining permission in order to put out a fire in a car parked outside of the building (a minor cost to the company but a great benefit to the owners of the cars parked in the lot). One problem with this approach is drawing the line—how large a monetary loss is enough to render an action unethical? If an organization locates a toxic waste dump in a poor neighborhood, the resulting decline in property values is much smaller than if it locates the dump in a wealthy neighborhood. Does that mean that the former action is ethical and the latter action is not? (By the way, this is not a hypothetical example; it is one of the core issues in a number of cases of "environmental racism" currently in the courts).

Another problem is selecting the appropriate continuum. Is it ethical to use expertise gained at one's former job to benefit one's new employer? Is it ethical to reveal as-yet-unpatented processes developed by one's former research team to one's new coworkers? If monetary value is used as the relevant criterion, the answer would depend on the monetary value of the expertise or patents. But is monetary value the appropriate criterion to use in these cases? Is it a more important criterion than others? Is it even relevant to either of these cases? Although "line drawing" (philosophers often use the term "**casuistry**" to describe this approach) *seems* to be a workable ethical system, it is very difficult to implement. It requires people to have a great deal of information available about all of the cases that make up the continuum; reduces a complex dilemma to one variable; and involves an arbitrary determination of what variable is most relevant and where the line should be drawn.[8] When does bribery (usually illegal and generally considered to be unethical) become "maintaining a customer's good will" (a business practice that can even be deducted from U.S. income taxes)? When do campaign contributions become bribes?

A second kind of dilemma occurs when ethical criteria conflict. What if a theft of intellectual property keeps a company from going bankrupt and protects the jobs of thousands of workers? What if downsizing actually does lead to improved competitiveness, and thus provides long-term economic stability for the remaining employees? What if one has signed a contract to never say anything negative about one's company in public, but one discovers long-term patterns of discrimination, fraud, or illegal activities that are known to and tolerated by one's supervisors? Presumably an employee can construct a hierarchy of ethical considerations and use it to sort out competing principles, or find a creative solution that meets all of the relevant ethical demands in part. But constructing a workable hierarchy is difficult. For example, there are obvious economic advantages to organizations that exploit their workers—profits are higher and, sometimes, the prices charged for products are lower, making the company more competitive and benefiting customers. When are these economic advantages offset by other considerations? Is it ethical for sporting goods companies to purchase soccer balls made by Pakistani children for pennies a day? Is it more or less ethical for Disney to pay adult workers in Haiti pennies a day to manufacture Mickey Mouse memorabilia? For Walmart to purchase its Kathie Lee Gifford line of clothes from U.S. sweatshops that pay immigrants in

California and New York as little as 70 cents an hour? For U.S. firms to market goods produced by political prisoners in mainland China? What countervailing ethical considerations are relevant in these cases, and are they more or less important than economic benefits?

Making ethical choices is an exceptionally complicated undertaking. Some of this complexity stems from the nature of ethical systems—some are more applicable in some situations than others, all are much more difficult to apply in concrete situations. Some of the complexity stems from the nature of organizational situations. Few situations provide simple, one-dimensional guidelines for acting. Most situations involve a complex maze of ethical concerns, some of which are dominant when viewed from one perspective, and others of which are dominant from other perspectives. And, as if these complexities were not enough, other complications stem from the characteristics of organizations.

ORGANIZATIONAL SITUATIONS AND ETHICAL DECISION-MAKING

Traditional views of organizational ethics are grounded in philosophy and focus on philosophical systems. Knowing about these systems and the ways they have developed in modern Western societies is valuable because it can help individual employees sort out their own ethical codes. But organizational ethics is much more a matter of power and politics than an exercise in applying philosophical systems.[9] As I have suggested throughout this book, employees' actions are strategic adaptations to the situations they encounter in their organizations. The particular strategy of organizing that exists in an organization creates a particular "ethical environment." The nature of that environment depends on almost all of the strategic and communicative processes that have been examined in this book.[10] For example, employees are more likely to act in ways that violate their personal ethical codes when (1) their organization (or unit) is a "closed system," isolated from and fearful about outside influences and pressures; (2) the organization's priorities are ambiguous or contradictory; (3) work groups are highly cohesive or employees have been socialized to identify with or otherwise not question the practices of the organization; (4) the organization is highly segmented and specialized; or (5) there are strong barriers to communicating across the formal boundaries of the organization. Commitment to strictly rational modes of decision-making also complicates ethical decision-making because human values (the "stuff" of which ethics is made), organizational politics, personal feelings, and interpersonal processes cannot be easily incorporated into the computations of the rational actor models.[11]

Factor #1: The Ambiguous Nature of Ethical Decision-Making

Almost every "traditional" analysis of organizational ethics concludes that a positive "ethical environment" will exist only when upper management is strongly committed to ethical action and persuasively communicates that commitment to their employees. However, studies of ethical dilemmas in employees' decision-making suggest that upper management rarely does. As important, when upper managers try to communicate their core values, they rely on "values codes" or "ethics statements" that are highly abstract or internally inconsistent. When "ethics codes" do exist they tend to focus on protecting the company from employees' actions, not protecting employees or outside interests from the company's actions. In short, it is much more likely that an ethics code will cover theft of paper clips than dumping untreated toxic wastes. Although these formal statements may reduce the legal liability of upper management, they provide employees with little guidance.[12] "Fair and equitable treatment" and "responsiveness to the customer" are common parts of formal organizational values statements, but they provide little guidance when an important customer asks you to "double our order in order to cope with an emergency" and you know that doing so would force you to delay a shipment to another customer. The manager of a U.S. Forest Service office may fully believe his or her organization's formal statement that forests should be managed "for the good of all the people today and tomorrow." But this value statement does little to help her or him decide whether to allow the clearcutting of rapidly vanishing old-growth timber when doing so will destroy the forest forever and not doing so will force more of his or her friends and neighbors out of jobs and onto public assistance.[13] Because formal values statements and policies are limited, abstract, and sometimes inconsistent, employees often find that they provide useful guidelines for decision-making in only very simple situations.[14]

To complicate the matter further, upper management also often discourages employees from discussing ethical issues, especially when possible illegal activities are involved.[15] Toffler's survey of employees' ethical choices concluded that upper management is even willing to fire employees in order to avoid *talking about* ethical issues. Then, if employees *do* act in unethical or illegal ways, management can plead ignorance of the activities and escape responsibility. (Operatives in the administration of President Reagan gave the name "plausible deniability" to this strategy.) Although more and more companies are stating publicly their commitment to ethics in management, few of their employees find it comfortable to raise such concerns in public (unless they can couch those concerns in terms of public relations or customer relations issues). Toffler concluded that "there seems to be a sense among managers that talking about ethics is 'just not done here.' And, unfortunately, they are usually right."[16]

The existence of these "gag orders" has two effects. First, the orders force employees to make complicated and difficult ethical decisions alone, in private, and in a context of ambiguity and uncertainty about the organization's values. In this context it is much easier to act in ways that ensure short-term profits for the firm (because that value is well understood by almost everyone) than to sacrifice profits for moral or ethical considerations. Second, if one employee acts in ways that are ethically questionable, it is difficult for other employees to challenge or resist their decision.[17] Most employees really do have strong personal moral codes, but because they are not allowed to talk to one another about ethical issues they rarely *realize* that other people share their values and would support their resistance. So they acquiesce, making it *seem* to everyone else that they do not oppose the unethical action. When all of the employees in a unit acquiesce, it *seems* that immoral or unethical decisions are supported by all of the employees. When communication about ethical issues is suppressed, the resulting ambiguities make it more likely that employees will act in ethically questionable ways.

Factor #2: "Hidden" Pressures Encouraging Unethical Decisions

In some cases the structure or "standard operating procedures" of an organization have the unintended effect of encouraging unethical decisions. For example, organizational theorists long have recognized that bureaucratic organizational structures allow people to avoid taking responsibility for unethical actions. Lower-level employees are allowed only to *implement* established policies and procedures, not to make them. As long as they act in ways that are consistent with those policies, they can claim not to be responsible for their actions, even if they are illegal or unethical. Upper-level employees also are able to deny responsibility because they only establish policies and procedures (which almost never are illegal or unethical in themselves), not make the illegal or unethical decision.[18] As a result, in bureaucratic organizations, it is easy to rationalize ethical considerations as "someone else's responsibility."

In addition, in very large or very complex organizations, tasks usually are broken into very small components. Each employee deals with such a small part of an overall process that she or he may not realize that the activity as a whole is improper. Secretaries shred paper, not knowing that the documents have been subpoenaed by a grand jury; truck drivers dump their loads in a county dump, not knowing their vehicles are filled with toxic wastes; accountants approve allowable cost increases in defense contracts, not realizing that some of the money will be used as kickbacks. Not only does the structure of large, complex organizations diffuse responsibility, it also diffuses the information necessary to realize that illegal or unethical activities are just that.

Third, aspects of organizational operations that on the surface seem to be ethically neutral can create pressures to engage in unethical activities. For example, during the early 1980s General Electric created its much-heralded "portfolio" model of managing its many divisions. In that system at a number of times during the year upper management computes the return (profits) that each of its divisions has generated and compares those returns to the amount of capital (money) that the company has invested in that division. Based on these computations management then labels the divisions "stars," "cash cows," "problem children," or "dogs." The divisions are treated differently depending on the category in which they are placed. Weaker divisions are denied needed capital in anticipation of their being eliminated, which further reduces their ability to move up from a lower classification.

Although the intent of this system is to provide a rational and objective means of prioritizing the divisions, it has the unintended effect of encouraging unethical behavior. If the manager of a division can artificially reduce its costs or artificially increase its income just before the accounting deadlines, she or he can ensure continued employment for the division's employees. One way of doing so is to refuse to pay bills to small suppliers until after the deadline has passed. Because the suppliers are small, they suffer significantly from the delays and have little ability to resist the tactic. In some cases the suppliers had insufficient reserves to cope with the delays and went out of business, but the managers were able to protect their jobs and those of their subordinates.[19] Of course, the portfolio management system is not intended to force small suppliers into bankruptcy or to place division managers in an ethical dilemma in which they must knowingly destroy someone else's jobs in order to protect those of their subordinates. But the unintended effect of the system is to create just that kind of ethical decision situation.

A final, "hidden" factor involves what earlier chapters called "identification" and "unobtrusive control." One characteristic of so-called "strong culture" organizations is the high level of commitment shown by their employees. During the late 1970s a group of employees of the Revco Drug Company in Indiana defrauded the state welfare department of millions of dollars. Interestingly, although the organization gained a great deal from their actions, the workers got little or no individual benefit from doing so. They acted illegally largely because they were loyal to their organization. They believed that the monies were legitimately owed to Revco, that a history of stalled negotiations between the firm and the welfare department proved that the company was being victimized by the bureaucracy, that the cost of correcting the situation through legal channels was greater than the likely return, and that they could significantly increase the firm's short-term profits if they were successful.[20] They were, in short, precisely the kind of employees that are "created" through cultural strategies of organizing—highly capable individuals who were committed to their organization and its success and willing to take risks and act creatively to ensure that it succeeds. Unless prohibitions against illegal or unethical activities is a core organizational value, cultural strategies of organizing may actually encourage it.

Of course, neither the bureaucratic structure of traditional organizations nor cultural strategies of organizing are *intended* to encourage employees to decide to act in illegal or unethical ways. But they create opportunities and incentives for them to do so. An *unintended consequence* of ethical environments in which ethical codes are confusing, ambiguous, and not discussed is to encourage employees to act in unethical ways and to do so *even if they have highly ethical personal moral codes.* As a result, employees become "ethical segregationists" who use one moral code at work and another in their outside lives. Negative ethical environments and rules of organizational survival overcome personal moral codes.[21]

CASE STUDY:
THE ETHICS GAME

There is a wonderful game that is designed to help people sort out their own ethical codes in business and personal situations.* It provides a series of situations in which a person engages in illegal or unethical behavior and asks the players to evaluate the acceptability of the action. For example, "Brent" faces four situations. In one he is the principal of a high school and accepts an expensive gift from a supply company with which he does business. In another he has spent most of his life savings on a lot on which he plans to build an apartment house, only to find that it is not quite big enough to include the number of parking spaces required by the city zoning ordinance. He offers a friend in the zoning office free rent for a year if he waives the requirement. In another Brent takes members of the city council on a hunting trip at company expense and while there lobbies them to relax an air-quality ordinance that is hurting his company's trade. In another case he wants to sell merchandise to a client in another country. The client tells him that if Brent gives him a $10,000 cash payment he will make sure that Brent gets the contract. The payment must be in cash because it is illegal in his country, although it is not illegal in Brent's country. Brent makes the payment.

In each of the cases Brent's actions involve offering or making a bribe in exchange for some kind of gain. Interestingly, whenever I have played the game, participants evaluate the situations differently. To the extent that the gain is *personal,* Brent's actions are judged to be unacceptable. But to the extent that only the organization benefits, people are much more accepting of his actions. And, during the last five years, if the action involves bribing a public official people see it as a normal and expected aspect of our political system. It doesn't seem to matter who the judges are (I have used it with undergraduates, graduate students, managers, and even lawyers), or what the specifics of the situation are (the game includes a number of other situations).

My results suggest that Americans have different ethical standards when they evaluate the actions of individuals acting alone and individuals acting as representatives of their organizations. A similar conclusion can be drawn from the results of court decisions: The average jail sentence for an individual who steals $10,000 or more is twelve years, but the average sentence for someone convicted of a comparable white-collar crime is only four years.

In a controversial article, Albert Carr argued that not only are there different ethical standards for individuals and for organizations, but also that there should

---

*It is called "Where Do You Draw the Line?" and is available from Simile II in Del Mar, California.

(continued)

(continued from the previous page)

be.** Lying (or bluffing) is expected in some areas of life, notably in poker, politics, and business. If an employee refuses to make conscious misstatements, conceal pertinent facts, or exaggerate—that is, if she or he feels obligated to tell the truth, the whole truth, and nothing but the truth—then his or her career, and his or her organization if she or he is an executive, is at grave risk. As one executive who Carr interviewed put it:

> So long as a businessman (sic) complies with the laws of the land and avoids telling malicious lies, he's ethical. If the law as written gives a man a wide-open chance to make a killing, he'd be a fool not to take advantage of it. If he doesn't, somebody else will. There's no obligation on him to stop and consider who is going to get hurt. If the law says he can do it, that's all the justification he needs. There's nothing unethical about that. It's just plain business sense.

The key, Carr argues, is recognizing that we are all "ethical segregationists" who use one code of ethics at work and a different one at home. Confusing the two can only needlessly complicate our lives.

Discussion Questions

1. Where would you "draw the line"? Which of Brent's actions was acceptable (or, in a more general sense, when are bribes acceptable)? When is it ethical to withhold key information (for instance, a major defect in the house you are trying to sell or the fact that the Ford Pinto's gasoline tank explodes in rear-end collisions)? Is it ethical to procure prostitutes for a client who asks you to? For a good friend? For a client from a country in which prostitution is legal? If you gave different answers, why? If not, why not?

2. Many people argue that, while unethical business practices may benefit an individual or organization in the short term, they fail over the long term. Assuming that this is accurate (although there is little evidence to support this assumption: Ford sales were not harmed by their unethical actions regarding the Pinto, and the guilty *Fortune* 500 firms mentioned at the beginning of this section still are *Fortune* 500 firms.), how would it affect employees' behaviors? Are they more likely to be ethical when they think about the long term? Why or why not?

**Albert Carr, "Is Business Bluffing Ethical?" *Harvard Business Review* (January-February 1968). For a critique of his position and Carr's response, see Timothy Blodgett, "Showdown on Business Bluffing" in Kenneth Andrews, ed. *Ethics in Practice* (Boston, MA: Harvard Business School Press, 1989).

FROM "CORPORATE SOCIAL RESPONSIBILITY" TO MULTIPLE STAKEHOLDER MODELS

As I indicated at the beginning of this chapter, most discussions of organizational ethics in the United States have de-emphasized *macro-ethical* questions about the existing business and economic system. With the economic dislocations of the 1980s and 1990s—declining real incomes, increasing maldistribution of wealth, evidence of continuing racism and sexism, job loss in the face of sky-rocketing corporate profits and compensation paid to upper managers—more and more people have started asking very serious questions about the relationship between organizations and the larger society. In some ways this tension is not new. Presumably, U.S. residents value both democracy and free enterprise. But historically, U.S. organizations have been decidedly undemocratic institutions. And throughout our history formal organizations have exerted strong influences on political decision-making, increasingly out of sight of the public eye. When combined with widespread acceptance of the assumptions underlying *laissez-faire* capitalism, these trends create a social situation in which very powerful political and economic institutions can operate freely, without being held responsible to the larger society. Stanley Deetz concludes that in the contemporary United States "commercial corporations function as public institutions but without public accountability."[22] This tension between a representative, democratic society and autonomous, nondemocratic organizations creates a wide range of *macro-ethical* questions.

From Social Responsibility to Social Responsiveness

Of course, some macro-ethical questions have been asked for decades. Writing at the turn of the century, Andrew Carnegie, founder of U.S. Steel, argued that two principles needed to be accepted if laissez-faire capitalism was to succeed over the long term. One was the **charity principle**, which required more fortunate members of the society to assist its less fortunate members, either directly or indirectly through corporate support of social service organizations. Second was the **stewardship principle**, which required businesses and wealthy people to attempt to increase the wealth of the society as a whole by wisely investing the resources they controlled. For the following fifty years Carnegie's assumptions were accepted and codified into a concept of "**corporate social responsibility**," the belief that organizations had a responsibility to assist in the solution of social problems, especially those that they helped create, in addition to making money. By the 1960s the social responsibility perspective was being challenged from almost every political perspective.

Conservative economist Milton Friedman (among others) argued that the only responsibility corporations have is to pursue their own economic self-interest. Managers have no particular expertise in defining social problems, no incentives for trying to solve them, and capitalism provides no means of holding them accountable for the effects of their purportedly "socially responsible" activities. To the extent that they *do* invest the organization's capital in such activities they make it vulnerable to competitors who invest all of their resources in enhancing the firm's economic position. Thus, in the long run, they threaten the jobs of their employees and violate the trust of their investors. In short, Carnegie's two principles are contradictory—in an economy defined by competitive, *laissez-faire* capitalism, corporate *charity* reduces the economic viability of a firm, thus violating the *stewardship* principle. In a democratic society, only government is responsible for dealing with social problems, because only government can be held accountable for doing or not doing so.[23] Debates over the "social responsibility" doctrine continued until the late 1970s, eventually leading to a new doctrine of "**social responsiveness**."

In the social responsiveness perspective, managers are responsible for monitoring an organization's environment and strategically responding to environmental pressures. Many of these pressures are primarily economic, as Unit I explained. But others are as much social as economic. For example, the growing environmental movement of the 1970s and 1980s placed new pressures on managers, pressures that, ironically, were enforced by governmental action. The advantage of the social responsiveness perspective is that it does give managers some guidelines for making socially relevant choices: obey the law, fulfill regulations, and placate powerful external interest groups. But it also is problematic in a number of ways. First, it establishes an adversarial relationship between managers and both government agencies and external interest groups. Instead of fostering a cooperative effort to deal with social and economic problems, it encourages competitive and hostile orientations (recall Chapter 9). Second, it encourages managers to find ways to proactively manage external pressures. In many cases it is easier to circumvent or overpower external pressures than to be responsive to them. Contributing to the political campaigns of candidates who promise to weaken environmental standards often is much less expensive than meeting those standards. Exploiting weaknesses in governmental monitoring or the legal system may be more cost-effective than acting in legal and ethical ways. For example, the record $100 million fine levied against Archer Daniels Midland for price fixing (described at the beginning of this chapter) pales in comparison to the estimated $200–$600 million in extra profits that ADM made by engaging in the illegal activities. In short, instead of moderating the conflict between "charity" and "stewardship" that was revealed in the debate over corporate social responsibility, the notion of "social responsiveness" magnifies it.

From Social Responsiveness to Multiple Stakeholders

Other critics have argued that the underlying assumptions of both the social responsibility and social responsiveness perspectives are flawed because they ignore *macro-ethical* questions about laissez-faire capitalism itself.[24] Advocates of multiple stakeholder perspectives argue that many groups have a legitimate stake in the decisions made by managers and the actions taken by the organizations they control. Workers, suppliers, consumers, host communities, stockholders, and the general community often have taken more risks and made greater long-term investments in their organizations than upper management has. Through their taxes, *they* have paid to educate the workers hired by the organization, built the infrastructure needed for the organization to function (roads, airports, electric systems, etc.), and invested *their* labor and capital in the organization. And *they* are harmed most when the organization downsizes, despoils the environment, engages in discriminatory actions, and so on. Although this observation is not new, it has become more salient during recent years because of three changes in the U.S. economy. First, the share of federal taxes paid by corporations has steadily fallen from approximately 50 percent during the 1950s to approximately 10 percent today, with the tax burden shifting to individuals, primarily people with middle or lower incomes. Consequently the indirect contributions that outside groups have made to organizational success have increased significantly.

Second, as Chapter 1 explained, both incomes and wealth have become increasingly concentrated at the top of the scale. Record corporate profits have not been distributed among workers, or even among investors. In 1996 dividends paid to stockholders fell to less than 2 percent, the lowest level in a generation. This shift was obscured by skyrocketing stock prices, but even those gains were concentrated at the top of the income pyramid (approximately 80 percent of the increase in portfolio values during the 1990s has gone to the richest 20 percent of U.S. residents). Record compensation packages for upper management and bonuses that rarely are tied to performance also create a perception that the economic system was inherently unfair.[25] And finally, corporate downsizing has disproportionately harmed middle- and lower-level workers while contributing relatively little to the long-term competitive position of U.S. organizations.[26]

Thus, neither the free market system nor government seems to be effectively protecting the interests of multiple stakeholders. Of course, doing so is not one of the goals of the free market system. Even if profit motives are supplemented by notions of social responsibility or responsiveness, they always will be in competition with one another. In the short term, profits will be a more salient value to managers than the more long-term interests of outsiders, especially during times of economic difficulty. According to multiple stakeholder models, the free market system simply does not provide any reason for managers to include stakeholders' values and interests in their decision-making.

In addition, the dynamics of free markets also are distorted by differences in power and control. In theory, in a free market everyone pursues his or her individual self-interests, and in doing so creates a mutually beneficial economy—checks and balances that are built into the system prevent any one individual or group of individuals from imposing their will on the others.[27] But economic power is not equitably distributed in *real* markets, so the system of checks and balances is upset. Presumably, government has the ability and right to intervene in markets to restore competitive balance, but differences in the political power of various stakeholder groups makes this kind of intervention unlikely. Even if political power was balanced, government agencies simply cannot successfully micro-manage managers' decisions, even with the extensive bureaucracies characteristic of "planned economies." More importantly, in the United States, government traditionally has acted primarily to serve managerial interests, increasingly so as political campaigns have relied on corporate contributions. Governmental discourse increasingly echoes managerial discourse, as the key assumptions of free market, manager-dominated economies become more deeply embedded in the taken-for-granted assumptions of U.S. society.[28] Thus, neither the structures, practices, nor communicative processes of government serve to ensure the interests of stakeholder groups.

The only ethically viable response to these trends, according to multiple stakeholder models, is to democratize U.S. organizations. Democratization involves two simple but radical steps: (1) encourage open and honest debate about the taken-for-granted assumptions about organizations and economic justice that dominate contemporary U.S. society, and (2) create systems, structures, and practices through which the voices of multiple stakeholders are raised and heard. Of course, many of these ideas have been discussed at various points in this book. Power relations are embedded in the taken-for-granted assumptions of a society, particularly involving those aspects of a society or economy that are perceived to be *normal* and *natural* (recall Chapters 1 and 7); definitions of key concepts (for example, "efficiency") are rarely challenged or even questioned, even though they result from arbitrary and value-laden choices that privilege the interests of some groups over the interests of others (Chapters 4 and 7); organizational power typically is used to suppress dissenting voices and interests (Chapters 7 and 9); and the strategic choices made by employees tend to reproduce the power relationships and situational constraints that the employees face (Unit I).

Democratization can succeed only if people challenge the societal myth that democratic governance is too inefficient to be used by organizations in highly competitive environments. Challenging this assumption begins by carefully examining the inefficiencies that are built into traditional, nondemocratic, strategies of organizing—the inevitable communication breakdowns described in Chapter 2, the alienation and resistance described in Unit I, the "nonrational" nature of organizational decision-making and suppression of conflicts described in Chapters 8 and 9, and the orientation toward short-term profit maximization and managerial control that are part of the traditional strategies of organizing (Chapter 2). But challenging the assumption also involves taking a new look at instances in which democratic processes have succeeded even within nondemocratic organizations (Chapters 5 and 11). For example, the Saturn automobile corporation was designed to foster a cooperative relationship between labor and management that focused on finding ways to increase product quality. This system was a radical departure from the adversarial, bureaucratic strategy that long had characterized U.S. auto manufacturers in general and General Motors in particular. The Saturn experiment was so successful that by 1992 the company needed to substantially increase production. Operating on the assumptions of traditional strategies of organizing, management proposed a strategy of short-term cost containment that would reduce economic rewards to workers and reduce product quality. Workers protested the strategy and responded with a work slowdown, forcing management to eventually negotiate systems that improved the production process, protected worker income, maintained high product quality, and ensured long-term customer satisfaction and loyalty. But the solution emerged only because workers had sufficient power to make their voices heard, and because both sides used integrative, problem-solving conflict management strategies to move beyond the preferences for short-term profit maximization that long have typified U.S. management. Other examples of successful democratic organizations were provided by the feminist organizations described in Chapter 11.

Once the assumption that democracy is inefficient is challenged, a number of steps can be taken to better represent the interests of multiple stakeholders. For example, limiting the size of organizations or units of organizations seems to encourage open debate and foster opportunities for multiple voices to be heard. Systems of employee "empowerment," including different versions of participatory decision-making (Chapter 3), are a first step toward democratizing organizations, but if they are employed within nondemocratic organizations, they tend to punish or unethically manipulate workers.[29] But the key shift is to take the long-standing U.S. preference for democratic governance seriously, so seriously that concepts of representation and accountability are applied *even* to formal organizations.

EPILOGUE: A PERSONAL NOTE

The times, they are a changin'

—BOB DYLAN

The 1990s have been dominated by a realization that the society, economy, and organizations of today's United States are both very different than they were a generation ago and even less like they will be a generation from now. As in all times of social and cultural change, the early 1990s have witnessed a great deal of anxiety and controversy about the directions that U.S. society, its economy, and its organizations will take. The increasing racial and ethnic diversity of our society, the increasing age of the population, and the increasing representation of women, African Americans, Latinos, Native Americans, Asian Americans, and disabled persons in our organizations are only part of that change. Equally important are changes in many of the "taken-for-granted" assumptions that Americans traditionally have held about their lives and their careers.

Two core assumptions of U.S. society have been that each successive generation will have a better standard of living than the previous one, and that committed, loyal, productive employees eventually will be rewarded by moving to progressively higher positions in their organizations or in other firms in their fields. Neither of these assumptions now seems to be true.[30] Disenchantment has set in even for those who have "made it"—fewer than half of the senior executives recently surveyed by the UCLA Graduate School of Business said that they would pursue the same career if they had it to do over again.[31] Companies no longer perceive that they have a "close, family-like" relationship with their employees, more than 70 percent of employees believe that they must be self-sufficient in managing their careers, rather than relying on their current firms for career growth or advancement—it's not only "Generation X" that realizes the "contract" has ended (recall Chapter 1).

This shift in expectations and values comes at precisely the time when organizations are asking, or demanding, that the employees they retain "do more with less." And, like all taken-for-granted assumptions, these shifts can easily become self-fulfilling. Employees who are disenchanted, self-oriented, and not committed to their firms tend to act in ways that support the perception that today's employees are disloyal and not to be trusted with significant responsibilities. Showing employees low levels of trust and refusing to assign them meaningful responsibilities tends to reduce commitment and increase disenchantment—which provides additional evidence of their lack of loyalty—and so on in a vicious cycle.

So it seems that both U.S. organizations and U.S. workers face a number of crucial challenges. The natures of these challenges are not especially surprising because they result from the fundamental tensions described in Chapter 1: a tension between societies' or organizations' needs for control and coordination and individuals' needs for autonomy, creativity, and sociability; and the tension between individuality and community that long has characterized U.S. society. The problem—and the challenge—is that a society and its organizations can deal with these fundamental tensions in one of two ways. They can focus on *individuality,* domination, and control, become more competitive and divided, with one group of members turning against another and magnifying long-held antagonisms based on organizational rank, class, race, ethnicity, and gender. Or they can focus on creating a meaningful *community* that represents the interests of multiple stakeholders and meets the needs of all of its members. But "societies" and "organizations" do not make choices—people do. Human beings are, after all, choice-making beings and it is our choices that will determine the road our society and our organizations take. As my generation moves into positions of political and organizational power, and as your generation moves into "the real world," we all face choices. The strategies that *we* choose will determine the kind of organizations that *we* live in for the rest of our lives, and the kind of society that *we* will create for ourselves and for our children. Make good choices.

NOTES

[1] This paraphrase of Professor Brief's comments appeared in Dawn Blalock (of *The Wall Street Journal*), "Workplace Ethics Take a Vacation," *Houston Chronicle,* March 31, 1996, D3; R. Edward Freeman and Jeanne Liedtka, "Corporate Social Responsibility: A Critical Approach," *Business Horizons* (July-August, 1991), p. 92.

[2] Amatai Etzioni, cited in C. Gorman, "Listen Here, Mr. Big!," *Time* (July 3, 1989): 40–45. Also see Lawrence Hosmer, "The Institutionalization of Unethical Behavior," *Journal of Business Ethics, 6* (1987): 439–447. The ADM case is summarized by Joseph Menn in "ADM Fine Criticized as Too Low," *Houston Chronicle,* December 1, 1996, C13.

[3] B.Z. Posner and W.H. Schmidt, "Values and the American Manager," *California Management Review, 26* (1984): 202–216. Also see M. Moser, "Ethical Conflict at Work," *Journal of Business Ethics, 7* (1988): 381–387; Robert Sims, "The Challenge of Ethical Behavior in Organizations," *Journal of Business Ethics, 11* (1992 501–513. The MBA study and the cost estimates are summarized in Jim Barlow, "Ethics Can Boost the Bottom Line," *Houston Chronicle,* October 31, 1996, C1; D. Robin, M. Giallourakis, F. David, and T. Mortiz examine the inadequacy of ethics codes in "A Different Look at Business Ethics," in P. Madsen and J. Shafritz (Eds.), *Essentials of Business Ethics* (New York: Meridian, 1990).

[4] See Otto A. Brener, John E. Logan, and Richard E. Wokutch, "Ethics and Values in Management Thought," in *Business Environment and Business Ethics,* Karen Paul (Ed.) (Cambridge, MA: Ballinger, 1987).

[5] William Frederick, "Review of Suresh Srivastva, *Executive Integrity,*" *Administrative Science Quarterly, 34* (1989): 490–492; also see G. Caiden and N. Caiden, "Administrative Corruption," *Public Administration Review, 10* (1977): 301–309. A representative case of the "bootstrap" theory is presented in Suresh Srivastva and Associates, *Executive Integrity* (San Francisco: Jossey-Bass, 1989). Frankly, I prefer a different metaphor for this theory, that of the religious revival. Many Protestant denominations hold annual or semiannual "revival" services at which people are encouraged to confess their sins and commit themselves to living a sin-free life. Unfortunately, the positive effects of revival experiences tend to be quite short-lived; most of the confessants return to their sinful lives soon after leaving the revival service. The ethics seminars and training programs that recently have become quite popular often are based on the same assumptions—if we just place employees in a setting in which they are encouraged to adopt a new religion of ethical organizational behavior, they will return to their organizations and change them forever. Although I do not know of any research on the long-term impact of these proposals, I suspect that their effects are much like those of religious revivals.

[6] Of course, I can only provide a very brief introduction to ethical theories in this section. An excellent brief summary is available in Ann Plamandon, "Ethics in the Workplace," in Peggy Yuhas Byars, (Ed.) *Organizational Communication: Theory and Behavior* (Boston: Allyn and Bacon, 1997).

[7] J. Gilchrest and Shirley Van Hoeven, "Employees' Accounts of Broken Organizational Promises," in J. Jaska (Ed.), *Proceedings of the 1992 National Communication Ethics Conference* (Annandale, VA: Speech Communication Association, 1992); Sissela Bok, *Lying: Moral Choice in Public and Private Life* (New York: Pantheon Books, 1978).

[8] See Albert Jonsen and Stephen Toulmin, *The Abuse of Casuistry* (Berkeley: University of California Press, 1988).

[9] This section is based on the introduction and first chapter of Charles Conrad, ed. *The Ethical Nexus* (Norwood, NJ: Ablex, 1993). The remaining chapters of that book provide a number of case studies of values-related decision-making in organizations. Also see J.A. Waters, "Catch 20.5: Corporate Morality as an Organizational Phenomenon," *Organizational Dynamics, 6* (1978): 2–19; and G.L. Pamental, "The Course in Business Ethics: Can it Work?" *Journal of Business Ethics, 8* (1989): 547–551. A number of authors have argued that the key to ethical behavior is the interaction between employees' personal moral codes and attributes of their organizations. This is the perspective that I will take in the following section. See William H. Hegerty and Henry P. Sims, "Some Determinants of Unethical Decision Behavior," *Journal of Applied Psychology, 63* (1978): 451–457, and "Organizational Philosophy, Policies, and Objectives Related to Unethical Decision Behavior," *Journal of Applied Psychology, 64* (1979): 331–338; Linda

Trevino and S.A. Youngblood, "Bad Apples in Bad Barrels," *Journal of Applied Psychology, 75* (1990): 378–385.

[10] For excellent summaries of the concept of ethical environments, see J.D. Pettit, Jr., B. Vaught, and K.J. Pulley, "The Role of Communication in Organizations: Ethical Considerations, *Journal of Business Communication, 27* (1990): 233–249; R.A. Cooke, "Danger Signs of Unethical Behavior," *Journal of Business Ethics, 19* (1991): 249–253; and John B. Cullen, Bart Victor, and C. Stephens, "An Ethical Weather Report," *Organizational Dynamics, 17* (1989): 50–62.

[11] Waters, "Catch 20.5." For a brief summary of the conflict between "rational" and "ethical" decision-making, see the final chapter of Charles Perrow, *Normal Accidents* (New York: Basic Books, 1984).

[12] J.A. Waters and F. Bird, "Attending to Ethics in Management," *Journal of Business Ethics, 8* (1989): 493–497; Bommer, C. Gratto, J. Gravander, and M. Tuttle, "A Behavioral Model of Ethical and Unethical Decision Making," *Journal of Business Ethics, 6* (1987): 265–280; and B.E. Toffler, *Tough Choices* (New York: John Wiley, 1986).

[13] Of course, changes in overall public policy could allow the forester to avoid being placed in this dilemma, but, as long as the policy is as it is, she or he must sacrifice one value in favor of another.

[14] Bommer, et al., p. 267; and Toffler, p. 333.

[15] Toffler; J. Waters and F. Bird, "The Moral Dimension of Organizational Culture," *Journal of Business Ethics, 6* (1987): 15–22.

[16] Toffler, p. 337. Also see Waters and Bird. Matthew Seeger has observed that when people *do* talk about ethics, it usually is to avoid taking responsibility for ethical choices ("Responsibility in Organizational Communication," in J. Jaska (Ed.) *Proceedings of the 1992 National Communication Ethics Conference* (Annandale, VA: Speech Communication Association, 1992).

[17] Herbert Kellman and L. Hamilton, *Crimes of Obedience* (New Haven, CT: Yale University Press, 1989).

[18] William G. Scott and D.K. Hart, *Organizational America* (Boston: Houghton Mifflin, 1979) and *Organizational Values in America* (New Brunswick, NJ: Transaction Publishers, 1989); C. Walton, *The Moral Manager* (Cambridge, MA: Ballinger, 1988); and Robert Jackall, "Moral Mazes: Bureaucracy and Managerial Work," *Harvard Business Review, 61* (September-October 1983): 99–123.

[19] Hosmer.

[20] Diane Vaughn, *Controlling Unlawful Organizational Behavior* (Chicago: University of Chicago Press). They also believed that they could get away with it.

[21] Jackall, "Terrain;" Sims, "Challenge."

[22] Stanley Deetz, "Transforming Communication, Transforming Business," *The International Journal of Value-Based Management* (1995, in press), p. 2. Also see Stanley Deetz. *Transforming Communication; Transforming Business* (Creskill, NJ: 1995).

[23] Milton Friedman, *Capitalism and Freedom* (Chicago: University of Chicago Press, 1962) and "The Social Responsibility of Business Is to Increase Profits," *New York Times Magazine,* September 13, 1970, pp. 122–126.

[24] The primary proponents of this perspective among organizational communication theorists are Stanley Deetz, *Transforming* and "Transforming," and George Cheney, "Democracy in the Workplace," *Journal of Applied Communication Research, 23* (1995): 167–200. Important proponents among organizational theorists are R. Edward Freeman, *Business as A Humanity* (New York: Oxford University Press, 1994) and *Business Ethics: The State of the Art* (New York: Oxford University Press, 1991); Russell Ackoff, *The Democratic Corporation* (New York: Oxford University Press, 1994); and Scott and Hart, *Values.* Even some economists have expressed concern for the conflict between individualism and community (see, for example, Amatai Etzioni, *The Moral Dimension* [New York: Free Press, 1988]; *New Communitarian Thinking* [Charlottesville, VA: University Press of Virginia, 1995]; *The New Golden Rule* [New York: Basic Books, 1996]).

[25] Excellent summaries of these trends are available in Sharon Cohen (AP), "Worker's American Dream Vanishing," *Bryan-College Station Eagle,* September 6, 1992, C3–5; David Gordon, *Fat and Mean* (Ithaca, NY: Cornell University/ILR Press, 1996); William Greider, *Who Will*

Tell the People? (New York: Simon and Schuster, 1992); a seven–part *New York Times* series on downsizing that was published during 1996; Thomas Moore, *The Disposable Work Force* (New York: Aldine de Gruyter, 1996); M. Scott Poole and Charles Conrad, eds., "Special Issue on Communication in the Age of the Disposable Worker," *Communication Research* (in press); and Edward N. Wolff, *Top Heavy: A Study of the Increasing Inequality of Wealth in America* (New York: The Twentieth Century Fund Press, 1995).

[26] Michael Hitt, Robert Hoskisson, R. Duane Ireland, and Jeffrey Harrison, "Effects of Acquisitions on R&D Inputs and Outputs," *Academy of Management Journal, 34* (1991): 693–706. Also see M. Hitt and R. Hoskisson, "Strategic Competitiveness," in *Advances in Applied Business Strategy,* L. Foster, ed. (Greenwich, CT: JAI Press, 1991) and M. Hitt, R. Hoskisson, and R.D. Ireland, "Mergers and Acquisitions and Managerial Commitment to Innovation in M-form Firms," *Strategic Management Journal, 11* (1990): 29–47.

[27] See Garrett Hardin, "The Tragedy of the Commons," *Science* (Dec. 13, 1968): pp. 1243–1248.

[28] James Aune, "Inevitability and Perversity: The Loci of Capitalist Arguments about Labor," paper presented at the Speech Communication Association convention, San Diego, CA, November 1996.

[29] Cheney, "Democracy," p. 168; Guillermo Grenier, *Inhuman Relations* (Philadelphia: Temple University Press, 1988).

[30] An excellent study of the sociocultural consequences of these trends is Katherine Newman, *Falling from Grace: The Experience of Downward Mobility in the American Middle Class* (New York: Free Press, 1988). Also see "Downward Mobility," *Business Week* (March 23, 1992): 56–63.

[31] Amy Saltzman, "Fast-Track Success Drops in Importance for Many," *Houston Chronicle,* Sept. 19, 1991, C1, C14.

BIBLIOGRAPHY

+Indicates particularly appropriate for graduate students

Abell, Peter. *Organizations as Bargaining and Influence Systems* London: Heinemann, 1975.

Abrahamsson, B. *Bureaucracy or Participation?* Beverly Hills, CA: Sage, 1977.

Aburdene, Patricia and Naisbitt, John. *Megatrends for Women.* NY: Villard Books, 1992.

Acker, Joan, The Gender Regime in Swedish Banks. *Scandinavian Journal of Management* (1994).

Acker, Joan. Feminist Goals and Organizing Processes, in *Feminist Organizations.* Myra Marx Ferree and Patricia Yancey Martin, eds. Philadelphia: Temple University Press, 1995.

Adams, J. Stacy. The Structure and Dynamics of Behavior in Organizational Boundary Roles, in *Handbook of Industrial and Organizational Psychology.* Marvin Dunnette, ed. Chicago: Rand-McNally, 1976.

Adams, Rebecca and Parrot, Roxanne. Pediatric Nurses' Communication of Role Expectations of Parents to Hospitalized Children. *Journal of Applied Communication Research, 22* (1994): 36-47.

Albrecht, Terrance. Communication and Personal Control in Empowering Organizations, in *Communication Yearbook 11.* James Anderson, ed. Beverly Hills, CA: Sage, 1987.

+Albrecht, Terrance. An Overtime Analysis of Communication Patterns and Work Perceptions, in *Communication Yearbook 8.* Robert Bostrom, ed. Beverly Hills, CA: Sage, 1984.

Albrecht, Terrance and Adelman, Mara. *Communicating Social Support.* Newbury Park, CA: Sage, 1988.

Albrecht, Terrance and Bach, Betsy. *Organizational Communication: A Relational Perspective.* Ft. Worth, TX: Harcourt Brace, 1996.

Albrecht, Terrance and Hall, Bradford. Facilitating Talk About New Ideas. *Communication Monographs, 58* (1991): 273-288.

Albrecht, Terrance and Hall, Bradford. Relational and Content Differences Between Elites and Outsiders in Innovation Networks. *Human Communication Research, 17* (1991): 535-561.

Albrecht, Terrance and Halsey, J. Mutual Support in Mixed Status Relationships. *Journal of Social and Personal Relationships, 9* (1992): 237-252.

Alderfer, Clayton, Alderfer, Charleen, Tucker, Leota, and Tucker, Robert. Diagnosing Race Relations in Management. *Journal of Applied Behavioral Science, 16* (1980): 135-166.

Alderton, S.M. and Frey, Larry. Effects of Reactions to Arguments on Group Outcomes. *Central States Speech Journal, 34* (1983): 88-95.

Aldrich, Howard. *Organizations and Environments.* Englewood Cliffs: Prentice-Hall, 1979.

+Aldrich, Howard and Herker, Diane. Boundary Spanning Roles and Organizational Structures. *Academy of Management Review, 2* (1977): 217-230.

Alexander, Elmore, Penley, Larry, and Jernigan, I Edward. The Effect of Individual Differences on Managerial Media Choice. *Management Communication Quarterly, 5* (1991): 155-173.

Alexander, Elmore, Penley, Larry, and Jernigan, I Edward. The Relationship of Basic Decoding Skills to Managerial Effectiveness. *Management Communication Quarterly, 8* (1992): 58-73.

Allen, Myria Watkins. The Relationship Between Communication, Affect, Job Alternatives, and Voluntary Turnover Intentions. *Southern Communication Journal, 61* (1996): 198-209.

+Allen, T.J. *Managing the Flow of Technology.* Cambridge, MA: M.I.T. Press, 1977.

+Alvesson, Mats. Cultural-Ideological Modes of Management Control: A Theory and a Case Study of a Professional Service Company, in *Communication Yearbook 16.* Stanley Deetz, ed. Newbury Park, CA: Sage, 1994.

+Alvesson, Mats. Organizations, Culture and Ideology. *International Studies of Management and Organization, 17* (1987): 4-18.

+Alvesson, Mats. *Organization Theory and Technocratic Consciousness.* New York: Walter de Gruyter, 1987.

+Alvesson, Mats and Wilmott, Hugh, eds. *Critical Management Studies.* Newbury Park, CA: Sage, 1992.

Amparano, Julie Lopez. Study Says Women Face Glass Walls as Well as Glass Ceilings. *Wall Street Journal,* March 3, 1992.

Andrews, Patricia Hayes and Herschel, Richard T. *Organizational Communication.* Geneva, IL: Houghton-Mifflin, 1996.

+Ansari, S. and Euske, K. Rational, Rationalizing, and Reifying Uses of Accounting Data in Organizations. *Accounting, Organizations, and Society, 12* (1987): 549-570.

Arendt, Hannah. *The Human Condition.* Chicago: University of Chicago Press, 1958.

Arvey, Richard and Ivanevich, John. Punishment in Organizations. *The Academy of Management Review, 5* (1980): 123-134.

Arvey, Richard, Davis, Gregory, and Nelson, Sherry. Use of Discipline in an Organization. *Journal of Applied Psychology, 69* (1984): 448-460.

Astley, Graham and Van de Ven, Andrew, Central Perspectives and Debates in Organizational Theory. *Administrative Science Quarterly, 28* (1983): 245-273.

Aune, James. Inevitability and Perversity: The Loci of Capitalist Arguments about Labor. Paper presented at the Speech Communication Association Convention, San Diego, CA, Nov., 1996.

Axelrod, R. *The Evolution of Cooperation.* New York: Basic Books, 1984.

Axley, Steve. Managerial and Organizational Communication in Terms of the Conduit Metaphor. *Academy of Management Review, 9* (1984): 428-437.

Bach, Betsy. Making a Difference by Doing Differently. Paper presented at the Arizona State University Conference on Organizational Communication: Perspectives for the 1990s, Tempe, AZ, April, 1990.

Bach, Betsy. The Effect of Multiplex Relationships Upon Innovation Adoption. *Communication Monographs, 56* (1991): 133-148.

+Bacharach, Samuel and Aiken, Michael. Communication in Administrative Bureaucracies. *Academy of Management Journal, 3* (1977): 365-377.

Bacharach, Peter and Baratz, Morton. Two Faces of Power. *American Political Science Review, 56* (1962): 947-952.

Bacharach, Samuel and Lawler, Edward. *Power and Politics in Organizations.* San Francisco: Jossey-Bass, 1980.

+Banks, Steve and Riley, Patricia. Structuration as an Ontology for Communication Research, in *Communication Yearbook 16.* Stanley Deetz, ed. Newbury Park, CA: 1993.

+Bantz, Charles and Smith, David. A Critique and Experimental Test of Weick's Model of Organizing. *Communication Monographs, 44* (1977): 171-184.

Barber, David. *Power in Committees.* Chicago: Rand-McNally, 1966.

Barge, J. Kevin and Musambria, G.W. Turning Points in Chair-Faculty Relationships. *Journal of Applied Communication Research, 20* (1992): 54-77.

Barkin, Steve and Gurvitch, Michael. Out of Work and On the Air. Critical Studies in Mass Communication, 4 (1987): 1-20.

Barker, James. Tightening the Iron Cage: Concertive Control in Self-Managing Teams. *Administrative Science Quarterly, 38* (1993): 408-437.

Barker, James and Cheney, George. The Concept and Practices of Discipline in Contemporary Organizational Life. *Communication Monographs, 61* (1994): 20-43.

Barker, James and Tompkins, Phillip. Identification in the Self-Managing Organization: Characteristics of Target and Tenure, *Human Communication Research, 21* (1994): 223-240.

Barker, James, Melville, Craig, and Pacanowsky, Michael. Self-Directed Teams at Xel. *Journal of Applied Communication Research, 21* (1993): 297-312.

+Barley, Steven and Kunda, Gideon. Design and Devotion: Surges of Rational and Normative Ideologies of Control in Managerial Discourse. *Administrative Science Quarterly, 37* (1992): 363-399.

+Barley, Steven, Meyer, G.W., and Gash, Debra. Cultures of Culture. *Administrative Science Quarterly, 33* (1988): 24-60.

Barlow, Jim. Ethics Can Boost the Bottom Line. *Houston Chronicle,* October 31, 1996, C1.

Barlow, Jim. Will Managers Follow Own Lead? *Houston Chronicle,* May 16, 1996, C1.

+Barnard, Chester. *The Functions of the Executive.* Cambridge, MA: Harvard University Press, 1938.

Barney, Jay. Organizational Culture: Can It Be a Source of Sustained Competitive Advantage?, *Academy of Management Review, 11* (1986): 656-665.

Baron, Stephanie and Clair, Robin P. From Coercion to Manipulation: Communication Competence as Disciplinary Discourse in the Organization. Paper presented at the International Communication Association Convention, Chicago, 1996.

Bartunek, Jean M. and Moch, Michael. Multiple Constituencies and the Quality of Working Life, in *Reframing Organizational Culture*. Peter Frost, et al., eds. Newbury Park, CA: Sage, 1991.

Bass, Bernard. *Bass and Stogdill's Handbook of Leadership*, 3rd ed. New York: The Free Press, 1990.

+Bass, Barnard and Avoilo, B.J. Transformational Leadership: A Response to Critiques. In Martin Chemers and R. Ayman, eds. *Leadership Theory and Research: Perspectives and Directions*. San Diego, CA: Academic Press, 1993.

Bastien, David. Change in Organizational Culture. *Management Communication Quarterly, 5* (1992): 403-442.

Baxter, Leslie. "'Talking Things Through' and 'Putting It In Writing'." *Journal of Applied Communication Research, 21* (1994): 313-328.

Bazerman, Max and Lewicki, Roy. *Negotiating in Organizations*. Beverly Hills: Sage, 1983.

Beatty, R.W. Blacks as Supervisors. *Academy of Management Journal, 16* (1973): 196-206.

Bell, Ella Louise. The Bicultural Experience of Career-Oriented Black Women. *Journal of Organizational Behavior, 11* (1990): 459-477.

Bellah, Robert, et al. *Habits of the Heart*, 2nd ed. Berkeley: University of California Press, 1995.

Bem, Daryl. *Beliefs, Attitudes and Human Affairs*. Belmont, CA: Brooks-Cole, 1972.

Benjamin, L. Black Women Achievers. *Sociological Inquiry, 52* (1982): 141-151.

Bennis, Warren. Beyond Bureaucracy. *Transaction, 2* (1965): 31-35.

Bennis, Warren and Naus, B. *Leaders: The Strategies for Taking Charge*. New York: Harper and Row, 1985.

Bennis, Warren, Parikh, Jagdish, and Lessem, Ronnie. *Beyond Leadership: Balancing Economics, Ethics, and Ecology*. Cambridge, MA: Basil Blackwell, 1994.

+Benson, J.K. Organizations: A Dialectical View. *Administrative Science Quarterly, 22* (1977): 1-21.

Berg, Ivar. *Education and Jobs*. New York: Praeger, 1970.

+Berger, Charles. Power, Dominance, and Social Interaction, in *Handbook of Interpersonal Communication*. Mark Knapp and Gerald Miller, eds. Beverly Hills, CA: Sage, 1994.

+Berger, Charles. Social Power and Interpersonal Communication, in *Handbook of In-*

terpersonal Communication. Mark Knapp and Gerald Miller, eds. Beverly Hills, CA: Sage, 1985.

Berger, Charles and Bradac, James. *Language and Social Knowledge*. London: Edward Arnold, 1982.

+Berger, Charles and Kellerman, Kathy. To Ask or Not to Ask, in *Communication Yearbook 7*. Robert Bostrom, ed. Beverly Hills, CA: Sage, 1983.

Berk, R. and Berk, S.F. *Labor and Leisure at Home*. Newbury Park, CA: Sage, 1979.

Bettman, J. and Weitz, B. Attributions in the Board Room. *Administrative Science Quarterly, 28* (1983): 165-183.

Beyer, Janice, Dunbar, Roger, and Meyer, Alan. Comment: The Concept of Ideology in Organizational Analysis. *The Academy of Management Review, 13* (1988): 438-489.

Bielby, William and Baron, James. Men and Women at Work. *American Journal of Sociology, 91* (1986): 87-90.

Bigoness, William. Effect of Applicant's Sex, Race, and Performance on Employers' Performance Ratings. *Journal of Applied Psychology, 61* (1976): 80-84.

Billingsley, Julie M. Nonverbal Communication in Organizations, in *Organizational Communication: Theory and Behavior*. Peggy Yuhas Byers, ed. Boston: Allyn and Bacon, 1997.

Bingham, Shereen. *Conceptualizing Sexual Harassment as Discursive Practice*. Westport, CT: Praeger, 1994.

+Bingham, Shereen and Burleson, Brant. Multiple Effects of Messages With Multiple Goals. *Journal of Applied Communication Research, 16* (1989): 184-216.

Bitzer, Lloyd. Functional Communication, in *Rhetoric in Transition*. Eugene White, ed. University Park, PA: Pennsylvania State University Press, 1980.

Bitzer, Lloyd. The Rhetorical Situation, *Philosophy and Rhetoric, 1* (1968): 1-14.

Blair, Anita. *Houston Chronicle*, July 8, 1996, 15A.

Blakenhorn, David, Bayme, Steven, and Elshtain, Jean Bethke. *Rebuilding the Nest*. Milwaukee, WI: Family Service America, 1990.

Blau, Peter and Alba, R. Empowering Nets of Participation. *Administrative Science Quarterly, 27* (1982): 363-379.

Blodgett, Timothy. Showdown on "Business Bluffing," in *Ethics in Practice*. Kenneth Andrews, ed. Boston, MA: Harvard Business School Press, 1989.

Blum, Linda and Smith, Vicki. Women's Mobility in the Corporation. *Signs, 13* (1988): 528-545.

Blumrosen, A.A. *Affirmative Action Programs and Claims of Reverse Discrimination.* New York: American Civil Liberties Union, 1995.

Boisseau, Charles. Ranks of Female Businesses Soar. *Houston Chronicle,* January 30, 1996, 1C.

Boisseau, Charles. Workers Foot the Bill for Boosts in Bosses' Pay. *Houston Chronicle,* June 9, 1996, A1.

Boje, David. The Storytelling Organization. *Administrative Science Quarterly, 36* (1991): 106–126.

Bok, Sissela. *Lying: Moral Choice in Public and Private Life.* New York: Pantheon Books, 1978.

Bok, Sissela. *Secrets: On the Ethics of Concealment and Revelation.* New York: Random House, 1982.

Bole, William. "Family Friendly:" Some Firms Make Slogan a Reality. *Houston Chronicle,* October 20, 1996, 8A.

Bommer, M., Gratto, C., Gravander, J., and Tuttle, M. A Behavioral Model of Ethical and Unethical Decision Making. *Journal of Business Ethics, 6* (1987): 265–280.

Bormann, Ernest. *Small Group Communication: Theory and Practice,* 3rd ed. New York: HarperCollins, 1990.

Bormann, Ernest. Symbolic Convergence Theory and Communication in Group Decision-making, in *Communication and Group Decision Making,* 2nd ed. Randy Hirokawa and M. Scott Poole, eds. Thousand Oaks, CA: Sage, 1996.

Boster, Frank and Mayer, Michael. Differential Argument Quality Mediates the Impact of Social Comparison Process of the Choice Shift. Paper presented at the International Communication Association Convention, San Francisco, 1984.

Bowman, W., Worthy, N.B., and Greyser, S.A. Are Women Executives People? *Harvard Business Review, 43* (July-August, 1965), 15–28, 164–178.

+Brands, H.W. Fractal History, or Clio and the Chaotics. *Diplomatic History* (1992): pp. 495–510.

+Brass, Daniel. Structural Relationships, Job Characteristics and Worker Satisfaction and Performance. *Administrative Science Quarterly, 26* (1981): 331–348.

Brener, Otto A. Logan, John E., and Wokutch, Richard E. Ethics and Values in Management Thought, in *Business Environment and Business Ethics.* Karen Paul, ed. Cambridge, MA: Ballinger, 1987.

Brenner, O.C., Tomkiewicva, Joseph, and Schein, Virginia. The Relationship Between Sex Role Stereotypes and Requisite Management Characteristics Revisited. *Academy of Management Journal, 32* (1989): 661–684.

Bridge, Karen and Baxter, Leslie. Blended Relationships: Friends as Work Associates. *Western Journal of Communication, 56* (1992): 200–225.

Brief, Arthur. Cited in Dawn Blalock (of the *Wall Street Journal*), Workplace Ethics Take a Vacation. *Houston Chronicle,* March 31, 1996, D3.

+Brief, Arthur. Differences in Evaluations of Employee Performance. *Journal of Occupational Psychology, 50* (1977):129–134.

Brief, Arthur and Aldag, Raymond. The Self in Work Organizations. *The Academy of Management Review, 6* (1981): 75–88.

+Brockner, Joel, House, Robert, Lloyd, Kathy, Nathanson, Sinaia, Birnbaum,. Gregg, Deitcher, Janet, and Rubin, Jeffrey. Escalation of Commitment to an Ineffective Course of Action. *Administrative Science Quarterly, 31* (1986): 109–126.

Broder, David. Congress *Sans* Personal Relationships Is Gridlock. *Houston Chronicle,* June 23, 1996:3C.

Broder, David. Retreat May Be a Tonic for Acrimonious Congress. *Houston Chronicle,* July 21, 1996, 3F.

Brown, D., Minor, C.W., and Jepsen, D.A. The Opinions of Minorities about Preparing For Work. *The Career Development Quarterly, 40* (1991): 5–19.

+Brown, Mary Helen. Defining Stories in Organizations. In *Communication Yearbook 12,* James Anderson, ed. Beverly Hills, CA: Sage, 1989.

+Brown, Michael. Identification and Some Conditions of Organizational Involvement. *Administrative Science Quarterly, 14* (1969): 346–355.

+Browning, Larry. Lists and Stories in Organizational Communication. *Communication Theory,2* (1992): 281–302.

+Browning, Larry. Diagnosing Teams in Organizational Settings. *Group and Organization Studies, 2* (1977): 187–197.

Browning, Larry, Korinek, J.T., and Cooper, M. Downplaying Formal Rules Negotiation in Military Cultural System. Paper presented at the International Communication Association Convention, Philadelphia, PA, May, 1979.

Brunnson, N. *The Irrational Organization.* Chicester, UK: Wiley, 1982.

Bryan-College Station (TX) Eagle, September 22, 1996, E2.

Bryant, Salatheia. Texaco Initiates Scholarship Program to Help Minorities," *Houston Chronicle,* November 12, 1996. 17A.

Bullis, Connie. At Least It's a Start, in *Communication Yearbook 16*. Stanley Deetz, ed. Newbury Park, CA: Sage, 1993.

Bullis, Connie and Bach, Betsy Wackernagel, Are Mentoring Relationships Helping Organizations? *Communication Quarterly, 37* (1989): 199–213.

+Bullis, Connie and Bach, Betsy Wackernagel. Socialization Turning Points. *Western Journal of Speech Communication, 53* (1989): 273–293.

Burawoy, Michael. *Manufacturing Consent.* Chicago: University of Chicago Press, 1979.

Burgoon, Judee and Saine, T.J. *The Unspoken Dialogue: An Introduction to Nonverbal Communication.* Boston: Houghton-Mifflin, 1978.

Burgoon, Judee, Buller, David, and Woodall, W. Gill. *Nonverbal Communication: The Unspoken Dialogue.* New York: Harper & Row, 1989.

+Burke, Kenneth. *Attitudes Toward History.* Boston: Beacon Press, 1937.

+Burns, Tom and Stalker, G.M. *The Management of Innovation.* London: Tavistock, 1961.

Burton, Clare. Merit and Gender, in *Gendering Organizational Analysis.* Albert Mills and Peta Tancred, eds. Newbury Park, CA: Sage, 1992.

Bush, David. Passive-aggressive Behavior in the Business Setting, in *Passive-Aggressiveness.* Richard Parsons and Robert Wicks, eds. New York: Brunner-Mazel, 1983.

Business Week, October, 1991.

+Butler, Richard, Astley, Graham, Hickson, David, Mallory, Geoffrey, and Wilson, David. Strategic Decision Making in Organizations. *International Studies of Management and Organization, 23* (1980): 234–249.

+Butler, Richard, Hickson, David, Wilson, David, and Axelsson, R. Organizational Power, Politicking and Paralysis. *Organizational and Administrative Sciences, 8* (1977): 108–126.

Buzzanell, Patrice. An Information Acquisition and Use Approach to Perceived Career Uncertainty, Transitional Events and Career Tracks. Doctoral dissertation, Purdue University, West Lafayette, IN, 1987.

Buzzanell, Patrice. Gaining a Voice: Feminist Organizational Communication Theorizing. *Management Communication Quarterly, 7* (1994): 339–383.

Buzzanell, Patrice. Reframing the Glass Ceiling as a Socially Constructed Process. *Communication Monographs, 62* (. 327–354.

Byrnes, Joseph. Review of In Search of E. lence. *Personnel Administrator, 28* (1983): 14–18.

Caiden, G. and Caiden, N. Administrative Corruption. *Public Administration Review, 10* (1977): 301–309.

Calas, Marta and Jacques, R. Diversity or Conformity? Paper presented at the Annual Conference on Women and Organizations, Long Beach, CA, August, 1988.

Calas, Marta and Smircich, Linda. Dangerous Liaisons: The "Feminine in Management" Meets "Globalization." *Business Horizons* (March/April, 1993): 106–132.

Calas, Marta, Jacobson, S., Jacques, R., and Smircich, L. Is a Woman-Centered Theory of Management Dangerous? Paper presented at the Academy of Management Convention, Miami, August, 1991.

+Caldwell, David and O'Reilly, Charles. Task Perceptions and Job Satisfaction. *Journal of Applied Psychology, 67* (1982): 361–369.

Cameron, Randolph. *The Minority Executive's Handbook.* New York: Warner, 1989.

+Campbell, John. Systematic Error on the Part of Human Links in Communication Systems. *Information and Control, 1* (1958): 334–369.

Campbell, John and Pritchard, Robert. Motivation Theory, in *Handbook of Industrial and Organizational Psychology.* Marvin Dunnette, ed. Chicago: Rand-McNally, 1976.

Canary, Daniel and Spitzberg, Brian. A Model of the Perceived Competence of Conflict Strategies. *Human Communication Research, 15* (1990): 630–649.

Carnegie, Simone. *The Hidden Emotions of Tourism: Communication and Power in the Caribbean.* M.A. Thesis, Texas A&M University, 1996.

Carr, Albert. Is Business Bluffing Ethical? *Harvard Business Review* (January-February, 1968).

Carroll, Daniel. A Disappointing Search for Excellence. *Harvard Business Review* (December, 1983).

Carter, Boslego. Women's Recent Progress in the Professions or, Women Get a Ticket to Ride After the Gravy Train Has Left the Station. *Feminist Studies, 7* (Fall, 1981): 477–514.

Catalyst, Inc., *Houston Chronicle,* October 18, 1996, 3C.

Catalyst. *Catalyst's Study of Women in Corporate America.* New York, 1991.

Cawelti, John. *Disciples of the Self-Made Man.* Cambridge: Harvard University Press, 1974.

Cervantes, Richard. Occupational and Economic Stressors Among Immigrant and United States-Born Hispanics, in *Hispanics in the Workplace.* P. Knouse, P. Rosenfeld, and A. Culbertson, eds. Newbury Park, CA: Sage, 1992.

Challenger, James. *Job Hunt.* Chicago, IL: Challenger, Gray & Christmas, Inc., 1995.

Chandler, Alfred. *The Visible Hand.* Cambridge: Harvard University Press, 1977.

Chandler, Alfred and Daems, H. eds. *Managerial Hierarchies.* Cambridge: Harvard University Press, 1980.

Chapa, Jeorge. Creating and Improving Linkages Between the Tops and Bottoms. Paper presented at the Organizational Innovation Conference, Humphrey Institute of Public Affairs, University of Minnesota, Minneapolis, September, 1992.

Chapple, E.E. Applied Anthropology in Industry, in *Anthropology Today.* A.L. Kroeber, ed. Chicago: University of Chicago Press, 1953.

Chase, J. and Panagopoulous, I. Environmental Values and Social Psychology, in Y. Gurrier, M. Alexander, J. Chase, and M. O'Brien, eds. *Values and the Environment.* Chicester, UK: John Wiley, 1995.

Chatman, Jennifer. Matching Person and Organization: Selection and Socialization in Public Accounting Firms. *Administrative Science Quarterly, 36* (1991): 459-484.

Chemers, Martin. Culture and Assumptions About Leadership, in *Small Group Communication.* Robert Cathcart and Larry Samovar, eds. Dubuque, IA: William C. Brown, 1984.

Cheney, George. The Corporate Person [Re]Presents Itself, in *Rhetorical and Critical Approaches to Public Relations.* Elizabeth Toth and Robert Heath, eds. New York: Praeger, 1992.

Cheney, George. Democracy in the Workplace. *Journal of Applied Communication Research, 23* (1995): 167-200.

Cheney, George. On the Various and Changing Meanings of Organizational Membership. *Communication Monographs, 50* (1985): 342-363.

Cheney, George. Organizational Identification as Process and Product. Master's Thesis, Purdue University, 1982.

Cheney, George. *Rhetoric in an Organizational Society: Managing Multiple Identities.* Columbia, SC: University of South Carolina Press, 1991.

Cheney, George. The Rhetoric of Identification. *The Quarterly Journal of Speech, 69* (1983): 143-158.

Cheney, George and Brancato, Jim. Scientific Management's Rhetorical Context and Enduring Relevance. Paper presented at the Speech Communication Association Convention, Chicago, November, 1990.

Cheney, George and Frenette, Greg. Persuasion and Organization, in *The Ethical Nexus.* Charles Conrad, ed. Norwood, NJ: Ablex, 1992.

+Cheney, George and Tompkins, Philip. Coming to Terms with Organizational Identification and Commitment. *Central States Speech Journal, 38* (1987): 1-15.

Cheney, George and Vibbert, Steve. Corporate Discourse, in *Handbook of Organizational Communication.* Fred Jablin, et al., eds. Beverly Hills, CA: Sage, 1987.

Chiles, Angella Michelle and Zorn, Theodore. Empowerment in Organizations: Employees' Perceptions of the Influences on Empowerment. *Journal of Applied Communication Research, 23* (1995): 1-25.

Clair, Robin Patric. The Bureaucratization, Commodification, and Privatization of Sexual Harassment Through Institutional Discourse. *Management Communication Quarterly, 7* (1993): 12-157.

Clair, Robin Patric. The Political Nature of the Colloquialism, 'A Real Job,' *Communication Monographs, 63* (1966): 249-267.

+Clair, Robin Patric. The Use of Framing Devices to Sequester Organizational Narratives. *Communication Monographs, 60* (1993): 113-136.

Clair, Robin Patric and Thompson, Kelly. Pay Discrimination as a Discursive and Material Practice. *Journal of Applied Communication Research, 24* (1996): 1-20.

+Clegg, Stewart. *Frameworks of Power.* Newbury Park, CA: Sage, 1989.

+Clegg, Stewart. *Modern Organizations.* Newbury Park, CA: Sage, 1990.

+Clegg, Stewart. *Power, Rule and Domination.* London: Routledge and Kegan Paul, 1975.

+Clegg, Stewart, Power, Theorizing and Nihilism. *Theory and Society, 3* (1976): 65-87.

+Cline, Tim and Cline, Rebecca. Risky and Cautious Decision Shifts in Small Groups. *Southern Speech Communication Journal, 44* (1979): 252-263.

Coffman, Stephen. "Staff Problems with Geriatric Care in Two Types of Health Care Organizations," *Journal of Applied Communication Research, 20* (1992): 292-307.

+Cohen, Michael and March, James. *Leadership and Ambiguity*, 2nd ed. Boston: Harvard Business School Press, 1974.

+Cohen, M., March, J. and Olson, J. A Garbage-can Model of Organizational Choice. *Administrative Science Quarterly, 17* (1972): 2-32.

Cohen, Sharon (Associated Press Reporter). Worker's American Dream Vanishing. *Bryan-College Station Eagle,* September 6, 1992, C3-5.

Collins, Patricia Hill. Learning From the Outsider Within: The Sociological Significance of Black Feminist Thought. *Social Problems, 33* (1986): S14-S32.

Comer, Debra. Organizational Newcomers' Acquisition of Information from Peers. *Management Communication Quarterly, 5* (1991): 64-89.

Connell, R.W. *Gender and Power: Society, the Person, and Sexual Politics.* Stanford, CA: Stanford University Press, 1987.

Connell, R.W. Theorizing Gender. *Sociology, 19* (1985): 260-272.

Conrad, Betty Webber. The Moving Experience. *The Waiting Room, 2* (1985): 12-18.

Conrad, Charles. Corporate Communication and Control, in *Rhetorical and Critical Approaches to Public Relations.* Elizabeth Toth and Robert Heath, eds. New York: Praeger, 1992.

Conrad, Charles, ed. *The Ethical Nexus.* Norwood, NJ: Ablex, 1992.

Conrad, Charles. Organizational Power: Faces and Symbolic Forms, in *Communication and Organizations.* Linda Putnam and Michael Pacanowsky, eds. Beverly Hills: Sage, 1983.

+Conrad, Charles. Power, Performance and Supervisors' Choices of Strategies of Conflict Management. *Western Journal of Speech Communication 47* (1983): 218-228.

Conrad, Charles. Power, Identity and Decision-making in Churches. *Journal for the Scientific Study for Religion, 27* (1988): 345-361.

Conrad, Charles. Review of *A Passion for Excellence. Administrative Science Quarterly, 30* (1985): 426-429.

Conrad, Charles. Was Pogo Right?, in *Communication Research in the 21st Century.* Julia Wood and Richard Gregg, eds. Creskill, NJ: Hampton Press, 1995.

Conrad, Charles. Work Songs, Hegemony, and Illusions of Self. *Critical Studies in Mass Communication, 5* (1988): 179-201.

+Conrad, Charles and Ryan, Mary. Power, Praxis and Person in Social and Organizational Theory, in *Organizational Communication.* Phillip Tompkins and Robert McPhee, eds. Beverly Hills: Sage, 1985.

Conrad, Charles and Taylor, Bryan. The Contexts of Sexual Harassment: Power, Silences and Academe, in *Conceptualizing Sexual Harassment as Discursive Practice.* Shereen Bingham, ed. Westport, CT: Praeger, 1995.

+Contractor, Noshir and Eisenberg, Eric. Communication Networks and New Media in Organizations, in *Organizations and Communication Technology.* Janet Fulk and Charles Steinfeld, eds. Newbury Park, CA: Sage, 1990.

Cooke, R.A. Danger Signs of Unethical Behavior, *Journal of Business Ethics, 19* (1991): 249-253.

Coopersmith, Jonathan. Facsimile's False Starts. *IEEE Spectrum* (February, 1993): pp. 46-49.

Corman, Abraham. Consideration, "Initiating Structure," and Organizational Criteria. *Personnel Psychology, 19* (1966): 349-361.

Corman, Steve. A Model of Perceived Communication in Collective Networks. *Human Communication Research, 16* (1990): 582-602.

Corporate Women. *Business Week,* June 8, 1992.

+Courtright, John, Fairhurst, Gail, and Rogers, L. Edna. Interaction Patterns in Organic and Mechanistic Systems. *Academy of Management Journal, 32* (1989): 773-802.

Cox, J. Robert. Symbolic Action and Satisfactory Choices. Paper presented at the Speech Communication Association Convention, New York, 1980.

Cox, Taylor, Jr. and Nkomo, Stella. Differential Performance Appraisal Criteria. *Group and Organization Studies, 11* (1986): 101-117.

Crozier, M. *The Bureaucratic Phenomenon.* Chicago: University of Chicago Press, 1964.

Culbert, Samuel and McDonough, John. *Radical Management: Power Politics and the Pursuit of Trust.* New York: The Free Press, 1985.

Cullen, John B., Victor, Bart, and Stephens, C. An Ethical Weather Report. *Organizational Dynamics, 17* (1989): 50-62.

Culp, Mildred. Child Care Issue Can Affect Work. *Houston Chronicle,* May 19, 1996, EE1.

Cupach, William and Metts, Sandra. *Facework.* Newbury Park, CA: Sage, 1994.

+Cussella, Louis. The Effects of Feedback Source, Message and Receiver Characteristics on Intrinsic Motivation. *Communication Quarterly, 32* (1985): 211-221.

+Cyert, M. and March, James. *A Behavioral Theory of the Firm*. Englewood Cliffs, NJ: Prentice-Hall, 1963.

+Czarniawska-Joerges, Barbara. *Exploring Complex Organizations*. Newbury Park, CA: Sage, 1992.

+Dachler, Peter and Wilpert, Bernhard. Conceptual Boundaries and Dimensions of Participation in Organizations. *Administrative Science Quarterly, 23* (1978): 1-39.

Daft, Richard. *Organization Theory and Design,* 3rd ed. St. Paul, MN: West, 1989.

+Daft, Richard and Lengel, R.H. Information Richness, in *Research in Organizational Behavior,* vol. 6. Larry Cummings and Barry Staw, eds. Greenwich, CT: JAI Press, 1984.

Daft, Richard and Macintosh, N. A Tentative Exploration into the Amount and Equivocality of Information Processing in Organizational Work Units. *Administrative Science Quarterly, 26* (1981): 207-224.

+Dandeker, Christopher. *Surveillance, Power and Modernity.* New York: St. Martin's Press. 1984.

D'Andrade, Richard. "Cultural Meaning Systems," in R. Schweder & R. LeVine, eds., *Culture Theory.* Cambridge: Cambridge University Press, 1984.

Dandridge, Thomas, The Life Stages of a Symbol, in *Organizational Culture*. Peter Frost, et al., eds. Beverly Hills, CA: Sage, 1985.

Daniels, Tom, Spiker, Barry, and Papa, Michael. *Perspectives on Organizational Communication*. Dubuque, IA: Brown and Benchmark, 1997.

+Danowski, James. Group Attitude Uniformity and Connectivity of Organizational Communication Networks for Production, Innovation and Maintenance Content. *Human Communication Research, 6* (1980): 299-308.

Davis, Keith. Management Communication and the Grapevine. *Harvard Business Review* (Sept.-Oct., 1953): pp. 43-49.

Deal, Terrance and Kennedy, Alan. *Corporate Cultures,* Reading, MA: Addison-Wesley, 1982.

+Deaux, K. and Emswiller, T. Explanations of Successful Performance on Sex-linked Tasks. *Journal of Personality and Social Psychology, 29* (1974): 80-85.

+de Certeau, Michel. *The Practice of Everyday Life*. Berkeley: University of California Press, 1984.

+DeDreu, Carstens. Gain and Loss Frames in Bilateral Negotiations. Diss., 1994.

+Deetz, Stanley. *Democracy in an Age of Corporate Colonization.* Albany, NY: SUNY Press, 1992.

+Deetz, Stanley. Transforming Communication, Transforming Business. *The International Journal of Value-Based Management* (1995, In Press).

Deetz, Stanley. *Transforming Communication; Transforming Business*. Creskill, NJ: 1995.

+Deetz, Stanley and Mumby, Dennis. Power, Discourse and the Workplace, in *Communication Yearbook 13.* James Anderson, ed. Beverly Hills, CA: Sage, 1990.

Della-Piana, Connie Kubo. Performing Community. Paper presented at the International Communication Association Convention, Chicago, 1996.

+DeSanctis, Gerardine and Gallupe, Brent. A Foundation for the Study of Group Decision Support Systems. *Management Science, 33* (1987): 589-609.

Deutsch, Morton. Conflicts: Productive or Destructive? *Journal of Social Issues, 25* (1969): 7-41.

Deutsch, Morton. *The Resolution of Conflict.* New Haven: Yale University Press, 1973.

Deutsch, Morton and Krauss, Robert. Studies in Interpersonal Bargaining. *Journal of Conflict Resolution, 61* (1962): 52-76.

+Dewar, Robert and Werbel, James. Universalistic and Contingency Predictions of Employee Satisfaction and Conflict. *Administrative Science Quarterly, 24* (1979): 426-447.

DeWine, Sue, Pearson, Judy, and Yost, Carol. Intimate Office Relationships and Their Impact on Work Group Communication, in *Communication and Sex Role Socialization.* Cynthia Berryman-Fink, D. Ballard-Reisch, and L.H. Newman, eds. New York: Garland Publishing Company, 1993.

Dickens, Floyd, Jr. and Dickens, Jacqueline B. *The Black Manager.* New York: AMACOM, 1991.

Dillard, James and Miller, Katherine. Intimate Relationships in Task Environments, in *Handbook of Personal Relationships.* Steve Duck, ed.

+Dillard, James, Hale, J.L., and Segrin, Chris. Close Relationships in Task Environments. *Management Communication Quarterly, 7* (1994): 227-255.

+Dolbear, T. and Lave, L. Inconsistent Behavior in Lottery Choice Experiments. *Behavioral Science, 12* (1967): 14-23.

Dolgoff, Thomas. Towards Understanding Morale. Working Paper, The Wil Menninger Center, Topeka, KS.

Donaghy, W.C. *The Interview.* Glenview, IL: Scott, Foresman and Company, 1984.

Donohue, William and Kolt, R. *Managing Interpersonal Conflict* Newbury Park, CA: Sage, 1992.

+Donohue, William, Diez, M., and Hamilton, M. Coding Naturalistic Negotiation Interaction. *Human Communication Research, 10* (1984): 403-425.

Douglas, Ann. *The Feminization of American Culture.* New York: Anchor Press, 1988.

Dovidio, John, Gaertner, Samuel, Anastasio, Phyllis, and Sanitioso, Rasyid. Cognitive and Motivational Bases of Bias, in *Hispanics in the Workplace.* Paul Knouse, Paul Rosenfeld, and Amy Culbertson, eds. Newbury Park, CA: Sage, 1992.

Downey, R. and Lahey, M.S. Women in Management, in *Career Growth and Human Resource Strategies.* M. London and E.M. Mone, eds. New York: Quorum Books, 1988.

Downey, R. and Lahey, M.S. Women in Management, in *Career Growth and Human Resource Strategies,* M. London and E.M. Mone, eds. New York: Quorum Books, 1988.

Downs, Anthony. *Inside Bureaucracy.* Boston: Little, Brown, 1967.

Downs, Cal and Conrad, Charles. A Critical Incident Study of Effective Subordinancy. *Journal of Business Communication, 19* (1982): 27-38.

+Downs, Cal, Johnson, Kenneth, and Barge, Kevin. Communication Feedback and Task Performance in Organizations, in *Organizational Communication,* v. 9. Howard Greenbaum, Raymond Falcione, and Susan Hellweg, eds. Beverly Hills, CA: Sage, 1982.

Downs, Timothy. Predictors of Communication Satisfaction with Appraisal Interviews. *Management Communication Quarterly, 3* (1990): 334-354.

Downward Mobility. *Business Week,* March 23, 1992, 56-63.

Dreheer, G.R. and Ash, R.A. A Comparative Study of Mentoring Among Men and Women in Managerial, Professional, and Technical Positions. *Journal of Applied Psychology, 75* (1990): 539-546.

Drucker, Peter. The Age of Transformation. *Atlantic Monthly* (September, 1994): 49-56.

Drucker, Peter. *The Changing World of the Executive.* New York: Times Books, 1982.

Duncan, K.D., Gruneberg, M.M. and Wallis, D. *Changing Values in Working Life.* New York: John Wiley, 1980.

Duncan, Robert B. Characteristics of Perceived Environments and Perceived Environmental Uncertainty. *Administrative Science Quarterly, 17* (1972): 313-327.

Dziech, B.W. and Weiner, L. *The Lecherous Professor,* 2nd. ed. Urbana, IL: University of Illinois Press, 1990.

Eadie, William and Wood, Julia, eds. *Journal of Applied Communication Research, 20* (1992): v-418.

Edwards, Audrey and Polite, Craig K. *Children of the Dream: The Psychology of Black Success.* New York: Doubleday, 1992.

Edwards, Renee. Sensitivity to Feedback and the Development of Self. *Communication Quarterly, 38* (1990): 101-111.

Edwards, Richard. *Contested Terrain.* New York: Basic Books, 1978.

+Edwards, Richard. The Social Relations of Production at the Point of Production, in M. Zey-Farrell and M. Aiken, eds. *Complex Organizations: Critical Perspectives.* Glenview, IL: Scott Foresman, 1981.

+Edwards, Ward. Subjective Probabilities Inferred from Decisions. *Psychological Review, 69* (1962): 109-135.

+Edwards, Ward. Utility, Subjective Probability, Their Interaction and Variance Preferences. *Journal of Conflict Resolution, 6* (1962): 42-50.

Eichenwald, Kurt. *New York Times,* November 4, 1966, A1, C4.

Eichenwald, Kurt. Texaco Reeling from Racial Scandal, *Houston Chronicle,* November 5, 1996, 1C.

Eisenberg, Eric. Ambiguity as Strategy in Organizational Communication. *Communication Monographs, 51* (1984): 227-242.

Eisenberg, Eric. Dialogue as Democratic Process, in *Communication Yearbook 17.* Stanley Deetz, ed. Thousand Oaks, CA: Sage, 1994.

Eisenberg, Eric and Goodall, H.L., Jr. *Organizational Communication.* New York: St. Martin's Press, 1993.

Eisenberg, Eric and Phillips, Steven. Miscommunication in Organizations, in *"Miscommunication" and Problematic Talk.* N. Coupland, H. Giles, and J. Wieman, eds. Newbury Park, CA: Sage, 1991.

Eisenberg, Eric and Riley, Patricia. Organizational Culture, in Linda Putnam and Fredric Jablin, eds. *The New Handbook of Organizational Communication.* Thousand Oaks, CA: Sage, 1997.

Eisenberg, Eric, Monge, Peter, and Miller, Kathleen. Involvement in Communication Networks as a Predictor of Organizational Commitment. *Human Communication Research 10* (1983): 179-201.

Eisenstein, H. *Gender Shock,* Boston: Beacon, 1991.

+Ellis, Beth. The Effects of Uncertainty and Source Credibility on Attitude About Organizational Change. *Management Communication Quarterly, 6* (1992): 34-57.

Emerson, Richard. Power-dependence Relations. *American Sociological Review, 27* (1962): 31–41.

Emmett, R. Vnet or Gripenet. *Datamation, 27* (1981): 48–58.

Emspak, Frank. Where Have All the Jobs Gone? *Chronicle of Higher Education,* April 4, 1996, B1–B2.

Enz, Cathy. *Power and Shared Values in the Corporate Culture.* Ann Arbor: UMI Research Press, 1986.

Enz, Cathy. The Role of Value Congruity in Intraorganizational Power. *Administrative Science Quarterly, 33* (1988): 284–304.

Essed, Philomena. *Everyday Racism.* Trans. Cynthia Jaffe. Claremont, CA: Hunter House, 1990.

Essed, Philomena. *Understanding Everyday Racism.* Newbury Park, CA: Sage, 1991.

Essed, Philomena. Understanding Verbal Accounts of Racism. *Text, 8* (1988): 5–40.

Etzioni, Amatai. Cited in C. Gorman. Listen Here, Mr. Big! *Time* (July 3, 1989): 40–45.

Etzioni, Amatai. *The Moral Dimension.* New York: The Free Press, 1988.

Etzioni, Amatai. *New Communitarian Thinking.* Charlottesville, VA: University Press of Virginia, 1995.

Etzioni, Amatai. *The New Golden Rule.* New York: BasicBooks, 1996.

+Etzioni, Amatai. Organizational Control Structures, in *Handbook of Organizations.* James March, ed. Chicago: Rand-McNally, 1965.

+Fairhurst, Gail. Dialectical Tensions in Leadership Research, in *The New Handbook of Organizational Communication.* Linda Putnam and Fredric Jablin, eds. Thousand Oaks, CA: Sage, 1997.

Fairhurst, Gail. Echoes of the Vision: When the Rest of the Organization Talks Total Quality. *Management Communication Quarterly, 6* (1993): 331–371.

Fairhurst, Gail and Sarr, Robert *The Art of Framing: Managing the Language of Leadership.* San Francisco: Jossey-Bass, 1996.

+Fairhurst, Gail, Graen, Stephen, and Snavely, Kay. Face Support in Controlling Poor Performance. *Human Communication Research, 11* (1984): 272–295.

+Fairhurst, Gail, Green, Stephen, and Snavely, B. Kay. Managerial Control and Discipline, in *Communication Yearbook 8.* Robert Bostrom, ed. Beverly Hills, CA: Sage, 1984.

+Fairhurst, Gail, Rogers, L. Edna, and Sarr, Robert. Manager-subordinate Control Patterns and Judgments about the Relationship, in *Communication Yearbook 10.*

Margaret McLaughlin, ed. Beverly Hills, CA: Sage, 1987.

Falbe, Cecilia and Yukl, Gary. Consequences of Managers of Using Single Influence Tactics and Combinations of Tactics. *Academy of Management Journal, 32* (1992): 638–652.

Faludi, Susan. *Backlash: The Undeclared War Against American Women.* New York: Crown, 1991.

Farace, Richard, Monge, Peter, and Russell, Hamish. *Communicating and Organizing.* Reading, MA: Addison-Wesley, 1977.

Farrell, Amy. "Like a Tarantula on a Banana Boat," in *Feminist Organizations.* Myra Marx Ferree and Patricia Yancey Martin, eds. Philadelphia: Temple University Press, 1995.

Farris, George. Groups and the Informal Organization," in *Groups at Work.* Roy Payne and Cary Cooper, eds. New York: John Wiley, 1981.

Fayol, Henri. *General and Industrial Management.* London: Pitman, 1949.

Feldman, Daniel. *Managing Careers in Organizations.* Glenview, IL: Scott, Foresman, 1988.

+Feldman, Daniel. The Multiple Socialization of Organization Members. *The Academy of Management Review, 6* (1981): 309–318.

+Feldman, Martha and March, James. Information in Organizations as Signal and Symbol. *Administrative Science Quarterly, 26* (1981): 171–186.

+Feldman-Summers, J. and Kiesler, J.B. Those Who Are Number Two Try Harder. *Journal of Personality and Social Psychology, 30* (1974): 846–855.

+Felsteiner, W.L., Abel, R.L., and Sarat, A. The Emergence and Transformation of Disputes. *Law and Society Review, 33* (1980/1981): 631–654.

Ferdman, Bernardo and Cortes, Angelica. Culture and Identity Among Hispanic Managers in an Anglo Business, in *Hispanics in the Workplace.* S. Knouse, P. Rosenfeld, and A. Culbertson, eds. Newbury Park, CA: Sage, 1992.

+Ferguson, Kathy. Feminism and Bureaucratic Discourse. *New Political Science, 11* (Spring, 1983): 61–62.

Ferguson, Kathy. *The Feminist Case Against Bureaucracy.* Philadelphia, PA: Temple University Press, 1984.

Fernandez, John. Racism and Sexism in Corporate America, in *Ensuring Minority Success in Corporate Management.* Donna Thompson and Nancy DiTomaso, eds. New York: Plenum, 1988.

Ferraris, Claire, Carveth, Rod, and Parrish-Sprowl, John. Interface Precision Benchworks: A Case Study in Organizational Identification. *Journal of Applied Communication Research, 21* (1993): 343–357.

Ferree, Myra Marx and Martin, Patricia Yancey. *Feminist Organizations.* Philadelphia: Temple University Press, 1995.

Finholt, Tom and Sproull, Lee. Electronic Groups at Work. *Organization Science, 1* (1990): 41–64.

+Finkelstein, Sydney. Power in Top Management Teams. *Academy of Management Journal, 35* (1992): 505–538.

Fiol, C. Marlene. A Semiotic Analysis of Corporate Language. *Administrative Science Quarterly, 34* (1989): 277–303.

Fish, Sandra. Preparation for the Year 2000: One Corporation's Attempt to Address the Issues of Gender and Race. *Howard Journal of Communication, 3* (1991): 61–72.

Fisher, Anne. When Will Women Get to the Top? *Fortune,* September 21, 1992, pp. 44–56.

+Fisher, B. Aubrey. The Process of Decision Modification in Small Discussion Groups. *Journal of Communication, 20* (1970): 51–64.

Fisher, Cynthia. On the Dubious Wisdom of Expecting Job Satisfaction to Correlate with Performance. *Academy of Management Review, 5* (1980): 607–612.

Fisher, R., and Ury, W. *Getting to Yes.* Boston: Houghton Mifflin, 1981.

Fisher, Walter. Narration as a Human Communication Paradigm. *Communication Monographs, 51* (1984): 1–22.

Fitt, L.W. and D.A. Newton. When the Mentor Is a Man and the Protege Is a Woman. *Harvard Business Review, 59* (March-April 1981): 3–4.

+Flax, Jane. Postmodern and Gender Relations in Feminist Theory. *Signs, 12* (1987): 621–643.

+Fleishman, Edwin and Associates, eds. *Studies in Personnel and Industrial Psychology.* Homewood, IL: Dorsey, 1961.

+Fleishman, Edwin and Associates, eds. *Studies in Personnel and Industrial Psychology,* 2nd ed., Homewood, IL: Dorsey, 1967.

+Fletcher, J. Feminist Standpoint Research and Management Science. Unpublished manuscript, Northeastern University, June, 1992.

Folger, Joseph, Poole, M. Scott, and Stuttman, Randall. *Working Through Conflict,* 3rd ed. New York: Longman, 1997.

+Follett, Mary Parker. *Creative Experience.* New York: Longmans, Green, 1924.

+Fombrun, Charles. Structural Dynamics Between and Within Organizations. *Administrative Science Quarterly, 31* (1986): 403–421.

Foreman, Chris. The Reality of Workplace Democracy: A Case Study of One Company's Employee Involvement Process. Paper presented at the International Communication Associations Convention, Chicago, IL, 1996.

+Foucault, Michel. *Discipline and Punish.* Harmondsworth, U.K.: Penguin, 1977.

+Foucault, Michel. *Power/knowledge.* C. Gordon, ed. Brighton, U.K.: Harvester Press, 1980.

+Forester, John. *Planning in the Face of Power.* Berkeley: University of California Press, 1989.

+Fox, F. and Staw, Barry. The Trapped Administrator. *Administrative Science Quarterly, 24* (1979): 449–456.

Francis, Bob. Tune in to Cheaper Videoconferencing, *Datamation, 39* (October 1, 1993): 48–51.

+Franz, Charles and Jin, K. Gregory. The Structure of Group Conflict in a Collaborative Work Group During Information Systems Development. *Journal of Applied Communication Research, 23* (1995): 108–127.

Frederick, William. Rev. of Suresh Srivastva, *Executive Integrity. Administrative Science Quarterly, 34* (1989): 490–492.

Freeman, Jo. The Tyranny of Structurelessness. *MS* (July, 1976).

Freeman, R. Edward and Liedtka, Jeanne. Corporate Social Responsibility: A Critical Approach. *Business Horizons* (July-August, 1991): 88–96.

French, J.R.P. and Raven, Bertram. The Bases of Social Power, in *Studies in Social Power.* Dorwin Cartwright, ed. Ann Arbor: University of Michigan Press, 1959.

Friedman, Milton. *Capitalism and Freedom.* Chicago: University of Chicago Press, 1962.

Friedman, Milton. The Social Responsibility of Business Is to Increase Profits. *New York Times Magazine,* September 13, 1970, pp. 122–126.

+Frost, Peter. Power, Politics and Influence, in *Handbook of Organizational Communication.* Fred Jablin, Linda Putnam, Karlene Roberts, and Lyman Porter, eds. Newbury Park, CA: Sage, 1987.

Frost, Peter, et al., eds. *Organizational Culture.* Beverly Hills, CA: Sage, 1985.

Frost, Peter, et al., eds. *Reframing Organizational Culture.* Newbury Park, CA: Sage, 1991.

+Frye, Northrop. *Anatomy of Criticism.* Princeton, NJ: Princeton University Press, 1957.

Fulk, Janet and DeSanctis, G., eds. *Information Technology and New Organizational Forms.* Thousand Oaks, CA: Sage, In press.

Fulk, Janet and Mani, Sirish. Distortion of Communication in Hierarchical Relationships, in *Communication Yearbook 9.* Margaret McLaughlin, ed. Newbury Park, CA: Sage, 1986.

Fulk, Janet, Steinfield, Charles W., Schmitz, Joseph, and Power, J. G. Power. A Social Information Processing Model of Media Use in Organizations. *Communication Research, 14* (1987): 529-552.

Gabarro, John. The Development of Trust, Influence, and Expectations, in *Interpersonal Behavior.* A.G. Athos & J.J. Gabarro, eds. Englewood Cliffs, NJ: Prentice-Hall, 1978.

Galbraith, Jay. Organizational Design, in *Handbook of Organizational Behavior.* J. Lorsch, ed. Englewood Cliffs: Prentice-Hall, 1987.

Galen, Michele and Palmer, Ann Therese. White, Male and Worried. *Business Week,* January 31, 1994, 50-55.

Gallupe, Brent, Bastianutti, Laura, and Cooper, W.H. Unblocking Brainstorms. *Journal of Applied Psychology, 76* (1991): 137-142.

Gamson, William. *Power and Discontent.* Homewood: Dorsey, 1968.

Garko, Michael. Persuading Subordinates Who Communicate in Attractive and Unattractive Styles. *Management Communication Quarterly, 5* (1992): 289-315.

Gaventa, J.P. *Power and Powerlessness: Quiescence and Rebellion in an Appalachian Valley.* Urbana, IL: University of Illinois Press, 1980.

Geerken, Michael and Gove, Walter. *At Home and at Work.* Beverly Hills, CA: Sage, 1983.

Geertz, Clifford. Common Sense as a Cultural System, in *Local Knowledge.* New York: Basic Books, 1983.

George, Claude. *The History of Management Thought.* Englewood Cliffs, NJ: Prentice-Hall, 1972.

Gephart, R.P., Jr. The Textual Approach: Risk and Blame in Disaster Sensemaking. *Academy of Management Journal, 36* (1993): 1465-1514.

+Giddens, Anthony. *Central Problems in Social Theory.* Berkeley: University of California Press, 1979.

+Giddens, Anthony. *The Constitution of Society.* Berkeley: University of California Press, 1984.

+Gifford, R., Ng, C.F., and Wilkinson, M. Nonverbal Cues in the Employment Interview. *Journal of Applied Psychology, 70* (1985): 729-736.

Gilchrest, J. and Van Hooven, Shirley. Employees' Accounts of Broken Organizational Promises, in *Proceedings of the 1992 National Communication Ethics Conference.* J. Jaska, ed. Annandale, VA: Speech Communication Association, 1992.

Gilligan, Carol. *In a Different Voice.* Cambridge, MA: Harvard University Press, 1982.

+Gioia, Dennis and Sims, Henry. Cognition-Behavior Connections: Attribution and Verbal Behavior in Leader-subordinate Interactions. *Organizational Behavior and Human Performance, 37* (1986): 197-229.

Goffman, Erving. On Face Work. *Psychiatry, 18* (1955): 213-231.

Goffman, Erving. *The Presentation of Self in Everyday Life.* New York: Doubleday, 1959.

+Goffy, G. Anthony and Scott-Morton, Michael S. A Framework for Management Information Systems, *Sloan Management Review, 13* (Fall 1971): 55-70.

Goldhaber, Gerald. *Organizational Communication,* 4th ed. Dubuque, IA: William C. Brown, 1986.

Goodall, H.L. Jr. *Small Group Communication in Organizations.* Dubuque, IA: W.C. Brown, Publishers, 1985.

+Goode, W.J. and Fowler, I. Incentive Factors in a Low Morale Plant. *American Sociological Review, 14* (1949): 618-624.

Gooding, Judson. *The Job Revolution.* New York: Macmillan, 1972.

Gordon, David. *Fat and Mean.* Ithaca, NY: Cornell University/ILR Press, 1996.

Gorman, C. Listen Here, Mr. Big!, *Time* July 3, 1989, pp. 40-45.

+Gottfried, H. and Weiss, P. A Compound Feminist Organization; Purdue University's Council on the Status of Women. *Women and Politics, 14* (1994): 23-44.

Gould, Jay. *Deadly Deceit: Low Level Radiation, High Level Coverup.* New York: Four Walls Eight Windows, 1990.

Gould, Jay and Sternglass, Ernest. *The Enemy Within: The High Cost of Living Near Nuclear Power,* forthcoming.

Gouldner, A. *Wildcat Strike.* Yellow Springs, OH: Antioch Press, 1954.

Gouran, Dennis. The Paradigm of Unfulfilled Promise, in *Speech Communication in the Twentieth Century,* T.W. Benson, ed. Carbondale, IL: Southern Illinois University Press, 1984.

+Gouran, Dennis and Fisher, B. Aubrey. The Functions of Communication in the Formation, Maintenance and Performance of Small Groups, in *Handbook of Rhetorical and Communication Theory,* C.C. Arnold and J.W. Bowers, eds. Boston: Allyn and Bacon, 1985.

Gouran, Dennis and Hirokawa, Randy. Functional Theory and Communication in Decision-Making and Problem-Solving Groups: An Expanded Perspective, in *Communication and Group Decision Making,* 2nd ed. Randy Hirokawa and M. Scott Poole, eds. Thousand Oaks, CA: Sage, 1996.

+Graen, G. B. Role-making Processes Within Complex Organizations. In *Handbook of Industrial and Organizational Psychology.* Marvin Dunnette, ed. Chicago: Rand McNally, 1976.

+Graen, G.B. and Scandura, T.A. Toward a Psychology of Dyadic Organizing, in *Research in Organizational Behavior,* vol. 9. B. Staw and L.L. Cummings, eds. Greenwich, CT: JAI Press, 1987.

Granovetter, Mark. *Getting a Job.* Cambridge, MA: Harvard University Press, 1974.

+Grant, August and Meadows, Jennifer Harmon, eds. *Communication Technology Update IV.* Boston: Focus Press, 1996.

Grant, Jan. Women as Manager: What They Can Offer to Organizations. *Organizational Dynamics* (Spring, 1988), pp. 56–63.

Gray, Barbara, Prudy, J., and Bouwen, R. Comparing Dispositional and Interactional Approaches to Negotiation. Paper presented at the International Association for Conflict Management Convention, Vancouver, 1990.

+Green, S.G. and Mitchell, T.R. Attributional Processes of Leaders in Leader-Member Interaction. *Organizational Behavior and Human Performance, 23* (1979): 429–458.

+Greenbaum, J. Division of Labor in the Computer Field. *Monthly Review, 28* (1976): 40–56.

+Greene, Charles and Podsakoff, Philip. Effects of Withdrawal of a Performance-contingent Reward on Supervisory Influence and Power. *Academy of Management Journal, 24* (1981): 527–542.

Greenhaus, J.H., Parasuraman, S., and Wormley, W.M. Effects of Race on Organizational Experiences, Job Performance Evaluations, and Career Outcomes. *Academy of Management Journal, 33* (1990): 64–86.

+Gregory, Kathleen. Native-view Paradigms. *Administrative Science Quarterly, 28* (1983): 360–372.

Greider, William. *Who Will Tell the People?* New York: Simon and Schuster, 1992.

Grenier, Guillermo. *Inhuman Relations.* Philadelphia: Temple University Press, 1988.

Gross, E. Some Functional Consequences of Formal Controls in Formal Work Organizations. *American Sociological Review, 19* (1954): 15–24.

+Guetzkow, Harold and Gyr, James. An Analysis of Decision-making Groups. *Human Relations, 7* (1954): 367–381.

Gusfield, Joseph, *Community.* New York: Harper and Row, 1975.

Guzley, Ruth. Organizational Climate and Communication Climate. *Management Communication Quarterly, 5* (1992): 379–402.

+Habermas, Jurgen. *Knowledge and Human Interests.* London: Heinemann Educational Books, 1972.

+Habermas, Jurgen. *Communication and the Evolution of Society.* London: Heinemann Educational Books, 1979.

Hackamach, L.C. and Solid, A.B. The Woman Executive—There Is Still Ample Room for Progress. *Business Horizons* (April, 1972): pp. 89–93.

Hackman, M.Z. and Johnson, C.E. *Leadership: A Communication Perspective.* Prospect Heights, IL: Waveland Press, 1991.

Hall, D. and Hall, F. Stress and the Two-Career Couple, in *Current Concerns in Occupational Stress.* Cary Cooper and Roy Payne, eds. New York: John Wiley, 1980.

+Hall, Stuart Hall. Encoding/decoding, in *Culture, Media, Language.* S. Hall, D. Hobson, A. Lowe, and P. Willis, eds. London: Hutchinson, 1982.

Hancock, Melissa and Papa, Michael. Employee Struggles with Autonomy and Dependence: Examining the Dialectic of Control through a Structurational Account of Power. Paper presented at the International Communication Association Convention, Chicago, 1996.

Hamner, Clay, Kim, J.S., Baird, L., and Bigoness, W.J. Race and Sex as Determinants of Ratings by Potential Employers in a Simulated Work-Sampling Task. *Journal of Applied Psychology, 59* (1974): 705–711.

Hannerz, Ulf. *Soulside.* Columbia University Press, 1969.

+Hansen, Karen and Philipson, Ilene, eds. *Women, Class, and the Feminist Imagination.* Philadelphia: Temple University Press, 1990.

+Hanser, Lawrence and Muchinsky, Paul. Performance Feedback Information and Organization Communication. *Human Communication Research, 7* (1980): 68–73.

Hardin, Garrett. The Tragedy of the Commons. *Science* (Dec. 13, 1968): pp. 1243–1248.

Harlan, Anne and Weiss, Carol. Sex Differences in Factors Affecting Managerial Career Advancement, in *Women in the Workplace.*

Phyllis Wallace, ed. Boston: Auburn House, 1982.

Harper, Nancy and Askling, L. Group Communication and Quality of Task Solution in a Media Production Organization. *Communication Monographs, 47* (1980): 77–100.

+Harris, Stanley and Sutton, Robert. Functions of Parting Ceremonies in Dying Organizations. *Academy of Management Journal, 29* (1986): 5–30.

Harrison, Teresa. Communication and Participative Decision Making. *Personnel Psychology, 38* (1985): 93–116.

Harrison, Teresa. Frameworks for the Study of Writing in Organizational Contexts. *Written Communication, 4* (1987): 3–23.

Hart, Roderick and Burks, Don. Rhetorical Sensitivity and Social Interaction. *Speech Monographs, 39* (1972): 75–91.

+Hart, Roderick, Carlson, Robert, and Eadie, William. Attitudes Toward Communication and the Assessment of Rhetorical Sensitivity. *Communication Monographs, 47* (1980): 1–22.

+Hartsock, Nancy. *Money, Sex and Power.* New York: Longman, 1983.

+Hawes, Leonard and Smith, David. A Critique of the Assumptions Underlying the Study of Communication and Conflict. *Quarterly Journal of Speech, 59* (1973): 423–435.

Hegerty, William H. and Sims, Henry P. Organizational Philosophy, Policies, and Objectives Related to Unethical Decision Behavior. *Journal of Applied Psychology, 64* (1979): 331–338.

Hegerty, William H. and Sims, Henry P. Some Determinants of Unethical Decision Behavior. *Journal of Applied Psychology, 63* (1978): 451–457.

+Heinen, J.S. and Jacobson, E. A Model of Task Group Development in Complex Organizations. *Academy of Management Review, 1* (1976): 98–111.

+Held, David. *Introduction to Critical Theory.* London: Hutchinson, 1980.

Helgessen, Sally. *The Female Advantage: Women's Ways of Leadership.* New York: Doubleday, 1990.

Hellman, Pamela. Her Push for Prevention Keeps Kids Out of ER. *Sunday Examiner and Chronicle Parade Magazine,* April 19, 1995, pp. 8–10.

Hellwig, Basia. The Breakthrough Generation. *Working Woman,* April, 1985.

Hennig, Margaret and Jardim, Ann. *The Managerial Woman.* New York: Pocket Books, 1976.

Hersey, Paul and Blanchard, Kenneth. *Management of Organizational Behavior,* 3rd

ed. Englewood Cliffs, NJ: Prentice-Hall, 1977.

Hess, Jon. Assimilating Newcomers Into an Organization: A Cultural Perspective. *Journal of Applied Communication Research, 21* (1993): 189–210.

Hewes, Dean, et al. "Second Guessing." *Human Communication Research, 11* (1985): 299–334.

+Hickson, David, Astley, W. Graham, Butler, Richard and Wilson, David. Organization as Power, in *Research in Organizational Behavior,* v. 3. Greenwich, NJ: JAI Press, 1981.

Hill, Linda and Kamprath, Nancy. Beyond the Myth of the Perfect Mentor. Teaching Note 9-491-096, Harvard Business School, 1991.

Hiltz, Starr Roxanne and Turoff, Murray. *The Network Nation: Human Communication via Computer.* Reading, MA: Addison-Wesley, 1978.

+Hirokawa, Randy. Discussion Procedures and Decision-Making Performance: A Test of a Functional Perspective. *Human Communication Research, 12:*203–224.

Hirokawa, Randy and Miyahara, A. A Comparison of Influence Strategies Used by Managers in American and Japanese Organizations. *Communication Quarterly, 34* (1986): 250–265.

Hirokawa, Randy and Poole, M.S., eds. *Communication and Group Decision Making,* 2nd ed. Thousand Oaks, CA: Sage, 1996.

Hirsch, Bryan. Psychological Dimensions of Social Networks. *American Journal of Community Psychology, 7* (1979): 263–277.

Hitt, Michael and Ireland, R. Duane. Peters and Waterman Revisited. *Academy of Management Executive, 1* (1987): 91–98.

Hitt, Michael and Hoskisson, Robert. Strategic Competitiveness, in *Advances in Applied Business Strategy.* L. Foster, ed. Greenwich, CT: JAI Press, 1991.

Hitt, Michael, Hoskisson, Robert, and Ireland, R.D. Mergers and Acquisitions and Managerial Commitment to Innovation in M-form Firms. *Strategic Management Journal, 11* (1990): 29–47.

Hitt, Michael, Hoskisson, Robert, Ireland, R. Duane, and Harrison, Jeffrey. Effects of Acquisitions on R&D Inputs and Outputs. *Academy of Management Journal, 34* (1991): 693–706.

Hitt, Michael, Keats, B.W., Harback, H.F., and Nixon, R.D. Rightsizing: Building and Maintaining Strategic Leadership and Long-Term Competitiveness. *Organizational Dynamics, 23* (1994): 18–32.

Hochschild, Arlie. *The Managed Heart.* Berkeley: University of California Press, 1983.

Hochschild, Arlie. *The Second Shift.* New York: Viking, 1989.

+Hoffman, L.R. Applying Experimental Research on Group Problem Solving to Organizations. *Journal of Applied Behavioral Science, 15* (1979): 375-391.

Hollander, E.P. *Leadership Dynamics.* New York: Free Press, 1978.

Hollihan, Thomas and Riley, Patricia. The Rhetorical Power of a Compelling Story. *Communication Quarterly, 35* (1987): 7-21.

Holmes, Michael. Phase Structure in Negotiation, in L. Putnam and M. Roloff, eds. *Communication and Negotiation.* Newbury Park, CA: Sage, 1993.

Homans, George. *The Human Group.* New York: Harcourt Brace, 1950.

hooks, bell. *Ain't I a Woman? Black Women and Feminism.* Boston: South End Press, 1981.

+hooks, bell. *Feminist Theory: From Margin to Center.* Boston: South End Press, 1984.

Hoover, Judith. NASA as a Myth System. Paper presented at the Speech Communication Association Convention, Boston, 1987.

Hosmer, Lawrence Hosmer. The Institutionalization of Unethical Behavior. *Journal of Business Ethics, 6* (1987): 439-447.

+House, Robert. A Path-Goal Theory of Leadership Effectiveness. *Administrative Science Quarterly, 16* (1971): 321-339.

Houston Chronicle, February 19, 1996, B1.

Houston Chronicle, October 18, 1996, 3C.

Howe, Louise Kapp. *Pink Collar Workers.* New York: Putnam's, 1977.

Huff, Anne. Politics and Argument as a Means of Coping with Ambiguity and Change, in *Managing Ambiguity and Change.* L.R. Pondy, et al., eds. New York: John Wiley, 1988.

Huff, Anne. Wives of the Organization. Paper presented at the Women and Work Conference, Arlington, TX, May 11, 1990.

Hughes, E.C. *Men and Their Work.* New York: Free Press, 1958.

+Huspek, Michael. A Language of Powerlessness. Ph.D. Dissertation, University of Washington, 1987.

+Iaffaldo, Michelle and Muchinsky, Paul. Job Satisfaction and Job Performance. *Psychological Bulletin, 97* (1985): 251-273.

Ianello, K.P. *Decisions Without Hierarchy.* New York: Routledge, 1992.

Ibarra, Herminia. Personal Networks of Women and Minorities in Management. *Academy of Management Review, 18* (1993): 56-87.

Ice, Richard. Corporate Publics and Rhetorical Strategies. *Management Communication Quarterly, 4* (1991): 341-362.

Infante, Dominic and Gordon, William. How Employees See the Boss. *Western Journal of Speech Communication, 55* (1991): 294-304.

+Ivanevich, John. High and Low Task Stimulating Jobs. *Academy of Management Journal, 22* (1979): 206-222.

Ivanevich, John. The Performance-Satisfaction Relationship. *Organizational Behavior and Human Performance, 22* (1978): 350-365.

+Jablin, Fredric. Assimilating New Members into Organizations, in *Communication Yearbook 8.* Robert Bostrom, ed. Beverly Hills, CA: Sage, 1984.

+Jablin, Fredric. Communication Competence and Effectiveness, in *The New Handbook of Organizational Communication.* Linda Putnam and Fredric Jablin, eds. Thousand Oaks, CA: Sage, 1997.

+Jablin, Fredric. An Exploratory Study of Subordinates' Perceptions of Supervisory Politics. *Communication Quarterly, 29* (1981): 269-275.

+Jablin, Fredric. Formal Organizational Structure, in *Handbook of Organizational Communication,* Fredric Jablin, Linda Putnam, Karlene Roberts and Lyman Porter, eds. Newbury Park, CA: Sage, 1987.

+Jablin, Fredric. Organizational Entry, Assimilation and Exit, in *The New Handbook of Organizational Communication.* Linda Putnam and Fredric Jablin, eds. Thousand Oaks, CA: Sage, 1997.

Jablin, Fredric. Superior-subordinate Communication, in *Communication Yearbook 2.* Brent Ruben, ed. New Brunswick, NJ: Transaction Books, 1978.

+Jablin, Fredric. Task/Work Relationships, in *Handbook of Interpersonal Communication.* Gerald Miller and Mark Knapp, eds. Beverly Hills, CA: Sage, 1985.

+Jablin, Fredric and Krone, Kathy. Organizational Assimilation, in *Handbook of Communication Science.* Charles Berger and Steve Chaffee, eds. Newbury Park, CA: Sage, 1987.

Jablin, Fredric and McComb, K.B. The Employment Screening Interview, in *Communication Yearbook 8.* Robert Bostrom, ed. Beverly Hills, CA: Sage, 1984.

+Jablin, Fredric and Siebold, David. Implications for Problem-solving Groups of Empirical Research on "Brainstorming." *Southern Speech Communication Journal, 43* (1978): 327-356.

+Jablin, Fredric and Sussman, Lyle. An Exploration of Communication and Productivity in Real Brainstorming Groups, *Human Communication Research, 4* (1978): 329-337.

Jablin, Fred and Sussman, Lyle. Organizational Group Communication, in *Organizational Communication Abstracts,* vol. 8. Howard Greenbaum, Ray Falcione, and Susan Hellweg, eds. Beverly Hills, CA: Sage, 1981.

Jackall, Robert. Business as a Social and Moral Terrain, in *Essentials of Business Ethics.* P. Madsen and J. Shafritz, eds. New York: Meridian, 1990.

Jackall, Robert. Life Above the Middle. *Harvard Business Review, 60* (September-October, 1982): 47-54.

Jackall, Robert. Moral Mazes: Bureaucracy and Managerial Work. *Harvard Business Review, 61* (September-October, 1983): 99-123.

Jamieson, David and O'Mara, Julie. *Managing Workforce 2000.* San Francisco: Jossey-Bass, 1991.

Janeway, Elizabeth. *Powers of the Weak.* New York: Morrow-Quill, 1980.

Janis, Irving. *Victims of Groupthink,* 2nd ed. Boston: Houghton Mifflin, 1982.

Janis, Irving. Sources of Error in Strategic Decision-making, in *Organizational Strategy and Change.* Johannes Pennings and Associates, eds. San Francisco: Jossey-Bass, 1985.

Janis, Irving and Mann, L. *Decision Making.* New York: Free Press, 1977.

Jarboe, Susan. Procedures For Enhancing Group Decision Making, in *Communication and Group Decision Making,* 2nd ed. Randy Hirokawa and M. Scott Poole, eds. Thousand Oaks, CA: Sage, 1996.

+Jarvenpaa, Sirkka, and Ives, Blake. The Global Network Organization of the Future: Information Management Opportunities and Challenges. *Journal of Management Information Systems, 10* (1994): pp. 25-57.

+Jehensen, Richard. Effectiveness, Expertise, and Excellence as Ideological Fictions. *Human Studies,* 7 (1984): 3-21.

Johansen, Robert, Vallee, Jacques, and Spangler, Kenneth. *Electronic Meetings: Technological Alternatives and Social Choices.* Reading, MA: Addison-Wesley, 1979.

Johansen, Robert. *Teleconferencing and Beyond.* New York: McGraw-Hill, 1984.

+Jermier, John and Albrecht, Terrance. New Directions in the Study of Communication, Power, and Domination. Paper presented at the International Communication Association Convention, Sydney, Australia, 1994.

Johnson, Haynes. *Divided We Fall: Gambling with History in the 1990s.* New York: W.W. Norton, 1994.

Johnson, Kirk. Many Companies Turn Workers Into High-Tech Nomads, *Minneapolis Star-Tribune,* April 3, 1994, 1J.

+Jonson, Albert and Toulmin, Stephen. *The Abuse of Casuistry.* Berkeley: University of California Press, 1988.

+Jones, E.E., Gergen, K.J., and Jones, R.G. Tactics of Ingratiation Among Leaders and Subordinates in a Status Hierarchy. *Psychological Monographs,* 77 (1963): 119-128.

+Jones, Gareth. Psychological Orientation and the Process of Organizational Socialization. *Academy of Management Review,* 8 (1983): 464-474.

+Kahneman, R., and Tversky, A. Prospect Theory. *Econometrica,* 47 (1981): 263-269.

Kalleberg, Arne and Leicht, Kevin. Gender and Organizational Performance. *Academy of Management Journal,* 34 (1991): 151-164.

Kanter, Donald and Mirvis, Philip. *The Cynical American: Living and Working in an Age of Discontent and Disillusionment.* San Francisco: Jossey-Bass, 1990.

Kanter, Rosabeth Moss. *Men and Women of the Corporation.* New York: Harper and Row, 1977.

Kanter, Rosabeth Moss. *A Tale of "O": On Being Different in an Organization.* New York: Harper and Row, 1980.

Karsten, M.F. *Management and Gender.* Westport, CT: Quorum Books, 1994.

+Katz, Daniel and Kahn, Robert. *The Social Psychology of Organizations,* 2nd ed. New York: John Wiley, 1978.

Kauffman, Herbert. *The Forest Ranger.* Baltimore: Johns Hopkins University Press, 1960.

Keele, A.K. Mentoring and Networking? in *Not as Far as You Think.* Linda L. Moore, ed. Lexington, MA: Lexington Books, 1986.

+Kelley, H.H., Berscheid, E. A., Christensen, J., Harvey, F., Huston, T., Levinger, G., McClintock, E., Peplan, L., and Peterson, D., eds. *Close Relationships.* New York: Freeman and Company, 1983.

Kellman, Herbert and Hamilton, L. *Crimes of Obedience.* New Haven, CT: Yale University Press, 1989.

Kennedy, George. *Classical Rhetoric in Its Christian and Secular Traditions from Ancient to Modern Times.* Chapel Hill: University of North Carolina Press, 1980.

Kerr, Elaine and Hiltz, Starr Roxanne. *Computer-mediated Communication Systems* (New York: Academic Press, 1982).

Kerr, Jeffrey and Slocum, John. Managing Corporate Culture Through Reward Systems. *Academy of Management Executive, 1* (1987): 99-108.

+Kersten, Astrid. Culture, Control, and the Labor Process, in Stanley Deetz, ed. *Communication Yearbook 16.* Newbury Park, CA: Sage, 1993.

Kessler, S., Ashenden, D.J., Connell, R.W., and Dowsett, G.W. Gender Relations in Secondary Schooling. *Sociology of Education, 58* (1985): 42-58.

Kiechel, Walter. Management Winners. *Fortune,* November 29, 1982, pp. 159-160.

+Kiesler, Sara, Siegel, Jane, and McGuire, Timothy W. Social Psychological Aspects of Computer-mediated Communication. *American Psychologist, 39* (1984): 1123-1134.

Kilborn, Peter T. For Many in Work Force, Glass Ceiling Still Exists. *New York Times,* 16 March, 1995.

+Kim, Ken, Park, Hun-Joon, and Suzuki, Nori. Reward Allocations in the United States, Japan, and Korea. *Academy of Management Journal, 33* (1990): 188-198.

Kim, Pan Suk and Lewis, Gregory. Asian Americans in the Public Service. *Public Administration Review, 54* (1994): 285-290.

+Kim, Young Yong and Miller, Katherine. The Effects of Attributions and Feedback on the Generation of Supervisor Feedback Message Strategies. *Management Communication Quarterly, 4* (1990): 6-29.

+Kipnis, David. *Technology and Power.* New York: Springer-Verlag, 1990.

+Knights, David and Willmott, Hugh. "Organizational Culture as Management Strategy: A Critique and Illustration from the Financial Service Industries," *International Studies of Management and Organization, 17* (1987): 40-63.

Korn/Ferry International. *The Decade of the Executive Woman.* New York: 1993.

Knouse, Paul. The Mentoring Process for Hispanics, in *Hispanics in the Workplace.* P. Knouse, P. Rosenfeld, and A. Culbertson, eds. Newbury Park, CA: Sage, 1992.

Knouse, Paul, Rosenfeld, Paul, and Culbertson, Amy, eds. *Hispanics in the Workplace.* Newbury Park, CA: Sage, 1992.

+Knuf, Joachim Knuf. "Ritual" in Organizational Culture Theory. In *Communication Yearbook 16.* Stanley Deetz, ed. Newbury Park, CA: Sage, 1994.

Kolb, Deborah, ed. *Hidden Conflict in Organizations.* Newbury Park, CA: Sage, 1991.

+Komorita, S.S. Negotiating from Strength and the Concept of Bargaining. *Journal of the Theory of Social Behavior, 7* (1977): 56-79.

Konar, E. Explanations of Racial Differences in Job Satisfaction. *Journal of Applied Psychology, 66* (1981): 522-534.

Kotter, John. *Power in Management.* New York: AMACOM, 1979.

Kouzes, J.M. and Posner, B.Z. *The Leadership Challenge: How to Get Extraordinary Things Done in Organizations.* San Francisco: Jossey-Bass, 1987.

+Kraiger, K. and Ford, J. A Meta-Analysis of Ratee Race Effects in Performance Ratings. *Journal of Applied Psychology, 70* (1985): 56-65.

Kram, Kathy. *Mentoring.* Chicago: Scott, Foresman, 1986.

+Kramer, Michael. Communication After Job Transfers: Social Exchange Processes in Learning New Roles. *Human Communication Research, 20* (1993): 147-174.

+Kramer, Michael. Communication and Uncertainty Reduction During Job Transfers: Leaving and Joining Process. *Communication Monographs, 60* (1993): 178-198.

+Kramer, Michael. Communication During Intraorganizational Job Transfers. *Management Communication Quarterly, 3* (1989): 213-248.

+Kramer, Michael. A Longitudinal Study of Superior-Subordinate Communication During Job Transfers. *Human Communication Research, 22* (1995): 39-64.

Kramerae, Cheris. *Women and Men Speaking.* Rowley, MA: Newbury House, 1984.

+Kreps, Gary. A Field Experimental Test of Weick's Model of Organizing, in *Communication Yearbook 4.* Dan Nimmo, ed. New Brunswick, NJ: Transaction, 1980.

Kreps, G., ed. *Sexual Harassment: Communication Implications.* Cresskill, NJ: Hampton Press, 1993.

Kritek, P.B. *Negotiating at an Uneven Table* (San Francisco: Jossey-Bass, 1994.

Lamude, Kevin, Daniels, Tom, and White, Kim. Managing the Boss. *Management Communication Quarterly, 1* (1987): 232-259.

Larkey, Linda and Morrill, Calvin. Organizational Commitment as Symbolic Process. *Western Journal of Communication, 59* (1995): 193-213.

+Lawler, Edwin. *High Involvement Management.* San Francisco: Jossey-Bass, 1986.

Lawler, Edwin. *Negotiation.* San Francisco: Jossey-Bass, 1980.

+Lawler, Edwin. *Pay and Organizational Effectiveness.* New York: McGraw-Hill, 1971.

+Lawler, Edward and Rhodes, John. *Information and Control in Organizations.* Pacific Palisades: Goodyear, 1976.

+Lawrence, Paul and Lorsch, Jay. *Organizations and Environment.* Boston: Harvard Business School, 1967.

Lears, T.J. The Concept of Cultural Hegemony. *American Historical Review, 90* (1985): 565-593.

Legg, Nina Anderson. Other People's Kids: Decision-making About Sexual Education,

Master's Thesis, Texas A&M University, 1992.

Lewicki, Roy. Lying and Deception, in *Negotiating in Organizations*. Max Bazerman and Roy Lewicki, eds. Newbury Park, CA: Sage, 1983.

Leyden, Peter. Teleworking Could Turn Our Cities Inside Out. *Minneapolis Star-Tribune,* September 5, 1993, 15A–16A.

+Liden, R.C. and Graen, G. Generalizability of the Vertical Dyad Linkage Model of Leadership. *Academy of Management Journal, 23* (1980): 451–465.

Likert, Rensis. *New Patterns of Management.* New York: McGraw-Hill, 1961.

+Lim, T. and Bowers, J.W. Face-work: Solidarity, Approbation, and Face. *Human Communication Research, 17* (1990): 415–450.

Lindblom, Charles. The Science of Muddling Through. *Public Administration Review, 19* (1959): 412–421.

+Lipman-Blumen, Jean. *Gender Roles and Power.* Englewood Cliffs, NJ: Prentice-Hall, 1984.

Lischeron, J.A. and Wall, T.D. Employee Participation. *Human Relations, 28* (1975): 863–884.

Locke, Edwin. The Ideas of Frederick Taylor. *The Academy of Management Review, 7* (1982): 14–24.

Locke, Edwin. The Nature and Causes of Job Satisfaction, in *Handbook of Industrial and Organizational Psychology.* Marvin Dunnette, ed. Chicago: Rand-McNally, 1976.

+Locke, Edwin, Shaw, Karyll, Saari, Lise, and Latham, Gary. Goal Setting an Task Performance: 1969–1980. *Psychological Bulletin, 90* (1981): 125–152.

Lodahl, T.M. and Mitchell, S.M. Drift in the Development of Innovative Organizations, in *The Organizational Life Cycle.* John R. Kimberly and Robert H. Miles, eds. San Francisco: Jossey-Bass, 1980.

Loden, Marilyn. *Feminine Leadership: How to Succeed Without Being One of the Boys.* New York: Times Books, 1985.

Lorde, Audre. Nobody Said It Was Simple, in *Common Differences: Conflicts in Black and White Feminist Perspectives.* Gloria Joseph and Jill Lewis, eds. New York: Anchor, 1981.

The Lordstown Auto Workers, in *Life in Organizations.* Rosabeth Moss Kanter and Barry Stein, eds. New York: Basic Books, 1979.

Lott, Cynthia. Redwood Records: Principles and Profit in Women's Music, in *Women Communicating.* Barbara Bate and Anita Taylor, eds. Norwood, NJ: Ablex, 1988.

Louis, Meryl Reis. Acculturation in the Workplace, in *Organizational Climate and Culture.* B. Schneider, ed. San Francisco: Jossey-Bass, 1990.

Louis, Meryl Reis. Surprise and Sense-making in Organizations. *Administrative Science Quarterly, 25* (1980): 226–251.

+Lucas, Henry. *The T-Form Organization.* San Francisco: Jossey-Bass, 1995.

+Lukes, Steven. *Power: A Radical View.* London: Macmillan, 1974.

Luthans, Fred and Larsen, Janet. How Managers Really Communicate. *Human Relations, 39* (1986): 161–178.

Macarov, David. *Incentives to Work.* Beverly Hills: Sage, 1981.

Macarov, David. *Worker Productivity: Myths and Reality.* Beverly Hills, CA: Sage, 1982.

+Madison, Dan, Allen, Robert, Porter, Lyman, Renwick, Patricia, Mayes, Bronston. Organizational Politics. *Human Relations, 33* (1980): 79–100.

+Mann, Michael. *The Sources of Social Power,* vol. 1. Cambridge: Cambridge University Press, 1986.

Mansnerus, Laura. Why Women Are Leaving the Law. *Working Woman,* April, 1993.

March, James. The Technology of Foolishness, in *Ambiguity and Choice in Organizations.* James March and Johann Olson, eds. Bergen: Universitetsforlaget, 1970.

+March, James and Olson, Johann. *Ambiguity and Choice in Organizations.* Bergen: Universitetsforlaget, 1970.

+March, James and Sevon, Guje. Gossip, Information, and Decision Making, in *Advances in Information Processing in Organizations,* v. 1. Lee Sproull and Patrick Larkey, eds. Greenwich, CT: JAI Press, 1982.

+March, James and Simon, Herbert. The Concept of Rationality, in *Human Behavior and International Politics.* David Singer, ed. Chicago: Rand-McNally, 1965.

+March, James and Simon, Herbert. *Organizations.* New York: John Wiley, 1958.

Marin, G. and Marin, B.V. *Research with Hispanic Populations.* Newbury Park, CA: Sage, 1991.

Marini, M.M. and Brinton, M.C. Sex Typing in Occupational Socialization, in *Sex Segregation in the Workplace.* B.F. Reskin, ed. Washington, D.C.: National Academy Press, 1984.

Marini, M.M. and Greenberger, E. Sex Differences in Occupational Aspirations and Expectations. *Sociology of Work and Occupations, 5* (1968): 147–178.

Marrow, Alfred, Bowers, David, and Seashore, Stanley. *Management by Participation.* New York: Harper & Row, 1967.

Marshall, Judi. Viewing Organizational Communication from a Feminist Perspective: A Critique and Some Offerings, in *Communication Yearbook 16.* Stanley Deetz, ed. Newbury Park, CA: Sage, 1993.

+Martin, Joanne. *Cultures in Organizations: Three Perspectives.* New York: Oxford University Press, 1992.

Martin, Joanne, Feldman, Marsha, Hatch, Mary and Sitkin, Sim. The Uniqueness Paradox in Organizational Stories. *Administrative Science Quarterly, 28* (1983): 438-453.

Martin, Joanne and Powers, Melanie. Truth or Corporate Propaganda: The Value of a Good War Story, in *Organizational Symbolism.* Louis Pondy, Peter Frost, Gareth Morgan and Thomas Dandridge, eds. Greenwich, CT: JAI Press, 1983.

Martin, Lynn. *Pipelines of Progress.* Washington, D.C.: U.S. Department of Labor, August, 1992.

Martin, Lynn. *A Report on the Glass Ceiling Initiative.* Washington, D.C.: U.S. Dept. of Labor, August, 1991.

Maslach, Christina. *Burnout, the Cost of Caring.* Englewood Cliffs, NJ: Prentice-Hall, 1982.

+Masuch, Michael and LaPotin, Perry. Beyond Garbage Cans. *Administrative Science Quarterly, 34* (1989): 38-68.

Matthews, Christopher. *Kennedy & Nixon.* New York: Simon & Schuster, 1996.

+May, Kenneth. Intransitivity, Utility and Aggregation of Preference Patterns. *Econometrica, 22* (1956): 1-36.

Mayo, Alton. *Social Problems of an Industrial Civilization.* Boston: Graduate School of Business Administration, Harvard University, 1945.

+McAllister, D.J. Affect- and Cognition-Based Trust as Foundations for Interpersonal Cooperation in Organizations, *Academy of Management Journal, 38* (1995): 24-59.

McCord, William, Howard, Joun, Friedberg, Bernard, and Harwood, Edwin. *Lifestyles in the Black Ghetto.* New York: Norton, 1969.

McCroskey, James and Richmond, Virginia Peck. The Impact of Communication Apprehension of Individuals in Organizations. *Communication Quarterly, 27* (1979): 55-61.

+McFarlin, Dean and Sweeney, Paul. Distributive and Procedural Justice as Predictors of Satisfaction with Personal and Organizational Outcomes. *Academy of Management Journal, 35* (1992): 626-637.

McLaughlin, Michael. *Conversation.* Beverly Hills, CA: Sage, 1984.

+McLeod, Raymond Jr. *Management Information Systems,* 6th ed. New York: MacMillan, 1990.

+McPhee, Robert. Vertical Communication Chains. *Management Communication Quarterly, 4* (1988): 455-493.

+McPhee, Robert and Poole, Marshall Scott. Organizational Forms and Configurations, in *The New Handbook of Organizational Communication.* Linda Putnam and Fredric Jablin, eds. Thousand Oaks, CA: Sage, 1997.

+Meindl, James. Managing to Be Fair. *Administrative Science Quarterly, 34* (1989): 252-276.

Menn, Joseph. ADM Fine Criticized As Too Low. *Houston Chronicle,* December 1, 1996, C13.

Meredith, Jack. *Project Management.* New York: John Wiley & Sons, 1989.

+Meyer, Alan. How Ideologies Supplant Formal Structures and Shape Responses to Environments. *Journal of Management Studies, 19* (1982): 45-61.

+Meyer, Alan. Mingling Decision Making Metaphors. *Academy of Management Review, 9* (1984): 231-246.

Meyer, Michael. Here's a "Virtual" Model for America's Industrial Giants. *Newsweek,* August 13, 1993, p. 40.

Meyers, H., Kay, E., and French, J.R.P. Split Roles in Performance Appraisals. *Harvard Business Review, 43* (1965): 21-29.

Meyerson, Debra. "Normal" Ambiguity?, in *Reframing Organizational Culture.* Peter Frost, et al., eds. Newbury Park, CA: Sage, 1991.

Meyerson, Debra. Interpretations of Stress in Institutions. *Administrative Science Quarterly, 39* (1994): 628-653.

Miceli, Marcia and Near, Janet. *Blowing the Whistle: The Organizational and Legal Implications for Companies and Employees.* New York: Lexington Books, 1992.

Miles, Raymond. *Theories of Management.* New York: McGraw-Hill, 1975.

Miles, Robert E. and Snow, Charles C. Organizations: New Concepts for New Forms. *California Management Review, 28,* 3(1986): 62-73.

Miller, Katherine. *Organizational Communication.* Belmont, CA: Wadsworth, 1994.

+Miller, Katherine and Monge, Peter. The Development and Test of a System of Organizational Participation and Allocation, in

Communication Yearbook 10. Margaret McLaughlin, ed. Beverly Hills, CA: Sage, 1987.

Miller, Lynn, Cooke, Linda, Tsang, Jennifer, and Morgan, Faith. Should I Brag? *Human Communication Research, 19* (1992): 364-399.

+Miller, Vernon and Jablin, Fredric. Information Seeking During Organizational Entry. *Academy of Management Review, 16* (1991): 92-120.

+Mintzberg, Henry. *The Nature of Managerial Work.* New York: Harper & Row, 1973.

+Mintzberg, Henry. *Power in and Around Organizations.* Englewood Cliffs, NJ: Prentice-Hall, 1983.

+Mintzberg, Henry. *Structuring in Fives.* Englewood Cliffs, NJ: Prentice-Hall, 1983.

+Mintzberg, Henry. *The Structuring of Organizations.* Englewood Cliffs, NJ: Prentice-Hall, 1978.

+Mintzberg, Henry and McHugh, Alexandra. Strategy Formation in an Adhocracy. *Administrative Science Quarterly, 30* (1985): 160-197.

+Mintzberg, Henry, Raisinghani, Duru, and Theoret, Andre. The Structure of 'Unstructured' Decision Processes. *Administrative Science Quarterly, 21* (1976): 246-275.

Missirian, A.K. *The Corporate Connection.* Englewood Cliffs, NJ: Prentice-Hall, 1982.

Moch, Michael K. and Bartunek, Jean. *Creating Alternative Realities at Work.* New York: Harper Business, 1990.

Mohrman, A.M., Resnick-West, S. and Lawler, Edwin. *Designing Performance Appraisal Systems.* San Francisco: Jossey-Bass, 1989.

Mohrman, Susan A., Cohen, Susan G., and Mohrman, Allan M. *Designing Team-Based Organizations: New Forms for Knowledge Work* San Francisco: Jossey-Bass, 1995.

+Monge, Peter and Contractor, Noshir. Emergent Communication Networks, in *New Handbook of Organizational Communication.* Linda Putnam and Fred Jablin, eds. (Thousand Oaks, CA: Sage, 1997).

+Monge, Peter, Edwards, Jane, and Kirstie, Kenneth. The Determinants of Communication and Communication Structure in Large Organizations, in *Communication Yearbook 2.* Brent Ruben, ed. New Brunswick, NJ: Transaction Books, 1978.

Mongeau, Paul and Black, Jennifer. Student Evaluations of Instructor Immediacy and Sexually Harassing Behaviors: An Experimental Investigation. *Journal of Applied Communication Research, 22* (1994): 256-272.

Moore, Thomas. *The Disposable Work Force.* New York: Aldine de Gruyter, 1996.

Morely, Dean and Shockley-Zalabak, Pamela. Conflict Avoiders and Compromisers. *Group and Organizational Behavior, 11* (1986): 387-402.

Morrill, Calvin. The Private Ordering of Professional Relationships, in *Hidden Conflict in Organizations.* Deborah Kolb and Jean Bartunek, eds. Newbury Park, CA: Sage, 1992.

+Morris, G.H. et al. Aligning Actions at Work. *Management Communication Quarterly, 3* (1990): 303-333.

Morris, Jim. Whistle-blower Claims Settled. *Houston Chronicle,* November 20, 1996, A24-25.

Morrison, Ann. *The New Leaders: Guidelines of Leadership Diversity in America.* San Francisco: Jossey-Bass, 1992.

Morrison, Ann and Von Glinow, Mary Ann. Women and Minorities in Management. *American Psychologist, 45* (1991): 200-208.

Morrison, Ann, White, Randall and Van Velsor, Ellen. *Breaking the Glass Ceiling.* Reading, MA: Addison-Wesley, 1987.

Moser, M. Ethical Conflict at Work. *Journal of Business Ethics, 7* (1988): 381-387.

Mowshowitz, K.W. Virtual Organization: A Vision of Management in the Information Age, *Information Society, 10* (1994): 267-288.

+Muchinsky, Paul. Organizational Communication. *Academy of Management Journal, 20* (1977): 592-607.

Mulder, Mauk. Power Equalization Through Participation? *Academy of Management Journal, 16* (1971): 31-38.

+Mulder, Mauk and Wilke, H. Participation and Power Equalization. *Organizational Behavior and Human Performance, 5* (1970): 430-448.

+Mumby, Dennis. *Communication and Power in Organizations.* Norwood, NJ: Ablex, 1988.

+Mumby, Dennis, ed. *Narrative and Social Control: Critical Perspectives.* Newbury Park, CA: Sage, 1993.

+Mumby, Dennis. Power, Politics, and Organizational Communication, in *The New Handbook of Organizational Communication.* Linda Putnam and Fredric Jablin, eds. Thousand Oaks, CA: Sage, In Press.

+Mumby, Dennis and Putnam, Linda. The Politics of Emotion: A Feminist Reading of Bounded Rationality. *The Academy of Management Review, 17* (1992): 465-487.

+Mumby, Dennis and Stohl, Cynthia. Power and Discourse in Organization Studies. *Discourse and Society, 2* (1991): 313-332.

Munoz, D. L. Myths, Facts, Reality on "The Hispanic Decade of the 80's." *La Prensa San Diego,* January 19, 1990.

+Murdock, J., Bradac, J., and Bowers, J. Effects of Power on the Perception of Explicit and Implicit Threats, Promises and Thromises. *Western Journal of Speech Communication, 48* (1984): 344–361.

Nadler, Marjorie and Nadler, Larry. Feminization of Public Relations, in *Communication and Sex-role Socialization.* Cynthia Berryman-Fink, D. Ballard-Reich, and L.H. Newman, eds. New York: Garland Publishing Company, 1993.

+Nathan, Barry, Mohrman, Allan, and Milliman, John. Interpersonal Relations as a Context of the Effects of Appraisal Interviews. *Academy of Management Journal, 34* (1991): 352–369.

Neal, Margaret and Bazerman, Max. Negotiating Rationally. *Academy of Management Executive, 6* (1992): 42–65.

Newman, Katherine. *Falling from Grace: The Experience of Downward Mobility in the American Middle Class.* New York: Free Press, 1988.

Nkomo, Stella. The Forgotten Case of the Black Female Manager, in *Women's Careers: Pathways and Pitfalls.* Suzanna Rose and Laurie Larwood, eds. New York: Praeger, 1988.

+Nkomo, Stella. The Emperor Has No Clothes: Rewriting "Race" in Organizations. *Academy of Management Review, 17* (1992): 487–512.

Noble, Barbara Presley. An Employee Rights Minefield. *New York Times,* May 30, 1993, E1.

Noe, Raymond. Women and Mentoring. *Academy of Management Review, 13* (1988): 65–78.

Nord, Walter and Durand, Douglas. What's Wrong with the Human Resources Approach to Management. *Organizational Dynamics* (Winter, 1978): pp. 13–25.

+Nunamaker, Jay F., Dennis, Alan R., Valacich, Joe, Vogel, Doug, and George, Joey. Electronic Meeting Systems to Support Group Work. *Communications of the ACM, 34* (1991): 40–61.

O'Barr and Atkins, B. Women's Language or "Powerless Language," in S. McConnell-Ginet, R. Borker and N. Furnam, eds. *Women and Language in Literature and Society.* New York: Praeger, 1980.

+O'Connor, Edward and Barrett, Gerald. Informational Cues and Individual Differences as Determinants of Perceptions of Task Enrichment. *Academy of Management Journal, 23* (1980): 697–716.

+O'Keefe, Barbara. The Logic of Message Design. *Communication Monographs, 55* (1988): 80–103.

+O'Keefe, Barbara. Variation, Adaptation, and Functional Explanation in the Study of Message Design," in *Developing Communication Theories.* G. Philipsen and T.L. Albrecht, eds. Albany, NY: SUNY Press, In Press.

O'Leary, V. and Hansen, R. Trying Hurts Women, Helps Men: The Meaning of Effort, in *Women in the Workforce.* H.J. Bernardin, ed. New York: Praeger, 1982.

+Olgren, C.H. and Parker, L.H. Teleconferencing Technology and Applications. Dedham, MA: Artech House, 1983.

Olivares, Frederica. Ways Men and Women Lead. *Harvard Business Review* (January-February, 1991).

+O'Reilly, Charles. Supervisors and Peers as Information Sources, Group Supportiveness, and Individual Decision-making Performance. *Journal of Applied Psychology, 62* (1977): 632–635.

+O'Reilly, Charles. Variations in Decision-makers' Use of Information Sources. *Academy of Management Journal, 25* (1982): 756–771.

+O'Reilly, Charles and Caldwell, David. Informational Influence as a Determinant of Task Characteristics and Job Satisfaction. *Journal of Applied Psychology, 64* (1979): 157–165.

O'Reilly, Charles, Chatman, Jennifer, and Caldwell, David. People and Organizational Culture: A Profile Comparison Approach to Assessing Person-Organization Fit. *Academy of Management Journal, 34* (1991): 487–516.

Organ, Dennis. Linking Pins Between Organizations and Environments. *Business Horizons, 14* (1971): 73–80.

Ospina, Sonia. *Illusions of Opportunity.* Ithaca, NY: Cornell University Press, 1996.

Ouchi, William. The Relationship Between Organizational Structure and Control. *Administrative Science Quarterly, 22* (1977): 95–113.

Ouchi, William and Wilkins, Alan. Efficient Cultures. *Administrative Science Quarterly, 28* (1983): 468–481.

Pacanowsky, Michael. Communication in the Empowering Organization. In *Communication Yearbook 11.* James Anderson, ed. Beverly Hills, CA: Sage, 1987.

Pacanowsky, Michael. Creating and Narrating Organizational Realities, in *Rethinking Communication,* vol. 2. Brenda Dervin, et al., eds. Beverly Hills, CA: Sage, 1989.

Pacanowsky, Michael and O'Donnell-Trujillo, Nick. Organizational Communication as Cultural Performance. *Communication Monographs, 50* (1983): 126–147.

Page, Paul. African Americans in Executive Branch Agencies. *Review of Public Personnel Administration, 14* (1994): 24-51.

+Palmer, Richard C. *Hermeneutics.* Evanston, IL: Northwestern University Press, 1979.

Paludi, M.A. and Barickman, R.B. *Academic and Workplace Sexual Harassment* Albany, NY: SUNY, 1991.

Pamental, G.L. The Course in Business Ethics: Can it Work? *Journal of Business Ethics, 8* (1989): 547-551.

+Papa, Michael and Tracy, Karen. Communicative Indices of Employee Performance with New Technology. *Communication Research, 15* (1988): 524-544.

Papa, Michael and Papa, Wendy. Competence in Organizational Conflicts," in *Competence in Interpersonal Conflict.* W.R. Cupach and D.J. Canary, eds. New York: McGraw-Hill, 1996.

Pardo, Mary. Doing it for the Kids, in *Feminist Organizations.* Myra Marx Ferree and Patricia Yancey Martin, eds. Philadelphia: Temple University Press, 1995.

+Parks, Malcolm. Interpersonal Communication and the Quest for Personal Competence, in *Handbook of Interpersonal Communication.* Mark Knapp and Gerald Miller, eds. Beverly Hills, CA: Sage, 1985.

+Parks, Malcom and Adelman, Mara. Communication Networks and the Development of Romantic Relationships. *Human Communication Research, 10* (1983): 55-80.

Parsons, Talcott and Clark, Kenneth, eds. *The Negro American.* Boston: Beacon, 1965.

Pascale, Robert, and Athos, A.G. *The Art of Japanese Management* New York: Warner, 1981.

Paskoff, Stephen. Ending the Workplace Diversity Wars. *Training: The Human Side of Business* (August, 1996), pp. 1-11.

+Pavitt, C., Whitchurch, G.C., McGlurg, H., and Peterson, N. Melding the Objective and Subjective Sides of Leadership: Communication and Social Judgements in Decision-Making Groups. *Communication Monographs, 62* (1995): 243-264.

Pearson, Judi, West, R.L., and Turner, L.H. *Gender and Communication.* Dubuque, IA: Brown and Benchmark, 1995.

Penelope, Julia, *Speaking Freely.* New York: Pergamon, 1990.

+Perelman, Chaim. *The Idea of Justice and the Problem of Argument.* London: Routledge and Kegan Paul, 1963.

Perrow, Charles. *Complex Organizations,* 3rd ed. New York: Random House, 1987.

Perrow, Charles. A Framework for the Comparative Analysis of Organizations, *American Sociological Review, 32* (1967): 194-208.

Perrow, Charles. *Normal Accidents.* New York: Basic Books, 1984.

Peters, Tom. The Best New Managers Will Listen, Motivate, Support: Isn't That Just Like a Woman? *Working Woman,* September 1990, p. 216.

Peters, Tom and Austin, Nancy. *A Passion for Excellence.* New York: Random House, 1985.

Peters, Tom and Waterman, Robert. *In Search of Excellence.* New York: Harper & Row, 1982.

+Peterson, D. R. Assessing Interpersonal Relationships by Means of Interaction Records. *Behavioral Assessment, 1* (1979): 221-236.

Peterson, L. and Albrecht, Terrance. Message Design Logics and Mixed Status Relationships. Paper presented at the Speech Communication Association Convention, Chicago, 1992.

Peterson, Tarla Rai and Choat Horton, Christi. Rooted in the Soil. *The Quarterly Journal of Speech, 18* (1995): 139-166.

Pettigrew, Andrew. Information Control as a Power Resource. *Sociology, 6* (1972): 187-204.

Pettigrew, Andrew. *The Politics of Organizational Decision-Making.* London: Tavistock, 1973.

Pettigrew, Thomas. New Black-White Patterns. *Annual Review of Sociology, 11* (1985): 329-346.

Pettit, J.D. Jr., Vaught, B. and Pulley, K.J. The Role of Communication in Organizations: Ethical Considerations. *Journal of Business Communication, 27* (1990): 233-249.

+Pfeffer, Jeffrey. The Bases and Uses of Power in Organizational Decision-making. *Administrative Science Quarterly, 19* (1974): 453-473.

+Pfeffer, Jeffrey. *Managing With Power.* Boston: Harvard Business School Press, 1992.

+Pfeffer, Jeffrey. *Organizations and Organization Theory.* Marshfield: Pitman, 1982.

+Pfeffer, Jeffrey. Power and Resource Allocation in Organizations, in *New Directions in Organizational Behavior.* Barry Staw and Gerald Salancik, eds. New York: St. Clair Press, 1977.

+Pfeffer, Jeffrey. *Power in Organizations.* Marshfield: Pitman, 1981.

+Pfeffer, Jeffrey and Davis-Blake, Alison. The Effect of the Proportion of Women on Salaries. *Administrative Science Quarterly, 32* (1987): 1-24.

+Pfeffer, Jeffrey and Langton, Nancy. Wage Inequality and the Organization of Work. *Administrative Science Quarterly, 33* (1988): 588-606.

+Pfeffer, Jeffrey and Salancik, Gerald. *The External Control of Organizations.* New York: Harper & Row, 1978.

Phillips, Don. *Houston Chronicle,* July 12, 1996, 6A.

+Pierce, Jon, Gardner, Donald G., Cummings, Larry, and Dunham, Randall. Organization-based Self-Esteem. *Academy of Management Journal, 32* (1989): 622-648.

+Pierce, J., Dunham, D., and Blackburn, R. Social Systems Structure, Job Design and Growth Need Strength. *Academy of Management Journal, 22* (1979): 223-240.

Plamandon, Ann. Ethics in the Workplace, in *Organizational Communication: Theory and Behavior.* Peggy Yuhas Byars, ed. (Boston: Allyn and Bacon, 1997).

Pondy, Louis. Organizational Conflict: Concepts and Models, *Administrative Science Quarterly, 12* (1967): 296-320.

Pondy, Louis. The Role of Metaphors and Myths in the Organization and the Facilitation of Change. In *Organizational Symbolism.* Louis Pondy, Peter Frost, Gareth Morgan and Thomas Dandridge, eds. Greenwich, CT: JAI Press, 1983.

Poole, M. Scott. Communication and Organizational Climates, in *Organizational Communication.* Robert McPhee and Phillip Tompkins, eds. Beverly Hills, CA: Sage, 1985.

+Poole, M. Scott. Decision Development in Small Groups, I. *Communication Monographs, 48* (1981): 1-24.

+Poole, M. Scott. Decision Development in Small Groups, II. *Communication Monographs, 50* (1983): 206-232.

+Poole, M. Scott. Decision Development in Small Groups, III. *Communication Monographs, 50* (1983): 321-341.

Poole, M. Scott and Baldwin, Carolyn. Developmental Processes in Group Decision-making, in *Communication and Group Decision Making,* 2nd ed. R. Hirokawa and M.S. Poole, eds. Thousand Oaks, CA: Sage, 1996.

Poole, Marshall Scott and Conrad, Charles, eds. Special Issue on Communication in the Age of the Disposable Worker. *Communication Research,* In Press.

+Poole, M. Scott and McPhee, Robert. Bringing Intersubjectivity Back In: A Change of Climate, in *Organizational Communication.* Linda Putnam and Michael Pacanowsky, eds. Beverly Hills, CA: Sage, 1983.

+Poole, Marshall Scott and Van de Ven, Andrew. Using Paradox to Build Management and Organizational Theories. *Academy of Management Review, 14*: 562-578.

+Porter, Lyman, Allen, Robert, and Angle, Harold. The Politics of Upward Influence in Organizations, in *Research in Organizational Behavior,* v. 3. JAI Press, 1981.

Posner, B.Z. and Schmidt, W.H. Values and the American Manager. *California Management Review, 26* (1984): 202-216.

Powell, Gary. *Women and Men in Management,* 2nd ed. Newbury Park, CA: Sage, 1993.

Powell, Gary and Butterfield, D.A. Investigating the "Glass Ceiling" Phenomenon. *Academy of Management Journal, 37* (1994): 68-86.

Prasso, Sheri. Study: Stereotypes Hinder Female Executives. *Houston Chronicle,* February 29, 1996, B1.

Pruitt, D.G. and Rubin, J. *Social Conflict.* New York: Random House, 1986.

Putnam, Linda. Conflict in Group Decision Making, in *Communication and Group Decision Making.* Randy Hirokawa and M. Scott Poole, eds. Newbury Park, CA: Sage, 1986.

+Putnam, Linda. Conflict and Dispute Management, in *New Handbook of Organizational Communication.* Linda Putnam and Fredric Jablin, eds. Thousand Oaks, CA: Sage, 1997.

+Putnam, Linda. Feminist Theories, Dispute Processes, and Organizational Communication. Paper presented at the Conference of Organizational Communication in the 1990s, Tempe, AZ, April, 1990.

+Putnam, Linda, ed. *Management Communication Quarterly, 2* (1988).

Putnam, Linda. Negotiation of Intergroup Conflict in Organizations. Hallie Mande Neff Wilcox Published Lecture. Waco, TX: Baylor University, 1987.

+Putnam, Linda. Preference for Procedural Order in Task-oriented Small Groups. *Communication Monographs, 46* (1979): 193-218.

Putnam, Linda. Reframing Integrative and Distributive Bargaining, in *Research on Negotiation in Organizations,* vol. 2. Roy Lewicki and Max Bazerman, ed. Greenwich, CT: JAI Press, Inc., 1990.

Putnam, Linda. Understanding the Unique Characteristics of Groups within Organizations, in *Small Group Communication.* Robert Cathcart and Larry Samovar, eds. Dubuque, IA: William C. Brown, 1984.

Putnam, Linda, and Holmer, Majia. Framing and Reframing, in *Communication and*

Negotiation. Linda Putnam and Michael Roloff, eds. Newberry Park, CA: Sage, 1992.

+Putnam, Linda and Jones, T. Reciprocity in Negotiations. *Communication Monographs, 49* (1982): 171–191.

+Putnam, Linda and Roloff, Michael, eds. *Communication and Negotiation.* Newberry Park, CA: Sage, 1992.

+Putnam, Linda and Sorenson, Ritch. Equivocal Messages in Organizations. *Human Communication Research, 8* (1982): 114–132.

Putnam, Linda and Stohl, Cynthia. Bona Fide Groups: An Alternative Perspective for Communication and Small Group Decision Making, in *Communication and Group Decision Making,* 2nd ed. R. Hirokawa and M.S. Poole, eds. Thousand Oaks, CA: Sage, 1996.

Putnam, Linda and van Hoeven, Shirley. The Role of Narrative in Teachers' Bargaining. Paper presented at the Temple University Discourse Conference on Conflict Intervention, Philadelphia, 1987.

Putnam, Linda and van Hoeven, Shirley. Teacher Bargaining as a Cultural Rite of Conflict Reduction. Paper presented at the Central States Speech Association Convention, Cincinnati, 1986.

+Putnam, Linda and Wilson, Charmaine. Communicative Strategies in Organizational Conflicts, in *Communication Yearbook 6.* M. Burgoon, ed. Newbury Park, CA: Sage, 1982.

Putnam, Linda, van Hooven, Shirley, and Bullis, Connie. The Role of Rituals and Fantasy Themes in Teachers' Bargaining. *Western Journal of Speech Communication, 55* (1991): 85–103.

Putnam, Linda, Wilson, S. and Turner, D. The Evolution of Policy Arguments in Teacher's Bargaining. *Argumentation, 4* (1990): 129–152.

Race in the Workplace, *Business Week,* July 8, 1991.

Radford, L.J. and Raines, C. *Twentysomething: Managing and Motivating Today's New Work Force.* New York: Master Media, Ltd., 1992.

+Rafaeli, S. *Electronic Message to Computer-mediated Hotline.* Comserve Electronic Information Service, April 26, 1990.

Ragins, Belle Rose. Barriers to Mentoring. *Human Relations, 42* (1989): 1–22.

Ragins, Belle Rose and McFarlin, D.B. Perceptions of Mentor Roles in Cross-Gender Mentoring Relationships. *Journal of Vocational Behavior, 37* (1990): 321–339.

+Rahim, M. Referent Role and Styles of Handling Interpersonal Conflict. *Journal of Social Psychology, 126* (1986): 79–86.

+Ralston, Steven and Kirkwood, William. Overcoming Managerial Bias in Employment Interviewing. *Journal of Applied Communication Research, 23* (1995): 75–92.

Ramstad, Evan [AP]. *Bryan-College Station Eagle,* September 22, 1996, E6.

Raven, Bertram and Kruglanski, Arie. Power and Conflict, in *The Structure of Conflict.* Paul Swingle, ed. New York: Academic Press, 1970.

Reardon, Kathleen Kelley. *They Don't Get It, Do They?* Boston: Little, Brown and Co., 1995.

+Redding, Charles. *Communication Within the Organization.* New York: Industrial Communication Council, 1972.

Redding, Charles. Rocking Boats, Blowing Whistles, and Teaching Speech Communication. *Communication Education, 34* (1985): 245–258.

Reimers, Cordelia W. Hispanic Earnings and Employment in the 1980s, in *Hispanics in the Workplace.* P. Knouse, P. Rosenfeld, and A. Culbertson, eds. Newbury Park, CA: Sage, 1992.

+Remland, Martin. Leadership Impressions and Nonverbal Communication. *Communication Quarterly, 19* (1987): 108–128.

+Renwick, Patricia. Perception and Management of Superior-Subordinate Conflict. *Organizational Behavior and Human Performance, 13* (1975): 444–456.

Report of the President's Commission on the Space Shuttle "Challenger." Washington, D.C.: U.S. Government Printing Office, 1986.

Reskin, Barbara and Roos, Patricia. Status Hierarchies and Sex Segregation, in *Ingredients for Women's Employment Policy.* C. Bose and G. Spitze, eds. New York: SUNY Press, 1987.

Reynolds, C.W. and Norman, R.V., eds. *Community in America: The Challenge of Habits of the Heart.* Berkeley: University of California Press, 1988.

+Rhenman, E., Stromberg, L., and Westerlund, G. *Conflict and Cooperation in Business Organizations.* New York: John Wiley, 1970.

+Rice, Ron. Evaluating New Media Systems, in *Evaluating the New Information Technologies.* J. Johnstone, ed. San Francisco: Jossey-Bass, 1984.

+Rice, Ron. *New Communication Technologies.* Beverly Hills: Sage, 1984.

+Rice, Ron and Associates. *The New Media: Communication, Research and Technology.* Newbury Park, CA: Sage, 1984.

+Rice, Ron and Aydin, Carolyn. Attitudes Toward New Organizational Technology. *Administrative Science Quarterly, 36* (1991): 219-244.

+Rice, Ron and Gattiker, Urs. Communication Technologies and Structures, in *The New Handbook of Organizational Communication.* Linda Putnam and Fredric Jablin, eds. Thousand Oaks, CA: Sage, 1997.

+Rice, Ron and Love, G. Electronic Emotion. *Communication Research, 14* (1987): 85-108.

Richmond, Virginia Peck and Roach, K. David. Willingness to Communicate and Employee Success in U.S. Organizations. *Journal of Applied Communication Research, 20* (1992): 95-115.

+Richmond, Virginia, McCroskey, James, and Davis, L.M. Individual Differences Among Employees, Management Communication Style and Employee Satisfaction. *Human Communication Research, 8* (1982): 170-188.

+Richmond, Virginia Peck, McCroskey, James, and Payne, S.K. *Nonverbal Behavior in Interpersonal Relationships.* Englewood Cliffs, NJ: Prentice-Hall, 1987.

Riger, S. and Galligan, P. Women in Management. *American Psychologist, 10* (1989): 902-910.

+Riley, Patricia. A Structurationist Account of Political Culture. *Administrative Science Quarterly, 28* (1983): 414-437.

Ring, Kathryn. Behind Every Successful Women . . . There's a Mentor. *Women in Business* (July-August, 1978): pp. 9-11.

Rizzo, A. and Mendez, C. *The Integration of Women in Management* New York: Quorum Books, 1990.

Robbins, Stephen. Conflict Management and Conflict Resolution Are Not Synonymous Terms. *California Management Review, 21* (1978): 67-75.

+Roberts, Karlene and O'Reilly, Charles. Failures in Upward Communication: Three Possible Culprits. *Academy of Management Journal, 17* (1974): 205-215.

+Roberts, Karlene and O'Reilly, Charles. Organizations as Communication Structures. *Human Communication Research, 4* (1978): 283-293.

Roberts, Karlene, Hulin, Charles, and Rousseau, Denise. *Developing an Inter-Disciplinary Science of Organizations.* San Francisco: Jossey-Bass, 1979.

+Roberts, Nancy. Organizational Power Styles. *The Journal of Applied Behavioral Science, 22* (1986): 443-45.

Robin, D., Giallourakis, M., David, F., and Mortiz, T. A Different Look at Business Ethics, in *Essentials of Business Ethics.* P. Madsen and J. Shafritz, eds. New York: Meridian, 1990.

Rogers, Everett and Argawala-Rogers, Rekha. *Organizational Communication.* New York: The Free Press, 1976.

+Rogers-Millar, Edna and Millar, Frank. Domineering and Dominance. *Human Communication Research, 5* (1979): 238-246.

Roloff, Michael. *Interpersonal Communication.* Beverly Hills, CA: Sage, 1981.

Roloff, Michael. Roloff's Modes of Conflict Resolution and Their Items, in *Explorations in Interpersonal Communication.* Gerald Miller, ed. Beverly Hills, CA: Sage, 1976.

+Roloff, Michael and Jordan, Jerry M. Achieving Negotiation Goals, in *Communication and Negotiation.* L. Putnam and M. Roloff, eds. Newbury Park, CA: Sage, 1993.

Rosen, Michael. Breakfast at Spiro's. *Journal of Management, 11* (1985): 31-48.

Rosen, Michael. You Asked for It: Christmas at the Bosses' Expense. *Journal of Management Studies, 25* (1988): 463-480.

Rosener, Judith. Ways Women Lead. *Harvard Business Review* (Nov.-Dec., 1990), pp. 119-125.

Ross, Roseanna, and Dewine, Susan. Interpersonal Conflict. Paper presented at the Speech Communication Association Convention, Washington, D.C., 1982.

Ross, Roseanna and Dewine, Susan. Interpersonal Needs and Communication in Conflict. Paper presented at the Speech Communication Association Convention, Chicago, 1984.

Rothschild-Whitt, Joyce and Whitt, J.A. *The Cooperative Workplace* (Cambridge: Cambridge University Press, 1986).

+Rotondi, Thomas, Jr. Organizational Identification. *Organizational Behavior and Human Performance, 13* (1975): 95-109.

+Rotondi, Thomas, Jr. Organizational Identification and Group Involvement. *Academy of Management Journal, 18* (1975): 892-897.

+Ruble, T. and Cosier, R. A Laboratory Study of Five Conflict-handling Modes, in *Conflict Management and Industrial Relations.* T. Bomers and R. Peterson, eds. Boston: Kluwer-Nijhoff, 1982.

Sacks, Karen. Networking: When Potluck Is Political. *MS, 11* (April, 1983): 97-98.

Salancik, Gerald. Commitment and the Control of Organizational Behavior and Belief, in *New Directions in Organizational Behavior.* B.M. Staw and G.R. Salancik, eds. Chicago: St. Clair, 1977.

Saltzman, Amy (Associate Press Reporter). Fast-Track Success Drops in Importance for Many. *Houston Chronicle,* September 19, 1991, C1, 14.

+Sambamurthy, V. and Poole, Marshall Scott. The Effects of Variations in Capabilities of GDSS Designs on Management of Cognitive Conflict in Groups. *Information Systems Research, 3* (1993): 224-251.

Sampson, Edward E. Justice, Ideology, and Social Legitimation, in *Justice in Social Relations.* H.W. Bierhoff, R.L. Cohen, and J. Greenberg, eds. New York: Plenum, 1986.

Sass, James and Canary, Daniel. Organizational Commitment and Identification. *Western Journal of Speech Communication, 55* (1991): 275-293.

Sayles, Leonard. Work Group Behavior and the Larger Organization, in *Research in Industrial Human Relations.* W.F. Whyte, ed. New York: Harper, 1957.

Schein, Edgar H. *Organizational Psychology,* 3rd ed. Englewood Cliffs, NJ: Prentice-Hall, 1980.

Schein, Virginia. The Relationships Between Sex-role Stereotypes and Requisite Managerial Characteristics. *Journal of Applied Psychology, 57* (1973): 95-100.

+Schenck-Hamlin, W. and Georgacarakos, G. Response to Murdock, Bradac, and Bowers. *Western Journal of Speech Communication, 50* (1986): 200-207.

Scherer, R. First National Survey of Minority Views Shows Deep Racial Polarization in the US. *Christian Science Monitor,* March, 1994.

Schiedel, Thomas. Divergent and Convergent Thinking in Group Decision-making, in *Communication and Group Decision-Making.* Randy Hirokawa and M. Scott Poole, eds. Beverly Hills, CA: Sage, 1986.

Schiedel, Thomas and Crowell, Laura. *Discussing and Deciding.* New York: Macmillan, 1979.

Schneider, B., Gunnarson, S., and Wheeler, J. The Role of Opportunity in the Conceptualization and Measurement of Job Satisfaction, in *Job Satisfaction.* C.J. Crannay, et al., eds. New York: Lexington Books, 1992.

Schrank, Robert. Two Women, Three Men on a Raft. *Harvard Business Review, 57* (May-June, 1977): 100-108.

+Schriesheim, Chester. and von Glinow, Mary Ann. The Path-Goal Theory of Leadership. *Academy of Management Journal, 20* (1977): 398-405.

Schwartz, E.B. and Rago, J.J. Beyond Tokenism. *Business Horizons,* December, 1973, pp. 69-76.

+Schweiger, David and Denisi, Angelo. Communication with Employees Following a Merger. *Academy of Management Journal, 34* (1991): 110-135.

Scott, Craig. Identification with Multiple Targets in a Geographically Dispersed Organization. Paper presented at the International Communication Association Convention, Chicago, 1996.

Scott, William G. and Hart, D.K. *Organizational America.* Boston: Houghton Mifflin, 1979.

Scott, William G. and Hart, D.K. *Organizational Values in America.* New Brunswick, NJ: Transaction Publishers, 1989.

Seeger, Matthew. Responsibility In Organizational Communication, in *Proceedings of the 1992 National Communication Ethics Conference.* J. Jaska, ed. Annandale, VA: Speech Communication Association, 1992.

Segura, Denise. Walking on Eggshells: Chicanas in the Labor Force, in *Hispanics in the Workforce.* Stephen B. Knouse, Paul Rosenfeld, and Amy L. Culbertson, eds. Newbury Park, CA: Sage, 1992.

Seibold, David and Meyers, Renee. Communication and Influence in Group Decision-making, in *Communication and Group Decision Making,* 2nd ed. Randy Hirokawa and Marshall Scott Poole, eds. Thousand Oaks, CA: Sage, 1996.

+Seibold, David and Shea, Christine. Participation and Decision-making," in *The New Handbook of Organizational Communication.* Linda Putnam and Fredric Jablin, eds. Thousand Oaks, CA: Sage, 1997.

+Seibold, David, Cantrill, James and Myers, Renee. Communication and Interpersonal Influence, in *Handbook of Interpersonal Communication.* Gerald Miller and Mark Knapp, eds. Beverly Hills, CA: Sage, 1985.

Seidenberg, Robert. *Corporate Wives, Corporate Casualties?* New York: AMACOM, 1973.

Sekaran, Uma. *Dual-Career Families.* San Francisco: Jossey-Bass, 1986.

Senge, Peter. *The Fifth Discipline.* New York: Doubleday, 1990.

Sewell, G. and Wilkinson, B. Something to Watch Over Me: Surveillance, Discipline, and the Just-in-time Labor Process. *Sociology, 26* (1992): 271-289.

+Sgro, Joseph, Worchel, Philip, Pence, Earl, and Orban, Joseph. Perceived Leader Behavior as a Function of Trust. *Academy of Management Journal, 23* (1980): 161-165.

Sharp, Rochelle. The Waiting Game. *Wall Street Journal,* March 29, 1994, p. A1.

+Shaw, James. An Information-processing Approach to the Study of Job Design. *Acad-*

emy of Management Review, 5 (1980): 41–48.

Shockley-Zalabak, Pamela. *Fundamentals of Organizational Communication: Knowledge, Sensitivity, Skills, Values,* 3rd ed. New York: Longman, 1995.

+Sias, Patricia. Constructing Perceptions of Differential Treatment. *Communication Monographs, 63* (1996): 171–187.

+Sias, Patricia and Jablin, Fredric. Differential Superior-Subordinate Relations, Perceptions of Fairness, and Coworker Communication. *Human Communication Research, 22* (1995): 5–38.

Siehl, Caren and Martin, Joanne. Organizational Culture: A Key to Financial Performance?, in *Organizational Climate and Cultures.* B. Schneider, ed. San Francisco: Jossey-Bass, 1990.

+Sillars, Alan. Stranger and Spouse as Target Persons for Compliance-gaining Strategies. *Human Communication Research, 6* (1980): 265–279.

Simon, Herbert. Making Management Decisions. *Academy of Management Executive, 1* (1987): 57–64.

+Simon, Herbert. *The New Science of Management Decision.* New York: Harper & Row, 1960.

+Simons, T. Speech Patterns and the Concept of Utility in Cognitive Maps. *Academy of Management Journal, 36* (1993): 139–156.

Sims, Robert. The Challenge of Ethical Behavior in Organizations. *Journal of Business Ethics, 11* (1992): 501–513.

Sims, Henry. Further Thoughts on Punishment in Organizations. *The Academy of Management Review, 5* (1980): 135–138.

+Sitkin, Sim B., Sutcliffe, Kathleen M., and Barrios-Choplin, J.R. A Dual-Capacity Model of Communication Medium Choice in Organizations. *Human Communication Research, 18* (1992): 563–598.

Sixel, L.M. *Houston Chronicle,* September 19, 1996, C1.

Sixel, L.M. Sincerity Needed for Diversity. *Houston Chronicle,* December 17, 1996, 1C.

Sixel, L.M. Workers Should Consider Themselves Free Agents. *Houston Chronicle,* November 20, 1995, 1C.

Sixel, L.M. Workplace Racism Cases Hard to Win. *Houston Chronicle,* November 13, 1996, 1C.

Sixel, L.M. Xers Want to be Their Own Bosses. *Houston Chronicle,* November 2, 1995, 1C.

Sless, David. Forms of Control. *Australian Journal of Communication, 14* (1988): 57–69.

+Slovic, Paul, Fischoff, Baruch, and Lichtenstein, Sarah. Behavioral Decision Theory. *Annual Review of Psychology, 28* (1977): 1–39.

+Smart, Charles and Veritsky, I. Designs for Crisis Decision Units. *Administrative Science Quarterly, 22* (1977): 640–657.

Smircich, Linda and Calas, Marta. Using the "F" Word: Feminist Theories and the Social Consequences of Organizational Research, in *Gendering Organizational Analysis.* Albert Mills and Peta Tancred, eds. Newbury Park, CA: Sage, 1992.

Smircich, Linda and Chesser, R. Superiors and Subordinates' Perceptions of Performance. *Academy of Management Journal, 24* (1981): 198–205.

+Smith, A. and Stewart, A. Approaches to Studying Racism and Sexism in Black Women's Lives. *Journal of Social Issues, 39* (1983): 1–15.

Smith, David. Stories, Values, and Patient Care Decisions, in *The Ethical Nexus.* Charles Conrad, ed. Norwood, NJ: Ablex, 1992.

+Smith, David H. Theoretical and Research Problems with the Concept of Utility. Paper presented at the International Communication Association Convention, Acapulco, 1980.

Smith, Kenwyn. The Movement of Conflict in Organizations. *Administrative Science Quarterly, 34* (1989): 1–20.

Smith, Kenwyn and Simmons, Valerie. The Rumpelstiltskin Organization. *Administrative Science Quarterly, 28* (1983): 377–392.

Smith, Ruth C. and Eisenberg, Eric. Conflict at Disneyland: A Root-Metaphor Analysis. *Communication Monographs, 54* (1987): 367–380.

+Smith-Lovin, L. and McPherson, M.J. You Are Who You Know, in *Theory on Gender/Feminism on Theory.* Paula England, ed. New York: Aldine, 1993.

+Snyder, Robert and Morris, James. Organizational Communication and Performance. *Journal of Applied Psychology, 69* (1984): 461–465.

Solomon, Charlene. Keeping Hate Out of the Workplace. *Personnel Journal* (July, 1992): 30–35.

+Sproull, Lee and Kiesler, Sara. *Connections: New Ways of Working in the Networked World.* Cambridge, MA: MIT Press, 1992.

+Sproull, Lee and Kiesler, Sara. Reducing Social Context Cues. *Management Science, 32* (1986): 1492–1512.

Srivastva, Suresh and Associates. *Executive Integrity.* San Francisco: Jossey-Bass, 1988.

Stagner, Robert and Rosen, H. *Psychology of Union-Management Relationships.* Belmont, CA: Brooks-Cole, 1965.

Stanfield, John H. II. Commentary: The Race Politics of Knowledge Production. *Research in Social Policy, 2* (1990): 177-194.

Stanfield, John H. II. Racism in America and in Other Race-Centered Nation-States. *International Journal of Comparative Sociology, XXXII* (1991): 243-260.

Starbuck, William. Acting First and Thinking Later. in *Organizational Strategy and Change.* Johannes Pennings and Associates. San Francisco: Jossey-Bass, 1985.

Starbuck, William and Milliken, E.J. Executives' Perceptual Filters, in *The Executive Effect.* D.C. Hambrick, ed. Greenwich, CT: JAI, 1988.

+Staw, Barry. Counterforces to Change, in *Change in Organizations.* P.S. Goodman & Associates, eds. San Francisco: Jossey-Bass, 1982.

Staw, Barry. Knee Deep in the Big Muddy. *Organizational Behavior and Human Performance, 16* (1976): 27-44.

+Staw, Barry and Ross, J. Commitment to a Policy Decision. *Administrative Science Quarterly, 23* (1978): 40-52.

+Staw, Barry, McKechnie, Pamela and Puffer, S. The Justification of Organizational Performance. *Administrative Science Quarterly, 28* (1983): 582-600.

+Staw, Barry, Sandelands, L., and Dutton, J. Threat-Rigidity Effects in Organizational Behavior. *Administrative Science Quarterly, 26* (1981): 501-524.

Steinfeld, Charles. Computer-mediated Communication in the Organizations, in *Cases in Organizational Communication.* Beverly Sypher, ed. New York: Guilford, 1991.

Stohl, Cynthia. *Organizational Communication: Connectedness in Action.* Thousand Oaks, CA: Sage, 1995.

Stohl, Cynthia. The Role of Memorable Messages in the Process of Organization Socialization. *Communication Quarterly, 34* (1983): 231-249.

+Stohl, Cynthia and Redding, Charles. Messages and Message Exchange Processes, in *Handbook of Organizational Communication.* Fred Jablin, Linda Putnam, Karlene Roberts and Lyman Porter, eds. Newbury Park, CA: Sage, 1987.

Stuttman, Randall. Denying Persuasive Intent. Paper presented at the Western Speech Communication Association Convention, San Diego, 1988.

Sussman, H. Is Diversity Training Worth Maintaining? *Business and Society Review, 89* (1994): 48-49.

+Sutcliffe, Cathy. Information Processing and Organizational Environments, in *The New Handbook of Organizational Communi-*

cation. Linda Putnam and Fredric Jablin, eds. Thousand Oaks, CA: Sage, 1997.

Sutton, Robert L. and Louis, Meryl Reis. How Selecting and Socializing Newcomers Influences Insiders. *Human Resource Management, 26* (1987): 347-361.

+Sypher, Beverly Davenport and Zorn, Theodore. Communication-related Abilities and Upward Mobility. *Human Communication Research, 12* (1986): 420-431.

Tannenbaum, Arnold. Control in Organizations. *Administrative Science Quarterly, 7* (1962): 17-42.

Taylor, Frederick. The Principles of Scientific Management, in *Classics of Organizational Theory.* Jay Shafritz and Philip Whitbeck, eds. Oak Park, IL: Moore, 1978.

+Tedeschi, James. Threats and Promises, in *The Structure of Conflict.* Paul Swingle, ed. New York: Academic Press, 1970.

+Terpstra, David and Baker, Douglas. Outcomes of Sexual Harassment Charges. *Academy of Management Journal, 31* (1988): 185-194.

+Therborn, Goran. *The Ideology of Power and the Power of Ideology.* London: Verso, 1980.

Thomas, David and Alderfer, Clayton. The Influence of Race on Career Dynamics, in *Handbook of Career Theory.* New York: McGraw-Hill, 1989.

+Thomas, David. The Impact of Race on Managers' Experiences of Developmental Relationships (Mentoring and Sponsorship). *Journal of Organizational Behavior, 2* (1990): 479-492.

Thomas, Kenneth. Conflict and Conflict Management, in *Handbook of Industrial and Organizational Psychology.* Marvin Dunnette, ed. Chicago: Rand-McNally, 1976.

Thomas, Kenneth. Where Do We Go From Here?, *Management Communication Quarterly, 1* (1988): 301-305.

Thompson, James. *Organizations in Action.* New York: McGraw-Hill, 1967.

+Thompson, John. *Studies in the Theory of Ideology.* Berkeley: University of California Press, 1984.

Thompson, Victor. *Modern Organizations.* New York: Knopf, 1967.

Thorngate, Warren. Must We Always Think Before We Act?, *Personality and Social Psychology Bulletin, 2* (1976): 31-35.

Tichy, Noel, Tushman, Michael, and Fombrun, Charles. Social Network Analysis for Organizations. *Academy of Management Review, 4* (1979): 507-519.

Ting-Toomey, Stella. Theory of Conflict and Culture, in *Communication and Culture.* William Gudykunst, ed. Beverly Hills, CA: Sage, 1985.

+Tjosvold, Dean. Affirmation of the High-power Person and His Position. *Journal of Applied Social Psychology, 8* (1978): 230-243.

+Tjosvold, Dean. Effects of Leader Warmth and Directiveness on Subordinate Performance on a Subsequent Task. *Journal of Applied Psychology, 69* (1984): 422-427.

Toffler, B.E. *Tough Choices.* New York: John Wiley and Sons, 1986.

Tompkins, Phillip. *Organizational Communication Imperatives: Lessons from the Space Program.* Los Angeles: Roxbury House, 1993.

Tompkins, Philip and Cheney, George. Communication and Unobtrusive Control in Contemporary Organizations, in *Organizational Communication.* Robert McPhee and Philip Tompkins, eds. Beverly Hills, CA: Sage, 1985.

Tompkins, Phillip, Fisher, J., Infante, D., and Tompkins, E. Conflict and Communication Within the University, in *Perspectives on Communication and Social Conflict.* G. Miller and H. Simons, eds. Englewood Cliffs, NJ: Prentice-Hall, 1974.

Toth, Elizabeth Lance and Heath, Robert, eds. *Rhetorical and Critical Approaches to Public Relations.* New York: Praeger, 1992.

+Tracy, Karen and Eisenberg, Eric. Giving Criticism. *Research on Language and Social Interaction, 24* (1990/1991): 37-70.

Trevino, Linda Klebe and Youngblood, S.A. Bad Apples in Bad Barrels, *Journal of Applied Psychology, 75* (1990): 378-385.

+Trevino, Linda Klebe, Lengel, Ralph, and Daft, Richard. Media Symbolism, Media Richness, and Media Choices in Organizations. *Communication Research, 14* (1987): 553-574.

Triandis, H.C., Kashima, Y., Hui, C.H., Lisansky, J., and Marin, G. Acculturation and Biculturalism Indices Among Relatively Acculturated Hispanic Young Adults. *Inter-American Journal of Psychology, 16* (1982): 140-149.

Trice, Harrison and Beyer, Janice. *The Cultures of Work Organizations.* Englewood Cliffs, NJ: Prentice-Hall, 1993.

Trice, Harrison and Beyer, Janice. Studying Organizational Cultures Through Rites and Ceremonials. *Academy of Management Review, 9* (1984): 653-669.

+Trombetta, John and Rogers, Donald. Communication Climate, Job Satisfaction, and Organizational Commitment. *Management Communication Quarterly, 4* (1988): 494-514.

+Tushman, Michael. Impacts of Perceived Environmental Variability on Work-Related Communication. *Academy of Management Journal, 22* (1979): 482-500.

+Tushman, Michael and Nelson, Richard, eds. *Administrative Science Quarterly, 35* (1990): 1-222.

Tushman, Michael and Scanlan, Thomas. Boundary Spanning Individuals. *The Academy of Management Review, 5* (1980): 123-138.

U.S. Bureau of the Census. *Population Reports.* Washington, D.C.: Government Printing Office, 1987.

U.S. Department of Labor. *The American Workforce: 1992-2005.* Washington, D.C.: Government Printing Office, USDL Bulletin N. 2452, 1994.

Vamos, M.N. ed. Business Week/Harris Executive Poll. *Business Week,* June 8, 1992, 77.

Vanderford, Marsha, Smith, David, and Harris, Willard. Value Identification in Narrative Discourse. *Journal of Applied Communication Research, 20* (1992): 123-161.

+Van de Ven, Andrew and Poole, M.S. Explaining Development and Change in Organizations. *Academy of Management Review, 20* (1995): 510-540.

van Maanen, John. The Smile Factory, in *Reframing Organizational Culture.* Peter Frost, et al., eds. Newbury Park, CA: Sage, 1991.

van Maanen, John, and Kunda, Gideon. Real Feelings: Emotional Expression and Organizational Culture. In L.L. Cummings & B.M. Staw, eds. *Research in Organizational Behavior,* vol. 11 Greenwich, CT: JAI, 1989.

+van Maanen, John and Schein, Edgar. Occupational Socialization in the Professions. *Journal of Psychiatric Research, 8* (1971): 521-530.

Vaughn, Diane. *The "Challenger" Launch Decision.* Chicago: University of Chicago Press, 1996.

Vaughn, Diane. *Controlling Unlawful Organizational Behavior.* Chicago: University of Chicago Press, 1983.

Vaughn, Diane. NASA and the "Challenger." *Administrative Science Quarterly, 35* (1990): 225-257.

Vaughn, E. and Siefert, M. Variability in the Framing of Risk Issues. *Journal of Social Issues, 48* (1992): 119-135.

+Vecchio, Robert. An Empirical Examination of the Validity of Fielder's Model of Leadership Effectiveness. *Organizational Behavior and Human Performance, 19* (1977): 180-206.

+Vecchio, Robert. Worker Alienation as a Moderator of the Job Quality-Job Satisfaction

Relationship. *Academy of Management Journal, 23* (1980): 479–486.

+Victor, Bart and Blackburn, Richard. Determinants and Consequences of Task Uncertainty. *Journal of Management Studies, 18* (1987): 108–132.

Violanti, Michelle. Hooked on Expectations: An Analysis of Influence and Relationships in the Tailhook Reports. *Journal of Applied Communication Research, 24* (1996): 67–82.

+von Neumann, John and Morganstern, Oskar. *Theory of Games and Economic Behavior.* New York: John Wiley, 1947.

+Wagner, John and Gooding, Richard. Effects of Societal Trends on Participation Research. *Administrative Science Quarterly, 32* (1987): 241–262.

+Waldron, Vincent. Achieving Communication Goals in Supervisor-Subordinate Relationships. *Communication Monographs, 58* (1991): 289–306.

Waldron, Vincent. Once More with Feeling: A Reconceptualization of Emotion in Organization. In *Communication Yearbook 17.* Stanley Deetz, ed. Newbury Park, CA: Sage, 1994.

+Waldron, Vince and Krone, Kathy. The Experience and Expression of Emotion in the Workplace. *Management Communication Quarterly, 4* (1991): 287–309.

Walker, Chip and Moses, Elissa. The Age of Self-Navigation," *American Demographics* (September, 1996): 36–42.

Walker, Katherine and Woods, Margaret. *Time Use.* Washington, D.C.: The American Home Economic Association, 1976.

Walsh, Sharon. Plaintiffs Say Texaco Tough in Bias Cases. *Houston Chronicle,* November 14, 1996, 1C.

+Walther, Joe B. Interpersonal Effects in Computer-mediated Interaction. *Communication Research, 19* (1992): 52–90.

Walton, C. *The Moral Manager.* Cambridge, MA: Ballinger, 1988.

Wanous, J. *Organizational Entry.* Reading, MA: Addison-Wesley, 1980.

Ware, B.L. And Linkugel, W.A. They Spoke in Defense of Themselves. *The Quarterly Journal of Speech, 59* (1973): 273–283.

Waters, J.A. Catch 20.5: Corporate Morality as an Organizational Phenomenon. *Organizational Dynamics, 6* (1978): 2–19.

Waters, J., and Bird, F. Attending to Ethics in Management," *Journal of Business Ethics, 8* (1989): 493–497.

Waters, J. and Bird, F. The Moral Dimension of Organizational Culture. *Journal of Business Ethics, 6* (1987): 15–22.

+Watzlawick, Paul, Beavin, Janet, and Jackson, Don. *Pragmatics of Human Communication.* New York: W.W. Norton, 1967.

+Weber, Max. *The Protestant Ethic and the Spirit of Capitalism.* New York: Charles Scribner's and Sons, 1958.

Weick, Karl. The Collapse of Sense-Making in Organizations: The Mann Gulch Disaster," *Administrative Science Quarterly, 38* (1993): 628–652.

+Weick, Karl. *Sensemaking in Organizations.* Thousand Oaks, CA: Sage, 1995.

Weick, Karl. *The Social Psychology of Organizing,* 2nd ed. Reading, MA: Addison-Wesley, 1979.

Weick, Karl. "Organizational Culture and High Reliability," *California Management Review, 29* (1987): 112–127.

Weick, Karl. The Vulnerable System: An Analysis of the Tenerife Air Disaster. *Journal of Management, 16* (1990): 571–593.

Weick, Karl and Browning, Larry. Argument and Narration in Organizational Communication. *Yearly Review of Management of the Journal of Management, 12* (1986): 243–259, ed. J.G. Hunt and J.D. Blair.

+Westerlund, G. and Sjostrand, S. *Organizational Myths.* New York: Harper & Row, 1979.

+Westley, Frances. Middle Managers and Strategy. *Strategic Management Journal, 11* (1990): 337–344.

Who's Excellent Now?, *Business Week,* November 5, 1984.

Whyte, William. *Money and Motivation: An Analysis of Incentives in Industry.* New York: Harper and Row, 1955.

Whyte, William. *The Organization Man.* New York: Simon and Schuster, 1956.

Wilkins, Alan. The Creation of Company Stories. *Human Resource Management, 23* (1984): 41–60.

Wilkins, Alan. *Managing Corporate Character.* San Francisco: Jossey-Bass, 1989.

Wilkins, Alan. Organizational Stories as Symbols Which Control the Organization. In *Organizational Symbolism.* Louis Pondy, Peter Frost, Gareth Morgan and Thomas Dandridge, eds. Greenwich, CT: JAI Press, 1983.

Wilkins, B.M. and Anderson, P.A. Gender Differences and Similarities in Management Communication. *Management Communication Quarterly, 5* (1991): 25–31.

+Wilson, Steven R. Face and Facework in Negotiation, in *Communication and Negotiation.* L. Putnam and M. Roloff, eds. Newbury Park, CA: Sage, 1993.

+Wilson, Steve and Putnam, Linda. Interaction Goals in Negotiation. In James Anderson, ed. *Communication Yearbook 13* Newbury Park, CA: Sage, 1990.

+Winter, Susan J. and Taylor, S. Lynne. The Role of IT in the Transformation of Work: A Comparison of Post-Industrial, Industrial, and Proto-Industrial Organizations. *Information Systems Research, 7* (1996): 5-21.

+Winter, Susan J. and Taylor, S. Lynne. Technology and the Past, *Information Systems Research, 7* (1996): 5-21.

Witte, Kim and Conrad, Charles. Some Emotional Roads Not Taken, in *Communication Yearbook 17* Stanley Deetz, ed. Newbury Park, CA: Sage, 1994.

Wolff, Edward N. *Top Heavy: A Study of the Increasing Inequality of Wealth in America.* New York: The Twentieth Century Fund Press, 1995.

Women and the Workplace: The Glass Ceiling. Hearings Before the Subcommittee on Employment and Productivity, Committee on Labor and Human Resources, U.S. Senate, October 23, 1991.

Wood, Julia and Pearce, Barnett. Sexists, Racists and Other Classes of Classifiers. *Quarterly Journal of Speech, 66* (1980): 239-250.

Wood, Julia, Phillips, Gerald, and Pederson, Douglas. *Group Discussion,* 2nd. ed. (New York: Harper and Row, 1989).

Wyatt, Nancy. Shared Leadership in the Weaver's Guild, in *Women Communicating: Studies of Women's Talk.* Barbara Bate and Anita Taylor, eds. Norwood, NJ: Ablex, 1988.

+Yates, Joanne and Orlikowski, Wanda J. Genres of Organizational Communication. *The Academy of Management Review, 17* (1992): 299-326.

+Young, Ed. On the Naming of the Rose. *Organization Studies, 10* (1989): 187-206.

+Youker, Robert. Organization Alternatives for Project Managers. *Project Management Journal, VIII* (March, 1977): 18-24.

Zak, M.W. It's Like a Prison in There. *Journal of Business and Technical Communication, 8* (1994): 282-298.

Zaldivar, R.A. Men Tiptoeing Their Way into Women's Work. *Houston Chronicle,* January 26, 1997, 1E.

Zalzenik, Abraham. Power and Politics in Organizational Life. *Harvard Business Review, 48* (May-June, 1970): 47-60.

+Zand, Dale E. Trust and Managerial Problemsolving. *Administrative Science Quarterly, 17* (1972): 229-239.

+Zimmerman, D. The Practicalities of Rule Use, in *Understanding Everyday Life.* J. Douglas, ed. Chicago: Aldine, 1970.

Zorn, Theodore. Implementing Self Management at Holiday Inn, in *Case Studies in Organizational Communication.* Beverly Sypher, ed. Guilford Press, 1991.

Zuboff, Shoshanna. *In the Age of the Smart Machine.* New York: Free Press, 1.

INDEX